The Cambridge Handbook of Social Theory

This ambitious two-volume handbook of social theory consists of forty original contributions. The researchers take stock of the state of social theory and its relationship to the canon, exploring such topics as the nature, purpose, and meaning of social theory; the significance of the classics; the impact of specific individuals and theory schools; and more. Both volumes reflect a mixture of what intellectual historian Morton White distinguished as the "annalist of ideas" and the "analyst of ideas," locating theoretical thought within the larger sociohistorical context that shaped it – within the terrain of the sociology of knowledge. Exploring the contemporary relevance of theories in a manner that is historically situated and sensitive, this impressive and comprehensive set will likely stand the test of time.

PETER KIVISTO is Richard A. Swanson Professor of Social Thought at Augustana College.

The Cambridge Handbook of Social Theory

Volume II: *Contemporary Theories and Issues*

Edited by

Peter Kivisto
Augustana College

CAMBRIDGE
UNIVERSITY PRESS

CAMBRIDGE
UNIVERSITY PRESS

University Printing House, Cambridge CB2 8BS, United Kingdom

One Liberty Plaza, 20th Floor, New York, NY 10006, USA

477 Williamstown Road, Port Melbourne, VIC 3207, Australia

314 321, 3rd Floor, Plot 3, Splendor Forum, Jasola District Centre, New Delhi – 110025, India

79 Anson Road, #06–04/06, Singapore 079906

Cambridge University Press is part of the University of Cambridge.

It furthers the University's mission by disseminating knowledge in the pursuit of education, learning, and research at the highest international levels of excellence.

www.cambridge.org
Information on this title: www.cambridge.org/9781107162693
DOI: 10.1017/9781316677452

First published 2021

Printed in the United Kingdom by TJ Books Limited, Padstow Cornwall

A catalogue record for this publication is available from the British Library.

ISBN Two-Volume Set 978-1-107-13170-5 Hardback
ISBN Volume I 978-1-107-16264-8 Hardback
ISBN Volume II 978-1-107-16269-3 Hardback

Contents

Figures

Tables

Contributors

ROBERT J. ANTONIO teaches sociology at the University of Kansas. He specializes in social theory, but also works on globalization, political economy, and the environment. Currently he is working on projects related to capitalism's crisis tendencies, especially concerning the intersection of increased economic inequality, ecological risk, and democratic and authoritarian responses.

RONALD L. BREIGER is Regents Professor and Professor of Sociology at the University of Arizona, where he holds affiliate appointments in Government and Public Policy, Statistics and Data Science, and Applied Mathematics. His interests include social network theory and methods, culture and networks, adversarial networks, and regression modeling as a network problem.

SHELLEY BUDGEON is Senior Lecturer in Sociology at the University of Birmingham. Her research analyzes how the constitution of gender relations and gender identification are being affected by sociopolitical change. This includes the formation of contemporary femininity and gendered subjectivities, the constitutive relations between different femininities and feminisms in late modernity, and the dynamics of postfeminist neoliberalism.

PETER BURKE is a winner of the American Sociological association's Cooley-Mead Award for Career Contributions to Social Psychology. He is Professor of the Graduate Division of the University of California, Riverside, Distinguished Professor (Emeritus) in the Department of Sociology, and a Fellow of both the AAAS and the APS.

BRETT CLARK is Professor of Sociology, Environmental Humanities, and Environmental and Sustainability Studies at the University of Utah. His research interests include social theory, political economy, and ecology.

PATRICIA HILL COLLINS is Distinguished Professor Emerita at the University of Maryland. An expert on race, gender, and class, her major works include *Black Feminist Thought: Knowledge, Consciousness, and the Politics of Empowerment* (Routledge, 1990), *Black Sexual Politics: African Americans, Gender, and the New Racism* (Routledge, 2004), and *Intersectionality as Critical Social Theory* (Duke University Press, 2019). She served as the 100th President of the American Sociological Association.

SHEILA CROUCHER is Distinguished Professor of Global and Intercultural Studies at Miami University. Trained in comparative politics, her research focuses on globalization's implications for cultural and political belonging. She is the author of *Globalization and Belonging: The Politics of Identity in a Changing World* (second edition 2018); *The Other Side of the Fence: American Migrants in Mexico* (2009); and *Imagining Miami: Ethnic Politics in a Postmodern World* (1997).

KEVIN GILLAN is Senior Lecturer in Sociology at the University of Manchester. He served as editor-in-chief of the journal *Social Movement Studies* from 2015 to 2019. His published work focuses primarily on the generation and communication of alternative ideas in movements opposing war and neoliberal capitalism.

KEVIN FOX GOTHAM is Professor of Sociology in the School of Liberal Arts (SLA) at Tulane University. He has research interests in real estate and housing policy, the political economy of tourism, and the intersections of crime, violence, and security.

CHRISTIAN JOPPKE holds a Chair in Sociology at the University of Bern. He is also a recurrent visiting professor in the Nationalism Studies Program at Central European University in Budapest, and an honorary professor in the Department of Political Science at Aarhus University. He is the author of *Is Multiculturalism Dead?* (2017).

MARGARETHE KUSENBACH is Associate Professor in the Department of Sociology at the University of South Florida. Her areas of publication include urban and community sociology, social psychology (identity and emotions), disasters and environment, and qualitative methods. For the past several years, her work has focused on issues of home and belonging among mobile-home residents and lifestyle migrants. Her most recent research investigates the intersection of street art and urban development.

DONILEEN R. LOSEKE is Emeritus Professor of Sociology at the University of South Florida. Her latest book, *Narrative Production of Meaning: Exploring the Work of Stories in Social Life* (Lexington, 2019) and her volume coedited with Sara A. Green, *New Narratives of Disability* (Emerald, 2019) focus on how stories construct cognitive, emotional, and moral meanings and how these meanings are central elements in all stages of social life.

DOUGLAS A. MARSHALL is Associate Professor of Sociology and Director of Honors Education at the University of South Alabama. He is currently at work on *Sociology Distilled: Science, Force, and Structure,* a supplemental text for introductory sociology, and a monograph, *The Moral Origins of God: Darwin, Durkheim, and Homo Duplex.*

BARBARA A. MISZTAL is Emeritus Professor of Sociology at the School of Media, Communication, and Sociology, University of Leicester. She has published on the topics of trust, memory, informality, vulnerability, multiple normalities, public intellectuals, political change, forgiveness, and later life. Currently she is researching narratives that make sense of the public sphere.

EWA MORAWSKA is Professor Emeritus in the Department of Sociology at the University of Essex. She is the author of 10 books and over 250 articles devoted to different aspects of past and present international migration in Europe and North America.

KARL-DIETER OPP is Professor Emeritus at the University of Leipzig and Affiliate Professor at the University of Washington in Seattle. His areas of interest include collective action, political participation, rational choice theory, the philosophy of the social sciences, social norms and institutions, and deviant behavior.

MARK C. PACHUCKI is Assistant Professor of Sociology at the University of Massachusetts, Amherst, and a core member of the UMass Computational Social Science Institute. His work investigates culture, social network dynamics, and health. He is particularly interested in relational mechanisms by which social forces interact with biological processes throughout the life course.

KLAUS RASBORG is Associate Professor in the Department of Social Sciences and Business, Roskilde University. He is the Danish translator of Ulrich Beck's *Risikogesellschaft* (1986), and has published several contributions to the discussion of modernity, risk, individualization, and inequality and class.

TIMOTHY RUTZOU studied under Roy Bhaskar, earning his Ph.D. in philosophy with a dissertation on the problem of structure and difference, in which he explored the complex relationship between critical realism and post-structuralism. He works at the intersection of philosophy and sociology, studying questions of ontology and models of causation in social science. He currently holds a teaching position at Western Sydney University.

CHRIS SHILLING is Professor of Sociology at the School of Social Policy, Sociology, and Social Research (SPSSR), University of Kent. He has published extensively in the areas of sociological theory and religion, and is one of the main figures in the development of "body studies." His recent books include *The Body and Social Theory*, 3rd edition (2012), *The Body: A Very Short Introduction* (2016), and with P. A. Mellor, *Sociology of the Sacred* (2014) and *Uncovering Social Life: Critical Perspectives from Sociology* (2018).

LYN SPILLMAN'S research interests focus on economic and political culture, qualitative methods, and cultural theory. Her most recent publication is *What Is Cultural Sociology?* (Polity, 2020). She is Professor of Sociology at the University of Notre Dame.

MICHAEL STRAND is Assistant Professor of Sociology at Brandeis University. His published work has appeared in *Theory and Society, Sociological Theory, History of the Human Sciences, American Journal of Cultural Sociology, Science, Technology & Human Values,* and *Thesis Eleven.* He is currently completing a book manuscript on social justice as a moral belief.

SIMON SUSEN is Professor of Sociology at City University of London. He is Associate Member of the Bauman Institute, and, together with Bryan S. Turner, is editor of the *Journal of Classical Sociology.*

STEPHEN VALOCCHI is Professor of Sociology at Trinity College, Hartford, Connecticut. His scholarly interests include social movements and the sociology of gender and sexuality. He has published research articles on the gay liberation, civil rights, and labor movements, queer theory, and social welfare policy. He is also author (along with Robert Corber) of *Queer Studies: An Interdisciplinary Reader* (2003) and *Social Movements and Activism in the USA* (2009).

PETER WAGNER is Research Professor of Social Sciences at the Catalan Institute for Research and Advanced Societies (ICREA) and at the University of Barcelona, as well as project director at Ural Federal University, Ekaterinburg. His research aims to combine globally oriented historical-comparative sociology with conceptual concerns in social theory and political philosophy. His recent books include: *Collective Action and Political Transformations: The Entangled Experiences in Brazil, South Africa, and Europe* (with Aurea Mota, 2019); *European Modernity: A Global Approach* (with Bo Stråth, 2017); and *Progress: A Reconstruction* (2016).

Preface

Social theory has a discovered and discoverable past and a complex, contested, dynamic, and anxious present. All of these adjectives save the last one – anxious – are reflected in various ways and with differing emphases throughout this handbook. I will say something about "anxious" below, but before doing so will offer a rationale for producing this multi-authored, two-volume overview reflecting the diversity of theory work in sociology and offering a sense of both how far the discipline has come and where it is today.

There is no univocal answer to the question, "What does social theory mean?" Since the institutionalization of sociology in the academy and its development of subfields, theory has found a place in the overall educational structure of the discipline, in a manner akin to the way that methodology has. That is to say, both theory and methodology have been viewed in some fashion as essential to sociological inquiry, and thus relevant to all of the substantive subfields within it. At the same time, it became clear early on that consensus regarding the meaning of theory has proven elusive. As World War II came to an end and the rapid expansion in higher education was about to commence, Robert K. Merton (1945), the protégé of Talcott Parsons, claimed that six types of analysis had come to be described as sociological theory. Over six decades later, Gabriel Abend (2008) identified seven distinct though sometimes overlapping meanings attributed to theory – a figure that Omar Lizardo (2014) thinks is at the lower end of the actual number of different meanings.

One way of understanding why this is the case is to turn to Jeffrey C. Alexander's (1982: 40) early work on theoretical logic in sociology. At the outset of his four-volume study, Alexander offers a diagram of the intellectual space in which theory happens, a capacious space located between two polar boundaries. He identifies one boundary as the nonempirical "metaphysical environment" characterized by an antiscientific relativism. The other boundary is the empirical physical environment, which is where positivism is drawn. Those who identify as theorists occupy the space between, where they can tilt, given their predispositions, either toward increased generality (the metaphysical boundary) or greater specificity (the physical environment boundary). The former move from definitions through concepts, models, and ideological orientations to the presuppositional. The latter move from definitions through classifications, laws, complex and simply propositions, methodological assumptions, to observational statements.

It is at key points along the continuum that the major debates over theory occur. While there are clearly debates at the definitional, conceptual, classificatory, and law-formulation nodes, Alexander points elsewhere to locate where the action – and the heat – can be found. Whereas the types of contestation headed toward specificity can take the form of debates over conflict versus equilibrium or within the realm of the philosophy of science, the types of contestation headed toward greater generality include systems debates, ideological critiques, and debates over order and action.

The inevitable question arising when confronted with this intellectual landscape is of whether this is good or bad for theory. Or is it neither? This question was first confronted in American sociology in the interwar years of the past century, coincidental with the waning of influence of the University of Chicago in the post–Robert Park era and the parallel rise in influence of the Department of Social Relations at Harvard under the direction of Parsons, along with sociology at Columbia University, shaped by Merton and Paul Lazarsfeld. Parsons, concurring with his mentor, Harvard biochemist L. J. Henderson, answered the question by forcefully contending that all sciences required a unified theoretical framework (Turner, 2009: 551–552). To that end, he set out to construct that framework, pursuing a two-step strategy. He had entered a discipline – a field – that had a history dating to the nineteenth century, without however having developed a singular theoretical framework.

The first step called for shaping the sociological canon, identifying who was important and dispensing with others. As *The Structure of Social Action* famously asks at its opening, "Who now reads Spencer?" (Parsons, 1937 [1968]: 3). In Parsons's view, Spencer, a widely read thinker during his lifetime, could be ignored, whereas the discipline could ill afford to ignore Émile Durkheim or Max Weber. The key to Parsons's work was to discover presumably heretofore hidden commonalities linking these two scholars. In the immediate postwar period more and more of their work was translated into English and they became the core of the sociological classics taught in theory courses. It is worth noting, however, that *Structure* included two other scholars also deemed to be important – Alfred Marshall and Vilfredo Pareto – whose subsequent reputations look more like that of Spencer than those of Durkheim and Weber. Despite not being entirely successful in his effort to stamp the canon with his imprimatur, Parsons did manage to convince many in the discipline of the ongoing value of engaging with the classics. I suspect my experience in an undergraduate theory course at the University of Michigan during the late 1960s was rather typical of elite public universities: we read and engaged in exegetical examinations of *Capital*, Volume 1, *Suicide,* and *The Protestant Ethic and the Spirit of Capitalism*. It is worth noting that, at least in Ann Arbor circa 1968, Marx had entered the canon.

The second step was more ambitious, calling as it did for the formulation of that unified theoretical framework the discipline was presumed to be in need of if it was to become a genuine science. With generous funding from the Carnegie Corporation, Parsons and Edward Shils brought together a group of scholars from not only sociology, but also psychology (Gordon W. Allport) and anthropology (Clyde Kluckhohn) in producing *Toward a General Theory of Action* (Parsons and Shils, 1951). And with evangelistic fervor Parsons sought to promote his theory, which as the subtitle made clear, was an attempt to provide the needed "theoretical foundations for the social sciences." In the same year that this book was published, Parsons's major theoretical scheme was published as *The Social System* (1951). He pushed and would continue to push what was pejoratively described as "grand theory" (Mills, 1959: 25–49), clearly dispositionally inclined toward Alexander's metaphysical boundary. His effort to shape the discipline at large was aided by the simultaneous move toward the physical environment boundary at Columbia, reflected in Merton's advocacy of middle-range theory and Lazarfeld's efforts to bring theory and methodology into dialogue.

Parsonian theory did not win over everyone in the discipline. Within his own department, George Homans suspected that Parsons was intent on making *Toward a General Theory of Action* (which in draft form was known colloquially as the "Yellow Book") the "official doctrine of the department," and forcefully spoke out against it. According to Homans, from that moment on the issue was no longer raised in departmental meetings (Homans, 1984: 303). Parsons's correspondence with Alfred Schutz, the Austrian émigré phenomenological sociologist at the New School for Social Research, revealed the gulf between their understandings of the meaning of theory (Grathoff, 1978). Likewise, Herbert Blumer, the major spokesperson for symbolic interactionism, remained unpersuaded by Parsons's entreaties. Located in elite Ivy League institutions, Parsons and his followers were far from successful in getting sociologists in other regions of the country to embrace structural functionalism. Stephen Turner (2014: 42) has pointed out that this was true in the Midwest, including the University of Chicago, where symbolic interactionism was strong. Turner also concluded that it did not gain traction in Southern Sociological Society, the largest of the regionals, writing that, "Many more sociologists were simply indifferent to this elite project."

Nevertheless, Parsons had a profound impact on sociology at the elite level, training a generation of students who would become prominent theorists and powerful disciplinary operatives. And he pursued his theoretical ambition to the end, as reflected in his posthumously published *American Society: A Theory of the Societal Community* (Parsons, 2007). And some prominent sociologists shared a similar vision for the sociological enterprise, as when Lewis Coser (1975: 691), in his American Sociological Association Presidential Address, decided to throw down the gauntlet, beginning his address as follows: "I am perturbed about present developments in American sociology which seem to foster the growth of both narrow, routine, activities and of sect-like, esoteric ruminations [the latter referring to ethnomethodology]."

During the last quarter of the past century grand theoretical ambitions, linked to the belief that a sociological center or mainstream was about to emerge as the discipline matured, gave way to increased fragmentation and persistent talk that in fact Alvin Gouldner's (1970) "coming crisis" had come to pass. What this meant for theory was that it became commonplace to refer to the discipline as a multiple paradigm science (Ritzer, 1975). This would be translated at the level of introductory sociology textbooks by informing the undergraduate audience that sociology was composed of three major theory schools: structural functionalism, conflict, and symbolic interaction. The situation was different among those who identified with and worked in the theory field. For them, two stark choices presented themselves. Either theorists could hunker down in their particular paradigmatic bunker and work to advance and deploy that theory while ignoring competing paradigms, or they could seek ways to overcome fragmentation and facilitate dialogue among competing theory camps. This was made all the more complicated by the internationalization of theory development and the emergence of new modes of theorizing, including but not limited to feminist theory, critical race theory, structuralism and post-structuralism, and postmodernism. These developments introduced new topical foci and, especially with efforts to theorize globalization, theorists were forced to reconsider the often implicit treatment of society as a synonym for nation-state.

The difficulty in pulling off an overcoming of the fractured state of theory was evident in the attempt to promote "metatheory," which George Ritzer (1990: 4) contended could accomplish three objectives. First, it could serve as a "means of attaining a deeper understanding of theory." Second, it could be a "prelude to theory development," and third, it could result in "the creation of an overarching metatheory." From the beginning, the call to metatheory was challenged, leading a frustrated Ritzer (1990: 3) to complain that it had barely been given a chance to develop before it was condemned – and often by leading lights in theory. What was clear was that theorists continued to go about their business. This included engaging with the classics, delving ever deeper into the work of Marx, Weber, and Durkheim, but expanding the range of classic figures deemed worthy of scholarly attention. Indeed, this period constituted something of a golden age in the Anglo-American world for scholarship in the history of sociological theory – with scholars describing their work in terms of intellectual history, the sociology of knowledge, exegetical examinations, hermeneutical inquiries, and the like. In short, they did what Ritzer's first objective of metatheory called for, but without a felt need to give it that label. Likewise with the second objective of metatheory. Parsons served as a model for subsequent theory developers who began with a period of exegetical work as a prelude to theory building. Two examples suffice: Jeffrey Alexander's early work paving the way first for his foray into neo-functionalism and later into cultural sociology, and similarly Anthony Giddens's exegetical preparation for his articulation of structuration theory. These examples are testament to the existence of a sociological theory tradition that theorists are expected not simply to be versed in, but to have a command of, and upon which they build their own theories – in an age more deferential to our predecessors, one might have said "on the shoulders of giants" (Merton, 1965).

But what about the grander objective of constructing an overarching theoretical perspective? To speak of this in the singular rather than the plural implies that the goal is to pursue the agenda of forging a univocal, all-encompassing theoretical scaffolding that could unite everyone who saw their vocation as theory, as well as informing the research agendas in sociology's substantive subfields. Did this mean that the multiple paradigm description advanced by Ritzer was to be overcome, rather than celebrated? Metatheory was framed in such a vague, imprecise way that it was difficult to know what its advocates had in mind. Stephen Turner and Jonathan Turner (1990: 170) summarized the situation near the *fin de siècle* by writing that "metatheorists talk primarily to each other, and so metatheorizing has not succeeded as an integrating effort." Thus, a more accurate assessment of the state of social theory at the cusp of the new century is reflected in Alan Sica's introduction to *What Is Social Theory? The Philosophical Debates* (1998). In this invited collection, he recognized that the diverse visions of theory represented in the book included some he did not find convincing given his own theoretical predilections. But the conclusion he drew from this situation is worth noting:

> However, since theory has always been a contentious business, this is hardly surprising, nor necessarily unfortunate. In fact, one might argue quite the contrary.... each [theory perspective] is argued with passionate regard for its own merit, yet none so dogmatically as to rule out the efficacy of other approaches. It is this happy confusion, this Babel-like quality, that will [prove valuable] for those interested in theory's immediate prospects, particularly as it positions itself with regard to philosophical problems. (Sica, 1998: 12)

An example of what Sica had in mind can be seen in Jeffrey C. Alexander's (1995) collection of essays from the same era in which he assesses contemporary currents of theorizing in terms of, as the subtitle indicates, "relativism, reduction, and the problem of reason." The goal of this project, despite being fiercely argued, was not to erase competing theoretical visions, but rather to serve as a corrective by highlighting the philosophical shortcomings he detected.

If this was the state of the field two decades ago, what has changed in the intervening two decades? For one thing, the deleterious implications of neoliberalism's intrusion into the university system – with its demand for market-driven metrics concerning efficiency, productivity, and real-world payoffs and with an assault on the professional autonomy of the professoriate – are now deeply imbedded in higher education. This is true not only of the United States, but to various degrees in all advanced capitalist societies. Combined with demographic shifts, the growth era in higher education has come to an end. This yields anxiety and uncertainty in both the humanities and in the social sciences most closely associated with the humanities – including sociology. Theory work has been especially hard-hit, as funding agencies and academic administrators look to empirical research that can have what they see as tangible external results – action being valued at the expense of contemplation, researching rather than theorizing.

Secondly, this is occurring along with the graying of the generation of theorists who came of age during the tumultuous decade of the 1960s, shaped by the civil rights movement, the Vietnam War, the woman's movement, and the cultural revolution. This "disobedient generation" (Sica and Turner, 2005) is gradually leaving the academy (though several members are represented herein). A new generation of theorists has emerged and are beginning to assume vaunted positions in theory at elite institutions, and are poised to set the agenda going forward. As an indication of their growing presence, a recent book edited by Claudio Benzecry, Monika Krause, and Isaac Ariail Reed (2017) reflects the generational shift underway, while offering a clear indication that they face the same challenge as their senior colleagues or former colleagues in determining the fundamental meaning(s) of theory.

That they do so is evident in the work of two younger theorists mentioned at the outset, Gabriel Abend and Omar Lizardo. Abend's (2008) effort to get at the meaning(s) of theory meant that he entered the territory previously trod by Merton and Ritzer, confronting the same issues but arriving at an assessment of the situation and a sketch of a path forward that is at odds with both. He takes as a given that the discipline comprises a multiplicity of theories and of ways in which doing theory is conceived. This is as it has always been. Abend is clear that this will not change, nor should it. What concerns him is the risk that theorizing is being and will continue to be done in a balkanized environment where different theory camps do their own thing, unconcerned about what others are doing. Abend wants to facilitate communication by focusing on what he calls the semantics question, one in which different approaches to theory need not be seen as disputes about what is and what isn't theory, but rather should be understood as a consequence of being interested in making sense of different social things. To accomplish this, he proposes the implementation of "semantic therapy," the application of practical reason, and the principle of ontological and epistemological pluralism (Abend, 2008: 192–195). This is not the place to unpack his ideas, merely to note that theorists continue to wrestle with what theory is and what it means to do theory. To date his article has provoked one sympathetic critique, that offered by Peeter Selg (2013: 1), who provides an alternative to what he sees as Abend's "deliberative-democratically oriented vision" of the community of theorists with an agonistic politics view.

The anxiety voiced by theorists, noted at the outset, is evident most clearly in Lizardo's (2014: 1–2) state-of-the-field lecture in which he confronts the changing conditions of theory production, which he frames in generational terms, writing, "If you are a theory person under the age of 45 you currently live and will live in a different theory world than your predecessors." Among the factors working against theory production, Lizardo identifies the deinstitutionalization of the teaching of theory, the devaluation of theory work in terms of career advancement, and a "rudderless heterodoxy, with various claimants for the title of preferred mode of doing theory but very little agreement as to the 'rules' of the theoretical game." If Abend's proposal amounts to a strategy to be conducted within the world of theory, Lizardo suggests that theorists need to rethink how they are connected to the rest of the discipline. Pointing to the role philosophers are playing in the realm of cognitive science, he sees a potential parallel for social theorists. Both are generalists whose capacity for generalization can assist more narrowly focused specialists due to their capacity to "detect, diagnose, and propose incipient solutions to common conceptual and substantive issues across seemingly disparate domains of inquiry" (Lizardo, 2014: 15).

Theorizing is a learned skill, a trained capacity to think like a theorist, the role of which, according to Lizardo (2014: 5), "essentially means engaging in the routine exploitation of the cultured capacities for consuming and producing theory." The acquisition of those cultured capacities requires developing knowledge of the history of social theory and its wide-ranging contemporary articulations. To that end, guides such as this two-volume collection are intended to assist in the process of becoming and being a theorist. In *Literature and Bibliography of the Social Sciences,* a book that is little known today, its editor, Thelma Freides, offered the following succinct rationale for handbooks, writing, "In the effort of the scholarly enterprise to synthesize a body of knowledge ... it is sometimes useful to pause and take stock of the accomplishments of the past and the foreseeable tasks of the future" (Freides, 1973: 1). This is precisely what this project sets out to accomplish. It is intended to reflect on the origins of modern social theory – the canon – and take stock of current developments, which includes locating these developments in terms of their respective relationships to a tradition of theorizing about what Charles Lemert (1997) would call "social things."

This is obviously not the first such stocktaking, and after surveying many previous efforts, it is clear that in a fundamental way the editors of those collections would agree with the general sense of what this enterprise is all about. That being said, not everyone necessarily sees eye to eye with my understanding about what makes the handbook a distinctive type of guide. In the landscape of reference books, one can find three basic types: handbooks (sometimes called something else, such as a "companion"), encyclopedias, and dictionaries. While all would agree that dictionaries are intended to offer relatively short definitions, sometimes the length of those definitions is similar to shorter encyclopedia entries. If there is one rule of thumb for dictionary editors, it is that the entries should be as ecumenical and impartial as possible, and that authorial voice should be muted. While the entries in encyclopedias generally call for more information and greater in-depth treatment, it is my understanding that they adopt a similar ecumenical and impartial style in which authors are more concerned with providing an overview of the topic than entering into sustained critiques and position taking. I note this because it is my sense that handbooks are – or should be – different. Specifically, they differ from encyclopedias in two ways. First, handbook articles should be significantly longer than those in encyclopedias. Second, authors enter into contested terrain where, while they must be as fair to competing sides as possible, they should nonetheless see their task as that of laying out an argument that tips one way or the other in the debates of the moment. In other words, while civility, fairness, comprehensiveness, and so forth are essential – facilitating mutually beneficial dialogue rather than winner-takes-all debate – the authors of handbook essays should be expected to articulate their own positions in terms of the issues they deem relevant to the topic at hand. The contributors whose work is presented in the following pages were encouraged to proceed accordingly and were permitted to write somewhat longer entries than is typical.

Volume I is concerned with the canon, that body of work that had received general – never universal – consensus as having built the foundation upon which contemporary theorizing proceeds, which is the topic of Volume II. Volume I begins with two framing chapters. Johan Heilbron presents an insightfully constructed historical account of the pre-disciplinary period of social theory, while Alan Sica, with his characteristic erudition and panache, explores the meaning of being a classic. This sets the stage for the remainder of Volume I, which begins by devoting six chapters to the three figures for whom there is little dispute about their classical or canonical status: Karl Marx, Émile Durkheim, and Max Weber. For each of these figures, a chapter is devoted to issues pertaining to intellectual biography: Kevin Anderson's chapter on Marx, Peter Kivisto's on Durkheim, and Lawrence Scaff on Weber. These are coupled with explorations of aspects of their subsequent legacies. Peter Beilharz's concise and engaging account examines the contradictory legacy of Marx. Durkheim's legacy differs insofar as in many respects it was not fully acknowledged by those influenced by his thought compared to those of Marx and Weber. This is clear in Simonetta Falasca-Zamponi's account of the ambiguous relationship that members of the Collège de sociologie had with the Durkheimian legacy. Finally, Austin Harrington traces the myriad ways in which Weber's protean thought has resonated with contemporary thinkers within sociology and beyond.

Georg Simmel's status in the canon is less secure than that of the preceding trio. This was evident in the 1930s when Talcott Parsons drafted a chapter on Simmel for *The Structure of Social Action*, but decided not to include it. Vincenzo Mele's chapter on the metropolitization of social life reveals the originality of Simmel's thought, concluding with a brief analysis of his intellectual inheritance as reflected in the Chicago School. Parsons's reputational trajectory differs from Simmel, for once he looked secure in the canon, but subsequently critics would ask, "Who now reads Parsons?" A. Javier Treviño offers a forceful defense of Parsons and a rebuttal of his critics in an attempt to rectify an unfortunate tendency to ignore his ongoing, consequential, and problematic contribution to social theory.

The distinctly American (indeed, Midwestern) theoretical orientation knows as symbolic interactionism is discussed by Lawrence Nichols, tracing its history from George Herbert Mead to the present. Though symbolic interactionists would like to claim his as their own, as Philip Manning makes clear, Erving Goffman was very much a theorist *sui generis* – and it is perhaps for that reason that his dramaturgical sociology has not resulted in a distinctive school founded by acolytes. Sandro Segre and Thomas Szanto responded to the parallel daunting challenges of providing overviews of the capacious theorizing associated respectively with structuralism and phenomenology – doing so in both cases by managing to be both concise and comprehensive. Sandwiched between these two chapters is the more focused topic of Norbert Elias and his approach to theory. Barbara Górnicka and Stephen Mennell provide readers with compelling accounts of Elias's theorizing of civilizing processes, but also explore the impact of his figurational sociology, particularly among British and Dutch sociologists.

The final four chapters rounding out Volume I focus on four prominent theorists. In the case of Pierre Bourdieu, David Swartz offers a broad overview of his work, linking it to the varied ways in which his legacy is shaping currents of contemporary theoretical work in fields such as, but not limited to, culture and education. Anne Rawls sets out to clarify the much misunderstood theoretical project of Harold Garfinkel that he defined as ethnomethodology, illustrating the impact of his earliest research projects on the theoretical work that would follow. Jürgen Habermas's work straddles the divide between social theory and philosophy, and Simon Susen provides readers with an instructive guide to the underlying philosophical grounding of Habermas's distinctive efforts in theory building. Finally, Rob Stones argues on behalf of the structuration theory developed by Anthony Giddens, using the theory to critique Giddens's political engagements on behalf of the "third way."

The twenty-one chapters contained in Volume II are meant to offer a broad overview of various currents of contemporary social theory, focusing both on particular theory schools and on a range of topical foci that preoccupy theorists today. The first two chapters examine respectively rational choice theory and network theory. It is instructive to contrast the two, given that the former tends to elicit polemical debates whereas the latter does not. Karl-Dieter Opp has produced a commendable overview of what rational choice theory purports to be and how it has been productively put to use – yielding light rather than heat. For their part, Mark Pachucki and Ronald Breiger present an instructive guide to the differing network traditions before turning to new developments in both the social and biological sciences.

The following three chapters – on cultural theory, identity, and emotions – focus on topics that have witnessed increased attention, and current theorizing often reflects cross-fertilization between and among them. Michael Strand and Lyn Spillman provide readers with an analysis of the basic components of cultural theory followed by an account that promotes a synthesis of competing perspectives advanced by theorists who have made the "cultural turn." Donileen Loseke and Margarethe Kusenbach wrestle with competing definitions of and approaches to emotions, shifting from there to in-depth analyses of two competing theory types, one stressing the individual and the other emphasizing culture. The two chapters that follow are also interrelated: Shelley Budgeon's on feminist social theory and Patricia Hill Collins on intersectionality. If the focus of Budgeon's chapter is on the sex/gender distinction, a singularly central concern to feminist theorizing, she indicates the ways in which feminist theorists have pushed past that point, as well. One such point is located in the development of what is Collins's topic: the emergence of intersectionality not simply as a definition of nodal points of inequality, but as the basis for a critical social theory.

Modernity has been a central topical focus of sociology from the beginning, but with the passage of time what we mean by the term has become increasingly clouded. Peter Wagner's engagement with the literature is both refreshing and original, pointing to a more tempered and conceptually productive way forward. Addressing the topic of realism – known more familiarly to many as critical realism – Timothy Rutzou's account of how those engaged in promoting this approach conceive theory is sympathetic, while raising questions about what it might mean for doing social theory – and indeed, doing sociology in general. Writing at a moment when various unsavory currents of nationalism have taken hold among authoritarian populists, Sheila Croucher's perceptive assessment of globalization offers a salutary viewpoint. Globalization, she argues, is a given that will not be wished or forced away. Rather, what is needed is a reckoning with the reality of the situation, which is that it is not an unmitigated good, but nor is it altogether bad. Related to the preceding chapter, Kevin Fox Gotham's exploration into time/space comprehensively and engagingly surveys the ways time/space has been conceptualized in social theory over time. If there is one area of sociology that has remained woefully – and inexplicably – undertheorized, it is ecology. Robert J. Antonio and Brett Clark have produced a historically grounded theoretical inquiry into the ecological crisis, rooted in the dynamics of capitalist development that has thus far stymied nation-states and transnational political bodies in their attempts to adequately address the potential shadow of catastrophe that looms over our future.

One consequence of sociology's distancing itself from biology is that the body has not been given its due in social theory. Chris Shilling offers an account of how this came to be in Western intellectual thought, before pointing to recent attempts by theorists to rectify this long-standing tendency, seeking to bring the body back in. Stephen Valocchi's topic is sexualities, locating it in such theoretical approaches as social constructionism, feminist theory, intersectionality, and queer theory.

Christian Joppke is one of the most original theorists of multiculturalism as a mode of incorporation. In this essay, his distinctive views on the subject are on display, complemented by judicious assessments of major theorists whose work diverges from his own. Associated in particular with the work of Anthony Giddens and Ulrich Beck, risk has grown as a crucial topic within social theory. Klaus Rasborg traces the significance of risk as a concept from the distant past through the rise of private insurance – and with it actuarial tables, forecasting, and so forth in efforts to measure risk – before locating it in contemporary efforts to theorize risk. Barbara Misztal addresses the topic of trust. Rather than delving into it in terms of deep history or outside of social theory, she instead examines the various ways differing theoretical traditions have addressed the topic. The divide between sociology and biology emerged over a century ago. Recently various voices in the discipline at large have called for initiating efforts to bridge the divide. Douglas Marshall take up that call in his chapter, which seeks to indicate the potential role of biosociology and evolutionary sociology in forging a sociology that recognizes the biological foundations of human social life. Civil society has had a long history in philosophy and sociology, with a burgeoning interest in it commencing near the end of the twentieth century. Aware of competing definitions of the term, Simon Susen is intent on clarifying what we talk about when we talk about civil society, doing so by tracing the term's use over time before developing the elements to be considered in constructing a critical theory of civil society.

Some sociological subfields have proven to offer distinctively dynamic programs in theorizing compared to other specialty areas. The final two chapters examine two subfields rich in theoretical work – immigration and social movements (one might add that economic sociology is another such subfield). Ewa Morawska, a theorist and historical sociologist of migration, looks at theorizing in immigration studies from both the micro and macro levels before engaging in sustained analyses of assimilation theory and transnationalism. Kevin Gillan's examination of theory development in social movements research is tightly focused on the varied ways social movement theorists have grappled with the temporal dimension inherent in social movements – a crucial consideration since movements have finite temporal parameters in which to accomplish their stated goals.

References

Abend, Gabriel. 2008. "The Meaning of 'Theory'." *Sociological Theory* 26(2): 173–199.

Alexander, Jeffrey C. 1982. *Positivism, Presuppositions, and Current Controversies. Vol. I of Theoretical Logic in Sociology*. Berkeley, CA: University of California Press.

    1995. *Fin de Siècle Social Theory: Relativism, Reduction, and the Problem of Reason*. London: Verso.

Benzecry, Claudio E, Monika Krause, and Isaac Ariail Reed (eds). 2017. *Social Theory Now*. Chicago, IL: University of Chicago Press.

Coser, Lewis. 1975. "Presidential Address: Two Methods in Search of a Substance." *American Sociological Review* 40(6): 691–700.

Freides, Thelma. 1973. *Literature and Bibliography of the Social Sciences*. Hoboken, NJ: Wiley & Sons.

Gouldner, Alvin W. 1970. *The Coming Crisis of Western Sociology*. New York: Equinox Books.

Grathoff, Richard (ed.). 1978. *The Theory of Social Action: The Correspondence of Alfred Schutz and Talcott Parsons*. Bloomington, IN: Indiana University Press.

Homans, George. 1984. *Coming to My Senses: The Autobiography of a Sociologist*. New Brunswick, NJ: Transaction Books.

Lemert, Charles. 1997. *Social Things: An Introduction to the Sociological Life*. Lanham, MD: Rowman & Littlefield.

Lizardo, Omar. 2014. "The End of Theorists: The Relevance, Opportunities, and Pitfalls of Theorizing in Sociology Today." Essay drawn from the Lewis Coser Memorial Lecture presented on August 17 at the American Sociological Association annual meeting in San Francisco. Open Book 010.

Merton, Robert K. 1945. "Sociological Theory," *American Journal of Sociology* 50(6): 462–473.

    1965. *On the Shoulders of Giants: A Shandean Postscript*. New York: The Free Press.

Mills, C. Wright. 1959. *The Sociological Imagination*. New York: Oxford University Press.

Parsons, Talcott. 1937 [1968]. *The Structure of Social Action*, Vols. 1 and 2. New York: The Free Press.

    1951. *The Social System*. New York: The Free Press.

    2007. *American Society: A Theory of the Societal Community*. Ed. and introduction by Giuseppe Sciortino. Boulder, CO: Paradigm Publishers.

Parsons, Talcott and Edward A. Shils (eds.). 1951. *Toward a General Theory of Action*. New York: Harper & Row.

Ritzer, George. 1975. *Sociology: A Multiple Paradigm Science*. Boston, MA: Allyn & Bacon.

    1990. "Metatheorizing in Sociology." *Sociological Forum* 5(1): 3–15.

Selg, Peeter. 2013. "The Politics of Theory and the Constitution of Meaning." *Sociological Theory* 31(1): 1–23.

Sica, Alan. 1998. "Introduction: Philosophy's Tutelage of Social Theory: 'A Parody of Profundity'?" In Alan Sica (ed.), *What Is Social Theory? The Philosophical Debates* (pp. 1–21). Malden, MA: Blackwell.

Sica, Alan and Stephen Turner (eds.). 2005. *The Disobedient Generation: Social Theorists in the Sixties*. Chicago, IL: University of Chicago Press.

Turner, Stephen. 2009. "The Future of Social Theory." In Bryan S. Turner (ed.), *The New Blackwell Companion to Social Theory* (pp. 551–556). Malden, MA: Wiley-Blackwell.

2014. *American Sociology: From Pre-Disciplinary to Post-Normal*. Basingstoke, UK: Palgrave Macmillan.

Turner, Stephen Park, and Jonathan H. Turner. 1990. *The Impossible Science: An Institutional Analysis of American Sociology*. Newbury Park, CA: Sage Publications.

1 Rational Choice Theory and Methodological Individualism

Karl-Dieter Opp

Introduction

This article is an introduction to, and a review and discussion of rational choice *theory* (RCT), also called the theory of rational action or the economic model of man, and the rational choice *approach* (RCA). RCT explains the behavior of individual actors. It is applied to explain *macro* phenomena (such as economic growth or revolutions), a major goal of the social sciences. The RCA, also called structural or methodological individualism, claims that RCT can and should be applied to explain macro phenomena. After introducing and reviewing RCT and the RCA, their strength and weaknesses and possible alternatives are analyzed.

What Is Rational Choice Theory About? The Basic Version

Critics of RCT usually attack "the" theory of rational action. This is highly problematic because there are several versions of RCT, and weaknesses of one version may not (and do not, as will be seen) hold for other versions. In this section we will present what one may call the core or basic version of RCT, that is, propositions that are shared by all versions.[1]

In this article, RCT is conceived as an empirical theory that addresses the causes of behavior. It must be sharply distinguished from *revealed-preference theory*, in which utility is not independently defined of choices. The theory gives up "any pretension to be offering a causal explanation of . . . choice behavior in favor of an account that is merely a description of the choice behavior of someone who chooses consistently. Our reward is that we end up with a theory that is hard to criticize because it has little substantive content" (Binmore, 2009: 20). In the present article this kind of theory is sharply rejected: the goal is to discuss a falsifiable theory (i.e. a theory that can be criticized), that has a high explanatory power and that can be applied to real-life phenomena.

RCT explains behavior (or, equivalently, action) that is not part of our biological endowment (such as the knee reflex). Voting, committing a crime, marrying, or

* I am grateful to Ivan Ermakoff (University of Wisconsin-Madison), Yuan Hsiao (University of Washington), and Peter Kivisto (Augustana College) for valuable comments on a former version of the article.

buying and selling are examples. "Behavior" often encompasses also "inner" actions such as thinking, categorizing objects, or processing information.

The theory consists of three propositions. The first – the *preference proposition* – posits that preferences or, equivalently, goals or motives determine behavior. Whether goals can be achieved depends on behavioral *constraints* or *opportunities* – this is the second proposition. Money is a constraint or opportunity for attaining many goals. A prison sentence blocks the realization of many goals. The third proposition claims that actors *maximize their utility*. This means that among the available options, the one with the highest utility is chosen.

It is important to distinguish between *egoism* or, equivalently *selfishness*, and *self-interest*. Egoism means that an individual is only interested in his or her own welfare; self-interest refers to utility maximization. Thus, Mother Teresa is not egoistic but altruistic (i.e. mainly interested in the welfare of others), but self-interested because she maximizes her own utility.

Preferences and constraints have *multiplicative effects*. This means that the effects of preferences depend on the extent to which constraints exist, and vice versa. A goal can only be realized if there are opportunities, and opportunities are seized only if there is some relevant goal.

Let us look at some *implications* of the theory: (1) The theory is *interdisciplinary*. Behavior is the subject of all social sciences such as economics, political science, and sociology. (2) RCT is *neither purely sociological nor purely psychological*. It neither focuses on social structures (constraints) nor on goals. (3) RCT implies that *behavior can be deliberate or spontaneous*. "Spontaneous" means that there is no deliberation involved. Before buying a computer most individuals will probably think about which model is best suited for their needs. But everyday goods are bought without deliberating (i.e. spontaneously): at an earlier time, after comparing different brands (i.e. after deliberating), a decision was made always to buy the same product and no longer think about it. Thus, a *habit* has been formed. This is only changed if the situation changes, for example if the brand deteriorates in quality.

Extending and Clarifying the Basic Version: The Wide and the Narrow Version of Rational Choice Theory

The version described in the previous section leaves several questions unanswered. For example, are internalized norms, that is the intrinsic motivation to conform to norms, among the preferences? Is altruism (i.e. worrying about the welfare of others) a possible preference? Different versions of RCT answer these questions differently.

Two versions of RCT are distinguished: a *narrow* and a *wide* version. Each version consists of assumptions that are not specified in the basic version. The narrow version resembles neoclassical economics, which focuses on egoistic preferences, full information, and "objective" utility maximization, that is, from the perspective of an informed observer. In a wide version such assumptions are not made.[2] The different assumptions are summarized in Table 1.1.

Table 1.1 *Assumptions of the wide and narrow versions of Rational Choice Theory*

Assumptions of the Narrow Version	Assumptions of the Wide Version
1a. Only egoistic preferences and preferences for material goods explain behavior.	1b. All kinds of preferences (including altruism) may be explanatory factors.
2a. Internalized norms are no determinants of behavior.	2b. Internalized norms may influence behavior.
3a. Only tangible or material constraints influence behavior.	3b. All kinds of constraints may influence behavior.
4a. Subjects have correct beliefs, at least in the long run.	4b. Subjects may, but need not, have correct beliefs.
5a. Objective constraints determine behavior.	5b. Perceived as well as objective constraints determine behavior.
6a. Only constraints explain behavior.	6b. Constraints and/or preferences may explain behavior.
7a. Individuals maximize their behavior, from the view of an informed observer.	7b. Individuals optimize or satisfice: They do what they *believe* is best for them.

Based on Opp (1999: 174)

An increasing number of scholars applying RCT use a wide version, albeit without mentioning this. An early advocate from *economics* is Herbert Simon with his idea of "satisficing" (i.e. finding satisfactory and not necessarily optimal solutions, e.g. Simon, 1997). Other economists broaden the range of application of the narrow economic model to explore, for instance, identity (Akerlof and Kranton, 2000), the impact of intrinsic and extrinsic motivation (Frey, 1997), the arts (Frey, 2003), and the kinds of incentives that explain human behavior (Fehr and Falk, 2002). *Game theorists* have included fairness norms in their explanations of behavior in ultimatum games. *Behavioral economics* (e.g. Thaler, 2015; Thaler and Sunstein, 2009), together with the work of D. Kahneman and A. Tversky, apply a wide version too. This also holds for a recent book from *social psychology*, *Why People Cooperate: The Role of Social Motivations*, which never refers to this fact (Tyler, 2013). Many *sociologists* use the wide version, again often implicitly. Examples include, beside work by the author of this article (Opp, 1999), Abell (2000), Boudon (1996, see the discussion in Opp, 2014), Coleman (1990), Diekmann (Diekmann et al., 2014), Ermakoff (2017), Esser (Esser and Kroneberg, 2015), Goldthorpe (1998), Kiser and Hechter (Kiser and Hechter, 1998), Hedström (2005, see the controversy: Opp, 2013a, 2013b; Manzo, 2013; Ylikoski, 2013), Homans (1974), and Lindenberg (2015). Although these and other authors apply a wide version, they are not a homogeneous group. They often express diverging views with regard to various issues connected with RCT.

Egoism, Altruism, and Internalized Norms

Let us now turn to the differences between the two versions. The narrow version assumes egoistic (or selfish) preferences (i.e. consideration only of one's own welfare); the focus is on material constraints such as money, and internalized norms, that is, felt obligations to behave in certain ways, are excluded (assumptions 1 and 2 of Table 1.1).

The wide version does not claim that egoistic preferences or preferences for material objects are entirely irrelevant. Because the wide version includes any preferences as possible explanatory factors, those preferences must be taken into account in explaining behavior. It may then turn out that they are irrelevant. Thus, the wide version does not contradict the narrow version. On the contrary, the *narrow version is a special case of the wide version.*

How do we know which preferences are relevant for explaining a certain behavior? The answer is that *it must be determined empirically which preferences (and constraints) influence a behavior.* For example, whether market transactions are influenced by norms (such as to fulfill contracts) must be measured by applying the existing methods of empirical research. Without measuring preferences, the application of RCT (the narrow as well as the wide version) becomes ad hoc. We will return to this issue later when the measurement problem is analyzed.

Reality and Beliefs: The Constraints

Assumption 3 addresses constraints or, equivalently, behavioral opportunities in return for realizing goals. Note that the kinds of preferences determine the kinds of constraints for a behavior. For example, the expected or real approval of others is a behavioral opportunity only for those who have a preference for approval.

The cognitive representation of constraints takes the form of beliefs. Proponents of the narrow version assume that beliefs adapt to reality because having false beliefs is costly. However, this is not always the case. If the likelihood of being arrested for a crime is overestimated and a person refrains from committing crimes, the false belief will probably not change. The wide version (assumption 4B) assumes that beliefs may be biased in the short as well as in the long run. These beliefs – even if they are wrong – are what influence behavior in the first place and not the real constraints (assumption 5b).

Economists in particular explain changing behavior as caused by changing constraints, and disregard preferences (assumption 6a). So the trend to smaller cars is often explained by a change in the price of gasoline. But in principle, as the wide version suggests, preferences could be relevant as well. The trend toward smaller cars may also be due to an increasing norm for environmentally friendly behavior. Again, whether this is the case must be determined empirically.

Subjective Utility Maximization

According to the narrow version, people do what is objectively best for them, from the viewpoint of an informed observer. The wide version assumes that *people do what they believe is best for them* (assumption 7). This may, but need not, coincide with the objectively best behavior. People may thus make mistakes.

Some Conceptual Clarifications: Costs, Benefits, and Rationality

RCT is often characterized as claiming that *costs* and *benefits* determine behavior. These terms have different meanings: (1) They refer to events that are valued by actors more or less positively. Punishment or approval from peers thus normally take the form of costs or benefits respectively. (2) Costs (or, equivalently, opportunity costs) refer to the utility forgone when an action is performed. The expression "opportunity benefits" is not used. (3) Costs often mean constraints, and benefits refer to behavioral opportunities. The term *incentives* denotes costs as well as benefits.

A frequent critique of RCT is that it assumes *rational* behavior. The critique argues that people are not rational. Because the rationality concept is often vague or has different meanings (see the discussion in Opp, 2017) this critique can only be evaluated if it is known what "rational" means. As a little exercise, the reader might judge whether the following statements are correct (the answers follow after the statements).

1. RCT's claim that people are *rational* is wrong because behavior is often spontaneous, that is, no consequences are considered.
2. RCT's claim that people are *rational* is wrong because action often does not yield the rewards people expect.
3. RCT's claim that people are *rational* is wrong because their behavior does often not yield the best possible outcome.

Each statement implicitly assumes a certain definition of "rational" and that RCT claims that people behave in a "rational" manner according to this definition. In statement 1 it is contended that "rational" in RCT means deliberate behavior, *and* it is held that RCT claims that people behave deliberately. However, RCT neither defines "rational" in this way nor claims that people only behave deliberately.

In statement 2, "rational" means that behavior should yield the expected reward, and in statement 3 "rational" refers to a behavior that is objectively utility maximizing. Again, RCT does not contain any of these definitions, and neither does it claim either that people behave in a "rational" manner according to these definitions.

In the previous presentation of RCT "rational" was not used, and there is no need to employ this term. Nonetheless, numerous authors define the concept, but no author provides detailed reasons for their definitions (see Opp, 2017).

In view of this fact it is very awkward that the denotation of RCT contains the word "rational." It is not clear how this label developed. To assign some meaning to it one might argue that "rational" means in some vague sense "reasonable" behavior. But "RCT" is generally accepted and a plea for changing it does not seem convincing. Neither are there any other terms that do not lead to misunderstandings. For example, one could speak of the "utilitarian" approach, but this term is associated with the philosophical school of utilitarianism.

Varieties of the Narrow and Wide Version

There are different varieties of RCT. Each consists of the basic assumptions described before, but each formulates them in different ways. In this section, two of these varieties will be presented.

Value Expectancy Theory (VET)

This well-known theory in social psychology is formally equivalent to "expected utility theory" or SEU theory (SEU for "subjective expected utility"). VET (also called expectancy-value theory; see, e.g., Fishbein and Ajzen, 2010: 96–128; for its history see Stigler, 1950a, 1950b) assumes that before any action is performed the actor perceives behavioral alternatives. Which action is chosen depends on the perceived behavioral *consequences* or outcomes O, their *subjective probabilities* p and their *utilities* U. The overall (or net) utility of an action a_i, its SEU, is defined as

$$SEU(a_i) = \sum_{j=1}^{N} p_{ij}U(O_j)$$

Thus, the SEU of an action i depends on the number j of outcomes O, their utility U, and the subjective probabilities of each outcome for a given action (p_{ij}). The probabilities depend on the kind of behavior chosen, whereas the utilities are general valuations of objects. The p's and U's stand in a multiplicative relationship: the impact of one of the variables depends on the values of the other variable and vice versa. For example, if p=0 the utility of the respective consequence has no effect on the behavior.

The previous equation is a *definition* of the concept "SEU." The *theory* asserts: if the SEU of a behavior a_i is greater than the SEU of any other behavior a_k, then a_i is chosen:

SEU(a_i) > SEU(a_k) ➔ a_i

Let us look at some implications of VET.

1. When we compare VET with the general (narrow or wide) version we see that VET is more informative: it states explicitly that p's and U's have multiplicative effects and that perceived behavioral options are important. The hypothesis that the action with the highest SEU is chosen refers to subjective utility maximization. The p's are the perceived constraints – the beliefs – and the U's the costs or benefits.
2. In social psychology VET is used as a wide version: p's and U's are subjective, and, thus, individuals do what is best from their perspective. Any kind of utility may be included, such as internalized norms or altruism. A behavior may have the consequence of violating a norm or affect the welfare of others. These consequences have a certain p and U.
3. The assumption that perceptions matter implies that an actor may drastically simplify situations and use various heuristic rules. A person who might take a vacation will not scrutinize all possible options. He or she might first decide to go on a skiing

vacation. The next relevant aspect may be distance to place of residence. This *elimination by aspects* is a common procedure to save (cognitive) costs and determines which consequences are considered and which decisions are made.

4. What the behavioral options, consequences, and values of p and U in specific situations are must be determined empirically. This is obvious for social psychologists, and there is no discussion of circularity or tautology, as in economics and sociology.

5. VET does not hold that individuals always deliberate, that is, weigh the advantages and disadvantages (p's and U's). Certain behaviors may have proved best in certain situations, have been stored in the memory, and then are activated in the respective situations and spontaneously performed.

6. The social environment is part of VET. Individuals may "care" more or less what the consequences of their behavior are for others. Furthermore, others' behavior (such as sanctioning) may be a behavioral consequence.

Prospect Theory

Prospect theory (PT, see Kahneman and Tversky, 1979)[3] is seen as an alternative to expected utility (EU) theory, as it was formulated by von Neumann and Morgenstern in 1944 and by Bernoulli in 1738. In presenting PT, proponents always attack EU theory; they never discuss VET. In this section, PT will be briefly presented and compared with VET.

PT and VET hold that behavior depends on its consequences, their utilities and probabilities, that the p's and U's are subjective, and that there is subjective utility maximization. Differences lie in the kinds of effects of utilities and probabilities.

PT claims that individuals consider *reference points* and thus *changes* of utilities and not the status quo. A reference point could be "the outcome that you expect, or perhaps the outcome to which you feel entitled" (Kahneman, 2011: 282). For example, the additional (marginal) utility of an income increase of $100 may be small when it is compared to the status quo; it may be negative if it is compared to the much higher increase of some reference group.

The assumption of reference points is not inconsistent with VET. Utilities are measured empirically, and actors may assign utilities in any way. The example of the previous paragraph is completely compatible with VET.

Another assumption of PT is that utilities differ for *gains and losses*. The "value function" (Kahneman and Tversky, 1979: 279) illustrates this (see Figure 1.1). It has the following properties: Values (or utilities) are defined as deviations from a reference point; the function is S-shaped, that is, concave for gains and convex for losses; and it is steeper for losses than for gains – it is steepest at the reference point.

In the right part of the figure, for gains, there is diminishing marginal utility. In contrast, for losses, a small loss decreases utility to a higher extent than a large loss – compare a loss of 100 and of 200.

The S-shaped curve implies different *attitudes toward risk* for gains and losses. The concave utility curve (right curve) implies that people are *risk averse*, i.e. the option with the certain outcome is preferred. For example, let students be presented with the following options (Kahneman, 2011: 279): (A) Get $900 for sure (i.e. with probability 1) or (B) a 90 per cent chance of getting $1000 (i.e. with probability .9). The expected values E are: (A) E_A=1 · 900 = *900*; (B) E_B=.9 · 1000 = *900*. Although both expected values are equal, most respondents choose the certain option. Thus, for gains PT hypothesizes that people are risk averse.

People are *risk seeking* when they prefer the risky option. For example, let there be two options (Kahneman, 2011: 279): (A) Lose $900 for sure or (B) a 90% chance of losing $1000. Again, both expected values are 900. But this time most respondents choose the risky option. In general, PT claims that for losses, people are risk seeking.

These results do not contradict VET, because this theory does not specify a utility function. Such functions can be empirically ascertained and so specify utilities and subjective probabilities.

VET consists of utilities and subjective probabilities. The findings of the previous examples are irrelevant for VET: they hold for monetary values and objective probabilities (presented in the experiment). They may differ from subjective values. For example, an "optimistic" person presented with a probability of .9 for a gain could consider this to be 1 if that person always thinks he or she will win.

Because of restrictions of space it is not possible to analyze the numerous other findings in the heuristics and biases research program and their relationship to VET. Such an analysis would be an important agenda for future research to follow. The result could be an integration of two theories that have so far been never compared systematically. At this point our conjecture is that PT's assumptions can be used as a heuristic reservoir for formulating assumptions about utilities and probabilities when VET is empirically applied.

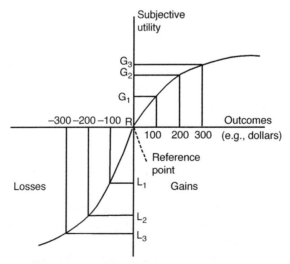

Figure 1.1 *Attitudes toward risk for gains and losses in prospect theory*
Based on: Kahneman (2011: 283)

It might be argued that VET should be replaced by PT. This is not to be recommended, for several reasons: (1) VET has been well confirmed in numerous natural situations (as for the explanation of protest, see Opp, 1986). (2) It is very difficult to apply PT in order to explain real-life phenomena such as voting, crime, punishment, collective action, cooperation, revolutions, marriage, exchange, or migration. Research that supports PT refers to gambling or lotteries. It is difficult to see which natural situations these results can be applied to (Barberis, 2013: 178–180). One problem is, for example, that "it is often unclear how to define precisely what a gain or loss is" (Barberis, 2013: 178). However, there are now many applications of PT in economics (see the review by Barberis, 2013) so that one might be optimistic about new possibilities in terms of applying the theory to real-world phenomena. Nonetheless, at this point it is not recommendable to replace VET.

Game Theory

Game theory models interactions between at least two actors. The question is which behavior by the actors has which "payoffs" (i.e. costs and benefits), given the behavior of other actors, and how actors jointly act (for an introduction see, e.g., Tadelis, 2013). We will illustrate game theory with the standard example: the prisoner's dilemma (PD).

Assume that two male prisoners are in separate cells. They cannot communicate, are selfish, have no internalized norms, and there is no possibility of external sanctioning. The attorney assumes they have committed a crime but he cannot prove it. He tells the prisoners that each has two options: to confess or not to confess. If both do not confess the attorney will charge them with some minor crime and each will receive 1 year in prison. If they both confess they get less than the most severe sentence, namely 5 years each. If one confesses and the other does not, the confessor will be free and the latter will be sentenced to 10 years in prison.

The reader might think for a moment how he or she would decide: confess or not confess? Take the perspective of A and let A assume B does not confess. "Confess" is best for A because then he will be free. If B confesses, it is best for A to confess as

Table 1.2 *Cooperation and defection in the prisoner's dilemma**

Behavioral Alternatives of Prisoner A	Behavioral Alternatives of Prisoner B	
	Not Confess (= Cooperate)	Confess (= Defect)
Not Confess (= Cooperate)	1 year in prison / 1 year in prison **1, 1**	10 years in prison / Free **−2, 2**
Confess (= Defect)	Free / 10 years in prison **2, −2**	5 years in prison / 5 years in prison **−1, −1**

*First entry in each cell is the payoff for A, second entry the payoff for B.

well, because he will serve a sentence of 5 years (instead of 10 years if he does not confess). Thus, whatever B does, it is best for A to confess. This holds for B as well. The "dilemma" is that not confessing would be better for both (1 year in prison each), but the prisoners will choose to confess (5 years in prison each) because this maximizes their utility. Thus, individual utility maximizing does not always lead to the best results for all actors.

Note that the example describes a certain situation – no communication etc. – and certain properties of the individuals (selfishness etc.). In terms of RCT, the individuals have certain behavioral options and preferences, and are subject to constraints (the situation). Assuming subjective utility maximization, the "outcome" of this situation is that both prisoners confess.

The situation of the prisoners can be described in a general way. The years in prison are transformed to (ordinal) payoffs: a low sentence has a relatively high payoff. The order of the payoffs for A runs from the lower-left cell (payoff 2) to the upper-left cell (payoff 1), to the lower-right cell (payoff −1), to the upper-right cell (payoff −2). The payoffs for B (second number in each cell) are highest in the upper-right cell. The alternative with the preferred payoff could be called "cooperation," whereas the payoff with the actually chosen payoff, "defection." Intuitively, "cooperation" yields the best result for both players, whereas "defection" is worse.

There are numerous natural situations that resemble this payoff structure. One is environmental pollution. Let "cooperation" mean not to pollute and "defection" to pollute. Assume now that A (a certain actor) assumes that the other members of the group (the B's) behave in an environmentally friendly manner. A would be best off polluting: the payoff is 2 instead of 1. If others defect ("confess"), A would get −2 when cooperation is chosen, otherwise (for defecting) A would get −1, which is higher. Again, pollution is the preferred behavior.

The assumptions of the PD are very restrictive. For example, there can be no threat of external sanctions. This would lower the payoff for defecting. Let the decrease be −5. For A, defecting would then have payoffs of −3 (2–5) and −6 (−1–5). Let this hold for B as well. Cooperation would then have the highest payoff and the PD would disappear. Similarly, strong altruistic motivations or an internalized norm to cooperate would make cooperation more beneficial.

This short outline illustrates the following points. Game theory is an application of RCT to a specific kind of situations. Inclusion of norms, altruism, and so on indicates that a wide RCT version could be used.

Agent-Based Modeling and Computer Simulation

Agent-based modeling refers to computer simulations of complex social processes with actors (agents) as basic units (e.g. Axelrod and Tesfatsion, 2016). These processes may be so complex that game theory and mathematical tools are not applicable. RCT can (but need not) guide the formulation of assumptions that explain the behavior of actors.

This is illustrated with Schelling's segregation model (Schelling, 1971). The question was why, in the United States, black people and white people live in different areas. This pattern originates spontaneously due to interactions and goals of the actors. For example, let 100 black people and 100 white people be distributed by chance in a space resembling a chessboard, each person on one square. Each person has the preference that a certain percentage of people with the same color live next to him or her. If this percentage is not reached, people move to the nearest place where this condition is fulfilled. In this case people are satisfied (i.e. they maximize their utility). There is thus an initial distribution of preferences and of constraints. The latter refer to the number and location of other people. Computer simulation then explores to what extent which degree of segregation (i.e. areas where blacks or whites concentrate) occurs under which conditions. For example, is the size of the group, the initial distribution, or the preferred percentage of similar neighbors relevant? The reader might explore these questions by downloading the computer program *Netlogo*.[4] After activating the program go to "File," then to "Models Library," to "Social Science," to "Segregation." Now you may insert different values for "number" (size of the group) and "%-similar-wanted." After choosing "your" values click on "setup" and then on "go." The program shows the resulting social processes.

This little exercise shows why agent-based modeling is useful for exploring complex social processes, based on rational choice (RC) assumptions. Modeling of these processes is a form of *thought experiment* ("Gedankenexperiment"). Simulations are thus *deductive arguments* answering the question of what follows from a set of assumptions, including the distribution of RC variables (preferences and constraints). Such simulations cannot replace empirical tests but are a first step in examining the plausibility of complex models.

Applying Rational Choice Theory to Explain Macro Phenomena: The Research Program of Methodological Individualism

So far RC *theory* has been addressed, which refers to propositions explaining individual behavior. RC theorists pursue a *research program*, namely to apply RCT in order to explain macro phenomena (such as the rise and decline of nations) or to explain relationships between macro phenomena (such as why we do not find central economic planning in democracies). This program is called the *RC approach*, structural individualism, the individualistic research program, or methodological individualism. It is thus important to distinguish between RC *theory* and the RC *approach*.

The procedure and problems of explaining macro phenomena can be illustrated with the widely quoted example by J. S. Coleman (1990: 8). He asks why the Protestant ethic was a cause for the advent of capitalism, as Max Weber claimed. "Protestantism" and "capitalism" are properties of collectives and not of individual actors. Figure 1.2 illustrates a micro-macro explanation. This explanation consists of assuming that the macro phenomena can be explained by the behavior (or properties)

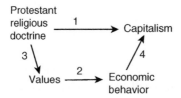

Figure 1.2 *The basic micro-macro model: The standard example*
See Coleman (1990: 8)

of individual actors. For example, the actions and interactions of numerous individual actors bring about a capitalist order (see relationship 4): members of parliaments make laws that allow market transactions and secure property rights; individuals who are motivated to earn an income set up firms and try to sell their products. These and other behaviors make up what is called "capitalism." This term thus refers to a complex of properties of individuals.

When individuals are the causal agents of the origins of capitalism, and when Protestantism is a cause of capitalism, then Protestantism should affect individual properties such as values which lead to activities that brought about a capitalist order. Max Weber argued that salvation was uncertain. This led to psychic tensions (which, it might be added, were costly). These tensions generated the belief that wealth accumulation was a signal of salvation. This is an empirical effect of Protestantism on individual values (relationship 3 of Figure 1.2). These values, in turn, have an empirical effect on the various activities of individuals (relationship 2) that bring about capitalism (relationship 4).

The *micro-macro model* in Figure 1.2 shows *in principle* how macro phenomena can be explained by considering their relationships to the "heart and minds" of individual actors. Although the scheme is simplified, more complicated explanations have the same structure.[5] There are several problems with this micro-macro model.

Relationship 1: The macro proposition. Figure 1.2 depicts this as a causal relationship. However, the macro relationship is completely explained by processes via the micro level: Protestantism leads to capitalism *because* it creates certain values, and so on. Protestantism thus has no additional causal effect on capitalism; its causal effects run via the micro level. Thus, the macro relationship is a correlation. If the micro-macro model is not specified it may *seem* that relationship 1 is causal: the *indirect* effects of Protestantism on capitalism seem to be direct causal effects.

Relationship 2: The micro relationship. In the RCA, this is RCT. The assumption is that macro phenomena affect incentives (costs and benefits) of actors that, in turn, lead to a behavior that aggregates to a macro phenomenon. However, the micro theory need not be RCT. Methodological individualism is not committed to RCT.

Relationship 3: The macro-to-micro relationship. As the example illustrates, this may be an *empirical* relationship. It may be a law (or set of laws), but also a singular causal relationship (that holds only for certain times and places).

Relationship 3 may also be *analytical* (i.e. logically true). Assume it holds: The larger a group, the less likely is the provision of public goods, that is, the realization of the common goals of the group members (Olson, 1965). In a large group an individual member has only a negligible influence on the realization of the common goals. This is the relationship of group size and individual influence (relationship 3 of Figure 1.2). "Influence" may be defined as 1 divided by the size of a group. In a group of 2 the influence of an individual is ½, in a group of 1000 it is 1/1000. In this case the relationship of group size and influence is analytical and not empirically: We can determine the relationship without any empirical research. If the micro variable is *perceived* influence, there is a causal effect: Given the size of a group, people may differ in regard to the extent to which they think they are influential.

Relationship 4: The micro-to-macro relationship. In the simplest case, this is an analytical aggregation. For example, the crime rate (macro property) is constructed by adding individual crimes, divided by the size of the group the individual is a member of. An empirical relationship would exist where there is individual sanctioning (micro property) which *leads* to a social norm (a macro property). Here sanctioning has the empirical effect that people exposed to sanctioning accept a norm not to pollute.

We do not find micro-macro modeling only in the work of rational choice proponents. Social scientists in general are often not satisfied with just stating macro propositions. One wants to know why such a relationship holds. Nobody is satisfied, for example, with simply stating that capitalism came about after Protestantism. The interesting question is why Protestantism led to capitalism. The answer is tantamount to specifying a micro-macro model.

What Is Wrong and What Is Right with Rational Choice Theory?

As is the case of every theory in the social sciences, RCT is heavily criticized. In this section those objections are discussed that seem particularly problematic for RCT. In contrast to the approach of most critics, the major question we address is whether objections hold for the wide version.

Rational Choice Explanations as Tautologies and Circular Explanations

Perhaps the most frequent objection is that RCT is tautological or circular. In formal logic a *tautology* (or an analytically true statement) exists if the truth of a statement can be determined by analyzing the meaning of its term. Take "all bachelors are unmarried"; "bachelor" means "an unmarried person," so the sentence is equivalent to "all unmarried persons are unmarried." This is certainly true, and the truth can be determined by analyzing the meanings of the terms. The sentence is thus a tautology or an analytically true sentence.

If RCT is a tautology, one could determine its truth just by analyzing the meaning of its terms. VET claims that behavior is determined by utilities, probabilities, and utility maximization. "Behavior" on the one hand and "utilities" on the other have clearly different meanings. Thus, there is no way to determine the truth of VET – and of RCT in general – by analyzing the meaning of its terms. An indicator for the non-tautological character of RCT is that many critics claim that it is falsified. But a tautology cannot, by definition, be wrong.

Critics who assert RCT is tautological often mean that it is *circular*. A statement is circular if the existence of the dependent variable is seen as evidence for the existence of the independent variables. Let somebody assert: "Person A's altruism led him to spend money." Another person could ask: "How do you know that A's generosity was caused by altruism?" The answer could be: "Don't you see that A spent money?" Such an argument could also be made for RC explanations. From a given behavior it could be "inferred" that its benefits were higher than its costs. It is obvious that circular arguments are against the canons of science. There is no question that the independent and dependent variables must be measured independently of each other. There is thus no circularity in RCT.

The Testability of the Theory

The vast majority of empirical research that tests RC hypotheses clearly shows that RCT is testable. However, there is one argument that seems to *immunize* RCT against falsification. Many different incentives may cause a phenomenon such as crime. Now assume that hypotheses claiming that certain incentives caused a behavior are falsified so that no incentives are found that explain crime. The researcher could argue that this is not a falsification because other incentives might have caused the behavior. If such arguments are accepted, RCT could never be falsified. The rule thus must be that a falsification of hypotheses derived from RCT is a falsification of RCT. However, if new research finds relevant incentives, the previous research cannot be counted as a falsification. Thus, finding no incentives that could explain a behavior is a possible *falsification* of RCT.

Measurement Issues: An Argument for the Narrow Version?

The narrow version of RCT, it could be argued, avoids measuring elusive subjective phenomena such as norms, altruism, or beliefs. Therefore, it is assumed that individuals have egoistic preferences, that beliefs reflect reality, and that people maximize their objective utility. All this can be ascertained in a reliable way.

This argument has several serious flaws:
1. As has been said before, there is a vast literature on the methods of empirical research that provide various reliable techniques and measurement instruments. They detect lying and social desirability and measure attitudes, altruism, norms, and beliefs. Obviously, there are situations where measurement is difficult or ethically problematic, such as formal interviews with victims of rape or small children. But a general claim that subjective phenomena cannot reliably be measured is clearly not tenable.
2. But assume that subjective phenomena cannot be measured. This would definitely not be an argument for the narrow version. Variables should only be eliminated

from a theory when they are theoretically irrelevant. If theoretically important variables cannot be measured, one should wait until measurement instruments are developed.

3. If subjective phenomena cannot be measured, this definitely does not provide an argument that only egoism should be included. This is also a subjective phenomenon. How do proponents of a narrow version know whether egoism is relevant or that reality is correctly perceived if all this cannot be measured?

Is Rational Choice Theory Wrong?

"Falsity" is a quantitative variable; that is to say, a theory may not be wrong in every situation. It may provide correct explanations in many situations but not in others. It seems that this holds for RCT. There is research that falsifies specific predictions of RCT. For example, RCT predicts: the higher the likelihood *and* severity of punishment, the less frequent is the punished behavior. However, this hypothesis is falsified in various studies.

The most spectacular falsifications seem to be the so-called anomalies (Frey and Eichenberger, 1989). In general, the "heuristics and biases" research program has shown that many assumptions of RCT are not empirically confirmed. It seems that much of this research only falsifies a narrow version. It is an open question which of the anomalies are in line with a wide version. A discussion of this question is not possible due to space restrictions and must be left as an important task for further research.

Assuming that there are falsifications of RCT, the question arises of what should or could be done. One possibility is to eliminate the theory from further discussion. However, as long as it provides many apparently valid explanations and as long as there is no superior theory it seems advisable to keep the theory and try to improve it. This is the argument of proponents of RCT and the RCA.

Can Every Factor Be Included in a Rational Choice Explanation?

It is argued that an explanation with the wide version of RCT may include *any* explanatory factor (see, e.g., Kroneberg, 2014: 111). Because we know that not every factor can be a cause for an explanandum, the theory is plainly false.

This argument is untenable (see Opp, 1999: 183–184). The selection algorithm of relevant explanatory goals and beliefs for a given action can be reconstructed in the following way (also Bohman, 1992: 212), as Figure 1.3 illustrates. Assume *action* A is to be explained: a group of students attend a class on calculus. Let the students have the *goal* G of getting a grade (in order to pass an exam). G is an explanatory variable because, from the perspective of the actor, A may satisfy goal G. Let a *belief* B of students be that attending the class regularly is the best way to get a grade. Thus, there is a clear *relevance* of G and B for A, from the perspective of the actor. This "relevance" is not given, for example, for the belief that apples are healthy and for the goal of traveling to Rome in a month. It is important to note that the selection is based on the perception of the actor.

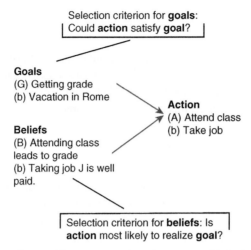

Figure 1.3 *Selection of preferences and beliefs in rational choice explanations*

Figure 1.3 depicts the example (the relevant belief and goal for action A as well as the action A are underlined). To further illustrate the relevance rule, look at the action (b) of taking a job. An actor will think that this could realize his or her goal of taking a vacation (goal b) but not of getting a grade. The belief (b) that the job will be well paid suggests that taking a job is most relevant for the goal of taking a vacation. Thus, the goal G of getting a grade is not relevant for the action (b) of taking a job but only for action A (attending the class).

Thus, there is a clear algorithm specifying which factors are to be included in a RC explanation. This rule implies that given goals or beliefs may be relevant for many actions. But, again, for a *given* behavior there is a clear selection rule.

Emotions and "Rationality"

A critique of RCT is that it does not say anything about the effects or origins of emotions. "Emotion" is a vague term, like "rationality," so a discussion of emotions and RCT first requires us to define "emotion." Since there are numerous definitions (Scherer, 2005) that cannot be addressed here, we proceed by looking at examples of emotions that are referents of most definitions. We ask how these examples fit into RCT.[6]

Figure 1.4 shows the variables of RCT (preferences, beliefs, behavior) and as an exogenous variable, "emotions." This variable could have causal effects on the independent RCT variables. For example, anger about government decisions could affect public goods preferences. RCT variables could also have causal effects on emotions. For example, low perceived influence could affect anger. Such relationships would not falsify but would extend RCT. Only if emotions have a direct causal effect on behavior would this be a falsification of RCT.

Often emotions *are* kinds of costs and benefits and thus can be subsumed under RCT. "Shame" at having committed a crime is an internal cost. "Hope" is a belief that certain events will take place.

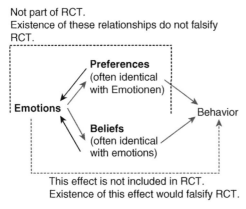

Not part of RCT.
Existence of these relationships do not falsify
RCT.

Preferences
(often identical
with Emotionen)

Emotions

Beliefs
(often identical
with emotions)

Behavior

This effect is not included in RCT.
Existence of this effect would falsify RCT.

Figure 1.4 *Emotions and Rational Choice Theory*

So far there is no rigorous research that shows that there are emotions that falsify RCT. Anyway, the simple critique that emotions invalidate RCT is not tenable.

Can Rational Choice Theory Explain Preferences and Beliefs?

Although there have been attempts to explain beliefs with RCT – the idea is that acquiring and changing beliefs depends, at least in part, on costs and benefits – it seems more difficult to explain preferences. At least there is, so far, no accepted version of RCT that explains preferences and beliefs.

It is important to note that RCT – or any other theory – is not falsified if its independent variables are not explained. Demanding this would lead to an *infinite regress*: assume we have explained preferences and beliefs. The next claim would be to explain the independent variables of this new theory, and so on.

If a researcher wants to explain beliefs or preferences, other theories are available. Cognitive theories such as dissonance theory (Festinger, 1957) or balance theory (Heider, 1958) are examples. Their basic idea is similar to RCT: Cognitive elements are likely to change if their simultaneous existence causes psychic strain or dissonance, that is, is costly.

How Specific Are Rational Choice Explanations? The Informative Content of RCT

An important criterion on which to judge scientific theories is their informative content (e.g. Popper, 1959). A theory has, among other things, a relatively high informative content if it can explain many relatively specific phenomena. For example the theory that frustration leads to aggression does not inform us about the *kind* of aggression that is to be expected if there is frustration. In contrast, RCT explains very specific actions because it assumes that the *kind* of action depends on the *kind* of incentives. Thus, it is not only able to explain whether people commit or do not commit a crime, but also the specific kind of crime.

Alternatives to Rational Choice Theory: Analytical Sociology, Dual-Process Theories, and Other Social Science Schools

The philosophical position of adherents of RCT and the RCA comes close to Karl Popper's Critical Realism (e.g. Popper, 1959). "Realism" means that scientists can in principle recognize reality as it is. "Critical" means that every hypothesis is preliminary and is open to revision. The aim of empirical science is to provide valid theories with high explanatory power, test them as rigorously as possible, and revise or replace them if they are falsified.

Much of contemporary social science is not based on this methodological program. Examples are Marxism, critical theory (Adorno, Habermas), functionalism (Parsons, Luhmann), postmodernism and (at least in part) qualitative approaches in sociology. Adherents of these schools strongly oppose RCT and the RCA. It is an open question to what extent these and other approaches contradict RCT and the RCA in regard to their *empirical* assumptions. To illustrate, a detailed analysis of Bourdieu's theory of practice, which is supposed to be entirely incompatible with RCT and the RCA, suggests that it has more similarities to them than had been previously thought (Ermakoff, 2010). Analytical Marxism (e.g. Mayer, 1994) is actually a transformation of Marxist ideas to empirically testable propositions. These works exemplify an important line of research that explores the fruitfulness of RCT and the RCA by comparing them with other approaches, finding new theoretical propositions and also possible problems.

In the remainder of this section a relatively new theoretical school will be briefly discussed that is similar to RCT and the RCA, namely analytical sociology (AS). Furthermore, a group of theories will be outlined that can extend RCT, namely dual-process theories.

Analytical Sociology (AS)

This relatively new school (Hedström, 2005; Hedström and Bearman, 2009; Hedström and Swedberg, 1998; Hedström and Ylikoski, 2014; Manzo, 2014) particularly emphasizes explanation by "mechanisms." This means that one should describe the social processes that bring about phenomena and not only bivariate causal relationships. The major mechanism is a micro-macro explanation. AS further emphasizes rigorous theoretical and empirical science. Proponents do not insist on applying a specific theory; they are open to the theory applied. They are very skeptical of RCT and emphasize the fruitfulness of theories of the middle range, that is, theories like theories of crime, which explain specific phenomena. Another focus is on agent-based modeling.

This short characterization suggests that AS and the RCA have several features in common. RC advocates subscribe to mechanism explanations, engage in agent-based modeling, and obviously demand a rigorous science. Apart from some methodological claims of AS that will not be discussed here the major disagreement consists in AS's rejection of the application of RCT as the major theory about individual behavior.

This critique is untenable for the following reasons: (1) It is based on a narrow version of RCT; (2) DBO theory (desire, beliefs, and opportunities), the AS alternative to RCT, is a deficient version of RCT; and (3) an analysis of work by AS proponents suggests that they actually apply a wide version of RCT without being aware of it (Opp, 2013a, 2013b; see also Ylikoski, 2013 and Manzo, 2013).

AS advocates reject the focus on any single theory. This "tolerance" of AS in regard to the theory applied seems tantamount to avoiding the dogmatism of the RCA. However, applying RCT is not dogmatism such as the belief in a religious dogma, but is based on evidence suggesting that there is no clearly superior theory. Furthermore, it has been found that RCT often modifies existing, more specialized theories. Not applying RCT would thus mean forgoing the opportunity to provide valid explanations.

If RCT is rejected in AS, one would expect that there are detailed comparisons of theories that show the deficiency of RCT. Such analyses are missing. For the time being it seems therefore meaningful to continue to apply RCT as a first option when social phenomena are to be explained.

If AS and the RCA are so similar, one would expect proponents of both approaches to cooperate. This is actually the case. For example, some of the annual AS conferences are organized by RC theorists. This organizational closeness confirms the similarity of the approaches.

Dual-Process Theories

These theories distinguish two kinds of decisions: spontaneous and deliberative actions.[7] For example, everyday norms are usually followed automatically, whereas buying a house is typically a deliberate act. Both theories assume that attitudes or goals and beliefs determine behavior. It seems that dual-process theories also implicitly assert subjective utility maximization.

In contrast to RCT, dual-process theories deal with *processes that occur before making a decision.* Attitudes, goals, and beliefs are stored in memory. They are more or less accessible. Only accessible cognitive elements can be activated by environmental stimuli. If they are categorized in a certain way they are aligned to stored cognitive elements. For example, assume a person all of a sudden perceives a cockroach (Fazio, 1990: 81). Perceiving such an object immediately activates existing beliefs, attitudes and behaviors. Different processes occur when a person wants to rent an apartment. Advertisements or personal communications will activate different mental elements. Often there is no spontaneous activation as in the example of the cockroach. Instead, people will deliberate and weigh the costs and benefits for renting a certain apartment.

The assumptions about situational cues that activate available goals and beliefs are compatible with RCT but usually not spelled out in detail. For example, voting is likely if, among other things, individuals think their participation makes a difference in providing desired public goods and if there is a perceived obligation to vote. In conducting research in which these variables are measured it is assumed that respondents have information about what time the election takes place, whether they have a right to cast a vote, and where they can cast it. RCT does not address accessibility and activation of these preferences and beliefs. RCT enters at the moment when these cognitive elements actually influence behavior. Hypotheses about these processes thus do not contradict RCT, they complement it. It would be an important task of future research to explore in much more detail the relationships between dual-process theories and RCT.

Assume the relevant cognitive elements are activated. When do people act spontaneously and when deliberately? In the MODE model (Motivation and Opportunity as DEterminants of the attitude/behavior relationship; see, e.g., Fazio, 1990) deliberate behavior is likely if "motivation" and "opportunity" are strong. The former variable refers to the "fear of invalidity" or costs of errors, while "opportunity" means "time and resources" available to an actor. These are variables from RCT. Furthermore, the theory clearly implies subjective utility maximization – either in the spontaneous or deliberate mode. In his review of dual-process theories (and of the *"heuristics and biases"-research program,* see, e.g., Thaler, 2015), Kahneman formulates a "law of least effort" that applies to cognitive as well as physical exertion. "The law asserts that if there are several ways of achieving the same goal, people will eventually gravitate to the least demanding course of action" (Kahneman, 2011: 35). This refers to subjective utility maximization.

Conclusion

This chapter provides an overview and discussion of RCT and the RCA. However, it could only cover a small part of the vast literature. For example, there are more versions of RCT than those described, and there are also more critiques. The numerous applications of RCT and the RCA could not even be adumbrated. I have focused on the mainstream in regard to the kinds of theory and approach that are widely applied and on what I regard as major critiques.

As this contribution shows, RCT and the RCA are, like every social science approach, controversial. Proponents of RCT and the RCA argue that despite existing problems there is no other social science school that is clearly superior. This judgment, which I share, suggests that in solving explanatory problems it is at least worthwhile *to consider* RCT and the RCA.

References

Abell, Peter. 2000 [1996]. "Sociological Theory and Rational Choice Theory." In B. S. Turner (ed.), *The Blackwell Compantion to Social Theory* (2nd ed.) (pp. 223–244). Oxford, UK: Blackwell.

Akerlof, George A., and Rachel E. Kranton. 2000. "Economics and Identity." *Quarterly Journal of Economics* 115 (CXV)(3): 715–753.

Axelrod, Robert, and Leigh Tesfatsion. 2016. "On-Line Guide for Newcomers to Agent-Based Modeling in the Social Sciences." www2.econ.iastate.edu/tesfatsi/abm read.htm.

Barberis, Nicholas C. 2013. "Thirty Years of Prospect Theory in Economics: A Review and Assessment." *Journal of Economic Perspectives* 27(1): 173–196.

Dinmore, Ken. 2009. *Rational Decisions*. Princeton, NJ, and Oxford, UK: Princeton University Press.

Bohman, James. 1992. "The Limits of Rational Choice Explanation." In J. S. Coleman and T. J. Fararo (eds.), *Rational Choice Theory: Advocacy and Critique* (pp. 207–228). Newbury Park, CA: Sage.

Boudon, Raymond. 1996. "The 'Cognitivist Model.' A Generalized 'Rational-Choice-Model.'" *Rationality and Society* 8(2): 123–150.

Buskens, Vincent, Werner Raub, and Marcel A. L. M. Van Assen. 2012. *Micro-Macro Links and Microfoundations in Sociology*. London and New York: Routledge.

Coleman, James S. 1990. *Foundations of Social Theory*. Cambridge, MA, and London: Belknap Press of Harvard University Press.

Diekmann, Andreas, Ben Jann, Wojtek Przepiorka, and Stefan Wehrli. 2014. "Reputation Formation and the Evolution of Cooperation in Anonymous Online Markets." *American Sociological Review* 29(1): 65–85.

Elster, Jon. 2007. *Explaining Social Behavior: More Nuts and Bolts for the Social Sciences*. Cambridge, UK: Cambridge University Press.

Ermakoff, Ivan. 2010. "Theory of Practice, Rational Choice, and Historical Change." *Theory and Society* 39(5): 527–553.

2017. "On the Frontiers of Rational Choice." In C. Benzecry, M. Krause, and I. A. Reed (eds.), *Social Theory Now* (pp. 162–200). Chicago, IL: Chicago University Press.

Esser, Hartmut, and Clemens Kroneberg. 2015. "An Integrative Theory of Action: The Model of Frame Selection." In E. J. Lawler, R. T. Shane, and J. Yoon (eds.), *Order on the Edge of Chaos: Social Psychology and the Problem of Social Order* (pp. 63–85). Cambridge, UK: Cambridge University Press.

Fazio, Russell H. 1990. "Multiple Processes by Which Attitudes Guide Behavior: The Mode Model as an Integrative Framework." In M. P. Zanna (ed.), in *Advances in Experimental Social Psychology* (pp. 75–109). San Diego, CA: Academic Press.

Fehr, Ernst, and Armin Falk. 2002. "Psychological Foundations of Incentives." *European Economic Review* 46(4–5): 687–724.

Festinger, Leon. 1957. *A Theory of Cognitive Dissonance*. Stanford, CA: Stanford University Press.

Fishbein, Martin, and Icek Ajzen. 2010. *Predicting and Changing Behavior: The Reasoned Action Approach*. New York and Hove: Psychology Press.

Frank, Robert H. 1988. *Passions within Reason. The Strategic Role of the Emotions*. New York: Norton.

Frey, Bruno S. 1997. *Not Just for the Money: An Economic Theory of Personal Motivation*. Cheltenham, UK: Edward Elgar.

2003. *Arts & Economics. Analysis & Cultural Policy*, 2nd ed. Berlin: Springer.

Frey, Bruno S., and Reiner Eichenberger. 1989. "Zur Bedeutung entscheidungstheoretischer Anomalien für die Ökonomik." *Jahrbücher für Nationalökonomie und Statistik* 206: 81–101.

Gawronski, Bertram, and Laura A. Creighton. 2013. "Dual Process Theories." In D. E. Carlston (ed.), *The Oxford Handbook of Social Cognition* (pp. 282–312). Oxford, UK, and New York: Oxford University Press.

Gilboa, Itzhak. 2010. *Rational Choice*. Cambridge, MA: MIT.

Goldthorpe, John H. 1998. "Rational Action Theory for Sociology." *British Journal of Sociology* 49(2): 167–192.

Hedström, Peter. 2005. *Dissecting the Social: On the Principles of Analytical Sociology*. Cambridge, UK: Cambridge University Press.

Hedström, Peter, and Peter Bearman. 2009. *The Oxford Handbook of Analytical Sociology.* Oxford, UK: Oxford University Press.

Hedström, Peter, and Richard Swedberg. 1998. *Social Mechanisms: An Analytical Approach to Social Theory.* Cambridge, UK: Cambridge University Press.

Hedström, Peter, and Petri Ylikoski. 2014. "Analytical Sociology and Rational-Choice Theory." In G. Manzo (ed.), *Analytical Sociology: Actions and Networks* (pp. 57–70) Chichester, UK: Wiley.

Heider, Fritz. 1958. *The Psychology of Interpersonal Relations.* New York: Wiley.

Homans, George C. 1974. *Social Behavior: Its Elementary Forms.* New York: Harcourt, Brace & World.

Kahneman, Daniel. 2011. *Thinking. Fast and Slow.* London: Allen Lane.

Kahneman, Daniel, and Amos Tversky. 1979. "Prospect Theory: An Analysis of Decision Under Risk." *Econometrica* 47(2): 263–291.

2000. *Choices, Values and Frames.* Cambridge, UK: Cambridge University Press.

Kiser, Edgar, and Michael Hechter. 1998. "The Debate on Historical Sociology: Rational Choice Theory and Its Critics." *American Journal of Sociology* 104: 785–816.

Kroneberg, Clemens. 2014. "Frames, Scripts, and Variable Rationality: An Integrative Theory of Action." In G. Manzo (ed.), *Analytical Sociology: Actions and Networks* (pp. 97–123). New York: Wiley.

Lindenberg, Siegwart. 2015. "Social Rationality and Weak Solidarity: A Coevolutionary Approach to Social Order." In E. J. Lawler, R. T. Shane, and J. Yoon (eds.), *Order on the Edge of Chaos: Social Psychology and the Problem of Social Order* (pp. 43–62). Cambridge, UK: Cambridge University Press.

Manzo, Gianluca. 2013. "Is Rational Choice Theory Still a Rational Choice of Theory? A Response to Opp." *Social Science Information* 52(3): 361–382.

2014. *Analytical Sociology: Actions and Networks.* Chichester, UK: Wiley.

Mayer, Tom. 1994. *Analytical Marxism.* Thousand Oaks, CA: Sage.

Olson, Mancur. 1965. *The Logic of Collective Action.* Cambridge, MA: Harvard University Press.

Opp, Karl-Dieter. 1986. "Soft Incentives and Collective Action. Participation in the Anti-Nuclear Movement." *British Journal of Political Science* 16(1): 87–112.

1999. "Contending Conceptions of the Theory of Rational Action." *Journal of Theoretical Politics* 11(2): 171–202.

2011. "Modeling Micro-Macro Relationships: Problems and Solutions." *Journal of Mathematical Sociology* 35(1–3): 209–234.

2013a. "What Is Analytical Sociology? Strengths and Weaknesses of a New Sociological Research Program." *Social Science Information* 52(3): 329–360.

2013b. "Rational Choice Theory, the Logic of Explanation, Middle-Range Theories and Analytical Sociology: A Reply to Gianluca Manzo and Petri Ylikoski." *Social Science Information* 52(3): 394–408.

2014. "The Explanation of Everything: A Critical Assessment of Raymond Boudon's Theory Explaining Descriptive and Normative Beliefs, Attitudes, Preferences and Behavior." *Papers. Revista de Sociologia* 99(4): 481–514.

2017. "Do the Social Sciences Need the Concept of 'Rationality'? Notes on the Obsession with a Concept." In F. Di Iorio and G. Bronner (eds.), *The Mystery of Rationality* (pp. 191–218). Wiesbaden: VS Springer.

Popper, Karl R. 1959. *The Logic of Scientific Discovery.* New York: Basic Books.

Sandler, Todd. 2001. *Economic Concepts for the Social Sciences.* Cambridge, UK: Cambridge University Press.

Schelling, Thomas C. 1971. "Dynamic Models of Segregation." *The Journal of Mathematical Sociology* 1: 143–186.

1978. *Micromotives and Macrobehavior.* New York & London: W. W. Morton and Company.

Scherer, Klaus R. 2005. "What Are Emotions? And How Can They Be Measured?" *Social Science Information* 44(4): 695–729.

Sherman, Jeffrey W., Bertram Gawronski, and Yaacov Trope. 2014. *Dual-Process Theories of the Social Mind.* New York: Guilford Press.

Simon, Herbert A. 1997 [1945]. *Administrative Behavior. A Study of Decision-Making Processes in Administrative Organizations*, 4th ed. New York: The Free Press.

Stigler, George J. 1950a. "The Development of Utility Theory. I." *Journal of Political Economy* 58(4): 307–327.

1950b. "The Development of Utility Theory. II." *Journal of Political Economy* 58(5): 373–396.

Tadelis, Steven. 2013. *Game Theory. An Introduction.* Princeton, NJ: Princeton University Press.

Thaler, Richard. 2015. *Misbehaving: The Making of Behavioral Economics.* New York: Norton.

Thaler, Richard, and Cass R. Sunstein. 2009. *Nudge: Improving Decisions About Health, Wealth, and Happiness.* London: Penguin Books.

Tversky, Amos, and Daniel Kahneman. 1992. "Advances in Prospect Theory: Cumulative Representation of Uncertainty." *Journal of Risk and Uncertainty* 5(4): 297–323.

Tyler, Tom R. 2013. *Why People Cooperate: The Role of Social Motivations.* Princeton, NJ: Princeton University Press.

von Neumann, John, and Oskar Morgenstern. 1944. *Theory of Games and Economic Behavior.* Princeton, NJ: Princeton University Press.

Ylikoski, Petri. 2013. "The (Hopefully) Last Stand of the Covering-Law Theory: A Reply to Opp." *Social Science Information* 52(3): 383–393.

Notes

1. There is a vast literature on the subject of RCT. It is described in textbooks of economics, game theory, and public choice theory. See, for example Gilboa (2010); Sandler (2001). What follows is based on Opp (1999), in which different versions of RCT are distinguished and objections discussed.

2. The narrow version is described in most of the literature cited in the previous footnote, but there is no detailed discussion of alternative versions of RCT. A detailed discussion of the two versions is provided in Opp (1999).

3. It was modified as "cumulative prospect theory," see Tversky and Kahneman (1992); see also Kahneman and Tversky (2000), Barberis (2013), and for a short summary, Kahneman (2011: 278–288).

4. Netlogo is available for free at https://ccl.northwestern.edu/netlogo/.

5. For details see Buskens, Raub, and Van Assen (2012). Numerous applications of the RC approach can be found in Schelling (1978). The following discussion in the remainder of this section is based on Opp (2011).

6. For discussions of emotions from a RC perspective see Elster (2007: 214–231); Frank (1988).

7. A good summary and review of dual-process theories is provided by Gawronski and Creighton (2013); Kahneman (2011: 19–108). See also Sherman, Gawronski, and Trope (2014).

2 Network Theories

Mark C. Pachucki and Ronald L. Breiger

Introduction: Three Traditions of Network Theory

Systematic research on the structuring of social relations – the analysis of social networks – has been increasing at an exponential rate in recent decades and has provided multiple foci of ever-expanding research interest across the social sciences as well as the biological and physical sciences and computational science (Borgatti and Halgin, 2011). And yet, along with this explosive growth and many generative research contributions have come repeated charges that the field is atheoretical (reviewed in Erikson, 2013: 219–220), and questioning of whether network theory has lived up to its promise (Galaskiewicz, 2007). Indeed, an influential and highly cited textbook on social network analysis (Wasserman and Faust, 1994) is subtitled *Methods and Applications*, highlighting the aspects of social network analysis that many consumers as well as practitioners see as the major contributions of network studies, with scant mention of theoretical advances. We find three broad perspectives on theories of social networks to be helpful in organizing our thinking.

Model-Based Theory

The first broad perspective that we consider to be helpful in organizing our thinking about network theory emphasizes theory as consisting of rigorous formulations of social relations and social structure. In this sense the methods, applications, concepts, and formal developments that have enabled the widely recognized scientific progress in network studies constitute in sum a highly significant, model-based theory. A non-exhaustive inventory of the most significant and highly influential contributions to this theory of networks would include the following: the distinction between strong and weak ties (the former tending to produce tightly connected clusters of actors but with clusters isolated from one another, while ties bridging clusters tend to be those of weak or specialized commitment); brokerage, centrality; transitivity of network connections; structural and more generalized forms of equivalence (leading to identification of positions in networks on the basis of relational configurations); homophily (the principle that interpersonal networks may be and often are structured by similarities on the sociodemographic, behavioral, and intrapersonal characteristics of network

---

* The authors would like to thank Chen-Shuo Hong for his research assistance on the topic of networks and geography.

actors); models of exchange networks (positing, for example, that the power of actor A over B is a function of resources that A controls and B desires); models for network structure arising from formal assumptions about actor rationality or strategy; models for multiple networks ranging from balance theory (for the interlinking of positive and negative affect) to role structures (algebraic modeling of rules for how different types of networks interrelate); and random graph models, including small worlds (network models in which the distance between any pair of nodes is relatively short while transitivity or clustering is high), and scale-free networks (models for networks in which the distribution of the number of connections per node follows a mathematical power law, at least asymptotically). These innovations are reviewed in reference works in the social sciences (Borgatti, Everett, and Johnson, 2018; De Nooy, Mrvar, and Batagelj, 2011; Scott, 2017, Wasserman and Faust, 1994) including economics (Jackson, 2008), the biological sciences (Junker and Schreiber, 2008), and the physical and computational sciences (Newman, 2010).

Ontological and Epistemological Underpinnings of Theory

A second perspective on network theory, in a sense the opposite of the first, emphasizes the articulation and development of thinking about the nature (ontology) of social networks, and the grounds for attaining knowledge about them (epistemology). Emirbayer's (1997) manifesto for a relational sociology focuses on ontology, by depicting the dilemma of "whether to conceive of the social world as consisting primarily in substances or processes" (281), "a choice of bedrock assumptions regarding the very nature of social reality itself" (311). The path an analyst chooses is consequential, for example, for whether the analyst conceptualizes "power" as a possession, something to be "seized" or "held" (291), or in contrast chooses to analyze societies as "constituted of multiple overlapping and intersecting sociospatial networks of power" (Emirbayer quoting Mann, 1986: 1). Martin (2009), in a book hailed as "the best work yet in network theory" (Collins, 2013), takes as his central point "that certain relationships have inherent structural potentials" (Martin, 2009: x). For example, the informal social relation of patronage tends toward network connections in the layout of (hierarchical) trees, which can then serve as "the backbone for more deliberate governance structures" (189). Reed (2017: 87), seeking an adequate analytical frame for the nature of power, puts forward "a basic theoretical vocabulary about power players and their projects." For Reed, power as the capacity for action, "reached via the social and physical organization of persons into networks, depends on understanding and misunderstanding, signs of trust and interactive engagement, and thus on the modes of thought that imagine persons as actors in the first place" (109). From the perspective on theory illustrated in this paragraph, the straightforward taking for granted of the existence of nodes (actors) and arcs (relations among nodes) that characterizes standard network analysis seems hopelessly naïve.

As an example of an intellectual movement within our second broad tradition, we consider the ontological and epistemological system of critical realism developed by philosopher Roy Bhaskar in collaboration with a number of British social theorists, including Margaret Archer (Gorski, 2013). Smith (2011) provides an extended critique of what the author sees as the reductionism inherent in analytic and model-based network theories. Smith's standpoint posits that a *"natural drive toward a sustained and thriving personal life broadly ... generates"* social structure (2011: 340, original italics). As Breiger and Puetz (2015) point out, Smith is sympathetic to the network structuralists' rejection of the variables paradigm and Parsonian theory. However, he portrays the pendulum as having swung too far, resulting in a network theory that is anti-humanist and person-annihilating. Smith (2011: 270, 272) argues that it is therefore necessary to redress network structuralism's neglect of human dignity, rights, respect, and rational deliberation.

Analytical sociology (Hedström and Bearman, 2009) provides another and quite different example of an intellectual movement within our second broad tradition. Inasmuch as research on social networks guided by this approach has led to a great deal of model-based quantitative empirical research (Moody, 2009), we were tempted to list analytical sociology under our first tradition. Nonetheless, analytical sociology emphasizes the ontological stance of individualism, as well as particular commitments to the concept of "mechanism" that "have more to do with philosophy of science than with sociology proper" (Hedström and Bearman, 2009: 4). This approach to social networks highlights individual entities, the activities of those entities, and the patterns of relations among them in elucidating mechanisms that bring about social facts. Here, social facts are explained as the result of individuals' actions, along with the social structures in which individuals are embedded (Hedström and Bearman, 2009; Hedström and Ylikoski, 2010; Pachucki, Jacques, and Christakis, 2011).

Theory Beyond Networks

The third approach to network theory that we find helpful in organizing our thinking is that networks are not sufficient unto themselves for depicting the social world, but that theorization is required to understand how networks are implicated in a wide array of institutions, language(s), cultural practices, and social and geographic spaces, and that the structuring of network ties cannot be separated from the contents of network relations. In this way "network structure is one ingredient in a recipe that depends upon the presence and quality of several other ingredients" (Galaskiewicz, 2007: 6). This third approach in a certain sense lies in between the other two, and in practice it often overlaps with one or (less commonly) both of them (i.e., with formal network analysis and/or explicitly ontological or epistemological formulations). We expect two recent streams of work subsumed under this third approach to become particularly influential.

Lazega and colleagues have developed a distinctive neo-structural theoretical and empirical approach to networks and institutionalization (reviewed in Lazega, 2017) that makes use of social and organizational network analyses, in combination with other methodologies, to better understand the roles of structure and culture in individual and collective agency. Lazega's neo-structural sociology (NSS) rests on theorization of multiple levels of agency and the problem of synchronization among levels (Lazega, 2016) while revitalizing the study of Selznick's (1949) concerns about the design and governance of public institutions in a world "where an institution becomes a different thing to different people, and where each stakeholder pushes towards goal drift" (Lazega, 2017: 13).

Padgett and Powell (2012), along with additional authors of several of the chapters comprising their book, exemplify our third tradition by having produced an analytic framework that spans historical research (fourteen case studies of the emergence of organizations and markets) and a modeling framework that applies concepts from biochemistry in order to understand the emergence of novelty in multiple domains (including language and national politics as well as markets and organizations). The authors view "inductive histories and deductive models . . . as complementary (not competitive) research strategies" (2). Networks are central to the book's arguments about transformation, for example in its framing of organizational inventions as "transpositions of relational logics from one domain to another, which attain new purposes in the new domain, whose reproduction is positively reinforced to the point that it alters interactions among others in the new domain" (Padgett and Powell, 2012: 201). Contrary to the approach of analytic sociology reviewed above, the mantra of Padgett and Powell (2) is that "in the short run, actors create relations; in the long run, relations create actors."

In this review we seek to build upon the efforts described in this section and focus on more recent integrative relational theoretical efforts in two areas: relational approaches to networks and culture, and recent work at the interface of biological and social organization. Then we highlight current challenges and horizons for network theory, including temporality and dynamism in networks, networks and geography, the treatment of missing data, and network experiments. As network methods are increasingly important to parsing large amounts of information (i.e. "big data"), analytic efforts must be undertaken with care relative to local context and meaning (Bail, 2014; Breiger, 2015).

Relational Approaches to Network Theory

The term "relational sociology" is itself highly contested (Dépelteau, 2018). In one of its senses the key idea is that interaction settings include meaningful orientations among actors, whereas network analysis tends to explicitly ignore actors' understandings in favor of a static and reductionist depiction of the nodes and network connections (Fine and Kleinman, 1983). In relational network approaches, the meaning that one actor assigns to another is the basis for the relation, and in fact the absence of meaning could easily be understood as the absence of the relationship (Erikson, 2013: 227). Thus, relational sociology analyzes networks as structures of relationships infused with meanings (Fuhse and Mützel, 2010).

Although it is compelling and generative, the above conception omits recognition that the formal network modeling of Boorman and White (1976) had a different, but also valuable, approach to the study of meaning in networks, but at a different level: for Boorman and White, the meaning of a type of tie (for example, advice-seeking) is given with respect to the patterning of its connections in comparison to the tie patterning in another type of network (for example, the network of friendship ties on the same population of actors). Moreover, the Boorman and White approach, but not the approach of relational sociology, is relevant to networks of impersonal interactions: for example, the network of world trade that takes nations as the nodes.

Nonetheless, in his book *Identity and Control* (White, 1992 revised ed. 2008) Harrison White made clear that formal network models were necessary but not sufficient for answering the question of how social forms emerge, and that formal network analysis captures poorly the shifting meanings and the switchings of context that characterize social ties and bound them (Fontdevila, 2018: 231). White's 1992 book upended existing formal network theory. As Fontdevila (2018: 236) relates, White now developed "story" as the subjective and phenomenological dimension of the network tie. He now contended that "networks are phenomenological realities as well as measurement constructs," and he opposed the simplistic view of social networks as "physical monads" and "lines" in Cartesian space (White, 1992: 65, quoted by Fontdevila, 2018: 236).

During the 1980s and 1990s other scholars were articulating theories of networks and meaning, including Donati (see Donati, 2018) and Emirbayer (1997; discussed earlier as a theorist of network ontology). In recent years, a number of scholars have identified productive tensions between relational theories of culture and networks (Mische, 2011; Mohr and Rawlings, 2015; Pachucki and Breiger, 2010; Rule and Bearman, 2015). This work focuses, for example, on bridging oppositions such as meanings and structure; symbols and practices; and categorization and boundaries. The authors of the present chapter offered one such contribution in proposing the heuristic of "cultural holes" in an attempt to value the range of social meanings by which individuals understand their lives and the patterns of connectivity and network position that mutually constitute social life (Pachucki and Breiger, 2010). In this formulation, network structure is highly contingent on cultural context, and these entities coevolve. Put another way, it is the constellation of cultural meanings, discourse, and practices that we suspect are most consequential in a particular actor occupying a structural position that bridges otherwise-disconnected network alters. Several empirical formalizations of this concept have recently been offered that extend our understanding of linkages between these realms.

As culture can be thought of in terms of similarities in communicative discourse, Vilhena and colleagues (2014) ambitiously analyzed the content of, and citation ties between, more than 1.5 million journal articles derived from 60 scientific fields contained in the JSTOR database between 1990 and 2010. Without shared culture and a common language, they posit, cultural holes exist between fields that impede the dissemination of ideas. Through the use of topographical mapping, the authors quantified the semantic distance (e.g. the size of the cultural hole) between aggregate bodies of field-specific technical language. Doing so allows for visualization of the landscape of shared culture – an illustration that intuitively and usefully communicates, for instance, the width of the gap between social science discourse and biological jargon.

Another empirical example illustrates different ways of bridging cultural forms and spanning cultural holes through a focus on cultural omnivorousness. Lizardo (2014), for instance, analyzed data from the Survey for Public Participation in the Arts with the use of two-mode network analysis methods to generate an index of the extent to which participants bridge musical and literary forms of culture. In doing so, Lizardo links one's propensity to bridge cultural holes with the notion of omnivorousness, and shows how previous measures of simple "omnivorousness by volume" (of distinct forms of culture) obscure the richness of actual patterns of cultural choice that may constitute varieties of omnivorous consumption.

Network Theories in Biological and Social Organization

Across a broad number of social animal and insect species, network methods have been used to document fundamental aspects of sociability and social processes that lead to coordinated action to obtain food and build shelter for survival. The relative scarcity of cross-species comparative work (though see, e.g., Faust and Skvoretz, 2002; Shizuka and McDonald, 2012) highlights the difficulty of the task as well as the promise of such efforts for theory-building. As Charbonneau, Blonder, and Dornhaus (2013) describe, social insects such as ants, termites, bees, and wasps are ecologically successful because of their abilities to coordinate a division of labor. Like other biological networks, social insect networks have scale-free characteristics, exhibiting local clustering around distinct nodes, and a large proportion of nodes with few ties. Faust (2011) offers an especially insightful review of the expansive topic of animal social networks, especially given the challenge of the existence of tens of thousands of social animal species. Identifying cross-species variation and similarity can be useful in systematizing processes of dominance and hierarchy, social roles, preferential attachment, assortativity, kinship, and network temporal dynamics of stability and change. Pinter-Wollman et al. (2014) offer an important review of properties of animal social networks from a behavioral ecology perspective that views social interactions not only shaping group-level behaviors, but fundamentally affecting evolutionary fitness. The authors compare common analytical methods used to study different species, and describe meta-analytic efforts across species, as well as surveying the state of network research on primates, ungulates, cetaceans, fish, and invertebrates. Importantly, they draw attention to the need for studying the evolution of networks over time within-species, as well as cross-species comparisons with an eye toward temporal dynamics, tie definition, and public availability of data for replication by others.

Scientists have also begun to gain new traction on the questions of how sociability – and different network substructures – shape, and are shaped by, cognitive processes and brain function in humans. Brashears and Quintane (2015) enrolled several hundred undergraduate students to conduct an experiment of the recall of fictional friendship groupings. In contrast to a great deal of established wisdom, they found that individuals tend to encode cognitive networks of social ties at the triadic and more complex group levels, rather than relying upon recall of simpler dyadic ties. Because network recall affects how individuals act to make, maintain, and dissolve ties in the real world, this finding suggests that cognitive encoding heuristics may take priority over taste preferences in directing network processes. Techniques for studying cognitive localization such as functional MRI (fMRI) also show promise in studying the foundations of status processes in network settings. Zerubavel and colleagues (2015) studied collegiate members (n=26) of two identically sized student voluntary organizations. Participants first rated sociometric popularity of other members, and then were shown pictures of members during fMRI scans, which tested for activation of the brain's social valuation system (ventromedial prefrontal cortex, ventral striatum, amygdala) and social cognition system (dorsomedial prefrontal cortex, temporoparietal junction, precuneus). Researchers found that sociometric popularity was differentially associated with activity in both of these cognitive systems. Additionally, mediation analysis showed that the social valuation system assumes a primary role, and that the valuation systems of popular participants were more sensitive to detection of status differences.

Further frontiers for network theorizing are the consideration of how social relationships with others – both perceived relationships and actual interactions – are fundamental to the human body's health, subjective well-being, and cellular maintenance (Berkman and Krisha, 2014; Cole, 2014; Holt-Lunstad and Smith, 2016). It is well recognized from studies across the social sciences, and increasingly, the biological sciences, that different aspects of our social networks can affect the body's function, and even our survival. For example, a meta-analysis of 148 studies that examined associations between structural and functional attributes of social network and mortality found that having more restricted networks on some dimension was linked with a 1.4–1.5 times greater mortality risk (Holt-Lunstad, Smith, and Layton, 2010). The World Health Organization considers social support networks and culture as key social determinants of health (WHO, 2018). Social scientists have identified a number of social-tie-related mechanisms that affect health outcomes, including social influence and social comparison, social control, having a sense of purpose and meaning, self-esteem, having a sense of mastery, belonging, and companionship, and perceived social support (Thoits, 2011). In addition, the structure of social ties can affect health behaviors over the life course through the content of social ties and the meanings that individuals attribute and derive from actions, but also through a reciprocal interaction between mental health and the body's physiological response (Umberson, Crosnoe, and Reczek, 2010).

At the cellular level, one stream of research demonstrates the promise of using network tools to identify connectivity between different functional systems in the body. For instance, Goh et al. (2007) used bipartite graphs to generate a typology of human disease (the "diseaseome") in which different forms of genetic disorder (e.g. Parkinson's disease, leukemia) are linked by shared genetic mutations. This work provides a useful visual heuristic for examining genetic links between disorders, with the promise of observing general patterns of disease that would not be possible to observe from discrete study of disorders alone. Even more granular than the genetic level, it is possible to examine how proteins within genes are interacting with one another. Menche and colleagues (2015) offer preliminary steps toward elaborating a complete map of this human "interactome," and show how a network approach to examining overlapping neighborhoods of proteins reveals unexpected relationships between diseases at the molecular level. This form of research could enable discovery of how gene interactions cause a particular ailment. Practically speaking, disrupting one disease could disrupt the potential for another before symptoms are experienced by a patient or diagnosed by a physician.

Separately, research on social genomics that investigates relationships between one's life circumstances and changes in gene expression illustrates how cells respond to socioenvironmental adversity and affect health and social behavior. Importantly, this work interrogates the roles that one's social network plays as a part of the broader social environment. This type of research is an especially important frontier of theorizing network processes because it provides evidence of how social connectivity may "get under the skin" to affect biological mechanisms, and vice versa. Robinson, Fernald, and Clayton (2008) formulate a model of how, across a range of different species, social interactions shape the genome through complex behavioral, epigenetic, evolutionary, and developmental pathways. Focusing on humans, Steven Cole (2014) theorizes two processes: social signal transduction, in which networks shape gene expression through cascading biological pathways; and reciprocal recursion, in which gene expression feeds back to the function of the central nervous system to affect social behaviors and networks. As an example, Cole and colleagues (2011) studied gene expression in chronically lonely individuals, and found that specific immune cells (plasmacytoid dendritic cells, monocytes, and B lymphocytes) mediate the effects of the social environment on immune function. Interestingly, gene expression was more strongly associated with subjective experiences of loneliness than one's actual social network size. This work suggests that the body's immune function has evolved in response to patterns of social interaction in order to reduce the likelihood of viral infection. Christakis and Fowler (2014) used genome-wide association study (GWAS) data to test a provocative hypothesis that humans tend to select friends with similar genotypes, theorizing that genetically similar friends might serve as a kind of functional kin. When they compared genotypes of friend pairs, they found these pairs to be more genetically similar than pairs of strangers. Friends are about as similar in terms of their genotype as fourth cousins are. Interestingly, the top quintile of single nucleotide polymorphisms (SNPs) shared by friends appear to have been more recently selected for by evolutionary processes, suggesting that friendship is evolutionarily adaptive for humans. Indeed, the interaction of social organization and culture at the locus of agriculture and diet has been shown through recent analysis of ancient DNA to influence evolutionary selection (Mathieson et al., 2015).

Further efforts to build models that integrate polygenic risk scores (Belsky and Israel, 2014) derived from thousands to millions of SNPs related to a given trait can help us identify how genetic factors interact with behavioral and social processes involving social networks to determine later-life outcomes (Domingue et al., 2018).

Where Theories of Networks Still Struggle

In many ways, theories involving networks are no different than any other theoretical endeavor, insofar as testing, verification, building, and falsification are part of our collective enterprise. However, several classes of problems that involve networks have been especially challenging, and we mention several persistently challenging concerns here.

Time and Network Evolution

One area where theories of networks could be meaningfully enriched would be by according closer attention to different meanings and dimensions of time. During the past decade there has been a transition away from a prototypical longitudinal research design that may involve multiple panels at yearly or semi-regular intervals, and toward continuous data streams gathered at the scale of nanoseconds (in the case of cellular signaling), microseconds (online data streams), or seconds (human behavioral interactions). Truly impressive progress has been made concerning models and methods for the study of large temporal networks (Batagelj et al., 2014). However, analyzing network dynamics across multiple successive life-course periods has proven challenging (Kreager, Felmlee, and Alwin, 2018; Pachucki and Goodman, 2015). There have, of course, been exciting discoveries that have emerged from large prospective cohort studies designed with a sociocentric focus such as Add Health (Bearman, Moody, and Stovel, 2004; Domingue et al., 2018), or egocentric studies such as the National Social Life, Health, and Aging Project (NSHAP) (Cornwell et al., 2009). Other studies contain dyadic network information, such as the Framingham Heart Study (Christakis and Fowler, 2007; Raghavan et al., 2016) or the Health and Retirement Study (Yang et al., 2016). Such datasets have long provided a substrate for developing and testing network hypotheses. But our understanding of how affiliations or network processes that are developed at an earlier point in life may shape outcomes much later is necessarily impoverished because of a paucity of this form of data.

Networks and Place

It is the case that humans socially interact with others in geographic space, that network structures vary geographically, and that propinquity is a stronger determinant of social ties than connections with far-off people. The fundamental dependence on geography and sociability for information diffusion is implicit in experimental findings dating back to Travers and Milgram's classic work (1967) on the average path length of social networks using messages forwarded by the postal service (and updated for the digital age by Liben-Nowell and Kleinberg, 2008; Liben-Nowell et al., 2005). Yet even in a sociocentric paradigm that bounds ties in a single space and theoretically controls for human movement, many analyses either ignore the spatial location of socially connected individuals or include information about it while not fully accounting for the difficult statistical challenge of the correlated nature of geographical location. This is problematic because in dynamic systems, social ties, individual-level characteristics, human behaviors, and spatial location can change and interact on different timescales and in nonlinear ways.

There are notable exceptions, and these theoretical and empirical lacunae have seen more attention in recent years. For one, research has revealed how physical location alone can be a proxy for sociability. Crandall et al. (2010) identified spatio-temporal co-occurrences based on over 85 million geo-tagged photographs, where a network tie was inferred between individuals based upon their precise location, and the inference of a tie was strengthened if there were multiple daily photographs at the shared location. Using mobile phone and texting data drawn from several million people in Europe, Onnela et al. (2011) also tested and confirmed that ties were less likely with greater geographic distance, but additionally sought to test whether distance was associated with different features of group structure. The authors found that physical centrality was uncorrelated with betweenness centrality, and that small groups were cohesive in terms of spatial clustering and geographical span. Yet these geographical effects decayed as the group size grew to exceed thirty people. These findings suggest that scholars should pay more attention to the heterogeneity of geographical effects at different levels of social organization.

A more fundamental question concerns what the functional form of the dependence structure between distance and friendship looks like. To evaluate this question, Preciado et al. (2012) turned to a panel network study of several hundred seventh-graders in Sweden and used generalized additive models (GAMs) and logistic regression to model the form of distance dependence. These models confirmed that the likelihood of friendships decreased as the distance between two individuals increased in a logarithmic fashion. Then, the researchers integrated the functional form of distance dependence in stochastic actor-oriented models (SAOMs) that modeled friendships, individual characteristics, endogenous network effects, and distance simultaneously to show that geographic influence was independent of other effects. Yet separate research by Daraganova et al. (2012: 16) among a suburban community of Australians modeled the simultaneous nature of network processes and geographic processes, and found that endogenous network processes were still at work even after adjusting for the effect of geographical proximity, which to the authors suggests a more limited influence of geographical proximity on network structures. Mathematically, this paper found that the functional form of the relationship between tie probability and distance was an "attenuated power law with baseline probability set to one."

The idea that individuals may be nested in multiple types of social context is a difficult set of threads to disentangle. Evans et al. (2016) investigate how the sometimes overlapping social contexts of adolescents' schools, neighborhoods, and friendship networks can differentially contribute to variance in body mass index (BMI). Using Bayesian Markov Chain Monte Carlo (MCMC) cross-classified models, the authors find that adolescents' friendship network communities contribute far more to BMI than geographic location (neighborhoods or schools). It is also the case that structural properties of social networks can vary depending upon geographic location. Using a variety of simulation approaches, Butts et al. (2012: 94) find that spatial variation is associated with network heterogeneity, but that certain network properties (aggregate mean degree, edge length, local clustering) can be ascertained by assessing geographic attributes of population size and land area within a given spatial context. As the authors eloquently put it, "[network] subgraphs in a spatial context have a dual existence: they can be considered on the one hand in terms of their network properties, and on the other in terms of the spatial positions of their members." It is our observation that scholars may productively benefit from giving greater analytic attention to this duality.

A further point at which network theories struggle has been highlighted by political and cultural geographers who have been working within place-based adaptations of post-structural, social constructivist, and actor-network theory (ANT) orientations. As described by Marshall and Staeheli (2015: 57), the problem is that there seem to be "irreconcilable epistemological differences between the structuralist empiricism of quantitative, formal approaches using SNA (social network analysis) and the post-structural constructivism of ANT and certain ethnographic approaches, which see networks as, in part, artefacts of the research process itself." Marshall and Staeheli present a tentative solution to this problem that involves iterative combinations of formal network visualization techniques and ethnography. Using civil society organizations as their example, the authors produce a formal network visualization that is then used to raise the sort of critical questions (concerning, for example, how this structure came about) that cannot be answered by the formal network methods but that can be addressed by means of grounded ethnographic work.

Missing Data

Another persistent challenge in estimating properties of, and associations with, networks involves missing data. Relative to missing data approaches in survey research (Rubin and Little, 2002), approaches for treating missing social network data for the purposes of causal inference are in their relative infancy, though this is starting to change (Gile and Handcock, 2017; Handcock and Gile, 2010; Koskinen, Robins, and Pattison, 2010; Kossinets, 2006; Krause, Huisman, and Snijders, 2018; Robins, Pattison, and Woolcock, 2004). Collecting complete data for social network analysis using survey approaches is a persistent challenge (Marin, 2004; Marsden, 2005, 2011). As a result, efforts often result in a substantial amount of missing data.

Missing network data present unique statistical challenges for causal inference because of the relational nature of the data. When a person (i.e. node) is missing, then relationships to others (i.e. social ties) can potentially be missing as well. Persons may be missing due to non-response, loss to follow-up, or informant inaccuracy, or they may be missing by design due to the sampling strategy (Rubin and Little, 2002). Relationship data may be missing due to boundary specification (noninclusion of relevant nodes or ties) and censoring by node degree (produced by fixed-choice survey questions) (Faust, 2008; Kossinets, 2006).

A variety of approaches exist to sample network data, ranging from snowball sampling and link-tracing/respondent-driven sampling designs, to probabilistic models (Chen, Crawford, and Karbasi, 2015; Crawford, Wu, and Heimer, 2015; Frank, 2005; Marsden, 2011). There has been relatively little research that might demonstrate how to infer a whole-network topology from incomplete network samples (Hanneke and Xing, 2009). Currently, network approaches to the problem of remediating missing data include missing link prediction from attribute or structural information (Lü and Zhou, 2011), network reconstruction of missing parts of networks (Guimerà and Sales-Pardo, 2009), and network completion of missing nodes and ties (Kim and Leskovec, 2011; Stork and Richards, 1992). Limited evidence suggests that hierarchical structure can also be used to predict missing ties in partially observed networks (Clauset, Moore, and Newman, 2008).

With respect to our other outstanding questions, we do not know whether effects of missingness on health are consistent across the life course. It may be that a certain amount of missing network data in a sample of adolescents yields relatively unbiased estimates of peer effects on certain health outcomes, while the same amount of missing data in a sample of adults results in highly skewed estimates of that same outcome. One illustrative example concerns cardiovascular disease, which only begins to develop during early and middle adulthood. Because rates of cardiovascular diseases (CVD) are so low during adolescence, missing network data would likely have little bearing. However, among adults, the same amount of missing network data may result in seriously biased estimates of peer associations in CVD.

Network Interventions and Experiments

There are far more observational network studies than network-based interventions (Valente, 2012). In sociocentric studies, this is typically because randomization encounters problems within a bounded community of individuals: many individuals tend to know one another. In studies of egocentric networks (or clusters of communities), there may be ties between clusters or between personal networks that interfere with appropriate discernment of the treatment effect (Staples, Ogburn, and Onnela, 2015; VanderWeele, Ogburn, and Tchetgen Tchetgen, 2012). Still, there is a growing literature on network experiments using Facebook or other social information platforms (Aral and Walker, 2014; Bond et al., 2012; Centola, 2011; Centola and Baronchelli, 2015; Kramer, Guillory, and Hancock, 2014; Muchnik, Aral, and Taylor, 2013; Phan and Airoldi, 2015), social games played by interacting participants (Han et al., 2017; Melamed, Simpson, and Harrell, 2017; Nishi, Christakis, and Rand, 2017; Shirado and Christakis, 2017), primary schools (Paluck et al., 2016), Honduran villages (Kim et al., 2015), and Ugandan organizations (Baldassarri, 2015), which seeks to discern mechanisms linking social relationships to a range of outcomes.

Klar and Shmargad (2017) studied how network structure influences preference formation on public issues. To do so, they designed an experiment involving 348 subjects assigned randomly to one of two carefully designed 144-person networks (plus 60 subjects in a control group): one a random network in which individuals reached others throughout the whole network with the same probability, the other a clustered lattice in which average path lengths were short and average distances between nodes in different regions of the network were long. Each person was by design connected to six others. Each network was designed to be like a social media network in that subjects received information about what their contacts were viewing. Information for and against two issues (GMO food and electric cars) was randomly seeded into each network, with two individuals receiving a "dominant" opinion and one a "minority" or "underdog" opinion. On each of the experiment's eight days, each subject received email notice of what information their contacts had viewed the day before, as information diffused through the networks. A basic finding was that "people connected to distant network regions [in the essentially random network] are exposed to dominant and underdog information at near equal rates" and, as a result, these subjects "learn about both sides of an issue and shift their attitudes toward the underdog." Those in the clustered lattice network, where contacts tend to be confined to the same network region, on the other hand, tend to exhibit a single perspective (pp. 717–718). Two additional rigorous examinations of the experimental findings were conducted: a simulation study, and three statistical analyses in which learning and support for the underdog were modeled. Given that the effects of network structure are difficult to locate with observational data, this study provides an exemplar of thoroughly rigorous research (experimental, simulation, and statistical) on how network structure affects preference formation.

Conclusions

As an aside, one final challenge posed by network theory is its resistance to being summarized succinctly in one handbook chapter! While researchers across the sciences and humanities (whether located in universities, government agencies, or the private sector) recognize the continued rapid acceleration of the rate of new empirical research publications on social networks, it is less appreciated that systematic theorization of social networks is also on the rise – and, we feel, more necessary than ever, given the increasingly interdisciplinary empirical study of social networks. We have endeavored to focus on the latter trend, emphasizing developments and problems in network theory that we think deserve enhanced attention, though these are but selected examples. With the 2018 revision of the Federal Policy for the Protection of Human Subjects (the Common Rule), in some ways network research is poised to become more accessible than ever, yet must always be balanced against ever-present concerns about data privacy, respect for persons, beneficence, and justice in the pursuit of knowledge of the complexity of human relationships.

References

Aral, S., and D. Walker. 2014. "Tie Strength, Embeddedness, and Social Influence: A Large-Scale Networked Experiment." *Management Science* 60 (6): 1352–1370.

Bail, Christopher A. 2014. "The Cultural Environment: Measuring Culture with Big Data." *Theory and Society* 43 (3–4): 465–482.

Baldassarri, D. 2015. "Cooperative Networks: Altruism, Group Solidarity, Reciprocity, and Sanctioning in Ugandan Producer Organizations." *American Journal of Sociology* 121 (2): 355–395.

Batagelj, Vladimir, Patrick Doreian, Natasa Kejzar, and Anuska Ferligoj. 2014. *Understanding Large Temporal Networks and Spatial Networks: Exploration, Pattern Searching, Visualization and Network Evolution*, Vol. 2. Hoboken, NJ: John Wiley & Sons.

Bearman, Peter S., James Moody, and Katherine Stovel. 2004. "Chains of Affection: The Structure of Adolescent Romantic and Sexual Networks." *American Journal of Sociology* 110 (1): 44–91.

Belsky, Daniel W., and Salomon Israel. 2014. "Integrating Genetics and Social Science: Genetic Risk Scores." *Biodemography and Social Biology* 60 (2): 137–155.

Berkman, Lisa F., and Aditi Krisha. 2014. "Social Network Epidemiology." In Lisa F. Berkman, Ichiro Kawachi, and M. Maria Glymour (eds.), *Social Epidemiology* (xvii, pp. 1–16). Oxford, UK: Oxford University Press.

Bond, R. M., C. J. Fariss, J. J. Jones, et al. 2012. "A 61-Million-Person Experiment in Social Influence and Political Mobilization." *Nature* 489 (7415): 295–298.

Boorman, S. A., and H. C. White. 1976. "Social-Structure from Multiple Networks. Role Structures." *American Journal of Sociology* 81 (6): 1384–1446.

Borgatti, Stephen P., and D. S. Halgin. 2011. "On Network Theory." *Organization Science* 22 (5): 1168–1181.

Borgatti, Stephen P., Martin G. Everett, and Jeffrey C. Johnson. 2018. *Analyzing Social Networks*, 2nd ed. Los Angeles: Sage.

Brashears, M. E., and E. Quintane. 2015. "The Microstructures of Network Recall: How Social Networks Are Encoded and Represented in Human Memory." *Social Networks* 41: 113–126.

Breiger, Ronald L. 2015. "Scaling Down." *Big Data & Society* 2(2): 2053951715602497.

Breiger, Ronald L., and Kyle Puetz. 2015. "Culture and Networks." In James D. Wright (ed.), *The International Encyclopedia of the Social and Behavioral Sciences* (pp. 557–562). Amsterdam: Elsevier.

Butts, C. T., R. M. Acton, J. R. Hipp, and N. N. Nagle. 2012. "Geographical Variability and Network Structure." *Social Networks* 34 (1): 82–100.

Centola, Damon. 2011. "An Experimental Study of Homophily in the Adoption of Health Behavior." *Science* 334 (6060): 1269–1272.

Centola, D., and A. Baronchelli. 2015. "The Spontaneous Emergence of Conventions: An Experimental Study of Cultural Evolution." *Proceedings of the National Academy of Sciences USA* 112 (7): 1989–1994.

Charbonneau, Daniel, Benjamin Blonder, and Anna Dornhaus. 2013. "Social Insects: A Model System for Network Dynamics." In Petter Holme and Jari Saramäki (eds.), *Temporal Networks* (pp. 217–244). Heidelberg/New York/Dordrecht/London: Springer.

Chen, Lin, Forrest W. Crawford, and Amin Karbasi. 2015. "Seeing the Unseen Network: Inferring Hidden Social Ties from Respondent-Driven Sampling." *arXiv preprint. arXiv:1511.04137.*

Christakis, N. A., and J. H. Fowler. 2007. "The Spread of Obesity in a Large Social Network over 32 Years." *New England Journal of Medicine* 357 (4): 370–379.

Christakis, N. A., and J. H. Fowler. 2014. "Friendship and Natural Selection." *Proceedings of the National Academy of Sciences USA* 111 Suppl 3: 10796–801.

Clauset, Aaron, Cristopher Moore, and Mark E. J. Newman. 2008. "Hierarchical Structure and the Prediction of Missing Links in Networks." *Nature* 453 (7191): 98–101.

Cole, S. W. 2014. "Human Social Genomics." *PLoS Genet* 10 (8): e1004601.

Cole, S. W., L. C. Hawkley, J. M. Arevalo, and J. T. Cacioppo. 2011. "Transcript Origin Analysis Identifies Antigen-presenting Cells as Primary Targets of Socially Regulated Gene Expression in Leukocytes." *Proceedings of the National Academy of Sciences USA* 108 (7): 3080–3085.

Collins, Randall. 2013. "Ten Major Theory Books Since 2000." *Contemporary Sociology* 42 (2): 160–166.

Cornwell, Benjamin, L. Philip Schumm, Edward O. Laumann, and Jessica Graber. 2009. "Social Networks in the NSHAP Study: Rationale, Measurement, and Preliminary Findings." *Journals of Gerontology Series B: Psychological Sciences and Social Sciences* 64 (suppl_1): i47–i55.

Crandall, D. J., L. Backstrom, D. Cosley, et al. 2010. "Inferring Social Ties from Geographic Coincidences." *Proceedings of the National Academy of Sciences of the United States of America* 107 (52): 22436–22441.

Crawford, Forrest W., Jiacheng Wu, and Robert Heimer. 2015. "Hidden Population Size Estimation from Respondent-Driven Sampling: A Network Approach." *arXiv preprint arXiv:1504.08349*.

Daraganova, G., P. Pattison, J. Koskinen, et al. 2012. "Networks and Geography: Modelling Community Network Structures as the Outcome of Both Spatial and Network Processes." *Social Networks* 34 (1): 6–17.

De Nooy, Wouter, Andrej Mrvar, and Vladimir Batagelj. 2011. *Exploratory Social Network Analysis with Pajek*, Vol. 27. Cambridge, UK: Cambridge University Press.

Dépelteau, François. 2018. *The Palgrave Handbook of Relational Sociology*: New York: Springer.

Domingue, Benjamin W., Daniel W. Belsky, Jason M. Fletcher, et al. 2018. "The Social Genome of Friends and Schoolmates in the National Longitudinal Study of Adolescent to Adult Health." *Proceedings of the National Academy of Sciences* 115 (4): 702–707: 201711803.

Donati, Pierpaolo. 2018. "An Original Relational Sociology Grounded in Critical Realism." In François Dépelteau (ed.), *The Palgrave Handbook of Relational Sociology* (pp. 431–456). New York: Springer.

Emirbayer, M. 1997. "Manifesto for a Relational Sociology." *American Journal of Sociology* 103 (2): 281–317.

Erikson, E. 2013. "Formalist and Relationalist Theory in Social Network Analysis." *Sociological Theory* 31 (3): 219–242.

Evans, C. R., J. P. Onnela, D. R. Williams, and S. V. Subramanian. 2016. "Multiple Contexts and Adolescent Body Mass Index: Schools, Neighborhoods, and Social Networks." *Social Science & Medicine* 162: 21–31.

Faust, Katherine. 2008. "Triadic Configurations in Limited Choice Sociometric Networks: Empirical and Theoretical Results." *Social Networks* 30 (4): 273–282.

Faust, Katherine. 2011. "Animal Social Networks." In John Scott and Peter J. Carrington (eds.), *The SAGE Handbook of Social Network Analysis* (pp. 146–166). Los Angeles, CA: Sage.

Faust, K., and J. Skvoretz. 2002. "Comparing Networks Across Space and Time, Size and Species." *Sociological Methodology* 32 (2002): 267–299.

Fine, Gary Alan, and Sherryl Kleinman. 1983. "Network and Meaning: An Interactionist Approach to Structure." *Symbolic Interaction* 6 (1): 97–110.

Fontdevila, Jorge. 2018. "Switchings Among Netdoms: The Relational Sociology of Harrison C. White." In François Dépelteau (ed.), *The Palgrave Handbook of Relational Sociology* (pp. 231–269). New York: Springer.

Frank, Ove. 2005. "Network Sampling and Model Fitting." In P. J. Carrington, J. Scott, and S. Wasserman (eds.), *Models and Methods in Social Network Analysis* (pp. 31–56). New York: Cambridge University Press.

Fuhse, Jan, and Sophie Mützel. 2010. *Relationale Soziologie*, Vol. 2. Wiesbaden: Springer.

Galaskiewicz, Joseph. 2007. "Has a Network Theory of Organizational Behaviour Lived Up to Its Promises?" *Management and Organization Review* 3 (1): 1–18.

Gile, Krista J., and Mark S. Handcock. 2017. "Analysis of Networks with Missing Data with Application to the National Longitudinal Study of Adolescent Health." *Journal of the Royal Statistical Society: Series C (Applied Statistics)* 66 (3): 501–519.

Goh, K. I., M. E. Cusick, D. Valle, et al. 2007. "The Human Disease Network." *Proceedings of the National Academy of Sciences USA* 104 (21): 8685–90.

Gorski, Philip S. 2013. What Is Critical Realism? And Why Should You Care?" *Contemporary Sociology* 42 (5): 658–670.

Guimerà, Roger, and Marta Sales-Pardo. 2009. "Missing and Spurious Interactions and the Reconstruction of Complex Networks." *Proceedings of the National Academy of Sciences USA* 106 (52): 22073–22078.

Han, X., S. N. Cao, Z. S. Shen, et al. 2017. "Emergence of Communities and Diversity in Social Networks." *Proceedings of the National Academy of Sciences USA* 114 (11): 2887–2891.

Handcock, Mark S., and Krista J. Gile. 2010. "Modeling Social Networks from Sampled Data." *The Annals of Applied Statistics* 4 (1): 5–25.

Hanneke, Steve, and Eric P. Xing. 2009. "Network Completion and Survey Sampling." International Conference on Artificial Intelligence and Statistics. April 16-19, 2009, Clearwater, FL.

Hedström, P., and P. Ylikoski. 2010. "Causal Mechanisms in the Social Sciences." *Annual Review of Sociology* 36 (36): 49–67.

Hedström, Peter, and Peter S. Bearman. 2009. *The Oxford Handbook of Analytical Sociology.* New York: Oxford University Press.

Holt-Lunstad, J., T. B. Smith, and J. B. Layton. 2010. "Social Relationships and Mortality Risk: A Meta-Analytic Review." *Plos Medicine* 7 (8): 1–2.

Holt-Lunstad, Julianne, and Timothy B. Smith. 2016. "Loneliness and Social Isolation as Risk Factors for CVD: Implications for Evidence-based Patient Care and Scientific Inquiry." *Heart*: heartjnl-2015–309242.

Jackson, Matthew O. 2008. "Social Networks in Economics." In J. Benhabib, A. Bisin, and M. O. Jackson (eds.), *Handbook of Social Economics* (pp. 511–586). New York: Elsevier.

Junker, B. H., and F. Schreiber. 2008. *Analysis of Biological Networks*. Hoboken, NJ: John Wiley and Sons.

Kim, D. A., A. R. Hwong, D. Stafford, et al. 2015. "Social Network Targeting to Maximise Population Behaviour Change: A Cluster Randomised Controlled Trial." *Lancet* 386 (9989): 145–153.

Kim, Myunghwan, and Jure Leskovec. 2011. "The Network Completion Problem:Inferring Missing Nodes and Edges in Networks." Conference Proceedings of the Eleventh SIAM International Conference on Data Mining, SDM, held April 28–30, 2011 in Mesa, AZ.

Klar, S., and Y. Shmargad. 2017. "The Effect of Network Structure on Preference Formation." *Journal of Politics* 79 (2): 717–721.

Koskinen, Johan H., Garry L. Robins, and Philippa E. Pattison. 2010. "Analysing Exponential Random Graph (P-star) Models with Missing Data Using Bayesian Data Augmentation." *Statistical Methodology* 7 (3): 366–384.

Kossinets, Gueorgi. 2006. "Effects of Missing Data in Social Networks." *Social Networks* 28 (3): 247–268.

Kramer, A. D. I., J. E. Guillory, and J. T. Hancock. 2014. "Experimental Evidence of Massive-Scale Emotional Contagion through Social Networks." *Proceedings of the National Academy of Sciences USA* 111 (24): 8788–8790.

Krause, Robert W., Mark Huisman, and Tom A. B. Snijders. 2018. "Multiple Imputation for Longitudinal Network Data." *Italian Journal of Applied Statistics* 30 (1): 33–57.

Kreager, Derek A., Diane H. Felmlee, and Duane F. Alwin. 2018. "Strategies for Integrating Network and Life Course Perspectives." In Duane F. Alwin, Diane H. Felmlee, and Kerek A. Kreager (eds.), *Social Networks and the Life Course* (pp. 479–486). New York: Springer.

Lazega, Emmanuel. 2016. "Synchronization Costs in the Organizational Society: Intermediary Relational Infrastructures in the Dynamics of Multilevel Networks." In Emmanuel Lazega and Tom A. B. Snijders (eds.), *Multilevel Network Analysis for the Social Sciences* (pp. 47–77). Cham, Switzerland: Springer.

         2017. "Networks and Institutionalization: A Neo-Structural Approach." *Connections* (37): 7–22.

Liben-Nowell, D., and J. Kleinberg. 2008. "Tracing Information Flow on a Global Scale Using Internet Chain-letter Data." *Proceedings of the National Academy of Sciences USA* 105 (12): 4633–4638.

Liben-Nowell, D., J. Novak, R. Kumar, P. Raghavan, and A. Tomkins. 2005. "Geographic Routing in Social Networks." *Proceedings of the National Academy of Sciences USA* 102 (33): 11623–11628.

Lizardo, Omar. 2014. "Omnivorousness as the Bridging of Cultural Holes: A Measurement Strategy." *Theory and Society* 43 (3–4): 395–419.

Lü, Linyuan, and Tao Zhou. 2011. "Link Prediction in Complex Networks: A Survey." *Physica A: Statistical Mechanics and Its Applications* 390 (6): 1150–1170.

Mann, Michael. 1986. *The Sources of Power. Volume 1: A History of Power from the Beginning to AD 1760.* Cambridge, UK: Cambridge University Press.

Marin, Alexandra. 2004. "Are Respondents More Likely to List Alters with Certain Characteristics? Implications for Name Generator Data." *Social Networks* 26 (4): 289–307.

Marsden, Peter V. 2005. "Recent Developments in Network Measurement." In Peter J. Carrington, John Scott, and Stanley Wasserman (eds.), *Models and Methods in Social Network Analysis* (pp. 8–30). New York: Cambridge University Press.

         2011. "Survey Methods for Network Data." In John Scott and Peter J. Carrington (eds.), *The Sage Handbook of Social Network Analysis* (pp. 370–388). London: Sage.

Marshall, David J., and Lynn Staeheli. 2015. "Mapping Civil Society with Social Network Analysis: Methodological Possibilities and Limitations." *Geoforum* 61: 56–66.

Martin, John Levi. 2009. *Social Structures.* Princeton, NJ: Princeton University Press.

Mathieson, I., I. Lazaridis, N. Rohland, et al. 2015. "Genome-wide Patterns of Selection in 230 Ancient Eurasians." *Nature* 528: 499–503.

Melamed, D., B. Simpson, and A. Harrell. 2017. "Prosocial Orientation Alters Network Dynamics and Fosters Cooperation." *Scientific Reports* 7: 357.

Menche, J., A. Sharma, M. Kitsak, et al. 2015. "Disease Networks. Uncovering Disease-disease Relationships through the Incomplete Interactome." *Science* 347 (6224): 1257601.

Mische, Ann. 2011. "Relational Sociology, Culture, and Agency." In John Scott and Peter J. Carrington (eds.), *The Sage Handbook of Social Network Analysis* (pp. 80–97). London: Sage.

Mohr, John W., and Craig Rawlings. 2015. "Formal Methods of Cultural Analysis." In James D. Wright (ed.), *International Encyclopedia of the Social & Behavioral Sciences* (pp. 357–367). New York: Elsevier.

Moody, James. 2009. "Network Dynamics." In Peter Hedström and Peter Bearman (eds.), *The Oxford Handbook of Analytical Sociology* (pp. 447–474). New York: Oxford University Press.

Muchnik, L., S. Aral, and S. J. Taylor. 2013. "Social Influence Bias: A Randomized Experiment." *Science* 341 (6146): 647–651.

Newman, Mark. 2010. *Networks: An Introduction*. New York: Oxford University Press.

Nishi, A., N. A. Christakis, and D. G. Rand. 2017. "Cooperation, Decision Time, and Culture: Online Experiments with American and Indian Participants." *Plos One* 12 (2): 1–9.

Onnela, J. P., S. Arbesman, M. C. Gonzalez, A. L. Barabasi, and N. A. Christakis. 2011. "Geographic Constraints on Social Network Groups." *Plos One* 6 (4): 1–7.

Pachucki, M. A., and R. L. Breiger. 2010. "Cultural Holes: Beyond Relationality in Social Networks and Culture." *Annual Review of Sociology* 36: 205–224.

Pachucki, M. A., P. F. Jacques, and N. A. Christakis. 2011. "Social Network Concordance in Food Choice Among Spouses, Friends, and Siblings." *American Journal of Public Health* 101 (11): 2170–2177.

Pachucki, Mark C., and Elizabeth Goodman. 2015. "Social Relationships and Obesity: Benefits of Incorporating a Lifecourse Perspective." *Current Obesity Reports* 4 (2): 217–223.

Padgett, John F., and Walter W. Powell. 2012. *The Emergence of Organizations and Markets*. Princeton, NJ: Princeton University Press.

Paluck, Betsy Levy, Hana H. Shepherd, and Peter Aronow. 2016. "Changing Climates of Conflict: A Social Network Experiment Survey." *Proceedings of the National Academy of Sciences of the United States of America* 113 (3): 566–571.

Phan, T. Q., and E. M. Airoldi. 2015. "A Natural Experiment of Social Network Formation and Dynamics." *Proceedings of the National Academy of Sciences USA* 112 (21): 6595–6600.

Pinter-Wollman, N., E. A. Hobson, J. E. Smith, et al. 2014. "The Dynamics of Animal Social Networks: Analytical, Conceptual, and Theoretical Advances." *Behavioral Ecology* 25 (2): 242–255.

Preciado, P., T. A. B. Snijders, W. J. Burk, H. Stattin, and M. Kerr. 2012. "Does Proximity Matter? Distance Dependence of Adolescent Friendships." *Social Networks* 34 (1): 18–31.

Raghavan, S., M. C. Pachucki, Y. C. Chang, et al. 2016. "Incident Type 2 Diabetes Risk is Influenced by Obesity and Diabetes in Social Contacts: A Social Network Analysis." *Journal of General Internal Medicine* 31 (10): 1127–1133.

Reed, Isaac Ariail. 2017. "Chains of Power and Their Representation." *Sociological Theory* 35 (2): 87–117.

Robins, Garry, Philippa Pattison, and Jodie Woolcock. 2004. "Missing Data in Networks: Exponential Random Graph (p^*) Models for Networks with Non-respondents." *Social Networks* 26 (3): 257–283.

Robinson, Gene E., Russell D. Fernald, and David F. Clayton. 2008. "Genes and Social Behavior." *Science* 322 (5903): 896–900.

Rubin, Donald B., and Roderick J. A. Little. 2002. *Statistical Analysis with Missing Data*. Hoboken, NJ: John Wiley & Sons.

Rule, Alix, and Peter Bearman. 2015. "Networks and Culture." In Laurie Hanquinet and Mike Savage (eds.), in the *Routledge International Handbook of the Sociology of Art and Culture* (pp. 161–173). London: Routledge.

Scott, John. 2017. *Social Network Analysis*, 4th ed. London: Sage.

Selznick, Philip. 1949. *TVA and the Grass Roots: A Study in the Sociology of Formal Organization*. Berkeley, CA: University of California Press.

Shirado, H., and N. A. Christakis. 2017. "Locally Noisy Autonomous Agents Improve Global Human Coordination in Network Experiments." *Nature* 545 (7654): 370–374.

Shizuka, D., and D. B. McDonald. 2012. "A Social Network Perspective on Measurements of Dominance Hierarchies." *Animal Behaviour* 83 (4): 925–934.

Smith, Christian. 2011. *What Is a Person? Rethinking Humanity, Social Life, and the Moral Good from the Person Up*. Chicago, IL: University of Chicago Press.

Staples, P. C., E. L. Ogburn, and J. P. Onnela. 2015. "Incorporating Contact Network Structure in Cluster Randomized Trials." *Scientific Reports* 5: 17581.

Stork, Diana, and William D. Richards. 1992. "Nonrespondents in Communication Network Studies Problems and Possibilities." *Group & Organization Management* 17 (2): 193–209.

Thoits, Peggy A. 2011. "Mechanisms Linking Social Ties and Support to Physical and Mental Health." *Journal of Health and Socoa; Behavior* 52 (2): 145–161.

Travers, Jeffrey, and Stanley Milgram. 1967. "The Small World Problem." *Psychology Today* 1 (1): 61–67.

Umberson, D., R. Crosnoe, and C. Reczek. 2010. "Social Relationships and Health Behavior Across the Life Course." *Annual Review of Sociology* 36: 139–157.

Valente, T. W. 2012. "Network Interventions." *Science* 337 (6090): 49–53.

VanderWeele, T. J., E. L. Ogburn, and E. J. Tchetgen Tchetgen. 2012. "Why and When 'Flawed' Social Network Analyses Still Yield Valid Tests of No Contagion." *Statistics, Politics, and Policy* 3 (1): 2151–1050.

Vilhena, Daril A., Jacob G. Foster, Martin Rosvall, Jevin D. West, James Evans, and Carl T. Bergstrom. 2014. "Finding Cultural Holes: How Structure and Culture Diverge in Networks of Scholarly Communication." *Sociological Science* 1: 221–238.

Wasserman, Stanley, and Katherine Faust. 1994. *Social Network Analysis: Methods and Applications*, Vol. 8. New York: Cambridge University Press.

White, Harrison C. 1992. *Identity and Control: A Structural Theory of Social Action*. Princeton, NJ: Princeton University Press.

    2008. *Identity and Control: How Social Formations Emerge*, 2nd ed. Princeton, NJ: Princeton University Press.

WHO. 2018. "The Determinants of Health." World Health Organization. www.who.int/hia/evidence/doh/en/.

Yang, Y. C., C. Boen, K. Gerken, et al. 2016. "Social Relationships and Physiological Determinants of Longevity across the Human Life Span." *Proceedings of the National Academy of Sciences USA* 113 (3): 578–583.

Zerubavel, N., P. S. Bearman, J. Weber, and K. N. Ochsner. 2015. "Neural Mechanisms Tracking Popularity in Real-World Social Networks." *Proceedings of the National Academy of Sciences USA* 112 (49): 15072–15077.

3 Cultural Sociology

Michael Strand and Lyn Spillman

Introduction

The concept of culture has been the principal source of theoretical innovation in sociology since the discipline began to fully take its own "cultural turn" starting in the 1980s (Alexander, 1988; Crane, 1994; Friedland and Mohr, 2004; Hall, Grindstaff, and Lo, 2010; Jacobs and Hanrahan, 2005; Jacobs and Spillman, 2005). The core problem of meaning making has inspired several path-breaking and paradigmatic theoretical discoveries and prompted the construction of concepts and categories that have traveled widely throughout the field. It has opened new avenues of empirical research in the discipline, making a significant imprint on nearly every subfield in sociology in a relatively brief space of time. Although theoretical inquiry and empirical investigations of culture in sociology tend to range broadly, it is possible to map theoretical approaches in the field by distinguishing three broad areas of topical concern and application – action, discourse, and production of culture – and their use at different levels of analysis.

Cultural sociology is arguably the subfield in sociology which has been most informed by diverse and interdisciplinary theoretical strands issuing from across the humanities and sciences. Significant theoretical influences include structuralism, hermeneutics, post-structuralism, cognitive neuroscience, phenomenology, and pragmatism, which have focused understandings of the culture concept around issues of internal complexity, active production, and practical use. Most of these themes remained unnoticed or undertheorized in older assumptions about culture in sociology, which tended to theorize culture as a qualitatively homogeneous property of specific groups. The reaction to this overgeneralization was theoretically productive, but the proliferation of conceptual refinements reinforced what Clifford Geertz (1973: 89) once called the "studied vagueness" of the concept, featuring a wealth of valuable references but a potentially baffling analytical eclecticism.

Cultural sociology at present tries to retain the productive comprehensiveness of the culture concept, but combine this with an emphasis on greater theoretical precision and analytical clarity. This often involves efforts to relate and render compatible or contextually specific what had been hitherto disconnected or opposed theoretical approaches to culture (Alexander, 2004; Lizardo, 2017; Patterson, 2014; Spillman, 1995). The conceptual emphasis in the field now tends to revolve around

---

* The authors thank Noah Rankins for his essential help reviewing the background literature.

a synthetic theoretical capital focused on establishing "both/and" frameworks rather than "either/or." This has proven theoretically fruitful in many crucial respects. Yet, in the process, cultural sociologists have tended to lose sight of important multilevel relationships by attending to micro-level processes in their meso-level settings while leaving macro-level cultural processes relatively neglected. To further strengthen cultural theory, sociologists need to strengthen their understanding of longer-term historical persistence, the relation of culture to issues of temporality and ontology, a finer-grained concern with emergent forms of discursive and performative power, and a renewal of macro-level empirical questions.

Elements of Cultural Theory

While the universe of cultural theory in sociology is fluid and expansive, it is possible to define specific dimensions that emerge from the organizing concern with meaning making in the field. These dimensions are action, discourse, and production, which remain irreducible and isolable from each other, but which are, arguably, implicit in any process of meaning making and are often fruitfully synthesized to more broadly specify its mechanisms (Spillman, 2016). Each of these dimensions also serves as the principal "trading zone" (Galison, 1997; Spillman, 2008) between cultural sociology and different theoretical and philosophical perspectives, as well as transdisciplinary arguments incorporated into (and exported from) the discipline. Cultural sociology is a field in which the full variety of theoretical vocabularies, methods, and data sources are brought together, "intercalated," and intermixed. This produces "full-fledged creoles or pidgin" thought styles more characteristic of an "interscience" than a field that trades only within a single disciplinary identity (Galison, 1997: 138).

Action

The action dimension encompasses those approaches to meaning making that foreground issues like interactional styles, cognition, embodiment, and motivation. Some cultural theorizing in this vein emphasizes the significance of group interaction processes in meaning making. Other influential approaches developed over the last few decades have incorporated influences from pragmatism and cognitive science into cultural sociology to deepen theories of individual action in processes of meaning making.

Some cultural theorists emphasize meaning making in group settings, prioritizing interactional process over individual action. For example, Matthew Norton (2014a) theorizes the importance of interactional settings, and for Nina Eliasoph and Paul Lichterman (2003; Lichterman and Eliasoph, 2014), group settings are finely differentiated according to informally generated group bonds, boundaries, and speech norms, and the particularities of these cultural forms shape specific cultural outcomes. This focus on analyzing group-level action has generated new understandings of public culture (Eliasoph, 1998; 2011; Lichterman, 1996; 2005). Conceived more broadly, attention to theorizing meaning-making processes in group interaction (see Hallett, 2010; Harrington and Fine, 2000) has also emerged in studies of a wide range of other groups, such as congregations (Becker, 1998), restaurants (Fine, 2008), and administrative subdivisions (Binder, 2007).

The classic Parsonian understanding of action as the means-ends "pursuit of ultimate values" has also been challenged through the pragmatist concepts of problem-solving, situational logic, and the creative construal of means and ends (Parsons, 1935; Parsons and Shils, 1951). This approach develops Ann Swidler's (1986; 2001a) influential argument against values as ends of action and in favor of the more flexible concept of cultural repertoires. For instance, in Richard Biernacki's (2002: 81) formulation, action consists of a "creative construal" that transposes schemas and tools between situations to solve meaningful problems. The "felicitous interplay between a puzzle and its solution" replaces "means-ends goal direction" as the primary model system of action, redefining how action serves as a locus of meaning making (see also Gross, 2009; Strand and Lizardo, 2015).

A similar reformulation has resulted from the inclusion of cognitive science into theories of action in cultural sociology. Unconscious mechanisms and processes (like schemas), new typologies and distinctions (public and private culture, "dual-process" models), and embodiment have all been new and ongoing points of focus for cultural sociologists (Cerulo, 2001; DiMaggio, 1997; Lizardo, 2014). Over the last several decades, the emergence of cognitive science has redefined the nature of cognition away from a classical focus on "internal symbol manipulation" toward a new emphasis on perception, embodiment, emotion, and the relation between motor capacities and higher-level cognitive processing (Ignatow, 2007; Lizardo and Strand, 2010; Shepherd, 2011; Vaisey, 2009). For cultural sociologists, action as the principal trading zone drawing these insights into the field has contributed to the development and resonance of concepts like habitus, practice, and cognition.

Building from the work of Pierre Bourdieu (1984; 1990), the concept of habitus has had a paradigmatic influence on research on topics like cultural taste, social class, education, and embodiment (Lamont and Lareau, 1988; Lareau, 2003; Lizardo, 2006; Wacquant, 2015). Bourdieu emphasizes the connection between habitus and "cognitive structures" that contribute most of all to an understanding of culture in action that is nonsymbolic and not consciously accessible or reportable. This offers a basis to critically revise traditional understandings of action that emphasize symbolic systems and consciously accessible meanings. The revisionist perspective has sparked debates in the field not only concerning the conceptual efforts to analytically respecify the nature of action, but also concerning issues of measurement and methodology, particularly the contrast between the more deliberate format of interview methods and the less deliberate measures of culture involving fixed-choice questions or large-N longitudinal patterns (Pugh, 2013; Vaisey, 2014).

Production of Culture

The production dimension of cultural sociology focuses on culture as a product in which the "mundane" influences of organizational context, legal infrastructure, and economic circumstances impact meaning making. As a trading zone, the production of culture has been a principal conduit for drawing insights, concepts, problematics, and frameworks from a variety of allied sociology subfields into cultural sociology, including organizations, networks, and the sociology of work, each drawing attention to factors that, alone or in combination, constrain or facilitate the nature and content of symbolic products.

Richard Peterson (1976) and Diana Crane (1976; 1992) pioneered the production-of-culture approach by drawing principles from organizational theory to emphasize how industry and organization structure, law and regulation, technology, and occupational careers impact the context in which culture is produced. This context directly affects innovation and diversity in popular culture (DiMaggio, 1982; Lopes, 1992; Peterson, 1997), and potentially affects the symbolic content of culture, as in Wendy Griswold's (1981) argument about the impact of copyright law on American literature. Paul Hirsch's (1972) paradigmatic early framework emphasized the "organization-set" and a multistage "flow" process that dictated the way in which organizations produced cultural products like books, films, and music. As Hirsch emphasized early on, a generalized uncertainty about reception plagues the production of culture and this generates a variety of organizational responses in terms of how (and how much) culture is produced by organizations. Scholars have further reiterated this claim, specifying more precisely the mechanisms that compensate for uncertainty (Bielby and Bielby, 1994).

Theorizing about social networks in cultural sociology has taken a variety of different forms. Important among them is the influence of social capital and "small worlds" on the production of culture. Eiko Ikegami (1998) broke new ground in this area with her study of "aesthetic networking" in the Tokugawa period of Japanese history around the *za* arts. This not only produced a flourishing aesthetic culture, but cultivated a civic sociability that was an important contributing factor to the dynamic political changes of the Tokugawa period. Social networks as a context for the production of culture have also been demonstrated in relation to world philosophy (Collins, 1998), Broadway musicals (Uzzi and Spiro, 2005), jazz music (Kirschbaum, 2015), and civic political communication (Mische and Pattison, 2000) to name just a few.

Fields have also emerged as a key structuring context for the production of culture, based largely on the groundbreaking work of Bourdieu (1993). The structure of field consists of relationally defined, competitive positions and "capital" as a dimension of power that dictates the symbolic content of cultural products and a hierarchical and quasi-hegemonic production context. The relative autonomy of fields is linked to the distinctiveness and transferability of their capital in relation to the larger social space and field of power. Fields as a context for the production of culture have been demonstrated in fashion (Mears, 2011), journalism (Benson, 2013), and poetry (Buyukokutan, 2011).

Institutions, meanwhile, have consistently been at the forefront of cultural theorizing within the sociology of organizations, and theorizing about institutions in cultural sociology has been innovative by helping integrate theories of networks and fields (Thornton, Ocasio, and Lounsbury, 2012). Indeed, the core concept of "institution" as consisting of both "patterns of activity" and "symbolic systems" often serves as a bridging concept in the field (Friedland and Alford, 1991: 232). Empirical investigation in both world-polity institutionalism (Meyer et al., 1997) and institutional field theory (DiMaggio and Powell, 1983; Fligstein and McAdam, 2012) has revealed strong tendencies for isomorphism to be transmitted through processes of meaning making, though isomorphism should not be understood to exclude local variation, change, and emergence (Clemens, 1997; Dobbin, 1994; Schneiberg and Clemens, 2006).

Discourse

The third irreducible dimension of cultural analysis involves the nature of cultural forms, and their expression of and influence on social life. Theories of cultural form have been a "trading zone" incorporating semiotic and structuralist theory, theories of performance, and material influences on meaning making. Arguably cultural sociology's most distinctive theoretical contribution, compared to other sociological perspectives, is its attention to the independent influence of cultural form on social action.

This became evident in the early application of "structuralist hermeneutics" to redefine the culture concept (Alexander and Smith, 2006; 1993), along with associated arguments by Jeffrey Alexander and his collaborators that emphasized the irreducibility of meaning making to social, political, or economic influences. This perspective maintains that both action and the production of culture *presuppose* cultural forms as a "landscape of meaning" (Reed, 2011). For example, the influence of semiotic presuppositions in the course of social relations has been investigated extensively in cases of scandal (Alexander, 1984; Reed, 2007), electoral outcomes (Alexander, 2004), social movements (Kane, 1997), state policy (Norton, 2014b; Smith, 2005), health-related sexual behavior (Tavory and Swidler, 2009), and innovation in industries (Weber, Heinze, and DeSoucey, 2008). From a different perspective but in a similar vein, Luc Boltanski and Laurent Thevenot (2006) analyze historically widespread situational logics and conventions of agreement constructing social relations.

Theories of performativity linking semiotic forms directly with action have offered further innovations for the analysis of cultural forms in social processes. Drawing from a broad synthesis of theories of performance and performativity, including those of Erving Goffman (1956), Judith Butler (1999), and Victor Turner (1974), but also theatrical studies by Richard Schechner (1977), Jeffrey Alexander (2004) offers a historically grounded theory of cultural performance in modernity. Meanwhile, Isaac Reed (2013) develops a theory comparing discursive and performative power as *sui generis* dimensions of power not reducible to material sources of power. These perspectives have enriched the study of social power in a variety of forms and manifestations, including its democratic expressions. For example, Alexander (2010) and Jason Mast (2013) offer rich analyses of conventional political power in the Obama and Clinton presidencies (respectively) in terms of cultural performance.

Contemporary cultural theorists are also exploring the influence of the material properties of cultural objects on meaning-making processes. Chandra Mukerji's (1997) study of the Garden of Versailles as a piece of material culture, with its elaborate earthworks, intricate architectural and engineering design, and immense wildlife preserve, is exemplary here. As Mukerji argues, the Garden's design reveals material practices that refigure the natural world for political effect, in this case generating a "naturalized" political territoriality assumed by the French state under King Louis XIV. Meanwhile, Terence McDonnell (2016, 2010) has developed a novel perspective on cultural materiality that draws on the notion of "cultural entropy" to emphasize the integral relation between materiality and variant interpretations of cultural objects. Dominik Bartmanski and Jeffrey Alexander (2012) also offer a theoretical approach for understanding the interplay of meaning and materiality in specifically iconic symbols. In each of these treatments, the materiality of cultural objects acts as a store for symbolism, energy, and forms of value that affect distinct sensory experiences of meaning making and communication (see Griswold, Mangione, and McDonnell, 2013). Perhaps ironically, as the material basis of symbol production becomes more remote from daily knowledge and experience, cultural theory is now reconsidering materiality.

All of these approaches emphasize the internally structured nature of cultural forms as sociologically significant over and above practical action and organized production in meaning making. They generate empirical analyses of the relative autonomy of culture, featuring specific informal logics, creative applications, and meaningful entailments. A discursive focus on cultural form in particular allows sociologists to offer specific analysis of "just how culture interferes with and directs what really happens" (Alexander and Smith, 2006: 14).

Lines of Synthesis

Clearly, there are many points of divergence between cultural theorists emphasizing action, production, or cultural forms, but these should not cloud the many points of synthesis between them, which have proven fruitful in recent years for using culture to solve empirical puzzles in a variety of topical areas and for developing new empirical questions. Much of this work integrates multiple levels of analysis, using concepts like fields, backgrounds, landscapes, and networks to situate micro-level phenomena within meso- and macro- contexts. Less common are efforts to synthesize levels in the *opposite* direction, from macro-levels to micro- and meso-levels.

Action and Cultural Production

The points of synthesis between action and production have revolved around concepts like fields, organizations, and networks and how these have shaped, and been shaped by, conventional "action"-related phenomena, like cognition, taste, decision-making, and interaction. Those studies that focus on these action phenomena in spaces of cultural production yield unique insights about how culture is produced by extending beyond the organization as the unit of analysis. Fields and social networks deploy an analogous theoretical logic in this respect, as they both emphasize the situatedness of action within larger social spaces.

A prominent example of this style of argument draws from field theory. Bourdieu's pioneering work on fields of cultural production emphasizes how cultural production takes place through action as "position-taking" by culture producers in a field structured by social relations. Bourdieu's (1996) own most prominent example involves a detailed "socio-analysis" of the writer Gustave Flaubert and how his aesthetic modernist ethic, "write the mediocre well," was a position-taking that tied together the contraries of "social art" and "bourgeois art." As Bourdieu argues, aesthetic modernism as a "generative formula" for the production of culture was not invented out of whole cloth by culture producers in literature, painting, and music. Rather, it was a "position to be made" in a field that historically situated culture producers. Its invention did not cause the autonomy of artistic fields but was symptomatic of changing social conditions for cultural production that allowed for greater field autonomy.

Subsequent examinations of fields as the structuring context for cultural production have drawn these arguments together with organizations as the context for cultural production (Boschetti, 1988; Spiro, 2013). Locating a "field effect" on cultural production remains the point of focus in research on fields that ranges far beyond Bourdieu's initial empirical focus on literature and painting. Monika Krause's (2014) study of NGOs and humanitarian relief is exemplary here. Krause reveals a transnational social field that shapes the "production of projects" by NGOs competing for a field-specific capital defined by the attention and resources given by institutional donors to humanitarian causes. Humanitarian intervention is not a direct logical extension of humanitarian principles but is subject to the (fragmented) representation of aid-worthiness by NGOs, a process which formally resembles the logic of cultural production because it exercises a field effect on the distribution of outcomes.

The synthesis of social networks with cultural production provides for a similar analytic focus in serving as a meso-level context for action phenomena (Emirbayer and Goodwin, 1994; McLean, 2016). Indeed, the further synthesis of networks with cultural production has led to a host of creative insights. Following the pioneering work by Diana Crane (1975) and Charles Kadushin (1974) on the role of creative networks in science, art, and intellectual life, network approaches have extended further into the production of culture by identifying multiply nested interpersonal-influence networks that affect both production and reception (Childress, 2017; Childress and Friedkin, 2012). Action phenomena like interaction, cognition, and judgment exercise a mutual influence over social networks and the composition of social groups as sites for aesthetic judgment and status evaluation (Erickson, 1996; Fuhse, 2009; Lizardo, 2006; Srivastava and Banaji, 2011; Wohl, 2015).

More broadly, the generative force of interaction in producing durable inequalities is uniquely revealed in cultural sociology that draws together all three dimensions of culture. Lauren Rivera's (2015) study of hiring decisions at elite professional services firms is an example. Hiring decisions are shaped by signals of cultural capital (class-based skills and presentation styles) that are an extension of economic privilege. Here Rivera extends the literature on the cultural reproduction of economic advantage into an organizational sociology of hiring practices. What is particularly novel about the study is how hiring decisions at elite firms are not only action phenomena but also serve as sites of cultural production, in this case about the discourse of what is "meritorious" and the contours of the symbolic boundaries that it generates.

Cultural Production and Discourse

The intersection of cultural production and discourse is also a significant point of focus for cultural sociology, as organizations, fields, and networks all serve as production venues for trans-individual discourses, knowledge, and policies. As anchoring points for discourse, cultural production venues of multiple sorts allow sociologists to specify in detail the processes of discursive change and patterns of broader circulation and resonance. Synthetic work here is more attuned to phenomena at the macro-level and large-scale patterns of meaning making than other types of synthesis.

Christina Simko's (2015) examination of public consolation in the aftermath of collective traumas like September 11 demonstrates these lines of synthesis. In this scenario, politicians become sources of cultural production as they fulfill cultural expectations to apply existing narratives and other cultural tropes to provide existential guidance during times of crisis, often by invoking collective memories. This sort of "consolation discourse" operates at a trans-individual level and is capable of reaffirming collective identities through the deployment of cultural forms. Here, politicians are the "carrier groups" reproducing larger and longer-term cultural narratives about collective trauma (Alexander et al., 2004).

The relation between discourse, cultural production, and policy has been a significant focus for cultural sociologists at least since Frank Dobbin's (1994) groundbreaking comparative study of industrial policy in Great Britain, the United States, and France. The dialectic between policy implementation and what is pre-established as "culturally conceivable" in a political context specifies in detail the role that cultural discourse plays in policy making. This research site includes the stages of conception of social policy concerned with anti-poverty protocol and the behavioral discourses that inform historical variation in the resonance of ideas about the causes of poverty, including culture itself (Guetzkow, 2010; Lamont and Small, 2010; Small, Harding, and Lamont, 2010). A production-of-culture perspective applied to "poverty knowledge" reveals how trans-individual discourses are marshaled by professional knowledge producers to shape and direct social policy in ways consistent with certain moral assumptions (O'Connor, 2010; Rodriguez-Muniz, 2015).

Cultural elites as influencers of tastes, dispositions, and cultural development have long been a point of reference for sociologists (Khan, 2012). More recently, elite social spaces have been recognized as sites of production for cultural discourse. In

Shamus Khan's (2011) study of an exclusive New England prep school, the problem of how to embody privilege despite anti-inequality and meritocratic discourse makes for a production-of-culture problem concerned with the redefinition of elite social status. In this circumstance, "privilege" is symbolically transformed from being a set of birth advantages leveraged for elite social reproduction to being a quasi-naturalized capacity to be successful in competitive environments that subsequently elides durable inequality. The school serves as an organizational context for the production of strategies and discourses that preserve privilege and advantage, despite growing resistance to the relentless extension of social inequality.

Discourse and Action

Lines of synthesis between discourse and action have proven to be among the most theoretically fruitful in sociology in recent years, as sociologists explore the role that cultural forms of various sorts (semiotic, cognitive, material) play in action and interaction. Dual-process models, performativity, motivation, cognition, and institutions have proven to be important venues for theoretical reformulations that synthesize action and discursive processes. In recent years, pragmatism, cognitive science, and science studies have all offered conceptual resources that break new ground at the intersection of meaning making and action, dealing with cross-domain mechanisms and processes that translate across different subfields.

A kind of Weberian revitalization is one direction of synthesis between discourse and action, as theorists have examined the way discourses shape internal mental states and motivations, thus linking the macro with the micro in novel formulations (Reed, 2011). The subjective moment of action from this perspective takes the form of beliefs and desires, but these are amorphous, "like melted bronze before it is poured into a case and allowed to harden into a real statue" (Reed, 2011: 158). Beliefs and desires may be conscious or subconscious, accessible to inquiry or not, but what is consequential for understanding action is the wider landscape of meanings that shape their expression (Pugh, 2013). Challenges to this view emphasize the importance of practical consciousness and preconscious dispositions in action (Lizardo and Strand, 2010; Vaisey, 2009). They have inspired finer-grained distinctions between personal and public, declarative and non-declarative types of culture (Lizardo, 2017; Patterson, 2014), and have reintroduced the distinction articulated here between culture as discourse and culture as action.

The strong revival of pragmatism, combined with the influence of science studies and sociological traditions of practice theory (Bourdieu, 1990; Reckwitz, 2002) have drawn increased attention to social practices as points of convergence between action and discourse (Camic, Gross, and Lamont, 2011; Lizardo and Strand, 2010; Swidler, 2001b). As public "ensembles of patterned activities," social practices provide an access point for understanding the meanings that motivate and render action "surprisingly regular" or patterned (Martin, 2011). Semiotic codes also articulate (or "suture together") preestablished practical understandings in ways that construct resonant cultural categories and "the social" as a built environment (Sewell, 2005). A more interactionist approach focuses on the semiotic spaces that locate action along discursively coded axes that signify and "give off" public meanings (Tavory and Swidler, 2009). Discourse and action are mutually specified here in ways that reveal their interconnection with the expression of both desired identities and "summoned" identities that surpass intended meanings (Tavory, 2016).

Ellen Berrey's (2015) study of the post–Civil Rights translation of racial progress as "diversity" brings many of these points together in a novel synthesis. Over the last thirty years, social policy focused on racial inequality has arrived at "selective inclusion" as a set of practices, social relationships, and symbolic constructs that signify diversity but pose little risk to established power structures. As a discourse, diversity articulates with moral identity as the desire not to discriminate against cultural difference, but this gives only certain ideas influence and "leaves advocates without a language for talking about inequality" (2015: 9). The institutional resonance of diversity discourse in universities and corporations and among local housing authorities in Berrey's study effectively precludes the advancement of a "radical race-class transformation" that could challenge the prevailing institutional logics and practices that reproduce racial domination.

Materiality has also become a point of focus for investigating relations between cultural forms and action in ways analogous to practice. McDonnell's (2016) study of anti-AIDS media campaigns in Ghana is exemplary of this trend. The materiality of the cultural objects at the center of these campaigns (posters, condoms, billboards) is basic to their communication of meaning and the larger effectiveness of campaign messages. Using a novel adaption of the thermodynamic concept of entropy, McDonnell emphasizes the materiality of meaning as revealing the "entropic unravelling" of cultural objects through unexpected usage and application (e.g. condom rings as bracelets). Cultural objects *as* (material) objects synthesize action and discourse as co-equal moments in meaning making (McDonnell, 2010). Combined with pragmatism, materiality makes the semiotic and practical "resonance" of cultural objects a critical mechanism (McDonnell, Bail, and Tavory, 2017; see also Boltanski and Thevenot, 2006).

Cultural Theory: From Meso/Micro to Macro/Meso

Cultural sociology has been uniquely concerned with drawing together phenomena at different units of analysis from the micro, meso, and macro. Issues generated by these efforts include how to "measure culture" (*Theory and Society*, Ghaziani and Mohr, 2014) questions of realism and ontology (Archer, 1995) and the problem of historical emergence. In recent years, micro/meso connections have been the most active area of synthesis, as fields and networks increasingly become meso-level research sites for explaining micro-level phenomena like action and cognition. However, this leaves unanswered questions about meso/macro connections, particularly ones that involve historical emergence and the historical persistence of fields.

Since cultural forms may be involved in many different settings over time, analysis of discourse is uniquely attuned to drawing meso/macro connections that counter the tendency to presuppose the existence of meso-level orders (like fields). It provides a way to account for the appearance of meso-level phenomena as parts of historical "formation stories" that capture a variable ontology (Hirschman and Reed, 2014). Philip Gorski (2013) provides a model of field emergence that emphasizes the discursive construction of "ultimate value" as a necessary accompaniment to the genesis of social fields. Shai Dromi's (2016) analysis of the nineteenth-century appearance of the humanitarian field demonstrates the appeal of discourse as a macro-level influence on meso-level orders like fields. He reveals how a very specific strand of Calvinist doctrine shaped the genesis of the humanitarian field through the efforts of activists associated with the International Red Cross. Michael Strand (2015, 2017) offers a similar analysis of the genesis of a field. Here, civil discourse and its early nineteenth-century moral coding of capitalist practices provides a co-determinant mechanism alongside multiply intersecting sets of social relations for the appearance of a field of social justice in late-nineteenth-century England.

The analysis of discourse also serves as a research focus that links lower-level meso or micro effects to macro-level explanations. Here the connection of discourse to social context and the structuring effects of organizations is a main point of focus. Christopher Bail (2014) explains the emergence of anti-Muslim discourse in the wake of September 11 as part of the evolution of a discursive field. Anti-Muslim "fringe organizations," and their fringe tendency to rhetorically deploy fear and anger, exercise a "gravitational pull" on the field that restructures the doxic contours of Muslim discourse in civil society (see also Berezin, 2009 on the influence of the far right in Europe). In the process, discourse reorganizes meso-level interorganizational networks. Gabriel Abend (2014), in his argument about the history of business ethics, shares similar concerns with discursive emergence. Here business ethics appears in America through the convergence of several discursive streams in the eighty years between the middle of the nineteenth century and the Great Depression. In Abend's argument, business ethics emerges as a "para-moral" element found in a second-order (macro) background that is presupposed by the first-order (meso/micro) morality of beliefs, behaviors, and norms that apply to evaluations and judgments of "good businesspeople."

These examples are consistent with Isaac Reed's (2011) broader theoretical concern with "landscapes of meaning" as the discursive spaces "upon which . . . human beings emerge [with] subjective motives that force action forward" (2011: 152). Landscapes of meaning provide a macro-level of discourse that is foundational in its extended effects on meaning making across time and space. It also provides a cultural model for causal explanation by identifying the effects of landscapes at the meso-level, through formation stories of social and cultural orders, and at the micro-level, by providing "forming causes" of action as explicit reasons and unconscious drives and desires. Arrangements of meaning and representation shape (or "form") the forceful causation exercised by mechanisms.

Social practices can play a similar role to that of macro foundation. Richard Biernacki's (1995; see also Alexander, 2002; Swidler 2001b) comparative study of labor in Britain and Germany from the seventeenth to the nineteenth centuries demonstrates how. Here, different practices of commodifying labor between the two countries (commodification of labor power in Germany; commodification of labor products in Britain) served as pragmatic "anchor" points for a variety of cultural forms (see also Swidler, 2001b). The practical "category of labor" systematically conveyed meanings at the meso- and micro-levels, affecting phenomena ranging from capital investments and workers' arguments about exploitation, to economic analyses (including Marx), perceptions of time, labor movement repertoires, and even the architectural design of factories.

Whether a discursive landscape or an anchoring practice serves in the role, macro foundations like these that extend across space and time and help explain both historical emergence and historical persistence – not to mention specifying cultural difference – are relatively neglected points of focus for cultural sociologists. The major difference between discourse and practice as ways of revealing the effects of macro-level cultural forms in this case is that discursive approaches tend to examine in detail the systematic components of these long-lasting cultural forms, while practice approaches tend to highlight the "experiential contexts and concrete histories of acquisition" that dictate the degree and type of systematicity that apply to them (Lizardo, 2017: 100; Sewell, 2005). More specifically, a focus on practice reveals historical configurations of practical activity in which culture is found in a "practical relation to the world" not mediated by explicit meanings or representations (Bourdieu, 1990: 27; Martin, 2011).

Drawing these arguments about macro-level foundations together with questions of temporality leads us to ask whether there might be multiple temporalities at work in social action, loosely in line with what Paul Ricoeur (1974) suggested as the "background" temporality of structure, combined with what we might refer to (following Sewell, 2005) as the "eventful" temporality of hermeneutics. In this case, a macro landscape or anchoring practice provides temporally persistent conditions of possibility for meso and micro phenomena. These are more proximately shaped by contingent events to produce specific formulations ("interpretations" in Ricoeur's terms) of what is available in the macro-level background. Meanwhile, the potential for "restless events" (Wagner-Pacifici, 2010) suggests a unit of analysis that allows cultural sociologists to understand how foundational discourses and practices can themselves be reorganized.

Because micro/meso syntheses have been the most active research site, cultural sociology still affords only a limited understanding of how meaning making occurs trans-situationally. Yet, meso-level situations and contexts remain critical units of analysis for cultural sociologists, not least because they serve as key empirical reference points for demonstrating macro-level influences on culture (Norton, 2014a; Strand and Lizardo, 2015). Two examples from economic and cultural sociology demonstrate how to draw non-reductive connections between macro-, meso-, and micro-levels by taking situations, contexts, and organizations as meso-level empirical research sites.

Luc Boltanski and Laurent Thevenot (2006) treat "critical situations" as integral points of synthesis between macro, meso, and micro phenomena. Here, macro-level and trans-situational "grammars" of social bonds or different "orders of worth" convey justifications that can start and end disputes and construct and reconstruct social bonds, through moral meaning making. In critical situations these grammars become evident in claims-making by actors seeking to construct justifiable denunciations and proofs. Political philosophy serves as a formal articulation of different grammars as sets of logically related propositions that mimic the form of everyday ("pragmatic") denunciations. Meanwhile, the micro-level exercise of "critical capacities" is brought into relief by critical situations, which Boltanski and Thevenot (2006) use to reflexively situate sociology and economics as themselves positive referents for moral grammars that construct social bonds.

Also linking macro- and micro- through meso-level contexts, Lyn Spillman's (2012) study examines trade associations as sites for the production and transmission of "business culture." The associations serve as points of articulation for reproducing a macro-level culture structure or discursive "grammar" that allows for the construction of vocabularies of motive and strategies of action whose solidaristic focus deviates from economistic assumptions about innate economic self-interest. The associations also serve as venues for meaning making in action as members acquire the business culture necessary for economic agency.

Increased attention to macro-level discourses and practices underpinning meso-level contexts and micro-level action seems particularly important if we are to further develop theories of cultural power. The synthesis between cultural theory and theories of power has arguably been a major focus ever since Steven Lukes (1974) identified a "third dimension" of power as the power to shape cognitions, preferences, and actions. Bourdieu's (1993) notion of "symbolic power" as naturalizing inequality is similar in its synthesis of misrecognition and perceptions of legitimacy. Recently, Reed (2013) has argued that this third dimension of power, or *cultural* power, operates through three distinct mechanisms: relational, discursive, and performative. He suggests that these cultural mechanisms serve as "forming" causes, setting the grounds and conditions for particular power relations that exercise "forceful" causes. More generally, this makes culture an integral part of an understanding of social ontology that focuses on the historical emergence of distinct social kinds with "causal powers" (Hirschman and Reed, 2014).

Conclusion

Cultural sociology remains at the forefront of theoretical discussions in sociology at large, not least because of the encompassing nature of culture as an object of research and the ambiguities that persist about it. Under the guise of cultural theory, sociology has been influenced by a range of broader theoretical and empirical trends, and it continues to be a trading zone between sociology and theoretical discourses from a wide range of different sources. Cultural sociology remains a subfield that often attracts the theoretically adventurous, and it is not surprising that most general theoretical debates are at least indirectly relevant to culture. Indeed, in many cases, they are directly inspired by the issues that circulate within it.

As we've argued, cultural sociology can be distinguished into three dimensions of meaning making: action, production of culture and discourse. Research in the subfield can be specified on these terms, and the new research in the subfield can be understood as different and novel integrations of these different types of cultural sociology. This helps overcome the prior "studied ambiguity" of the concept that Geertz (1973) noticed early on, and it remains a fruitful theoretical endeavor to draw more distinctions, to decipher more analytically specific frameworks, to draw further boundaries within culture, that clarify the concept even more. The argument here is that blanket generalizations about culture or dismissals of it for its lack of fixed precision are theoretically retrograde.

Issues on the horizon of cultural sociology include further advancements in those that have remained consistent points of focus, including discourse, production of culture and action, and those that have driven innovation in the subfield over the last couple of decades, including cognition, performativity, and meso-level production contexts like fields and networks. Newer issues that should gain a greater foothold in the field in the future include materiality, power, ontology, temporality, and (we claim) levels of analysis. The latter might not seem as theoretically novel as the former set of issues, but we argue that paying specific attention to distinctions between macro-, meso-, and micro-level phenomena, and placing cultural forms at each of these levels, remains a theoretically productive endeavor.

What becomes especially clear is the highly active area of drawing meso/micro relationships with concepts like fields and networks and their impact on action and cognition. What also becomes clear is the relative dearth of research that explores the effects of macro phenomenon on meso and micro phenomenon. This level of analysis presses the culture concept into the terrain of temporality and questions about emergence and persistence, and the arguably slower-moving timescale of macro cultural forms in comparison with the more eventful temporal horizons found at meso- and micro-levels.

References

Abend, Gabriel. 2014. *The Moral Background: An Inquiry into the History of Business Ethics*. Princeton, NJ: Princeton University Press.
Alexander, Jeffrey. 1984. "Three Models of Culture and Society Relations: Toward an Analysis of Watergate." *Sociological Theory* 2: 290–314.
    1988. "The New Theoretical Movement." In Neil J. Smelser (ed.), *Handbook of Sociology* (pp. 77–101). Newbury Park, CA: Sage
    2002. "On the Social Construction of Moral Universals." *European Journal of Social Theory* 5: 5–85.
    2004. "Cultural Pragmatics: Social Performance between Ritual and Strategy." *Sociological Theory* 22: 527–573.
    2010. *The Performance of Politics*. New York: Oxford University Press.
Alexander, Jeffrey C. and Philip Smith. 1993. "The Discourse of American Civil Society: A New Proposal for Cultural Studies." *Theory and Society* 22: 151–207.

2006. "The Strong Program in Cultural Sociology." In *The Meanings of Social Life* (pp. 11–27). New York: Oxford University Press.

Alexander, Jeffrey, Ron Eyerman, Bernhard Giesen, Neal Smelser, and Piotr Sztompka. 2004. *Cultural Trauma and Collective Identity*. Berkeley, CA: University of California Press.

Archer, Margaret. 1995. *Realist Social Theory: The Morphogenetic Approach*. New York: Cambridge University Press.

Bail, Christopher. 2014. *Terrified: How Anti-Muslim Fringe Organizations Became Mainstream*. Princeton, NJ: Princeton University Press.

Bartmanksi, Dominik, and Jeffrey C. Alexander. 2012. "Materiality and Meaning in Social Life: Toward an Iconic Turn in Cultural Sociology." In Jeffrey C. Alexander, Dominik Bartmanski and Bernhard Giesen (eds.), *Iconic Power: Materiality and Meaning in Social Life* (pp. 1–12). New York: Palgrave.

Becker, Penny Edgell. 1998. *Congregations in Conflict: Cultural Models of Local Religious Life*. London: Cambridge University Press.

Benson, Rodney. 2013. *Shaping Immigration News: A French-American Comparison*. London: Cambridge University Press.

Berezin, Mabel. 2009. *Illiberal Politics in Neoliberal Times: Culture, Security and Populism in the New Europe*. New York: Cambridge University Press.

Berrey, Ellen. 2015. *The Enigma of Diversity: The Language of Race and the Limits of Racial Justice*. Chicago, IL: University of Chicago Press.

Bielby, William, and Denise Bielby. 1994. "'All Hits Are Flukes': Institutionalized Decision Making and the Rhetoric of Network Prime-Time Program Development." *American Journal of Sociology* 99: 1287–1313.

Biernacki, Richard. 1995. *The Fabrication of Labor: Germany and Britain, 1640–1914*. Berkeley, CA: University of California Press.

2002. "The Action Turn? Comparative-Historical Inquiry Beyond the Classical Model of Conduct." In Julia Adams, Elisabeth Clemens, and Ann Shola Orloff (eds.), *Remaking Modernity* (pp. 75–104). Durham, NC: Duke University Press.

Binder, Amy. 2007. "For Love and Money: Organizations' Creative Responses to Multiple Environmental Logics." *Theory and Society* 36: 547–571.

Boltanski, Luc, and Laurent Thevenot. 2006. *On Justification: Economies of Worth*. Princeton, NJ: Princeton University Press.

Boschetti, Anna. 1988. *The Intellectual Enterprise: Sartre and Les Temps Modernes*. Chicago, IL: Northwestern University Press.

Bourdieu, Pierre. 1984. *Distinction: A Social Critique of the Judgment of Taste*. Cambridge, MA: Harvard University Press.

1990. *The Logic of Practice*. Stanford, CA: Stanford University Press.

1993. *Field of Cultural Production*. New York: Columbia University Press.

1996. *The Rules of Art*. Stanford, CA: Stanford University Press.

Butler, Judith. 1999. *Gender Trouble: Feminism and the Subversion of Identity*. New York: Routledge.

Buyukokutan, Boris. 2011. "Toward a Theory of Cultural Appropriation: Buddhism, the Vietnam War and the Field of US Poetry." *American Sociological Review* 76: 620–639.

Camic, Charles, Neil Gross, and Michele Lamont (eds.). 2011. *Social Knowledge in the Making*. Chicago, IL: University of Chicago Press.

Cerulo, Karen (ed.). 2001. *Culture in Mind*. New York: Routledge.

Childress, Clayton. 2017. *Under the Cover: The Creation, Production and Reception of a Novel*. Princeton, NJ: Princeton University Press.

Childress, Clayton, and Noah Friedkin. 2012. "Cultural Reception and Production: The Social Construction of Meaning in Book Clubs." *American Sociological Review* 77: 45–68.

Clemens, Elisabeth. 1997. *The People's Lobby: Organizational Innovation and the Rise of Interest Group Politics in the United States, 1890–1925*. Chicago, IL: University of Chicago Press.

Collins, Randall. 1998. *Sociology of Philosophies*. Cambridge, MA: Harvard University Press.

Crane, Diana. 1975. *Invisible Colleges*. Chicago, IL: University of Chicago Press.

   1976. "Reward Systems in Art, Science and Religion." *American Behavioral Scientist* 19: 719–734.

   1992. *The Production of Culture: Media and Urban Arts*. Beverly Hills, CA: Sage.

Crane, Diana (ed.). 1994. *Sociology of Culture: Emerging Theoretical Perspectives*. London: Blackwell.

DiMaggio, Paul. 1982. "Cultural Entrepreneurship in Nineteenth Century Boston: The Creation of an Organizational Base for High Culture in America." *Media, Culture and Society* 4: 33–50.

   1997. "Culture and Cognition." *Annual Review of Sociology* 23: 263–287.

DiMaggio, Paul, and Walter Powell. 1983. "The Iron Cage Revisited: Institutional Isomorphism and Collective Rationality in Organizational Fields." *American Sociological Review* 48: 147–160.

Dobbin, Frank. 1994. *Forging Industrial Policy: The United States, Britain and France in the Railway Age*. Cambridge, MA: Harvard University Press.

Dromi, Shai. 2016. "Soldiers of the Cross: Calvinism, Humanitarianism and the Genesis of Social Fields." *Sociological Theory* 34: 196–216.

Eliasoph, Nina. 1998. *Avoiding Politics: How Americans Produce Apathy in Everyday Life*. New York: Cambridge University Press.

   2011. *Making Volunteers: Civic Life After Welfare's End*. Princeton, NJ: Princeton University Press.

Eliasoph, Nina, and Paul Lichterman. 2003. "Culture in Interaction." *American Journal of Sociology* 108: 735–794.

Emirbayer, Mustafa, and Jeff Goodwin. 1994. "Network Analysis, Culture and the Problem of Agency." *American Journal of Sociology* 99: 1411–1454.

Erickson, Bonnie. 1996. "Culture, Class and Connections." *American Journal of Sociology* 102: 217–251.

Fine, Gary Alan. 2008. *Kitchens: The Culture of Restaurant Work*. Berkeley, CA: University of California Press.

Fligstein, Neil, and Doug McAdam. 2012. *A Theory of Fields*. New York: Oxford University Press.

Friedland, Roger, and Robert Alford. 1991. "Bringing Society Back In." In Walter Power and Paul DiMaggio (ed.), *New Institutionalism in Organizational Analysis* (pp. 232–267). Princeton, NJ: Princeton University Press.

Friedland, Roger, and John Mohr. 2004. "The Cultural Turn in American Sociology." In Roger Friedland and John Mohr (eds.), *Matters of Culture* (pp. 1–71). Chicago, IL: University of Chicago Press.

Fuhse, Jan. 2009. "The Meaning Structure of Social Networks." *Sociological Theory* 27: 51–73.

Galison, Peter. 1997. *Image and Logic: A Material Culture of Microphysics*. Chicago, IL: University of Chicago Press.

Geertz, Clifford. 1973. *Interpretation of Cultures*. New York: Basic Books.

Ghaziani, Amin, and John W. Mohr (eds.). 2014. Measuring Culture (Special Issue). *Theory and Society* 43(3–4).

Goffman, Erving. 1956. *Presentation of Self in Everyday Life*. New York: Scribner's.

Gorski, Philip. 2013. "Bourdieusean Theory and Historical Analysis." In Philip Gorski (ed.), *Bourdieu and Historical Analysis* (pp. 327–367). Durham, NC: Duke University Press.

Griswold, Wendy. 1981. "American Character and the American Novel: An Expansion of Reflection Theory in the Sociology of Literature." *American Journal of Sociology* 86: 740–765.

Griswold, Wendy, Gemma Mangione, and Terence McDonnell. 2013. "Objects, Words and Bodies in Space: Bringing Materiality into Cultural Analysis." *Qualitative Sociology* 46: 343–364.

Gross, Neil. 2009. "A Pragmatist Theory of Social Mechanisms." *American Sociological Review* 74: 358–379.

Guetzkow, Joshua. 2010. "Beyond Deservingness: Congressional Discourse on Poverty 1964–1996." *Annals of the American Academy of Political and Social Science* 629: 173–196.

Hall, John, Laura Grindstaff, and Ming-Cheng Lo (eds.). 2010. *Handbook of the Sociology of Culture*. London: Routledge.

Hallett, Tim. 2010. "The Myth Incarnate: Recoupling Processes, Turmoil and Inhabited Institutions in an Urban Elementary School." *American Sociological Review* 73: 52–74.

Harrington, Brooke, and Gary Alan Fine. 2000. "Opening the Black Box: Small Groups and Twenty-First Century Sociology." *Social Psychology Quarterly* 63: 312–323.

Hirsch, Paul. 1972. "Processing Fads and Fashions: An Organization-Set Analysis of Culture Industry Systems." *American Journal of Sociology* 77: 639–659.

Hirschman, Daniel, and Isaac Reed. 2014. "Formation Stories and Causality in Sociology." *Sociological Theory* 32: 259–282.

Ignatow, Gabriel. 2007. "Theories of Embodied Knowledge: New Directions for Cultural and Cognitive Sociology?" *Journal for the Theory of Social Behaviour* 37: 115–135.

Ikegami, Eiko. 1998. *Bonds of Civility: Aesthetic Networks and the Political Origins of Japanese Culture*. New York: Cambridge University Press.

Jacobs, Mark, and Nancy Hanrahan (eds.). 2005. *The Blackwell Companion to the Sociology of Culture*. New York: Wiley-Blackwell.

Jacobs, Mark D., and Lyn Spillman. 2005. "Cultural Sociology at the Crossroads of the Discipline." *Poetics* 33(1): 1–14.

Kadushin, Charles. 1974. *The American Intellectual Elite*. New Brunswick, NJ: Transaction Publishers.

Kane, Anne. 1997. "Theorizing Meaning Construction in Social Movements: Symbolic Structures and Interpretation during the Irish Land War, 1879–1882." *Sociological Theory* 15: 249–276.

Khan, Shamus. 2011. *Privilege: The Making of an Adolescent Elite at St Paul's School*. Princeton, NJ: Princeton University Press.

2012. "Sociology of Elites." *Annual Review of Sociology* 38: 61–77.

Kirschbaum, Charles. 2015. "Categories and Networks in Jazz Evolution: The Overlap between Bandleaders' Jazz Sidemen from 1930 to 1969." *Poetics* 52: 154–178.

Krause, Monika. 2014. *The Good Project: Humanitarian Relief NGOs and the Fragmentation of Reason*. Chicago, IL: University of Chicago Press.

Lamont, Michele, and Annette Lareau. 1988. "Cultural Capital: Allusions, Gaps and Glissandos in Recent Theoretical Developments." *Sociological Theory* 6: 153–168.

Lamont, Michele, and Mario Small. 2010. "Cultural Diversity and Anti-Poverty Policy." *International Social Science Journal* 61: 169–180.

Lareau, Annette. 2003. *Unequal Childhoods: Class, Race, and Family Life*. Berkeley, CA: University of California Press.

Lichterman, Paul. 1996. *The Search for Political Community: American Activists Reinventing Commitment*. New York: Cambridge University Press.

2005. *Elusive Togetherness: Church Groups Trying to Bridge America's Divisions*. Princeton, NJ: Princeton University Press.

Lichterman, Paul, and Nina Eliasoph. 2014. "Civic Action." *American Journal of Sociology* 120: 798–863.

Lizardo, Omar. 2006. "How Cultural Tastes Shape Personal Networks." *American Sociological Review* 71: 778–807.

2014. "Beyond the Comtean Schema: The Sociology of Culture and Cognition versus Cognitive Social Science." *Sociological Forum* 29: 983–989.

2017. "Improving Cultural Analysis: Considering Personal Culture in Its Declarative and Nondeclarative Modes." *American Sociological Review* 82: 88–115

Lizardo, Omar, and Michael Strand. 2010. "Skills, Toolkits, Contexts and Institutions: Clarifying the Relationship between Different Approaches to Cognition in Cultural Sociology." *Poetics* 38: 205–238.

Lopes, Paul. 1992. "Innovation and Diversity in the Popular Music Industry, 1969 to 1990." *American Sociological Review* 57: 56–71.

Lukes, Steven. 1974. *Power: A Radical View*. New York: Oxford University Press.

Martin, John Levi. 2011. *The Explanation of Social Action*. New York: Oxford University Press.

Mast, Jason. 2013. *The Performative Presidency: Crisis and Resurrection during the Clinton Years*. New York: Cambridge University Press.

McDonnell, Terence. 2010. "Cultural Objects as Objects: Materiality, Urban Space and the Interpretation of AIDS Campaigns in Accra, Ghana." *American Journal of Sociology* 115: 1800–1852.

2016. *Best Laid Plans: Cultural Entropy and the Unraveling of AIDS Media Campaigns*. Chicago, IL: University of Chicago Press.

McDonnell, Terence, Christopher Bail, and Iddo Tavory. 2017. "A Theory of Resonance." *Sociological Theory* 35: 1–14.

McLean, Paul. 2016. *Culture in Networks*. Cambridge, UK: Polity.

Mears, Ashley. 2011. *Pricing Beauty: The Making of a Fashion Model*. Berkeley, CA: University of California Press.

Meyer, John, John Boli, George Thomas, and Francisco Ramirez. 1997. "World Society and the Nation State." *American Journal of Sociology* 103: 144–181.

Mische, Ann, and Philippa Pattison. 2000. "Composing a Civil Arena: Publics, Projects and Social Settings." *Poetics* 27: 163–194.

Mukerji, Chandra. 1997. *Territorial Ambitions and the Garden of Versailles*. New York: Cambridge University Press.

Norton, Matthew. 2014a. "Mechanisms and Meaning Structures." *Sociological Theory* 32: 162–187.

2014b. "Classification and Coercion: The Destruction of Piracy in the English Maritime System." *American Journal of Sociology* 119: 1537–1575.

O'Connor, Alice. 2010. *Poverty Knowledge*. Princeton, NJ: Princeton University Press.

Parsons, Talcott. 1935. "The Place of Ultimate Values in Sociological Theory." *International Journal of Ethics* 45: 282–316.

Parsons, Talcott, and Edward Shils. 1951. *Toward a General Theory of Action*. New Brunswick, NJ: Transaction Publishers.

Patterson, Orlando. 2014. "Making Sense of Culture." *Annual Review of Sociology* 40: 1–30.

Peterson, Richard. 1976. *Production of Culture*. Thousand Oaks, CA: Sage.

1997. *Creating Country Music: Fabricating Authenticity*. Chicago, IL: University of Chicago Press.

Pugh, Allison. 2013. "What Good Are Interviews for Thinking about Culture?" *American Journal of Cultural Sociology* 1: 42–68.

Reckwitz, Andreas. 2002. "Toward a Theory of Social Practices." *European Journal of Social Theory* 5: 243–263.

Reed, Isaac. 2007. "Why Salem Made Sense." *Cultural Sociology* 1: 209–234.

2011. *Interpretation and Social Knowledge*. Chicago, IL: University of Chicago Press.

2013. "Power: Relational, Discursive and Performative Dimensions." *Sociological Theory* 31: 193–218.

Ricoeur, Paul. 1974. "Structure and Hermeneutics." In *Conflict of Interpretations* (pp. 27–62). Evanston, IL: Northwestern University Press.

Rivera, Lauren. 2015. *Pedigree: How Elite Students Get Elite Jobs*. Princeton, NJ: Princeton University Press.

Rodriguez-Muniz, Michael. 2015. "Intellectual Inheritances: Cultural Diagnostics and the State of Poverty Knowledge." *American Journal of Cultural Sociology* 3: 89–122.

Schechner, Richard. 1977. *Ritual, Play, and Social Drama*. New York: Seabury Press.

Schneiberg, Mark, and Elisabeth Clemens. 2006. "The Typical Tools for the Job: Research Strategies in Institutional Analysis." *Sociological Theory* 24: 195–227.

Sewell, William. 2005. *Logics of History*. Chicago, IL: University of Chicago Press.

Shepherd, Hana. 2011. "The Cultural Context of Cognition: What the Implicit Association Test Tells Us About How Culture Works." *Sociological Forum* 26: 121–143.

Simko, Christina. 2015. *The Politics of Consolation: Memory and the Meaning of September 11*. New York: Oxford University Press.

Small, Mario, David Harding, and Michele Lamont. 2010. "Rethinking Culture and Poverty." *Annals of the American Academy of Political and Social Science* 629: 6–27.

Smith, Philip. 2005. *Why War? The Cultural Logic of Iraq, the Gulf War and Suez*. Chicago, IL: University of Chicago Press.

Spillman, Lyn. 1995. "Culture, Social Structure and Discursive Fields." *Current Perspectives in Social Theory* 15: 129–154.

2008. "Message from the Chair: Cultural Sociology and Its Others." *Culture* 22: 1–4.

2012. *Solidarity in Strategy: Making Business Meaningful in American Trade Associations*. Chicago, IL: University of Chicago Press.

2016. "Culture." In George Ritzer (ed.), *The Blackwell Encyclopedia of Sociology*, 2nd edition. Oxford, UK: Blackwell Publishing.

Spiro, Gisele. 2013. "Structural History and Crisis Analysis." In Philip Gorski (ed.), *Bourdieu and Historical Analysis* (pp. 266–286). Durham, NC: Duke University Press.

Srivastava, Sameer, and Mahzarin Banaji. 2011. "Culture, Cognition and Collaborative Networks in Organizations." *American Sociological Review* 76: 207–233.

Swidler, Ann. 1986. "Culture in Action: Symbols and Strategies." *American Sociological Review* 51: 273–286.

2001a. *Talk of Love: How Culture Matters*. Chicago, IL: University of Chicago Press.

2001b. "What Anchors Cultural Practices." In Theodore Schatzki, Karen Knorr-Cetina, and Eike von Savigny (eds.), *The Practice Turn in Contemporary Theory* (pp. 74–92). New York: Routledge.

Strand, Michael. 2015. "The Genesis and Structure of Moral Universalism: Social Justice in Victorian Britain, 1834–1901." *Theory and Society* 44: 537–573.

2017. "Historicizing Social Inequality: A Victorian Archive for Contemporary Moral Discourse." *American Journal of Cultural Sociology* 5: 225–260.

Strand, Michael, and Omar Lizardo. 2015. "Beyond World Images: Belief as Embodied Action in the World." *Sociological Theory* 33: 44–70.

Tavory, Iddo. 2016. *Summoned: Identification and Religious Life in a Jewish Neighborhood*. Chicago, IL: University of Chicago Press.

Tavory, Iddo, and Ann Swidler. 2009. "Condom Semiotics." *American Sociological Review* 74: 171–189.

Thornton, Patricia, William Ocasio, and Michael Lounsbury. 2012. *The Institutional Logics Perspective*. New York: Oxford University Press.

Turner, Victor. 1974. *Dramas, Fields, and Metaphors: Symbolic Action in Human Society*. Ithaca, NY: Cornell University Press.

Uzzi, Brian, and Jarret Spiro. 2005. "Collaboration and Creativity: The Small World Problem." *American Journal of Sociology* 58: 447–504.

Vaisey, Stephen. 2009. "Motivation and Justification: A Dual-Process Model of Culture in Action." *American Journal of Sociology* 114: 1675–1715.

2014. "Is Interviewing Compatible with the Dual-Process Model?" *American Journal of Cultural Sociology* 2: 150–58.

Wacquant, Loic. 2015. "For a Sociology of Flesh and Blood." *Qualitative Sociology* 38: 1–11.

Wagner-Pacifici, Robin. 2010. "Theorizing the Restlessness of Events." *American Journal of Sociology* 115: 1351–1386.

Weber, Klaus, Kathryn Heinze, and Michaela DeSoucey. 2008. "Forage for Thought: Mobilizing Codes in the Movement for Grass-fed Meat and Dairy Products." *Administrative Science Quarterly* 53: 529–567.

Wohl, Hanna. 2015. "Community Sense: The Cohesive Power of Aesthetic Judgment." *Sociological Theory* 33: 299–326.

4 Identity

Peter Burke

Introduction

Within identity theory, an identity is a set of meanings defining who one is in a role (e.g., father, plumber, student), in a group or social category (e.g., member of a church or voluntary association, an American, a female), or a unique individual (e.g., a highly moral person, an assertive person, an outgoing person) (Burke and Stets, 2009). Identities answer the question of what it means to an individual to be, for example, a blacksmith, or an Israeli, or a moral person. Identities tell us who we are and they announce to others who we are. Identities guide behavior that is in accord with the meanings defining the identity. Thus, fathers act like "fathers," nurses act like "nurses," and dominant people act "dominant." People protect their identities, actively working to maintain being defined by themselves and others in the way they are as a father, or Israeli, or moral person.

People have multiple identities. Each identity tells what it means to the individual to be, as examples, a father, a Muslim American, or an outgoing person. And, when identities are activated, people behave in ways that are consistent with these meanings. If several identities are activated at the same time, people try to portray all of the relevant meanings, either simultaneously or serially. People act in ways that confirm the meanings of who they are. For example, acting more fairly if they have a high fairness identity or less fairly if they have a low fairness identity. And, people react to any suggestion that they are not coming across in a situation in a manner that is consistent with their identity. If a person with a high dominance identity thinks others see them as not very dominant, they become upset and work to change how they are coming across so that others will see them the way they see themselves.

Our identities tie us as individuals to the groups, the social categories, and the roles that make up society. Identities are the link between the individual and society or social structure. Identities tell us who we are, give us existential meaning, and tell us how to act. Identities tell others who we are so that they know how to act toward us and what to expect of us. In this chapter we will review the concept of identity as seen in identity theory and show how it is related to the many aspects of the self, to interaction with others, and to the creation and maintenance of society.

Origins of Identity Theory

Identity theory as a set of ideas has been developing since its basic outlines were independently developed in the 1960s by McCall and Simmons (1966) and Stryker (1968). McCall and Stryker both drew upon the symbolic interaction tradition and the work of Mead (1934) to understand the social origins of the self as well as the development and function of identities in society. The term "symbolic interaction" was coined by Herbert Blumer (1962, 1969), in his exegesis of the thinking of Mead, to denote a perspective that focuses on the unique character of human interaction, which centers on meaning and the shared use of symbols. Symbols can be used to represent objects and events in the situation (including other symbols) even when the objects and events are not present. Words are symbols, for example, that are used to communicate ideas and meanings.

Symbolic interaction makes note of the fact that when people interact, the exact behaviors are not what's important; it's the meaning behind these behaviors that is important. By sharing a common symbolic framework, people share an understanding of the words and gestures (symbols) they use and can thus communicate, share ideas, and collectively plan and organize themselves. When people talk, they respond to their own words in the way that others who share the symbolic culture also respond to those words. By sharing the same response to words and gestures, meaning is shared.

The use of symbols, as Mead acknowledges, is possible because of the development of the self; that is, the ability of the mind of a person to perceive and reflexively recognize the self and treat the self as an object, much like any other object in the situation. This ability allows the mind/self to think about and both act toward and react to the self in the same way that the self can think about and act on and react to any other part of the social environment. Perception of the social situation and action in the situation are intertwined and related through a mind that has been socially developed to respond, not just to the environment, but also to the relationship between the person and the environment, adjusting each to meet the needs, goals, and desires of the person. This connection between perception and action or behavior is central to identity theory, as is the understanding that behavior is always engaged in in the pursuit of the goals of the person.

Being part of a culture, one comes to learn the concepts, the categories and classifications, the meanings and expressions that are used by others in that culture to understand the world. Stryker (2002 [1980]) has noted this in his statement of the set of assumptions underlying the structural version of symbolic interactionism within which identity theory is set. He states that behavior is dependent on a named and classified world. The names point to aspects of the environment and carry meaning in the form of expectations about those aspects of the environment that are shared with others. One learns how to classify and name objects and how to behave with respect to those objects and their names through interactions with others in the community. Among those class terms, Stryker suggests, are the names that are used to designate shared understanding of the positions in the social structure such as teacher, student, truck driver, African American, police officer, and so on. As applied to the self, these shared understandings or meanings become one's identities.

Because these meanings are shared within the culture, actions by the self based on them will be understood commonly by the self and by others. As Mead has made clear, the meaning conveyed by symbols is shared in society by general consensus. The meaning of a symbol is the shared reaction to the symbol. People understand the word "fire" because they have the same reaction as others to the word (symbol) "fire." Thus, we can communicate by using symbols (words and gestures), and both we and our communication partner know what we are saying. The actions/meanings conveyed in an identity both tell us who we are and tell others who we are. If I am in the social position named "sister," I label myself "sister," and others know I am a "sister." Because we hold the meanings/identities of sister for ourselves, we know how to act and how we fit in to society. Because the positions/identities we hold for ourselves are related to other positions in society that are held by others (e.g., "brother") who have identities based on those other positions, they know how to act toward us and we know how to act toward them. Because we share the meanings within a common culture, we can interact with others in meaningful ways, understand each other, communicate with each other, and plan together. Through meanings, then, identities tie people to each other, to groups, and to society (Burke and Reitzes, 1981).

Identity Characteristics

In addition to the meanings that define an identity, each identity has several other characteristics. The characteristics of identities that are most generally discussed in research are the *salience* (or the general probability that the identity will be activated in a situation), *commitment* (or the strength of one's ties to others through the identity), and *prominence* of the identity (or the importance of the identity to the self). Two people may have a spouse identity, but each may differ on one or more of these three characteristics: one may be more or less salient than the other, more or less prominent, or more or less committed (Stryker, 1968; Stryker and Serpe, 1982, 1994).

Each of these characteristics modifies the way identities impact our behavior. Because we have many identities, for the roles we play, for the groups and organizations to which we belong, for the social categories which place us in society, and for the many individuating characteristics that make us unique individuals, it is impossible for all identities to be active at once. Most identities that we have are turned off most of the time, and activated only as needed. Different identities are activated at different times, and some identities are activated more frequently than others. The term *salience* of an identity refers to how frequently the identity is activated. A highly salient identity is likely to be relevant in many situations and therefore activated frequently. If the grandfather identity of a person is highly salient, the person may find opportunities to activate this identity, even in situations that normally may not call it up. For example, at the office one may hear, "Did I show you the latest pictures of my grandkids?" Other identities may have very low salience and become activated only occasionally, as, for example, the organizer identity of the person who organizes the year-end company picnic.

In addition to salience, identities also differ in *commitment*, or the strength of the individual's ties to others because of their identity. The more people who know you because of an identity, the more people who have expectations for you in terms of that identity. These expectations and ties to others link you more strongly to the social structure as people generally try to live up to their expectations. Being tied to more or fewer other people because of your identity is the quantitative part of commitment: more people, more commitment. Another, more qualitative part of commitment has to do with the quality of the ties to the others who know you because of your identity. The stronger those ties to others, the stronger your commitment to the identity. Again, commitment to an identity is something that varies from identity to identity. Some identities link you to only a few others, while some identities link you to many others. One of the dicta of identity theory is that the stronger the commitment to the identity, the more salient the identity will be. Having positive and strong relations with lots of people in terms of an identity gives one many opportunities to activate that identity.

The *prominence* of an identity, which is to say, how important the identity is to you, is another important aspect of identities that varies from one identity to another. A golfer identity may be very important to one person and not very important to another. For some, a worker identity may be more important than a spousal identity, while for others the reverse may be true. Prominence, like commitment, leads to salience. More important identities are more likely to be enacted in situations. Knowing the prominence, commitment, and salience of identities can help explain why, for example, two persons with the same work identity, for example an accountant, may differ in their approach to work, with one running home at quitting time, while the other stays on, continuing to work and get ahead.

The Content of Identities

Identities contain the meanings that tell us and others who we are when those meanings are displayed in our behavior. If we have the identity of a teacher, we act like a teacher, we dress like a teacher and we do the things that teachers do. The meanings that individual teachers hold for themselves may vary to a certain extent. Teachers may be more or less strict, more or less compassionate, more or less child-centered. Identity theory developed a set of procedures that allow us to measure the meanings that people hold for themselves in terms of their identities (Burke and Tully, 1977). Based on the work of Osgood, Suci, and Tannenbaum (1957), meanings are understood as mediational responses to a stimulus. It is mediational in the sense that it is an internal cognitive/emotional process that stands between the stimulus and a behavioral response to the stimulus. It gives us a moment to categorize and understand the stimulus so that we can take appropriate action rather than simply react to the stimulus. In measuring meaning, the responses that people have to stimuli are measured and the underlying dimensions of those responses are discovered.

For example, Burke and Tully (1977) measured the gender identity of sixth-, seventh-, and eighth-grade boys and girls. The children responded to questionnaires that asked them to separately rate "boys are ..." and "girls are ..." on a series of thirty-four adjective pairs. The dimensions that most discriminated between what it means to be a boy and what it means to be a girl for these schoolchildren were captured by responses to the adjective pairs soft/hard, weak/strong, girlish/boyish, emotional/not emotional, and smooth/rough. Girls were seen as more soft, weak, girlish, emotional, and smooth while boys were seen as more hard, strong, boyish, not emotional, and rough. The boys and girls then rated themselves on the same thirty-four adjective pairs in response to "as a boy I am ..." or "as a girl I am ..." The self-ratings on the most discriminating items were then used to calculate gender-identity scores for each person, ranging from the more masculine (-3) to the more feminine ($+3$). The gender behaviors of the children were then found to match the gender-identity scores (Burke and Tully, 1977). School performance in language arts, math, social studies, and other subjects was also predictable from their gender-identity scores, with both boys and girls with "girlish" identities doing better at language arts and both boys and girls with "boyish" identities doing better at math and science (Burke, 1989).

In a similar way, Burke and Reitzes (1980, 1981) measured what it means to be a college student. Following the Burke-Tully method, using adjective pairs relevant to being a student, they discovered four different dimensions of meaning along which students saw themselves. These were academic responsibility, intellectualism, sociability, and personal assertiveness. They found that students who were planning to go to graduate school were higher on academic responsibility and intellectualism than those planning to work after school. Similarly, those students involved in more social activities were higher on sociability and personal assertiveness than those students who were less involved in social activities. Again, we see the correspondence between the meanings held in the identity and the behaviors that are manifested by those meanings.

In addition to gender identity and the student identity, these same procedures have allowed the measurement of meanings associated with several other identities and allowed those identities to be related to the meaningful behaviors resulting from the specific identity. These include the spouse identity, with meanings having to do with the roles of husbands and wives (Burke and Stets, 1999), old-age identity, with meanings of isolation and being useless (Mutran and Burke, 1979a, b), moral identity, with meanings of fairness and care (Savage et al., 2016; Stets and Carter, 2011, 2012), ethnic identity, with meanings pertaining to both heritage and personal dimensions (Burke, Cerven, and Harrod, 2009), and a leadership identity (Burke, 2016; Riley and Burke, 1995). In each case, people are seen to behave in such ways that the meanings behind their behavior are congruent with the identity meanings. By using the same procedures that measure self/identity meanings, the meanings of different behaviors can be assessed. It was, in fact, the development of the measurement procedures that allowed identity theory to grow and develop as a theory, through test and retest.

The Bases of Identities

Three bases for identities have been recognized: social identities, role identities, and person identities (Burke and Stets, 2009). First, in common with social identity theory, identity theory recognizes that many identities are based on the social categories and groups recognized by society and understood in the culture. These include identities such as racial and ethnic identities, gender identity, country region, and geographic identities such as American or Israeli or Midwesterner. But, also included are identities based on belonging to particular organizations and groups, such as member of the local parent-teacher association (PTA) or student at the university of X. Unlike identities based on social categories, identities based on group membership generally involve more direct interaction with others in the group and a feeling of being accepted in the group. Again, the content of any of these identities is meaning: what it means to be an American or a female or a member of the PTA. By portraying these meanings, whether in actions or rituals, such as going to prayer meetings, or costume or dress, such as wearing the school uniform, one affirms the identity, and announces the identity to both the self and to others.

The second basis for identities consists of the roles people play in groups, organizations, and society in general. The role-based identities include identities such as firefighter, truck driver, professor, and student. Unlike social identities that are generally conveyed by *being* an American or a Midwesterner, role identities involve performing the role, doing the things that someone in the role does such as engaging in the activities and behaviors of a firefighter or going to classes and studying as a student. Often, too, for any role there are one or more counter-role relationships that are necessary for the role performance. For example, husband is understood with respect to wife, teacher to student, but also teacher to principal. Performing any role involves interacting with persons in these counter-roles; each depends upon the other in order to enact the role. Meanings are not only about who you are, but what you do.

While both social and role identities tie a person to the social structure as a member of a category or group or in a role relationship with others, the third basis of an identity is more individualistic. Person identities are based on the unique individual that one is. Person identities distinguish between individuals, for example, whether a person is dominant or submissive (or somewhere in between), the level of morality that a person holds for him or herself, or the level of fairness a person tries to maintain. Each person has identities, the meanings of which are set at certain levels of, for example, dominance, or fairness, or risk-taking. These meanings are not tied to the social structure in terms of being a group member or a role player, but characterize the individual across situations, across groups, and across roles. The meanings and the way in which these meanings are understood, of course, are given in the shared culture. People share an understanding of being moral or dominant and can understand and interpret the meanings of actions that indicate dominance or morality.

Identity Processes

The meanings relevant to each identity, whether it is a social identity, a role identity, or a person identity, are held in what is termed the *identity standard*. This standard is used to select behaviors when an identity is activated, behaviors that have meanings congruent with the meanings in the identity standard. When the identity is not activated, the meanings are dormant. The intellectual student may not act "intellectual" at a dinner party where the student identity is not activated. The person with a high moral identity may not act in a "moral" way when the identity is not activated. Depending upon the salience of the identity, some identities may be activated more often than others, but the meanings people attempt to portray in their behavior will be congruent with the meanings in the identity standard when the identity is activated. Further, they will try harder to enact appropriate meanings when the identity is highly committed, as when many people know the individual in terms of the identity, or when the identity is prominent, or important to the individual.

People do not just automatically behave in ways that are consistent with their identities, however. Rather, the meanings of their behavior are constantly monitored to be sure they are congruent with those in the identity standard. People may find that at times they are behaving in ways that are, for example, more fair or less fair than the level of fairness in their moral identity due to situational factors or others' expectations. When this happens, people adjust the level of, in this case, the perceived fairness of their behavior until it matches the level in their identity standard. This is the *identity-verification* process, and it is the main dynamic of how identities operate (Burke and Stets, 2009, 2015).

In the identity-verification process, people become aware of the meanings of their behavior through their own perceptions of their behavior and its consequences (direct appraisals) and, even more importantly, through their perceptions of how others interpret the meanings of their behavior (reflected appraisals). Other's views are important because symbolic meaning is socially constructed and maintained; the views of others matter (Mead, 1934). If the meanings in the direct and reflected appraisals do not match that of one's identity (the identity standard), the person will feel distress and negative emotions and, as a consequence work to change their behavior to change how they are coming across in the situation (Burke, 1991, 1996). They are successful in this verification process only when their reflected-appraisal meanings match the identity-standard meanings. Identity theory makes it clear that people do not control their behavior; rather they control their perceptions of how they are coming across in the situation, what meanings they are portraying as understood in their reflected appraisals (Powers, 1973). When the action is successful in bringing their perceptions of self-relevant meanings into alignment with their identity standard, identity verification has occurred. If people are practiced and skilled at verifying an identity, their perceptions of identity-relevant meanings are brought to alignment with the standard meanings and maintained, in most cases without them being aware that a control process is going on.

The actual behavior used to control the perceptions is not relevant except for its effects on the meanings that are perceived, and this may change from time to time to maintain control of perceptions. For example, if we are controlling to stay in the middle of our lane while driving a car, we may have to turn the wheel left or right depending upon the way the road turns, the wind gusts, lane-marking changes, and so on. We only know what to do by noting our perception of the current position of the car relative to our standard of where it should be, and then taking appropriate action. The action needed is not constant and cannot be foreseen. The same is true for the identity-verification process. We need to increase or decrease meanings constantly to keep the meanings in the situation consistent with the identity meanings.

By measuring identity meanings and reflected-appraisal meanings on the same scale, it is possible to calculate the degree to which an identity is not verified as the difference between the two measures. This difference or discrepancy is calculated as the reflected-appraisal measure minus the identity-standard measure. If the reflected-appraisal measure of the academic responsibility meaning of the student identity were, for example, 1.97 and the identity standard were 1.37, the difference, +.60, would indicate that the reflected appraisals were higher than the identity; the person saw herself as less academically oriented than she thought others saw her as being. Research has indicated that when this happens the person will feel distressed and will act in an even less academically oriented fashion in an attempt to convince others that she is less academically oriented than they had thought. This will continue until the reflected appraisals become 1.37, the same as the identity standard. If the person overcorrects, the process reverses itself, again to bring perceived meanings to match identity-standard meanings.

Notice that when the discrepancy is in the positive direction, the person acts in the negative direction to counteract the disturbance that pushed the reflected appraisals too positive. Similarly, if the discrepancy is in a negative direction (the reflected appraisals are less than the identity standard), the person will behave in a more positive fashion, again to counteract the disturbance (Burke, 2003). Thus, the direction of the discrepancy is important in guiding behavior to counteract the disturbance. The emotional reaction to the discrepancy, however, is negative whether the reflected appraisals are higher than the identity standard or lower than the identity standard. The squared discrepancy is the measure that captures this since it is always a positive number, and it is the squared discrepancy that predicts the level of negative emotion that people feel when their identity is not verified (Burke and Harrod, 2005; Stets and Burke, 2014a). The intensity of the emotion felt from the discrepancy becomes stronger as the discrepancy moves away from zero. A two-unit discrepancy is felt four times as much as a one-unit discrepancy. People work harder to avoid larger discrepancies and move their perceptions of identity-relevant meanings in the situation closer to the identity standard.

This model of behaving to control one's perceptions of identity-relevant meanings in the situation in order to verify one's identity was an important addition to identity theory based on the work of Powers (1973), who recognized that human behavior is an outcome of the control of perceptions. People act pragmatically, in whatever way achieves the goal of keeping perceptions of meaning in congruence with the identity standard. This is very much in keeping with the pragmatism of Mead (1934). This accounts for the multitude of ways in which people can achieve the same goal of verification; by keeping perceptions focused on the goal, we continue doing what we have to do to achieve the goal.

This does not mean that people are free to do whatever they want with no constraints, but that we are constrained by the many identities we have. Stealing, a behavior that may advance us toward verifying one identity (getting money to support a family) may move us away from verifying another identity (being a moral person). Identity theory suggests that people act to keep all of their identities verified as best they can, with more emphasis on those identities that have more commitment or more prominence (importance).

As people verify their identities by making perceived self-relevant meanings in the situation consistent with the meanings in their identity standards, more is happening than creating meanings in the situation to which others respond. If the identity is a social identity, those meanings may manifest to the self and others the group or category to which the individual belongs (in-group), and in doing so, distinguishes the group or category from other groups or categories to which the individual does not belong (out-groups). Group boundaries are maintained and people know who is in the group and who is not. What it means to be in one group and not the other is made clear. Republicans are distinguished from Democrats, males from females, blacks from whites, my group from your group. Such in-group and out-group distinctions are both manifested and maintained by people verifying their social identities.

If the identity is a role identity, verification accomplishes the role or job to be done. If I am a delivery-truck driver, for example, verifying my role involves delivering the packages, taking care of the truck, interacting with the dispatcher, getting delivery signatures, and so on. Verification accomplishes this in spite of disruptions and things that go wrong. Behaviors change to accomplish the verification in the best way possible. Looking at this across society, all of the functions of society are maintained by people verifying their role identities. Each person performing their role interacts with others performing their role in the vast network that is society.

Finally, the verification of person identities keeps us through time as the persons we are. We get to know what kind of person we are. Others get to know what kind of person we are. We avoid situations that make it difficult to verify our person identities. If we have an identity that is outgoing and social, we may avoid taking on a job or role in which we have little contact with others. If our identity is not at all dominant, we may avoid leadership roles. In this way, person identities guide individuals into roles and groups which allow them to verify their person identities. Person identities become sorting mechanisms that help to guide persons into positions in society where they will be happy (verifying their person identity) and not be distressed or likely to leave. Stability at the societal level is maintained.

Identity Change

Keeping identities verified is the main identity process that drives behavior, but this is not always possible. Some disturbances are not easily controlled; sometimes the source of the disturbance to identity-relevant meanings has more power than the person, for example, and the employer has more power than the employee, and changes in situational meanings by the employer that are relevant to the employee's identity may not be (easily) changed. If those meanings set by the employer are at odds with the employee's identity standard, and the employee cannot act to bring them into alignment with the employee's identity standard, the discrepancy will persist. Under these conditions, identity theory suggests that the employee's identity standard will slowly shift and change to be more like the meanings set by the employer. The identity changes and will ultimately bring the perceived meanings into agreement with the (modified) identity standard.

This process of identity change, however, is slow compared to the usual adjustment of meanings to align them with the identity. Burke and Cast studied changes in the gender identities of newly married couples (1997) over a period of three years. Part of the criteria for being included in the study was that the couple did not already have any children. The gender identities of these newly married individuals were measured at the beginning of the study and again a year later, during which time several of the couples had had children. A third measurement of the gender identities was made after another year, and during this period more children were born. Burke and Cast reasoned that the birth of a child provided a disturbance or change to the situational meanings that were relevant to the gender identities of the individuals, a change that could not be easily counteracted. Compared to the couples that did not have children during the first year, those couples that did have children experienced change in their gender identities. The husbands became more masculine and the wives became more feminine with the birth of a child. This change also occurred in the next year for those additional couples who had a child during that year. The amount of change was not large, though it was significant, occurring slowly over the period of a year.

The change in the gender identities was not deliberate or conscious. It did not produce a recognizable difference immediately, but persistently and slowly over time, the gender identities shifted. This suggests that identities are never "fixed." They are generally unchanging because the meanings that support and verify the identities in the situation are maintained so as to be congruent with the identity standards. But, should the meanings in the situation no longer be congruent with the identity standard, change begins to occur. The identities change in the direction of the disturbance even for small temporary disturbances, but the amount is so slight it is not apparent. It only becomes apparent if the discrepancy between situational meanings and identity meanings persists long enough, because the situational meanings cannot be altered (as with the birth of a baby). Thus, the change in the gender identity of the newly married couples who had a baby could be measured after the six or eight months that elapsed after the birth until the gender identities were again measured.

Self-Esteem

When identities are not verified, it has been pointed out that people have a negative emotional response. Burke and Harrod (2005) showed that when the identities of newly married couples were not verified they felt increased distress, depression, and anger. Stets and Burke (2014a) replicated this work and showed that non-verification produced strong negative emotions (a combined scale including happiness [reversed], fear, disgust, anger, sadness, shame, guilt, and empathy [reversed]). These negative emotions help motivate a response in terms of acting to change meanings in the situation so that the reflected appraisals again match the identity standard and restore verification.

Continued verification, on the other hand, has positive effects – people feel good. More than that, however, research has shown that identity verification enhances one's self-esteem. Indeed, Cast and Burke (2002) suggested that the source of self-esteem was, in fact, the verification of identities, and that once built up through the verification process, self-esteem diminished the negative emotion that occurs when self-verification is problematic, thus allowing continued interactions and continuity in the structural arrangements provided by role and group membership. In this way, persons who had high self-esteem could persist longer in the achievement of verification than those without high self-esteem.

Stets and Burke (2014b) developed this idea further, pointing out that self-esteem had three different dimensions. The first dimension is *self-worth* or feeling good about oneself because one is in communion with others; one belongs and is worthy. Second is *self-efficacy*, or the feeling that one is competent and capable; one is effective in one's actions. And third is *authenticity*, based on individual strivings for meaning, coherence, and understandings about the self; one is able to enact one's "true self," be who one really is. Together, these three dimensions make up global self-esteem. Falling short on any of these dimensions is to have lower global self-esteem. Boosting any of these dimensions increases the level of global self-esteem.

Stets and Burke (2014b) point out that the idea that identity verification increases self-esteem, as in the theory earlier put forth by Cast and Burke (2002), can be elaborated. They show that it is the verification of group (social) identities that increases self-worth, the verification of role identities that increases self-efficacy, and the verification of person identities that increases a feeling of authenticity. In this way, Stets and Burke linked the different bases of identities to the different dimensions of global self-esteem. They showed, for example, that the verification of one's gender identity (a social identity) increases feelings of self-worth but not self-efficacy. They also showed that the verification of the role identity of student (among college students) increased self-efficacy but not self-worth or authenticity. And finally, they showed that verification of one's moral identity (a person identity – whether it was high or low) increased feelings of authenticity (Stets and Burke, 2014b).

In this way, there is a general alignment of the different bases of identities and the different dimensions of self-esteem. However, this may be more of an analytic alignment than an empirical one because in any situation, a person with a role identity may be part of a group or organization, with its own identity, within which that role is defined. And there may be other person identities the individual has that are activated. Since the person identities are almost always relevant and roles are frequently within groups, there may be few situations in which a single identity with a single basis is ever activated. To measure the different effects of any identity basis is technically difficult, requiring the measurement of the multiple identities across different bases along with the degree of verification of each. Although the early research cited above is promising, more research is clearly needed.

Multiple Identities

The fact that several identities with different bases may be activated at the same time raises the question of the relationships among the multiple identities that individuals in contemporary society hold. Whatever number of identities an individual has that influence behavior, there is still only one individual whose behavior is influenced. And, the more identities that are activated at one time, the more identities that are vying for control of that behavior to maintain a state of verification. It is, perhaps a good thing that most identities are dormant or not activated most of the time.

If the meanings that are relevant for a particular identity are not manifested in a situation, then that identity is likely to not be activated unless the identity is highly salient. If that identity is highly salient, it may become activated, and the person may generate and control meanings that are consistent with the identity. It is possible, however, that such meanings may be deemed inappropriate by others in the situation. For example, if someone brings out vacation pictures of their spouse during a business meeting, this could result in the non-verification of their spouse identity, but it could also result in the non-verification of their business identity. Thus, even salient identities may not be activated too often.

If two identities control some of the same meanings, and the identity standard for each is set to the same value – for example, I am a fair person (9 out of 10) and I am a fair county judge (also 9 out of 10) – then acting as a judge with a fairness level of 9 will verify the judge identity as well as the person identity. However, if my fairness person identity is a 9 and my identity as a county judge is only a 7 and both identities are activated, I have created a conflict situation for myself. If my behavior is 7, my judge identity is verified, but my person identity is not verified. Indeed, there is no behavior that can verify both identities. For this reason, people generally select groups and roles which will also verify their person identities and the above scenario is not likely to arise too often.

It may be that initially both the judge and the person identity were highly fair (9 out of 10), but situational pressures and demands may have caused the judge identity to be a 7 on one or more occasions. If that situation persists, and the person cannot counteract these pressures on the judge role, the persistent non-verification will produce distress, and over time, the person identity of fairness may change toward the lower level of the judge. In all likelihood, the person will both act to counteract the situational pressures on the judge identity and will experience identity change over time in the person identity so that the two identity-standard levels will come to be in agreement, perhaps at an 8 (somewhere between the lower levels demanded by the situation and the 9 demanded by the person identity). It is also possible that the person learns to inactivate their fairness person identity when sitting on the bench and to activate the judge role identity. It is also possible that the person chooses to leave the judge role and no longer have that identity. It is only when both identities are activated that the conflict manifests itself.

When two identities have the same meaning dimension, such as fairness in the above example, then the two identities can help each other control the meaning if both standards are set to the same level. If the meaning is at different levels in the two identities then the two identities are in conflict, each trying to set the meanings in the situation at different levels. If, however, the meanings controlled by one identity are irrelevant for the meanings controlled by the other identity, then both meanings can be brought to the level indicated in the identity standards and there is no conflict. Nor is there any cooperation. In this case, if the two identities are activated at the same time, the one individual holding the two identities must act in such a way as to control both meanings – multitasking, so to speak, in such a way that controlling one meaning occurs without disturbing the other meaning. For example, if one identity requires that I wear a suit and tie, that can be done without interference with my being more or less fair as my fairness identity requires. Verifying both identities is thus possible and I will act to counteract disturbances to the verification of either identity and do my best to verify both at the same time. If one identity is more prominent or important, it may be verified before the other, or I may work harder to verify that identity. Nevertheless, identity theory says that both identities must be verified. Similarly, if there are more than two identities that are activated at the same time, a way must be found the verify all of them as much as possible.

The multiple identities discussed above are assumed to exist side by side, at the same level, so to speak, with each controlling perceptions of meaning relevant to its standards. However, identities also can be arranged in a hierarchical fashion, with one above the other. In this arrangement, the output of the higher identity is (part of) the standard of the lower identity. In this case the higher identity is one step removed from directly controlling perceptions. Rather than the output of the higher identity controlling perceptions by meaningful behavior, the higher identity helps to set the meanings in the identity standard of the lower identity. In this way, the higher identity controls its perceptions indirectly by controlling the meanings that the lower identity seeks to verify. A higher-level identity can help to set the standards of several lower-level identities. For example, one's gender identity is often at a higher level than many of the role identities one holds. Being female helps set the meanings that define being a student, or a friend, or a truck driver. That is to say, what it means to be a friend varies by the kind of gender identity one has.

In this hierarchical arrangement of the identity control system, the higher identity achieves verification indirectly through the lower identities that it controls. The higher identity does not verify itself directly, but, in a sense, gets the lower-level identities to do that. In the above example of a female gender identity, this identity is manifested in being, for example, a female student, a female friend, or a female truck driver, the gender identity is verified through the way in which the student, friend, or truck-driver identity is manifested. If the perceptions at the higher, gender-identity level do not match the meanings in the gender-identity standard, the output from the gender identity modifies the meanings of the student, friend, or truck-driver identities, and through that modifies the student, friend, or truck-driver role performances to bring about the verification of the gender identity (as well as verification of the lower-level identities of student, friend, or truck driver).

A study by Tsushima and Burke (1999) illustrated some of these principles of the hierarchical levels of control in identities. They examined the parent identity and found that some of the meanings of being a parent were at a higher level, concerned with general principles such as raising children to be independent, than other meanings of the parent identity that were concerned with the lower-level procedures for accomplishing particular tasks such as getting the children to make their bed. They found that parents who focused their parenting on controlling perceptions relevant to the more abstract principles such as being independent and taking responsibility for oneself had an easier and less stressful time of it than parents who focused entirely on the lower-level perceptions relevant to getting the children to make their bed, be ready for school on time, clean up their rooms, and so on, without attending to the more general principles. In effect, by focusing on the lower-level perceptions without having them be manifestations of higher-level principles such as being independent, both parents and children jumped from one little task to another without rhyme or reason. Parents had to control the children accomplishing each and every little task rather than accomplishing all of them as part of the process of being independent.

In general, the multiple identities that people have are not independent of one another. There can be conflict among them when the meanings are at odds with one another as well as cooperation among them when the meanings align. When there is conflict, the meanings in the conflicting identities prevent verification, which leads to distress and a tendency for the identities to change slowly over time to be in accord and thus reduce the conflict. There can also be a control relationship among identities at different levels, where higher-level identities set the identity-standard meanings of the lower-level identities. When this is the case, conflict is minimized and verification of the lower identities helps to indirectly verify the higher-level identities.

Conclusion

Identities tell us what it means to be who we are. They tell us how to act and they tell others how to act toward us. Identities ties us as individuals to society in terms of the groups, the social categories, and the roles we are born into, take on, or join. The identity meanings that define us – as Americans or family members or in terms of the jobs we have or the associations to which we belong – these meanings, when verified, provide our life with meaning, make us feel good, and give us self-esteem. And, when these identity meanings are not verified, we become distressed, depressed, and life seems meaningless and void. The key is verification, a largely social process that depends upon others and how we perceive their reactions toward us. If we are successful in verifying our identities, we not only feel good, but we are doing our part to maintain the structure of society, maintaining the social divisions and categories, the groups and organizations, and the roles that connect us to others.

References

Blumer, Herbert. 1962. "Society as Symbolic Interaction." In Arnold M. Rose (ed.), *Human Behavior and Social Processes* (pp. 179–192). Boston, MA: Houghton Mifflin Co.

1969. *Symbolic Interactionism.* Englewood Cliffs, NJ: Prentice-Hall.

Burke, Peter J. 1989. "Gender Identity, Sex, and School Performance." *Social Psychology Quarterly* 52(2): 159–169.

1991. "Identity Processes and Social Stress." *American Sociological Review* 56(6): 836–849.

1996. "Social Identities and Psychosocial Stress." In Howard B. Kaplan (ed.), *Psychosocial Stress: Perspectives on Structure, Theory, Life-Course, and Methods* (pp. 141–174). San Diego, CA: Academic Press.

2003. "Relationships Among Multiple Identities." In Peter J. Burke, Timothy J. Owens, Richard T. Serpe, and Peggy A. Thoits (eds.), *Advances in Identity Theory and Research* (pp. 195–214). New York: Kluwer Academic/Plenum.

2016. "The Emergence of Status Structures." In Jan E. Stets and Richard T. Serpe (eds.), *New Directions in Identity Theory and Research.* New York: Oxford.

Burke, Peter J., and Alicia D. Cast. 1997. "Stability and Change in the Gender Identities of Newly Married Couples." *Social Psychology Quarterly* 60(4): 277–290.

Burke, Peter J., Christine Cerven, and Michael M. Harrod. 2009. "Measuring Ethnic Identity." Pacific Sociological Association Meetings, Seattle, April.

Burke, Peter J., and Michael M. Harrod. 2005. "Too Much of a Good Thing?" *Social Psychology Quarterly* 68: 359–374.

Burke, Peter J., and Donald C. Reitzes. 1980. "College Student Identity: Measurement and Implications." *Pacific Sociological Review* 23: 46–66.

1981. "The Link Between Identity and Role Performance." *Social Psychology Quarterly* 44: 83–92.

Burke, Peter J., and Jan E. Stets. 1999. "Trust and Commitment through Self-Verification." *Social Psychology Quarterly* 62: 347–366.

2009. *Identity Theory.* New York: Oxford University Press.

2015. "Identity Verification and the Social Order." In Edward J. Lawler, Shane R. Thye, and Jeongkoo Yoon (eds.), *Order on the Edge of Chaos: Social Psychology and the Problem of Social Order* (pp. 145–164). New York: Cambridge.

Burke, Peter J., and Judy C. Tully. 1977. "The Measurement of Role Identity." *Social Forces* 55(4): 881–897.

Cast, Alicia D., and Peter J. Burke. 2002. "A Theory of Self-Esteem." *Social Forces* 80(3): 1041–1068.

McCall, George J., and J. L. Simmons. 1966. *Identities and Interactions.* New York: The Free Press.

Mead, George H. 1934. *Mind, Self, and Society.* Chicago, IL: University of Chicago Press.

Mutran, Elizabeth, and Peter J. Burke. 1979a. "Feeling 'Useless': A Common Component of Young and Old Adult Identities." *Research on Aging* 1: 188–212.

1979b. "Personalism as a Component of Old Age Identity." *Research on Aging* 1: 37–64.

Osgood, Charles E., George J. Suci, and Percy H. Tannenbaum. 1957. *The Measurement of Meaning.* Urbana, IL: University of Illinois Press.

Powers, William T. 1973. *Behavior: The Control of Perception.* Chicago, IL: Aldine.

Riley, Anna, and Peter J. Burke. 1995. "Identities and Self-Verification in the Small Group." *Social Psychology Quarterly* 58 (2): 61–73.

Savage, Scott V., Jan E. Stets, Peter J. Burke, and Zachary L. Sommer. 2016. "Identity and Power Use in Exchange Networks." *Sociological Perspectives.* DOI:http://dx .doi.org/10.1177/0731121416644788

Stets, Jan E., and Peter J. Burke. 2014a. "Emotions and Identity Non-Verification." *Social Psychology Quarterly* 77: 387–410.

2014b. "Self-Esteem and Identities." *Sociological Perspectives* 57: 1–25.

Stets, Jan E., and Michael J. Carter. 2011. "The Moral Self: Applying Identity Theory." *Social Psychology Quarterly* 74: 192–215.

2012. "A Theory of the Self for the Sociology of Morality." *American Sociological Review* 77: 120–140.

Stryker, Sheldon. 1968. "Identity Salience and Role Performance." *Journal of Marriage and the Family* 4: 558–64.

2002 [1980]. *Symbolic Interactionism: A Social Structural Version.* Caldwell, NJ: The Blackburn Press.

Stryker, Sheldon, and Richard T. Serpe. 1982. "Commitment, Identity Salience, and Role Behavior: A Theory and Research Example." In William Ickes and Eric S. Knowles (eds.), *Personality, Roles, and Social Behavior* (pp. 199–218). New York: Springer-Verlag.

1994. "Identity Salience and Psychological Centrality: Equivalent, Overlapping, or Complementary Concepts?" *Social Psychology Quarterly* 57: 16–35.

Tsushima, Teresa, and Peter J. Burke. 1999. "Levels, Agency, and Control in the Parent Identity." *Social Psychology Quarterly* 62(2): 173–189.

5 Emotions Theory

Donileen R. Loseke and Margarethe Kusenbach

Introduction

Classical philosophers, from Aristotle to Plato, from Hobbes to Descartes, "all thought it necessary to understand emotion in order to explore human nature and our capacity for politics" (Marcus, 2000: 221). More recent social theorists, including Comte, Durkheim, Simmel, Weber, Freud, and members of the Frankfurt School, likewise have argued that emotion is central to social life (Beatty, 2005; Schilling, 2002). While continental philosophy retained a strong interest in emotion (Solomon, 2006), from the late nineteenth to the mid-twentieth century, Western ideas promoting body–mind dualism became embedded in the social sciences and served to reduce attention to emotion, theorizing it as inferior to cognition, as irrational and subjective, and therefore as not worthy of "scientific" attention (Harré, 1986; Lutz, 1986). That has changed within the last forty years as social science observers and professional practitioners alike converged on returning to the classical understanding of emotion as a foundation of social life. Scholars now argue that emotions are the glue that holds society together (Von Scheve and Von Luede, 2005) and are the internal constraints that make social order possible (Barbalet, 2002). Emotions are called a key ingredient of "social order and action" (Schilling, 2002: 11), and an "inextricable element of thinking, speaking, and acting" (Beatty, 2014: 546). Emotion has been theorized as the core of democratic politics (Marcus, 2002) and as a "constitutive dimension of the economy – even if we only collectively recognize it in times of crisis" (Berezin, 2009: 336). Observers of globalization maintain that there is a "geopolitics of emotion" (Moïsi, 2009) that drives cross-cultural interactions of all types, and that we must explore "how emotions can be theorized to create a better understanding of people's experiences in an increasingly globalized and interconnected world" (Svašek and Skrbiš, 2007: 368).

Despite such widespread agreements about the centrality of emotion in social life, our goal of summarizing social science theories of emotion is complicated. Most simply, the literature is vast and ever-expanding. More critically, there are numerous conceptual confusions surrounding this topic and the study of emotion has been fragmented both within and between academic disciplines.

Summarizing the current state of emotion theory is difficult because the topic is characterized by conceptual confusions. Indeed, there is not even agreement about how to define emotion, which is sometimes conceptualized as the same as – and sometimes as different from – "feeling," "mood," "affect," and "sentiment" (Bericat, 2015; Dixon, 2012; Mulligan and Scherer, 2012; Robinson, 2014; Thoits, 1989). Further confusion results from a lack of agreement on the definitions of central concepts: Robinson, Smith-Lovin, and Wisecup (2006), for example, detail how the concepts of affect, emotion, sentiment, and mood have different meanings in Affect Control Theory than in other theories of emotion; Gendron and Barrett (2009) describe how the term "emotion appraisal" is used in very different ways. Observers also argue that seemingly similar emotions such as "compassion," "sympathy," and "pity" are dissimilar in important respects (Boltanski, 1999); there are continuing debates about differences between, for example, the emotions of "patriotism" and "nationalism" (Skitka, 2005), and between "anger" and "rage" (Lewis, 1993).

Still further, because there are countless specific emotions, a classification scheme is necessary, yet there are several such competing systems. One common contemporary system, for example, distinguishes between *primary* emotions, defined as "universal, physiological, of evolutionary relevance and biologically and neurologically innate," and *secondary* emotions, which are "socially and culturally conditioned" (Bericat, 2015: 2). Others categorize emotions in terms of their behavioral and environmental preconditions, relationships between particular emotions, associated behavioral adaptations, or the "directionality of emotion" as toward the self or as toward others. There are multiple ways to categorize emotion, yet no agreements on what type of categorization is the best (Thamm, 2006).

In brief, it is challenging to discuss emotion theorizing given the myriad conceptual confusions surrounding what emotion is and how it should be studied. Indeed, some observers argue that the term of emotion as well as the category of phenomena it designates are simply too fuzzy to be of much use in social science (Dixon, 2012), while others contend that pursuing a general theory of emotion is less useful than developing theories of particular emotions, or of particular types of emotions (Barbalet, 2001).

Second, it also is difficult to summarize emotion theories because, as variously conceptualized, emotion is about human biology, individual psychology, face-to-face interaction, formal and informal organizations, social structure, and culture. Emotion at each level of social life – from the microbiological to the macro-political – raises different sorts of questions and requires different types of conceptualizations and contextualization. This multidimensionality of emotion also has led it to be of interest in a variety of academic disciplines, from primatology to cultural studies, which brings further confusion associated with differences among disciplines in epistemologies and characteristics of theoretical frameworks. Cunningham (2013), for example, describes differences between "constructionism" as viewed psychologically and sociologically; Beatty (2013) describes differences between psychological and anthropological understandings of "emotional embodiment." Still further fragmentation stems from tendencies within disciplines for interest to be targeted specifically and narrowly to emotion in particular topics (such as social movements or research methods) and/or to emotion in particular sites (such as family, work, and politics). Unfortunately, there is very little cross-disciplinary or cross-topic conversation, so theorists and researchers alike tend to draw primarily from – and therefore contribute primarily to – dialogues that have fairly narrow audiences of like-minded others. Our task of summarizing theories about emotion therefore is complicated by a literature that is fragmented by discipline, and within disciplines separated into specific frameworks or topics.

Given these complexities, as well as the sheer volume of attention to emotion, we will limit our review in several ways. First, two topics are too complex to include in a review of this sort: We will not attend to theories of relationships between emotion and psychological troubles (e.g. the psychogenic theories of Freud, Adler, Maslow, Rogers, Lacan, etc.), nor will we consider how underlying philosophical and epistemological paradigms (such as phenomenology, naturalism, constructionism, feminism, critical race theory) inform theoretical frameworks of emotion. Second, we will focus on "emotion" in general and not attend to myriad theories surrounding specific emotions such as sympathy (Clark, 1997), shame (Scheff, 2003), fear (Altheide, 2002; Tudor, 2003; Witte and Allen, 2000), jealousy (Stearns, 1989), grief and sadness (Charmaz and Milligan, 2006; Lofland, 1985), love (Cancian, 1987; Swidler, 2001), disgust (Nussbaum, 2006), humiliation (Saurette, 2006), or anger (Lambek and Solway, 2001). Third and finally, although many theories of emotion are distinctly evidence-based, we will not explore the vast empirical literature on emotion nor will we evaluate the soundness of evidence for particular theories. Most clearly, there is much about emotion that we do not cover, yet even with such bracketing, we made many trade-offs in what we covered – and what we ignored. Our hope is to offer a general sense of the kinds of social theories useful in the study of emotion.

There were multiple alternatives for organizing our review. We rejected an organization based on disciplinary boundaries because work coming from various disciplines is not always easily identified and, more importantly, we do not want to further the practice of disciplinary segregation that greatly impedes knowledge building. Likewise, we decided against highlighting differences between "positivist" and "social constructionist" views on emotion (see Stearns, 1995 and Von Scheve and Von Luede, 2005 for descriptions of these perspectives) because, while a common feature of work in emotion, concern with differences in these underlying epistemological frameworks often reflects quite stale debates within the social sciences that advance neither theoretical nor substantive understandings.

Here we use a quite minimalist classification and sort theories into two broad categories in terms of the *center of theoretical interest*. By far, the most common practice among Western scholars is to theorize emotion as a property of *individuals*, which leads to questions about the experiences, causes, and consequences of emotion that are empirically examined by the research techniques of introspection, interview, observation, or experiment. In contrast, although receiving less attention, interest can be in emotion as an element of *culture*, as socially circulating systems of meaning. Empirical work relying on document analysis (historical records, public policy documents, popular culture, etc.) examines the sources, circulations, social uses, and consequences of these systems of meaning.

Emotion Theory I: The Centrality of Individuals

Called "ethnopsychologies" (Kirkpatrick and White, 1985), "indigenous theories" (Abu-Lughod and Lutz, 1990: 17), or "ethnotheories" (Lutz, 1986), Western folk beliefs about emotion are a "EuroAmerican set of unspoken assumptions embedded in the concept of emotion" (Lutz, 1986: 287). These beliefs, ordered around assumptions of body–mind dualism and the primacy of individual well-being, lead to understanding emotion as something that is both personal and private. Emotions are "messages from a private place within the individual" (Reddy, 1999: 258). Many scholarly observers carry these ethnopsychologies into their studies by claiming, for example, that "[w]ithout doubt, the 'self,' the feeling subject, constitutes the central reference upon which emotions turn" (Bericat, 2015: 3) and that the study of emotion is a "subarea in social psychology" (Rogers and Kavanaugh, 2010: 333). This focus leads to questions about how individuals experience emotion as well as about the causes and consequences of emotion experienced by individuals.

Questions about the experience of emotion, about emotion as embodied "feeling," have long been of interest in phenomenological philosophy, which draws insights from theorists including Heidegger, Scheler, Levinas, Sartre, Merleau-Ponty, Marcel, Ricoeur, and others (see Solomon, 2006 for a review). Yet phenomenological frameworks have not made many inroads into other social science disciplines (however see Denzin, 1984 and Katz, 1999 for sociological frameworks; see Heavey, Hurlburt, and Lefforge, 2012 for a psychological framework). In the social sciences, most interest in the individual experience of emotion has been in what is called the *lived experience* perspective (Ellis and Flaherty, 1992) which eschews theory and focuses on simply describing "what emotion feels like and how it is experienced" (Ellis, 1991: 23).

Social theory surrounding emotion as an individual phenomenon tends to focus on questions about causes and consequences. Answers to causal questions range from those framing emotion totally – or almost totally – as biological (the traditional "nature" framework), to those framing emotion totally – or almost totally – as environmental (the traditional "nurture" framework). We begin with the most inward-facing formulations of the causes of emotion and move to the increasingly outward-facing.

Emotion and Biology

The biological framework begins with the work of Charles Darwin (1872), who maintained that emotion in humans arose in the process of evolution. At the extreme, some social observers conceptualize emotion *only* as biological. These are called *somatic* theories, or the *basic emotion* approach. Most common in psychology, where its origin is traced to William James (1884) and Paul Ekman (1972), this approach theorizes that certain kinds of emotion are "biologically privileged and are automatically triggered by objects and events in the world" (Gendron and Barrett, 2009: 318). Basic emotions, traditionally called "instincts" and now called "neurological activity" (Barrett et al., 2007; Chiao, 2015; Izard, 2009), originate in that part of the brain humans share with other primates (the "old brain"), and are "funda-mental to human mentality and adaptive behavior" (Izard, 2009: 7–9). While there is considerable disagreement about what particular emotions are "basic" (compare, for example, Ekman, 1992 and Izard, 2009), sadness, anger, disgust, fear, and happiness appear on most lists.

More recent work conceptualizing emotion as solely biological is "embodiment," or "modality-based emotion" theory. Embodiment theories are a counter to cognitive theories (we discuss these next) and are fueled by neuroscience claims that emotion as experienced is solely biological and does not require cognition (see Smith-Lovin and Winkelman, 2010 for a review).

Emphasizing biology as the *foundation* of emotion is in keeping with a general movement throughout the social sciences advocating bringing biology into social theorizing. This call typically begins with arguing that sophisticated new technolo-gies are allowing researchers to ask distinctly social questions about biological processes, and because of this, understandings of human biology increasingly acknowledge the profound effects of social experience. If biology is becoming social, it follows that social theory must become more biological (Chiao, 2015; Meloni, 2014; Rose, 2013; B. Turner, 2009). For example, Douglas Massey's Presidential Address to the American Sociological Association was about the evolu-tionary role of emotion in human social life. In it he criticized social scientists who "have allowed the fact that we are social beings to obscure the biological foundations upon which our behavior ultimately rests" (Massey, 2002: 1). Other reviewers of sociological theories of emotion also have complained that failures to examine "the evolutionary forces that have shaped human emotions" have led to sociologists holding "an overly constructionist view of emotions as the product of culture" (Turner and Stets, 2006: 46). In sum, sociologists can join psychologists in theoriz-ing that biology is the sole (or at least primary) basis of emotion in individuals.

Emotion and Cognition

Despite the current trend emphasizing the importance of biology, it remains most common for observers in the social sciences to argue that "emotions are, *at the same time*, socially constructed and biologically evident" (Barrett, 2012: 413, emphasis in original), or that there are "mutual interdependencies between biological and micro- and macro-level social processes" (Rogers and Kavanagh, 2010: 334). The basis of many theories conceptualizing emotion as at least somewhat social is the assertion that emotion is not possible without *cognition*. This is the argument that – to a greater or lesser degree – bodily sensations are unintelligible until they are cognitively interpreted (Averill, 1980; Hochschild, 1979; McCarthy, 1989; Shott, 1979). Theories focused on the cognitive evaluations of events, objects, and people revolve around the general social psychological process called *appraisal* (see Boiger and Mesquita, 2012 and Bericat, 2015 for reviews).

Appraisal theories of emotion have been advanced by both psychologists (e.g. Scherer, 2009) and sociologists (e.g. Heise, 1979; Hochschild, 1983). With appraisal defined as the cognitive interpretation of the meanings of events, the domain assumption is that how emotions will be internally experienced as well as how they will be behaviorally expressed depends upon "appraisal" (see Mesquita and Walker, 2003). Stated more formally: "All experience (including social experiences, like emotional responses) have to be first transduced from their modality-based form (including perceptual, somatosensory and motor systems) into symbolic, language-like representations" (Smith-Lovin and Winkelman, 2010: 329).

An example of appraisal theories is Conceptual Act Theory (CAT), associated with Lisa Feldman Barrett. According to CAT, "emotions emerge when physical sensations in the self and physical actions in others are meaningfully linked to situations during a process that can be called both cognitive and perceptual ... [bodily indications of emotion] become real as emotion (as fear, anger, etc.) when they are categorized as such using emotion knowledge within a perceiver" (Barrett, 2014: 292).

Another example of appraisal theories is Affect Control Theory (ACT). Associated with David Heise and Lyn Smith-Lovin (Heise, 1979; Smith-Lovin, 1990; Smith-Lovin and Heise, 1988), the core of ACT is the traditional symbolic interactionist notion that actors react to situations in terms of meanings, particularly meanings associated with self-identity. Within ACT, emotions are signals of how events are maintaining or challenging those identities. As a formal mathematical model, ACT extends traditional social constructionism from George Herbert Mead's (1934) interest in cognitive meanings to the realm of emotional meanings (Robinson, Smith-Lovin, and Wisecup, 2006).

Another variation of appraisal theories is the category of *rational choice* theories, although this might seem odd because the cores of these theories are "behavioral and rational choice assumptions" about practical actors (Lawler and Thye, 1999: 218). Rational choice theory, popular in criminology, views individuals as self-interested, goal-maximizing actors who undertake cost–benefit calculations before deciding to either conform with, or deviate from, societal norms (Cornish and Clarke, 2014). Emotion plays a key role in these calculations because rational actors view positive feelings, such as the "thrill" of getting away with a crime, as an action's benefit, whereas negative feelings, such as the fear of getting caught, are evaluated as a cost. Emotion also is a part of rational choice theories because it is thought to limit rationality, leading to "bounded rationality" (Kaufman, 1999).

Exchange theories are a variant of rational choice theories. Assuming "self-interested actors who transact with other self-interested actors to accomplish individual goals they cannot achieve alone" (Lawler and Thye, 1999: 217), recent work has emphasized how emotions "arise from completed social exchanges" and, in turn, how resulting emotions affect future exchanges (Robinson, Clay-Warner, and Everett, 2008: 6).

Many theories conceptualize emotion as involving appraisal, and appraisal as rooted in cognition. This is the foundation for a number of theories positing social environmental activations for emotion. In these cases, emotion is a dependent variable, so to speak, the product of distinct social influences (Thoits, 1989). These approaches include theories claiming that emotions primarily occur within the context of interactions, that the management of emotion is a requirement for society's members, and that emotions are shaped by social structure. In various ways, such theories are the "nurture" side of answers to questions about emotion as a property of individuals. Although we present these as separate theories, their development over time has led to much cross-fertilization.

Emotion and Interaction

Interactional frameworks focus exclusively on emotion generated in face-to-face interactions, conceptualized by Erving Goffman (1952, 1956, 1967), as the foundation of social life. Drawing heavily from Emile Durkheim's (1965/1915) insights about the importance of ritual encounters in religious life, Goffman argued that daily life itself is highly ritualized, containing predictable patterns of interaction. Interaction theories of emotion center on how "emotions emerge from social interactions and relationships, which they in turn constitute, shape, and change ... [S]ocial interaction and emotions form one system of which the parts cannot be separated" (Mesquita and Boiger, 2014: 298).

Interaction Ritual (IR) theories, or *Interaction Ritual Chain* (IRC) theories, associated with Randall Collins (1975, 1981, 2004), are variants of interactional theories which partially emphasize emotion. Borrowing from Durkheim and Goffman, Collins defines all focused interaction as ritual. Rituals depend on a number of factors: the physical copresence of two or more interactants, a mutual awareness and common "mood," and bodily synchronization. While successful rituals generate group "emotional energy," failed rituals deplete it. IRC theory claims that while flowing from situation to situation, individuals are drawn to interactions that provide the best emotional energy payoff for their personal and social attributes.

Emotion and Emotion Management

Originally developed by Arlie Hochschild (1979, 1983), emotion management theory begins with several beliefs: Emotions arise from inside individuals; emotion is governed by "feeling rules" (normative ideas on what we should feel), "framing rules" (evaluations of the social meaning of these feelings), and "expression" rules (ideas on how to express our feelings); and it is not uncommon for there to be disjunctures between what is spontaneously felt and what should be felt. This gap calls for *emotion management* or *emotion work*, which is "typically performed for the purposes of bringing nonnormative feelings and expressions back in line with culturally agreed-upon emotion norms" (Lively and Weed, 2014: 202). *Emotion work* is thus the act of "trying to change in degree or quality an emotion or feeling," which might involve "evoking or shaping as well as suppressing feeling in oneself" (Hochschild, 1979: 561). While Hochschild developed her theory to account for the emotion work required of employees in service occupations, the framework now is used to explore emotion management throughout social life as well as to answer questions about how social actors attempt to manage the emotions of others (Thoits, 1996; see Lively and Weed, 2014 for a review).

Emotion and Social Structure

While emotions are created through, and managed in, face-to-face interactions, these interactions take place within social structures. The center of interest in many sociological theories of emotion is "the social context and how the consensus of meaning and the structural forms of that context shape (and are shaped by) emotional experience" (Smith-Lovin and Thoits, 2014: 188). In contrast to interactional and emotion management theories, social structural theories characterize human actors as more acted upon than acting because the core of such theories is the assertion that particular structural positions lead to particular emotions in individuals. While there are myriad and often interlocking theories, the most common frameworks are power-status, expectation states, and identity theories.

The *power-status* theory of emotion developed by Theodore Kemper is often called the exemplar social structural theory of emotion. Its foundation is Kemper's argument that a "large class of emotions results from real, imagined or anticipated outcomes in social relationships" (Kemper, 1978: 43) and that these outcomes, invariably and without exception, revolve around issues of power (the ability to enforce compliance) and status (honor/deference). Power-status theory posits that emotions result from actors' perceived evaluations of the power and status of self and other in interactions. For example, having power, or gaining power, is associated with positive emotions while not having power, or losing power, is associated with negative emotions.

Expectation states theory, part of a larger family of group process theories, is centered on understanding the "way that power and prestige orders develop, evolve and are legitimated" (Robinson, Clay-Warner, and Everett, 2008: 5; also see this for a description of multiple variants of such theories). Retaining a focus on social structural characteristics of power and status, these theories apply to social groups where members interact around accomplishing a specific task; the theories are about how emotion is intertwined with hierarchy by way of "expectations," which are the "task specific anticipation for the quality of future performances" (Webster and Walker, 2014: 128). Similar to ideas developed by Kemper (1978) and Collins (1975, 1981), the central assertion is that "people's positions of power and regard in social groups and changes to those positions are basic determinant of the emotions they feel" (Ridgeway, 2005: 348). Again, emotion is both an outcome of structural positions of power and a creator of such structure because "status and expectation affect behavior and behaviors affect status and expectations" (Webster and Walker, 2014: 128).

A final example of structural theories of emotion is *identity* theory. Drawing from symbolic interactionism, identity theories link the evaluation of identity performance (conceptualized as a set of meanings attached to the self) with perceived evaluations of others. Positive emotions are associated with identity being perceived as confirmed by others; negative emotions result when identity is perceived as not confirmed by others (Stets and Trettevik, 2014).

Theoretical Limits of Conceptualizing Emotion as a Property of Individuals

Reflecting Western ethnopsychologies privileging the importance and centrality of individuals, most social science attention is devoted to the individual experiences, causes, and consequences of emotion. While this orientation has led to countless empirical studies and a considerable accumulation of knowledge, we will continue our tour through theories of emotion by changing the center of theoretical attention from individuals to *culture*. Conceptualizing emotion as cultural serves to historically and socially contextualize questions about emotion as a property of individuals; cultural frameworks also lead to a more complete understanding of how emotion works and the work emotion does in social life.

First, theories of the experiences, causes, and consequences of individual emotion tend to be relatively silent about the meanings and workings of larger cultural contexts informing individuals, interactions, and social structure. Yet, while culture, defined as "historically transmitted patterns of meanings embodied in symbols" (Geertz, 1973: 89), is ignored or undertheorized, understandings of culture nonetheless are embedded in these theories. Goffman's dramaturgical actors, for example, engage in impression management in order to present themselves in a favorable light. Doing so assumes actors who more or less share images of what types of performances are expected and preferred. In the same way, to be sensible, expectation states theory and social identity theory assume some measure of agreement about what is valued. And, while the feeling rules, framing rules, and expression rules of emotion management theories are cultural objects, these theories take these systems of meaning as givens in order to focus on how social actors respond to them. In brief, it is not possible to fully comprehend emotion as a property of individuals without attending more to cultural notions of cultures surrounding individuals, interactions, and social structures.

Second, changing social and historical conditions raise questions about emotion that are not about individual experience. For example, centering attention on individuals has led to a primary theoretical interest in face-to-face interactions, yet the "face-to-face domain ... simply no longer has the structural importance it once had" (Knorr Cetina, 2009: 63). An increasing share of interaction is mediated, targeted to large audiences, and transmitted through technologies of various sorts. Understanding what emotion does in social life requires attending to the characteristics and workings of what Boltanski (1999) called "communication at a distance," a mediated communication encouraging particular forms of cognitive and emotional evaluations of *strangers*. Further, it would not be much of an overstatement to claim that all theories of emotion as a property of individuals reflect distinctly Western ethnopsychologies (see Solomon, 1995; Stearns, 2010). Countless anthropological studies showing the idiosyncrasies of Western ethnopsychologies cannot be dismissed as being merely of "academic" interest given that we live in a world increasingly characterized by globalization and mass migrations. Focusing on emotion as a property of individuals does not easily lead to theorizing the social and political work of emotion in this world (Moïsi, 2009; Svašek and Skrbiš, 2007).

In summary, although placing individuals in the center of theoretical interest has led to an accumulation of considerable knowledge, it is not sufficient to fully comprehend the meanings and importance of emotion in social life. We move now to frameworks that place culture in the center of attention.

Emotion Theory II: The Centrality of Culture

When theories of emotion center on culture, it leads to questions about individuals remaining in a murky background. We will begin with an idealistic conception of emotion as consisting of systems of ideas, and then move to the social and political uses of these ideas.

Emotion and Discourse

Emotion discourse is talk that performs social actions (Edwards, 1999), talk that is a "tool for shaping the social construction of reality" (White, 2000: 39). There are two varieties of this discourse: talk *about* emotions (revealing how social actors think about feeling), and talk that "seems to have some affective content or effect" (Abu-Lughod and Lutz, 1990: 10; see also Bickford, 2011). While observers of emotion as a property of individuals view such talk in terms of its personal, psychological, and interactional work (Edwards, 1999), proponents of cultural perspectives broaden this meaning to include "pragmatic acts and communicative performances" (Abu-Lughod and Lutz, 1990: 11) found in *all* spoken and written forms of human communication, from poetry to public policy, from songs to scientific arguments.

The concept of emotion discourse can be enlarged into an idea variously called *emotion codes* (Loseke, 2009), *emotion cultures* (Gordon, 1990), *emotionologies* (Stearns and Stearns, 1985), *emotion schemas* (White, 1990), or *feeling rules, framing rules, and expression rules* (Hochschild, 1979). These are cultural ways of feeling (Solomon, 1995), *cognitive* models about which emotions are expected when, where, and toward whom or what, as well as about how emotions should be inwardly experienced, outwardly expressed, and morally evaluated (see Loseke and Kusenbach, 2008 for a review). When viewed within ethnomethodology, these systems of meaning, often embedded in narratives that circulate throughout social life (Kusenbach and Loseke, 2013), are resources that "allow members of a society to identify and discuss emotions, evaluate them as desirable or undesirable, and regulate them in line with values and norms" (Gordon, 1990: 29). As such, they are a part of the "cultural tool kit" (Swidler, 1986), the "structuring and constituting resources which we utilize in expressing our own emotional states and in responding to those of others" (Tudor, 2003: 241).

Further, in any given time and place there are "specific modes of emotionality that are widely practiced, actively traded upon, and routinely expected by members of a social collectivity" (Tudor, 2003: 243). Such *emotional climates* result from emotion codes that are both widely shared and evaluated as important. Hence, it is possible to talk about the "the emotional climate of advanced capitalist societies" (Hunt, 2012: 137), or the emotional climate in the United States in the late twentieth century characterized by prohibitions against the emotions of guilt and anger (Irvine, 1997), an expectation of constant "cheerfulness" (Kotchemidova, 2010), an increasing production of "synthetic" emotions such as those stirred by Valentine's Day or Mother's Day, and so on (Hunt, 2012).

Emotion and Persuasion

When emotion discourse is evaluated as having affective content, it is *persuasive* discourse. While theorists from the classical philosophers onward have been interested in persuasion, understanding how persuasion works is increasingly important given characteristics of our modern world, where mass migrations, loss of traditional authority, heterogeneity, and accompanying social and moral fragmentation have made meaning in general, and shared meaning in particular, difficult to attain and sustain (see Calhoun, 1994). Observers argue that such environments have served to "relativize" truth and, as a consequence, social actors, at least those in the Western world, have become very "emotion conscious," meaning that how social actors "feel" can be evaluated as more important than how they "think" (McCarthy, 1989). As a consequence, persuasion of all types becomes more oriented toward appeals to feeling than to thinking (see Loseke and Kusenbach, 2008 for a review) and there is considerable interest in theorizing how, precisely, discourse can achieve persuasiveness in mass, heterogeneous audiences and on multiple stages of social life (see, for example, Loseke, 2009; Richards, 2004; Witte and Allen, 2000).

Emotion and Social Structure

When emotion is conceptualized as a property of individuals, social structure causes individual emotional experience. When rather conceptualized as a property of culture, emotion causes social structure. That is, as an element of culture, emotion discourse is a "superstructure of mental life" that can become "sewn into the fabric of the economy, society, and the state" (Starr, 1992: 264). This happens in three ways.

First, emotional *climates* can create social structure. The primary example fueling modern attention is the "culture of fear" in the Western world. Observers argue that a culture of fear refers to far more than a collective way of feeling, for it has led to massive increases in surveillance and massive decreases in privacy for citizens in general; fears about uncontrolled immigration have led to political upheavals; and an increasing number of citizens are taking refuge from perceived urban dangers behind fences and gates. Many industries and government agencies are dedicated to producing fearfulness, while many others are dedicated to offering protection against it (Altheide, 2002; Furedi, 1997; Tudor, 2003). Discourse becomes social structure when it fuels social actions of particular sorts.

Second, embedded in emotion discourse are assumptions, values, and biases that permit or prohibit, encourage or discourage particular types of moral evaluations and behaviors toward particular types of people, objects, and events. There is a long-standing interest in understanding how such discourse justifies inequalities. Consider, for example, Western emotionologies that associate emotion with bodies (not minds), with irrationality (not rationality), and with subjectivity (not objectivity). This emotion discourse, in turn, is mapped onto a binary system of ideas called "gender" that identifies emotion with women and cognition with men. Within Western social orders prizing rationality and cognition, this emotion/gender discourse reinforces the ideological and structural subordination of women (Abu-Lughod and Lutz, 1990; Cancian, 1987). In much the same way, emotion discourse serves as a normative device for judging the mental health of culturally different people (Lutz, 1986: 288). Such normative judgments lead to freedom or confinement, to the presence or absence of rights and privileges.

Third, moral evaluations and biases within emotion discourse create *symbolic boundaries*, "conceptual distinctions ... to categorize objects, people, practices" (Lamont and Molnár, 2002: 168; Zerubavel, 1996) that can become embedded in social policy and organizational structures (Fischer, 2003; Stone, 1997).

A common interest in the structural consequences of symbolic boundaries focuses on relationships between emotion discourse, assignments of morality, and social policy. Because morality is something that is felt more than it is thought, the politics of morality is the politics of emotion (Loseke, 2003; Pizarro, Inbar, and Helion, 2011). Observers have theorized both micro- and macro-politics of sympathy (Clark, 1997), pity (Boltanski, 1999), grief (Ahmed, 2015), and disgust (Hancock, 2004). These politics are cultural, in that socially circulating emotion discourses assign moral evaluations to *types* of people: They are designations of the type of person who is a worthy recipient of sympathy or grief, the type of person who deserves pity, the type of person who is disgusting. Such socially circulating systems of meaning become images of people, who will be the "targets" of social policy, and they influence the extent to which policy seeks to "help" or "punish" (Schneider and Ingram, 1993). Real people then receive the benefits or burdens of policy that becomes embedded in rules and regulations, in organizations and groups.

In summary, placing culture in the center of interest is important because it shows the cultural context surrounding individuals, interactions, and social structures. In addition, theorizing beginning with culture leads to exploring the uses and consequences of emotion discourse, which generates insight into how the "production of emotional meaning in discourse ... enters into wider spheres of power and violence" (White, 2004: 294).

Theoretical Limits of Conceptualizing Emotion as a Property of Culture

As with frameworks conceptualizing emotion as an individual-level phenomenon, cultural frameworks yield important insights about relationships between emotion and social life. We do not need to belabor the obvious limitations of this perspective: By foregrounding culture, this framework moves the individual experience of emotion into the background. As such, it assumes, yet does not interrogate, how individuals use culture and, critically, it ignores feelings which stand at the center of the "guts" of emotion (Leavitt, 1996; Lyon, 1995). Hence, when frameworks center on individuals, culture remains in a murky, under-theorized background; and when frameworks center on culture, individuals all but disappear.

Final Reflections on Emotion Theory

In this chapter we developed a minimalist categorization system that was capable of including theories of emotion generated in several social science disciplines. Because our system distinguished theories only in terms of their focus on emotion as a property of individuals or as a property of culture, it did not make visible the many differences between theoretical approaches in each category. Yet our system did have the benefit of demonstrating how individual and cultural frames each serve to raise specific questions about emotions while ignoring others. Although it is fairly common for observers to "choose sides" and argue for one framework and against the other, our review has led us to believe that *both* frameworks are characterized by strengths and by weaknesses, that *both* are necessary if we want to understand the full range of relationships between emotion, culture, and individual selves.

While much theoretical and empirical work remains in developing individual and cultural views of emotion, an important project is to bridge the two frameworks, to focus specifically on *reflexive* relationships between cultural meanings and individual experiences, on *reflexive* relationships among emotions in individuals, relationships, social structure, and culture. One such promising topic is "collective emotions," because these are emotions experienced by individuals but that are not individual phenomena because they are widely shared. Observers argue that such collective emotions lead to social and political change (Stearns, 1995), that collective emotions of electorates *always* have been a central component of democratic politics (Marcus, 2002), that entire countries or geographical regions can be characterized in terms of collective emotions, and that these are evoked by processes of global politics (Moïsi, 2009; Saurette, 2006). On one hand, observers argue that collective emotion is a neglected topic within the framework of emotion as a property of individuals (Barbalet, 2001). On the other hand, collective emotion is about culture. Widely shared emotion sheds light on underlying emotional climates and it highlights emotion as a *cultural* ways of feeling (Loseke, 2009).

We end where we began: After a long period of neglect in the social sciences, there now is enormous interest in the topic of emotion. There are countless theories centering on emotion as a property of individuals and emotion as a property of cultures and these most typically are segregated by discipline and, within discipline, by topic with little cross-fertilization. While emotion theorists have accomplished a great deal, there is much that needs to be done. Some of the most basic questions upon which theorizing rests remain surrounded by disagreements: What *is* emotion? What are its most important properties? What are the most important questions to ask? What are the reflexive relationships between individual, interactional, organizational, structural, and cultural levels of emotion?

Finally, the observations of Andrew Beatty (2013: 545) about emotion researchers apply equally well to emotion theorists:

> Emotion researchers, it often is said, irresistibly call to mind the fable of the blind men and the elephant, each right in his own way, none getting the whole beast. Where does emotion begin and end? Is it a matter of interpretation, feeling, category, response, expression, or some or all of these? ... The definitional problem can't be made to go away by putting all the parts together, because the parts may be only contingently related; some parts may be more essential than others (an elephant is still an elephant without its tail).

References

Abu-Lughod, Lila, and Catherine A. Lutz. 1990. "Introduction: Emotion, Discourse, and the Politics of Everyday Life." In Catherine A. Lutz and Lila Abu-Lughod (eds.), *Language and the Politics of Emotion* (pp. 1–23). New York: Cambridge University Press.

Ahmed, Sara. 2015. *The Cultural Politics of Emotion*. New York: Routledge.

Altheide, David L. 2002. *Creating Fear*. New York: Aldine deGruyter.

Averill, James R. 1980. "A Constructivist View of Emotion." In Robert Plutchik and Henry Kellerman (eds.), *Emotion: Theory, Research, and Experience. Volume 1: Theories of Emotion* (pp. 305–340). New York: Academic Press.

Barbalet, Jack. 2002. "Introduction: Why Emotions are Crucial." In Jack Barbalet (ed.), *Emotions and Sociology* (pp. 1–9). Cambridge, MA: Blackwell Publishing.

Barbalet. Jack M. 2001. *Emotion, Social Theory, and Social Structure: A Macrosociological Approach*. New York: Cambridge University Press.

Barrett, Lisa Feldman. 2012. "Emotions Are Real." *Emotion* 12: 413–429.

2014. "The Conceptual Act Theory: A Précis." *Emotion Review* 6: 292–297.

Barrett, Lisa Feldman, Batja Mesquita, Kevin N. Ochsner, and James J. Gross. 2007. "The Experience of Emotion." *Annual Review of Psychology* 58: 373–403.

Beatty, Andrew. 2005. "'Feeling Your Way in Java:' An Essay on Society and Emotion." *Ethnos* 70: 53–78.

2013. "Current Emotion Research in Anthropology: Reporting the Field." *Emotion Review* 5: 414–422.

2014. "Anthropology and Emotion." *Journal of the Royal Anthropological Institute* 20: 545–563.

Berezin, Mabel. 2009. "Exploring Emotions and the Economy: New Contributions from Sociological Theory." *Theoretical Sociology* 38: 335–346.

Bericat, Eduardo. 2015. "The Sociology of Emotions: Four Decades of Progress." *Current Sociology* 64(3): 1–23.

Bickford, Susan. 2011. "Emotion Talk and Political Judgment." *The Journal of Politics* 73: 1025–1037.

Boiger, Michael, and Batja Mesquita. 2012. "The Construction of Emotion in Interactions, Relationships, and Cultures." *Emotion Review* 4: 221–229.

Boltanski, Luc. 1999. *Distant Suffering: Morality, Media and Politics*. Cambridge, UK: Cambridge University Press.

Calhoun, Craig. 1994. "Social Theory and the Politics of Identity." In Craig Calhoun (ed.), *Social Theory and the Politics of Identity* (pp. 9–36). Cambridge, MA: Blackwell

Cancian, Francesca M. 1987. *Love in America: Gender and Self-Development*. Cambridge, UK: Cambridge University Press.

Charmaz, Kathy, and Melinda Milligan. 2006. "Grief." In Jan E. Stets and Jonathan H. Turner (eds.), *Handbook of the Sociology of Emotions* (pp. 516–543). Boston, MA: Springer.

Chiao, Joan Y. 2015. "Current Emotion Research in Cultural Neuroscience." *Emotion Review* 7: 280–293.

Clark, Candace. 1997. *Misery and Company: Sympathy in Everyday Life*. Chicago, IL: University of Chicago Press.

Collins, Randall. 1975. *Conflict Sociology: Toward an Explanatory Science*. New York: Academic Press.

   1981. "On the Micro-Foundations of Macro-Sociology." *American Journal of Sociology* 86: 984–1014.

   2004. *Interaction Rituals*. Princeton, NJ: Princeton University Press.

Cornish, Derek B., and Ronald V. Clarke (eds.). 2014. *The Reasoning Criminal: Rational Choice Perspectives on Offending*. New Brunswick, NJ: Transaction Publishers.

Cunningham, William A. 2013. "Introduction to Special Section: Psychological Constructivism." *Emotion Review* 5: 333–334.

Darwin, Charles. 1872. *The Expression of the Emotions in Man and Animals*. London: Murray.

Denzin, Norman K. 1984. *On Understanding Emotion*. San Francisco, CA: Jossey-Bass.

Dixon, Thomas. 2012. "'Emotion': The History of a Keyword in Crisis." *Emotion Review* 4: 338–344.

Durkheim, Emile. 1965/1915. *The Elementary Forms of Religious Life*. New York: Free Press.

Edwards, Derek. 1999. "Emotion Discourse." *Culture & Psychology* 5: 271–291.

Ekman, Paul. 1972. "Universal and Cultural Differences in Facial Expressions of Emotions." In J. K. Cole (ed.), *Nebraska Symposium on Motivation, 1971* (pp. 207–283). Lincoln, NE: University of Nebraska Press.

   1992. "Are There Basic Emotions?" *Psychological Review* 99: 550–553.

Ellis, Carolyn. 1991. "Sociological Introspection and Emotional Experience." *Symbolic Interaction* 14: 23–50.

Ellis, Carolyn, and Michael G. Flaherty. 1992. "An Agenda for the Interpretation of Lived Experience." In Carolyn Ellis and Michael G. Flaherty (eds.), *Investigating Subjectivity: Research on Lived Experience* (pp. 1–16). London: Sage.

Fischer, Frank. 2003. *Reframing Public Policy: Discursive Politics and Deliberative Practices*. New York: Oxford University Press.

Furedi, F. 1997. *Culture of Fear: Risk-taking and the Morality of Low Expectation*. London: Cassell.

Geertz, Clifford. 1973. *The Interpretation of Cultures*. New York: Basic Books.

Gendron, Maria, and Lisa Feldman Barrett. 2009. "Reconstructing the Past: A Century of Ideas About Emotion in Psychology." *Emotion Review* 4: 316–339.

Goffman, Erving. 1952. "On Cooling the Mark Out: Some Aspects of Adaptation to Failure." *Psychiatry* 15: 451–463.

   1956. "Embarrassment and Social Organization." *American Journal of Sociology* 62: 264–274.

   1967. *Interaction Ritual: Essays on Face-to-Face Behavior*." Garden City, NY: Anchor Books.

Gordon, Steven L. 1990. "Social Structural Effects on Emotions." In Theodore D. Kemper (ed.), *Research Agendas in the Sociology of Emotions* (pp. 134–179). Albany, NY: State University of New York Press.

Hancock, Ange-Marie. 2004. *The Politics of Disgust: The Public Identity of the Welfare Queen*. New York: New York University Press.

Harré, Rom. 1986. "An Outline of the Social Constructionist Viewpoint." In Rom Harré (ed.), *The Social Construction of Emotions* (pp. 2–13). New York: Basil Blackwell.

Heavey, Christopher L., Russell T. Hurlburt, and Noelle L. Lefforge. 2012. "Toward a Phenomenology of Feelings." *Emotion* 12: 763–777.

Heise, David R. 1979. *Understanding Events: Affect and the Construction of Social Action*. Cambridge, UK: Cambridge University Press.

Hochschild, Arlie R. 1983. *The Managed Heart: Commercialization of Human Feeling*. Berkeley, CA: University of California Press.

Hochschild, Arlie Russell. 1979. "Emotion Work, Feeling Rules, and Social Structure." *American Journal of Sociology* 85: 551–575.

Hunt, Alan. 2012. "The Civilizing Process and Emotional Life: The Intensification and Hollowing Out of Contemporary Emotions." In Dale Spencer, Kevin Walby, and Alan Hunt (ed.), *Emotions Matter: A Relational Approach to Emotions* (pp. 137–160). Toronto: University of Toronto Press.

Irvine. Leslie. 1997. "Reconsidering the American Emotional Culture: Co-dependency and Emotion Management." *Innovation* 10: 345–359.

Izard, Carroll E. 2009. "Emotion Theory and Research: Highlights, Unanswered Questions, and Emerging Issues." *Annual Review of Psychology* 60: 1–25.

James, William. 1884. "What Is an Emotion?" *Mind* 9: 188–205.

Katz, Jack. 1999. *How Emotions Work*. Chicago, IL: University of Chicago Press.

Kaufman, Bruce E. 1999. "Emotional Arousal as a Source of Bounded Rationality." *Journal of Economic Behavior & Organization* 38: 135–144.

Kemper, Theodore. 1978. *A Social Interactional Theory of Emotions*. New York: Wiley.

Kirkpatrick, John, and Geoffrey M. White. 1985. "Exploring Ethnopsychologies." In Geoffrey M. White and John Kirkpatrick (eds.), *Person, Self, and Experience: Exploring Pacific Ethnopsychologies* (pp. 1–32). Berkeley, CA: University of California Press.

Knorr Cetina, Karin. 2009. "The Synthetic Situation: Interactionism for a Global World." *Symbolic Interaction* 32: 61–87.

Kotchemidova, Christina. 2010. "Emotion Culture and Cognitive Constructions of Reality." *Communication Quarterly* 58: 207–234.

Kusenbach, Margarethe, and Donileen R. Loseke. 2013. "Bringing the Social Back In: Some Suggestions for the Qualitative Study of Emotions." *Qualitative Sociology Review* 9: 20–38.

Lambek, Michael, and Jacqueline S. Solway. 2001. "Just Anger: Scenarios of Indignation in Botswana and Madagascar." *Ethnos* 77: 49–72.

Lamont, Michéle, and Virag Molnár. 2002. "The Study of Boundaries in the Social Sciences." *Annual Review of Sociology* 28: 167–95.

Lawler, Edward J., and Shane R. Thye. 1999. "Bringing Emotions into Social Exchange Theory." *Annual Review of Sociology* 25: 217–244.

Leavitt, John. 1996. "Meaning and Feeling in the Anthropology of Emotions." *American Ethnologist* 23: 514–539.

Lewis, Michael. 1993. "The Development of Anger and Rage." In Robert A. Glock and Steven P. Roose (ed.), *Rage, Power, and Aggression* (pp. 148–168). New Haven, CT: Yale University Press.

Lively, Kathryn J., and Emi A. Weed. 2014. "Emotion Management: Sociological Insight into What, How, Why, and to What End?" *Emotion Review* 6: 202–207.

Lofland, Lyn H. 1985. "The Social Shaping of Emotion: The Case of Grief." *Symbolic Interaction* 8: 171–190.

Loseke, Donileen R. 2009. "Examining Emotion as Discourse: Emotion Codes and Presidential Speeches Justifying War." *The Sociological Quarterly* 50: 497–524.

2003. *Thinking About Social Problems: An Introduction to Constructionist Perspectives*, 2nd edition. New York: Aldine DeGruyter.

Loseke, Donileen R., and Margarethe Kusenbach. 2008. "The Social Construction of Emotion." In Jaber Gubrium and James A. Holstein (eds.), *Handbook of Social Construction* (pp. 511–530). New York: Guilford Press.

Lutz, Catherine. 1986. "Emotion, Thought, and Estrangement: Emotion as a Cultural Category." *Cultural Anthropology* 1: 287–309.

Lyon, Margot. 1995. "Missing Emotion: The Limitations of Cultural Constructionism in the Study of Emotion." *Cultural Anthropology* 10:244–263.

Marcus, George E. 2000. "Emotions in Politics." *Annual Review of Political Science* 3: 221–250.

2002. *The Sentimental Citizen: Emotion in Democratic Politics*. Pennsylvania, PA: The Pennsylvania State University Press.

Massey, Douglas S. 2002. "A Brief History of Human Society: The Origin and Role of Emotion in Social Life." *American Sociological Review* 67:1–29.

McCarthy, E. Doyle. 1989. "Emotions are Social Things: An Essay in the Sociology of Emotions." In David D. Franks and E. Doyle McCarthy (eds.), *The Sociology of Emotions: Original Essays and Research Reports, Volume 9* (pp. 51–72). Greenwich, CT: JAI Press.

Mead, George Herbert. 1934. *Mind, Self, and Society*. Chicago, IL: University of Chicago Press.

Meloni, Maurizio. 2014. "How Biology Became Social, and What It Means for Social Theory." *The Sociological Review* 62: 593–614.

Mesquita, B., and R. Walker. 2003. "Cultural Differences in Emotions: A Context for Interpreting Emotional Experiences." *Behaviour Research and Therapy* 41: 777–793.

Mesquita, Batja, and Michael Boiger. 2014. "Emotions in Context: A Sociodynamic Model of Emotions." *Emotion Review* 6: 298–302.

Moïsi, Dominique. 2009. *The Geopolitics of Emotion: How Cultures of Fear, Humiliation, and Hope are Reshaping the World*. New York: Anchor Books.

Mulligan, Kevin, and Klaus R. Scherer. 2012. "Toward a Working Definition of Emotion." *Emotion Review* 4: 345–357.

Nussbaum, Martha C. 2006. *Hiding from Humanity: Disgust, Shame, and the Law*. Princeton, NJ: Princeton University Press.

Pizarro, David, Yoel Inbar, and Chelsea Helion. 2011. "On Disgust and Moral Judgment." *Emotion Review* 3: 267–268.

Reddy, William M. 1999. "Emotional Liberty: Politics and History in the Anthropology of Emotions." *Cultural Anthropology* 14: 256–288.

Richards, Barry. 2004. "The Emotional Deficit in Political Communication." *Political Communication* 21: 339–52.

Ridgeway, Cecilia. 2005. "Expectation States Theory and Emotion." In Jan E. Stets and Jonathan H. Turner (eds.), *Handbook of the Sociology of Emotions* (pp. 347–354). New York: Springer.

Robinson, Dawn T. 2014. "The Role of Cultural Meanings and Situated Interaction in Shaping Emotion." *Emotion Review* 6: 189–195.

Robinson, Dawn T., Jody Clay-Warner, and Tiffany Everett. 2008. "Introduction." In Jody Clay-Warner and Dawn T. Robinson (eds.), *Social Structure and Emotion* (pp. 1–7). New York: Elsevier.

Robinson, Dawn T., Lynn Smith-Lovin, and Allison K. Wisecup. 2006. "Affect Control Theory." In Jan E. Stets and Jonathan H. Turner (eds.), *Handbook of the Sociology of Emotions* (pp. 179–202). New York: Springer.

Rogers, Kimberly B., and Liam Kavanaugh. 2010. "Bridging Emotion Research: From Biology to Social Structure." *Social Psychology Quarterly* 73: 333–334.

Rose, Nikolas. 2013. "The Human Sciences in a Biological Age." *Theory, Culture & Society* 30: 3–34.

Saurette, Paul. 2006. "You Dissin Me? Humiliation and Post 9/11 Global Politics." *Review of International Studies* 32: 495–522.

Scheff, Thomas. 2003. "Shame in Self and Society." *Symbolic Interaction* 26: 239–262.

Scherer, Klaus R. 2009. "The Dynamic Architecture of Emotion: Evidence for the Component Process Model." *Cognition & Emotion* 23: 1307–1351.

Schilling, Chris. 2002. "The Two Traditions in the Sociology of Emotions." In Jack Barbalet (ed.), *Emotions and Sociology* (pp. 10–31). Oxford, UK: Blackwell.

Schneider, Anne, and Helen Ingram. 1993. "Social Construction of Target Populations: Implications for Politics and Policy." *American Political Science Review* 87: 334–347.

Shott, Susan. 1979. "Emotion and Social Life: A Symbolic Interactionist Analysis." *American Journal of Sociology* 84: 1317–1334.

Skitka, Linda J. 2005. "Patriotism or Nationalism? Understanding Post-September 11, 2001, Flag-Display Behavior." *Journal of Applied Social Psychology* 35: 1995–2011.

Smith-Lovin, Lynn. 1990. "Emotion as the Confirmation and Disconfirmation of Identity: An Affect Control Model." In Theodore D. Kemper (ed.), *Research Agendas in the Sociology of Emotions*. Albany, NY: State University of New York Press.

Smith-Lovin, Lynn, and David R. Heise. 1988. *Analyzing Social Interaction: Advances in Affect Control Theory*. New York: Gordon and Breach.

Smith-Lovin, Lynn, and Piotr Winkelman. 2010. "The Social Psychologies of Emotion: A Bridge that Is Not Too Far." *Social Psychology Quarterly* 73: 327–332.

Smith-Lovin, Lynn, and Peggy A. Thoits. 2014. "Introduction to the Special Section on the Sociology of Emotions." *Emotion Review* 6: 187–188.

Solomon, Robert C. 1995. "Some Notes on Emotion: East and West." *Philosophy East & West* 45: 171–202.

2006. "Emotions in Continental Philosophy." *Philosophy Compass* 1/5: 413–431.

Starr, Paul. 1992. "Social Categories and Claims in the Liberal State." *Social Research* 59: 263–295.

Stearns, Peter N. 1989. *Jealousy: The Evolution of an Emotion in American History*. New York: New York University Press.

1995. "Emotion." In Rom Harré and Peter Stearns (ed.), *Discursive Psychology in Practice* (pp. 37–54). Thousand Oaks, CA: Sage.

2010. "Dare to Compare: The Next Challenge in Assessing Emotional Cultures." *Emotion Review* 2: 261–264.

Stearns, Peter N., and Carol Z. Stearns. 1985. "Emotionology: Clarifying the History of Emotions and Emotional Standards." *American Historical Review* 90: 813–836.

Stets, Jan E., and Ryan Trettevik. 2014. "Emotions in Identity Theory." In Jan E. Stets and Jonathan H. Turner (eds.), *Handbook of the Sociology of Emotions: Volume II* (pp. 33–39). New York: Springer Science.

Stone, Deborah. 1997. *Policy Paradox: The Art of Political Decision Making.* New York: W.W. Norton and Company.

Svašek, Maruška, and Zlatko Skrbiš. 2007. "Passions and Powers: Emotions and Globalization." *Identities: Global Studies in Culture and Power* 14: 367–383.

Swidler, Ann. 2001. *Talk of Love: How Culture Matters.* Chicago, IL: University of Chicago Press.

1986. "Culture in Action: Symbols and Strategies." *American Sociological Review* 51: 276–286.

Thamm, Robert A. 2006. "The Classification of Emotions." In Jan E. Stets and Jonathan H. Turner (eds.), *Handbook of the Sociology of Emotions* (pp. 11–37). New York: Springer.

Thoits, Peggy A. 1989. "The Sociology of Emotions." *Annual Review of Sociology* 15: 317–342.

1996. "Managing the Emotions of Others." *Symbolic Interaction* 19: 85–109.

Tudor, Andrew. 2003. "A (Macro) Sociology of Fear?" *The Sociological Review* 51: 238–256.

Turner, Bryan S. 2009. "Introduction: A New Agenda for Social Theory?" In Bryan S. Turner (ed.), *The New Blackwell Companion to Social Theory* (pp. 1–16). Malden, MA: John Wiley & Sons.

Turner, Jonathan H., and Jan E. Stets. 2006. "Sociological Theories of Human Emotions." *Annual Review of Sociology* 32: 25–52.

Von Scheve, Christian, and Rolf Von Leude. 2005. "Emotion and Social Structures: Towards an Interdisciplinary Approach." *Journal for the Theory of Social Behaviour* 35: 303–328.

Webster, Murray, Jr., and Lisa Slattery Walker. 2014. "Emotions in Expectation States Theory." In Jan E. Stets and Jonathan H. Turner (ed.), *Handbook of the Sociology of Emotions, Volume II* (pp. 127–153). New York: Springer.

White, Geoffrey M. 1990. "Moral Discourse and the Rhetoric of Emotions." In Catherine A. Lutz and Lila Abu-Lughod (eds.), *Language and the Politics of Emotion* (pp. 46–68). New York: Cambridge University Press.

2000. "Representing Emotional Meaning: Category, Metaphor, Schema, Discourse." In Michael Lewis and Jeanette M. Haviland-Jones (eds.), *Handbook of Emotions*, 2nd ed. (pp. 30–44). New York: The Guilford Press.

2004. "National Subjects: September 11 and Pearl Harbor." *American Ethnologist* 31: 293–310.

Witte, Kim, and Mike Allen. 2000. "A Meta-Analysis of Fear Appeals: Implications for Effective Public Health Campaigns." *Health Education & Behavior* 27(5): 591–615.

Zerubavel, Eviatar. 1996. "Lumping and Splitting: Notes on Social Classification." *Sociological Forum* 11: 421–433.

6 Theorizing Sex/Gender: Feminist Social Theory

Shelley Budgeon

This chapter is concerned with the question of what happens to 'social theory' when the term 'feminist' is used to qualify it? Feminist social theory will be located in its relationship to mainstream social theory highlighting, the significance of its key critical interventions. Feminist interventions have disturbed many of the traditional assumptions underpinning social theory and have profoundly affected how we think about the social world. It is now 'impossible to study society without at the same time studying how society is constructed through male and female, masculinity and femininity' (Evans, 2003: viii). This chapter is also concerned with questions such as: what is theory and who is it for? Feminist social theory has articulated a vision of theory that is distinctive due to its critique of external, dominant disciplinary conventions, and, has also pursued a project driven by internal, self-reflexive dialogues. Feminist social theory has developed as much as a critique of those ways of explaining the social that are associated with male-dominated knowledge production *and* as the product of a reflexive and critical discussion amongst different feminist perspectives. As such this chapter will explore the generative nature of feminist social theory by surveying a range of issues which have arisen out of those analyses and debates.

Feminist thought will be contextualized by discussing its relation to the tradition of sociological theory which sought to apprehend the nature of modernity. Feminist critiques of this body of mainstream theory have demonstrated how key thinkers ignored the centrality of gender to social relations and, yet, at the same time proffered a very particular construction of gender by defining women as being outside the social and firmly in the realm of nature. Strategies for denaturalizing women's status and bringing their experiences fully into the social are outlined, then followed by those critiques which emanated from within feminist thought itself, taking aim at its own problematic assumptions. These interrogations have come from various quarters and are exemplified by challenges made by postcolonial and postmodernist feminist critiques of dominant theorizations of women's experiences. Understanding feminist social theory begins with the recognition that it always operates in a 'double register': 'it will both contest other ways of understanding the world (those theories that are often not seen as theories as they are assumed to be "common sense"), and it will *contest* itself, as a way of interpreting the world (or of "making sense" in a way which contests what is "common")' (Ahmed, 2000: 101). The final section focuses on three significant areas that have recently developed as a result of debates within feminist thought – intersectionality, new materialism, and transgender theory. Feminist thought is characterized by diversity and variations which defy easy capture by a single definition and, therefore, an important caveat framing this chapter is that in places the discussion will make both generalizations and exclusions out of practical necessity.

What Is Feminist Social Theory?

Witz and Marshall (2004: 1) state 'If we round up the usual suspects, then it appears that it is largely straight white men who get to do the abstract, universally generalizable thinking that counts as sociological theory with a big T.' The production of knowledge has been inherently gendered, and for this reason, both the very nature of knowledge, and what becomes established as legitimate expertise, are questions at the heart of feminist epistemological approaches to established social theory. The set orientations towards mainstream social theory shared by feminist theory show that the enterprise of theorizing has long been seen as a masculinist preserve which produces biased accounts while purporting to offer objective, impartial, and abstract generalizable knowledge of the social world. Scepticism towards foundational principles of social theory has meant that feminists have questioned both the form and content of what becomes recognized as knowledge. Butler and Scott (1992: xiii) acknowledge that the relationship between feminism and theory is often challenging because 'theory' is a highly contested term within feminism discourse.

> What qualifies as 'theory'? Who is the author of 'theory'? Is it singular? Is it defined in opposition to something which is atheoretical, pretheoretical, or posttheoretical? What are the political considerations of using 'theory' for feminist analysis, considering that some of what appears under the sign of 'theory' has marked masculinist and Eurocentric roots? Is 'theory' distinct from politics? (Butler and Scott, 1992: xiii)

The relationship between feminist thought and malestream social, political, and cultural theory is defined by the view that 'there is something inadequate and unjust about traditional theory' (Beasley, 1999: 15). Feminist social theory proceeds from the insistence that the categories we work with must recognize sexual difference; however, the responses which follow on from this primary criticism are diverse, hence, feminist theory is characterized by perspectives which vary in their approach. These differences are reflected in debates regarding the very nature of what feminist social theory is and what it aims to achieve. Because privileged ways of knowing have so long been called 'theory' and associated with a quintessentially male discourse, feminists have often 'prioritized *doing* sociology in new ways, by pioneering new methodologies and foci of sociological investigation, as well as redefining and expanding the conventional male-centred, sociological problematic' (Witz and Marshall, 2004: 1–2).

Debates about the current status of feminist social theory are characterized by several key points. Following Winter (2000: 105) we may accept that the concept of theory is defined quite straightforwardly as 'a set of coherent principles that explain and inform practice'. The term 'feminist', however, must necessarily remain contested and open-ended in order to recognize that one of the legacies of the women's liberation movement and the theories that informed feminist practice has been that the category 'woman' does not represent a unified or stable constituency which exists prior to its naming (Butler, 1990). That being said it is possible, and indeed necessary to name feminist social theory, despite contingencies, for as Winter (2000) reminds us, if specialists refuse to define theory by naming it out of fear of imposing closure, and thereby excluding some experiences, then it becomes a 'non-concept'. This leads to relativism (is everything/ nothing feminist?) or leaves feminist social theory as an object for naming by non-specialists who may simplify, distort, or disregard key dimensions of this complex body of thought. As a starting point for discussions it is beneficial to sign up to the view advanced by Stanley and Wise (2000: 265) that feminist social theory is tied to feminism in a foundational manner through a common political orientation, 'that is, the belief that "something is wrong" and that it can and should be changed, even though there is disagreement as to the content of the "something wrong" and the nature of the "change required".'

Feminist thought questions the 'transcendental knower'; it insists that ways of knowing emanate from concrete social locations and that those who produce knowledge are immersed in hierarchical sets of social relations which have a material and historical specificity. Therefore, that which comes to be recognized as knowledge or 'theory', and that person who enjoys the status of an expert, and who is in turn positioned as the intended consumer of theory is the product of social processes shaped by power. We must attend carefully to defining what counts as feminist knowledge.

> Part of the work that is done by 'feminist theory' may be, then, *the posing of a critical challenge to the criteria that operate within the academy about what constitutes theory per se.* Feminist definitions of theory might emphasize, for example, the intimate relationship between theory and practice, as well as the grounded nature of theoretical work (the fact that theory, like other writing and knowledge is produced). If theory is produced, as well as being about producing different ways of understanding and interpreting the world, then feminist theorizing might involve recognizing that theory is produced 'outside' the spaces in which it is recognized as being produced within the academy. (Ahmed, 2000: 99)

Thus feminist theorizing is necessarily framed by meta-theoretical issues. Stanley and Wise (2000: 276) argue that if feminist thought is to stay true to its *raison d'être*, particularly as it becomes institutionalized within the academy, it must not commit the mistakes of malestream social theory but remain committed to the principles that: knowledge is always 'partial, local and grounded'; it is produced as a shared, communal enterprise and is not the preserve of an elite; it draws upon and represents a range of different experiences; it is marked by a refusal to reinstate an alternative privileged 'canon' produced by specific feminist 'theorists'; it strives to remain relevant by speaking to the everyday lives of women; and that it retains a self-reflexive stance to its own production as a site of knowledge/power.

Refusing a Singular Feminist History

These guiding principles have made the task of representing feminist social theory, in a chapter such as this, a potentially problematic endeavour, for they challenge us to approach the subject in ways that resist authorizing a particular version of feminism over alternatives. These principles encourage us to refuse a singular telling of what feminist theory is at present and how it has come to be that way. And yet, the value of seeking to represent, explain, review and appreciate this body of knowledge remains paramount to the study of feminism. Hemmings (2005, 2011) warns of the pitfalls associated with narrating the history of feminist theory and argues that too often, Western feminism is constructed through a teleological, developmental narrative 'where we move from a preoccupation with unity and sameness, through identity and diversity, and on to difference and fragmentation. These shifts are broadly conceived of as corresponding to the decades of the 1970s, 1980s and 1990s respectively' (Hemmings, 2005: 116).

Adopting this linear structure creates the impression that it is possible to condense feminist thought into a set of primary stages that are coherent, unitary and successive in their approach to theorizing gender relations. This significant oversimplification has contributed to the characterization of feminist thought as either a story of linear progress or as one of loss (Hemmings, 2011). The former version constructs feminism as moving from an essentialist theory of monolithic patriarchal oppression and 'universal sisterhood' on to an awareness of difference and the recognition that feminism had been exclusionary, through to a chronological move towards greater fluidity and greater sophistication culminating in the embrace of difference beyond the categories of sexuality and 'race' to a condition of general fragmentation, indeterminacy, and multiplicity – a set of conditions deemed the preserve of post-structuralist feminists. The implied progressive structure of this narrative allows particular types of theory, and specific authors as evidenced by citation practices, to emerge as delivering superior forms of knowledge while disregarding the wide range of contributions that constitute feminist theory (Hemmings, 2005). Alternatively, this linear account may be interpreted as a process of loss. In this version feminism moves away from its constitution as a 'political unity' towards an 'apolitical individualism' producing a nostalgic yearning for a time in the past when feminist thought was tied more firmly to the everyday, material 'reality' of women's lives; was not institutionalized and mainstreamed, hence more radical in intent; and not the sole enterprise of professional, 'superstar' theorists (Hemmings, 2005).

Explorations of feminist theory should proceed according to the sensitizing principle that the history of feminist thought is 'a series of ongoing contests and relationships rather than a process of imagined linear displacement' in which many continuities and interconnections exist (Hemmings, 2005: 131). To achieve an understanding of the complex nature of feminist social thought we should be attuned to the consequences our 'technologies' of storytelling have. This reflexive awareness and the resulting practice of self-critique are defining features of feminist thought. Other continuities include a deconstructive impulse which challenges the taken-for-granted 'nature' of gender relations; a critical interrogation of gendered binaries that privilege the masculine over the feminine; a concern with the materiality of gender relations in its fullest sense; an awareness of difference and diversity within the category of 'woman'; and a commitment to linking theory and practice. The aim in this chapter is to represent these key elements as they have materialized within specific approaches to theorizing gender relations at different times. Despite the risks of 'telling' a particular story that fails to be inclusive, these elements do represent meaningful dimensions which are central to the body of thought we name as feminist theory. The aim is to perform this while avoiding a representation which 'fixes' its character and impact. In the following discussion key themes are identified as exemplary of feminist theory and are offered as a method for understanding where feminist theory sits within the field of social theory more widely, and to illuminate ways feminist thinkers have engaged each other in an ongoing internal dialogue to formulate, appraise, and rework key ideas and debates.

Mainstream Social Theory

Social theory is concerned with establishing systematic and coherent understandings of the social world and has two primary, distinctive objectives. The first concerns critical reflection upon how and why we may develop ways of knowing the social world. The second is more substantive in nature and seeks to theorize 'social structures, institutions, practices and ideas – and their implications for groups and individuals – in the context of large scale dynamics of stability and change' (Leggett, 2017: 5). The origins of social theory are associated with the emergence of modernity. As Harrington (2005: 16) suggests, 'the rise of a scientific way of studying society is itself a product of the particular kinds of social conditions called "modern,"' and has cultural, political, and socio-economic dimensions. The Industrial Revolution and emergence of capitalism, the impact of Enlightenment thought as it culminated in the French Revolution, and the scientific revolution are routinely identified as central to theorizing the conditions associated with modern social life. Together these created a new orientation of the social order based upon the values of reason over superstition; a belief that both the natural and the social world could be brought under control; an emphasis on the individual over the collective; and a commitment to the ideals of liberty, progress, and freedom. The unfolding of modern social conditions out of those associated with traditional social forms provided the basis for new experiences, ideas, behaviours, sets of social relations, and orientations. This foundational context for modern social theory, identified with eighteenth- and nineteenth-century Europe, has been a key point of critical entry for feminist thinkers and an important starting point if we are to appreciate the profound critical import of feminist thought today.

Feminism and Modernity

Feminist theory has interrogated a range of assumptions underpinning classical social theory on the grounds that it is constituted by the exclusion of women and, therefore, the resulting distortions and partial accounts require 'correction'. For example, where industrialization moved production into the factory and created new social relations associated with modern capitalism, classical theory responded with an analysis of paid labour but failed to appreciate that the transformation of production also created separate spheres of gendered productive activity, with both equally significant to the operation of the capitalist system and each one reflecting changes associated with modernity. Feminist revisions of Marxist theory have required rethinking class relations and the forces of labour required to reproduce capitalism, notably the role of unpaid domestic labour. In addition to revising mainstream theory it has been necessary to produce original conceptual frameworks particularly in the case where areas of social life have been ignored. For this reason studies of the so-called 'private sphere', including studies of housework, sexuality, the body, and domestic violence have been central to the contributions made by feminist theory to fully understand the social world.

In addition to correcting absences in key texts feminist critiques have also mined these theories to glean insights into the views held by classical theorists. Their texts communicate prescriptive and normative views of what women *ought to be*, rather than accounting for their actual experiences of modernity. For the classical theorists 'modernity was seen as primarily problematic for men and the overriding concern was with how *men* were to live under the new, troubling and challenging condition of the modern' (Witz and Marshall, 2004: 3). Approaching these texts from a historical perspective situates the authors within the gender relations of their particular time, revealing hegemonic ideals associated with the conditions within which the theories were written. In another critical method the process of canonization has been analysed in order to recover absent female voices and to give a critical account of how it is that particular texts acquire their status when others, although offering substantive contributions to knowledge, disappear from view.

A further strategy of immanent critique reveals gender is always present in these texts, as masculinity is drawn upon to constitute the social in modernity, where women are aligned with nature (Felski, 1995; Smith, 1999; Sydie, 1987; Wolff, 2000). Women's experiences are not merely absent from canonical works; where women are discussed it is not only that 'the founding fathers' passively drew upon the dominant ideas about women's nature circulating in their culture at that time. Their writings 'actively *constructed* a theory of sexual difference, ultimately rooted in "nature" and its variable relationship to the "social". Classical theorists mobilized the "natural" in strategic ways to epistemologically carve out the distinctive contours of the social' (Witz and Marshall, 2004: 20–21). Theorists such as Durkheim and Simmel wrote about gender relations in terms which polarized men and women as categorical opposites. Being male and being female were constructed as exclusively different modes of being reflecting a particular structure of thought rooted in a Western humanist philosophical tradition – the Cartesian definition of the subject founded upon a separation of mind and body. To think was to overcome the flesh and bodily passions and was, therefore, a precondition for claiming the status of a self-defining and self-sufficient subject (Cranny-Francis et al., 2003: 179). This subject, central to imagining modern political life and the social contract which established the conditions for governance, was implicitly a transcendent subject not bound by 'irrational' passions (Gatens, 1996: 50). Within these constitutive dualisms woman is 'always the Object, a conglomeration of attributes to be predicted and controlled along with other natural phenomena. The place of the free-willed subject who can transcend nature's mandates is reserved exclusively for men' (Alcoff, 1995: 434–435).

> Woman in fact never makes the transition from the mythical 'state of nature' to the body politic. She becomes nature. She is necessary to the functioning of cultural life, she is the very ground which makes cultural life possible, yet she is not part of it . . . (Gatens, 1996: 51)

Feminist social theory has analysed how, time and again, a series of exclusionary dichotomies, which map onto sexual difference, are deployed in the course of theorizing modernity. These include culture/nature; reason/irrationality; mind/body; public/private; and individual/collective. This dualist ontology runs throughout theorizing of the social whereby the social is constituted in a relation with the non-social or that which is outside of, or separate from, the social. Classical social theory concerns itself explicitly with the social, which is the realm of masculinity as defined by a capacity for reason and by implication autonomy and self-determination. Witz (2001) has revealed how this masculine ontology of the social provided a point of departure for constructing modernity. It is men who are the subjects of the modern social while women are defined as belonging to the state of nature; trapped by their essential qualities and the constraints of corporeality, they are relegated accordingly to a position outside the social.

In Durkheim's writings, for example, repeated constructions of the social as a realm marked in its civility by its separation from nature may be found. He writes, 'man is man only because he is civilized', and civilization is that which is achieved by liberation from one's senses (Durkheim, 1960: 325). This capacity is denied to women, who are 'naturally' emotional and irrational (Witz and Marshall, 2003: 343–344). Women, he asserts, are 'instinctive creatures' controlled by their biology (Durkheim, 1964: 272). The social emerges out of, and thereby transcends the state of nature, whose domination is a measure of civilization. Adkins (2005) similarly analyses the work of Weber and Simmel and finds recurrent instances where the social is conflated with the masculine. Simmel explicitly genders the social and cultural forms of modernity by deploying a dualist ontology of a priori male and female modes of being (Witz, 2001: 359). In his writings women do not experience modernity with its 'alienating, contradictory and dizzying' effects like men do, because they possess a 'non-differentiated wholeness' and therefore are able to remain grounded (Adkins, 2005: 236). It is this nature, however, which also limits women in being able to achieve the detachment and critical capacity for reflection that is essential to participating in the social and cultural institutions of modern social life.

Feminist theory proceeds from its critique of malestream theory with two basic aims. Firstly, to produce knowledge from a different standpoint thus making an epistemological challenge to whomever may legitimately claim the position of the 'knower', and secondly, to produce knowledge about a female subject, thereby challenging the narrow definition of what should be 'known' when studying the social world. To achieve this, feminist theorists have had to redraw the conceptual map used in conventional social theory.

Theorizing Gender

Classical social theory made the distinctive claim that the individual did not exist prior to society but was significantly shaped by society. Feminists have insisted that since this individual is gendered as part of social processes, but not recognized as such in classical social thought, a theory which accounts for the socialization of women is necessary. The concept of gender has provided a language for speaking about the significance of sexual difference and the very real, material effects it has upon the lives of men and women, without relying upon essentialism to address differences. It has provided a conceptual foundation for understanding that constructing gender as a relationship between fundamentally different types of human beings, men and women, has been used to explain and justify unequal treatment, and that this convention is not the product of nature but of social relations, processes, and structures.

Simone de Beauvoir's classic text *The Second Sex* (1953), in which she conceptualized the dualistic relation of the masculine and the feminine, laid the groundwork for further deconstruction of naturalized understandings of sexual difference. She explained 'how the social position, identity, and consciousness of women are products of interaction which systematically position woman as Other to a universal subject, a subject marked as Man' (Adkins, 2005: 243). Oakley built upon this foundational understanding when insisting that gender and sex have distinctly different referents. In what became a standard designation, sex referred to biological difference while gender, in contrast, referred to the social meanings and norms imposed upon those different bodies. Although often conflated these are two separate processes. 'Sex' refers to the visible and functional biological differences of male and female bodies, while 'gender' operates as a sociocultural system of classification into 'masculine' and 'feminine'. Oakley stated 'the constancy of sex must be admitted, but so too must the variability of gender', thereby providing evidence of the social rather than the natural origins of gender roles (Oakley, 1985: 16). This formulation allowed feminist critique to identify those interests served by particular constructions of gender, thereby enabling a political analysis of the power relations secured by versions of difference in which women's 'natural' qualities were cited as evidence of their inferiority.

The Social Construction of Gender

Making a distinction between sex and gender separated off space to develop theories which would challenge the marginalization of women within existing social theory and enable analyses of the social world which by making gender relations an explicit feature, became more comprehensive and illuminating. For the political project of feminism it also provided the possibility that intervention into existing social relations could alter those conditions. This approach did not deny that biological differences between men and women existed. Indeed as argued by Nicholson (1994: 80) '*gender* was introduced as a concept to supplement *sex,* not to replace it'. Real biological phenomena which differentiated men from women and provided the basis for a binary distinction of male/female were accepted. While not determinate of gender relations, these differences nevertheless provided a meaningful and constant *foundation* for gender difference across time and space. Biological foundationalism 'expresses itself in the claim that distinctions of nature, at some basic level, manifest themselves in or ground sex identity, a cross-culturally common set of criteria for distinguishing women and men' (emphasis in original, Nicholson, 1994: 82). Gender is a coherent response to given and stable biological difference. Socially constructed reactions to those stable differences have enough in common to generate meaningful categories of 'women' and 'men'. For instance, society reacts to commonly manifest bodily differences such as reproductive functions. Identifying a constant base makes it possible to develop systematic theories of patriarchal oppression whereby two distinct groups, men and women, are conceptualized as hierarchically related.

Theorizing gender has facilitated multidimensional analyses in which the socially constructed distinction between male and female organizes a wide range of social processes and practices. Risman (2004: 433) argues gender should be conceptualized as a social structure and provides the basis for stratification, and is deeply embedded in the individual, interactional, and institutional dimensions of our society. According to Lorber (1994: 2) gender 'establishes patterns of expectations for individuals, orders the social processes of everyday life, is built into the major social organizations of society, such as the economy, ideology, the family, and politics, and is also an end in and of itself'. It is a 'system' which creates and maintains distinctions and organizes relations of inequality on the basis of these distinctions, so it does not just assign meaning to difference. It is a socially constructed product of patriarchal hierarchies, and therefore, reflects the materialization of gendered power differences.

Key Phases

The concept of gender has provided the basis for comprehensive theories of women's oppression. The 1970s, when we witnessed a burgeoning of feminist theories, often features in accounts of feminism as a period dominated by 'the big three' positions, named as liberal feminism, radical feminism and Marxist feminism (Hines, 2015; Maynard, 1995). The tendency to characterize the development of feminist theory in this period in terms of three coherent and unified categories does a disservice to the intricacy and diversity of thought developed at this time (Hemmings, 2005). The long-standing impulse to classify feminist thought by applying various conventions has found none of sufficient calibre to capture the complexity that exists. As such 'there is no real consensus as to which categories are the most meaningful, how many there are and which writers are to be located within each' (Maynard, 1995: 262). With that critique in mind, categories are used here to illustrate tendencies or patterns found, broadly speaking, within different approaches which have emerged. They are not invoked to suggest continuities do not exist between approaches or that differences within categories are not also apparent. By examining these paradigms we can assess what has been achieved by theorizing patterns of male and female difference.

The premises of liberal feminism draw upon the long tradition of Western liberal political philosophy which, like other bodies of thought, has been constructed with an androcentric bias. Feminists argue that the principles of liberal theory, namely that all men (*sic*) are equal based upon their equal potential for exercising reason, and should be afforded the right to autonomy on that basis, has not been applied to women. Instead of being treated as individuals, as men are, women are discriminated against because they are judged first as a group, and only secondly as individuals. The implication is that gender should not be deemed relevant in the allocation of, and competition for, social goods. Achieving equality, therefore, is a matter of challenging sexist stereotypes and prejudice; asserting that the qualities associated with masculinity are achievable by women; and relying upon legislation to reform key social institutions so that women are free to compete alongside men according to the same set of criteria. Liberal feminism has been highly influential particularly in the American context, with some commentators suggesting that it has become the dominant paradigm because of its compatibility with the rise of neoliberal capitalism (Fraser, 2009).

Critics have argued that many of its key principles, such as: emphasizing individual rights over the common good; placing value on attributes that are essentially associated with the masculine, such as reason; encouraging women to be 'just like men' instead of demanding that masculinity be remade; and advocating a conservative politics based upon reform, rather than a more far-reaching analysis of overarching social structures, contradict feminist values.

Materialist approaches, in contrast, are explicitly concerned with theorizing systematic power relations between men and women by emphasizing the structural features of the social world which create gendered pathways within society. Structural features of the social world have a material reality observable in areas such as paid work, the legal system, education, and institutions such as the family. Two main paradigms take this view that social relations of gender are essentially exploitative and oppressive due to the operation of overarching systems of power – these are radical feminism and Marxist feminism. Radical feminism theorizes structure in terms of patriarchal power, as inscribed within the totality of the social formation, creating a universal system in which all women, as women, are subject to oppression by men, thereby creating a commonality amongst women, embodied in the notion of 'universal sisterhood'. Areas such as sexual reproduction, sexuality, and the body are theorized as central to men's exploitation and control of women. In the 1970s this analysis offered new understandings of sites for political engagement including heterosexual marriage; mothering and motherhood; health and reproductive rights; sexual and domestic violence; and sexual harassment and pornography. Whelehan (1995: 69) notes that radical feminists 'possessing no single core doctrine which informed their theories, were fragmented from the start', making it difficult to 'isolate a central governing principle' compared to other strands. Instead radical feminism rejected available modes of theorizing, as these were perceived as masculine ways of knowing.

Early writings 'displayed a marked reluctance to adopt the analytical frameworks or "jargon" of established patriarchal academic discourse' (Whelehan, 1995: 69). Instead women's experiences provided the focus, hence the significance of practices such as consciousness-raising, which were intended to encourage women to understand the pervasiveness of patriarchal power in every aspect of their lives. The creation of women-only spaces free of patriarchal domination where women could reconceive and resist their positioning within social structures constituted a key political strategy. Given the diversity of radical feminist thought, critiques focus on a range of issues, but generally it became evident that the conceptualization of patriarchy as a monolithic, undifferentiated, universal structure lacked sufficient nuance to serve as a workable theory of power. Charges were also made that the theory was essentialist and often reductionist, relying upon unitary categories of 'men' and 'women'.

The feminist critique of Marxist thought revealed the extent to which existing theory failed to understand women's situation within capitalism. Like radical feminism, the aim was to provide insights into an overarching structure of women's oppression. Where patriarchy provided this for radical feminism, Marxist feminists looked to the class relations of capitalist production to explain the systematic exploitation of women's labour, both paid and unpaid, as socially necessary for the reproduction of capitalism. Gender inequality in this view is a form of class inequality accounted for by understanding the sexual division of labour. For some critics, however, the categories of conventional Marxist theory were too gender-blind to simply be reformed, and could not provide adequate explanations for the nature of women's oppression. From this perspective gender and class relations held equal significance, therefore, both systems had to be considered in an integrated analysis. Socialist/dual-systems theory argues that within the class system those in power are typically male and, therefore, class and patriarchy work in concert across the public and private spheres. These theories were also subject to the criticism that they relied upon gender categories which were not internally differentiated and, therefore, insufficient. They implied for example, that all men were in positions of structural advantage over all women when it was clear that some women had greater access to power and resources compared both to other women and some men too.

The 'Waves'

Another feature common to accounts that trace the development of feminist theory is the image of 'waves' to depict phases perceived as sufficiently distinct to warrant demarcation. The paradigms discussed above are collectively assigned to the second wave of the 1970s, with a third wave emerging in the late 1980s and early 1990s and a fourth in the early part of the twenty-first century. This method, like other strategies, has been met with unease and a demonstrable lack of consensus towards conventions used to represent feminist thought. The wave metaphor invites one to view feminism through the lens of a reproductive temporality in which one wave is succeeded by the next one. This often leads to the notion that waves map onto different generations, thereby setting up difficult relations between feminists (Budgeon, 2011). New generations of feminists are expected to perform the role of 'dutiful daughters' and be held to account for performing feminism according to established conventions. When they don't, it may appear that feminism has not been 'passed on' successfully, creating a sense of failure and loss (Adkins, 2004). The generational metaphor also suggests knowledge from the past is no longer relevant, that older feminists are out of sync with the present, and that for feminism to 'progress' these theories need to be relegated to the past. It is questionable, therefore, whether the 'wave' device is a useful one because it necessarily requires the imposition of categorizations and drawing distinctions when in practice the diversity of feminist thought resists such easy, chronological boundaries.

It remains unclear what the substantive referents of these terms are and as Dean (2009: 191) argues, for example, the label 'third wave' might be more helpfully deployed as a discursive resource or 'empty signifier' which brings 'a modicum of unity and coherence to an otherwise diverse set of feminist issues, while at the same time maintaining a degree of openness providing critical exchanges among feminists'. This strategy limits the impact of a narrative that represents feminism as fragmented and 'in crisis'. The self-reflexive autocritique and questioning that is central to the practice of feminist theorizing has at times been unproductive (Wiegman, 1999/2000). As feminist theory has become more self-conscious it has become increasingly anxious about its direction and beset by concerns about its focus and who it speaks to (Elam and Wiegman, 1995). A perceived failure of feminism's present tense is attributed to various factors. Foremost amongst these has been the assertion that the object of feminism along with its goals and self-definition are less coherent and less transparent than once thought.

> Feminism ain't what it used to be. Perhaps with some nostalgia, many of us who call ourselves feminists look back to the peak of the second wave in the 1970s, to a feminism that in retrospect seems to have had a clear object (women), a clear goal (to change the fact of women's subordination), and even a clear definition (political struggle against patriarchal oppression). Such clarity is a trick of memory, no doubt ... (Kavka, 2001: ix).

Kavka's quote insightfully disrupts the linear narrative which has become part of the mythology of feminist storytelling (Hemmings, 2011). As suggested, that coherence perhaps is the effect of partial remembering. The diverse character of feminist thought has now been firmly established due to contributions such as that made by feminist postcolonial theory. This body of work exemplifies the critique of exclusion which feminist thought is charged with having perpetuated through the use of universalizing conceptualizations of women's oppression across cultural, economic, and political divides. The project of postcolonial feminist theory has made several significant interventions (Mills, 1998). Firstly, it exposes the exclusion of gender from mainstream postcolonial theory, which resonates with feminist critiques of androcentric tendencies in theories of modernity. As argued by McClintock (1995: 6–7) 'gender dynamics were, from the outset, fundamental to the securing and maintenance of the imperial enterprise', but are absent in hegemonic theories.

Secondly, theorists such as Mohanty (1988), Sandoval (1991), Spivak (1988), and Trinh (1989) reveal that the structure of Western feminist theorizing relies upon a binary logic associated with Western Enlightenment thought that constructs a dominant subject position for white, middle-class, English-speaking women through the exclusion of women from different national and cultural contexts, whom it constitutes as Other. These analytical categories perform a discursive colonization of the 'material and historical heterogeneities of the lives of women in the third world, thereby, producing/representing a composite, singular "third-world woman"' (Mohanty, 1988: 62). This homogenized image depicts third-world woman as leading 'an essentially truncated life based on her feminine gender (read, sexually constrained) and being "third world" (read, ignorant, poor, uneducated, tradition-bound, religious, domesticated, family-oriented, victimized, etc.)' (Mohanty, 1988: 65). In contrast Western women are positioned as 'educated, modern, as having control over their own bodies and sexualities, and the "freedom" to make their own decisions', and are authorized to speak for and act on behalf of third-world women.

Thirdly, alongside the critique of exclusionary tendencies of dominant theory, postcolonial feminism offers a situated standpoint from which to develop conceptual frameworks that challenge the hegemony enacted by particular forms of feminist theorizing. Sandoval (1991), for example, explores white women's official histories of modes of oppositional consciousness, by which that movement understands itself, and argues a narrative has been built that effectively erases the long-standing presence of US Third World feminists. In contrast she theorizes a distinct type of political consciousness embodied by US Third World feminists – one created by a 'citizenry compelled to live within similar realms of marginality' (1991: 10). Marginalization contributes to the development of a common culture across multiple differences – cultural, racial, class, and gender – such that women of colour have been present and involved in the women's movement in the United States while simultaneously engaged in other struggles. This requires operating from a perspective of 'differential consciousness'. Sandoval's work highlights that from the beginning of the women's movement US Third World feminists were insisting that the binary gender division of male/female did not fully capture the lived experience of women's oppression and that 'interactions between social categories produce other genders within the social hierarchy' (1991: 4). Sandoval illustrates that the act of presenting feminist history sets limits on how feminist activity can be conceptualized 'while obstructing what can be perceived or even imagined by agents thinking within its constraints' (1991: 10). In critical stances such as this we witness the ongoing challenge of making women's experiences visible using conceptual tools that allow us to say something about gender without in the act of doing so misrepresenting or marginalizing particular experiences. Critiques of feminist conceptual frameworks such as that offered by postcolonial feminism have contributed to an ongoing theoretical project of refining and revising the concept of 'gender'.

Deconstructing Gender

Theorizing the sex/gender system has been an extremely effective enterprise for feminist theory and has resulted in the production of a rich and diverse body of literature that continues to have much to offer. However, theories of gender have developed in ways which refuse the sex and gender distinction, offering significant interventions into established feminist thought. In rethinking the relationship between sex and gender it is recognized that 'society not only shapes personality and behaviour, it also shapes the ways in which the body appears. But if the body is itself always seen through social interpretation, then sex is not something that is separate from gender but is, rather, that which is subsumable under it' (Nicholson, 1994: 79). Scott elaborates, 'gender is the knowledge that establishes meanings for bodily differences ... We cannot see sexual differences except as a function of our knowledge about the body and that knowledge is not "pure", cannot be isolated from its implication in a broad range of contexts' (Scott, 1988: 2, quoted in Nicholson, 1994: 79–80). Once unmoored from the body, who or what is represented by the term gender is less certain. Furthermore, when taken to its logical conclusion, 'gender' as a social construction can be seen to actually constitute that which it purports to represent. Taking up this position, Butler (1990: 1) argues that the 'very subject of women is no longer understood in stable or abiding terms ... there is very little agreement after all on what it is that constitutes, or ought to constitute, the category of women'. Whereas many thinkers had proceeded with confidence on the basis that the category of 'women' could be theorized in a relation to the category of 'men' based on sex, the deconstruction of gender suggests an overestimation of the commonality of women's experience (Hanssen, 2001) and the need for feminism to 'be willing to understand the necessity of indeterminacy' (Elam, 1994).

The radical deconstruction and further denaturalization of gender has been facilitated by the engagement of feminist theory with 'post-Enlightenment' values expressed by post-structuralism and postmodernism, and 'the cultural turn', which has had a significant impact on social theory more widely (Adkins, 2005: 233; Weedon, 1997). Feminist theory was always already sensitive to these values as they were embodied by feminist critiques of the truth claims made by mainstream social theory. These include a scepticism towards grand narratives, an understanding of the relationship between truth claims and power, a questioning of the norms of knowledge production including definitions of objectivity, an appreciation of the plural and fluid nature of subjectivity, a mistrust of linear representations of history as a story of progress, and insights into the role of language in constituting the social world (see Barrett and Phillips, 1992; Butler and Scott, 1992; Nicholson, 1990).

While productively generating a series of critical insights, feminist social theory has also had to reflect upon the usefulness of fully adopting post-structuralist principles (Adkins, 2005; Hines, 2015; Jackson, 1998). Maynard (1995) for instance contends feminism need not abandon the notion of a self or the possibility of a collective identity based on a shared experience and should instead recognize that making general statements is not the same as making universalizing claims. The 'category' of woman may be deployed in a non-unitary and yet still meaningful way.

Nor should feminist social theory uncritically privilege the cultural in its analyses, and discount material processes that influence cultural practices.

Developments

Continuing debates within feminist social theory drive new ideas and innovations. In the remainder of the chapter three of these will be briefly outlined, drawing attention to linkages with previous debates, and an assessment of their contributions to the field.

Intersectionality

Intersectionality is an influential construct, even deemed 'the most important theoretical contribution that women's studies, in conjunction with related fields, has made so far' (McCall, 2005: 1771) and cited as having 'become a central paradigm in feminist theory' (Geerts and van der Tuin, 2013: 171). Despite the significance accorded to it, there is little consensus on its defining features and focus (Collins and Chepp, 2013; Davis, 2008; Geerts and van der Tuin, 2013). For Davis (2008: 68) intersectionality 'refers to the interaction between gender, race, and other categories of difference in individual lives, social practices, institutional arrangements, and cultural ideologies and the outcomes of these interactions in terms of power'. Similarly Collins and Chepp (2013: 13) define it as a theoretical framework that 'recognizes how race, class, gender, and sexuality function in the structural bases of domination and subordination and, therefore, how these systems of power get institutionalised in society'.

Its roots lie within key two areas – critiques of the exclusion of difference from theories of gender, and anti-foundational, post-structuralist feminist critiques of representational practices underpinning identity politics. Therefore, it provides a conceptual strategy for carrying on feminist analyses that are able to recognize and address critiques made of feminist theory. Crenshaw (1989) introduced the term in her analyses of the failure of dominant feminist and anti-racist theories to account for violence against women of colour and the specificity of their vulnerability. It has been utilized to understand complex power dynamics by applying a framework which emphasizes multiplicity, variability, interaction, and irreducibility as analytical tools. Systems of intertwined power are analysed as co-productive and maintained through their interrelations. These constellations produce distinct material realities and matrices of domination that reflect the specificities of a given time and space (Collins and Chepp, 2013). The limits of identity politics are addressed by challenging an either/or logic and refusing to reduce identity to a single category such as 'woman'. Instead binaries are subverted to capture simultaneity. The epistemic value of this theory is that intersections of power structures shape knowledge, and as a result of simultaneous and multiple positioning, feminist standpoints will not be reducible to a single experience. Intersectionality, therefore, provides a platform for the recognition of subjugated knowledge.

There are many criticisms of the theory, however. Its vagueness is an issue and as Davis (2008: 68) states, 'it is not clear whether intersectionality should be limited to understanding individual experiences, to theorizing identity, or whether it should be taken as a property of social structures and cultural discourses'. A methodology for applying the concept has yet to be worked out (McCall, 2005) and as an analytical strategy it is not clear which differences to take into account. Are all differences equally salient? There is also a danger that class, race, and gender are taken for granted as always relevant and reified, as a result, leading researchers to adopt a focus that is inappropriate. Furthermore, this approach might obscure the specificity of separate systems of power. Finally, it has been argued that intersectional thinkers, by adopting social constructivism, have accentuated the epistemological dimensions of social categories while neglecting their ontological and material status (Geertz and van der Tuin, 2013).

Materialism

The call for a return to the material gestures towards a renewed engagement on the part of some feminist theorists to counteract the excesses of the 'cultural turn' that marked the take-up of post-structuralist principles. The relationship between the cultural and the material has been the focus of many exchanges (Benhabib et al., 1995; Butler, 1998). Fraser (1995, 2009) for example is highly critical of the shift in focus in feminist analyses from issues of material inequalities towards those of identity, difference, cultural domination, and a politics of recognition (1995: 68), which she asserts has over time meant that feminist theory has overextended its 'critique of culture, while downplaying the critique of political economy' (2009: 108).

A body of thought called 'new materialism' is not necessarily 'new' where feminism is concerned, as feminist thought has a substantial tradition of theorizing the material (see Ahmed, 2008). However, this body of thought brings materiality into an analysis which also extends the principles of post-structuralism and, in so doing, attempts to transcend the nature/culture divide and the hierarchical structuring of binaries which have long worked to naturalize the privilege of the masculine (mind, culture, reason) over the feminine (body, nature, emotion). As noted by Frost (2011: 76), 'Feminists have been more comfortable with denaturalizing nature than with what we might call "deculturalizing culture" – or admitting that matter or biology might have a form of agency or force that shapes, enhances, conditions, or delimits the agency of culture'. A core concern then, which feminist new materialists address, is that dualisms of Western thought are a 'thoroughly gendered phenomenon' which feminists have been highlighting since de Beauvoir's *The Second Sex* (Hinton and van der Tuin, 2014: 4). Post-structuralism set out to deconstruct constitutive binaries; however, it often failed to fully do so because meaning was held as determinate over the material (Hekman, 2014). Therefore new materialism is often seen to deliver fully on the promise of post-structuralism (Barad, 2007).

Unlike dialectical materialism in which ontological primacy is assigned to the material, new materialism collapses boundaries and grants equal status to the material and the semiotic. Where cultural theory often did not address materiality adequately and instead emphasized the linguistic as constitutive of the material, new materialism seeks to reconceptualize matter as an active force, operating in concert with cultural representations to produce reality. This orientation is embodied in concepts that include 'transversality' – a mode of analysis which refuses modernist dualisms (van der Tuin and Dolphijn, 2010); 'transcorporeality' – boundaries of the human body open out into a more-than-human world (Alaimo, 2008), and 'agential realism' – an insistence on the intra-action of matter of discourse (Barad, 2003).

While the influence of new materialism on critical and cultural theory has been extensive, is there anything in its approach which makes it a feminist theory? A substantial range of literature (Alaimo and Hekman, 2008; van der Tuin, 2011) now explores the extent to which a productive relationship has been forged. First, new materialism invites us to think critically about how knowledge is produced from a material location and recognize that subjectivity is embodied, a position consistent with previous feminist critiques of mainstream epistemology (Hinton, 2014). It allows us to question the separation of the empirical world from the inquiring subject and to think about *who* can claim the status of a knowing subject, along with interrogating the nature of our relationship with that which is known. Recognizing the materiality of subjectivity also allows feminist theory to address the reality of women's bodies and their experiences in a patriarchal world while avoiding the threat of essentialism, as in this model nature is not determinate nor is it determined by discourse. It is important for feminism to engage with women's embodiment without the risk of naturalizing gender difference or equating the feminine with the body. Secondly, undermining the subject/object dualism carries an ethical impetus to recognize a range of subjectivities and refuse imposing the status of 'Other' (Alaimo, 2010). This is based on a relational ontology and is consistent with feminist ethics of care. Thirdly, this insight is derived from the commitment to think relations through non-negating logics, opening space for the existence of difference, not defined as lack, but as difference in itself; as an ontological condition (Thiele, 2014).

Difference is reconceptualized as immanent; as a multiplicity of differing and irreducible forces in contrast to a model of power as repressive and exclusionary. Fourthly, new materialism facilitates the interest feminist theory has had in deconstructing the sex/gender system and is consistent with attempts to think about the role of the body in the meanings of gender, a question previously posed by corporeal feminism (Grosz, 1994). Finally, building upon insights gleaned by intersectionality, materialist analyses can accommodate multiple, non-linear relations and avoid explanations that rely upon unidirectional causality.

Transgender

A further area of theory which builds upon and challenges feminist theorizing of sex/gender comes from transgender studies, which has problematized normative links between the body, experience, sexuality, gender, and identity – categories intrinsic to feminist thought. The term 'transgender' incorporates a wide range of identities. Principally it encompasses 'anyone whose expression of gender disrupts conventional assumptions of the gender order and who identifies as such' (Elliot, 2010: 1). It incorporates 'practices and identities such as transvestism, transsexuality, intersex, gender queer, female and male drag, cross-dressing and some butch/femme practices. Transgender may refer to individuals who have undergone hormone treatment or surgery to reconstruct their bodies or to those who cross gender in ways that are less permanent' (Hines, 2015: 32). Like Third World US feminism and post-structuralism, transgender theory radically destabilizes the sex/gender binary by throwing further into question the coherence of gender categories and assumptions about who these categories represent and/or exclude. It also raises questions about the materiality of the body and the role of the body in theorizing gender. Feminist responses to these questions are not uniform. Some non-trans feminists' encounters with transsexuality are conflictual in nature and remain unresolved, while others express an affinity with the transgender subversion of the enforced cultural binaries found within the nexus of sex, sexuality, and gender. The transsexual body 'remains a battlefield' and site of much debate for trans and non-trans theorists of gender and sexuality in complex ways, and 'are far from being settled' (Elliot, 2010: 3). As observed by Heyes (2003: 1098), 'whether appropriated to bolster queer theoretical claims, represented as the acid test of constructionism, or attacked for suspect political commitments, transgender has been colonized as a feminist testing ground'.

Jeffreys (2014: 36) firmly occupies a hostile position, as articulated in *Gender Hurts: A Feminist Analysis of the Politics of Transgenderism*, where she writes 'transgender theory and practice contradict the very basis of feminism, since feminism is a political movement based on the experience of persons who are women, born female and raised in the female sex caste'. For her the question of identity politics and the role gender categories play in granting recognition to particular experiences goes to the heart of feminist theory. This position, recently named TERF (trans-exclusionary radical feminism) reflects a long-standing antagonism expressed in the late 1970s by writers such as Raymond in *The Transsexual Empire* (cited in Hines, 2015: 32), who argued that biological sex did matter when it came to the lived experience of being subject to patriarchal domination: 'If chromosomal sex is taken to be the fundamental basis for maleness and femaleness, the man who undergoes sex conversion is *not* female.' This views sex and gender as inherently co-dependent and on that basis one cannot claim to be a 'real' woman if not born one, implying that trans women cannot be legitimate subjects of feminism. Further criticisms claim that by performing conventional femininity or masculinity and/or by engaging in the surgical modification of sex, trans people reinforce hegemonic, dimorphic models of gender; bolster gender essentialism; and are complicit with medical experts' sexist norms, all of which are anathema to feminism (Heyes, 2003: 1101).

Alternatively, feminists who seek to deconstruct the sex/gender binary embrace transgender practices because of their transgressive potential to disrupt the regulatory force of the dominant gender order which insists that sex, sexuality, and gender adhere to a binary code (Halberstam, 2005). Subversion in this view creates the possibility of dismantling normative gender architecture and making transcendence achievable and, therefore, is fundamentally compatible with feminist aims.

Furthermore, claims made on behalf of transgendered experience are consistent with the feminist epistemological project of rendering subjugated knowledge visible. Finally, encounters between trans and non-trans feminists have illustrated the need for feminist theory to remain reflexive in its practices. Cisgendered feminists, when writing about trans issues, have had to acknowledge their privileged positioning within the sex/gender system, which renders such encounters productive for furthering the practice of feminist theory.

Conclusion

The aim of this chapter has been to convey the dynamism, complexity, and creativity of contemporary feminist social theory and offer insights into how these characteristics have manifested throughout its development. These attributes are born from operating in a 'dual register' of interrogating dominant, mainstream social theory, which is often gender-blind or the source of distortion, *and* engagement in reflexive autocritique in which core assumptions and principles of feminist thought are continuously interrogated. Of particular importance, the binary conceptualization of sex/gender has garnered continued engagement from a range of different perspectives and theoretical traditions. Key dimensions of theories which develop this tool have been outlined, illustrating that while a continuous focus on understanding gender as a central structuring force in society constitutes feminist theory, the tools for doing so have been the source of much careful consideration and ongoing questioning.

The task of presenting key elements of feminist thought has been performed here with the knowledge that depictions of feminist theory must avoid evolutionary narratives or tales of succession and relegation. Indeed, while feminism in the early twenty-first century is now more than ever constituted by diversity, a 'fourth wave' of feminism has been identified which, arguably, draws upon similar critiques and political practices to those of second-wave feminism, with campaigns addressing everyday sexism, violence against women, sexualization and distorted cultural representations of women, the gender pay gap, and the feminization of poverty amongst others. This is a politics, however, which is simultaneously harnessing the potential of new media platforms and social media thereby creating 'a global community of feminists who use the internet both for discussion and activism' within and across digital spaces (Munro, 2013: 23). Furthermore, this enterprise incorporates diversity and recognizes gender is multifaceted and intersectional. Fourth wave, therefore, despite the temptation to read 'waves' through the lens of replacement, forcefully demonstrates continuities with existing approaches to feminist theory *and* potential to break new ground in promising and productive ways.

References

Adkins, Lisa. 2004. 'Passing on Feminism: From Consciousness to Reflexivity?' *European Journal of Women's Studies* 11(4): 427–444.

2005. 'Feminist Social Theory.' In Austin Harrington (ed.), *Modern Social Theory: An Introduction* (pp. 233–251). Oxford, UK: Oxford University Press.

Ahmed, Sara. 2000. 'Whose Counting?' *Feminist Theory* 1(1): 97–103.

2008. 'Imaginary Prohibitions: Some Preliminary Remarks on the Founding Gestures of the "New Materialisms".' *European Journal of Women's Studies* 15(1): 23–39.

Alaimo, Stacey. 2008. 'Trans-corporeal Feminisms and the Ethical Space of Nature.' In Stacey Alaimo and Susan Hekman (eds.), *Material Feminisms* (pp. 237–264). Bloomington, IN: Indiana University Press.

2010. *Bodily Natures*. Bloomington, IN: Indiana University Press.

Alaimo, Stacey, and Susan Hekman. 2008. *Material Feminisms*. Bloomington, IN: Indiana University Press.

Alcoff, Linda. 1995. 'Cultural Feminism Versus Post-Structuralism: The Identity Crisis in Feminist Theory.' In Nancy Tuana and Rosemary Tong (eds.), *Feminism and Philosophy* (pp. 434–456). Oxford, UK: Westview Press.

Barad, Karen. 2003. 'Posthuman Performativity.' *Signs* 28(3): 801–831.

2007. *Meeting the Universe Halfway: Quantum Physics and the Entanglement of Matter and Meaning*. Durham, NC: Duke University Press.

Barrett, Michele, and Anne Phillips (eds.). 1992. *Destabilizing Theory*. Stanford, CA: Stanford University Press.

Beasley, Chris. 1999. *What Is Feminism? An Introduction to Feminist Thought*. London: Sage.

Benhabib, Seyla, Judith Butler, Drucilla Cornell, and Nancy Fraser. 1995. *Feminist Contentions*. London: Routledge.

Budgeon, Shelley. 2011. *Third Wave Feminism and the Politics of Gender in Late Modernity*. Basingstoke, UK: Palgrave.

Butler, Judith. 1990. *Gender Trouble*. London: Routledge.

1998. 'Merely Cultural.' *New Left Review* I (227): 33–44.

Butler, Judith, and Joan W. Scott (eds.). 1992. *Feminists Theorize the Political*. London: Routledge.

Collins, Patricia Hill, and Valerie Chepp. 2013. 'Intersectionality.' In Georgina Waylen, Karen Celis, Johanna Kantola, and Laurel S. Weldon (eds.), *The Oxford Handbook of Gender and Politics*. Oxford, UK: Oxford University Press. www.oxfordhandbooks.com.

Cranny-Francis, Anne, Wendy Waring, Pam Stavropoulos, and Joan Kirby. 2003. *Gender Studies*. Basingstoke, UK: Palgrave.

Crenshaw, Kimberley. 1989. 'Demarginalizing the Intersection of Race and Sex: A Black Feminist Critique of Antidiscrimination Doctrine, Feminist Theory, and Antiracist Politics.' *University of Chicago Legal Forum* 14: 538–554.

Davis, Kathy. 2008. 'Intersectionality as Buzzword: A Sociology of Science Perspective on What Makes a Feminist Theory Successful.' *Feminist Theory* 9(1): 67–85.

De Beauvoir, Simone. 1953. *The Second Sex*. New York: Knopf.

Dean, Jonathan. 2009. 'Who's Afraid of Third Wave Feminism?' *International Feminist Journal of Politics* 11(3): 334–352.

Durkheim, Emile. 1960. 'The Dualism of Human Nature and Its Social Conditions.' In K. H. Wolff (ed.), *Emile Durkheim, 1858–1917: A Collection of Essays* (pp. 325–340). Columbus, OH: Ohio State University Press.

1964. *Suicide*. New York: Free Press.

Elam, Diane. 1994. *Feminism and Deconstruction*. London: Routledge.

Elam, Diane, and Robyn Wiegman (ed.). 1995. *Feminism Beside Itself*. New York: Routledge.

Elliot, Patricia. 2010. *Debates in Transgender, Queer and Feminist Theory*. Farnham, UK: Ashgate.

Evans, Mary. 2003. *Gender and Social Theory*. Buckingham, UK: Open University Press.

Felski, Rita. 1995. *The Gender of Modernity*. Cambridge, MA: Cambridge University Press.

Fraser, Nancy. 1995. 'From Redistribution to Recognition? Dilemmas of Justice in a "Post-Socialist" Age.' *New Left Review* I(212): 68–93.

    2009. 'Feminism, Capitalism and the Cunning of History.' *New Left Review* 56: 97–117.

Frost, Samantha. 2011. "The Implications of the New Materialisms for Feminist Epistemology." In Heidi E. Grasswick (ed.), *Feminist Epistemology and Philosophy of Science: Power in Knowledge* (pp. 69–84). Dordrecht and New York: Springer.

Gatens, Moira. 1996. *Imaginary Bodies*. London: Routledge.

Geerts, Evelien, and Iris van der Tuin. 2013. 'From Intersectionality to Interference: Feminist Onto-epistemological Reflections on the Politics of Representation.' *Women's Studies International Forum* 41: 171–178.

Grosz, Elizabeth. 1994. *Volatile Bodies: Toward a Corporeal Feminism*. Bloomington, IN: Indiana University Press.

Halberstam, Judith. 2005. *In a Queer Time and Place: Transgender Bodies, Subcultural Lives*. New York: New York University Press.

Hanssen, Beatrice. 2001. 'Whatever Happened to Feminist Theory?' In Elisabeth Bronfen and Misha Kavka (eds.), *Feminist Consequences* (pp. 58–100). New York: Columbia University Press.

Harrington, Austin (ed.). 2005. *Modern Social Theory: An Introduction*. Oxford, UK: Oxford University Press.

Hekman, Susan. 2014. *The Feminine Subject*. Cambridge, UK: Polity Press.

Hemmings, Clare. 2005. 'Telling Feminist Stories.' *Feminist Theory* 6(2): 115–139.

    2011. *Why Stories Matter*. London: Duke University Press.

Heyes, Cressida. 2003. 'Feminist Solidarity after Queer Theory: The Case of Transgender.' *Signs* 28(4): 1093–1120.

Hines, Sally. 2015. 'Feminist Theories.' In Victoria Robinson and Diane Richardson (eds.), *Introducing Gender & Women's Studies*, 4th ed. (pp. 23–39). Basingstoke, UK: Palgrave.

Hinton, Peta. 2014. '"Situated Knowledges" and New Materialism(s): Rethinking a Politics of Location.' *Women: A Cultural Review* 25(1): 99–113.

Hinton, Peta, and Iris van der Tuin. 2014. 'Preface.' *Women: A Cultural Review* 25(1): 1–8.

Jackson, Stevi. 1998. 'Feminist Social Theory.' In Stevi Jackson and Jackie Jones (eds.), *Contemporary Feminist Theories* (pp. 12–22). Edinburgh: Edinburgh University Press.

Jeffreys, Sheila. 2014. *Gender Hurts*. Abingdon, UK: Routledge.

Kavka, Misha. 2001. 'Introduction.' In Elisabeth Bronfen and Misha Kavka (eds.), *Feminist Consequences* (pp. ix–xxxi). New York: Columbia University Press.

Leggett, Will. 2017. *Politics and Social Theory: The Inescapably Social and the Irreducibly Political*. Basingstoke, UK: Palgrave MacMillan.

Lorber, Judith. 1994. *Paradoxes of Gender*. New Haven, CT: Yale University Press.

Maynard, Mary. 1995. 'Beyond the "Big Three": The Development of Feminist Theory into the 1990s.' *Women's History Review* 4(3): 259–281.

McCall, Leslie. 2005. 'The Complexity of Intersectionality.' *Signs* 30(3): 1171–1800.

McClintock, Anne. 1995. *Imperial Leather: Race, Gender and Sexuality in the Imperial Context*. London: Routledge.

Mills, Sara. 1998. 'Post-Colonial Feminist Theory.' in Stevi Jackson and Jackie Jones (eds.), *Contemporary Feminist Theories* (pp. 98–112). Edinburgh: Edinburgh University Press.

Mohanty, Chandra Talpade. 1988. 'Under Western Eyes, Feminist Scholarship and Colonial Discourses.' *Feminist Review* 30: 61–88.

Munro, Ealasaid. 2013. 'Feminism: A Fourth Wave?' *Political Insight* 4: 22–25.

Nicholson, Linda (ed.). 1990. *Feminism/Postmodernism*. London: Routledge.

Nicholson, Linda. 1994. 'Interpreting Gender.' *Signs* 20(1): 79–105.

Oakley, Ann. 1985. *Sex, Gender and Society, Revised Edition*. Aldershot, UK: Gower.

Risman, Barbara. 2004. 'Gender as a Social Structure.' *Gender & Society* 18(4): 429–450.

Sandoval, Chela. 1991. 'US Third World Feminism: the Theory and Method of Oppositional Consciousness in the Postmodern World.' *Genders*, 10: 1–24.

Scott, Joan. 1988. *Gender and the Politics of History*. New York: Columbia University Press.

Smith, Dorothy. 1999. *Writing the Social, Critique, Theory and Investigations*. Toronto: University of Toronto Press.

Spivak, Gayatri Chakravorty. 1988. 'Can the Subaltern Speak?' In Cary Nelson and Lawrence Grossberg (eds.), *Marxism and the Interpretation of Culture* (pp. 271–313). Urbana, IL: University of Illinois Press.

Stanley, Elizabeth, and Susan Wise, 2000. 'But the Empress Has No Clothes!' *Feminist Theory* 1(1): 261–288.

Sydie, Rosalind. 1987. *Natural Women and Cultured Men*. Toronto: Methuen.

Thiele, Kathrin. 2014. 'Pushing Dualism and Differences: From "Equality versus Difference" to "Nonmimetic Sharing" and "Staying with the Trouble."' *Women: A Cultural Review* 25(1): 9–26.

Trinh, T. Minh-ha. 1989. *Woman Native Other: Writing Postcoloniality and Feminism*. Bloomington, IN: Indiana University Press.

van der Tuin, Iris. 2011. 'New Feminist Materialisms.' *Women's Studies International Forum* 34: 271–277.

van der Tuin, Iris, and Rick Dolphijn. 2010. 'The Transversality of New Materialism.' *Women: A Cultural Review* 21(2): 153–171.

Weedon, Chris. 1997. *Feminist Practice and Poststructuralist Theory*, 2nd ed. Oxford, UK: Blackwell.

Whelehan, Imelda. 1995. *Modern Feminist Thought*. Edinburgh: Edinburgh University Press.

Wiegman, Robyn. 1999/2000. 'Feminism, Institutionalism, and the Idiom of Failure.' *Differences* 11(3): 107–136.

Winter, Bronwyn. 2000. 'Who Counts (or Doesn't Count) What Is Feminist Theory.' *Feminist Theory* 1(1): 105–111.

Witz, Anne. 2001. 'George Simmel and the Masculinity of Modernity.' *Journal of Classical Sociology* 1(3): 353–370.

Witz, Anne, and Barbara L. Marshall. 2003. 'The Quality of Manhood: Gender and Embodiment in the Classical Tradition.' *Sociological Review* 51(3): 339–56.

Witz, Anne, and Barbara L. Marshall. 2004. 'Introduction: Feminist Encounters with Sociological Theory.' In Barbara L. Marshall and Anne Witz (eds.), *Engendering the Social* (pp. 1–15). Maidenhead, UK: Open University Press.

Wolff, Janet. 2000. 'The Feminine in Modern Art: Benjamin, Simmel and the Gender of Modernity.' *Theory, Culture and Society* 17(6): 33–53.

7 Intersectionality as Critical Social Theory

Patricia Hill Collins

The varying ways in which people understand intersectionality are more often assumed than explored, leaving definitions of intersectionality open to interpretation (Collins, 2015; 2019). Some scholars conceptualize intersectionality as a perspective (Browne and Misra, 2003; Steinbugler, Press, and Dias, 2006), a concept (Knapp, 2005), a type of analysis (Nash, 2008; Yuval-Davis, 2006), or as a nodal point for feminist theorizing (Lykke, 2011). Other scholars emphasize intersectionality's placement in the research process, with some approaching intersectionality as a methodological approach (Steinbugler, Press, and Dias, 2006; Yuval-Davis, 2006), a research paradigm (Hancock, 2007a; 2007b), or a measurable variable and a type of data (Bowleg, 2008). Many scholars categorize intersectionality as a theory, suggesting that intersectionality is already a social theory and that all we need to do is apply it. These definitional debates identify important areas of emphasis for exploring intersectionality's relationship to social theory, yet beyond laying down some provocative avenues of investigation, the field itself has yet to systematically develop them.

Intersectionality's emerging relationship to social theory constitutes one important definitional dilemma with potentially important implications for both areas. Social theory brings explanatory power to social phenomena, casting light on certain dimensions of reality while obscuring others. Moreover, because intersectionality and social theory both operate in dual registers, namely, the epistemological register of explaining social phenomena, and the ontological register of participating in and shaping the social relations that it aims to explain, they potentially have important intellectual, social, and political effects.

This two-part essay explores the connections between intersectionality and critical social theory. The first section provides a brief overview of intersectionality's emerging canon, paying careful attention to its understandings of and approaches to social inequality. The second section positions intersectionality in a landscape of traditional and critical social theory that is alternatively contentious and complementary. Contemporary intersectionality and social theory are both in flux, with their meanings shaped by how varying social actors use them for varying purposes across heterogeneous social contexts. In this context, few definitive answers exist as to whether intersectionality is a social theory and if so, whether it engages its traditional and/or critical dimensions. Rather, this essay provides some navigational tools for investigating the shifting relationship between intersectionality and critical social theory.

Intersectionality's Emerging Canon

Many current debates about intersectionality investigate what kind of knowledge and/or political project intersectionality is and/or might be (Collins, 2015). Philosopher John Stuhr's description of American pragmatism parallels my approach to intersectionality as a discourse, field of study, or knowledge project:

> it may be defined by its exponents' common attitudes, purposes, philosophical problems, procedures, terminology, and beliefs. It is in virtue of such a shared complex of features that we identify, understand, and differentiate philosophical developments, movements, and "schools of thought." Such a unity of character, we must recognize, is not a single and simple essence, some necessary and sufficient feature of classical American philosophy, some property present always and only in classical American philosophy. Instead, it is an identifiable configuration, a characteristic shape, a resemblance, an overlapping and interweaving of features (present to differing degrees in the writings of the individual philosophers) that, as a relational whole, pervades and constitutes this philosophy and these philosophers. (Stuhr, 2000: 2–3)

Following Stuhr, I approach intersectionality as a knowledge project that has "developments, movements, and 'schools of thought'" within it such that there is no essential intersectional essence. As a pragmatist philosopher, Stuhr understands knowledge construction by examining how people use ideas to make meaning in their lives and, through those meaning-making processes, give meaning to the terms they use. Within this logic, pragmatism (and intersectionality) is "defined by its exponents' common attitudes, purposes, philosophical problems, procedures, terminology, and beliefs." Pragmatism and intersectionality both have communities of practitioners, or in pragmatist terms, communities of inquiry that shape the knowledge produced through using it. A focus on people as knowledge creators and consumers permeates his definition of pragmatism, one taken up in varying ways across American pragmatism itself (Bernstein, 2010; Joas, 1993). Via this incorporation of a community of practitioners, intersectionality is neither solely a scholarly endeavor nor an activist undertaking, but rather constitutes a form of critical inquiry and praxis (Collins, 2019; Collins and Bilge, 2016).

Here I draw on pragmatism's interpretive frameworks, yet unlike Stuhr, I stress how power relations shape knowledge construction processes. Intersecting power relations provide social contexts that house intersectionality's heterogeneous communities of inquiry as well as shape the meanings attributed to intersectionality's arguments. Because social theories have universalizing tendencies, they can feel far removed from actual politics. Even in social theories that show the connections between discourse and actual power relations – which is the case, for example, within Michel Foucault's studies of medicine, the disciplinary practices of prisons, and the centrality of religion to the regulation of sexuality – connections between this grounding in social context and the focus on meaning making within a specific context can be negated; see for example, how subsequent scholars have used Foucault's arguments about knowledge and power (Foucault, 1980).

Following Foucault's genealogical methodology, I approach intersectionality as a knowledge project that emerges in tandem with the diverse forms that historically specific power relations of decolonization and desegregation took locally, regionally, nationally, and globally. Intersectionality, or more accurately, the constellation of knowledge projects that have been assembled under the term intersectionality, reflect the current fluidity and flux of power relations that produce a host of knowledge projects that aim to explain the erosion of long-standing patterns of social hierarchy and/or the installation of new ones. Social relations of colonization relied on segregation, the bedrock of social hierarchies of nation, race, gender, ethnicity, religion, sexuality and age, which installed various strategies of separating, categorizing, and ranking people. In contrast, decolonization and its imperfect desegregation erodes these borders of colonial power relations. Not only have social groups long thought to be separate and unequal been brought into common space, but the knowledge projects associated with group histories have also become more visible and/or contentious. Because intersectionality emerges from, attends to, and reflects these social conditions, both the power relations of a decolonizing and desegregating world, and the contours of intersectionality as a knowledge project are interrelated.

By now, a general consensus exists about intersectionality's general contours in academic and nonacademic settings. As a working definition, intersectionality consists of a constellation of ideas and practices that maintain that gender, race, class, sexuality, age, ethnicity, ability, and similar phenomena constitute a mutually constructing constellation of power relationships. They produce unequal material realities and distinctive social experiences for individuals and groups positioned within them. This insight creates analytic space for a more robust understanding of the privileges and penalties associated with intersecting systems of oppression, as well as a multifaceted conception of standpoint epistemologies and knowledges. Vivian May's definition of intersectionality, one more closely aligned with intersectionality's activist roots, tells a slightly different story:

> Intersectionality is a form of resistant knowledge developed to unsettle conventional mindsets, challenge oppressive power, think through the full architecture of structural inequalities and asymmetrical life opportunities, and seek a more just world. It has been formed in the context of struggles for social justice as a means to challenge dominance, foster critical imaginaries, and craft collective models for change. (May, 2015: xi)

These working definitions emphasize distinctive aspects of intersectionality's positionality as inquiry and praxis, thereby having different implications for social theory.

A sociology of knowledge analysis of intersectionality thus attends not only to the substance of intersectionality's ideas, but also to the specific sites where it is developed and practiced. In this regard, the academy constitutes an important venue in which intersectional scholarship has been produced. Recognized by academic actors in the early 1990s, intersectionality as a form of inquiry moved quickly into the scholarly mainstream (Collins and Bilge, 2016: 63–87). Yet intersectionality has never been just another academic discourse. Intersectionality has been associated with the intellectual production of African-American women intellectual activists as well as the intellectual production of women, indigenous people, Latinos and Latinas, immigrant groups, LGBT people, and similar social actors who have done intellectual work within "struggles for social justice as a means to challenge dominance, foster critical imaginaries, and craft collective models for change" (May, 2015: xi). This intellectual work produced across varying venues provides a framework not only for the contemporary scholars cited at the beginning of this essay, but also for teachers, social workers, parents, policy advocates, university support staff, community organizers, clergy, lawyers, graduate students, nurses, and other practitioners who confront contemporary social inequalities. These social actors engage the ideas of intersectionality, if not intersectionality's formal scholarship, in myriad ways. It is important to point out that, given its wide-ranging approaches and concerns, intersectionality has been taken up within activist, policy, social media, and academic venues (Collins and Bilge, 2016).

Because conceptions of social theory are so closely tied to power relations within academia, this broader understanding of intersectionality as a form of critical inquiry and praxis also informs intersectionality's canon formation. Intersectionality has within it, to paraphrase Stuhr, an identifiable configuration, a characteristic shape, a resemblance, an overlapping and interweaving of features that are present to differing degrees in the writings of the large number of individual scholars who claim intersectionality. Understanding intersectionality as a knowledge project honed within critical inquiry and praxis highlights several core themes from this identifiable configuration, namely, attentiveness to (1) intersecting power relations; (2) relationality; (3) situated knowledge production; and (4) complexity. These themes are not all present in a given work, their treatment of these themes varies considerably, and they are not unique to intersectionality. Because intersectionality has been influenced by multiple social theories, it often shares their basic terminology and sensibility, but its use of a common vocabulary does not mean that intersectionality is derivative of extant social theories. Rather, intersectionality's intellectual and political association with social relations of decolonization and desegregation suggests that intersectionality may take up its core themes of power relations, relationality, situated knowledge production, and complexity in particular ways.

The significance both of power relations generally, and intersecting power relations in particular, constitutes one core idea that permeates intersectional knowledge projects. Intersecting power relations produce social divisions of race, gender, class, sexuality, ability, age, country of origin, and citizenship status that are unlikely to be adequately understood in isolation from one another. Non-intersectional scholarship assumes that race, class, and gender are unconnected variables or features of social organization that can be studied as singular phenomena, for example, gender or race as discreet aspects of individual identity, or patriarchy or racism as mono-categorical systems of power. Intersectionality posits that systems of power coproduce one another in ways that reproduce both unequal material realities (social locations) and the distinctive social experiences that characterize people's experiences within social hierarchies. Stated differently, racism, sexism, class exploitation, and similar oppressions may mutually construct one another by drawing upon similar and distinctive practices and forms of organization that collectively shape social reality.

For any given social context, intersecting power relations constitute a specific matrix of domination that reflects the particularities of a given time and place (Collins, 2000). Some aspects of intersecting power relations may be more salient than others across time and place, for example, intersections of gender, sexuality and race within twenty-first-century US political campaigns, or the growing centrality of religion and ethnicity within immigration debates in Europe. Intersectional analyses are not better or worse based on the number of categories they incorporate. Rather, intersectional analyses begin with the most salient forms of intersectionality in a given social context, and deepen analysis by looking within that context for additional categories that explain power relations, as well as outside that context (through history and/or geographic space) for insight about the power relations of interest.

Relationality constitutes a second core idea that underpins intersectional knowledge projects (Phoenix and Pattynama, 2006: 187). This emphasis on relationality shifts focus away from the essential qualities that seemingly lie in the center of categories and toward the relational processes that sustain categories. Race, gender, class, and other systems of power are constituted and maintained through relational processes, gaining meaning through the nature of these relationships. The analytic importance of relationality in intersectional scholarship demonstrates how various social positions (occupied by actors, systems, and political/economic structural arrangements) necessarily acquire meaning and power (or a lack thereof) in relationship to other social positions.

This focus on relationality highlights the intersecting and co-constructing nature of social systems and structures organized around power and inequality. Intersecting power relations occur on multiple levels of social analysis, from the micro-level of identities to the macro-level processes of public policy. For example, Collins (2010) addresses the political implications of intersectionality's conceptualization of social groups as fundamentally characterized by interrelationships across power differences. Indeed, the very prefix given to the term intersectionality marks an important departure away from the binary Western thinking that classifies idea systems and eras according to pre- and post- (e.g., pre-modern, post-structuralism); instead, prefixes such as inter- and trans- reflect the interrelated nature of social power relations that is increasingly recognized in social and political theory, as well as in intersectionality. Intersectionality's ability to draw attention to and account for inter-social locations – including those on the margins – challenges binary thinking, shifting the analytic focus onto the fluidity among, interrelationships between, and coproduction of various categories and systems of power.

A third core idea of intersectionality concerns the theme of situated knowledge production, namely, how intersecting power relations of social inequality catalyze varying standpoints, epistemologies, and knowledges (Stoetzler and Yuval-Davis, 2002). Intersectional knowledge production emphasizes how the distinctive social locations of individuals and groups within intersecting power relations catalyze multiple experiences and perspectives on social phenomena. Building on

Foucault's thesis that knowledge and power relations are co-forming (Foucault, 1980), intersectionality provides a more robust power analytic that draws from multiple interpretive traditions, for example, racism as a system of power, hetero-patriarchy as a system of power, and so on drawing from Marxist social thought's commitment to standpoint epistemology in order to suggest that multiple knowledge projects characterize intersectionality's heterogeneity. This knowledge/power framework has been criticized as a simple reversal of the privileged standpoint that formerly accrued to Western social thought, granting, for example, Latinas versus elite White men a superior analysis of power relations. Yet this criticism is disingenuous, projecting onto less powerful groups the mindset and behaviors of the more powerful. Whereas an individual thinker may fall victim to the same fallacies as elite intellectuals, the field of intersectionality is sufficiently inclusive and dynamic to keep these tendencies at bay. Efforts to install a privileged standpoint from within intersectionality runs headlong into multiple perspectives that characterize intersectionality as a critical form of inquiry and praxis.

One important dimension of situated knowledge production concerns what is visible and invisible to differently situated actors. Intersectionality speaks not just to what can be seen, but also what can be experienced within varying social locations. These differences in experience and self-reflexivity concerning one's own actions and those of others can catalyze dramatically different interpretations of social phenomena that may share a common vocabulary but have a markedly different worldview. For example, for those involved in praxis and in much intersectional scholarship, social justice lies at the heart of intersectionality's purpose. A normative goal of intersectionality lies in not simply understanding social inequality, or multiple discriminations against an individual, or how power works, but also problem-solving about the injustices that these phenomena signal. Quite simply, people who are closer to the bottom of any social hierarchy are more likely to develop different analyses of social injustice and social justice than those who are privileged within these same systems. Intersectionality makes these relations more complex, arguing for multiplicity that places individuals and groups as differentially disadvantaged and privileged within intersecting power relations, with equally complex standpoints concerning the meaning of social justice.

Finally, the complexities of actual social relations, a complexity catalyzed by decolonization and desegregation in a global context, fosters complexity within intersectionality as a knowledge project. In a widely cited article, "The Complexity of Intersectionality," McCall provides a provisional template for thinking through the relationship between complexity and intersectionality (McCall, 2005). McCall identifies three methodological approaches that scholars of intersectionality use when making sense of analytic "categories" (such as race, class, gender, etc.); each approach treats the complexity of such categories differently. While anticategorical analyses deconstruct categorical boundaries by exposing their socially constructed nature, intercategorical complexity strategically assumes the reality of such categories in an effort to document social inequalities between different categorical groups. The third approach, intracategorical complexity, adopts analytic features of anti- and intercategorical complexity by deconstructing categories while strategically accepting their existence in an effort to document social inequalities within a "master" category. McCall points to the work of Crenshaw (1991) and other feminists of color as working within this intracategorical register of analysis (McCall, 2005: 1779). Notably, McCall (2005) recognizes that varying types of methodological approaches shape different intersectional knowledge projects (2005: 1774). Intersectional knowledge projects achieve greater levels of complexity because they are iterative and interactional, always examining the connections among seemingly distinctive categories of analysis.

Within the academy, these dimensions of intersectionality have changed the discourse on social inequality, recasting the main ideas of inequality more broadly than through race-only or gender-only frameworks as well as challenging standard assumptions about social inequality in a desegregating world. While previous research on inequality focused largely on those bearing the brunt of that inequality (e.g., women, minorities, the poor), intersectionality's emphasis on the complex and co-constructing relationship between systems of power highlights the importance of researching the privileged as well as the disadvantaged in order to more fully address the complex and multifaceted dynamics of inequality (Choo and Ferree, 2010). Overall, intersectionality's focus on intersecting power relations, relationality, situated knowledge, and complexity has expanded the optics that the field can use to deepen its analyses of many issues.

The Social Problem of Social Inequality: Intersectionality's Object of Investigation?

The previous section introduces four distinguishing features of intersectionality as a knowledge project, pointing to intersectionality as an interpretive framework that can be used to make meaning of the world, and to intersectionality's placement in a set of social practices that articulate with power relations. Self-reflexivity is crucial to the kind of intellectual and political work that intersectionality sets out to do. Casting a self-reflexive eye on intersectionality as a knowledge project highlights the contested nature of intersectionality's canon formation within the intellectual, political, and social context of the neoliberal university. Contextualizing intersectionality within power relations sheds light not just on the thematic content of intersectionality's emerging canon, but also on the political significance of canon formation. Vivian May's (2014) understanding of intersectionality as a form of resistant knowledge that is dedicated to unsettling conventional scholarship and challenging prevailing power hierarchies envisions a particular pathway for intersectionality. Whether intersectionality can actualize this approach and do so within the strictures of canon formation in the academy remains an open question. How might this particular understanding of intersectionality as a resistant knowledge work with processes of canon formation?

Prevailing stories of the emergence of intersectionality routinely claim that Kimberlé Crenshaw "coined" the term intersectionality in her *Stanford Law Review* article "Mapping the Margins: Intersectionality, Identity Politics, and Violence Against Women of Color" (Crenshaw, 1991). These narratives rarely include prior periods of social movement politics and their social justice projects, and instead, confine themselves to locating a point of origin within the academy. Despite the centrality of Black feminism to intersectionality, as well as ignoring the decade or so of race/class/gender studies that maintained visible ties with social justice projects outside the academy and paved the way for intersectionality within it (see, e.g., Dill, 2009), contemporary narratives concerning the emergence of intersectionality as an academic discourse within American higher education situate its origins within academia. This framing of intersectionality's emerging canon suggests that the ideas that are now categorized under the umbrella of intersectionality remained unimportant until they came to the attention of powerful institutional actors. Naming intersectionality seemingly legitimated it. This framing also suggests that any theorizing that might be associated with intersectionality could not have occurred outside the academy, among derogated social actors that are associated with social movement activism and, and most importantly, using a broad array of theoretical tools of academic knowledge production. This framing assumption of canon formation limits understanding of the scope and significance of intersectionality and suppresses its aspirations toward resistant knowledge (Alexander-Floyd, 2012).

As is often noted, intersectionality remains closely associated with Black feminism, the intellectual production of African-American women, as well as with Latinas, indigenous peoples, and similar social actors who were subordinated within intersecting systems of oppression. Yet the more interesting question is why Marx, Weber, Durkheim, Simmel, Bourdieu, Foucault, and a long list of elite Western social theorists failed to advance intersectional arguments? These figures had academic training and credentials, access to publishing venues, and intellectual legitimacy that far exceeded anything that was available to women of color. Yet these figures consistently failed to analyze racial, gender, sexual, ethnic, and similar forms of social inequality. Were they capable of seeing and understanding intersectionality, yet chose to look the other way? Or did they simply not need it?

The parallel question is, how and why might social actors in less powerful social locations be more apt to advance intersectional analyses than social actors in more powerful ones? African-American women's intellectual history provides an important context for teasing out the knowledge/power relations of intersectionality as a knowledge project (Bay et al., 2015; Collins, 2000). African-American social and political thought had long analyzed racial inequality as its primary focus, with an eye toward understanding it and dismantling it. Three focal points underlay the logic of African-American social and political thought: (1) African Americans as a collectivity faced distinctive social problems that took a particular form because of race; (2) racial inequality had a distinctive political organization (e.g., slavery, de jure and de facto racial segregation in the United States, and colonialism in continental Africa and the Caribbean), as well as throughout school, jobs, housing, and other social institutions that collectively organized racial inequality; and (3) racism as a system of power with ideological and material components explained both the social problems that confronted African Americans and the institutional forms they took. Black women intellectuals drew upon this foundational framework, and expanded it beyond racial inequality in response to actual social problems that they faced as Black people, as women, as poor people, and as second-class citizens.

As the growing corpus of scholarship on Ida B. Wells-Barnett, Anna Julia Cooper, and other Black women intellectuals suggests, some saw gender early and often but initially framed their intersectional analysis within the political context of projects for racial justice. Theorizing had a practical dimension, in this case conceptualizing gender as both an addition to and a necessary corrective for projects for racial equality. Over time, for many African-American women intellectuals, it became clear that analyzing racial inequality by itself could deliver neither adequate explanations for the social problems Black women encountered, nor adequate guidance for action. This deepening complexity of Black feminist analysis mirrors complexity as a core theme of intersectionality itself. Intersectionality was neither a replacement for racial analysis, nor was it opposed to it. Rather, analyzing the social problems, social organization, and power relations that produced racial inequality required additional analytical lenses that might provide better theoretical insight. For example, violence, an endemic global social problem that occurs on all levels of social analysis and that touches all people in different ways, constituted one important social problem that preoccupied Black women intellectuals and was a catalyst to their intersectional analysis (Cooper, 1892; Giddings, 2008). Decades later, Kimberlé Crenshaw deepened an intersectional analysis, naming it as such, by arguing that an intersectional analysis was needed to address violence against women of color (Crenshaw, 1991). Violence persists as a catalyst for inquiry and praxis that draws upon intersectional frameworks (Collins and Bilge, 2016: 48–55).

Using intersectionality as a way of making meaning of the world took specific form across varying periods of African-American women's history, yet only came into public view in the context of post–World War II global power upheavals. During the 1950s–1970s, many groups found themselves facing similar political challenges with social inequalities to those of Black women, encountering variations of similar social problems and using distinctive tools from their social contexts to deal with them. For example, Chicana feminist theory and practice had a distinctive history and organizational framework that also embraced intersectional complexity. The core features of intersectionality took special form within each group's history, yet how individuals and groups analyzed their own social location and political aspirations within intersecting systems of power is more generalizable. Desegregation catalyzed the increasingly visibility granted the ideas of intersectionality, but also the meaning of these ideas for resistant knowledge projects.

In an era of neoliberalism, Black feminism, intersectionality, and similar social justice projects encounter new challenges within the academy. For one, diagnosing and remedying social inequality and its concomitant social problems, the object of investigation long associated with intersectionality's emergence, has been increasingly supplanted by a focus on identity as intersectionality's primary object of investigation. For another, rather than seeing intersectionality as a broad, expansive framework that encompasses race, gender, class, sexuality, and other key categories, intersectionality has been increasingly cast as a feminist project or theory within the framing assumptions of feminism. This framing of intersectionality as the progeny of feminism recasts the function of intersectionality as one of making contributions to feminist theory (Davis, 2008). Combining these two focal points re-presents intersectionality as a feminist theory of identity, with varying critiques of intersectionality stemming from this limited understanding. Increasingly, Black feminist scholars and others who reject these framing assumptions, either in whole or in part, have launched sustained criticisms of these critiques of intersectionality (see, e.g., Alexander-Floyd, 2012; Bilge, 2013; Cooper, 2015; May, 2014). The approach taken here, namely, viewing intersectionality as a knowledge project that is broadly defined as a form of critical inquiry and praxis, counteracts these academic debates, which seem overly confined to women's and gender studies. Myriad social actors, both inside and outside the academy, draw upon intersectionality for a variety of projects, including those concerning identity. Within the broad parameters of intersectionality, actors are far more engaged in inquiry and praxis that uses and evaluate intersectionality to speak to social inequality.

In this context, can contemporary intersectionality in academic venues sustain its focus on social inequality as an object of investigation? If so, how might intersectionality incorporate the complexities of heterogeneous interpretive traditions of inequalities associated with racism, sexism, class exploitation, homophobia, nationalism, and xenophobia, spelling out the interconnections among the theoretical traditions that accompany these areas of investigation as well as their collective contributions to intersectionality as social theory? When it comes to thinking through intersectionality's standing as social theory, these questions lie at the heart of intersectionality as a form of critical inquiry and praxis. It's tempting to treat intersectionality just like any other social theory, hoping that when it is appropriately mainstreamed it will settle down and take its place at the table of Western social theory. All social theories in the academy encounter the common challenge of gaining legitimation within prevailing academic norms, and, as a result, the impetus to make intersectionality conform is strong. Scholars are well aware of the stiff penalties attached to social theories that cannot properly be disciplined to academic norms. Yet as the brief genealogy of intersectionality presented here suggests, intersectionality is not a typical knowledge project.

In the self-reflexive approach to intersectionality taken thus far, I have taken pains to point out how contextualizing intersectionality in the intersecting power relations that house it catalyzes an intellectual and political complexity that other social theories can simply ignore. In theorizing, I doubt that Pierre Bourdieu or Judith Butler, for example, paid serious attention to how their social location as privileged intellectuals shaped what they were able to say as well as how their conformity to preexisting academic norms catalyzed the seemingly effortless reception of their ideas. Ideas such as habitus or performativity may seem to be the product of their individual brilliance, but they were only able to advance these ideas in a context where they were already empowered to do so. Neither Foucault nor Butler had to work to make the conditions of their intellectual work possible. My sense is that, even if either thought about the hierarchical power dynamics that surrounded their work, such relations were of minor concern and not a major barrier to their being able to do intellectual work in the first place. Philosopher Jose Medina's discussion of "active ignorance and the epistemic vices of the privileged" (Medina, 2013: 30–40) speaks to this sense of what can be taken for granted and rendered unimportant within intellectual work. Intersectionality has had no such luxury. The difficulties of introducing a power analytic into the process of doing intellectual work shapes intersectional inquiry and praxis.

Because social theory is so closely tied to epistemology, an entity which itself is implicated in reproducing social inequality, intersectionality finds itself in a complex interpretive space regarding its relation to social theory. Power relations that privilege certain groups of social actors and penalize others apply differential standards to the knowledge projects that are associated with differentially empowered groups. Social theory itself has been the purview of educated Western elites whereby the value of a theory can rest less on the integrity of the theory itself, than on the ability of privileged intellectuals to legitimate their worldviews. Despite efforts to democratize social theory, the binary thinking that underlies social hierarchy, for example, theory/practice, or theory/application or theory/stories, has been difficult to dislodge.

Intersectionality originates in resistant knowledge projects that took aim at social inequalities produced by racism, sexism, heterosexism, capitalism, nationalism, and similar systems of power. Ironically, many of these dissident knowledge projects criticized how social theory upheld social hierarchy by aiming to provide a corrective to current practices, thereby decentering Western social theory itself (see, e.g., the essays in Go, 2013), as well as valorizing the oppositional knowledge projects advanced by subordinated groups. Ironically, during intersectionality's institutional incorporation, feminist philosophers took aim at the very foundations of Western knowledge, providing concise analyses of issues of the power relations of standpoint epistemology and of social justice (Harding, 1986; Hartsock, 1983; Young, 1990). Many of these heterogeneous sites of critique aimed not just to deconstruct existing power relations but also to generate new ways of knowing and theorizing the social world (Santos, 2007).

Social theory constitutes a site of intellectual and political contestation. Theory is neither objective nor outside of politics; rather, social theories participate in intersecting power relations by contributing explanations for and justification of the social inequalities that underpin social hierarchies. What might it mean for intersectionality to function as a social theory in this context?

Positioning Intersectionality in a Theoretical Landscape

Social actors who advance resistant knowledge projects consistently distinguish them from mainstream or dominant projects using the prefix critical. While many scholars, including myself, use this rubric, calling something "critical" doesn't necessarily make it so. It may not even make it social theory. In my prior work, I deploy an earlier version of the sociology of knowledge approach deployed here that situates social theory within power relations and aligns critical social theory with the knowledge projects of African-American women and similarly subordinated groups (Collins, 1998). In *Fighting Words*, I offered the following definition of critical social theory: "critical social theory encompasses bodies of knowledge and sets of institutional practices that actively grapple with the central questions facing groups of people differently placed in specific political, social, and historic contexts characterized by injustice. What makes critical social theory 'critical' is its commitment to justice, for one's own group and/or for other groups" (Collins, 1998: xiv). While this working definition still rings true for me, the changing political context and the broadening scope of how intersectionality has traveled into a variety of venues suggests that my working definition's emphasis on social justice would not be supported by many scholars of intersectionality as being central to what they do.

In this context, investigating intersectionality's relationship to social theory generally, and critical social theory in particular, becomes vital. The meaning of critical social theory is surprisingly unspecified, ranging from a relatively narrow focus on the critical theory of the Frankfurt School to a broader categorization that incorporates a plethora of intellectuals and theories that are deemed to be doing critical scholarship. The term critical theory has been closely associated with the Frankfurt School, a group of philosophers, sociologists, social psychologists, and cultural critics who primarily worked in the 1930s (see, e.g., Held, 1980). European scholars build on this foundation, tracing the ideas of the Frankfurt School into the contemporary period as exemplary of critical theory (Held, 1980). Piet Strydom provides an especially comprehensive treatment of critical theory, identifying how its main ideas were carried forward into contemporary expressions, fostering a useful engagement with pragmatism (Strydom, 2011).

The term critical social theory seemingly builds on the orienting scaffold of the Frankfurt School yet often goes far beyond its intellectual roots in Marxist social theory (Calhoun, 1995). Despite a widely shared language, the meaning of critical social theory as an entity unto itself remain unspecified. Some authors identify social theories that they categorize as being "critical" of some aspect of mainstream social theory as archetypes for critical social theory. For example, Calhoun identifies poststructuralist and feminist theory in such fashion, privileging the idea of difference drawn from the seeming preoccupations of these particular theories as the core theme for contemporary critical social theory writ large (Calhoun, 1995). Agger takes a similar path, identifying feminist theory and cultural studies as critical social theories, also positioning them in relation to Marxist social thought as a seemingly foundational critical social theory (Franklin, 2014). In other cases, the boundaries of critical theory are established by focusing on the "Other"; this can be seen, for example, in Gerard Delanty's attempt to revitalize critical social theory by introducing the idea of cosmopolitanism (Delanty, 2009).

Still others claim a looser framework for critical theory itself, one that resembles Calhoun and Agger's expansive renditions of critical social theory. Jon Simons' edited volume of fifteen essays on key contemporary theorists assembles a list of seemingly canonical figures who stand for the ideas that make theory "critical." The opening paragraph to his introduction provides a concise statement of how he approaches critical theory: "The type and range of 'critical theory' covered in this volume refers to the broad sense of that term as it is used in Anglophone academia as a catch-all phrase for a divergent set of theories that distinguish themselves from conventional or traditional theories" (Simons, 2010: 1). Taking a canonical approach to theory, Simons specifies the criteria he uses for selection as follows: "The thinkers covered in this volume are those who had established significant trans-disciplinary reputations in the Anglophone world since about 1990, though they are likely to have been well known in some circles before then" (Simons, 2010: 3). This sample by reputation within the anglophone world yields a list of "critical thinkers" including, among others, Giorgo Agamben, Zygmunt Bauman, Homi Bhabha, Judith Butler, Donna Haraway, Antonio Negri, and Slavoj Žižek. Collectively, these approaches suggest that we imagine a constellation of social theories and/or social thinkers who are inherently "critical" of something, in the case of Simons, those with reputations within the anglophone world, then extrapolate the defining criteria of critical social theory from this small sample.

In this definitional context, which seems biased toward the epistemological frameworks of Western social theory itself, how "critical" are theories that carry the designated mantle of critical social theory? Certainly post-structuralism, feminist theory, and cultural studies have critical elements that are deployed via theoretical mechanisms, but in the absence of any specified criteria for what distinguishes critical social theory from other forms of theory, it is difficult to see exactly how these forms of social inquiry constitute benchmarks for critical social theory itself. Moreover, this list many not be exhaustive. Some forms of theorizing may or may not result in recognizable social theories that may be equally if not more "critical" than these agreed-upon benchmarks. Furthermore, social theories that seem to be inherently critical may engage in practices that pay far less attention to criticizing social inequality itself in favor of arguments on issues that most concern individual theorists, for example, personal identity.

Intersectionality faces a difficult task in specifying those of its actual and potential connections to critical social theory that stem from its own ideas and practices. Taking a predefined definition of critical social theory and seeing how intersectionality measures up constitutes one way to proceed. A more iterative approach places both intersectionality and social theory in the processes of knowledge production that are provisional and contextual. In other words, both projects aim to make meaning about specific aspects of the social world in particular times and places. This approach to knowledge construction conceptualizes genealogies of intersectionality as emergent, and views extant definitions of social theory, critical and otherwise, as provisional and contextual. The first section's summary of intersectionality's history and its growth within the academy, its main ideas, and its standing within academic venues provides a brief genealogy for positioning intersectionality within a theoretical landscape.

When it comes to conceptualizing both intersectionality and social theory as provisional and contextual, Max Horkheimer's 1937 classic essay "Traditional and Critical Theory" offers a useful rubric for cutting into the expansive discourses of both forms of inquiry. Horkheimer's rubric takes us closer to the epistemological underpinnings of theory itself, versus using the content of a knowledge project as the primary criteria with which to analyze its theoretical contours. While this particular essay draws from Marxist social thought, and reflects the tenor of the times, it articulates well with a sociology of knowledge perspective that takes knowledge and power relations into account in examining any knowledge project.

The scholarly content of Horkheimer and other members of the Frankfurt School was resistant, yet here I emphasize the epistemological criteria that underpinned their work. In this essay, Horkheimer sketches out what he sees as important epistemological distinctions among social theories that alternately claim and reject the status of critical (Horkheimer, 1982). Using Horkheimer's framing of the distinctions between traditional and critical theory as a jumping-off point for identifying issues concerning the connections between intersectionality and critical social theory, I ask, how might treating the categories of traditional and critical social theory as themselves provisional and contextual shed light on the critical nature of theory generally and of intersectionality in particular?

What Makes a Traditional Social Theory "Traditional"?

Within Western social sciences, the definition of theory has been relatively straightforward. For most researchers, theory consists of the sum total of propositions about a subject that are linked with each other such that a few remain basic and the rest derive from them. The fewer primary principles there are in any given theory, the better the theory. Containing conceptually formulated knowledge on the one hand and the facts to be subsumed under it on the other, traditional theory in the sciences evolves by trying to ensure that derived propositions remain consonant with actual facts. If theory and the so-called facts contradict each other, one or both must be re-examined because either the scientist has failed to observe correctly or something is wrong with the principles of the theory (Horkheimer, 1982: 188).

This general understanding of social theory has had an important impact on the contemporary social sciences. Social science theories typically examine a particular issue or social phenomenon, for example, a social question, an ongoing debate, a philosophical concept, or an important social problem. Moreover, theories within Western social science typically deploy distinctive epistemological frameworks in the process of theorizing, specifically, maintaining a division between a context of discovery and a context of justification. Methodologies reflect epistemological assumptions concerning criteria for legitimation, for deciding what counts as evidence, and even who is qualified to do social theory in the first place. Social theories gain legitimacy via their universalism, namely, their ability to explain cases across many topics and often fields of study.

Horkheimer wrote during a period when the promise of positivist science was increasingly subject to ideological challenges. Horkheimer's defense of traditional theory seems wedded to his refusal to relinquish Enlightenment ideals that brought informed scientific knowledge to bear on important social issues. Theory in its traditional form engages in the critical examination of data with the aid of an inherited apparatus of concepts and judgments. Yet Horkheimer also recognized the necessity of a self-reflexive impetus within Western science. Science might make substantial contributions to human well-being when its traditional theory concentrated on the problems raised within its own internal technical development and, addressed these problems by either changing its theoretical assumptions and/or by searching for new data (Horkheimer, 1982: 205). In this sense, applying traditional theory to social problem-solving might catalyze a positive social function.

Horkheimer wrote in the context of a nation state run by an elected Nazi party, the expansion and legitimation of eugenics as a global science, and the encroaching nature of ideology and politics on what had been science as a noble endeavor. Writing two decades later in the US context, C. Wright Mills was far less sanguine about traditional theory's contributions to social betterment. Mills launched two key criticisms of what he called grand theory, again focused on the social sciences, that might be applied more broadly to any social theory that garners standing as traditional. The first criticism concerns intelligibility: "We really must ask: Is grand theory merely a confused verbiage or is there, after all, also something there?" (Mills, 2000: 27). Mills's second criticism concerns the significance of abstraction:

> The basic cause of grand theory is the initial choice of a level of thinking so general that its practitioners cannot logically get down to observation. They never, as grand theorists, get down from the higher generalities to problems in their historical and structural contexts. The absence of a firm sense of genuine problems, in turn, makes for the unreality so noticeable in their pages. One resulting characteristic is a seemingly arbitrary and certainly endless elaboration of distinction, which neither enlarges our understanding nor make our experience more sensible. (Mills, 2000: 33).

In essence, the attention to details could generate a swamp of particularities that might make it difficult to see the big picture.

Social science research that examines social inequality draws from the tenets of traditional theory in order to produce knowledge for social betterment. The issue becomes the use to which research is put, primarily how it becomes incorporated into and potentially transforms traditional theories of social inequality. Here intersectionality has had substantial impact, adding more complexity to standard analyses of social inequality. For example, Charles Tilly's durable inequality creatively examines why inequalities themselves persist (Tilly, 1998). Yet Tilly's analysis of inequality-generating mechanisms clarifies some questions and raises others. He notes, "students of inequality must still examine whether such historical accumulations have such regularity and power that exploitation, opportunity hoarding, emulation, and adaptation work differently depending on which categorical distinctions they employ" (Tilly, 1998: 241). As in the case of other social theories with universalizing tendencies, Tilly suggests that explanations might vary if categories such as race, gender, sexuality, and the like were used to test his theory, yet the overall, universal analysis would remain valid. An intersectional contrast, in comparison, would begin with the particularities of these categories and see whether Tilly's model could be built at all from the data he marshals. Working both ways would still advance traditional theory's goal of bringing its theoretical model and empirical findings into alignment.

Positivist social science is often categorized as the grand theory that has influenced Western traditional theory, yet not all traditional social theory has come through science. Using the tools of philosophy, post-structuralism, identified by both Calhoun and Agger as inherently critical, has launched a very important critique of Western social theory, much of it initially aimed at the positivist dimensions of Western science. For many post-structuralist theorists, positivism's scientific theory constitutes the traditional grand narrative to be overcome. Yet whereas post-structuralism may justifiably claim the resistant intent of its content in relation to the traditional social theory that was its Other, the political economy of its production and consumption raise questions about whether post-structuralism increasingly functions as another kind of traditional theory, for example, a hegemonic social theory that serves the same purpose of the theory it displaced.

Post-structuralism has theorized differently about social inequality, often by not paying much attention to it at all, or situating issues of structural social inequality within apolitical identity debates. More importantly, its rules of engagement with power relations seemingly stand in the same relation to subordinated populations as a traditional scientific theory. In this sense, theories of scientific truth organized via technologies of discovery and justification and post-structuralist theories of difference that, for Calhoun, underpin critical social theory itself, perform important, political gatekeeping functions. For science, only those who can uphold the tenets of science itself can produce and consume scientific theory. For post-structuralism, only those who can understand and manipulate post-structuralism's often unintelligible prose and abstractions can gain admission into its inner circle.

Whether scientific or post-structural, within the tenets of traditional theory, the placement of the individual intellectuals within a web of group-based social relations that are typically White, male, well-educated and Western, and the effects that these relationships might have on theoretical knowledge and on the processes of producing it, are of little concern to knowledge outcomes. Science erases the individual in defense of avoiding bias. Individuals need to deny their race, class, gender, or other aspects of their placement within intersecting power relations, as a way to protect the integrity of the research process. In contrast, individuals and individualism are ever-present within post-structuralism's particularity. Race, gender, sexuality, class, citizenship status, and other aspects of identity arrive as categories that can be reassembled and given multiple meanings. This idea resembles the meaning making of pragmatism, but far too often, post-structural analysis remain untethered from structural power relations. More ominously, post-structuralism obscures the privileged social location of its own intellectuals by refusing to consider how it operates as an elite discourse, particularly regarding intelligibility and abstraction. While claiming a language of critique, theorizing the impossibility of stable identities and social groups, post-structuralist theories provide sustained arguments against the categories themselves.

When it comes to social inequality, traditional social theories of science and post-structuralism both yield mixed results. Their meaning is contextual and contingent. Because grand theories of social science and post-structuralism both demonstrate universalizing ambitions, albeit with different objects of investigation and tools of analysis, they both function in some settings as traditional theories and in others as more closely aligned with critical social theory within intersecting power relations. Social inequality may form the content of such universalizing theory, yet the theory itself becomes inherently traditional if not hegemonic as it fails to disrupt social inequality itself. Stated differently, one can make a career of theorizing social inequality, using the tools of science and post-structuralism alike, with little impact on social inequality itself.

What Makes Critical Social Theory "Critical"?

Traditional social theory often fails to take a critical posture either toward its own scientific project or the processes that legitimate it. In contrast, critical theory takes into consideration the entire knowledge production and consumption process, often casting a self-reflexive eye not only on its own assumptions and practices, but also on the effects it generates (Collins, 2019). Horkheimer's essay provides an important touchstone for social theory because he positions traditional and critical social theory within relational frameworks of how these forms of theory inform one another, as well as how each is situated within broader political, epistemological, and ethical contexts. Because Horkheimer's essay examines the epistemological underpinnings of Western social theory that consider the relationship between inquiry and praxis, it provides a useful framework for assessing intersectionality's aspirations toward critical social theory.

Horkheimer spells out what he means by the term critical:

> The critical attitude of which we are speaking is wholly distrustful of the rules of conduct with which society as presently constituted provided each of its members. The separation between individual and society in virtue of which the individual accepts as natural the limits prescribed for his activity is relativized in critical theory. The latter considers the overall framework which is conditioned by the blind interaction of individual activities (that is, the existent division of labor and the class distinctions) to be a function which originated in human action and therefore is a possible object of planful decision and rational determination of goals. (Horkheimer, 1982: 207)

Here, Horkheimer clearly embraces the positive benefits of reason for bettering society – a shared dimension of traditional and critical theory – yet rejects traditional theory's tendency to naturalize and thereby justify existing forms of social organization.

Horkheimer identifies elements of critical social theory with special implications for intersectionality that distinguish it from its more traditional counterparts. Critical social theories seemingly share several epistemological tenets: (1) a dialectical analysis that recognizes and takes into account their positionality within the specific spatial and temporal power relations in which they are situated; (2) adherence to an ethical social justice framework that aspires to better society; (3) reflective accountability concerning their own practices in producing intersectional knowledge; (4) a distinctive theory of how social change has been and might be brought about. How does intersectionality articulate with each of these tenets?

First, because actual social relations are inherently power relations, critical social theory engages in a dialectical analysis that is cognizant of structures of power as well as its own relationship to them. Horkheimer contends that critical theory originates not in the "idealist critique of pure reason" but rather in a dialectical process that is critical of the ways that the political economy is organized (Horkheimer, 1982: 206). By implication, this dialectical approach criticizes the outcomes of current social arrangements, among them social inequality, which for Horkheimer meant class inequality. This framework rejects the epistemological stance of traditional theory – that science operates as a mirror of the world – in favor of a dialectical conception of knowledge whereby what counts as theories and/or facts are part of an ongoing historical process in which the way we view the world (theoretically or otherwise) and the way the world is are reciprocally determined.

Neither critical social theory nor intersectionality are embedded exclusively within academic disciplines, and thus shaped solely by them. Rather, both critical social theory under Horkheimer's definition and intersectionality's reach within and across academic disciplines and outside the academy are also embedded within a web of relational power relations. The material for dialectical engagement is vast, suggesting that the singular scholar could not possibly do intellectual work alone and that broader interdisciplinary, dialogical engagements are essential. By bringing different disciplines together, the scholars of the Frankfurt School modeled this process, positing that working on social issues across disciplinary boundaries would yield insights that were unobtainable by working within narrow and increasingly specialized academic domains. Via this commitment to interdisciplinary work, they modeled an intellectual synergy across academic disciplines, but also potential synergies among theoretical approaches of traditional and critical theory that foreshadow intersectionality and similar contemporary interdisciplinary projects.

Second, critical social theory has an explicitly ethical or normative dimension – it aspires to better society by both understanding and transforming it. This impetus for social transformation is more evident within broader Marxist social theory that influenced the Frankfurt School, but Horkheimer's initial framing of critical theory expresses the nucleus of a social justice ethos. In the 1937 essay, Horkheimer mentions social justice, pointing to critical social theory as a potential site of resistance to epistemic injustice: "For all its insight into the individual steps in social change and for all the agreement of its elements with the most advanced traditional theories, the critical theory has no specific influence on its side, except concern for the abolition of social injustice" (Horkheimer, 1982: 242). Horkheimer suggests that grappling with social injustice is a central activity of critical theory: "But the transmission will not take place via solidly established practice and fixed ways of acting but via concern for social transformation. Such a concern will necessarily be aroused ever anew by prevailing injustice, but it must be shaped and guided by the theory itself and in turn react upon the theory" (Horkheimer, 1982: 241). Because social theories can be marshaled for oppressive or emancipatory purposes, questions of ethics explicitly or, more often, implicitly, permeate all scholarship.

These ideas add an ethical component that identifies the diagnostic and reconstructive dimensions of critical social theory. Knowledge for knowledge's sake speaks to the normative goal of truth. Traditional social theory contents itself with deconstructing and/or diagnosing social problems; critical social theory aims to remedy those social problems, seeing reconstructing society from the rubble of deconstruction as just as if not more important than analysis. Here a framework that valorizes ethics replaces the value neutrality of traditional theory.

Third, critical social theory expresses a reflective accountability concerning its own practice. On the surface, critical social theory and traditional social theory share this core value. Yet what is included in the scope of self-reflexivity matters. Because traditional social theory brackets out the effects of power relations on its own practices, it focuses on the standards of a much smaller, historically homogeneous community of practitioners in science or philosophy. Self-reflexivity may occur but also produces important blind spots. In contrast, critical social theory would contain a critical reflexivity both about its own practices and how its social location within power relations shape those practices. This attentiveness to social location mandates that intersectionality should take into account its own participation in creating the society that it aims to understand and shape. For intersectionality, a theory engaged in a dialectical analysis would recognize that its own knowledge claims and practices cannot be benign, but instead contribute to and reflect intersecting systems of power in which it is situated. Jose Medina provides a greatly expanded understanding of how the concept of reflexivity links to an epistemology of resistance.

Finally, critical social theory advances a distinctive theory of how social change has been and might be brought about. As Horkheimer describes it, "theory has a historically changing object which, however, remains identical amid all the changes" (Horkheimer, 1982: 239). Critical theory views change as inherent to society; it also posits that societies all contain certain core principles that remain the same even though they may change form and expression. Building on Horkheimer's logic, intersecting power relations shape changing-same social formations grounded not in linear, evolutionary processes, but rather in human agency. Change may be vital for critical social theory, but the question is, which aspects of the changing same merit critical social theory's attention? Intersectional projects that focus on social inequality, the power relations that catalyze them, and the social problems that show social inequality in action constitute the entity that merits change.

This issue of a commitment to social change seems to be an important distinction between traditional and critical social theory. Craig Calhoun (1995) identifies the idea of sameness and difference as the overarching theme for contemporary social theory, and certainly one that would be endorsed by Simon's contemporary critical theorists (Simons, 2010). Whereas social change and difference constitute important objects of investigation, in this essay, I have explicitly pointed to the theme of social inequality as a competing object of investigation for intersectionality, precisely to challenge the seemingly hegemonic identity frame and its spinoff of similarities and differences and its implications for individual change. Yet when it comes to critical social theory, Calhoun's more important point lies in identifying change as a process of imagining new possibilities for society. Calhoun suggested that critical social theory "exists largely to facilitate a constructive engagement with the social world that starts from the presumption that existing arrangements . . . do not exhaust the range of possibilities. It seeks to explore the ways in which our categories of thought reduce our freedom by occluding recognition of what could be" (Calhoun, 1995: xviii).

Many scholars increasingly turn to the idea of imagination as an important vehicles for knowledge production within communities of inquiry generally, and for oppressed people in particular. Within critical race theory, historian Robin D. G. Kelley organizes his monograph on African-American activism under the theme of a "black radical imagination" that is focused on change (Kelley, 2002). Stoetzler and Yuval-Davis (2002) discuss the situated imagination as a crucial component of feminist standpoint theory (2002: 316), pointing to the ways in which social positioning shapes knowledge as well as the imagination. This approach yields one important insight for critical social theory: individuals and groups are differently positioned in a distinctive matrix of domination, which has implications for how we experience society including not only what we know but also what we can imagine (Collins, 2000; see also Collins, 2019).

Implications

First, because knowledge projects change and shift over time, we should be cautious of categorizing the ideas of any given social theory, especially intersectionality, as inherently traditional or critical. Instead, ideas such as intersectionality gain meaning though their use. Theories of positivist science can be alternately traditional and critical, depending on the use to which they are put. Similarly, post-structuralism is situated in a creative yet conflicted tension between aspirations toward both critical social theory and traditional social theory. The meaning of the theory lies in its use, not solely in the substance of its ideas. Building a theory of what constitutes critical social theory using the content of a given theory or set of social theorists is shortsighted. Instead, the standards applied to intersectionality itself, instead of focusing on what it means to do intersectionality may be a better frame for theory in general and for understanding critical social theory in particular.

Second, this essay suggests that critical intent or simply claiming that intersectionality is critical is insufficient for intersectionality's engagement as critical social theory. A project can vociferously proclaim to be "critical," yet its practices may undermine its proclamations. Intersectionality may thus dispute dominant social theory concerning social inequality from within the putative political safety provided by working within traditional norms. In this fashion, intersectionality as social theory can have critical intentions without meeting the additional risk-taking criteria of self-reflexive political engagement, claiming an ethical stance, or imagining new social possibilities that are associated with critical theory. Much empirical work that draws on intersectional frameworks with critical intent is situated within the overarching framework of traditional social theory.

Finally, intersectionality's theoretical dimensions will deepen not only via internal dialogues, but also through critical engagement with multiple social theories that speak to varying aspects of its *raison d'être*. Placing intersectionality in dialogue with a range of social theories, traditional and critical, provides multiple lenses for specific intersectional projects as well as intersectionality writ large. Rushing prematurely to choose one theory and force it on intersectionality as the so-called answer to its theoretical deficiencies or worse yet, using one hegemonic theory to criticize intersectionality in order to move beyond it seems shortsighted. With relationality as a core premise of intersectionality, intersectionality's relationship to multiple social theories remains open and ongoing. This approach is aligned with drawing important ideas from more than one theory to see what is of value to an intersectional project (a better understanding of social inequality and what can be done to dismantle it). Developing intersectionality as social theory involves placing the ideas in dialogue with a range of social theories, traditional and critical, both inside and outside the academy, that further its goals. Via these dialogues, intersectionality would be in a better position to criticize both the substance and the terms of its own practice, with an eye toward changing them.

References

Alexander-Floyd, Nikol G. 2012. "Disappearing Acts: Reclaiming Intersectionality in the Social Sciences in a Post-Black Feminist Era." *Feminist Formations* 24(1): 1–25.

Bay, Mia, Farah J. Griffin, Martha S. Jones, and Barbara D. Savage (eds.). 2015. *Toward an Intellectual History of Black Women*. Chapel Hill, NC: University of North Carolina.

Bernstein, Richard J. 2010. *The Pragmatic Turn*. Malden, MA: Polity.

Bilge, Sirma. 2013. "Intersectionality Undone: Saving Intersectionality from Feminist Intersectionality Studies." *Du Bois Review* 10(2): 405–24.

Bowleg, Lisa. 2008. "When Black + Lesbian + Woman (Does Not Equal) Black Lesbian Woman: The Methodological Challenges of Qualitative and Quantititave Intersectionality Research." *Sex Roles* 59(5–6): 312–325.

Browne, Irene, and Joya Misra. 2003. "The Intersection of Gender and Race in the Labor Market." *Annual Review of Sociology* 29: 487–513.

Calhoun, Craig. 1995. *Critical Social Theory: Culture, History, and the Challenge of Difference*. Malden, MA: Blackwell Publishers.

Choo, Hae Yeon, and Myra Marx Ferree. 2010. "Practicing Intersectionality in Sociological Research: A Critical Analysis of Inclusions, Interactions, and Institutions in the Study of Inequalities." *Sociological Theory* 28(2): 129–149.

Collins, Patricia Hill. 1998. *Fighting Words: Black Women and the Search for Justice*. Minneapolis, MN: University of Minnesota Press.

   2000. *Black Feminist Thought: Knowledge, Consciousness, and the Politics of Empowerment*. New York: Routledge.

   2010. "The New Politics of Community." *American Sociological Review* 75(1): 7–30.

   2015. "Intersectionality's Definitional Dilemmas." *Annual Review of Sociology* 41 (August): 1–20.

   2019. *Intersectionality as Critical Theory*. Durham, NC: Duke University Press.

Collins, Patricia Hill, and Sirma Bilge. 2016. *Intersectionality*. London: Polity.

Cooper, Anna Julia. 1892. *A Voice from the South: By a Black Woman of the South*. Xenia, OH: Aldine.

Cooper, Brittney C. 2015. "Intersectionality." In Lisa Jane Disch and Mary Hawkesworth (eds.), *The Oxford Handbook of Feminist Theory*. Oxford Handbooks Online.

Crenshaw, Kimberlé Williams. 1991. "Mapping the Margins: Intersectionality, Identity Politics, and Violence Against Women of Color." *Stanford Law Review* 43(6): 1241–1299.

Davis, Kathy. 2008. "Intersectionality as a Buzzword: A Sociology of Science Perspective on What Makes a Feminist Theory Successful." *Feminist Theory* 9(1): 67–85.

Delanty, Gerard. 2009. *The Cosmopolitan Imagination: The Renewal of Critical Social Theory*. Cambridge, UK: Cambridge University Press.

Dill, Bonnie Thornton. 2009. "Intersections, Identities, and Inequalities in Higher Education." In Bonnie Thornton Dill and Ruth Zambrana (eds.), *Emerging Intersections: Race, Class, and Gender in Theory, Policy, and Practice* (pp. 229–52). New Brunswick, NJ: Rutgers University Press.

Foucault, Michel. 1980. *Power/Knowledge: Selected Interviews and Other Writings, 1972–1977*. New York: Pantheon.

Franklin, Sekou M. 2014. *After the Rebellion: Black Youth, Social Movement Activism, and the Post-Civil Rights Generation*. New York: New York University Press.

Giddings, Paula. 2008. *Ida: A Sword Among Lions: Ida B. Wells and the Campaign Against Lynching*. New York: Amistad.

Go, Julian (ed.). 2013. *Decentering Social Theory*. Bingley, UK: Emerald Group Publishing.

Hancock, Ange-Marie. 2007a. "Intersectionality as a Normative and Empirical Paradigm." *Politics and Gender* 3(2): 248–55.

2007b. "When Multiplication Doesn't Equal Quick Addition: Examining Intersectionality as a Research Paradigm." *Perspectives on Politics* 5(1): 63–79.

Harding, Sandra. 1986. *The Science Question in Feminism*. Ithaca, NY: Cornell University Press.

Hartsock, Nancy. 1983. "The Feminist Standpoint: Developing the Ground for a Specifically Feminist Historical Materialism." In Sandra Harding and Merrill B. Hintikka (eds.), *Discovering Reality* (pp. 283–310). Boston, MA: D. Reidel.

Held, David. 1980. *Introduction to Critical Theory: Horkheimer to Habermas*. Berkeley, CA: University of California Press.

Horkheimer, Max. 1982. "Traditional and Critical Theory." In Max Horkheimer (ed.), *Critical Theory: Selected Essays* (pp. 188–243). New York: Continuum Publishing.

Joas, Hans. 1993. *Pragmatism and Social Theory*. Chicago, IL: University of Chicago Press.

Kelley, Robin D. G. 2002. *Freedom Dreams: The Black Radical Imagination*. Boston, MA: Beacon.

Knapp, Gudrun-Alexi. 2005. "Race, Class, Gender: Reclaiming Baggage in Fast Travelling Theories." *European Journal of Women's Studies* 12(3): 249–265.

Lykke, Nina. 2011. "Intersectional Analysis: Black Box or Useful Critical Feminist Thinking Technology?" In Helma Lutz, Maria Teresa Herrera Vivar, and Linda Supik (eds.), *Framing Intersectionality: Debates on a Multi-Faceted Concept in Gender Studies* (pp. 207–220). Burlington, VT: Ashgate Publishing Company.

May, Vivian M. 2014. "'Speaking into the Void'? Intersectionality Critiques and Epistemic Backlash." *Hypatia* 29(1): 94–112.

2015. *Pursuing Intersectionality, Unsettling Dominant Imaginaries*. New York: Routledge.

McCall, Leslie. 2005. "The Complexity of Intersectionality." *Signs* 30(3): 1771–1800.

Medina, Jose. 2013. *The Epistemology of Resistance*. New York: Oxford University Press.

Mills, C. Wright. 2000. *The Sociological Imagination*. New York: Oxford.

Nash, Jennifer C. 2008. "Rethinking Intersectionality." *Feminist Review* 89: 1–15.

Phoenix, Ann, and Pamela Pattynama. 2006. "Intersectionality." *European Journal of Women's Studies* 13(3): 187–192.

Santos, Boaventura de Sousa (ed.). 2007. *Another Knowledge Is Possible: Beyond Northern Epistemologies.* New York: Verso.

Simons, Jon (ed.). 2010. *From Agamben to Žižek: Contemporary Critical Theorists.* Edinburgh: Edinburgh University Press.

Steinbugler, Amy C., Julie E. Press, and Janice Johnson Dias. 2006. "Gender, Race and Affirmative Action: Operationalizing Intersectionality in Survey Research." *Gender and Society* 20(6): 805–825.

Stoetzler, Marcel, and Nira Yuval-Davis. 2002. "Standpoint Theory, Situated Knowledge and the Situated Imagination." *Feminist Theory* 3(3): 315–333.

Strydom, Piet. 2011. *Contemporary Critical Theory and Methodology.* New York: Routledge.

Stuhr, John J. 2000. "Introduction: Classical American Philosophy." In John J. Stuhr (ed.), *Pragmatism and a Classical American Philosophy: Essential Readings and Interpretive Essays* (pp. 1–9). New York: Oxford University Press.

Tilly, Charles. 1998. *Durable Inequality.* Berkeley, CA: University of California Press.

Young, Iris Marion. 1990. *Justice and the Politics of Difference.* Princeton, NJ: Princeton University Press.

Yuval-Davis, Nira. 2006. "Intersectionality and Feminist Politics." *European Journal of Women's Studies* 13(3): 193–210.

8 Modernity

Peter Wagner

Within social theory, the term 'modernity' is most often, albeit frequently implicitly, used to refer to societies that are built on the principles of individual freedom and instrumental mastery. At the same time, it is assumed that such societies start to emerge in Western Europe and North America from the late eighteenth century onwards. All debate and dispute notwithstanding, this is and has remained something like the core understanding of modernity. Even critical positions have mostly been developed against the backdrop of some such notion of modernity. The main objective of this essay is neither to portray the rich debate nor to add a further nuance to the positions advanced. Rather, by contextualizing the existing debates, it aims to widen the horizon of thinking about modernity.

Talking about Modernity at the Supposed End of Modernity

The necessity of such an endeavour can be gathered from the observation that the term 'modernity' came into explicit use in social theory at the very moment when the end of modernity as a social formation was announced. That moment was the publication of Jean-François Lyotard's *La Condition postmoderne* in 1979, a small 'report on knowledge' written on commission for the government of Quebec that immediately received wide attention. Arguably, this was due to the fact that Lyotard combined the analysis of a major social transformation with a critique of social theory. Seeing social life as a coexisting plurality of language games, he seemed to be saying both that socio-theoretical attempts of making the social world intelligible had ultimately failed and that 'modern societies' were undergoing a profound transformation, not least due to the diffusion of information and communication technology. How the two components of his diagnosis were precisely related was rather unclear. But their combination stimulated both conceptual reflection and sociological analysis, both of which often came to use 'modernity' as the key term to frame the discussion.

With hindsight one can say that Lyotard's proposal, rather than being accepted, provoked discussion based on need for clarification. Tellingly, the two elements of his diagnosis were soon treated rather separately again. To give only two key examples: Participating in the focus on language often called 'the linguistic turn', Jürgen Habermas (1985) reconstructed the philosophical discourse of modernity as being turned towards intersubjective communication rather than the isolated individual subject. Thus he suggested that the critique of individual autonomy and instrumental mastery does not necessarily lead to abandoning the commitment to modernity. This reasoning is compatible with, but completely disconnected from, the sociological diagnosis of the present time provided a few years earlier by the same author in *Theory of Communicative Action* (1981) and never updated since. In turn, Ulrich Beck's *Risk Society: Towards Another Modernity* (1986) takes up the idea of an ongoing major transformation of modernity, but it uses as a backdrop precisely the Parsonian-Luhmannian ways of making social life intelligible that were criticized by Lyotard, without going back to his own preceding work in the philosophy of the social sciences.

Even though this debate from the closing years of the twentieth century has in many respects been superseded, to refer to it is useful for several reasons. First, as already said above, this is the debate in which the noun 'modernity' is introduced in social theory (the adjective 'modern' and the processual noun 'modernization' have longer trajectories in the field). Secondly, it permits us to make the distinction between two aspects of the use of the term, one pertaining to conceptual reflection in social philosophy, the other requiring empirical points of reference typical of sociological analysis. At a closer look, thirdly, one recognizes that both sub-debates are indeed about 'modernity' in the broad sense of aiming to define their own present, and doing so by distinguishing it from some different past. Thus, a historical-comparative perspective is adopted, even though not always very explicitly or concisely, and the question of the appropriate temporal comparison is raised. The comparison, finally, does not only operate in time, but also in space. All three above-mentioned authors connect the experience of modernity with a focus on Europe (or the West), a perspective unquestioningly shared by most contributors to the debate, but in need of a reconsideration that goes beyond mere resistance to Eurocentrism.

In other words, much of the debate was marked by firmly locating modernity in space and time – a space that could be as small as only parts of north-western Europe or as large as Europe and North America together, and a time that could reach from the early sixteenth century, at the very earliest, or from the late eighteenth century to the present, or to just before our present, if one believes the suggestion that the end of modernity has already happened. This spatio-temporal determination of modernity has led to rather barren debates about the differences between supposedly modern and non-modern social configurations. Modernity's particular location in the named spatio-temporal envelope, furthermore, gave rise to the largely futile disputes between 'post-' or 'decolonial' thinkers and those accused of 'Eurocentrism'. The generally problematic nature of the conflation between a socio-theoretical concept, 'modernity', and a particular historical constellation was widely overlooked or underestimated.

To overcome the limitations of those recent debates about modernity, one needs to contextualize both the socio-philosophical and the historico-sociological debate and relate them to each other. This is what this essay will aim to do. To anticipate the result in a nutshell, it will become clear that modernity is most fruitfully understood as a self-understanding, a way of being in the world, rather than as an institutional arrangement of a socio-historical constellation. Further, a modern self-understanding indeed centres on some notion of autonomy, but not necessarily on individual autonomy and the related quest for instrumental mastery. Rather, the modern self-understanding is open to interpretation, the variety of which creates the space for generating what has been called 'multiple modernities' (Eisenstadt, 2000). Furthermore, tracing the fate of such modern self-understanding through history, one recognizes that the history of modernity is neither marked by the realization of freedom and autonomy, nor by an ideological conceit hiding domination, but by struggles over claims to autonomy and justifications for domination. Transformations of modernity, like the one on which the late-twentieth-century debate focused, are the outcome of such struggles.

The Historico-Sociological Account of Modernity

The 'Great Transformation' and the Social Theory of Modernity

Although the term itself was not used at that time, the historico-sociological notion of modernity originated during the nineteenth century, but was based on the diagnosis of an earlier rupture. At the end of the nineteenth century, the notion that European societies were in some way ahead of others was widespread. To have embarked on a steady trajectory of progress was part of the European self-understanding; and elites in other societies were often observing Europe with a view to identifying which aspects of them could and should be emulated to catch up with Europe, or be it rather to better resist Europe. Within Europe, the sense of superiority was expressed in distinctions between one's own social organization and the traditional or primitive ones, as employed in early sociology and anthropology. Vice versa, the concepts of European sociology were translated into other languages, such as Chinese or Japanese, to enable their application in those contexts (see recently Mishima, 2016). Searching for the roots of what he called occidental rationalism, Max Weber would famously ask in the early twentieth century, 'what concatenation of circumstances has led to the fact that in the Occident, and here only, cultural phenomena have appeared which – as at least we like to imagine – lie in a direction of development of universal significance and validity?'

These 'phenomena' are those that would later summarizingly be called 'modernity', and Weber himself used the adjective when speaking of 'modern capitalism' in this context. Weber was a rather late contributor to the view that some significant rupture with past sociopolitical organization had occurred, putting social life on new foundations, and that this had happened in 'Europe' or 'the West'. As a first step, we can proceed to understand what 'modernity' came to mean by looking at the thinking about social relations during the long European nineteenth century, lasting from 1789 to 1914, and referring to a range of scholars reaching from Henri de Saint-Simon and G. W. F. Hegel through Alexis de Tocqueville and Karl Marx to Emile Durkheim, Max Weber, and Georg Simmel. Across all differences between them, these authors had in common that they identified a profound rupture in social life that had brought about, or was to bring about, a radically new form of social relations and social structure. Even though they chose different terms for characterizing the rupture and the ensuing social transformation, and varied in the identification of the events that they saw as most significant for that transformation (we come back to these issues below), they made the analysis of the emergent social formation their key concern, both because it was new and because it would mark the present and the future.

Modernity, in the sum of these authors' views, was characterized by a number of features that had been absent from the social world before the rupture or at least only of marginal importance. Modernity supposedly brought with itself novel attitudes to the world as well as to other human beings, which were captured by terms such as abstract freedom, individual instrumental rationality ('egotistical calculation', in Marx and Engels's words), individualism, and occidental rationalism. The novel social constellation within which human beings found themselves and within which these attitudes grew, in turn, was captured by terms such as industry, division of labour, democracy, bourgeois society, class struggle, and capitalism. Even though earlier developments are sometimes mentioned, all these authors claimed that these attitudes and constellations emerged, or arose to dominance, in Europe (and North America) from the late eighteenth and early nineteenth centuries onwards.

It is important to note, however, that, rather than developing an institutional analysis of 'modernity' as an established novel social configuration, these historically minded scholars aimed to grasp the meaning and consequences of the 'great transformation' (Karl Polanyi) that they had been witnessing and for which they were in need of new concepts. In other words, those scholars to whom we now refer as theorists of modernity tried to understand the European nineteenth century. But they were not entirely aware that doing this was possibly not the same as 'theorizing modernity'. As a consequence, one has tended to conflate 'modernity' with the European nineteenth century. Before reflecting in more detail on the theoretical programmes of these authors, we shall therefore briefly explore the historical context that they were addressing.

The Nineteenth Century: Confronting Notes from Social Theory and Historiography

What was Europe in the nineteenth century? To answer this question, we need to go beyond that which these authors knew about their contemporary world and use the information we have at our hands today, most importantly contributions to the recently developed area of 'world history' (see, among others, Bayly, 2004; Darwin, 2007; Osterhammel, 2008; Pomeranz, 2000).

In this current view, there was little difference in social and economic life between Europe and at least some other regions in the world, in particular in Asia, by 1800. By 1900, however, the world was dominated by European powers, through a combination of superior military force, actual colonial occupation and settlement of non-European territories, and by economic exchange the conditions for which were often determined by the Europeans. It was partly as a consequence of this domination that elites in non-European societies saw themselves as lagging behind, as mentioned above, and often considered the absence of European ideas and concepts as the cause for their weakness and slowness to change.

Today, we have good reasons to assume that 'the great divergence' (Kenneth Pomeranz) between Europe and other world regions that emerged in the course of the nineteenth century was less determined by prior, 'endogenous' European history than has often been assumed. Neither legal regimes, in particular concerning property rights, nor technological advances emerging from the later so-called Scientific Revolution, nor the rise of universities in the early second millennium CE as autonomous sites for debate and exploration or of cities as sites for politico-economic organization, nor the power divide between Pope and Emperor, mark such a difference between Europe and other world regions that they could explain nineteenth-century developments. Rather, the European 'take-off' (Rostow, 1971) was highly conditioned by the triangular commercial relations across the Atlantic that had slowly evolved over the preceding three centuries, using African labour and American soil to liberate Europe from earlier constraints to economic 'development' (Stråth and Wagner, 2017).

Furthermore, it seems now less persuasive to see the 'cause' of the historical rupture in the combination of a socio-economic and an intellectual event, namely the rise of the bourgeoisie and the emergence of political economy and the associated idea of market freedom. Regardless of whether one considers the former as determining the latter or the latter as opening the path for the former, the transformative powers of both have been overestimated. In the early nineteenth century, the new economic possibilities created by the Atlantic connections came to be perceived. But no entirely new world with new dominant actors arose. Rather, in response to the new possibilities, the old aristocratic elites gradually changed outlook and started building new alliances, containing any radical new visions as created in the French Revolution and in political economy and imposing their power in the novel constellation through violence at home and abroad. The period between the Vienna Congress of 1815 and the Versailles Peace Treaty of 1919 was neither as peaceful nor as revolutionary in Europe as has often been suggested. True, it witnessed the rise of industry, and with it, of wealth and power, both highly asymmetrically distributed. But the sociopolitical transformation that has often been seen to accompany the techno-economic transformation remained very limited (Halperin, 2004; Mayer, 1981; Stråth, 2016).

Thus, the fundamental change between 1800 and 1900 was the rise of Europe to world domination, based on the exploitation of new techno-economic possibilities enabled by the emergence of the Atlantic division of labour. In principle, this was recognized by, for instance, Marx and Engels, who in their short and forceful account of recent social transformations in *The Communist Manifesto* asserted that the 'discovery of America [and] the rounding of the Cape' gave an 'impulse never before known' to the revolutionary bourgeoisie. But even in their text, this is an opening remark without consequences for the further analysis. Scholars tended to see the changes in Europe as self-propelled, either determined by a logics of history, reaching from functional accomplishments and selection of superior solutions to the dynamics of class struggle, or at the least as producing inescapable results of a path once entered. In other words, by now we can say that the nineteenth-century social theorists misconceived the causes of the European social transformations of the same period. What does this entail for their view of the modernity that they saw as being produced by those alleged causes?

Rethinking the Historico-Sociological Account of European Modernity

Thus, we take a second brief look at the notion of modernity that emerged during the long nineteenth century (for more detail on the following, see Wagner, 2014). Two observations were crucial to the early social theory of modernity: First, these scholars perceived a rather radical *rupture* in history, exemplified by the Industrial Revolution and the French Revolution – even though the relation between the two remained underexplored, and the latter under-theorized, with few exceptions such as Tocqueville and to some extent Lorenz von Stein. Second, as alluded to above, they perceived a *dynamics* of history, which may not have been sociologically explicit in Hegel, but became evident from the middle of the nineteenth century onwards, with the *Communist Manifesto* of 1848 as a prime example. In connection of the two perceptions, the social theory of modernity diagnosed a radical destruction of the existing fabric of social relations, which in turn unleashed an unprecedented dynamics.

As a consequence, the early social theory of modernity provided predominantly an analysis of movement; it offered few 'portraits' of modernity. Emile Durkheim is the main European exception on which Talcott Parsons and the USA-based sociology of 'modern society' would build after the Second World War. Now that we have come to think of 'modernity' with the Parsonian image of 'modern society' in mind, such a claim may seem erroneous at first sight. But we can interrogate its validity by briefly looking backwards from Parsons's viewpoint. Parsons offered an institutional image of society as differentiated into subsystems with their own logics, including an economic system based on market exchange regulated by money and a politico-administrative system underpinned by the formal, impersonal rules of rational administration. The image used elements of the early social theory of modernity, but it assembled them towards a coherence and stability that cannot be found in the original version, again with the partial exception of Durkheim. Following the political economists, Marx analysed money-regulated market exchange, but he insisted on the antagonism in the underlying social relations that would prevent any market from stabilizing into an economic system. Weber's 'dwelling-place of steel' (rather mistranslated as 'iron cage') is a 'portrait', indeed working with a visual metaphor to illustrate the outcome of rationalization, but Weber was sceptical about the stability of this construction, and rather expected it to be challenged and possibly dismantled because of its lack of desirability.

Why the early social theory of modernity emphasized tendencies rather than providing an institutional model of society can easily be understood in the context of the time. If one applies the post–Second World War view of 'modern society', for example, European societies did not look very modern at all by 1900, as shown above. Resorting to tendencies could make these empirical problems acceptable by projecting the full realization of modernity into an indefinite future. We may say that the early social theory of modernity engaged with the opening of the time horizon effected by sociopolitical thought from the late eighteenth century onwards (Koselleck, 1979), oscillating between more determinist, teleological projections of a future modernity, on the one side, and indecisiveness and scepticism, on the other. Sociologists certainly participated in the broadly evolutionist mode of thinking triggered by the apparently unstoppable rise of Europe during the nineteenth century. Few of them, however, adopted a blunt linear view of progress across history, and of Europe as the territorial site of such progress. Let us just recall the tension in Marx's work between identification of the laws of class struggle and capitalist competition, on the one hand, and the concern about the possible 'common ruin of the contending classes', on the other; and similarly Weber's analysis of the ongoing rationalization processes, on the one side, as opposed to his conjecture about the return of old values or the rise of new prophets, on the other. The observation of novel social forms (structures) and novel human beings (rational individuals) constituted an agenda for thought and for action; it did not lead straight into a theory of modernity because the observed 'modernity' was too unstable and tension-ridden (see Wagner, 2015 for more detail).

By the early years of the twentieth century, Weber being a key example, the tone of the self-diagnosis of modernity had indeed changed. The now so-called classical sociologists – such as Weber, Durkheim, Georg Simmel, Vilfredo Pareto – were struggling with a social transformation that we can now recognize as a first crisis of the kind of modernity that had emerged from nineteenth-century events, entailing not least the development of capacities for collective action – by states, nations, classes – to counteract the problematic consequences of trends set in motion (Wagner, 1994; see also Mota and Wagner, 2019 for a view going beyond Europe). These scholars were no longer, in their own view, writing at the dawn of a new era, as Saint-Simon, Hegel, Tocqueville, and even Marx had had some reason to assume they were. They were looking back at a major transformation and were trying to assess its outcomes. Significantly, they were uncertain about both how such an assessment could proceed and what its results would be. The former uncertainty led to writings in the philosophy and methodology of the social sciences, often of a high level of sophistication; the latter to the ambivalence-ridden diagnoses that we have referred to above. The 'modernity' that the 'classical sociologists' were experiencing was anything but stable; and they knew this. Whether it would stabilize depended very much on what the future would look like.

To put it briefly, that future began to look bleak. The experience of the First World War, totalitarianism, Great Depression, and the Second World War shook any remaining optimistic expectations. Those who continued their contemporary critical historico-sociological investigations along the lines set out by the earlier scholars could not fail to take these events into account. In 1935, Karl Mannheim published *Man and Society in an Age of Reconstruction* (1940 [1935]), which proposed to see 'fundamental democratization' as the key force in sociopolitical change of the time. He linked up to Tocqueville's observation, a century earlier, that the democratic imaginary was so powerful in contemporary societies that inclusive-egalitarian participation had become the telos of politico-institutional change. At the same time, he recognized that this change could occur in such a form and at such speed that democracy was at risk of self-cancellation (Karagiannis, 2016). A few years later, in 1944, Karl Polanyi's *The Great Transformation* provided a similar analysis, focusing on the instability created by the dynamics of economic change. The idea of market self-regulation, the dominant economic ideology during the first half of the nineteenth century, entailed commodification, including the tendency to turn goods into commodities that were not – and could not be – produced with the purpose of being sold, most importantly labour, land; and money. Against such inappropriate commodification, which was destructive of social life, the 'self-defence of society' arose, and Polanyi analysed social transformations between the middle of the nineteenth and the middle of the twentieth centuries from this angle. His key concern was, having witnessed the rise of fascisms and of Soviet socialism, in how far such necessary self-defence of society could be pursued without endangering freedom. Yet a few years later, after the end of the Second World War, in *The Origins of Totalitarianism* (1951), Hannah Arendt combined an analysis of an ever-expansive capitalism in the form of imperialism with an analysis of the nation state that required a stable framework for political action to understand the tensions in European societies that had exploded and given rise to totalitarianism.

These authors provided powerful diagnoses of their time by employing selective elements from the earlier social theory of modernity, but simultaneously interrogating and questioning any previous assumptions about the regularity and predictability of trends of modern evolution. Building on detailed historical reconstruction, they recognized the inherent tensions in, and the fragility of, modern sociopolitical arrangements and emphasized the contingency of historical outcomes, the ever-present possibility that things could have turned out otherwise had human beings acted differently at key moments in history.

From the vantage point of the present, one can identify two key insights in terms of the social theory of modernity in these mid-century writings. First, the authors of these works stayed with the focus on freedom, democracy, and capitalism that had characterized the debate on the new social constellation throughout the long nineteenth century, but they abandoned any kind of determinist perspective, be it weak or strong, linear or dialectical. And, second, they did so because they saw societies as being shaped by underlying commitments but recognized that these commitments did not neatly translate into stable institutional forms. Rather, they gave rise to open-ended struggle over the interpretation of those commitments. In terms that these authors did not use, they recognized that 'modernity' is more appropriately seen as a societal self-understanding than as an institutional arrangement. While any such self-understanding expresses normative principles, no specific institutional arrangement could be 'derived' from them. The modern self-understanding turned out to be rather widely open to interpretation, and the range of interpretations was enlarged in the struggle over interpretations when dealing with societal problems in specific historical situations.

There was little follow-up on these insights during the first three post–Second World War decades, almost none at all within sociology. But there is a bridge that these works provide to political philosophy. They can be read as showing how fascism and totalitarianism arose from sociopolitical constellations committed to freedom and democracy. Rather than its opposite and antagonist, those regimes should be seen as interpretations of modernity. But if this could be so, what then is exactly the modern societal self-understanding; how far does its openness to interpretation reach? Posing the question this way means moving from the historico-sociological to the socio-philosophical account of modernity. For this reason it is useful to leave the historico-sociological account at this point, returning to it later, and move to the socio-philosophical account of modernity that unfolded in parallel.

The Socio-Philosophical Account of Modernity

The Standard Account: Individual Autonomy and Instrumental Mastery

As mentioned above, there is a standard theoretical understanding of modernity based on the key concepts of individual freedom and instrumental mastery. In this view, the combination of the commitment to these two principles defines what it means to be modern. Far from being arbitrary, this double commitment is seen to result from the radical search for the foundations on which to base human social life. There are two main authors and events that stand at the origins of philosophical modernity: on the one side, René Descartes and his *Discours de la méthode* (1637), which grounds the certainty of knowledge in the thinking subject alone; and on the other side, Thomas Hobbes and his *Leviathan* (1651), which grounds political order in individual human beings' interest in self-preservation. In both cases, preceding ways to reach certainty and political stability are criticized as speculative or unviable, and the individual human being is placed in the centre as the only possible source for such achievements. Freed from illegitimate constraints, this human being will make use of their capacity for reason to place knowledge and politics on firm grounds.

In this standard account, further on, the US Declaration of Independence (1776) and the French Revolution (1789), on the one side, and the Industrial Revolution (mid-eighteenth- to mid-nineteenth centuries), on the other, are considered evidence of the societally transformative effects of the new commitments. The political revolutions apply social contract theory, according to which a legitimate and stable political order arises from the agreement between the individual members of this polity. In turn, the Industrial Revolution applies the new forms of knowledge that systematic investigation of the laws of nature had provided to increase human mastery over nature.

Between the mid-nineteenth and the mid-twentieth centuries, as mentioned above, the assessment of these transformations became increasingly ambivalent. What we now know as critical social theory emphasized the negative consequences of building social orders on individual freedom and instrumental mastery. While Marx resolved the ambivalence by resorting to dialectical reasoning, Weber laid it bare, and Adorno and Horkheimer concluded negatively on the complete self-cancellation of the original promise of enhanced freedom and mastery. Across this entire critical tradition, however, the assumption that 'modern' societies were based on the principles of individual freedom and instrumental mastery was taken for granted.

Affirmative versions of such modernist thinking emerged gradually from the late nineteenth century onwards, and this with an increasing degree of formalism and rigour. Neoclassical economics from the 1890s, versions of analytical philosophy from the early twentieth century, and the revival of social contract theory with John Rawls's *Theory of Justice* (1971) are key examples of such developments. In many respects, rational choice theorizing with its explicit grounding on individuals and their rationality brings together those elements to form a social philosophy based on such modernist assumptions, which has spread across most social-science disciplines (Wagner, 2000). These affirmative versions often combine, though mostly implicitly, an idea of superior, because more clear, thinking and reasoning with the notion of social institutions being superior to others if they are arranged according to such reasoning. Thus, they support a triumphant interpretation of the history of modernity as the increasing commitment to individual freedom and instrumental rationality.

Two additional observations are in order before continuing our review of the socio-philosophical account. First, beyond the critical social theory tradition mentioned earlier, with its dialectics and ambiguities, other, mostly more recent forms of critical thinking tended to portray European societies as being straightforwardly shaped by the commitments to individual autonomy and instrumental mastery and having turned these principles into tools of domination by reserving autonomy to male Europeans and by employing an instrumental attitude also to other human beings, in particular subjects of colonial domination. Such approaches from feminism and postcolonial studies considerably widen the critical perspective. But they also create a very one-dimensional picture of European thinking and European societies.

Second, namely, individual autonomy and rational mastery never became the uncontested foundation of the European philosophy of modernity. In their time, obviously, Descartes and Hobbes were radical innovators, strongly deviating from commonly held views. At the end of the eighteenth century, true, the combination of freedom and reason had become the centrepiece of then-widespread Enlightenment thought. But widespread does not mean uncontested. To the contrary, intellectual opposition to such thinking arose in new forms. Among them, romanticism in the broad sense objected to the atomist version of individualism and the instrumentalist version of rationality, while remaining committed to the principles of freedom and reason, more widely understood. Thus, considering the combination of individual freedom and instrumental rationality as the core of the European philosophy of modernity is a caricature, portraying some features in a highly exaggerated way while omitting others.

Contextualizing the Socio-Philosophical Account of Modernity (1): The Other and the Divided Self

Rather than remaining within philosophical debates, though, we will continue our account by contextualizing them historically, as we did with the historico-sociological account before. A widespread view sees the philosophy of modernity, conceived in the wake of Descartes and Hobbes, as a European achievement that contributed to the global European superiority in the centuries to come. A contextual reading, however, does not support this triumphant view at all.

It is widely accepted that Descartes and Hobbes were searching for certainty, epistemic and political respectively. It is much less widely understood, however, that their search was motivated by the concern about prevailing uncertainty, about loss of certainty. Once one considers the political context of their writings, namely the period of the religious wars in Europe, this concern is easily understood (Toulmin, 1990 explicitly provides such a reasoning for Descartes; see Shapin and Schaffer, 1985 for Hobbes). In epistemic terms, the success of the Reformation in parts of Europe had destroyed the common cosmology on which knowledge had been based. In political terms, the consequence was that one could not rely any longer on shared values and principles. The profound doubts about having anything in common with others led Descartes and Hobbes to resort to the individual as the only source of certainty, in epistemic terms, and as the only immediate holder of rights, in political terms. Having taken this step, which seemed inevitable to them, they first of all had only displaced the problem. If all certainty and right resided in individuals, how would understanding others and acting in concert with others be possible? The capacity for reason was the answer to this question, thus establishing the combination of individuality and rationality as the new ground for epistemology and political philosophy, triggered by the profound crisis of the destruction of the earlier common ground.

There had been a precedent to the crisis of cosmology produced by the scission of Christianity. When the seafarers for the Spanish crown landed in what became known as America, they encountered people whom they had not expected and who were completely unknown to Europeans. Thus, the question as to how to interact with these people arose. To answer this question, one needed to determine whether they were to be considered as human beings and, if so, what followed from the fact that they were human beings. These questions were at the core of what became known as the Valladolid–Salamanca debates of 1550–1551 between Bartolomé de las Casas and Juan Ginés de Sepúlveda, during which Las Casas developed what can be seen as the first explicit formulation of abstract human rights. Like for Descartes and Hobbes a century later, the starting point was a novel situation for which existing concepts and understandings were insufficient. And similarly, new knowledge and certainty could only be established by referring to the human being itself, since no other commonality appeared to exist between the Native Americans and the Europeans. The 'colonial' origins of this new understanding have long been overlooked (see now Dussel, 2003), placing the beginnings of the philosophy of European modernity in the seventeenth century. But their far-reaching impact on an entirely new way of thinking is recognizable when, for instance, John Locke suggested in the *Second Treatise on Government* that 'in the beginning all the world was America'. The encounter with the Native Americans provided the experiential underpinnings for thinking the possibility of a social contract between individuals as the foundation of the modern polity.

Saying this does not mean downplaying the intellectual novelty created by Enlightenment thinkers. To resort to individuals and their rationality is a radical and unprecedented step in intellectual history. But the contextualization helps us recognize that this step should not be seen as an unequivocal breakthrough in solving fundamental problems of humanity, which sprang from great European minds. It was a response to novel and highly critical experiences that demanded explicit answers to questions that had never been posed before in fundamental terms. These new answers had a considerable impact on the ways in which basic questions of living together would be addressed in the future. But they were neither uncontested nor did they provide straightforwardly superior solutions.

Contextualizing the Socio-Philosophical Account of Modernity (2): The Misunderstood Rise of Freedom

This latter claim, though, is exactly what is suggested in the core understanding of modernity, as we presented it at the outset. The historical narrative that is used to support this claim starts at around 1800, when humanity is seen as exiting from self-incurred immaturity and societies as starting to be built on the principle of freedom. This principle is indeed increasingly enshrined in constitutions, which provide the basic laws of society and begin to emerge from some kind of social contract. Supposedly, these are the origins of what would later be called liberal-democratic societies. From a range of otherwise very different perspectives, this is still regarded as the beginning of the historical rise of freedom as a guiding principle of social organization (Honneth, 2011; Welzel, 2013).

Though it is not without validity, such a view considerably distorts the picture. As evidenced in the preceding presentation of the historico-sociological account, European societies deviated so strongly from this picture that their socio-philosophical interpretation cannot remain unaffected. On the one side, liberties were always limited to parts of the population and to certain expressions of freedom. And far from modernity just remaining 'incomplete', as Jürgen Habermas used to state, justifications of principle were explicitly provided for these restrictions of liberty across the whole region and the entire nineteenth century, even a considerable part of the twentieth century. At the same time, the so-called 'democratic revolution' did not just fail temporarily either. Rather, the conclusion of the revolutionary decades by 1815 was that democracy was explicitly rejected as untenable by the European – and even to a large extent by the North American – elites (Wagner, 2013).

Thus, a social philosophy of freedom is inadequate for interpreting the historical experience of modernity. This is even the case if such a philosophy includes an evolutionary component and suggests that freedom is not realized immediately but shapes the evolutionary trajectory of modernity, since it would impose a reading of history on a multitude of events many of which resist such interpretation. The proposal to see modernity as driven by a 'politics of liberation' (Dussel, 2003) opens the interpretative perspective more widely, but not sufficiently so.

How should one then deal with the nevertheless indubitable presence of a political imaginary of freedom and democracy in world history over the past two centuries?

The most promising avenue seems to be to indeed see these principles at work in political imagination (Castoriadis, 1989 and elsewhere; Arnason, 1989). But this imagination does not operate with the expectation of realizing these principles, which are far too abstract to guide expectations. Rather, it works under conditions of domination, which is characterized by the absence of possibilities for personal self-realization and collective self-determination. Thus, the guide to interpreting the political history of modernity is a notion of emancipation as aiming to overcome domination. Such a notion is distinct from one of liberation or democratization since it leaves interpretative space for a variety of outcomes of what successful emancipation could mean.

If one looks in this light at the historical experience of modernity, then one recognizes that emancipation has come to be predominantly interpreted as the achievement of equal rights, both individual and political rights. By the end of the Second World War, such equality was achieved in much of the 'West', and by the late twentieth century on much of the globe. But this current 'outcome' would be misinterpreted as a telos of political modernity. This becomes evident from ongoing disputes over that which was achieved. In terms of individual rights, there is an open debate about the relation between equality and the recognition of difference, emerging from feminism but also from claims about recognition of cultural communities. In terms of political rights, there is a time-honoured debate about the distinction between formal or procedural democracy, on the one hand, and substantive democracy, on the other. With regard to both aspects, these debates overlap with concerns about effective capacities for self-realization and self-determination, which are often seen to require economic or social conditions beyond formal equality (for more detail, see Wagner, 2017).

Contextualizing the Socio-Philosophical Account of Modernity (3): 'Modern Society' in One World Region

The misidentification of the achievement of formal equal freedom with the completion of the project of modernity is one key problem of the socio-philosophical account of modernity. Nevertheless, the fact that 'Western' societies begin after the Second World War to resemble the image that had been provided of modernity needs to be acknowledged. Such acknowledgement would open a debate about the place of formal equal freedom within the larger field of possible – and viable – interpretations of the modern commitment to autonomy (see Arnason, 2018, for reflections on this question).

The 'completion' of modernity also becomes an issue in the spatial sense, namely due to the fact that the term 'modern' had long been reserved for societies in the northwest of the globe. During the 1960s and 1970s, other societies were considered to be in the process of 'modernization and development', thus on their way to 'completing' modernity. Only recently has the term 'global modernity' come to be used. The recent transformation of modernity that entailed a reconsideration of what 'modernization' might mean under conditions of 'globalization' will be discussed in the subsequent section, thus relinking the historico-sociological with the socio-philosophical account of modernity. Before doing so, a conceptual issue needs to be addressed regarding what one might call the possibility of modernity in one world region (paraphrasing the time-honoured question of the possibility of 'socialism in one country').

This question would not emerge if indeed we could consider the trajectory of modernity as one of liberation. In such a reading, liberation could just occur earlier in some world regions than in others, but no conceptual problem would arise with subsequent liberation processes elsewhere. As discussed above, though, it is more appropriate to interpret the trajectory of modernity as one of struggles for emancipation, or to overcome domination, rather than as liberation. Such an understanding entails the possibility that domination in one world -region will be overcome – or, at least, altered and mitigated – by displacing (aspects of) the conflict between dominant and dominated groups elsewhere. This 'elsewhere' can be in another space on the globe or in another time, a time of the future.

An interpretation that assumes that those supposedly modern societies in which formal equality reigned after the Second World War had reached this accomplishment largely by such displacement has considerable plausibility. Those societies combined equal rights to political participation and relatively low degrees of social inequality with relative affluence and high levels of industrialization. Industrialization was supposed to entail increasing mastery of nature, but today we have come to recognize that this supposed mastery was in fact a form of exploitation of nature the consequences of which have an impact on the living conditions for human beings on the earth, both due to resource depletion and– more urgently an issue than ever – due to climate change. Thus, north-western societies have 'mortgaged the future', as an English expression has it. They have been 'buying time' (Streeck, 2013), but have been doing so on credit, not knowing whether there will be an occasion to reimburse the loan. In parallel, those societies have largely closed their borders to people from other parts of the world, or at least opened them in only very restrictive ways, thus creating and maintaining a differential of affluence and well-being to their outside. They have done so historically through outright colonial domination, depriving other people of their right to self-determination. More recently, they have continued to do so through their economic and political power of setting the terms of trade in their own favour, sometimes called neocolonial domination. Regarded in this light, that which is often seen as a success of emancipatory social movements, in particular the workers' and the women's movement in the north-west, needs to be understood at the same time as a displacement of lines of conflict from the domestic to the global arena (Mota and Wagner, 2019). A recent study calls those societies 'externalization societies', using the economic term for acquiring and securing benefits by imposing the cost on accounts external to one's own 'business' (Lessenich, 2016; Mota and Wagner, 2018).

Transformations of Modernity: The Past Half-Century

With these observations, we have pushed the socio-philosophical account somewhat further in time than the historico-sociological account, which we had left hanging in the middle of the twentieth century, and have also started to reconnect the two. These two tasks will be further pursued by a concluding look at the most recent past and, in this context, by reflections on the logic of transformations of modernity.

By the beginning of the 1970s, the theory of modernity seemed to have reached its apogee in the most coherent formulations that had ever been provided. The sociological version was offered by Talcott Parsons in his *System of Modern Societies* of 1971; and the political theory of modernity was crowned by John Rawls's *Theory of Justice* of the same year. In contrast to earlier attempts, these were indeed portraits of modernity, suggesting that a stable state had been reached, or at least could be coherently outlined. Both the concern with potentially overwhelming dynamics, which had marked the theorization of modernity during the nineteenth century, and the worry about fragility and instability at the core of modern arrangements which was characteristic of mid-twentieth-century diagnoses, seemed to have been laid to rest. But even though sociology and political theory would discuss these works for decades to come, a transformation of modernity was already underway that would alter the terms of debate. The updated restating of modernity's strongest claims by Parsons and Rawls was indeed closely followed by Lyotard's announcement of the postmodern condition, mentioned at the outset.

Logic of Transformations

In the wake of Lyotard's report, a sociological debate ensued that by now can be seen as having led to wide consensus about the notion that modernity undergoes transformations, thus is not a single and superior form of sociopolitical organization, and that one major such transformation started happening from the 1960s and 1970s onwards. There is much less agreement about the ways to investigate and identify such transformations. Methods include survey research about values and orientations, featuring the thesis that 'postmaterial' values arise once material needs are largely satisfied, initially launched by Ronald Inglehart; as well as institutional analysis, focusing on the decline of the nation state and the extension of practices beyond institutional boundaries. Neither of these approaches is incompatible with an emphasis on changing societal self-understandings, but both of them have a more narrow focus. Furthermore, there is very little explicit debate about the dynamics behind transformations of modernity in either of them. Both appear to resort to technical change in the last instance, be it by leading to a higher satisfaction of material needs or be it through the 'time-space compression' (David Harvey, 1996) achieved by new technologies, in recent decades particularly in information and communication technologies. At the same time, they are little suited to capturing varieties of interpretations of modernity. Indicator-based analysis lends itself more to recognizing trends than to making distinctions of category. Proponents of such approaches, therefore, tend to operate within a paradigm of neo-modernization rather than of variety of modernity (see, e.g., Schmidt, 2014). Similarly, institutional analysis is inclined to overestimate convergence, at least in our time in which, for instance, 'varieties of capitalism' (Hall and Soskice, 2000) are more systematically explored than alternatives to capitalism.

In contrast, the approach to modernity as a societal self-understanding is based on the fundamental insight into the openness to interpretation of the modern commitment to autonomy. It considers every existing 'modern' sociopolitical constellation as a specific interpretation of this commitment rather than its realization. Any such interpretation can be contested from the angle of other possible interpretations. A 'crisis' of modernity arises when such contestation is widely seen as persuasive, indicated by the perception that a sociopolitical constellation fails to satisfactorily fulfil its functions and/or normative commitments. It is triggered by 'critique' that unveils and denounces such shortcomings, leading to mobilizations that potentially bring about a social transformation. These concepts go back to Reinhart Koselleck's early works on reform in nineteenth-century Prussia, later to be enhanced by his historiography of concepts. They have been applied to transformations of modernity by Wagner (1994; 2010) and systematically employed for transformations of capitalism by Boltanski and Chiapello (1999). To identify a crisis, it is certainly not sufficient to merely identify critical discourses. Rather, those discourses would need to be analysed, on the one hand, with regard to the kind of critique they raise, namely whether they consider a sociopolitical institution falling short of its explicit purpose or regard it as pursuing an inadequate purpose (see Boltanski, 2009). And thus, on the other hand, the critical discourses would also need to be confronted with the sociopolitical constellation they are addressing, to be analysed through more standard sociological analysis. In other words, the approach to modernity as a societal self-understanding is not to be pursued as an alternative to institutional or indicator-based analysis, but as a frame into which to insert the latter.

Globalization of Modernity

The broad sociological debate about the exit from 'organized modernity' (Wagner, 1994) that was led from the mid-1980s through the 1990s had two components that remained far too little connected. On the one hand, efforts were made to understand what was conceived as a transformation of Western modernity (for a recent contribution, see Reckwitz, 2017). On the other hand, it was recognized that modernity was much less centred on the Western experience than had mostly been assumed and that a broadening both of the concept and of historical-comparative investigation was required. This latter strand was opened by Shmuel Eisenstadt's conceptualization of 'multiple modernities' (Eisenstadt, 2000), being inspired by Weber's comparative sociology of world religions and elaborating a broad-ranged interpretative analysis of societal self-understandings (without using the term). This approach yielded important analyses of Eurasian societies, but tended to overestimate both the long-term cultural continuity and internal homogeneity of the classical civilizations (for a most perceptive discussion, see Arnason, 2003). Accordingly, subsequent steps were to broaden the comparative perspective by including societies that had emerged from the 'colonial encounter' (Talal Asad, 1973), and that thus could not possibly be analysed in terms of continuity and homogeneity (for instance, Domingues, 2008; Larrain, 2000), and to analyse 'Old World' societies in terms of transformations rather than interpretative continuity (for instance, Kaya, 2004; Mazlovskiy, 2018).

This whole comparative approach to varieties of modernity, including quite a range of different perspectives, sat uneasily with the mainstream sociological debate about 'globalization' and 'individualization' of the 1990s, to which it was to some extent also a response (Karagiannis and Wagner, 2007). This mainstream debate took account of the transformation of modernity from the 1970s onwards and the challenges to the theory of 'modern society', but it returned to reasoning in terms of long-term historical trends with evolutionary implications, without being overly concerned with operationalization (for an early critique of the standard sociology of social change, see Boudon, 1984, ch. 1). In turn, the comparative approach may be said to have been rather unconcerned about the problem of the 'unit of analysis', assuming that 'societies' can still be analysed as being rather closed to the outside and thus separate from each other, as was typical of the period in which, as regards Europe, societies coincided with the boundaries of nation states due to the 'nationalisation of European societies' (Noiriel, 1991).

The connection between the approaches would need to be made through an explicit consideration of the degrees of connectedness of social relations across the globe. While there has been some debate about 'waves of globalization' and their reversals, thus placing the current constellation in historical context, the ways in which degrees of connectedness enable and constrain action in particular world regions have rarely been analysed in detail (but see Osterhammel, 2008; and also Mota and Wagner, 2019). From such an angle, one can recognize how what has been discussed as a recent major transformation of modernity is indeed conditioned by an intensification of connectedness, leading to what some call 'global modernity' (Bringel and Domingues, 2015; Domingues, 2012; see also Arjomand, 2014; and Arjomand and Reis, 2014). In connection with the rising field of transnational history or *histoire croisée*, the term 'entangled modernity' (Randeria, 1999) has been proposed, allowing us to link comparative analyses with globalizing analyses without merging the one into the other (see also Dlamini, Mota, and Wagner, 2016). Thus, the analysis of the recent major transformation of modernity, brought about in a variety of ways in the different world regions, could lead over into an understanding of the emergence of a novel social formation, which has a global range in many respects, but keeps being marked by differences in the interpretations of modernity and struggles over such interpretations.

References

Arendt, Hannah. 1951. *The Origins of Totalitarianism*. New York: Schocken.

Arjomand, Said (ed.). 2014. *Social Theory and Regional Studies in the Global Age*. Stony Brook, NY: SUNY Press.

Arjomand, Said, and Elisa Reis (eds.). 2014. *Worlds of Difference*. London: Sage (ISA series 'SAGE Studies in International Sociology').

Arnason, Johann. 1989. 'The Imaginary Institution of Modernity.' *Revue européenne des sciences sociales* 27(86): 323–337.

2003. *Civilizations in Dispute*. Leiden: Brill.

2018. 'Questioning Progress: Retreat, Revision or Revival?' *Social Imaginaries* 4(2): 171–189.

Asad, Talal (ed.). 1973. *Anthropology and the Colonial Encounter*. Reading, UK: Ithaca Press.

Bayly, C. A. 2004. *The Birth of the Modern World, 1780–1914*. Oxford, UK: Blackwell.

Beck, Ulrich. 1986. *Risikogesellschaft*, Frankfurt am Main: Suhrkamp.

Boltanski, Luc. 2009. *De la critique*. Paris: Gallimard.

Boltanski, Luc, and Eve Chiapello. 1999. *Le nouvel esprit du capitalisme*. Paris: Gallimard.

Boudon, Raymond. 1984. *La Place du désordre*. Paris: PUF.

Bringel, Breno, and José Mauricio Domingues (eds.). 2015. *Global Modernity and Social Contestation*. London: Sage (ISA series 'SAGE Studies in International Sociology').

Castoriadis, Cornelius. 1989. 'Fait et à faire.' In Giovanni Busini et al. (eds.), *Autonomie et autotransformation de la société*. Geneva: Droz.

Darwin, John. 2007. *After Tamerlane: The Rise and Fall of Global Empires, 1400–2000*. London: Allen Lane.

Dlamini, Jacob, Aurea Mota, and Peter Wagner (eds.). 2016. *Trajectories of Modernity: Towards a New Historical-Comparative Sociology*. Special issue of *Social Imaginaries* 2(2).

Domingues, José Mauricio. 2008. *Latin America and Contemporary Modernity*. London: Routledge.

2012. *Global Modernity, Development, and Contemporary Civilization*. London: Routledge.

Dussel, Enrique. 2003. *Política de la liberación*. Madrid: Trotta.

Eisenstadt, Shmuel N. 2000. 'Multiple Modernities.' *Daedalus* 129(1): 1–29.

Habermas, Jürgen. 1981. *Theorie des kommunikativen Handelns*. Frankfurt am Main: Suhrkamp.

1985. *Der philosophische Diskurs der Moderne*. Frankfurt am Main: Suhrkamp.

Hall, Peter A., and David Soskice (eds.). 2000. *Varieties of Capitalism*. Oxford, UK: Oxford University Press.

Halperin, Sandra. 2004. *War and Modern Europe*. Cambridge, UK: Cambridge University Press.

Harvey, David. 1996. *Justice, Nature, and the Geography of Difference*. Malden, MA: Blackwell.

Honneth, Axel. 2011. *Das Recht der Freiheit*. Berlin: Suhrkamp.

Karagiannis, Nathalie. 2016. 'Democratic Surplus and Democracy-in-Failing: On Ancient and Modern Self-Cancellation of Democracy.' In Gerard Rosich and Peter Wagner (eds.), *The Trouble with Democracy*. Edinburgh: Edinburgh University Press.

Karagiannis, Nathalie, and Peter Wagner (eds.). 2007. *Varieties of World-Making: Beyond Globalization*. Liverpool, UK: Liverpool University Press.

Kaya, Ibrahim. 2004. *Social Theory and Later Modernities: The Turkish Experience*. Liverpool, UK: Liverpool University Press.

Koselleck, Reinhart. 1979. *Vergangene Zukunft*. Frankfurt am Main: Suhrkamp.

Larrain, Jorge. 2000. *Identity and Modernity in Latin America*. Cambridge, UK: Polity.

Lessenich, Stephan. 2016. *Neben uns die Sintflut. Die Externalisierungsgesellschaft und ihr Preis*. Munich: Hanser.

Lyotard, Jean-François. 1979. *La Condition postmoderne*. Paris: Minuit.

Mannheim, Karl. 1940 [1935]. *Man and Society in an Age of Reconstruction*. London: Routledge.

Mazlovskiy, Mikhail. 2018. 'Russia against Europe: A Clash of Civilizations?' *European Journal of Social Theory.* https://doi.org/10.1177/1368431018768623.

Mayer, Arno. 1981. *The Persistence of the Old Regime.* Princeton, NJ: Princeton University Press.

Mishima, Kenichi. 2016. 'The Long Shadow of European Self-Interpretation in Another Modernity.' *Social Imaginaries* 2(2): 183–197.

Mota, Aurea, and Peter Wagner. 2018. 'The Amazon, the Rhino and the Blue Sky over the Ruhr: Ecology and Politics in the Current Global Context.' *Changing Societies and Personalities* 2(4): 6–21.

2019. *Collective Action and Political Transformations: The Entangled Experiences of Brazil, South Africa and Europe.* Edinburgh: Edinburgh University Press.

Noiriel, Gérard. 1991. *La tyrannie du national.* Paris: Calmann-Lévy.

Osterhammel, Jürgen. 2008. *Die Verwandlung der Welt.* Munich: Beck.

Parsons, Talcott. 1971. *The System of Modern Societies.* Englewood Cliffs, NJ: Prentice-Hall.

Polanyi, Karl. 1944. *The Great Transformation.* New York, NY: Farrar and Rinehart.

Pomeranz, Kenneth. 2000. *The Great Divergence.* Princeton, NJ: Princeton University Press.

Randeria, Shalini. 1999. 'Geteilte Geschichte und verwobene Moderne.' In J. Rüsen, H. Leitgeb, and N. Jegelka (eds.), *Zukunftsentwürfe. Ideen für eine Kultur der Veränderung.* Frankfurt am Main: Campus.

Rawls, John. 1971. *A Theory of Justice.* Cambridge, MA: Harvard University Press.

Reckwitz, Andreas. 2017. *Die Gesellschaft der Singularitäten.* Frankfurt am Main: Suhrkamp.

Rostow, W. W. 1971. *The Stages of Economic Growth: A Non-Communist Manifesto*, 2nd ed. Cambridge, UK: Cambridge University Press.

Schmidt, Volker H. 2014. *Global Modernity.* London: Palgrave Macmillan.

Shapin, Steven, and Simon Schaffer. 1985. *Leviathan and the Air-Pump.* Princeton, NJ: Princeton University Press.

Stråth, Bo. 2016. *Europe's Utopias of Peace.* London: Bloomsbury.

Stråth, Bo, and Peter Wagner. 2017. *European Modernity: A Global Approach.* London: Bloomsbury.

Streeck, Wolfgang. 2013. *Gekaufte Zeit.* Berlin: Suhrkamp.

Toulmin, Steven. 1990. *Cosmopolis: The Hidden Agenda of Modernity.* Chicago, IL: The University of Chicago Press.

Wagner, Peter. 1994. *A Sociology of Modernity.* London: Routledge.

2000. 'The Bird in Hand: Rational Choice as the Default Mode of Social Theorising.' In Margaret Archer and Jonathan Tritter (eds.), *Challenging Rational Choice* (pp. 19–35). London: Routledge.

2010. 'Successive Modernities and the Idea of Progress.' *Distinktion: Scandinavian Journal for Social Theory* 21 (October): 9–24.

2013. 'Transformations of Democracy: Towards a History of Political Thought in Long-Term Perspective.' In Johann P. Arnason, Kurt Raaflaub, and Peter Wagner (eds.), *The Greek Polis and the Invention of Democracy: A Politico-Cultural Transformation and Its Interpretations* (pp. 47–68). Oxford, UK: Blackwell.

2014. 'Europe and the Sociology of Modernity.' In Alexandros-Andreas Kyrtsis and Sokratis Koniordis (eds.), *Handbook of European Sociology.* London: Routledge.

2015. 'Autonomy in History: Teleology in Nineteenth-Century European Social and Political Thought.' In Dipesh Chakrabarty, Sanjay Subrahmanjan and

Henning Trüper (eds.), *Historical Teleologies in the Modern World*. London: Bloomsbury.

2017. 'The Question of Freedom: Social and Political Progress under Conditions of Modernity.' *Revue internationale de philosophie* 3(281): 281–297.

Welzel, Christian. 2013. *Freedom Rising: Human Empowerment and the Quest for Emancipation*. Cambridge, UK: Cambridge University Press.

9 Realism

Timothy Rutzou

Few positions in philosophy or social theory have drawn more controversy than realism. It is generally perceived that realism is a naïve if not completely indefensible position that rests upon outdated or dogmatic claims about the nature of reality (perhaps most famously Rorty, 1979). With various degrees of hostility, its critics suggest that realism ignores epistemology, sidelines interpretation, neglects language and discourse, relies on outdated notions of truth, or fails to realize the extent to which the "out there" is constructed through practice (Latour and Woolgar, 1986; Law, 2004; Martin, 2014; Reed, 2011). And yet, realism is a position that has received considerable attention and, in spite of the protests to the contrary, has been particularly attentive to the problematics raised by its critics. Far from being naïve, realism has, overwhelmingly, been critical.

As a distinct position in social theory, realism began to gain shape in the 1970s in the wake of the discussions concerning the nature of scientific explanation and, in particular, the scientific relativism introduced by Thomas Kuhn, Paul Feyerabend, and the linguistic turn. The shaking of the philosophical foundations of scientific knowledge initiated by these philosophical and sociological examinations of scientific knowledge prompted a suitably philosophical response in social theory, directed toward problems of ontology and epistemology from a generation of particularly theoretically inclined scholars who proceeded to develop and apply realist theories, concepts, and research across a large number of subfields in social theory. The impact of this realist turn became quickly apparent and gained steam in the 1980s and 1990s alongside the rise of "postmodernism" and "post-structuralism," prompting a series of responses, discussions, and debates about the viability or infeasibility of realism (e.g. Latour, 1999; Potter, 1997; Shotter, 1996), including recent updates (e.g. Martin, 2014; Reed, 2011).

In spite of the barrage of criticism directed its way, realism can be found prominently defended across social theory; in the philosophy of social science (Benton, 1977; Benton and Craib, 2010; Roy Bhaskar, 1998 [1979]; Rom Harré, 1979; Keat and Urry, 1975; Little, 2016; Manicas, 1987, 2006; Putnam and Conant, 1990; Searle, 1995), "continental" philosophy (DeLanda, 2006, 2016; Frost and Coole, 2010; Harman, 2016), sociology (Archer, 1995; Danermark et al., 1997; Sayer, 2010 [1984]), the sociology and philosophy of religion (Schillbrack, 2014; Smith, 2017), ethnography (Decoteau, 2017; Fine, 1999; Fine and Hallett, 2014; Rees and Gatenby, 2014), anthropology (Graeber, 2015), feminist theory (Assiter, 1996; Haslanger, 2012), comparative historical studies (Gorski, 2008; Steinmetz, 1998, 2003), international relations (Wendt, 1999; Wight, 2006), political theory (Callinicos, 2006; Shapiro, 2005; Wright, 1994), discourse analysis (Fairclough, 1995), education (Scott, 2000), literary criticism (Norris, 1985, 1995), economics (Lawson, 1997, 2003), law (Norrie, 1993), management and organization studies (Ackroyd and Fleetwood, 2000; Edwards, O'Mahoney, and Vincent, 2014), and policy studies (Pawson, 2006, 2013; Pawson and Tilley, 1997). Many of these positions have built upon the early work of Rom Harré, Roy Bhaskar, Margaret Archer, and Andrew Sayer who (alongside others) collectively established the most organized and enduring platform for realism in social theory under the banner "critical realism," complete with its own international organization, journal, and research centers.[1] Other traditions of realism emerged or converged from discussions within Marxism and critical theory about the role of science, the nature of explanation, and the place of the extra-discursive within social analysis (Callinicos, 2006; Outhwaite, 1987; Porpora, 1993; Wright, 1994). Among other traditions is one that is influenced by a pragmatist orientation (Dreyfus and Taylor, 2015; Manicas, 2006; Putnam, 1978; Putnum and Connant, 1990; Shapiro, 2005). Most of these positions draw heavily from philosophy and the philosophy of science in particular and are heavily invested in debates about the implications of ontology and epistemology, especially the nature of causal explanation.

At least one of the problems when it comes to realism is the long and complicated philosophical history of the term and its use across different disciplines, which burdens the name itself with considerable historical baggage (Williams, 1983: 257). Throughout history realism has been counterpoised against nominalism to defend the objective existence of universals and essences, against idealism to defend the objective existence of the material world, against appearance to defend the existence of underlying structures, against romanticism in art to defend the portrayal of real-world people and situations, against ideology to defend science, and against relativism and social construction to defend truth. Insofar as this history weighs like a nightmare, it is perhaps not surprising then that there has been so much controversy and misapprehension surrounding realism.

It could easily be said that realism is not what many people think it is, that it is weighed down by the baggage of past debates, and that this misconception prevents realism from getting a just hearing or a just critique. It is all too quickly discussed in monochromatic and monolithic terms that rely upon lazy caricatures. In general, the nature of this caricature would suggest that all realism involves a god-trick, a foundationalism that lays hold of an Archimedean standpoint to claim a privileged access to the one and only "Reality" and the one and only "Truth," when generally realists explicitly reject such claims, arguing against foundationalism and basing realism on the fallibility rather than the certainty of knowledge (Sayer, 2000: 1). While it is often presented as a single coherent position, realism is more truly a variety of claims ranging from the more general philosophical affirmation of the mind-independent existence of reality, through to positions that emphasize the historical and material dimension of social reality, through to the epistemological position that suggests the aim of science is to provide explanations of phenomena which *correspond* to reality, and can and should be judged accordingly. Within its broad banner, some of the positions that lay claim to realism emphasize ontology and are more philosophical by nature, while others are more invested in empirical work and closely follow the lead of the natural sciences, being timid or restrained about ontological discourse: following the precept "if ontology, then make the least of it." In short, realism comes in more than one form and represents a spectrum of claims of different strength. At the modest end realism is concern with more general assertions about ontology, through to stronger positions that some statements in certain domains are more or less truth-apt, while the stronger form would assert that ontology and realism are grounded in categories that are not arbitrary but cut reality at the joints.

The Mind-Independent Existence of Reality

In what follows I will discuss and hopefully render clear the contours and logic of a position in social theory that continually (and perhaps necessarily) haunts the field. The chief concern of this essay will be delineating what exactly realism is, how it has been used, what it implies, its themes and genres, and why it has drawn considerable heat.

At its core, I want to propose that the best way to understand realism in social theory is by reference to claims about the mind-independent existence of reality. Any position that orients itself toward or draws meaning or significance from the existence of a mind-independent reality can be fairly labeled realism. This can be said to be the basic foundational claim and defining feature of realism and the point which forms the anchor for all the claims and positions made within realism concerning the nature of ontology, epistemology, methodology, and science. In whatever form, realism always refers back to the mind-independent existence of reality as the necessary grounding thesis for a theoretical position.

There is, of course, something inherently puzzling about a theoretical position that stakes its claim on the mind-independent existence of reality and its independence from our conceptions of it. Kant called it the scandal of philosophy that there was no cogent proof of the existence of the external world, while Heidegger called it the scandal of philosophy that such proofs should be needed in the first place, and worse, that such proofs should be attempted again and again. A similar argument could be made about realism in social theory. In responding to his critics Bruno Latour (1999) reflects this bewilderment when confronted with the question (and accusation!) "Do you believe in reality?" The attempt to elicit a commitment or condemn ambivalence to the mind-independent existence of reality is an odd performance; is a belief in reality something that needs to be affirmed, let alone proved?

Similarly, or in contrast, it might be argued that most social science operates within a tacitly realist framework which makes "realism" a redundant position. There are few social theorists who would deny that at some level social science is concerned with uncovering social "realities" from patterns of behavior to structures of oppression, whether these are explicitly constructed in "realist" terms or not. Few would deny that much of the social world exists independently from our understanding. Few would deny that there is more to the social than language or discourse. When placed in such terms, the core observations and implications of realism seem obvious and perhaps even prosaic, making realist claims seem naïve, redundant, or ridiculous prima facie. What is added by claiming the mantle "real"? The realist claim is that these seemingly inane observations have important and profound theoretical consequences in establishing the basis of a necessary meta-theoretical platform for social theorizing when it comes to both empirical and conceptual work. The mind-independent existence of reality becomes a crucial regulative ideal for social theory and without this explicit basis, so the realist argues, social theory is liable to fall into the trappings of reductionisms of one sort or another.

By its nature the claim to the mind-independent existence of reality can be understood as a "reactive" gesture: realism is always a response. The appeal to the mind-independent existence of reality occurs against a background in which realism or reality has come under question in one form or another. Indeed, both historically and substantively, realism can be seen as a corrective against relativism. While many of the discussions within realism are concerned with empiricism and positivism, substantively and historically realism as a position gains steam as a critique against the crisis caused by the emergence of some form of epistemological relativism, generally characterized by positions that sideline ontology or deny the possibility of objective knowledge or truth – in other words, access to the mind-independent existence of reality. Realist arguments target both "irrealism," which is apathetic to the mind-independent existence of reality in favor of epistemic pluralism, and "anti-realism," which is critical of the possibility of realism *tout court*. These take on two prototypical forms; "positivism," which asserts that knowledge is achieved through inductive warrant and empirical generalizations (or particular forms of phenomen-ology), which deny the possibility of ontology and reduce reality to human "obser-vation"; and "social constructionism," a cluster term encompassing interpretivism, neo-Kantianism, hermeneutics, post-structuralism, and postmodernism, which are seen to emphasize perspectivism, interpretation, or discourse without objectivity or an "outside," and in doing so reduce the world to an array of discourses and interpretations. If we understand realism as a regulative ideal that operates reactively or as a response to relativism, the appeal to the mind-independent existence of reality functions as a coded shortcut to short-circuit positions that are perceived to reduce reality (or our access to reality) to one dimension (notably empiricism or idealism).

As a corrective, realism presents itself as offering a third way or *via media* between empiricism on the one hand and the various forms of relativism on the other, taking on the insights of both while avoiding their excesses, and it does so characteristically by resituating these positions vis-à-vis the mind-independent exis-tence of reality. Exactly what this means takes on different expressions, with the relationship between realism and social constructionism being perhaps the most contested boundary within realism (see Elder-Vass, 2012; Haslanger, 2012; Sayer, 2000; Searle, 1995). But, broadly construed, as a response realism can be understood as a position that eschews global claims about empiricism or construction and focuses upon embodied and situated knowledges, concrete context, materiality, causal complexity, and social structures, while simultaneously revindicating the place of ontology and social metaphysics (c.f. Haslanger, 2012: 197).

This gesture provides realism with a characteristic and seemingly contradictory movement that simultaneously moves to the most abstract spheres of philosophy to discussions about the nature of being (ontology), while also orienting itself toward concrete contextual analysis. In placing a strong emphasis on the importance of ontology, realism draws its coherence as a position by way of orientation to ontological structures, being critically attentive to the referents contained within theoretical positions, and attending to what is being presupposed, signified, or implied by a theory. And yet, alongside this ontological motion is a movement placing firm emphasis upon the explanation of historical and contextual concrete reality (Jessop, 2015, see also Reed, 2011). While the gesture appears contradictory, one operates in service of the other, with ontology paving the way or clearing a path for contextual analysis. In both cases the orientation is toward uncovering the structures of reality.

If this can be understood as the substantive orientation generated by the mind-independent existence of reality, it becomes imperative to see realism as comprised of not one but two related-but-separate theses concerning the mind-independent existence of reality, which are often combined or conflated, sowing further confusion as a result. While all realism gains its force by orienting itself to the mind-independent existence of reality, there are two distinct but related theses: an ontological thesis and an epistemological thesis. The ontological thesis simply states that there exists a mind-independent reality that is separate from our representations. This operates as a regulative ideal that revindicates the importance of ontology as a necessary theoretical enterprise and a limit on one-dimensional constructions of reality. In other words, the ontological thesis is best understood as a means of invoking a degree of priority or fundamentality to matters of ontology.

The epistemological thesis builds on this and suggests that theories, if true, need to be understood and judged by their approximate truth to the mind-independent existence of reality; that is to say, realism is concerned with statements or models that relate to some reality that exists independently of our knowledge, but does so in such a way that that reality renders each statement not only warranted but determinately true or false (c.f. Dummett, 1982). The epistemological thesis is therefore best understood as a claim about how social facts can be grounded, examined, and justified in terms of warrant, adequacy, or truth. While this often entails a correspondence theory of truth (Little, 2016; Searle, 1995), this is not necessarily the case (e.g. Bhaskar, 2008 [1975]) with many realists advocating a more pragmatic criterion of truth (most notably Dreyfus and Taylor, 2015).

The Ontological Thesis

To say the mind-independent existence of reality is a means of invoking a degree of priority or fundamentality to ontology is at one level simply to highlight that all forms of social inquiry rest on beliefs about what counts as an explanation of a social phenomenon and what makes up the social world. As such, ontology requires a degree of priority within theory. Social objects are always already described and given functions and properties that create background conditions that are taken for granted by any social theory or explanation. These form the ontological conditions of possibility that makes a theory or an explanation intelligible or meaningful by laying the ontological ground rules of a theory, or in other words by asking what the world must be like for this theory to hold true.

At the very least theories have minimal social references that presuppose a social context in which certain actors, actions, behaviors, beliefs, contexts, and structures are given particular form and significance. These may be thick or thin concepts, or posit general or specific types of "things," but nevertheless theories presuppose or entail particular accounts, propositions, or models about the social world. At a very crude level, to say person is a slave is to presuppose a certain type of social order, just as the cashing of a check implies a banking order, money, and rules of lending and borrowing (Manicas, 1987: 271; Sayer, 2000: 18; Searle, 1995). But this not only extends to accounts of particular social institutions and forms of life, but to philosophical definitions about the nature of structures, agents, and causation, which may not presuppose or entail any particular propositions directly. What makes capitalism capitalism? Racism racism? What gives the Supreme Court its powers? These are ontological questions: ones which bear and entail empirical surveying, but ontological nevertheless.

This logic applies equally to methodologies. As an approach to studying social phenomena, methodological individualism makes certain assumptions or presuppositions about the social world (ontological individualism) that make methodological individualism plausible for Friedrich Hayek, while simultaneously making Durkheim react by claiming that "every time that a social phenomenon is directly explained by a psychological phenomenon, we may be sure that the explanation is false" (Durkheim cited in Lukes, 1968: 124). Similarly, a mechanism-based account of causal explanation creates a very different background to the social world than accounts that define causality in terms of regularities or laws without inherently, or rather without directly, affecting particular social theories (Bhaskar, 2008 [1975], see also Hedström and Ylikoski, 2010). Background conditions can therefore be understood as non-intentional or pre-intentional theoretical conditions that frame social theories (Searle, 1995). These framings form the reference points of an ontological landscape in which a social theory operates, a broader "picture" of reality that is taken for granted in the course of theorizing, often tacitly and unintentionally, and that necessarily structures descriptions, understanding, and explanation. Within this landscape certain types of objects will seem normal, and as such can be understood as constituting ontological norms imbedded in our research or theorizing that will either resonate and harmonize with compatible background assumptions in other theories or generate discord and dissonance. In any case, certain ontological landscapes are taken for granted.[2]

In this ontological mode realism, as many have suggested, is not a general or a specific theory about social entities or phenomenon (Archer, 1995; Manicas, 2006). As an ontological thesis, neither is it a theory of truth, language, semantics, or knowledge, let alone one advocating a view from nowhere. Insofar as it is ontological, it implicitly has a relatively open stance toward epistemology and varieties of realism based on the ontological thesis are compatible with multiple epistemic traditions (Outhwaite, 1987; Searle, 1995). The appeal to the mind-independent existence of reality does not inherently (or directly) affirm the reality of anything in particular; it is the philosophical and meta-theoretical view that there is a way that things are that is independent from human representation and as such realism does not say *what* things are in fact, but simply that *there is a way* that they are (Searle, 1995: 155). These can be understood as framing principles, background conditions, or landscapes, but they are characterized by assertions or impressions, implicit or explicit, about the nature of mind-independent reality. They are not inherently built from philosophical argument alone, but are built from, implied by, and extended from, empirical social research (Kaidesoja, 2015).

As an ontological thesis it is clear, then, that one can be a realist about the existence of particular things and not others. Moreover this is necessarily the case. Methodological individualism may be necessarily tied to an account of ontological individualism, but it is not necessary for anyone to be a methodological or ontological individualist, let alone for it to be a consistent or tenable thesis, or one that has empirical warrant (Lukes, 1968). Furthermore, while someone may have a general inclination toward realistic views within social theory or about the existence of particular ontological entities, there is arguably no coherent philosophical position which consists in being an ontological realist *tout court,* although there are inconsistent positions (Dummett, 1982). At the very minimum, realism then can be held to involve an existential commitment to the mind-independent existence of reality as an ontological project, an orientation to "reality," and a constraint on theoretical inquiry holding that some realities exist independently of our knowledge. Insofar as we are only concerned here with ontology, we can suggest that while the affirmation of particular realities may lend warrant to a theory, or be a necessary presupposition or implication for a theory, this does not inherently entail whether we know, or can know, the truth-value of it.

This has a further implication. The mind-independent existence of reality also suggests that a large part of reality does not depend upon human intentionality in any shape. The "real world" is indifferent to how we describe it and remains, in some respects, a "brute" fact (Searle, 1995: 163). This is certainly true of the natural world. The sheer existence of a physical object such as a molecule or a stone does not depend on human activity for its existence and is itself largely unaffected in its *intrinsic* existence by the attitudes or descriptions of observers or users. It has a mass, chemical structure, and composition granting it a certain degree of "objectivity" that secures the possibility of scientific knowledge. As the philosophy-of-science tradition has been increasingly sympathetic toward forms of scientific and structural realism as a means of accounting for the success of the natural sciences (Bhaskar, 2008 [1975]; Harré, 1979; Psillos, 1999; Putnam, 1978), this debate and its contours plays an important role within realism concerning the extent of the possible analogy between realism in natural science and realism in the social sciences, often called the problem of naturalism (see Bhaskar, 1979).

Adopting a slavishly "brute" approach to realism is significantly more difficult when it comes to objects in the social world, and creates a barrier to any strong correlation between natural science and social science (Bhaskar, 1998 [1979]; Little, 2016). Unlike their counterparts in the natural world, social objects (such as money, property, and economies) are generally dependent for their existence upon human activity and are affected by human intentionality. Without constant activity to maintain those structures, even if that activity is non-intentional, unintentional, or accidental, many "social realities" would simply cease to exist. Nevertheless, while these realities are dependent upon human activity, there is a sense in which they become relatively autonomous from human activity and have causal affects upon human behavior. People adjust themselves to social structures, and not necessarily consciously or intentionally. Examples of this can be seen in Marx's analysis of commodity fetishism and in Durkheim who, while often aligned with positivism, famously suggests that the social world is made up of social facts that have the special characteristic of "existing outside of individuals." As such, within many realist discourses, reality is not simply something that is presupposed by theories but is also couched in terms that draw on the language of resistance and sometimes external compulsion or causal efficacy, often cashed out in terms of the causal criterion of reality: if it has an effect it is real. Accordingly, realism asserts the mind-independent existence of reality (including the social world) has many features that do not directly depend on the attitudes of observers or users, but exist relative to or outside the intentionality of agents (as individuals or collectives), and this often takes on a causal dimension. This both serves as a check to unconstrained theorizing and provides an orientation to social theory (Searle, 1995: 10).

Causal Realism: Causal Structures and Generative Mechanisms

Front and center, then, in most realist discussions are causation and explanation (Bhaskar, 2008 [1975]; Danermark et al., 1997; Sayer, 2010 [1984]; Steinmetz, 1998). One of the crucial implications drawn from the mind-independent existence of reality is the conviction that the world consists of causal structures and/or generative mechanisms[3] that exist independently of our awareness or our study, and that the goal and method of social science is to understand their characteristics, properties, and operations, which includes discerning their effect upon us. These causal structures and mechanisms function as capacities, abilities, dispositions, tendencies, relations, dynamics, and forces more generally that give form, enable, constrain, or inspire social agents and social activities. These structures encompass beliefs, desires, rules, discourse, material distributions, intentional states, groups, hierarchies, human capabilities, indeed, any forces that affect social life (the causal criterion). Here it is helpful to separate out scientific ontology as distinct from philosophical ontology: the former being modeling of particular entities based upon empirical research, the latter being conceptual work concerning background conditions and landscapes.

Underlying the emphasis upon casual mechanisms is an opposition to any form of instrumentalism or covering-law mentality (Gorski, 2004; Hedström and Ylikoski, 2010). Against the abstractions represented by causal laws and empirical generalities, realism emphasizes concrete forms of causation grounded in the overdetermined interaction between structures and entities. Central to causal realism is the critique of the so-called Humean causation and accompanying ontology which posits causation wholly in terms of regularities, constant conjunctions, or "if x then y" causal formulations which, by their nature, are ambivalent to ontology, the nature of the object, reference, and context.[4]

In contrast to the ontologically minimalist language of regularities, the realist emphasis on mechanisms and powers makes strong ontological claims that play an important role in distinguishing between spurious and real associations or descriptions and explanations. Realism holds that not only does the world consist of mechanisms and structures, but that our explanations should reflect the causal processes actually responsible for the observations of regularities and that these must be understood as grounded in structures and the "nature" of "things." Social theory gains its warrant from the reference to one of various generative structures, understood in terms of "shifting constellations of causal mechanisms" that are historical and delineated in space and time (Lawson, 1997: 149). Explanation on this account becomes the concrete explanation of the intersection of causal structures and relations, or as Bhaskar puts it "differentiation and stratification, production and reproduction, mutation and transformation, continual remolding and incessant shifting, of the relatively enduring relations presupposed by particular forms and structures [point to where] sociology's distinctive theoretical interest lies" (Bhaskar, 1998: 44). The paradigmatic case studies of such structures are fields, economies, and capitalism, each of which are characterized by structured relations, roles, practices, and material distributions that are not reducible to either individuals (beliefs, practices) or to structures (distributions, roles) but rely upon the interaction of both as distinct causal agents.

As with ontology in general, the ontology of causation itself plays an important regulatory roles vis-à-vis methodology and explanations by conceptualizing social reality in certain terms while rejecting others (Archer, 1979: 17). Accounts of causation – tacit or explicit – inherently govern what is accepted as admissible and encourage theorizing in particular directions, including what concepts can be used, and how a theorist goes about their research. The realist account of causation suggests that scientific work cannot remain content with either providing descriptions or highlighting regularities and placing hope that through inductive or deductive warrant these empirical results will automatically (magically) yield theoretical insights (Hedström and Wittrock, 2009: 6). Rather, science is viewed as always making ontological assumptions and building theories about causal mechanisms and structures which may not be directly observable, may be invisible, or known only through their effects, but which may be real none the less, and this is necessarily so and inescapable. This places an emphasis upon "depth" explanations suggesting warrant lies in theory construction drawing upon the loose criterion of explanatory

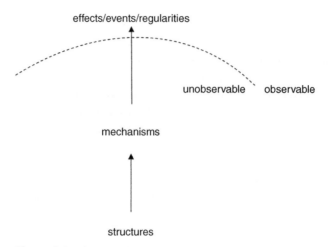

Figure 9.1 *The causal realism iceberg effect*

power and generating the important distinction between appearance (phenomena) and the things appearing (the things referred to) crucial to realist logics.

By focusing on depth, the logic of realism suggests reading events almost as signifiers or symptoms by which we are able to gain access to examine the generative mechanism and structures operative behind the scenes producing events and regularities. This is particularly illustrative for the realist account of causation insofar as symptoms by nature are often idiosyncratic, different diseases generate similar symptoms, the same disease generates different symptoms, and so on. Finding a diagnosis requires moving beyond manifestations and symptoms to uncover the pathological causes. As an extension of ontological realism, causal realism can then be seen as a prescription for realist forms of explanation, asserting that no purported explanations of social phenomena truly count as explanations (or as realist explanations), unless they are cashed out in terms of ontology, structures, mechanisms, and contexts. Realists aim to identify and explain the concrete combinations of contexts, mechanisms, and effects (Sayer, 2000: 23). This depth model of explanation can be represented in terms of the iceberg metaphor (Figure 9.1).

The Epistemological Thesis

Insofar as ontology and the logic of the mind-independent existence of reality increasingly moves into the realm of explanation, often through analogy to natural science, we begin to move into the terrain of the epistemological thesis. As has been mentioned, at one level realism need not entail a theory of truth beyond a general logic of epistemological relativism, world-making, or coherence and an orientation to "reality." However, realism often moves from ontology into epistemology and does so in particular directions that emphasize the truth-aptness of statements and the possibility of convergent reference.

In its weaker form the epistemological thesis suggests that just as positions have certain ontological commitments, ontologies possess epistemological and methodological implications, some of which are better or more truthful than others. As such, operating with faulty background assumptions is liable to derail explanations by being misleading, distorting, incoherent, inchoate, juvenile, or just plain wrong. Bad ontology leads to bad science and ontological mistakes lead to scientific mistakes. The Lysenko affair stands as the paradigmatic case in natural science, but the adoption of ontologies drawn from physics, chemistry, biology, or psychology have equally led to crude forms of explanation from social behaviorism, crass sociobiology, grand theories of history that never eventuate and, in general, accounts which paint human actors as passive players on the social stage. Similarly, misidentifying, overstating, or mischaracterizing the nature and characteristics of the social world by recourse to, for example a paradigmatic or grand social ontology is liable to lead to distortion, as the many critiques of Parsons have suggested (even if it is not placed in directly ontological terms). Within realism the structure–agency problem has served as an important site upon which epistemological and methodological arising from ontology are given force (Archer, 1995; Bhaskar, 1998 [1979]; Wendt, 1999; Wight, 2006). The emphasis upon the mind-independent existence of reality acts to guarantee the relative autonomy of different social spheres, serving as an ontological corrective that constitutes a form of epistemological vigilance: forcing reflexivity about the presuppositions and implications of a theoretical paradigm for epistemology and methodology. Acting to clarify the nature of ontological referents and the role and origin of those referents raises questions about their truth-aptness.

Somewhat ironically, within realist epistemological discussions much is made of the fallibility rather than the certainty of knowledge. In particular, the mind-independent existence of reality serves as the basis for an epistemological corrective against epistemic realism; the independence of objects from knowledge serves to undermine complacent assumptions about our theories and the real world in any one-to-one equation. Just as knowledge may converge on particular accounts, the experience of getting things wrong, or having expectations confounded serves as the basis for realist epistemology (Sayer, 2000: 1). The emphasis moves to a qualified realism by which theories are known only under particular descriptions, and we communicate about the world with only a partial grasp: references are not always clear, and the criteria are not always clear, but the mind-independent existence of reality serves to constrain inquiries (Haslanger, 2012: 14; Sayer, 2000: 1). As Haslanger highlights, "the whole point of speaking of an independent reality is to emphasize that there is no necessary connection between what's real and what human beings know or can (in practice) know" (Haslanger, 2012: 111). This leads to the crucial tension within realism which, it must be said, is not always maintained. On the one hand realism must differentiate itself from foundationalism and tendencies which tend to limit the vision of what is real, while also being careful to avoid perspectivist accounts or global claims of construction (Haslanger, 2012: 111). This positions realism close to standpoint theory in terms of its emphasis on perspectivism, situation, and structural context (Harding, 1991). However, we might also note the strong role ontology plays as a means by which epistemological claims and adequate explanations are moderately enabled, constrained, and motivated.

In a stronger form, the epistemological thesis is seen to entail scientific realism usually under the banner of the correspondence theory of truth. Unfortunately, both "scientific realism" and "correspondence" are awkward, elusive, and much-disputed concepts, particularly as regarding social entities. Simply put, scientific realism holds that the (unobservable) causes, entities, and structures postulated by scientific theories are approximately correct or adequately represent reality, or in other words we do in fact succeed in faithfully inscribing the world into accurate representations, and that our attempt to articulate real forces, structures, and mechanisms results in both genuine objective knowledge (Little, 2016; Searle, 1995). The promise of realism then rests in the possibility of convergent and even fixed reference points. On this account science, including social science, can be said to depend upon judgments that rely upon evidence and argumentation and forms the basis on which to judge whether certain claims ought to be accepted as correct, or at least warranted, granting the possibility (but not necessity) of progress in our knowledge of social reality. Accordingly, either Robert Merton is correct that deviancy is a response to an acute disjunction between cultural norms, goals, and socially structured capacities of members to realize or attain those norms and goals, or he is mistaken, not uncovering the whole truth in what amounts to an outdated approach. This can be borne out by empirical investigations that corroborate or challenge theoretical propositions, and models that provide accounts of particular and contextual mechanisms at work (Little, 2016; Merton, 1968). In either case, social theory is said to progress by studying the ontological implications of successful well-confirmed theories and not only through the accumulation of empirical hypotheses. The question this raises is one on which the controversies of realism have rested: what lends warrant to a theory? What makes a theory true (i.e. representative of reality)? And why lay claim to the mantle of reality?

In general, realists do not hold to a commonsensical or naïve objectivism which roots meaning between terms and their referents in a simple one-to-one correspondence or supposes that knowledge mirrors the world (Sayer, 2000: 36). Given predictive success is not possible to the same extent as in the natural sciences, if at all, the burden lies on theory generally. If theory is conceived merely as an instrument for organizing data and experience, rather than a reference to real causal structures or mechanisms, it is suggested that the character of the derived explanations are unable to shed light on the social world but rather "save the phenomena" that need explanation (Shapiro, 2005: 25). The goal of theory or research encompasses accounting for the procedures for discovering, identifying, and understanding the entities, processes, and structures to which a theory is referring and drawing epistemic warrant from this. For realism, the implication is that the plausibility of a theory is not based on empirical verification but primarily by reference to a theorized underlying reality (Reed, 2011). The validity of a theory is interpreted as grounded on the extent to which the expectations and practices that inform that theory are intelligible, reliable, thick, and answer the question posed to the world. As such, realist theory draws its warrant from ontology and its system of referents, namely the explanatory power of structures and mechanisms.

This is perhaps best seen in contrast. Realism critiques positivism for avoiding contextualized explanation in favor of description and for providing thin explanations constituted by correlations and regularities rather than thick explanations constituted by claims about mechanisms, structures, and ontology. In a similar vein, realism critiques social constructionism for treating the realm of intentionality and discourse as given or determinative in such a way as to obscure or fail to account for underlying causal processes and mechanisms that ground social conventions or discursive formations. In particular, unlike social constructionism, realism claims that discourses, beliefs and well-established theories do refer to, are situated within, and are constrained by, external reality (Sayer, 2000; Shapiro, 2005). Here, by external reality, what is primarily on view are social structures and specific historical forms that constrain, enable, and motivate particular individual actions and ground discourses, rules, or ideologies in such a way that social construction is conditioned in multiple and varying ways across social contexts (Haslanger, 2012: 11). Notably, this encompasses material forms (Porpora, 1993) and embodiment (Archer, 2000; Haslanger, 2012). Theory, then, must also be sensitive to this situational complexity such that focusing simply on agents or structures or culture is insufficient, and social theory must be attentive to the intersection of agents, structures, and cultural forms (Archer, 1995). As one might expect, this has led to the heavy favoring of intensive and qualitative methods within realism and often skepticism toward extensive and quantitative methods (Olsen and Morgan, 2005).

The Methodological Implications of Realism

With the focus firmly on ontology, realism reserves its strongest critiques for approaches in social theory that place emphasis upon methodology, which substitutes theory, ontology, origins, and ends, for means; in short, approaches which eclipse or elide the object. In such cases, rather than being a function of the object, method becomes the basis of the scientific endeavor itself and the basis for the justification of knowledge and the attainment of reality for a theory. The most virulent critique is then merited by positivism, understood as a self-enclosed and autonomous method that guarantees truth through the rigorous use of applied methodologies to arrive at "generalities." But, this critique applies to any form of abstract empiricism that prioritizes description, science, the clarification of logic, and the theoretical justification of particular forms of inference, namely the problem of causation and correlation. Understanding and explanation are then subordinate to description, or rather warrant is closely tied to description and generally renounces speculation beyond the confines of methodologically proscribed limits. This is not exclusively limited to quantitative accounts, although these have historically been the target of realist ire, but applies to quantitative accounts that express similar tendencies, sticking close to methods by maximizing description and minimizing theory and explanation, thereby removing all color from both the object and the researcher.

Realism, in contrast, presents itself as object-oriented: concrete explanation of concrete phenomena. It begins by suggesting that the nature of what exists is closely tied to the manner in which it is studied and theorized: the object determines the approach. The methods and forms of explanation adopted by realists must be adequate and beholden to the distinctive character of their objects, arriving at theorizing that is appropriate to the nature of their investigations (Benton, 1977: 137, see also Durkheim, 1982: 46). While what is held to exist may not strictly or logically determine the use of a method or a form of explanation, it must influence considerations about method, explanation, and theory along with the problematic (Archer, 1995: 16). Following this emphasis upon the primacy of both ontology and the concrete results is a critique of monochromatic applications of methodological and theoretical approaches. The universalization of particular modes generates either reductive monovalence in which the social world becomes one-dimensional; conflation which rejects the possibility of distinctions between features of the social world, resulting in the collapse of one dimension of the social into others; or atheoretical privileging of empirical methodologies, which retreat into the universal application of particular methods or theories regardless of the idiosyncrasies of a particular context (Aviles and Reed, 2017). In each case the distinctness of the object loses out to formulaic a priori prescriptions.

As a critique of abstract methodological applications, realism generally advocates a dialectical approach to theory and methodology, in which method functions to provide a systematic means for the theorist or researcher to clearly see what they are doing and how they are proceeding, with the intended purpose of bringing the object into greater clarity. Again, here we see realism functioning as a regulatory ideal that endorses diverse explanatory and methodological programs, rejecting cookbook prescriptions, and providing a theoretical counterpoint to any attempt at methodological unity. Hand in hand with ontology, realism then operates as a regulative ideal for social theory and social research. The nature of the social reality that is held to exist cannot but influence how it is studied, which places ontology firmly in the driver's seat. In other words, as Archer suggests "there is always a connection between social ontology and explanatory methodology (however covert and however unhelpful)" (Archer, 1995: 13).

Likewise, forms of theorizing are considered in terms of circumscribed descriptions of social realities that are predicated on the possibility of making intelligible and explaining something through sufficiently adequate accounts that are autonomous from, rather than justified by methodological precepts. Here description, explanation, and theorizing are seen to go hand in hand. Explanation cannot proceed without prior descriptions within the context of theory, which necessarily circumscribes any further theoretical or explanatory projects (Archer, 1995: 20). This generally means, social realism implies the necessity of "analytical dualism" in which understanding and explanation of social things depends upon separating an account of how the properties and powers of the "people" causally intertwine with those of the "parts." The goal is to avoid reducing or conflating distinct ontological realities into a blancmange by maintaining the distinction between persons and social structures, materiality and discourse (Archer, 1995: 15). Maintaining the distinctness of the object against reduction and conflation remains a central concern within realism.

The emphasis on a dialectical approach to the object is somewhat vague, but places emphasis upon theory rather than method to do the work. Theoretical warrant lies in the criteria of explanatory power rather than correct use of method. In general, realism appeals to abduction or retroduction, meaning (crudely) "inference to the best explanation" (Danermark et al., 1997). This forms the main criterion governing and legitimating any realist social theory. Emphasis is placed upon the systematic discovery of deep structures known only through theoretical reconstructions: reasoning from mature theories and from observed effects to unobservable structures and causes (Shapiro, 2005: 39). The realist's goal then is to describe accurately the causal mechanisms and structures by reference to which questions about reality can be answered (Shapiro, 2005: 40). On this view conceptual specification and theoretical articulation are more important than matters of methodology. Inquiry should be conducted systematically and in keeping with the object of inquiry, with the questions of the researcher taking priority over inductive or deductive warrant, which is seen only to proffer evidence in service of a theory. While this may be critiqued not only as vague but as being a priori, or departing from empirical inquiry into philosophical speculations, the focus upon concrete, historical, and contextual rather than abstract causes and structures operates as a regulative ideal that grounds realist forms of inquiry. The logic of realism implies non-reductive concrete research performed to identify, specify, and investigate substantial connections grounded by the orientation to the mind-independent existence of reality.

Concluding Remarks

To echo Donna Haraway, the problem of realism is how to have simultaneously an account of contingency for all knowledge claims and knowing subjects, a critical practice for recognizing our own ontological landscapes and how they structure our accounts, and a no-nonsense commitment to faithful accounts of a "real" world (Haraway, 1988: 579). To this end, the unquestionable contribution of realism to social theory is the emphasis upon ontology, its focus upon referents, and the attention to ontological landscapes presupposed by theories. While the mind-independent existence of reality does a lot of work, it efficiently functions as a regulative ideal for ontology, epistemology, and methodology that provides an antireductive normative constraint for what concepts and approaches are deemed fitting for social theory and research, determining what constitutes a valid theory, explanation, or description in relation to a "real" world. It contains evaluations of particular ontological and epistemological judgments about the ultimate constituents of social reality, and what concepts, practices, approaches, and responses are deemed appropriate within that context. Rather than being regulative in the strict sense, and creating strong criteria of demarcation about what constitutes the real versus the unreal, realism entails a commitment to the autonomy of social entities. These are understood according to a causal criterion of existence that can be used to generate discussion about the nature and relationship between the various realities of the social world and the best means of weighing and adjudicating particular claims. It does, however, forcibly imply that certain concepts and approaches are illegitimate insofar as they fail to head attention to ontology and neglect certain features of the social, resulting in reduction or conflation. As such, realism presents ontology and ontological discourse as a guardian or backstop against reductionism in social theory, and in so doing provides social theory with different forms of explanation and understanding.

At this point, it should be said, insofar as realism has been "reactive," it has often been polemical, quick to characterize certain positions as irrealist or antirealist, particularly those that focus on language, discourse, and culture. In so doing, it often fails to attend to these dimensions as an over-corrective, at the very least giving the impression that it is overlooking certain currents or consigning certain positions to the trash can of history (not to mention trying to have both its realist and relativist cake and eat it too). In short, realism doth protest too much methinks, and in doing so falls into overstatement and exaggeration. All too often the realist seems to claim that social science is immersed in a swamp of positivism and relativism and in need of deliverance appealing to reality, paying lip service to the social and situated character of knowledge without fleshing out the exact nature of the epistemic burden of realism. The result is a tendency toward caricatures of both positivism and social construction – and of social theory in general in the process. This gives realism the sheen of the indefatigable savior of social theory with grand promises and a privileged access to the one true meta-theoretical position, whether fairly or unfairly and in spite of its internal logic. Similarly, with a firm focus on philosophy, particularly concerning matters of causation, realism tends to engage in large historical battles, which often results in engagements that are either out of vogue or seem removed from present-day contexts. In many cases, theory has moved on and many of the stronger programs of positivism and social construction have either been abandoned or have been replaced by more sophisticated positions that have responded to their critics. While it can be argued that the influences of various philosophies (such as positivism) implicitly linger and still inform the field, charges about the overwhelming but implicit legacy of a position are difficult to argue or support, often having the appearance of jousting at windmills.

And yet while realism falls into caricature of positivism and social construction-ism, positivism and social constructionism have similarly relied on caricatured accounts of realism: all too willing to attribute to realism an unsophisticated naivety, collapsing it into cartoonish versions of foundationalist ontologies and correspondence theories. The result is a disorganized stalemate in social theory between three rival philosophical foundations conveniently represented by the three mythological founding fathers of modern social science: Saint Marx, Saint Weber, and Saint Durkheim, respectively the canonized representatives of realism, interpretivism, and empiricism. The debates circle around and around: realism correcting social constructionism and empiricism by appealing to the mind-independent existence of reality; social constructionism responding by highlighting the role of language and discourse in shaping "reality"; positivism retreating from the theoretical debates, stressing the need for stronger empirical projects to rein in realism and social construction. In each case there is a tendency for one pole of the social world to triumph over the others; the game is rigged in advance, one dimension is always fated to win. In each position, the social world is fundamentally characterized by a particular feature or domain. Whether this is methodological, discursive, cultural, practical, or structural, the social world is always already predetermined by an existential commitment to a given genre or logic. That is to say, there is always already a paradigmatic resolution of the theoretical problematic and a preexisting commitment to a particular version of social reality that underpins our understanding of the social world. Reference to one form of social fact, be it discourse, regularities, or structures, becomes the dominant and hegemonic logic, or rather, the dominant form of reality in our explanations, explicitly or otherwise.

This stalemate raises important questions about the limits of realism as a position and a logic. At one level, if realism is indeed grounded in a particular logic of reference (namely the external world, ontology, and causal structures), contexts of ontological and semantic vagueness create situations in which realism seems to spin its wheels, unable to lay claim to a fixed or coherent point that would ground its analysis. Arguably social construction and empiricism have an analytical advantage in such situations as they are able to reference certain fixities, be it in language or empirical regularities, that have the effect of naturally smoothing over ambiguity, whereas realism lacks such a possibility. Perhaps this can particularly be seen in issues of gender and race. Here assumptions about reality, that is to say ideology, are precisely that which make certain realities real. In such situations operating with a realist logic risks either the proliferation of realities and points of reference or acts to lay claim to such reference points as biology, as extra-ideological representatives of the external world. The structures in such situations seem more naturally those of discourse, in which the language, logic, and baggage of ontology can be seen to hinder rather than illuminate such realities. While realism and ontology can assist to clarify the nature of referents and the role and origin of referent, realism must tread carefully in order to avoid the process of fixing reference and sense in such situations, and act to retain ambiguity and vagueness where necessary. If we take the promise of realism as ultimately the promise of the possibility of ontology and even convergent reference, realness and ontological commitment must be understood as a matter of degree, real and yet vague, in which the limits of realism and reference in certain domains is recognized and realism becomes realistic about its own logic. Yet, once this limitation is recognized, in such situations the logic of realism can function to illuminate the contingent ontologies and structural mechanisms at work: drawing out underpinning ontological structures and landscapes, and highlighting their contingency, incoherencies, contradictions, and functions.

Unfortunately, it seems that all too often the tendency in social theory is to build positions on enduring stereotypes that force opponents into simple dichotomies. While this is often done to highlight particular and important stakes, the ongoing challenge within social theory must be to find a way to move beyond this disorganized stalemate and avoid the self-perpetuating polemics so characteristic of the sociological enterprise today – although this too might just be yet more quixotic jousting of an unreconstructed realist still trying to rescue reality from theory. In any case, realism has an important role to play within social theory.

References

Ackroyd, Stephen, and Steve Fleetwood (eds.). 2000. *Realist Perspectives on Management and Organizations*. London: Routledge.

Archer, Margaret. 1979. *Social Origins of Educational Systems*. London: Sage.
  1995. *Realist Social Theory*. Cambridge, UK: Cambridge University Press.
  2000. *Being Human: The Problem of Agency*. Cambridge, UK: Cambridge University Press.

Assiter, Alison. 1996. *Enlightened Women: Modernist Feminism in a Postmodern Age*. London: Routledge.

Aviles, Natalie, and Isaac Reed. 2017. "Ratio via Machina: Three Standards of Mechanistic Explanation in Sociology." *Sociological Methods and Research* 46(4): 715–738.

Ayer, A. J. 1970. "What Is a Law of Nature" In B. A. Brody (ed.), *Readings in the Philosophy of Science*. Englewood Cliffs, NJ: Prentice-Hall.

Bhaskar, Roy. 1998 [1979]. *The Possibility of Naturalism*. London: Routledge.
  2008 [1975]. *A Realist Theory of Science*. London: Verso.

Benton, Ted. 1977. *Philosophical Foundations of the Three Sociologies*. London: Routledge and Kegan Paul.

Benton, Ted, and Ian Craib. 2010. *Philosophy of Social Science: The Philosophical Foundations of Social Thought*. Basingstoke, UK: Palgrave Macmillan.

Callinicos, Alex. 2006. *Resources of Critique*. Cambridge, UK: Polity Press.

Danermark, Berth, Mats Ekström, Lisolette Jakobsen, and Jan Ch. Karlsson. 1997. *Explaining Society: Critical Realism in the Social Sciences*. London: Routledge.

Decoteau, Claire. 2017. The AART of Ethnography: A Critical Realist Explanatory Research Model. *Journal for the Theory of Social Behaviour* 47(1): 58–82.

Delanda, Manuel. 2006. *A New Philosophy of Society: Assemblage Theory and Social Complexity*. London and New York: Continuum.
  2016. *Assemblage Theory*. Edinburgh: Edinburgh University Press.

Dreyfus, Hubert, and Charles Taylor. 2015. *Retrieving Realism*. Cambridge, MA: Harvard University Press.

Dummett, Michael. 1982. "Realism." *Synthese* 52: 55–112.

Durkheim, Emile. 1982. *The Rules of Sociological Method*. New York: The Free Press.

Edwards, Paul, Joe O'Mahoney, and Steve Vincent (eds.). 2014. *Studying Organizations Using Critical Realism*. Oxford, UK: Oxford University Press.

Elder-Vass, Dave. 2012. *The Reality of Social Construction*. Cambridge, UK: University of Cambridge Press.

Fairclough, Norman. 1995. *Critical Discourse Analysis*. Boston, MA: Addison-Wesley.

Fine, Gary Alan. 1999. "Field Labor and Ethnographic Reality." *Journal of Contemporary Ethnography* 28: 532–539.

Fine, Gary Alan, and Tim Hallett. 2014. "Stranger and Stranger: Creating Theory through Ethnographic Distance and Authority." *Journal of Organizational Ethnography* 3: 188–203.

Frost, Samantha, and Diana Coole (eds.). 2010. *New Materialisms: Ontology, Agency, and Politics*. Durham, NC: Duke University Press.

Gorski, Philip. 2004. "The Poverty of Deductivism: A Constructive Realist Model of Sociological Explanation." *Sociological Methodology* 34(1): 1–33.

2008. "The ECPRES Model: A Critical Realist Approach to Causal Mechanisms in the Social Sciences." In Björn Wittrock and Peter Hedström (eds.), *The Frontiers of Sociology* (pp. 147–194). Leiden: Brill.

Graeber, David. 2015. "Radical Alterity Is Just Another Way of Saying 'Reality': A Reply to Eduardo Viveiros de Castro." *HAU: Journal of Ethnographic Theory* 5: 1–41.

Haraway, Donna. 1988. "Situated Knowledges: The Science Question in Feminism and the Privilege of Partial Perspective." *Feminist Studies* 14(3): 575–599.

Harding, Sandra. 1991. *Whose Science/Whose Knowledge?* Milton Keynes, UK: Open University Press.

Harman, Graham. 2016. *Immaterialism: Objects and Social Theory*. Malden, MA: Polity Press.

Harré, Rom. 1979. *Social Being*. Oxford, UK: Basil Blackwell.

Haslanger, Sally. 2012. *Resisting Reality: Social Construction and Social Critique*. Oxford. UK: Oxford University Press.

Hedström, Peter, and Björn Wittrock (eds.). 2009. *The Frontiers of Sociology*. Leiden: Brill.

Hedström, Peter, and Petri Ylikoski. 2010. "Causal Mechanisms in the Social Sciences." *Annual Review Sociology* 36: 49–67

Hume, David. 1777. *An Enquiry Concerning Human Understanding*, ed. A. Selby-Biggs. Oxford, UK: Clarendon Press.

Jessop, Bob. 2015. "The Symptomatology of Crises, Reading Crises and Learning from Them: Some Critical Realist Reflections." *Journal of Critical Realism* 14(3): 238–271.

Kaidesoja, Tukka. 2015. *Naturalizing Critical Realist Social Ontology*. London: Routledge.

Keat, Robert, and John Urry. 1975. *Social Theory as Science*. London: Routledge and Kegan Paul.

Latour, Bruno. 1999. *Pandora's Hope: Essays on the Reality of Science Studies*. Cambridge, MA: Harvard University Press.

Latour, Bruno, and Steve Woolgar. 1986. *Laboratory Life: The Construction of Scientific Facts*. Princeton, NJ: Princeton University Press

Law, John. 2004. *After Method: Mess in Social Science Research*. London: Routledge.

Lawson, Tony. 1997. *Economics and Reality*. London: Routledge.

2003. *Reorienting Economics*. London: Routledge.

Little, Daniel. 2016. *New Directions in the Philosophy of Social Science*. Lanham, MD: Rowman & Littlefield.

Lukes, Steven. 1968. "Methodological Individualism Reconsidered." *The British Journal of Sociology* 19(2): 119–129.

Manicas, Peter. 1987. *A History and Philosophy of the Social Sciences*. New York: Basil Blackwell.

2006. *A Realist Philosophy of Social Science: Explanation and Understanding*. Cambridge, UK: Cambridge University Press.

Martin, John Levi. 2014. *Thinking through Theory*. New York: W. W. Norton & Company.

Merton, Robert K. 1968. *Social Theory and Social Structure*. New York: The Free Press.

Norrie, Alan. 1993. *Crime, Reason and History: A Critical Introduction to Criminal Law*. London: Weidenfeld & Nicolson.

Norris, Christopher. 1985. *The Contest of Faculties*. London: Methuen & Co.

1995. *Truth and the Ethics of Criticism*. Manchester, UK: Manchester University Press

Olsen, Wendy, and Jamie Morgan. 2005. "A Critical Epistemology of Analytical Statistics: Addressing the Skeptical Realist." *Journal for the Theory of Social Behaviour* 35 (3): 255–284.

Outhwaite, William. 1987. *New Philosophies of Social Science: Realism, Hermeneutics and Critical Theory*. New York: St. Martin's.

Pawson, Ray. 2006. *Evidence-Based Policy: A Realist Perspective*. London: Sage.

2013. *The Science of Evaluation: A Realist Manifesto*. London: Sage.

Pawson, Ray, and Nick Tilley. 1997. *Realistic Evaluation*. London: Sage.

Porpora, Douglas. 1993. "Cultural Rules and Material Relations." *Sociological Theory* 11(2): 212–229.

Potter, Jonathan. 1997. *Representing Reality*. London: Sage.

Psillos, Stathis. 1999. *Scientific Realism: How Science Tracks Truth*. London: Routledge.

2014. "Regularities, Natural Patterns and Laws of Nature." *Theoria* 79: 9–27.

Putnam, Hilary. 1978. *Meaning and the Moral Sciences*, London: Routledge & Kegan Paul.

Putnam, Hilary, and James Conant. 1990. *Realism with a Human Face*. Cambridge, MA: Harvard University Press.

Reed, Isaac A. 2011. *Interpretation and Social Knowledge: On the Use of Theory in the Human Sciences*. Chicago, IL: University of Chicago Press.

Rees, Chris, and Mark Gatenby. 2014. "Critical Realism and Ethnography." In Paul K. Edwards, Joe O'Mahoney, and Steve Vincent (eds.), *Studying Organizations Using Critical Realism* (pp. 132–147). Oxford: Oxford University Press.

Rorty, Richard. 1979. *Philosophy and the Mirror of Nature*. Princeton, NJ: Princeton University Press.

Sayer, Andrew. 2000. *Realism and Social Science*. London: Sage.

2010 [1984]. *Method in Social Science: A Realist Approach*. London: Routledge.

Schillbrack, Kevin. 2014. *Philosophy and the Study of Religions: A Manifesto*. Chichester, UK: John Wiley & Sons.

Scott, David. 2000. *Realism and Educational Research: New Perspectives and Possibilities*. London: Routledge.

Searle, John. 1995. *The Construction of Social Reality*. London: Penguin Books.

Shapiro, Ian. 2005. *The Flight from Reality in the Human Sciences*. Princeton, NJ: Princeton University Press.

Shotter, John. 1996. *Conversational Realities: Constructing Life through Language*. London: Sage.

Smith, Christian. 2017. *Religion: What It Is, How It Works, and Why It Matters*. Princeton, NJ: Princeton University Press.

Steinmetz, George. 1998. "Critical Realism and Historical Sociology." *Comparative Studies in Society and History* 40(1): 170–186.

2003. "Odious Comparisons: Incommensurability, the Case Study, and 'Small N's' in Sociology." *Sociological Theory* 22(3): 371–400.

Wendt, Alexander. 1999. *Social Theory of International Politics*. Cambridge, UK: Cambridge University Press.

Wight, Colin. 2006. *Agents, Structures and International Relations: Politics as Ontology*. Cambridge, UK: Cambridge University Press.

Williams, Raymond. 1983. *Keywords*. Oxford, UK: Oxford University Press.

Wright, Erik Olin. 1994. *Interrogating Inequality: Essays on Class Analysis, Socialism and Marxism*. London: Verso.

Notes

1. It should be noted that critical realism is so named against naïve realism and in continuity with critical theory and not, as some commentators have suggested, as a combination of Bhaskar's transcendental realism (1975) and critical naturalism (1979). This should also not be confused with the distinct forms of critical realism of Haslanger (2012) or indeed, Wilfred Sellars and Arthur Lovejoy, all of which converge on many similar ideas in distinct and importantly different ways.

2. We might here note that these landscapes are also social. They are influenced not only by theory, but forms of life. Following Wittgenstein, we might suggest there is no private ontology and ontological landscapes must be understood as shared landscapes.

3. Sometimes called causal powers instead of mechanisms.

4. Humean causation, named for the British empiricist and sceptic David Hume who was famously "cautious" of all metaphysical claims and appeals to "occult powers" in matters of causation, consigning everything that wasn't wholly empirical or logical to the flames as sophistry and illusion (Hume, 1777). This characteristic Humean approach would be picked up in the early twentieth century under the name logical positivism and form the basis of Humean causation, cautious about anything beyond the identification of regularities (see, for example, Ayer, 1970). Similarly, modern neo-Humeanism in the philosophy of science argues for patterns and regularities without the need for regularity-enforcers: empirical patterns and regularities alone are enough without needing ontology or theories of causation: if ontology, make the least of it (Psillos, 2014: 29 c.f. Hedstrom and Ylikoski, 2010: 53).

10 Globalization: Not Good, Bad, or Over

Sheila Croucher

"Globalization is a fact of life." Former Secretary-General of the United Nations (UN) Kofi Annan offered this observation before the 1999 World Economic Forum in Davos, Switzerland. Annan was speaking at the turn of a new millennium, when contemporary globalization was in full swing. The World Trade Organization (WTO), formally established four years earlier, boasted 134 members from around the world and was preparing for its third ministerial conference in Seattle, Washington later that year. European Union members had just adopted the euro as the single currency of the European Monetary Union, and the North American Free Trade Agreement (NAFTA) was marking five years of tariff-free trade between Canada, Mexico, and the United States. Foreign Direct Investment (FDI) worldwide jumped 27 percent in 1999 alone, reaching a record high of US $865 billion (Yester, 2009). The number of Internet users worldwide had grown to 240 million in 1999, more than tripling the 70 million users just two years prior in 1997 (Internet World Stats, 2018), and flows of international migrants were increasing sharply (SOPEMI, 2001).

Annan's assessment of globalization was an ambivalent one. He and a few other analysts expressed concerns about the growth in global inequality. Harvard economist Dani Rodrick warned that economic integration seemed likely to beget troubling social disintegration, as low-skilled workers in developed economies throughout the Western world experienced declining wages and growing job insecurity (Rodrick, 1997). Related concerns were echoed by thousands of activists who protested the meeting of the WTO in Seattle, Washington at the end of 1999. Despite evident dissent, the general consensus at the turn of the new millennium was that growing global interconnectedness would generate economic, political, and social progress worldwide. Moreover, arguing against globalization seemed, as Annan remarked, like "arguing against the laws of gravity" (Crossette, 2000).

Barely two decades into the dawning of the new millennium, the global landscape had changed in ways that few would have predicted in 1999. A series of watershed events beginning in 2001 highlighted both the reality of global interconnectedness and the ambiguities surrounding it. On September 11, 2001, nineteen al-Qaeda-affiliated hijackers used commercial airliners to unleash terror on the United States. In the years following the attacks on New York and Washington, radical jihadists committed similar atrocities in cities around the world. By 2007, a different sort of terror took hold as a global financial crisis spread around the world. The crisis started in the US housing market, but quickly evolved into the

Great Recession of 2008 – characterized as the worst economic disaster since the Great Depression of 1929. Eight years later, in 2016, the global economic upheaval had subsided, only to be replaced by a political one. A tide of nationalist populism swept across Europe and the United States, resulting in Britain's withdrawal from the European Union (EU) and the election of nationalist leaders like Donald Trump in the United States, Sebastian Kurz in Austria, and Viktor Orbán in Hungary – all of whom capitalized on and fomented exclusionary attitudes toward immigrants.

Debate continues regarding the underlying causes and consequences of these different events, but globalization figures centrally. For some, the 9/11 terrorist attacks signaled not only a backlash against Westernization, but the end of globalization. John Gray of the London School of Economics opined: "After the attacks on New York and Washington, the conventional view of globalisation as an irresistible historical trend has been shattered. We are back on the classical terrain of history, where war is waged not over ideologies, but over religion, ethnicity, territory and the control of natural resources" (Gray, 2001). Yet, while al-Qaeda, and later ISIS, rejected key tenets of globalization, their rise and success confirmed the condition of globality. This was the case in terms of: (1) the effective transnational mobilization of global terror networks, (2) the ease with which these terrorists breached nation-state borders, and (3) the nature of the grievances that they claimed motivated their attacks – namely the global cultural, political, and economic hegemony of the West. Seven years later, the Great Recession of 2008 prompted similar declarations of globalization's demise, while also simultaneously attesting to its achievement. The world had become so closely intertwined that our economic fortunes rose and fell as one (Eichengreen et al., 2012).

In 2016, globalization surfaced again as the primary explanation for widespread resurgent nationalism. Yet, the nationalists themselves acted globally in building upon and supporting each other's movements and ideas. United States presidential candidate Donald Trump praised Britain's decision to leave the EU. His top advisor, Steve Bannon, made speeches throughout Europe offering encouragement to supporters of far-right movements in France, Germany, and Italy. In the United States, when devout conservatives showed up at the 2017 Conservative Political Action Conference, among the many speakers they cheered were Marion Maréchal-Le Pen, niece of French far-right leader Marine Le Pen, and Nigel Farage, British champion of the Brexit movement. Farage used his keynote address to anticipate the "very exciting elections" in the Netherlands, France, and Germany, and described the spread of nationalist populism as "the beginning of a great global revolution" (Owen and Smith, 2017). Meanwhile, Nobel laureate Joseph Stiglitz, whose 2002 book *Globalization and Its Discontents* analyzed widespread dissatisfaction with globalization in the developing world, revisited his thesis to explain that by 2016, the discontent with globalization had itself been globalized (Stiglitz, 2017).

Despite globalization's prominent place in analyses of contemporary issues, it is a concept plagued by competing definitions, assumptions, and assessments. The pages that follow shed light on what globalization is, when it emerged, and how it might be assessed. Like gravity, aspects of globalization may be inescapable, but not inexplicable or unmanageable.

Globalization: What Is It?

When British economist Martin Wolf described globalization as "a hideous word of obscure meaning" (2004: 13), he captured frustration over a term that is ubiquitous but not well understood. The countless definitions of globalization range from the very general, such as Roland Robertson's definition of globalization as "the intensification of the world as a whole" (1992: 8), to the highly specific:

> "Globalisation" is the growth, or more precisely the accelerated growth, of economic activity across national and regional political boundaries. It finds expression in the increased movement of tangible and intangible goods and services, including ownership rights, via trade and investment, and often of people, via migration. It can be and often is facilitated by a lowering of government impediments to that movement, and/or by technological progress, notably in transportation and communications. The actions of individual economic actors, firms, banks, people, drive it, usually in the pursuit of profit, often spurred by the pressures of competition. Globalisation is thus a centrifugal process, a process of economic outreach, and a microeconomic phenomenon. (Oman, 1996: 5)

Definitions of globalization also vary in emphasis from the economic and technological to the sociocultural and political. Some definitions aim simply for description, while others entail assessment, or indictment: "Globalization is what we in the Third World have for several centuries called colonization" (M. Khor, quoted in Scholte, 2005: 16).

Further complicating efforts to define globalization is the complex web of interrelationships that exists between different aspects and dimensions of global change. Economics provides an obvious engine of globalization, as worldwide production and exchange led by transnational corporations (TNCs) tie together far-flung regions of the world. The dynamics of the global marketplace do not, however, occur in a political vacuum. States still facilitate and/or resist globalization, as do a large and growing number of international governmental and non-governmental organizations (NGOs). Meanwhile, global interconnectedness in the economic and political realms relates directly to significant technological innovations. And, culture both shapes and is shaped by all of the processes identified above. Popular definitions capture this multidimensionality by referring to globalization as a "package of changes" (Giddens, 2003: 3), or "a set of social processes" (Steger, 2017: 12).

Many of the changes and processes discussed under the umbrella of globalization can arguably be, and have been, accounted for by other terminology: internationalization, liberalization, universalization, and Westernization. For this reason, Jan Scholte (2000: 17) has argued that the introduction of "globalization" is redundant at best and confusing at worse if it fails to capture a fundamental characteristic of the contemporary world, namely, far-reaching transformations in the nature of social space. Globalization, for Scholte, entails the "spread of supraterritoriality" or "a reconfiguration of geography, so that social space is no longer wholly mapped in terms of territorial places, territorial distances, territorial borders." Distilling these insights, globalization can be defined as:

a cluster of related changes that are increasing the interconnectedness of the world. These changes occur in, but are not limited to, the economic, technological, cultural, and political realms. Nor is globalization restricted to merely enhancing the interdependence of already existing entities or the intensification of established networks and flows. It is also creating and facilitating the creation of new ones. (Croucher, 2018: 14)

What follows are examples or evidence of globalization in these four realms.

Economic Interconnectedness

Adam Smith's 1776 *Wealth of Nations* never mentions the term globalization, but the power of the marketplace to integrate far corners of the globe was central to Smith's theory, and the role of economics has figured centrally into definitions of globalization since. The Institute for National Strategic Studies (INSS) defines globalization as "anchored in economic dynamics" (Flanagan, Frost, and Kugler, 2001: 5). The Organization for Economic Cooperation and Development deems it: "a dynamic and multidimensional process of economic integration" (OECD, 2005: 11); and economists routinely use the term "globalization" to describe international integration in commodity, capital, and labor markets (Bordo, Taylor, and Williamson, 2003).

Ample data attest to the central role of global trade and investment in linking countries and regions throughout the world. World trade expanded rapidly, at more than 8 percent per year, between 1950 and 1970 (WTO, 2008), and by the early 1980s, it was growing at twice the rate of world economic output (Mittelman, 2000: 21). Trade as a proportion of gross domestic product (GDP) increased steadily beginning the 1970s, and by 2000 reached ratios as high as 30 percent and higher in advanced industrialized countries (Held, 2000: 97). In 1960 global imports of goods and services as a percentage of GDP totaled 12.7 percent. By 2008 that percentage had reached 30.2 ("Imports of Goods and Services" 2017). FDI also climbed during the same period. In 1982, FDI inflows and outflows were $58 billion and $37 billion respectively. By 1990 both figures had quadrupled to $209 billion and $245 billion, and by 2000, they had again more than quadrupled to $1,271 billion and $1,150 respectively (UNCTAD, 2001). By 2007, before the onset of the Great Recession, global FDI flows reached historic highs of around $2 trillion (Poulsen and Hufbauer, 2011).

This intensification of trade and exchange applies not only to goods and services, but also to money. World foreign exchange transactions climbed from US$15 billion a day in the 1970s to US$900 billion a day in the early 1990s. By 2001, financial markets were moving US$1.5 trillion around the world every day, and in the United States, cross-border flows of bonds and equities were fifty-four times higher than they had been in 1970, fifty-five times higher for Japan, and sixty times higher for Germany (Foreign Policy, 2001: 58). International bank lending also grew dramatically during the same period, moving from $265 billion in 1975 to $4.2 trillion by 1995, and continuing that growth pattern through the early 2000s. International bank lending as a share of GDP – a key proxy for economic globalization – almost doubled between 2002 and 2008 (Committee on the Global Financial System, 2010). The INSS concluded, at the turn of the new millennium, that "the *integration of capital and commodity markets* has surpassed all previous levels and is still spreading" (Flanagan, Frost, and Kugler, 2001: 8, emphasis in the original).

Some of these trends were halted (if only temporarily) when the 2008 global economic crisis wreaked havoc worldwide. In industrialized countries, GDPs plunged and unemployment rose – in some cases to double digits. The volume of world trade dropped by more than 40 percent in the second half of 2008 (Alfaro and Chen, 2010), and the twenty-year rates of steady growth in trade and overseas investments declined. FDI flows which had reached historic highs in 2007 plummeted by 16 percent in 2008 (Poulsen and Hufbauer, 2011). Imports of goods and services as a percentage of GDP, which had climbed 30.2 in 2008, fell to 25.8 in 2009 – the sharpest drop since 1960 ("Imports of Goods and Services," 2017). The crisis prompted widespread declarations of globalization's demise, but ultimately, as Pankaj Ghemawat explained in 2017: "The sentiments have moved around more than the actual numbers" (Brancaccio, 2017).

Technological Interconnectedness

The high degree of integration among the world's markets helps account for the globality of economic swings, but the dynamics described above would not have been possible without the increased sophistication of communication and information technologies. The introduction of satellites and fiber optics, and the accompanying proliferation of cellphones, laptops, and fax machines led to a massive increase in transborder communications. In fact, breaking with the central emphasis on economics, theorist Anthony Giddens (1995: 10) identified communications media as "the leading influence in the globalisation of society over the past 20 or 30 years." The INSS concurred: "Globalization would not be occurring in its present form were it not for the business application of the knowledge revolution – for example, computers, e-mail, satellites, and other innovations" (cited in Flanagan, Frost, and Kugler, 2001: 8).

The Internet and its numerous social media platforms are prime examples of technology connecting the planet. In 1995, less than 1 percent of the world's population had an Internet connection. By 2017, that proportion reached 51 percent. Between 2000 and 2017, worldwide Internet usage grew an astonishing 962.5 percent, with the number of users reaching the first billion in 2005. By 2018, over 4 billion people worldwide were using the Internet (Internet World Stats, 2018). It took radio broadcasting 38 years from the time of its inception to reach 50 million people, and television 13 years. The Internet did so in only four years (Simon, 2001: 615). The devices (cellphones, laptops, tablets, etc.) through which people access the Internet have proliferated at similarly astonishing rates. In 2014, the number of mobile devices in the world, estimated at 7.22 billion, officially surpassed the number of people in the world – estimated at 7.19 billion (Boren, 2014). The number of cellular subscriptions climbed from 738 million in 2000 to over 7 billion in 2015; and an estimated 95 percent of the world's population now lives in an area covered by a cellular signal (Central Intelligence Agency, 2015).

Launched in 2004, with a mission to "bring the world closer together," in 2018 Facebook boasted 2.20 billion monthly active users from almost every country of the world (Facebook, 2018). The company achieved an unprecedented benchmark of 1 billion users in a single day on August 24, 2015 – equal to about one in seven people on Earth. Mark Zuckerberg, cofounder and CEO remarked: "This was the first time we reached this milestone, and it's just the beginning of connecting the whole world" (Wattles, 2015). Meanwhile, WeChat, China's mobile messaging service, counted 1 billion monthly active users in 2018 – up 12 percent from two years prior (Hollander, 2018). Technological innovation has always unleashed profound change, since the invention of the printing press, and even the wheel. Yet, what is arguably different today "is the sheer ubiquity of technology in our lives and the speed of change" (Dobbs, Manyika, and Woetzel, 2015).

Cultural Interconnectedness

Revolutionary changes in communications and information technology not only support economic globalization, but also spur the global circulation of cultural goods – defined as "special goods which carry symbolic, aesthetic, artistic, or cultural value" (UIS, 2016). People, information, ideas, and symbols are moving and interfacing worldwide more freely, rapidly, and at greater distances than ever before, and this interface profoundly affects the globalization of culture. The value of cultural imports and exports, measured in terms of printed matter, music, visual arts, cinema and photographic, and radio and television equipment, almost tripled from an estimated $67 billion in 1980 to $200 billion in 1991 (UNDP, 1999: 33). This impressive growth slowed during the Great Recession of 2008, but had resumed by 2010. By 2013, the value of world trade in cultural goods and services had reached $212.8 billion, nearly doubling from $108.4 billion in 2004 (UIS, 2016). The United States dominates much of this trade, particularly in the areas of film and television, and saw its export and import of cultural goods and services grow steadily from $20 billion in 1998 to $60 billion by 2012 (ACPSA, 2015). Although the United States remains the world's largest importer of cultural goods, China was the leading exporter of cultural goods in 2010 (UIS, 2016).

The exchange of cultural ideas, practices, and artifacts fuels and is fueled by the spread and exchange of people. In 1970, 310 million passengers were carried by air transport. By 2006, that number had soared to 2.073 billion, and 10 years later to a record 3.696 billion. In 2017, the International Air Transport Association (IATA) reported the strongest increases in more than five years in the demand for global air travel. Attributing this higher-than-expected growth to the establishment of more than 700 new routes in 2016, and to an upturn in the global economic cycle following the 2008 recession, the IATA has predicted growth in global air travel will continue to exceed expectations (International Air Transport Association, 2017).

Beyond business travel and tourism, recent decades have witnessed a profound increase in more permanent forms of human migration. Currently, more than 244 million migrants are estimated to be living outside of their country of birth, marking a 41 percent increase from 2000, and revealing that the number of international migrants has grown faster that the world's population. Included in the 244 million are millions of refugees – a group whose numbers have soared in recent years. Some are pushed from their homes by natural disasters, but the majority are fleeing violent conflicts related to various forms of sectarian belonging. By the end of 2017, a record 68.5 million people had been forcibly displaced from their homes due to conflict and persecution (Edwards, 2016).

This global movement of human beings results in an increasing number of foreign-born residents living in countries around the world. In France, Germany, and the United States, that proportion ranges between 12 to 13 percent of the total population. In Canada and Australia, the foreign-born make up 20 and 27.7 percent respectively. Cities are often the main destinations for migrants, and since the 1990s, many metropolises throughout the world (including Auckland, Brussels, London, Los Angeles, Singapore, and Toronto) have seen their percentage of foreign-born residents exceed one third, and sometimes half, of the total population (Ambrecht, 2016). International migrants have long maintained ties to their homelands, but the various technologies noted above now make it even easier to stay connected to country and kin. The result is that identifications crisscross and transcend established geopolitical borders, and culture – the shared patterns, behaviors, beliefs, and interpretations that are thought to help us distinguish among human groupings. These patterns, while never tightly or territorially bounded, are even less so now.

Political Interconnectedness

Economic, technological, and cultural globalization do not occur in a political vacuum. The term "political" in this context encompasses circumstances that range from interstate relations to trans-state organizations and networks. Because the political formation of the modern nation state has predominated since the eighteenth century, much of what constitutes global interaction and exchange is mediated through nation states, but also increasingly transcends them. In this regard, political interconnectedness relates closely to what international relations (IR) scholars have termed interdependence.

During the 1970s, many IR theorists began to recognize that realism, a theory positing an anarchic international system of competitive relations among autonomous states, did not account for the multiple ways that states, even the very powerful ones, were dependent upon other states (Keohane and Nye, 1977). Some of that interdependence relates to resource needs, such as oil or water; but there is also evidence of coordination and cooperation among states that is not reducible to the realist model of brute power relations. In fact, the international system comprises an array of regimes, sometimes deliberately codified in formal agreements or organizations and other times the result of less formal but widely accepted practices that serve to manage activities and address policy problems that transcend the boundaries and capacities of individual states. These regimes range in focus from human rights and refugee issues to the control of natural resources and weapons systems.

Governance, then, is not the sole purview of the sovereign nation state, but is dispersed across international, suprastate, and substate agencies. International associations that engage in global governance are not new, but they expanded significantly in number and charge throughout the twentieth century. In 1909, only thirty-seven international governmental organizations (IGOs) existed. By 1960, the number of IGOs had reached 154, and by 2012, had reached 262 (Blanton and Kegley, 2017). Similarly, in the middle of the nineteenth century, the congresses sponsored by IGOs numbered only 2 or 3 per year; by 1988, more than 4,000 were being held annually (Held, 1998: 20). The WTO, created in 1995, is a marked example of the degree to which individual states commit themselves to comply with international law. Under WTO rules, a Trade Policy Review Body monitors member governments' commercial activities. Alleged violations of WTO regulations are reviewed by a panel, whose decisions are binding, and the consensus principle that prevailed under the General Agreement on Tariffs and Trade (GATT) has been replaced by one of majority rule. Nonetheless, there has been no shortage of states around the world lining up for membership in the WTO. As of June 2016, the organization boasted 164 members, with additional countries and IGOs enjoying observer status.

The increasing interconnectedness of states in the world system is a testament to political globalization, but so, too, are the growing number and transborder activities of NGOs. Whether the International Red Cross, Amnesty International, Oxfam, or the International Planned Parenthood Federation, associations whose mission and membership are not tied to a state have proliferated. In 1909, international nongovernmental organizations (INGOs) numbered 176; by 1960, that number had soared to 1,255, and by the year 2012 to 8,382 (Blanton and Kegley, 2017). Meanwhile, many NGOs with a previously domestic focus have expanded their reach to incorporate issues and clientele extending beyond the sovereign state. Instead what exists are complex, ad hoc, non-territorial social formations and allegiances that exist outside of and largely disconnected from the nation state (Appadurai, 1996). These associations recognize the transborder nature of the issues that concern them, and their transborder or extra-state responses further contribute to global political interconnectedness.

Beyond international IGOs and NGOs, extralegal or illegal networks also demonstrate growing worldwide interconnectedness. Global criminal activity includes worldwide trade in arms and drugs, intricate money-laundering schemes, international financial fraud, trade in biological and chemical technology and human organs, and the smuggling of illegal migrants and endangered species (Thachuk, 2001: 746). By 2017, the global value of transnational crime averaged between $1.6 trillion and $2.2 trillion per year – comprising an estimated 3.6 percent of the world's GDP (May, 2017). The drug trade makes up approximately half a trillion dollars of that total, and "is becoming truly more global" (Ellyatt, 2013). Human trafficking, estimated to be a $150 billion business, has also become a global enterprise affecting every region of the world. So, too, with terrorism. Writing in 2001, the *Christian Science Monitor* compared al-Qaeda to a "terrorist NATO" (Grier, 2001: 1), and Robert Jervis remarked: "Were this a peaceful enterprise, we would celebrate it as showing the ability of people from different countries, social classes, and experiences to work together" (2002: 40). As a successor to al-Qaeda, ISIS, too, has been recognized as an international organization which succeeded in establishing a "global network of killers" (Callimachi, 2016).

Although some observers continue to emphasize one specific dimension of globalization, whether economic, technological, cultural, political, or otherwise, most acknowledge its multidimensionality, and few discount the abundant evidence indicating that the contemporary world is a tightly interconnected one, and will likely continue to be.

Globalization: Old or New?

Often implicit in definitions of globalization are assumptions regarding its inception. If globalization is defined in terms of "the intensification of consciousness of the world as a whole" (Robertson, 1992: 8), then it is possible to trace its origin to the second century BC, when Greek historian Polybius wrote in reference to the rise of the Roman Empire: "Formerly the things which happened in the world had no connection among themselves . . . . But since then all events are united in a common bundle" (quoted in Robertson, 1992: 54). Global consciousness is also evident in various religious faiths dating as far back as the fifth and sixth centuries BC (Scholte, 2005: 87). If, on the other hand, globalization refers to increased economic interconnectedness among states, then Christopher Columbus' arrival in the Americas in 1492 marks an important beginning of market integration, transcontinental trade, and human migration. If more extensive worldwide exchange is the indicator, globalization's birth might be set in the mid-nineteenth century, when a series of technological innovations (steamships, railways, telegraph cables, and telephones) facilitated global economic and political integration by dramatically reducing the costs of transportation and communications (O'Rourke and Williamson, 1999). Two world wars and the Great Depression marked an end to that period of interconnectedness, leading many to consider globalization a distinctly contemporary phenomenon that emerged in the 1970s with the rise of TNCs, the solidification of neoliberal ideology in the 1980s, and the exponential spread of Internet access since the 1990s.

Rather than offer a definitive response to the question "old or new," some analysts map the evolution of globalization through distinct phases. Roland Robertson described five phases. Phase 1, the *Germinal Phase,* takes place in Europe between the early fifteenth and mid-eighteenth centuries and entails the emergence and growth of national communities, the accentuation of concepts of the individual, and growing awareness of humanity. Phase 2, the *Incipient Phase,* occurs between the mid-eighteenth century and the 1870s, also mainly in Europe, and entails a "sharp shift towards the idea of the homogenous, unitary state," and the "crystallization of conceptions of formalized international relations" (Robertson, 1992: 58). Phase 3, the *Take-Off Phase,* occurs between the 1870s and the mid-1920s. This period witnesses increasingly global conceptions of what constitutes an "acceptable" national society, the inclusion of some non-European societies in "international society," a pronounced increase in the number and speed of global forms of communications, and the founding of the League of Nations. Phase 4, the *Struggle for Hegemony Phase*, lasts from the early 1920s until the mid-1960s and features "disputes and wars about the fragile terms" of globalization (Robertson, 1992: 59), and the founding of the UN. The final *Uncertainty Phase* begins in the 1960s with a heightening of global consciousness, and includes a dramatic increase in the number of global institutions and movements, a growing interest in world civil society, and the consolidation of a global media system. It also witnesses the end of the Cold War, the spread of nuclear weapons, and the increase in problems related to multiculturality in societies worldwide.

Geographer Jan Scholte also maps globalization by reference to distinct phases, in his case three. His first phase, the "emergence of a global imagination" (Scholte, 2000: 63), describes a long gestation period up to the eighteenth century. Religious faiths dating back to the fifth and sixth centuries BC, such as Buddhism, were premised on the notion of supra-territorial world community. Writers and thinkers spanning from the fourteenth to the eighteenth centuries, and ranging from Dante and Shakespeare to Enlightenment thinkers, evinced secular global thinking. Nonetheless, Scholte (2000: 65) concludes that "prior to the nineteenth century actual globality had little existence outside the mind." Phase 2, "incipient globalization," began in the 1850s and lasted through the 1950s. This period saw the emergence and consolidation of global communications technologies, global markets, and some degree of globality in finance and organization. As a result of the gold standard, some national currencies – most notably the British pound – circulated globally, and several worldwide organizations and movements also emerged. The International Red Cross was started in 1863; the International Telecommunication Union was founded in 1865, and the labor movement maintained its First International from 1864 to 1872, with two more before 1943 (Scholte, 2005: 97).

Because Scholte (2005: 101) defines globalization as the growth of supra-territorial spaces, he marks its "full-scale" emergence, phase 3, in the 1960s, and its most significant qualitative expansion in the decades since. "These years have seen far and away the greatest increase in the number, variety, intensity, and influence of global social phenomena." Among those phenomena are the vast array of global products that appeared in markets, the burgeoning growth in electronic commerce, the unprecedented global circulation and exchange of national currencies, and the emergence of suprastate currencies such as the International Monetary Fund's (IMF) Special Drawing Rights (SDR), and the euro.

Ultimately, what these chronologies of globalization reveal is that more helpful than debating whether or not the processes and patterns of contemporary worldwide interconnectedness are fundamentally new or different from those of the past, is acknowledging that they have certainly intensified. The implications of that intensification comprise another area of significant debate.

Globalization: Good or Bad?

Generally more contentious than disagreements about when globalization began are disputes about its implications: is globalization good or bad, in what sense, and for whom? The norms around which the debates revolve vary, but typically include: equality, diversity, and democracy.

Equality

Debates about globalization's implications for equality typically focus on economic and social justice issues. For example, are the costs and the benefits of globalization being fairly distributed between countries and between groups within countries? Is globalization a force for greater social and economic equity, or is it an ever more sophisticated mechanism for exploitation? Proponents or defenders of globalization, like defenders of trade liberalization more generally, have long argued that the deregulation of trade, of investment, and of the movement of capital improves market efficiency and greatly benefits both producers and consumers (Bhagwati, 2004; Wolf, 2000). When inequalities have persisted, globalization's defenders typically direct blame elsewhere, arguing, for example, that income disparity in an economy likely has "more to do with history, economic growth, price and wage controls, welfare programs, and education policies than it does with globalization or trade liberalization" (Foreign Policy, 2001: 64). As such, many policymakers and politicians, have argued, as did former President of Mexico Ernesto Zedillo in 2001, that, "more, not less, globalization is the answer." Globalization, Zedillo insisted, should not be viewed as a cause of worldwide poverty or economic disparity, but rather as "a vital part of the solution" (Zedillo, 2001).

Despite such optimism, opponents point to the increase in income inequality that has accompanied the intensification of globalization. In 1999, the UN issued a report on globalization revealing that the combined wealth of the world's three richest families was greater than the annual income of 600 million people in the least developed countries. In 1960, the gap between the richest fifth of the world's people and the poorest was 30 to 1. By 1990, it had widened to 60 to 1, and in 2000, stood at 74 to 1 (Held, 2000: 112).

As the new millennium wore on, evidence mounted that economic globalization was producing benefits, but only for a relatively few (Broad, 2016). In 2015, the World Economic Forum named income inequality the most significant global trend: "This affects all countries around the world. In developed and developing countries alike, the poorest half of the population often controls less than 10% of its wealth" (World Economic Forum, 2015). Oxfam International reported that in 2017, 8 individuals owned the same wealth as half of the world's 3.6 billion people. Stark differences in wealth and opportunity persisted between countries, but the greater increases in inequality occurred within countries. In the United States, for example, income inequality, measured by the Gini coefficient, began increasing steadily in the 1970s and each decade thereafter. Between 1979 and 2007, the average household income for the top 1 percent rose by 275 percent. The majority of the population in the middle of the scale saw growth of only 37 percent, and income for those at the very bottom grew by only 18 percent. In 1965, a corporate CEO in the United States earned, on average, more than twenty times a typical worker. In 2011, that ratio reached 383 to 1 (Markovich, 2014).

Other significant disparities exist alongside those in income and wealth. In 1999, the UN reported that 88 percent of all Internet users in the world live in the West (Held, 2000: 112). By 2016, global Internet access had improved markedly, but the World Bank confirmed in a 2016 report on digital technologies that more than half of humanity still remained offline (Sengupta, 2016). While 87 percent of the US population uses the Internet at least occasionally, that number drops to only 8 percent in Pakistan, for example (Poushter, Bell, and Oates, 2015). Even in the United States, one of the wealthiest and most developed countries in the world, access to broadband is still distributed unequally. In 2013, only 54 percent of US households with annual incomes less than $30,000 had broadband in the home, compared to 88 percent of households with incomes over $75,000 (Zickuhr and Smith, 2013).

After the worldwide financial shock of the 2008 recession, even globalization's supporters conceded that the benefits in terms of wealth creation had hit only a small proportion of the world's population. Their solution, however, was not less globalization, but fairer globalization. Christine Lagarde, Director of the IMF, suggested: "We can raise the income floor only by coming together and moving quickly to build a stronger, more inclusive global economy" (2017: 62). Martin Wolf, chief economics commentator for the *Financial Times,* proffered: "Globalization must not be made a scapegoat for all our ills ... a stalling would slow economic progress and reduce opportunities for the world's poor" (Wolf, 2016).

This debate will continue, even as the specific winners and losers of economic globalization shift. But, alongside globalization's implications for economic well-being are equally poignant questions about its consequences for cultural autonomy.

Diversity

"The central problem of today's global interactions," theorist Arjun Appadurai (1990: 295) explains, "is the tension between cultural homogenization and cultural heterogenization." Advances in communications and transportation technology have unquestionably led to a rapid and intensified exchange of ideas, information, cultural symbols, and modes of behavior. Less clear is whether the outcome of this interchange is convergence around a Western-dominated and commodity-driven world culture, or a more dialectical and multilateral process whereby individual, groups, and locales negotiate and reshape the local meaning and significance of global cultural symbols.

The former position posits increased levels of homogenization and points to a global culture industry with roots in the United States that has people worldwide, from Johannesburg to Rio de Janeiro, wearing Levis, drinking Coca-Cola, and visiting, or dreaming of visiting, a Disney theme park. Benjamin Barber (1992: 53) coined the term "McWorld," to capture this "onrush of forces that demand integration and uniformity and that mesmerize the world with fast music, fast computers, and fast food," while sociologist George Ritzer (2007: 11) popularized the related concept of "McDonaldization" to describe "forces bringing increasing sameness, or homogeneity, to much of the world." Cultural globalization, from this perspective, represents nothing more than a form of cultural imperialism.

Frequently cited examples of how globalization facilitates Westernization at the expense of global cultural diversity include Hollywood's global dominance of the film industry, and the global dominance of the English language (Steger, 2017). For many decades, on any list of the top-ten grossing films worldwide, Hollywood has dominated all of the top-ten slots in all but a few cases. In 2009, the twenty top grossing films in the world were predominantly American productions (Crane, 2014); and every year between 2009 and 2014, the top twenty box-office performers in the world were films by US companies and their partners (Cieply, 2014).

Alongside the pervasiveness of American popular culture is the status of English as the predominant language in global culture. Currently, more than 380 million people in the world speak English as a native language, and another 250 million speak it as a second language. An estimated 1 billion people in the world are learning English, and experts anticipate that by 2050, half of the world's population will be proficient in the language (Xue and Zuo, 2013). English is the main language for communication on the Internet, within and between global organizations, and among the world's scientists. In 1880, 36 percent of scientific publications used English. In 1980, the percentage had increased to 64 percent, and by 2000, 96 percent of the scholarly journals recognized by *Journal Citation Reports* were published in English (Pickels, 2016). As English continues its global ascendency, the diversity of languages spoken in the world declines. In the year 1500, 14,500 different languages were spoken worldwide. By 2012, the number had dropped to 6,500. At this rate, anywhere between 50 to 90 percent of the world's current languages will have disappeared by the end of the twenty-first century (Steger, 2017: 86).

Reacting to the predominance of US culture, many countries such as France, Canada, and more recently Russia, have mounted campaigns against Americanization. In 1998, Canada sponsored a two-day International Meeting on Cultural Policy during which Canadian cultural heritage minister Sheila Copps insisted, "Americanization of cultures is a major concern" (quoted in Stewart, 1998: A10). In 1999, French farmer José Bové achieved hero-like status after he was arrested for vandalizing a local McDonald's. And in 2014, as tensions mounted between the United States and Russia over Ukraine, Russia ordered the closure of McDonald's restaurants in Moscow. At that time, the fast food giant was serving more than 1 million customers per day in over 400 stores throughout Russia (Gorst, 2014).

The cultural homogenization thesis is compelling, but many analysts question whether this conceptualization captures reality. Sociologist Jan Nederveen Pieterse (2015), for example, argues that globalization, rather than being viewed in terms of standardization, should be recognized as a process of "hybridization" that gives rise to "translocal mélange cultures." To view globalization as a process of homogenization obscures its fluid, indeterminate, open-ended, and multidimensional nature. Roland Robertson (1995) proposes that instead of focusing on the global and the local as opposing forces, we employ the term "glocalization" to capture the dialectical and contingent interchange between local cultures and global trends. Cultures are not static, uniform, organic entities highly vulnerable to imposed alteration by outside forces. Instead, when different cultures interact over an extended time period, even if on unequal terms, what typically emerges are new cultural forms that are not merely derived from one or the other culture. The potentially homogenizing tools of communications and information technology can also serve to preserve and promote indigenous languages, local cuisines, and ancestral art forms. In this way, globalization facilitates diversity rather than squelching it (Cowen, 2004).

Democracy

Related to how globalization might impinge on cultural autonomy is the broader issue of how the global compression of time and space affects political rights, and particularly democracy. This question is complicated by the fact that democracy itself is a contested concept. Typically defined as "rule by the people," and based on the principle that members of a polity should have the capacity to shape decisions that affect their lives, disagreement ensues as to: who constitutes the people, and what precisely does it mean to rule? Nevertheless, in the aftermath of the Cold War, leaders and observers, particularly in the West, presumed that globalization would lead to widespread democratization. A number of political scientists proclaimed the "twilight of authoritarianism" (Pye, 1990), or the "end of history" (Fukuyama, 1989), arguing that liberal democracy had triumphed over competing ideologies, that its appeal was universal, and that the increasing interconnectedness of the world would facilitate a global democratic contagion. Expanding membership in global governance regimes was expected to facilitate the spread of intrinsically valuable democratic norms and new and multiple levels of access through which individuals could pursue rights and participate in politics. Advances in communications and information technology would aid social movements fighting for political opening in authoritarian regimes, and help to fortify an emerging "global civil society" (Keane, 2003). Economic liberalization was expected to spur social pressure for political reform in countries throughout the world. In some cases, this occurred, in others not (Dalpino, 2001).

Respect and accountability for human rights has become more global, as evinced, for example, by the success of the International Criminal Tribunals on the former Yugoslavia and Rwanda, and the subsequent creation and ratification of the International Criminal Court. The post–Cold War political openings, particularly in Eastern Europe, were remarkable, as has been the role of communications technologies in supporting social movements worldwide. Chinese protestors in Tiananmen Square in 1989 made skillful use of fax machines. During the early 1990s, the Zapatista rebels in Mexico relied on the then-revolutionary Internet to transmit daily e-mail updates worldwide from the remote jungle areas of Chiapas. Twenty years later, much more advanced and globally dispersed technology and social media platforms played a central role in social uprisings in Egypt, Tunisia, and other Arab countries in what came to be known as the Arab Spring; and, in 2014, protestors in Hong Kong resisting Chinese control over elections skillfully used social media applications to avoid the Chinese government's Internet censoring.

The current record on democracy is not, however, a uniformly rosy one. Worldwide *awareness* of the democratic norms of human rights has been heightened much more than *compliance* (IIGGP, 2012). In Eastern Europe, many of the countries that were considered "poster children for post-communist democratization," Hungary and Poland among them, have recently experienced a dramatic rise of nationalist populist leaders who came to power promoting policies that are at best indifferent to key tenets of liberal democracy, and at worst openly hostile to them (Krastev, 2018). Meanwhile, technological innovation clearly has the capacity to support democratization, but, as noted above, access to advanced information and communications technology is not equally distributed around the world, and the same technology that assists social movements in their pursuit of democracy also assists states in their subversion and surveillance of these movements.

As the Internet gained in popularity, many governments sought, and often secured, control over its use and content. China has been remarkably effective at controlling information and access to it – resorting, for example, to the massive shutdown of Internet cafés. And software companies, most of them American, have found a lucrative market in helping countries throughout the Middle East, particularly Saudi Arabia, block access to websites the government deems inappropriate (Lee, 2001: C1). Russia has recently mounted concerted, and successful, efforts to use technology to undermine democratic elections in the United States and Europe. And the same technological tools available to pro-democracy movements are equally available to and utilized by extremist groups actively opposed to Western liberal democracy.

Finally, the assumption, a largely Western one, that global economic integration would beget political liberalization is contradicted by the number of countries experiencing impressive economic growth under solidly authoritarian regimes. Singapore consistently ranks high on indices of globalization, but with little challenge to a semi-authoritarian state. China benefits from economic globalization without fundamentally altering its political system. Russian dissidents complain that the country's greater economic internationalization has worsened official corruption (Dalpino, 2001). Moreover, when global economic crises erupt, countries that had begun instituting political reforms often halt them in the name of maintaining order. Globalization can boost authoritarianism rather than weaken it.

Signs of ascendant autocracy and a crisis of democracy are evident in many parts of the world today – including in the established liberal democracies of Western Europe, and the US Survey data show that although two thirds of Americans over the age of sixty-five consider living in a democracy as "absolutely important" to them, only one third of Americans under the age of thirty-five agree. Meanwhile, in France, Germany, and Italy, the proportion of the population willing to support military rule more than tripled from 1995 to 2017 (Mounk and Foa, 2018: 29–30). The efficacy of these attitudes is confirmed by recent electoral support for authoritarian leaders in those same regions. Mounk and Foa attribute the contemporary disillusionment with democracy to the declining ability of liberal democratic states to satisfy the economic expectations of their citizenries, while a growing number of authoritarian states have improved their ability to do so (2018). From this perspective, it seems that neither capitalism nor globalization naturally spread democracy.

Debates about the normative implications of globalization will likely persist, due in part to the fact that the debates involve value judgments around which consensus rarely exists, and to the fact that the multifaceted processes that comprise globalization are experienced differently around the world. For an Indian software designer, globalization may look like a good thing. For an American autoworker it may not. That same autoworker may, however, appreciate the supply of low-cost imported goods available at Wal-Mart, and the opportunity to chat with a far-away grandchild via Skype. A French child who grew up loving Mickey Mouse might have been thrilled when Disney opened its theme park just outside of Paris. Her parents who feel strongly attached to the French culture and language likely were not. Young people in China enjoy easy access to material and cultural products unimaginable to their elders. Such freedom to choose remains elusive, however, at election time. In this regard, Kofi Annan's comparison between globalization and gravity works: gravity feels like a positive thing while walking securely on the Earth's surface, and less so when you trip and fall.

Conclusion: The End?

Globalization's obituary has been written multiple times, and perhaps most emphatically in relation to the economic and political fallout from the Great Recession of 2008. *Fortune* magazine pronounced in 2012 that globalism was going "backward" (Ramo, 2012). In a 2016 article for the World Economic Forum, "Globalization Is Dead: What Now?" Paul Laudicina, Chairman, A. T. Kearney Global Business Policy Council, wrote: "Charting the seven years since the global financial crisis, my colleagues and I . . . posit the effective end of the period of world history known as globalization" (Laudicina, 2016). Matthew Rooney of the George H. W. Bush Institute shared that assessment, although invoking a different indicator: "The outcome of the presidential election [of 2016] marks the end of globalization" (Rooney, 2017), and in December of 2016, the British *Guardian* ran a headline: "It's too late for hand-wringing. Globalisation is already dead" (Swarup, 2016).

Yet, alongside every proclamation of globalization's demise is an equally compelling insistence that it lives on. Using data from the IMF, a *Wall Street Journal* post in 2016 responded to the query, "Is Globalization Dead?" with a definitive "no:" "Globalization hasn't hit the skids . . . a careful study of cross-border finance, trade, immigration and data flows reveals strong evidence the global economy is still integrating at a steady pace" (Talley, 2016). Indeed, within years of the onset of the Great Recession some of the key indicators of global economic integration, including cross-border bank lending, had again turned positive (McCauley, 2015), and by 2017, world trade was again on the rise, leading outlets like *Bloomberg View* to acknowledge: "OK, Maybe Globalization Isn't Dead" (Fox, 2017).

Ultimately, whether globalization is pronounced dead or not depends on how it is defined. Only if defined in very narrow terms can globalization be convincingly deemed dead, and perhaps not even then. Decelerations in specific measures of economic interconnectedness do not sound a death knell for globalization; nor does a crack in what might once have appeared as political consensus regarding the benefits of globalization. Speaking to this latter point, Ariadna Estévez maintained that "globalization isn't dead, it's just shed its slick cover story" (2017). For Estévez, that the political shine seems to have recently worn off globalization for many people particularly in the developed world does nothing to counter the fact that it is and always has been essentially neoliberalism. That free-market orthodoxy is alive and well and deeply embedded in policies and practices worldwide.

Globalization is not in retreat. As analysts Susan Lund and Laura Tyson (2018: 130) explain, it is "continuing its forward march, but along new paths." It is less Western-led, as the locus of its activity and dynamism shifts toward China and other emerging economies. Its form is less a "series of lines connecting major trading hubs," and more of a "complex, intricate, sprawling web" (Dobbs, Manyika, and Woetzel, 2015). And it is driven less by traditional trade, and more by digital technology. As has been the case since the beginning of time, the implications of such dynamic and multifaceted processes will vary widely, and none are solidly foreseeable. It is in this respect that Annan's analogy to the laws of gravity is somewhat flawed, as gravity's consequences are more scientifically predictable. Nevertheless, globalization, like gravity has a distant beginning, about which disagreement persists. As with gravity, globalization's ubiquity and complexity confound attempts at normative assessment of its consequences. Finally, even though gravity adheres to certain laws, humankind has continually discovered ways to better understand and manage that powerful force. That globalization is arguably more malleable enhances the opportunity for its constructive management. The challenge, and not a small or new one, is for humans to negotiate a shared vision for what constitutes constructive management.

References

ACPSA. 2015. *Arts and Cultural Production Satellite Account, Brief #5: Imports and Exports of Arts and Cultural Goods and Services*. Washington, DC: Office of Research & Analysis National Endowment for the Arts, January, 2015. www.arts.gov/sites/default/files/ADP6-5_ImportsandExports.pdf

Alfaro, Laura, and Maggie Chen. 2010. "Surviving the Global Financial Crisis: Foreign Direct Investment and Establishment Performance." *Harvard Business School: Working Paper* (June 2010): 10–110.

Ambrecht, Arwen. 2016. "Where are the Global Cities of the Future?" *World Economic Forum* (February 1). www.weforum.org/agenda/2016/02/who-has-the-largest-migrant-population/

Annan, Kofi. 1999. "Secretary-General Proposes Global Compact on Human Rights, Labour, Environment, in Address to World Economic Forum in Davos." United Nations Press Release SG/SM/6881 (February 1). New York: United Nations. www.un.org/press/en/1999/19990201.sgsm6881.html

Appadurai, Arun. 1990. "Disjuncture and Difference in the Global Cultural Economy." *Theory, Culture and Society* 7: 295–310.

1996. *Modernity at Large: Cultural Dimensions of Globalization*. Minneapolis, MN: University of Minnesota Press.

Barber, Benjamin. 1992. "Jihad vs. McWorld." *Atlantic Monthly* (March): 53–63.

Bhagwati, Jagdish. 2004. *In Defense of Globalization*. Oxford, UK: Oxford University Press.

Blanton, Shannon L., and Charles W. Kegley. 2017. *World Politics: Trends and Transformations*. Boston, MA: Cengage Learning.

Bordo, Michael D., Alan M. Taylor, and Jeffrey G. Williamson. 2003. "Globalization in Historical Perspective." *National Bureau of Economic Research*. Chicago, IL: University of Chicago Press.

Boren, Zachary D. 2014. "There are Officially More Mobile Devices than People in the World." *The Independent*, October 7. www.independent.co.uk/life-style/gadgets -and-tech/news/there-are-officially-more-mobile-devices-than-people-in-the- world-9780518.html

Brancaccio, David. 2017. "Is Globalization in Decline?" *MarketPlace*, August 18. www .marketplace.org/2017/08/18/world/trade-stories-globalization-and-backlash/globa lization-decline

Broad, Mark. 2016. "Why Is Globalisation Under Attack?" *BBC News*, October 6. www .bbc.com/news/business-37554634

Callimachi, Rukmini. 2016. "How a Secretive Branch of ISIS Built a Global Network of Killers." *The New York Times*, August 3. www.nytimes.com/2016/08/04/world/middleeast/isis- german-recruit-interview.html?emc=edit_th_20160804&nl=todaysheadlines&n lid=69662753&_r=1

Central Intelligence Agency (CIA). 2015. "Total Number of Mobile Cellular Telephone Subscribers as of July 2015: 7 billion." *CIA World Factbook*. Previously available at: www.cia.gov/library/publications/the-world-factbook/fields/2151.html

Committee on the Global Financial System (CGFS). 2010. *Long-Term Issues in International Banking*. Paper No. 41 (July). Report submitted by a study group established by the Committee on the Global Financial System, Basel, Switzerland. www.bis.org/publ/ cgfs41.pdf

Cieply, Michael. 2014. "Hollywood Works to Maintain Its Dominance." *The New York Times*, November 3. www.nytimes.com/2014/11/04/business/media/hollywood-works-to- maintain-its-world-dominance.html?mcubz=0

Cowen, Tyler. 2004. *Creative Destruction: How Globalization Is Changing the World's Cultures*. Princeton, NJ: Princeton University Press.

Crane, Diana. 2014. "Cultural Globalization and the Dominance of the American Film Industry." *International Journal of Cultural Policy* 20(4): 365–382.

Crossette, Barbara. 2000. "Globalization Tops 3-day U. N. Agenda for World Leaders." *The New York Times*, September 3: www.nytimes.com/2000/09/03/world/globalization -tops-3-day-un-agenda-for-world-leaders.html

Croucher, Sheila. 2018. *Globalization and Belonging: The Politics of Identity in a Changing World*. Lanham, MD: Rowman and Littlefield.

Dalpino, Catharin E. 2001. "Does Globalization Promote Democracy?" Washington, DC: Brookings Institution, September 1. www.brookings.edu/articles/does -globalization -promote-democracy-an-early-assessment/

Dobbs, Richard, James Manyika, and Jonathan Woetzel. 2015. "The Four Global Forces Breaking All the Trends." *McKinsey Global Institute*, April. www.mckinsey.com /business-functions/strategy-and-corporate-finance/our-insights/the-four-global -forces-breaking-all-the-trends

Edwards, Adrian. 2016. "Forced Displacement at Record 68.5 Million." United Nations High Commissioner on Refugees (UNHCR). www.unhcr.org/en-us/news/stories/2018/6/5b222c494/forced-displacement-record-685-million.html

Eichengreen, Barry, Ashoka Mody, Milan Nedelikovic, and Lucio Sarno. 2012. "How the Sub-Prime Crisis Went Global." *Journal of International Money and Finance* 31(5): 1299–1318.

Ellyatt, Holly. 2013. "Global Drug Trade 'as Strong as Ever' as Fight Fails." *CNBC Europe*, August 13. www.cnbc.com/id/100957882

Estévez, Ariadna. 2017. "Globalization Isn't Dead, It's Just Shed Its Slick Cover Story." *Huffington Post*, May 27. www.huffingtonpost.com/entry/globalisation-isnt-dead-its-just-shed-its-slick_us_5926f2f8e4b090bac9d46c05

Facebook. 2018. "Company Info." FB.com, May 30. https://newsroom.fb.com/company-info/

Flanagan, Stephen, Ellen L. Frost, and Richard L. Kugler. 2001. *Challenges of the Global Century: Report of the Project on Globalization and 'National Security*. Washington, DC: National Defense University Press.

Foreign Policy. 2001. "Measuring Globalization." *Foreign Policy*, January/February: 56–66.

Fox, Justin. 2017. "OK, Maybe Globalization Isn't Dead." *Bloomberg View*, April 25. www.bloombergquint.com/opinion/ok-maybe-globalization-isn-t-dead

Fukuyama, Francis. 1989. "The End of History." *National Interest* (Summer): 3–18.

Giddens, Anthony. 1995. "The New Context of Politics." *Democratic Dialogue* 1: 8–23.

2003. *Runaway World*. New York and London: Routledge.

Gorst, Isabel. 2014. "Russia to McDonald's: We're Closing It." *Los Angeles Times*, August 20. www.latimes.com/world/europe/la-fg-russia-to-mcdonalds-were-closing-it-20140820-story.html

Gray, John. 2001. "The Era of Globalisation is Over." *The New Statesman*, September 24. www.i-p-o.org/globalization-gray.htm

Grier, Peter. 2001. "A Terrorist Version of NATO?" *Christian Science Monitor*, February 2, p. 1.

Held, David. 1998. "Democracy and Globalization." In D. Archibugi, D. Held, and M. Köhler (eds.), *Re-imagining Political Community* (pp. 11–27). Stanford, CA: Stanford University Press.

Held, David (ed.) 2000. *A Globalizing World? Culture, Economics, Politics*. London: Routledge.

Hollander, Rayna. 2018. "We Chat has hit 1 billion monthly active users." *Business Insider*, March 6. www.businessinsider.com/wechat-has-hit-1-billion-monthly-active-users-2018-3?r=DE&IR=T

"Imports of Goods and Services as a Percentage of Gross Domestic Product." 2017. *World Bank Data*. http://data.worldbank.org/indicator/NE.IMP.GNFS.ZS

International Air Transport Association (IATA). 2017. "Passenger Demand Growth Hits Five-Year Peak in January." March 7. www.iata.org/pressroom/pr/Pages/2017-03-07-01.aspx.

IIGGP (International Institutions and Global Governance Program). 2012. "The Global Human Rights Regime." *Council on Foreign Relations*, May 11. www.cfr.org/report/global-human-rights-regime

Internet World Stats. 2018. "Usage and Population Statistics." www.internetworldstats.com/stats.htm

Jervis, Robert. 2002. "An Interim Assessment of September 11: What Has Changed and What Has Not?" *Political Science Quarterly* 117(1): 37–55.

Keane, John. 2003. *Global Civil Society*. Cambridge, UK: Cambridge University Press.

Keohane, Robert, and Joseph Nye. 1977. *Power and Interdependence: World Politics in Transition*. Boston, MA: Little, Brown.

Krastev, Ivan. 2018. "Eastern Europe's Illiberal Revolution." *Foreign Affairs* 97(3): 49–59.

Lagarde, Christine. 2017. "The Challenge of Economic Inclusion." *Project Syndicate*, January 11. www.project-syndicate.org/onpoint/the-challenge-of-economic-inclusion-by-christine-lagarde-2017

Laudicina, Paul. 2016. "Globalization Is Dead: What Now?" *World Economic Forum* (January 20). www.weforum.org/agenda/2016/01/globalization-is-dead-what-now/

Lee, Jennifer. 2001. "Companies Compete to Provide Internet Veil for the Saudis." *New York Times*, November 19, p. C1.

Lund, Susan, and Laura Tyson. 2018. "Globalization is Not in Retreat." *Foreign Affairs* 97 (3): 130–140.

Markovich, Steven J. 2014. "The Income Inequality Debate." *Council on Foreign Relations*, February 3. www.cfr.org/backgrounder/income-inequality-debate

May, Channing. 2017. "Transnational Crime and the Developing World." *Global Financial Integrity*, March 27. www.gfintegrity.org/report/transnational-crime-and-the-developing-world/

McCauley, Robert. 2015. "International Banking Since the Crisis: Four Trends." Panel Remarks at the Symposium on "What *Has* Happened to Cross-Border Banking Since the Crisis?" April 21, London. London: Brevan Howard Centre for Financial Analysis. Previously available at: https://workspace.imperial.ac.uk/business-school/Public/brevan-howard-centre-for-financial-analysis/The%20Clearing%20House%20Symposium/Bob%20McCauley.pdf

Mittelman, James H. 2000. *The Globalization Syndrome: Transformation and Resistance*. Princeton, NJ: Princeton University Press.

Mounk, Yascha, and Roberto S. Foa. 2018. "The End of the Democratic Century." *Foreign Affairs* 97(3): 29–38.

OECD. 2005. *Handbook on Economic Globalisation Indicators*. Paris, France: OECD.

Oman, Charles. 1996. "The Policy Challenges of Globalisation and Regionalisation." OECD Development Centre, Policy Brief 11. Paris, France: OECD.

O'Rourke, Kevin, and Jeffrey G. Williamson. 1999. *Globalization and History*. Cambridge, MA: The MIT Press.

Owen, Paul, and David Smith. 2017. "Nigel Farage says Brexit and Trump win are 'Beginning of Global Revolution.'" *The Guardian*, February 24. www.theguardian.com/us-news/2017/feb/24/nigel-farage-cpac-speech-trump-brexit-global-revolution.

Pickels, Matt. 2016. "Could the Dominance of English Harm Global Scholarship?" *BBC News*, January 20. www.bbc.com/news/business-35282235.

Pieterse, Jan Nederveen. 2015. *Globalization and Culture: Global Mélange*. Lanham, MD: Rowman and Littlefield.

Poulsen, Lauge S., and Gary C. Hufbauer. 2011. *Foreign Direct Investment in Times of Crisis* (Working Paper Series WP11-3). Washington, DC: Peterson Institute for International Economics. https://ideas.repec.org/p/iie/wpaper/wp11-3.html

Poushter, Jacob, James Bell, and Russ Oates. 2015. "Internet Seen as Positive Influence on Education but Negative on Morality in Emerging and Developing Nations." Pew

Research Center, March 19. Previously available at: www.pewglobal.org/files/2015/03/Pew-Research-Center-Technology-Report-FINAL-March-19–20151.pdf

Pye, Lucian. 1990. "Political Science and the Crisis of Authoritarianism." *American Political Science Review* 84(1): 3–19.

Ramo, Joshua Cooper. 2012. "Globalism Goes Backward." *Fortune Magazine*, November 20. http://fortune.com/2012/11/20/globalism-goes-backward/

Ritzer, George. 2007. *The Globalization of Nothing 2*. Thousand Oaks, CA: Pine Forge Press.

Robertson, Roland. 1992. *Globalization: Social Theory and Global Culture*. London: Sage.
1995. "Glocalization: Time-Space and Homogeneity-Heterogeneity." In Mike Featherstone, Scott Lash, and Roland Robertson (eds.), *Global Modernities* (pp. 25–44). London: Sage.

Rodrick, Dani. 1997. *Has Globalization Gone Too Far?* New York: Columbia University Press.

Rooney, Matthew. 2017. "Globalization Is Dead, Long Live Globalization." *The Catalyst* (Issue 5): www.bushcenter.org/catalyst/whats-next/rooney-globalization-is-dead-.html

Scholte, Jan A. 2000. *Globalization: A Critical Introduction*. New York: St. Martin's Press.
2005. *Globalization: A Critical Introduction*, 2nd ed. New York: St. Martin's Press.

Sengupta, Somini. 2016. "Internet Yields Uneven Dividends and May Widen Inequality." *The New York Times*, January 13. www.nytimes.com/2016/01/14/world/asia/internet-yields-uneven-dividends-and-may-widen-inequality-report-says.html?_r=1

Simon, Leslie D. 2001. "The Net: Power and Policy in the 21st Century." In R. L. Kugler and E. L. Frost (eds.), *The Global Century: Globalization and National Security* (pp. 613–633). Washington, DC: National Defense University Press.

SOPEMI. 2001. *Continuous Reporting System on Migration. Trends in International Migration.* Annual Report. Organization for Economic Cooperation and Development. www.oecd.org/migration/mig/2508596.pdf

Steger, Manfred B. 2017. *Globalization: A Very Short Introduction*. Oxford, UK: Oxford University Press.

Stewart, Elizabeth. 1998. "Push on for Cultural Diversity." *Toronto Star*, June 28, p. A10.

Stiglitz, Joseph. 2017. *Globalization and Its Discontents Revisited*. New York: W. W. Norton and Co.

Swarup, Bob. 2016. "It's Too Late for Hand-Wringing. Globalisation Is Already Dead." *The Guardian,* December 2. www.theguardian.com/business/economics-blog/2016/dec/02/too-late-for-hand-wringing-globalisation-dead.

Talley, Ian. 2016. "Is Globalization Dead? A Different View of the Data Says No." *The Wall Street Journal*, November 30. https://blogs.wsj.com/economics/2016/11/30/is-globalization-dead-a-different-view-of-the-data-says-no/.

Thachuk, Kimberly L. 2001. "The Sinister Underbelly: Organized Crime and Terrorism." In R. L. Kugler and E. L. Frost (eds.), *The Global Century: Globalization and National Security* (pp. 743–760). Washington, DC: National Defense University Press.

UIS (United Nations Institute for Statistics). 2016. *The Globalisation of Cultural Trade: A Shift in Consumption: International Flows of Cultural Goods and Services 2004–2013*. New York: UIS. Previously available at: http://uis.unesco.org/sites/default/files/documents/the-globalisation-of-cultural-trade-a-shift-in-consumption-international-flows-of-cultural-goods-services-2004-2013-en_0.pdf

UNCTAD (United Nations Conference on Trade and Development). 2001. *World Investment Report 2001*. Geneva: United Nations Conference on Trade and Development.

UNDP. 1999. *Human Development Report*. United Nations Development Program. New York: Oxford University Press.

Wattles, Jackie. 2015. "Facebook Hits 1 Billion Users in a Single Day." *CNN Tech*, August 28. http://money.cnn.com/2015/08/27/technology/facebook-one-billion-users-single-day/

Wolf, Martin. 2000. "Why This Hatred of the Market." In F. J. Lechner and J. Boli (eds.), *The Globalization Reader* (pp. 9–11). Oxford, UK: Blackwell.

2004. *Why Globalization Works*. New Haven, CT: Yale University Press.

2016. "The Tide of Globalization Is Turning." *Financial Times*, September 6. www.ft.com /content/87bb0eda-7364-11e6-bf48-b372cdb1043a

World Economic Forum. 2015. "Top Ten Trends." *Outlook on the Global Agenda, 2015*. Geneva, Switzerland. http://reports.weforum.org/outlook-global-agenda-2015/top -10-trends-of-2015/1-deepening-income-inequality/

WTO. 2008. *World Trade Report 2008: Trade in a Globalizing World*. Geneva, Switzerland: World Trade Organization.

Xue, Jiao, and Wenjing Zuo. 2013. "English Dominance and Its Influence on International Communications." *Theory and Practice in Language Studies* 3(12): 2262–2266.

Yester, Katherine. 2009. "Measuring Globalization." *Foreign Policy*, November 20. http:// foreignpolicy.com/2009/11/20/measuring-globalization/.

Zedillo, Ernesto. 2001. "More, Not Less, Globalization Is the Answer." *Vital Speeches of the Day* 67(17) (June 15): 514–518.

Zickuhr, Kathryn, and Aaron Smith. 2013. "Home Broadband 2013. Internet and Technology." August 26. Washington, DC: Pew Research Center. www .pewinternet.org/2013/08/26/home-broadband-2013/

11 Time/Space

Kevin Fox Gotham

Introduction

Over the past several decades, theoretical and empirical research on the causes, impacts, and consequences of time/space restructuring has proliferated across the natural and physical sciences, art and humanities, and social sciences. Broad transformations in politics, migration, culture, identity, technology, and socioeconomic relations have given rise to several sets of phenomena related to time/space. One is the development of a globalized economy involving new systems of production, finance, and consumption (Held and McGrew, 2007). A second is the rise of new transnational cultural patterns and practices that both reflect and reinforce trends toward cultural homogenization and diversification (Appadurai, 1996; Featherstone, 1990). A third is the cross-scale spread of global governance and authority structures (Brenner, 2004; McGrew and Held, 2002). A fourth is the unprecedented movement of people around the world involving new patterns of cross-border migration and formation of new identities and communities (May and Thrift, 2003; Sassen, 1999). A fifth is the development of new forms of social-spatial hierarchies, inequalities, and relations of domination and subordination both within nation states and across the nation-state system as a whole (Robinson, 2008; Sassen, 2001). These strands of research reflect an enormous variety of topics, from transnational sexualities to global tourism, changes in the state, the restructuring of work, globalization and crime, the global media, and so on. This explosion of research points to the ubiquity of time/space conceptualizations, empirical indicators, ontologies, epistemologies, and theorizations.

Since the 1980s, scholars have begun to rethink traditional social categories such as class, race, gender, and power through the prism of space and time (Gieryn, 2000; Liggett and Perry, 1995; Lobao, Hooks, and Tickamyer, 2007). For Urry (1995: 378–379) "space makes a clear difference to the degree to which [...] the causal powers of social entities (such as class, the state, capitalist relations, patriarchy) are realized." Related, Henri Lefebvre (1991b: 416) argued that "groups, classes, or fractions of classes cannot constitute themselves, or recognize one another, as 'subjects' unless they generate (or produce) a space." The fact that time and space matters, according to geographer Doreen Massey (1984: 14), requires us to consider that "processes take place over space, the facts of distances, closeness, of geographic variation between areas, of individual character and meaning of specific places and repair – all these are essential in the operation of social processes themselves."

Gotham (2014 [2002]) has developed the concept *racialization of space* to refer to the linkages between discriminatory practices of the real-estate sector and the creation and development of racial residential segregation. In discussing relationships between gendered space and women's status, Spain (1992, 1993) argues that gender stratification in homes, workplaces, and schools reduces women's access to socially valued knowledge and services to reproduce prevailing status differences. The more pronounced the degree of spatial gender segregation, according to Spain, the lower is women's status related to men's status (see also DeSena, 2008; Massey, 2013).

This essay addresses major debates involving time/space relationships and processes of socio-spatial, techno-economic, and cultural transformation. I first introduce and discuss conceptions of time/space in classical social theory. Next, I describe contributions and conceptual innovations related to accounts of time/space distanciation, compression, and intensification. I then discuss recent scholarship on the causal impacts, developmental trajectories, and consequences of various rescaling processes. In the fourth section of the chapter, I focus on recent debates on the relationship among fixity and liquidity in scholarship on the political economy of real estate and finance. Next, I devote attention to specifying the major topics of research in tourism, entertainment, and spectacle related to the homogenizing impacts and diversification features of temporal-spatial restructuring. In all the debates I cover, scholars recognize that social interaction takes place "in" time and space and "across" time and space. At the same time, humans are agents of change that are constantly acting upon and transforming time/space relationships through individual and group decision-making. Indeed, just as constructed meanings of social life have time/space components, time/space is a constitutive feature of human agency and social structure. Quoting Slevin (2011: 650), "The ordering of social life comes about because social practices are routinely made to come together across time/space as shared experiences." Thus, people construct and express notions of time/space in the ways in which they create and organize social structures, institutions, groups, and communities.

Conceptions of Time/Space in Classical Social Theory

Time/space has always been a central topic of sociological concern. For decades scholars have noted that the rise of classical social theory from the 1880s to World War I coincided with the emergence of new conceptions of space and time, embodied not only in artistic and cultural modernism but in the rise of bureaucratic forms of administration and such scientific innovations as relativity theory and quantum mechanics. In the *Manifesto of the Communist Party*, Marx and Engels (1978 [1848]) theorized how capitalist industrialization promoted rapid urbanization and restructured work relations, thus transforming small agrarian towns with their chain of venerable traditions into highly populated cities in which "all that is solid melts into air." In theorizing the rise of disciplined "clock time," Marx argued that the rationalization of time is inseparable from the commodification of labor:

schedules, quotas, and deadlines separate and organize workers' time into abstract quantities of work time, home time, and leisure time. In turn, each of these zones of time are bounded off from one another, assigned a discrete beginning time and ending time, and valued using the abstract measure of money (Marx, 1993 [1957]: 37). For Marx, clock time is thus seen primarily as a tool of economic power relations that facilitates the transformation of "life-time" into "working time" and the domination of capital over the meaning and use of "time" in modern society (1977: 799)

Later Marxian theorists elaborated on critical Marxist insights. Influenced by Marx's theory of capitalism, E. P. Thompson (1967: 69) argued that the imposition of time-discipline upon workers marked "the transition to mature industrial society [and] a severe restructuring of working habits – new disciplines, new incentives, and a new human nature upon which these incentives could bite." As a result, "a general diffusion of clocks and watches is occurring at the exact moment when the industrial revolution demanded a greater synchronization of labor." For Thompson, the internalization of time-discipline by workers suffices as a form of domination and subordination of the worker to the work and time demands of industrial capital (1967: 91). Extending the theory of time/space as a mechanism of social domination and control, Postone (1996) argues that clock time evolves historically as the wage-labor relationship becomes a global tendency. Like Marx, Postone views clock time as a mechanism of social domination that acts as a form of compulsion. Drawing on Marx's theory of alienated labor, Postone suggests that clock time reflects and reinforces the alienation of workers from the product of labor, from the means of production, from workers themselves, and from human-species being. The mechanism of alienation in modern society, according to Postone, is the discipline of the clock. Clock time estranges workers from knowing about and understanding other possible ways of relating to time and thereby assigns and controls to them a fixed routine of activity in the service of capital.

Max Weber's historical analytical investigations of the rise of Protestantism, the city as economic market, and political military development reflect a concern with understanding the origin of modern Western rational capitalism and its impacts on the organization of space and time (Weber, 1958). In the *Protestant Ethic and the Spirit of Capitalism*, Weber (2011) argued that modern clock time is a cultural practice permeated by the "this-worldly asceticism," an ideology that valorizes active life and denigrates inactivity. Weber showed that before industrialists and bureaucrats used clocks and schedules to order individuals' lives, religious leaders associated with the early Protestant sects developed an ideology of temporal conduct that was reflected symbolically in the constant beat of the mechanical clock and the methodical routine of the schedule (Weber, 2011: 130–132). In developing a neo-Weberian approach to clock time, Snyder (2013: 243) argues that clock time is a "moral institution that shapes social action in modernity through two 'time disciplines': regularity and density. Where regularity supports a methodical life, density maintains a life of constant activity." Clock time facilitates the construction of meaningful action in time-space and enables social actors to creatively organize and direct mental and physical energy to the production of social life. A neo-Weberian approach to time/space theorizes clocks and schedules as bearers of socio-spatial meanings. Once people internalize notions of time and space in their psyche, clock time shapes behavior by disciplining different dimensions of temporal conduct – standardization, coordination, regularity, and density.

In the *Division of Labor in Society*, Emile Durkheim theorized that the dissolution of segmental social structures and increased frequency of contact among different groups of people is associated with the emergence of new categories of spatial and temporal knowledge associated with modern society (Durkheim, 1964 [1893]: 259–260). With the development of the modern division of labor characterized by specialization, differentiation, and complexity, previously insular and autonomous communities gradually became interrelated parts of a single systemic whole defined by organic solidarity. For Durkheim, new spatial and temporal representations come to dominate modern life and these representations mirror dominant patterns of social organization. In developing a sociohistorical approach to the standardization of time, Zerubavel (1982) draws on Durkheim's theory of time/space to explain the rise of standard time within the context of the establishment of national and international communication networks following the introduction of railway transportation and telegraphic communication. From a Durkheimian perspective, standard time is thus among the most essential coordinates of intersubjective reality and one of the defining features of modern society. Indeed, as Zerubavel (1982: 2) notes, "social life would probably not have been possible at all were it not for our ability to relate to time in a standard fashion." Quoting Durkheim (1965 [1912]: 30), from his classic book, the *Elementary Form of the Religious Life*, "If men . . . did not have the same conception of time . . . all contact between their minds would be impossible, and with that, all life together."

In the "Metropolis and Mental Life," Georg Simmel (1971 [1903]) elaborated a theory of the modern city in which its distinct modes of socio-spatial representation – that is, amusement, consumption, architecture, and forms of exhibition and cultural products – encourages the growth of individual freedom while promoting an urban personality that is reserved, detached, and blasé. In Simmel's general thesis, the development of a mature money economy resulted in a progressive estrangement of social relations from space (i.e. an emancipation of the social from geographic location). In addition, new communication technologies (e.g. the telegraph in the nineteenth century) enabled people for the first time to communicate and exchange information without being hampered by time constraints or spatial barriers. According to Simmel, the unique spatial form and organization of the modern metropolis permits the growth individuality as different people meet others through new contacts, connections, and networks. At the same time, the modern metropolis is based on the money economy, which is the source and expression of individual personality, rationality, and intellectualism. The money economy has two major transformative impacts on time/space. First, money transforms people into calculating agents and helps nurture a concern with punctuality and exactness. Second, the money economy – whose concentrated and expanding network is the modern metropolis – contributes to a "reduction of qualitative values to quantitative ones . . . a new precision, a certainty in definition of identities and differences, an unambiguousness in agreements and arrangements" (1971 [1903]: 177).

As noted by many scholars, the transformative shifts in the historical geography of capitalism dovetailed with the emergence of new modes of urban imagery and representation – photography, commercial advertisement, popular journalism, and postcards – linked with the commodification and rationalization of space and time (Cocks, 2001; Cox, 2011; Shaffer, 2013). In his book, *The Culture of Time and Space, 1880–1918*, Stephen Kern (1983: 34) explains how the growth of the telegraph, railroads, and photography "made it possible for more people to read about new distant places in the newspaper, see them in movies, and travel more widely. As human consciousness expanded across time and space people could not help noticing that in different places, there were vastly different customs." Importantly, photographic technology and image-making allowed people to visually represent urban reality at one fixed point in time and space. This new mode of representation valorized the notion of cities as having distinctive urban "personalities" that could be interpreted through film and visual imagery (Gotham, 2007a; 2007b).

Later, US sociologists focused attention on interactions of time and space, using spatial and temporal concepts to understand and explain the basis of social action, stability, and change. These issues were present in Talcott Parsons' writings on the dimensions of "action space" (Parsons and Bales, 1953) and in Pitrim Sorokin's (1964) theorization of sociocultural "distance" and "nearness." The early Chicago School sociologists devoted much effort to examining the social forces behind the spatial and temporal ordering of urban communities, land-use conflicts and social movement networking. Robert Park, Ernst Burgess, and Roderick McKenzie focused on developing a set of propositions that could explain the spatial ordering of different groups in the city, and specify linkages between the internal differentiation of the city and the process of growth (Park, Burgess, and McKenzie, 1925).

Compression, Distanciation, and Intensification

One of the most wide-ranging and influential debates on time/space restructuring is the emergence of a globalized economy involving new systems of production, finance, and consumption. Globalization is not a new issue or research topic, however. Although the intensity and impact of globalization appear novel today, generations of scholars have acknowledged the interconnectedness of globalization, capitalist development, and transformations of time and space (Arrighi, 1994; Harvey, 1989). Karl Marx made this point emphatically in his youthful comments on capitalism, pointing out in the *Manifesto of the Communist Party* that the "need of a constantly expanding market for its products chases the bourgeoisie over the whole surface of the globe. It must nestle everywhere, settle everywhere, establish connections everywhere" (Marx and Engels, 1978 [1848]: 476). Similarly, postwar-era Marxian theorists stressed capitalism's growing international scope and the advent of "monopoly" capitalism (Baran and Sweezy, 1966; Mandel, 1978: 310–376). Recession and deindustrialization brought global competition to the center of US public-policy debates in the 1970s and 1980s, while scholars drew attention to the increasing proletarianization of third-world populations (Phillips, 1991). Later in the decade, Bennett Harrison and Barry Bluestone's influential *Great U-Turn* (1988) identified globalization as a core corporate strategy that enhanced profitability and "flexibility" through "capital mobility," helping to weaken labor unions, reduce wages, avoid regulation, and cut production costs. In the 1990s, Manuel Castells (1996) developed a far-reaching theory of the "network society" to explain the rise of a new and qualitatively different historical epoch where networks and flows, rather than agents and structures, constitute the new global economy.

A number of scholars have focused on the disruptive and destabilizing effects of time/space restructuring, using concepts such as disembedding, distanciation, compression, and intensification to describe the spatial-temporal transformations affecting society and human experience. For Anthony Giddens (1991), the current round of time/space restructuring is occurring through a process of *time-space distanciation* – where time and space are universalized and "lifted out" or disembedded from their local contexts of interaction and meaning making. Distanciation, according to Giddens, suggests that social relations and interactions are no longer confined or restricted to immediate contexts but become controlled or coordinated over longer periods, over longer distances, and over more spheres of activity. The effect of this is to "link distant localities in such a way that local happenings are shaped by events occurring many miles away and vice versa" (1991: 64). Giddens argues that local activities are increasingly abstracted or delocalized from temporal and spatial contexts. At the same time, new electronic forms of communication and information dissemination can serve as coordinating mechanisms for long-distance social relations and forms of interaction.

Giddens' emphasis on time/space distanciation draws attention to the ways in which the integration and coordination of different aspects of society and social organization increasingly operate at a distance rather than in situations of closeness, nearness, and propinquity. The point here is that contemporary social practices and activities can no longer be primarily defined by their grounding, or embeddedness, in a local context of a restricted place and time. For Giddens (1991: 21, 27), there are two disembedding mechanisms that allow for time/space distanciation. The first is *symbolic tokens* like money that enable people to engage in transactions and exchanges with others who are separated by time and/or space. The second is *expert systems*, defined as "systems of technological accomplishment or professional expertise that organize large areas of material and social environments" (1991: 27). Time/space distanciation and related disembedding processes do not produce a diminution of social integration or collective identity per se. Rather, disembedding mechanisms foster both trust and ontological insecurity. Expert systems and symbolic tokens could not survive without people establishing a series of stable routines based on the trust of each other in interactions and exchanges. At the same time, new and dangerous risks – nuclear war, disasters, contamination – threaten our trust and can promote skepticism, cynicism, and collective anxiety about social institutions and the future.

Other scholars have argued that time and space relations have contracted and shrunk in a process of *time-space compression*. According to David Harvey (1989), recent decades have witnessed a "compression" of time and space as new communication and information technologies eliminate the spatial barriers to the circulation of capital, the "annihilation of space through time," in Karl Marx's (1993 [1857]: 539) famous statement in the *Grundrisse*. For Harvey, the major driver of time/space compression is the relentless determination by capitalists to reduce the temporal and spatial constraints to profit making, a conflictual and contested process that "has a disorienting and disruptive impact upon political-economic practices, [and] the balance of class power, as well as upon cultural and social life" (Harvey, 1989: 284). Although Harvey stresses the novelty and destabilizing effects of time/space compression, he suggests that there are continuities between past and present rounds of capitalist investment and disinvestment in the built environment. His major conclusion is that "there has certainly been a sea-change in the surface appearance of capitalism since 1973 . . . [but] the underlying logic of capitalist accumulation and its crisis tendencies remain the same" (1989: 189).

Time/space compression is akin to the increasing velocity or speeding up of communication, transportation, fashion cycles, commodity life spans, and associated shrinking of distances and spaces – all of which radically transform codes of transmission of social values and meanings. As an example of time/space compression, Harvey (1989) refers to the ability of supermarkets and restaurants in cities such as London or Los Angeles to offer foods from all over the world. Cuisines that used to be spatially bounded and restricted to particular locales and indigenous groups are now created, transported, and assembled in different places irrespective of geography, place-based culture, or political borders. Moreover, the accelerated circulation of images, capital, commodities, and technologies on a global scale reduces the world's geographical complexity to a series of dramatic media images that people can visually consume any time during the day or night. The increasing speed of image production and dissemination makes it possible for people to experience the putative geography, history, environment, and culture of any particular place vicariously through the consumption of images or simulacra (Baudrillard, 1983).

More recently, Riain (2014, 2006) has advanced the concept of *time/space intensification* as an as an alternative heuristic device to long-standing notions of time/space distanciation and time/space compression. Like Giddens and Harvey, Riain seeks to explain the restructuring of time and space in contemporary advanced capitalism. This concept suggests time and space are intensified in the contemporary period in three ways. First, the social *experience* of time and space becomes more crucial to socioeconomic actors' lives. Time and space become more explicit elements of human experience and awareness of difference across scales. Second, time and space are *mobilized* more explicitly in individual and corporate action. While all social practices have a spatial and temporal dimension, according to Riain (2006: 511), "explicitly spatial and temporal practices become more critical to social and political action as social actors attempt to mobilize time and space strategically within global connections and in protection against the pressures of time–space compression." Third, time and space become more *politicized* through conflicts pitting labor against capital for access to and control over wages, profits, and corporate resources – all of which are linked to collective struggles over meanings of space and time.

In sum, the concepts of time/space distanciation, compression, and intensification signify the broad shift in understanding of space and time that has occurred in social theory since the 1970s. Shifts in temporal and spatial relations and interactions are the result of several interrelated processes: accelerating turnover time in production; increased pace of change and ephemerality of fashion; greater availability of products from distant and obscure places; increased temporariness of products (planned obsolescence), relationships, and contacts; greater importance of advertising and rapidly changing media images; and proliferation of new technologies of information and communication which transcend space. These extraordinary changes have motivated scholars to theorize and analyze the rescaling of social activities and power, the political economy of finance and real estate, and the impact of tourism, entertainment, and spectacle on everyday life.

Rescaling and the Explosion of Spaces

Theorizations of time/space compression, intensification, and distanciation dovetail with the growth of a burgeoning literature on the causal impacts, developmental trajectories, and consequences of various rescaling processes. Rescaling is a process that involves a reconfiguration of cultural and economic flows, networks of socioeconomic activities, and forms of territorial governance across various spatial and temporal scales. Rescaling is associated with a shift of institutional/regulatory arrangements from the national scale, both upward to supranational or global scales and downward to regional or local scales. Rescaling also posits that economic activities and interfirm networks are becoming simultaneously more localized and transnational (Swyngedouw, 2004: 25). In the work of Neil Brenner and colleagues, rescaling encompasses several processes including the rescaling of state space, rescaling of capital accumulation, the rescaling of urbanization processes, and the rescaling of contentious politics (Brenner, 2004; Brenner and Theodore, 2002). The proliferation of research on rescaling has opened up fertile areas of research and theorizing linked to several concerns including the various political sites of rescaling, the etiology of rescaling processes, and the socio-spatial patterns and consequences of rescaling for the cities and political-economic life (Brenner, 2004; Cox, 2009; Sassen, 2006; Swyngedouw, 2004). In addition, temporal and spatial metaphors now permeate major strands of social science research on time and space: for example, "deterritorialization" (Agnew, 2014; Brenner, 1999a), "glocalization" (Robertson, 1995), "grobalization" (Ritzer, 2004), and "indigenization" (Appadurai, 1996). The popularity of these terms reflects scholarly interest in understanding how global-level processes interact with the restructuring of time/space relations to affect cities and everyday life.

The rich intellectual work of Henri Lefebvre (1991b) has inspired much empirical and theoretical research on time/space restructuring and rescaling processes. Throughout his major works in the 1970s, Lefebvre elaborates on the major time/space transformations affecting the world and focuses specifically on globalization as an intensely contradictory process of integration, fragmentation, polarization and redifferentiation of social spaces. Lefebvre conceptualizes time/space restructuring as a conflictual "explosion of spaces" in which an enormous diversity of connections and linkages permeate geographical scales and proliferate struggles over access to cultural, political, and economic resources. The conceptual phrase "explosion of spaces" refers to the simultaneous destabilization and restabilization of geographies of industrialization, state power, urbanism, and everyday life. Processes of destabilization/restabilization of time/space relations are evident in the following worldwide trends: global economic enmeshment, consolidation of new supranational and cross-border institutions, and increased importance of localized agglomeration economies. Central to this framework is the idea that spatial boundaries, identities, and meanings are negotiated, defined, and produced through social interaction, social conflict, and struggles between different groups. As a component of social organization, spatial patterns and conflicts permeate social relations at the personal, collective, regional, and global levels.

In the decades since Lefebvre developed his prescient insights, scholars have mined his theoretical ideas and employed his heuristic devices to explain the broad societal transformations that are reorganizing cities and urban life. Mark Gottdiener's (1994 [1985]) *Social Production of Urban Space* drew upon Lefebvre's pioneering insights on urban space to launch a polemical attack against structural determinism and functionalism in Marxian analyses of socio-spatial restructuring. For Gottdiener, Lefebvre's work serves as the theoretical foundation for the Socio-Spatial Perspective (SSP), which emphasizes the role of human agents and organized interests in the production of the built environment; the centrality of conflict and struggle in shaping urban space; and the reflexive and dialectical relation between space and social action and organization. Gotham (2014 [2002]) has drawn on Lefebvre's insights to explain how race and racial inequalities are central dimensions of the organization and reproduction of rescaling processes. Lefebvre's ideas have become popular among Marxist intellectuals seeking to theorize and explain the proliferation of new manifestations of alienation, reification, and rationalization in society (Butler, 2012; Elden, 2004; Gardiner, 2000; Goonewardena et al., 2008; Merrifield, 2006; Shields, 1999; Stanek, 2011).

Since the 1990s, Lefebvre's insights have motivated scholars to develop new theories to examine the different processes of upscaling, downscaling, and outscaling. Rescaling processes are diverse and have uneven impacts and consequences. They also manifest differently in different institutional political forms around the world. Scholars suggest, for example, that there has been an upscaling of capitalist control capacities toward the global and supranational levels combined with a downscaling of productive capacities and competitive assets toward the regional and urban levels of metropolitan agglomerations (Brenner, 2004; Sassen, 2006). Upscaling processes are akin to the deterritorialization of socioeconomic activity whereby social actors and activities become disembedded or "uprooted" from local- or national-based social conditions and restructured across time and space (Brenner, 1999a, 1999b; Cetina and Bruegger, 2002; Giddens, 1990: 21–29; Sites, 2003). Downscaling processes are analogous to the vertical decentralization or devolution of national-level policy implementation and regulatory responsibilities to regional and local governments (Brenner, 2004: 62). Scholars have also argued that state institutions are rescaling socioeconomic relations outward to create new decentralized and multi-node networked forms of governance that involve horizontal linkages with nongovernment organizations and private firms. Upscaling, downscaling, and outscaling processes do not represent a contraction or diminution of state power but rather express state efforts to enhance place-specific and territory-specific competitive advantages to attract investment and consumers.

Overall, a major contribution from rescaling scholarship is that time/space compression, distanciation, and intensification do not entail the construction of a placeless or distanceless space of flows. One popular argument promulgated by scholars such as Castells (1996) and Hardt and Negri (2001), among others, is that the current round of time/space restructuring in the form of globalization and rescaling is tantamount to the formation of a borderless "space of flows." The problem with such an argument is that strategies to avoid or subvert place-based constraints on capital accumulation do not involve the subversion or elimination of space but the reinvention of place at a different scale. Brenner (2004: 59) has noted that the "transcendence of national scale regulatory systems in recent decades has been inextricably bound up with the production of new subnational and supra-national scales of accumulation and state regulation that provide the place- and territory-specific conditions for accumulation." In arguing for the continuing significance of space and time, scholars suggest that temporal and spatial configurations are being reconstituted at different scales as some political-economic activities are upscaled, other activities are outscaled, and still others are downscaled.

Fixity, Liquidity, and the Political Economy of Real Estate and Finance

Another major strand of scholarship on time/space restructuring focuses on the relationship between the circulatory and nomadic nature of capital, and the fixity of property and real estate in the built environment. On the one hand, real estate is by definition illiquid, spatially fixed and immobile, and defined by local particularities and idiosyncrasies. Further, once built, the built environment provides access to certain resources to some groups of people rather than others; spatially embeds classes, races, and ethnic groups in particular locales; and restricts and channels the spatial growth and movement of capital. On the other hand, capital is abstract, itinerant, and placeless. Insofar as possible, capital seeks to eradicate local peculiarities and place distinctions that characterize the buying and selling of commodities and thereby eliminate the spatial barriers to the circulation of capital. It is this duality, or inherent contradiction, between immobile properties and mobile capital that defines the political economy of real estate and finance.

During the 1960s and 1970s, Henri Lefebvre and David Harvey drew attention to the built environment as a generator, site, and barrier to capital accumulation. For Harvey (2001 [1975]: 247) capitalism's "crowning glory" is the creation of a built environment that reflects and reproduces accumulation. At the same time, this built environment anchors capital into place, a condition that can discourage profit making as preexisting time/space relations can stifle market creation and obstruct capital circulation. As a contingent and volatile process of time/space spatial restructuring, capitalist development thereby has to negotiate a "knife-edge path" between preserving the fixed social structures that underpinned and supported past capital investments and destroying these structures in order to create new opportunities for investment. As a consequence, according to Harvey, we "witness a perpetual struggle in which capitalism builds a physical landscape appropriate to its own condition at a particular moment in time, only to have to destroy it, usually in the course of a crisis, at a subsequent point in time" (2001 [1975]: 247). Thus, the mobilization of space and time as forces of production and consumption serve as both cause and effect of the crisis-prone nature of modern capitalism.

Over the decades, other leading scholars have elaborated on the links between production and consumption in the creation of space and time, the temporal influences on the realization of profits, and the geographical opportunities and constraints on the organization of production and consumption. The matter of transformation in the socio-spatial dynamics and institutional arrangements of global capitalism is taken up by Saskia Sassen, whose works have generated new theorizations of time/space restructuring. Sassen's oft-cited book *The Global City* (2001) argues that a new temporal and spatial order has been emerging under over the last several decades based on a network of "global cities" led by New York, London, and Tokyo. Global cities are places of highly specialized services for transnational financial firms that provide the investment capital to fuel the global economy. This global economy involves the decentralization of production combined with the centralization of command-and-control functions of the global production system within global cities. In particular, Sassen argues that the increasing complexity, differentiation, and specialization of global economic activities involves the formation of new networks of time/space coordination. Global cities linked to one another constitute nodes or "command posts" of an increasingly complex and globally fragmented production/consumption system. Global cities contain a variety of financial services, mechanisms of capital availability, and amenities to regulate the global economy. According to Sassen, "the combination of spatial dispersal and global integration has created a new strategic role for major cities" (2001: 3). At the same time, the new transnational structure reflects and reinforces new political-economic linkages between different geographic regions premised on a global hierarchy of cities in which low-income groups increasing face the specter of displacement, casualization, and informalization of work (for an overview, see Brenner and Keil, 2006).

Global cities approaches draw our attention to another leading theme in time/space studies: how the state shapes temporal and spatial relations and transformation through the creation and control of liquid resources. As noted by Gotham (2006, 2009), a liquid asset or resource has homogeneous, predictable, and standardized features that enable financial actors to convert it into cash quickly and easily. Exchangeability and marketability define liquid commodities. Liquidity is neither a psychological phenomenon nor a static and immutable feature of an asset. Rather, as a social construction, liquidity is variable, contingent, and dependent on state actions and legal and regulatory frameworks to support the standardization, homogenization, and exchangeability of commodities. In contrast, an illiquid asset or resource is non-transportable and possesses the conditions of non-exchangeability and nontransferability. There is a close relationship between commodities that are spatially fixed and commodities that are illiquid. Commodities that are spatially fixed have diverse, idiosyncratic, and inconsistent properties such that it is difficult for buyers and sellers in different places to know the value and property of what they are exchanging.

Cross-border flows and exchange networks depend on the creation of liquidity, which is a product of an elaborate and complex set of rules, regulations, and institutions that are established by the state. Institutions do the legal and organizational work to enhance liquidity by homogenizing and standardizing knowledge of assets. Gotham's (2006, 2009) analyses of real estate focus on state efforts to increase the liquidity of residential and commercial property, attract new sources to finance real estate, and territorially disembed or "delocalize" real estate by enmeshing the financing of residential and commercial property within global capital markets. Importantly, the production of liquidity is a policy creation that is essential for establishing global flows and cross-scale networks of activity. The distinguishing features of real estate, local specificity and heterogeneity, make it difficult to communicate information about assets, liabilities, and opportunities to a large audience of investors in a clear and credible manner. Given these problems, the creation of liquidity to facilitate cross-border exchange would seem to be a formidable obstacle. Thus, creating liquidity out of spatial fixity is a problem of creating shared agreements and stable social relations that allow economic exchange to occur in a transparent manner. These agreements and relations produce generalized knowledge so that a variety of market actors can comprehend value and risk, interpret the behaviors of other buyers and sellers, and act to control situations.

Gotham's analysis of the US real-estate sector dovetails with recent debates on the "financialization" of the economy and the impact of state legal-regulatory actions on the post-2008 "Great Recession" and global financial crisis. Cetina and Preda (2012: 1) note that financial activities are a defining characteristic not only of the corporate economy, but also of politics, the welfare and social security system, and general culture. Financialization is a pattern of accumulation in which profit making occurs increasingly through financial channels rather than through trade and commodity production (Aalbers, 2012) As a multidimensional, contested, and conflictual process, financialization refers to the growth of financial actors (banks, lenders, private equity corporations, etc.), new financial tools (mutual funds, asset backed securities, hedge funds, etc.), and the increasing significance of financial firms in different areas of the economy such as real estate (Krippner, 2011) and post-disaster reconstruction (Gotham, 2016). The financial system and the financialization process interconnect with the state through fiscal and regulatory policies that impact housing markets and try to promote liquidity within the residential, commercial, and industrial real-estate sectors. The state plays a key role in the dialectics of spatial fixity and liquidity

through a variety of policies, legal-regulatory actions, and infrastructural investment that can reinforce territorial coherence and promote flows between cities and
regions.

Tourism, Entertainment, and Spectacle

Reference to the pace, trajectories, and impacts of temporal-spatial
restructuring abound in interdisciplinary scholarship on tourism, entertainment,
and spectacle (for a recent overview, see Hughes, 2013). Scholars have drawn
attention to how tourism has evolved into a global industry dominated by transnational hotel firms, entertainment corporations, gaming casinos, and professional
sports franchises (Gottdiener, 2000; 1997; Hannigan, 1998; Chatterton and
Hollands, 2003). These firms and their networked connections with the finance
and real-estate sectors have been at the forefront of the shift from an economy
based on manufacturing of industrial goods to an economy based on the production
and consumption of images, spectacles, and entertainment-based consumption
experiences (Coleman and Crang, 2002; Hoffman, Fainstein, and Judd, 2003).
Tourism corporations are simultaneously placeless and place-full. They accentuate
the place-theme in their products and operations by valorizing the milieu where
they are located, using place images and symbols that connect the locale with
pleasurable experiences. Unlike other commodities, the tourism commodity and
related services are spatially fixed and consumed by tourists at the place of
production. Whereas the circulation of commodities among people dominated
time/space relations during the stage of industrial capitalism, the circulation of
people to specific locations that are consumed as spaces – spaces of amusement,
leisure, sport, recreation, "nature," "history," or simply "otherness" – expresses the
nature of time/space relations today (Gotham, 2007a).

Meanings of time and space are central to the production and consumption of
tourism activities and entertainment spectacles. Today, the production of spectacles is subservient to rigid clock time, a phenomenon that constitutes a critical form
of alienation from what would be the ordinary course of social events and festival
not dictated by clocks. In premodern societies, Lefebvre 1991a [1958]: 201–227)
asserts, everyday life was not separated by specialized activities or differentiated
by time. Popular celebrations, festivals, and collective rituals were fully integrated
into a relatively undifferentiated totality of human practice (1991a [1958]: 30–31).
Today, however, all consumer-based tourism activities and entertainment spectacles are produced and organized to occupy precisely the length of clock time given
for them and to end on time, regardless of the desires of the consumers and
participants. By reifying clock time, modern spectacles are the antithesis of
spontaneity, creativity, and originality. Like all social activities in modern society,
including work and leisure, spectacles are fragmented, rationalized, and specialized. As a result, people confront and experience spectacles as external forces that
constitute them as atomized consumers rather than as collective and creative beings
(Gotham, 2011b).

In the *Society of the Spectacle,* Guy Debord (1994 [1973]) drew attention to the significance of "spectacular time," where the qualitative value and use-value of time is erased and transformed into a quantified, homogenized, and exchangeable unit (1994 [1973]: #149). Under the conditions of modern production and consumption, the packaging and the selling of "'fully equipped' blocks of time" (1994 [1973]: #152) become part of the expanding economy of leisure activities. Debord's critique of time-as-commodity is based on his observation that time as lived and experienced, as a sequence of qualitative events that constitute traditions and community, has been replaced by the image of time, the advertisement of time, and consumable pseudo-cyclical time. As more and more aspects of social life become defined by clock time, people come to expect and value routinized control of spectacles, as evident from the anger and frustration people feel when scheduled events and spectacles are delayed, postponed, or canceled. Once time and space are commodified, it becomes possible to mass-produce festivals and celebrations that incite people to spend money while producing only an illusion of community, a phenomenon discussed by Michael Sorkin and colleagues (1992) in their interrogations of the adaptation of theme-park characteristics to contemporary urban redevelopment projects (see also Bryman, 2004; Eeckhout, 2001).

There are two areas of theoretical debate over the significance of space and time in critical scholarship on tourism, entertainment, and spectacle. First, the idea that "consumption" is taking precedence over "production," one of the most widely debated facets in tourism studies, maintains that the expansion and deepening of commodity markets has transferred the logic and rationality of "production" to the sphere of "consumption" (Gotham, 2002). Several scholars describe a broad shift from production-centered capitalism, rooted in work and coercion, to consumer capitalism, based on leisure, market "seduction," and spectacle (for overviews, see Bauman, 1992; Ritzer, 1998; Urry, 1995). For Gottdiener (2000; 1997), the historical development of consumer society is an organized extension of production relations with the "new means of consumption" as a crucial productive force of capital itself. Focusing on the increasing commodification of reality, other scholars argue that we have moved from society organized on the basis of an "immense accumulation of commodities," to quote Marx, to a society dominated by "an immense accumulation of spectacles," according to Debord (1973: #1). Framed as style, taste, travel, and "destination," the world of tourism and tourist experience is one in which image, advertising, and consumerism take primacy over production per se (for an overview, see Aitchison et al., 2014). Thus, tourism has decentered and localized consumption, replacing work with entertainment and lifestyle as the pivotal facets of sociocultural life (Lloyd, 2010; Lloyd and Clark, 2001). Stressing the emergence and centrality of new forms of consumption, thinkers draw attention to the role that tourism plays as a form of commodified pleasure, tourism-as-spectacle, which defines individual travelers and tourists as consumers, and the impact of the tourism "industry" in using advertising and marketing to constitute and then exploit consumer desires and needs for profit (Gotham, 2002).

Second, scholars have argued that one trend associated with processes of time/space compression and distanciation is the replacement of real authenticity with a "staged" authenticity in which local cultures and traditions become manufactured or simulated for tourist consumption (Cohen, 1988; MacCannell, 1992, 1973). As many scholars have argued, tourism and entertainment corporations seek to transfer the logic of commodity production to the production of tourist places, the effect of which is to transform space into a saleable object and therefore destroy authentic cultural spaces. Such an account dovetails with Manuel Castells' (1996) argument that we are moving from a world characterized by "space of places" to one dominated by "spaces of flows" and "timeless times," two foundational concepts that describe the network society. The space of places are unique settings marked by rich emotional ties, a well-defined culture and history, and long-standing and venerable traditions. In contrast, discontinuity, ephemerality, and lack of stability define the space of flows. As far as possible, the space of flows seeks to crush the space of places, creating an environment without significant places. Going further, Castells (2000) argues that virtual media and information and communication technologies like the Internet construct a new symbolic environment in which "virtuality" becomes a "reality." With these new communications systems, time is erased, since "past, present, and future can be programmed to interact with each other in the same message" (1996: 406) thus superseding the rationalized clock time of the industrial era. Other novel technologies, such as biotechnologies and reproductive technologies, eradicate the biological sense of time, eliminate logical sequences of time, and blur life-cycle patterns in conditions of parenting by either slowing down or speeding up the life cycle.

The homogenizing features of time/space restructuring are discussed at length by George Ritzer (2004) in his oft-cited book, *The Globalization of Nothing*. According to Ritzer (2004: 105), "one of the best examples" of the "globalization of nothing" is in the realm of tourism which involves the global production of non-places (Disneyland), non-things (mass-manufactured souvenirs), and non-people (clerks at souvenir shops). For Ritzer, tourism is about the production of "nothing," which refers to a "social form that is generally centrally conceived, controlled, and comparatively devoid of distinctive content" (2004: 3). In Ritzer's explanation, flows of people, information, and signs and symbols that characterize the temporal-spatial transformations associated with tourism disembed or delocalize culture, making it difficult for people to develop meaningful interactions, or individual and communal identities. In its extreme form, this argument describes a world in which particular cultures have been assimilated into a homogenized "monoculture," driven by a process of McDonaldization (Ritzer, 1998) or Disneyization (Bryman, 2004), one that transforms all places into ageographical theme parks devoid of local identity and cultural authenticity (Sorkin, 1992). Disneyization (or Disneyfication) is the process by which the principles of the Disney theme parks are incorporated into the operation and functioning of major social institutions. McDonaldization is a process by which the principles of the fast-food restaurant come to dominate different aspects of society. In each case, the processes of standardization, rationalization, and homogenization are employed by organizations and institutions to increase the efficiency, predictability, and calculability of consuming goods and services.

Scholars have identified several limitations with accounts that conceive a world increasingly alike everywhere, where processes of standardization and rationalization dominate and subsume local realities. First, critics contend that such accounts employ hyperbolic rhetoric and exaggerated claims that ignore or downplay the complexity and nuances of time/space restructuring. Studies of cultural homogenization tend to make sweeping generalizations and absolute conclusions about time/space relations and conditions, without the requisite supporting evidence and empirical substance. People everywhere may be increasingly exposed to and subject to many of the same cultural stimuli, tourist attractions, and places of consumption. But there is no guarantee that all people will react to these standardized activities and practices in the same way. Consequently, every local context involves its own appropriation and reworking of global influences, thus encouraging diversity, variety, hybridity, and synthesis. Thus, contemporary tourism embodies both these contrasting tendencies at once – it can be a force of homogenization and heterogeneity (Gotham, 2005).

Second, the homogenization approach is problematic because it suggests the "death of distance" or the "end of geography," as time presumably wipes out space as a meaningful dimension of human experience, whether in the short term or the long term. Yet, as many theorists have shown, the processes of bureaucratic rationalization, McDonaldization, and Disneyfication may actually strengthen the power of place so that specific places emerge to occupy specific nodes in the global economy (for an overview, see Agnew, 2014). The power of place intersects with each places' global connections as pressures of time/space restructuring manifest themselves in struggles and contestations within different workplaces, communities, and institutions.

A third limitation of homogenization accounts is the view that consumers are passive "recipients" of commodity-images, or cultural dupes that are "seduced" and "distracted" by the titillating images of entertainment and spectacle. In contrast, more critical studies and analyses have focused attention on the diverse forms of action and resistance that consumers engage in to challenge corporate attempts to induce them to conform to established patterns of consumer behavior. Indeed, spectacles and related spaces of entertainment are sites of struggle where powerful economic and political interests are often forced to defend what they would prefer to have taken for granted. That is, the process of ideological production and transmission is not a one-way or top-down process of indoctrination, but rather, is an active process of negotiation that groups of consumers can resist or transform to suit their own needs and interests. While the production of spectacles connects to issues of political and economic power, the interpretation of spectacles is filtered through prior experience, one's social location and identity (race, class, gender, and so on), and one's conversations and engagement with others (Gotham, 2015; 2011a; Gotham and Krier, 2008).

Conclusions

Throughout the social sciences, diverse theories have informed empirical research into time/space processes, helped recast varied current social science agendas in light of time/space restructurings, and provided paradigmatic points of reference for studying social change in the twenty-first century. Today, scholars conceptualize and analyze time/space in a variety of ways using different methods and research designs. Conceptualizations include time/space as instruments of labor control; strategies of state economic development; elements of the lived reality of socioeconomic life; major factors in the social construction of collective identity; and sites of social conflict, contestation, and political struggle. While all social practices have a spatial and temporal dimension, over the last several decades explicitly spatial and temporal practices have become more critical to social and political action, as different actors and groups have attempted to mobilize time and space to confront the opportunities and pressures of broad and sweeping macro-structural changes.

Comprehending the temporality and spatiality of social life and social change encourages us to fashion sociological explanations that are not just a restatement of social action taking place in time or space (i.e., reference to time and space as context, background, or setting). As explanation becomes permeated with temporality and spatiality, processes and concepts themselves become increasingly temporalized and spatialized. The implication is that we should understand causes of changes in the organization of time/space relations as "conjunctive combinations" (Ragin, 2014) and sequences of events (Abbott, 2001). In this formulation, time/space "change" appears as discontinuous, indeterminate, and open, and time/space "stability" as temporary, fleeting, and ephemeral. Such an approach has the additional merit of conceptualizing agency as a spatially and temporally embedded process of social engagement (Emirbayer and Mische, 1998; Gotham, 2003; Gotham and Brumley, 2002). Underscoring the importance of space and time in theoretical and empirical research means that any explanation of *why* and *how* human actions and processes happen will need to take account of *where* and *when* they happen.

References

Aalbers, M. (ed.). 2012. *Subprime Cities: The Political Economy of Mortgage Markets.* New York: John Wiley & Sons.

Abbott, A. 2001. *Time Matters: On Theory and Method.* Chicago, IL: University of Chicago Press.

Agnew, J. A. 2014. *Place and Politics: The Geographical Mediation of State and Society.* London: Routledge.

Aitchison, C., N. E., MacLeod, N. E., Macleod, and S. J.Shaw. 2014. *Leisure and Tourism Landscapes: Social and Cultural Geographies.* London: Routledge.

Appadurai, A. 1996. *Modernity At Large: Cultural Dimensions of Globalization.* Minneapolis, MN: University of Minnesota Press.

Arrighi, G. 1994. *The Long Twentieth Century: Money, Power, and the Origins of Our Times.* London: Verso.

Baran, P. and P. Sweezy. 1966. *Monopoly Capital.* New York: Monthly Review Press.

Baudrillard, J. 1983. *Simulations.* New York: Semiotext(e).

Bauman, Z. 1992. *Intimations of Modernity.* London: Routledge.

Brenner, N. 1999a. "Globalization as Reterritorialization: The Re-scaling of Urban Governance in the European Union." *Urban Studies* 36(3): 431–451.

    1999b. "Beyond State-Centrism? Space, Territoriality, and Geographical Scale in Globalization Studies." *Theory and Society* 28(1): 39–78.

    2004. *New State Spaces: Urban Governance and the Rescaling of Statehood.* New York: Oxford University Press.

Brenner, N., and R. Keil (eds.). 2006. *The Global Cities Reader.* New York: Routledge.

Brenner, N., and N. Theodore (eds.). 2002. *Spaces of Neoliberalism: Urban Restructuring in North America and Western Europe.* Cambridge, MA: Blackwell.

Bryman, A. 2004. *The Disneyization of Society.* New York: Sage.

Butler, C. 2012. *Henri Lefebvre: Spatial Politics, Everyday Life, and the Right to the City.* New York: Routledge.

Castells, M. 1996. *The Rise of the Network Society.* Vol. I of *The Information Age: Economy, Society, Culture.* Oxford, UK: Blackwell.

    2000. "Materials for an Exploratory Theory of the Network Society." *British Journal of Sociology* 51(1): 5–24.

Cetina, K. K., and U. Bruegger. 2002. "Global Microstructures: The Virtual Societies of Financial Markets." *American Journal of Sociology* 107(4): 905–950.

Cetina, K. K., and A. Preda (eds.). 2012. *The Oxford Handbook of the Sociology of Finance.* Oxford, UK: Oxford University Press.

Chatterton, P., and R. Hollands. 2003. *Urban Nightscapes: Youth Cultures, Pleasure Spaces and Corporate Power.* New York: Routledge.

Cocks, C. 2001. *Doing the Town: The Rise of Urban Tourism in the United States, 1850–1915.* Berkeley, CA: University of California Press.

Cohen, E. 1988. "Authenticity and Commodification in Tourism." *Annals of Tourism Research* 15: 371–386.

Coleman, S., and M. Crang (eds.). 2002. *Tourism: Between Place and Performance.* London: Berghahn Books.

Cox, K. L. 2011. *Dreaming of Dixie: How the South Was Created in American Popular Culture.* Chapel Hill, NC: University of North Carolina Press.

Cox, K. R. 2009. "'Rescaling the State' in Question." *Cambridge Journal of Regions, Economy and Society* 2: 1–15.

Debord, G. 1994 [1973]. *The Society of the Spectacle.* Translated by Donald Nicholson-Smith. New York: Zone Books.

DeSena, J. N. (ed.). 2008. *Gender in an Urban World.* New York: Emerald Group Publishing.

Durkheim, E. 1964 [1893]. *The Division of Labor in Society.* New York: Free Press.

    1965 [1912]. *The Elementary Forms of the Religious Life.* New York: Free Press.

Eeckhout, B. 2001. "The 'Disneyfication' of Times Square: Back to the Future?" In K. F. Gotham (ed.), *Critical Perspectives on Urban Redevelopment* (pp. 379–428). New York: Elsevier.

Elden, S. 2004. *Understanding Henri Lefebvre: Theory and the Possible.* London/New York: Continuum.

Emirbayer, M., and A. Mische. 1998. "What Is Agency?" *American Journal of Sociology* 103 (4): 962–1023.

Featherstone, M. 1990. *Global Culture: Nationalism, Globalization and Modernity.* Thousand Oaks, CA: Sage.

Gardiner, M. 2000. *Critiques of Everyday Life: An Introduction.* New York: Routledge.

Giddens, A. 1984. *The Constitution of Society.* Berkeley, CA: University of California Press.

1990. *The Consequences of Modernity*. Cambridge, UK: Polity.

1991. *Modernity and Self-Identity*. Cambridge, UK: Polity.

Gieryn, T. 2000. "A Space for Place in Sociology." *Annual Review of Sociology* 26: 463–496.

Goonewardena, K., S. Kipfer, R. Milgrom, and C. Schmid (eds.). 2008. *Space, Difference, Everyday Life: Reading Henri Lefebvre*. New York: Routledge.

Gotham, K. F. 2002. "Marketing Mardi Gras: Commodification, Spectacle, and the Political Economy of Tourism in New Orleans." *Urban Studies* 39(10): 1735–1756.

2003. "Toward an Understanding of the Spatiality of Urban Poverty: The Urban Poor as Spatial Actors." *International Journal of Urban and Regional Research* 27(3): 723–737.

2005. "Tourism From Above and Below: Globalization, Localization, and New Orleans's Mardi Gras." *International Journal of Urban and Regional Research* 29(2): 309–326.

2006. "The Secondary Circuit of Capital Reconsidered: Globalization and the US Real Estate Sector." *American Journal of Sociology* 112(1): 231–275.

2007a. *Authentic New Orleans: Tourism, Culture, and Race in the Big Easy*. New York: New York University Press.

2007b. "Destination New Orleans Commodification, Rationalization, and the Rise of Urban Tourism." *Journal of Consumer Culture* 7(3): 305–334.

2009. "Creating Liquidity Out of Spatial Fixity: The Secondary Circuit of Capital and the Subprime Mortgage Crisis." *International Journal of Urban and Regional Research* 33(2): 355–371.

2011a. "Resisting Urban Spectacle: The 1984 Louisiana World Exposition and the Contradictions of Mega Events." *Urban Studies* 48(1): 197–214.

2011b. "Theorizing Carnival: Mardi Gras as Perceived, Conceived, and Lived Space." In J. Braun and L. Langman (eds.), *Alienation and the Carnivalization of Society* (pp. 93–118). New York and London: Routledge.

2014 [2002]. *Race, Real Estate, and Uneven Development: The Kansas City Experience*, 2nd ed. Albany, NY: SUNY Press.

2015. "Beyond Bread and Circuses: Mega-Events as Forces of Creative Destruction." In R. Gruneau and J. Horne (eds.), *Mega Events and Globalization: Capital and Spectacle in a Changing World Order* (pp. 31–47). New York: Routledge.

2016. "Re-anchoring Capital in Disaster-Devastated Spaces: Financialization and the Gulf Opportunity (GO) Zone Program." *Urban Studies*. Special Issue: Financialization and the Production of Urban Space. 53(7): 1362–1383.

Gotham, K. F., and K. Brumley. 2002. "Using Space: Agency and Identity in a Public-Housing Development." *City & Community* 1(3): 267–289.

Gotham, K. F., and D. A. Krier. 2008. "From the Culture Industry to the Society of the Spectacle: Critical Theory and the Situationist International." *Current Perspectives in Social Theory* 25: 155–192.

Gottdiener, M. 1994 [1985]. *Social Production of Urban Space*, 2nd ed. Austin, TX: University of Texas Press.

1997. *The Theming of America: Dreams, Visions, and Commercial Spaces*. Boulder, CO: Westview Press.

Gottdiener, M. (ed.). 2000. *New Forms of Consumption: Consumers, Culture, and Commodification*. Lanham, MD: Rowman & Littlefield.

Hannigan, J. 1998. *Fantasy City: Pleasure and Profit in the Postmodern Metropolis*. New York: Routledge.

Hardt, M., and Negri, A. 2001. *Empire*. Cambridge, MA: Harvard University Press.

Harrison, B., and Bluestone, B., 1988. *The Great U-Turn: Corporate Restructuring and the Polarizing of America*. New York: Basic Books.

Harvey, D. 1989. *The Condition of Postmodernity*. New York: Free Press.

2001 [1975]. *Spaces of Capital: Towards a Critical Geography*. New York: Routledge.

Held, D., and A. G. McGrew (eds.). 2007. *Globalization Theory: Approaches and Controversies*. Cambridge, UK: Polity Press.

Hoffman, L. K., S. Fainstein, and D. R. Judd (eds.). 2003. *Cities and Visitors: Regulating People, Markets, and City Space*. Malden, MA: Blackwell Publishing.

Hughes, H. 2013. *Arts, Entertainment and Tourism*. New York: Taylor & Francis.

Kern, S. 1983. *The Culture of Space and Time, 1880–1918*. London: Weidenfeld and Nicolson.

Krippner, G. R. 2011. *Capitalizing on Crisis*. Cambridge, MA: Harvard University Press.

Lefebvre, H. 1991a [1958]. *Critique of Everyday Life*. Volume 1: Introduction. Translated by J. Moore. London and New York: Verso.

1991b [1974]. *The Production of Space*. Oxford, UK: Basil Blackwell.

Liggett, H., and D. C. Perry (eds.). 1995. *Spatial Practices: Critical Explorations in Social/Spatial Theory*. Thousand Oaks, CA: Sage.

Lloyd, R. 2010. *Neo-Bohemia: Art and Commerce in the Postindustrial City*. New York: Routledge.

Lloyd, R., and T. N. Clark. 2001. "The City as an Entertainment Machine." In K. F. Gotham (ed.), *Critical Perspectives on Urban Redevelopment*. New York: Elsevier.

Lobao, L. M., G. Hooks, and A. R. Tickamyer (eds.). 2007. *The Sociology of Spatial Inequality*. Albany, NY: SUNY Press.

MacCannell, D. 1973. "Staged Authenticity: Arrangements of Social Space in Tourist Settings." *American Journal of Sociology* 79(3): 589–603.

1992. *Empty Meeting Grounds: The Tourist Papers*. New York: Routledge.

Mandel, E. 1978. *Late Capitalism*. London: Verso.

Marx, K. 1977. *Capital, Volume One: A Critique of Political Economy*. Translated by B. Fowkes. New York: Vintage Books.

1993 [1857]. *Grundrisse: Foundations of the Critique of Political Economy*. Translated by M. Nicolaus. New York: Penguin Classics.

Marx, Karl, and Friedrich Engels. 1978 [1848]. "The Manifesto of the Communist Party." In R. C. Tucker (ed.), *The Marx-Engels Reader* (pp. 469–500). New York: W. W. Norton.

Massey, D. 1984. *Spatial Divisions of Labour: Social Structures and the Geography of Production*. New York and London: Methuen and Macmillan.

2013. *Space, Place and Gender*. New York: John Wiley & Sons.

May, J., and N. Thrift (eds.). 2003. *Timespace: Geographies of Temporality*. New York: Routledge.

McGrew, A., and D. Held. 2002. *Governing Globalization: Power, Authority and Global Governance*. Cambridge, UK: Polity Press.

Merrifield, A. 2006. *Henri Lefebvre: A Critical Introduction*. London: Routledge.

Park, R. E., E. Burgess, and R. D. McKenzie (eds.). 1925. *The City*. Chicago, IL: University of Chicago Press.

Parsons, T., and R. Bales. 1953. "The Dimensions of Action Space." In T. Parsons, R. Bales, and E. Shils (eds.), *Working Papers in the Theory of Action*. Glencoe, IL: Free Press.

Phillips, K. 1991. *The Politics of Rich and Poor: Wealth and the American Electorate in the Reagan Aftermath*. New York: Basic Books.

Postone, M. 1996. *Time, Labor, and Social Domination: A Reinterpretation of Marx's Critical Theory*. New York: Cambridge University Press.

Ragin, C. C. 2014. *The Comparative Method: Moving Beyond Qualitative and Quantitative Strategies*. Berkeley, CA: University of California Press.

Riain, S. Ó. 2006. "Time–Space Intensification: Karl Polanyi, the Double Movement, and Global Informational Capitalism." *Theory and Society* 35(5–6): 507–528.

2014. *The Rise and Fall of Ireland's Celtic Tiger: Liberalism, Boom and Bust*. Cambridge, UK: Cambridge University Press.

Ritzer, G. 1998. *The McDonaldization Thesis: Explorations and Extensions*. Thousand Oaks, CA: Sage.

2004. *The Globalization of Nothing*. Thousand Oaks, CA: Pine Forge Press.

Robertson, R. 1995. "Glocalization: Time-Space and Homogeneity-Heterogeneity." In M. Featherstone, S. Lash, R. Robertson (eds.), *Global Modernities* (pp. 25–44). London: Sage.

Robinson, W. I. 2008. *Latin America and Global Capitalism: A Critical Globalization Perspective*. Baltimore, MD: The Johns Hopkins University Press.

Sassen, S. 1999. "Making the Global Economy Run: The Role of National States and Private Agents." *International Social Science Journal* 51(3): 409–416.

2001. *The Global City: New York, London, Tokyo*. Princeton, NJ: Princeton University Press.

2006. *Territory, Authority, Rights*. Princeton, NJ: Princeton University Press.

Shaffer, M. 2013. *See America First: Tourism And National Identity, 1880–1940*. Washington, DC: Smithsonian Institution.

Shields, R. 1999. *Love and Struggle – Spatial Dialectics*. London: Routledge.

Simmel, G. 1971 [1903]. "Metropolis and Mental Life." In D. Frisby and M. Featherstone (eds.), *Simmel on Culture*. London: Sage Publications.

Sites, W. 2003. *Remaking New York: Primitive Globalization and the Politics of Urban Community*. Minneapolis, MN: University of Minnesota Press.

Slevin, J. 2011. "Time-Space." In G. Ritzer and J. M. Ryan (eds.), *Concise Encyclopedia of Sociology* (pp. 650–651). Malden, MA: Wiley Blackwell.

Snyder, B. H. 2013. "From Vigilance to Busyness A Neo-Weberian Approach to Clock Time." *Sociological Theory* 31(3): 243–266.

Sorkin, M. (ed.). 1992. *Variations on a Theme Park: The New American City and the End of Public Space*. New York: Hill and Wang.

Sorokin, P. 1964. *Sociocultural Causality, Space, and Time*. New York: Russell and Russell.

Spain, D. 1992. *Gendered Spaces*. Chapel Hill, NC: University of North Carolina Press.

1993. "Gendered Spaces and Women's Status." *Sociological Theory* 11(1): 137–160.

Stanek, L. 2011. *Henri Lefebvre on Space: Architecture, Urban Research, and the Production of Theory*. Minneapolis, MN: University of Minnesota Press.

Swyngedouw, E. 2004. "Globalisation or 'Glocalisation'? Networks, Territories and Rescaling." *Cambridge Review of International Affairs* 17(1): 25–48.

Thompson, E. P. 1967. "Time, Work-Discipline, and Industrial Capitalism." *Past and Present* 38: 56–97.

Urry, J. 1995. *Consuming Places*. London and New York: Routledge.

Weber, M. 1958. *The City*. Translated and edited by D. Martindale and G. Neuwirth. New York: Free Press.

2011. *The Protestant Ethic and the Spirit of Capitalism: The Revised 1920 Edition*. Translated by S. Kalberg. New York: Oxford University Press.

Zerubavel, E. 1982. "The Standardization of Time: A Sociohistorical Perspective." *American Journal of Sociology* 88(1): 1–23.

12 Social Theory in the Anthropocene: Ecological Crisis and Renewal

Robert J. Antonio and Brett Clark

> There is an urgent need for a new paradigm that integrates the continued develop-
> ment of human societies and the maintenance of the Earth system . . . .
> (Steffen, Richardson, et al., 2015: 736)

Modern social theory emerged when natural resources and environmental sinks seemed infinite, and ecological problems were primarily local, as a response to epochal changes, crises, and possibilities driven by nascent capitalism with its unparalleled economic growth and remarkable technical, sociocultural, and political innovations. Free-market liberals proposed that synergies of markets and science, despite periodic downturns, would sustain ever-expanding capitalism, urbanism, industrialism, and human populations ad infinitum. Even as ecological problems mounted during the enormous post–World War II economic expansion or "Great Acceleration," they contended that markets and exponential growth would sustain and advance widely shared human well-being and a habitable, verdant planet. However, nearly worldwide consolidation of late twentieth-century neoliberal capitalism massively increased the speed and volume of resource utilization and waste production, and thus the scale of ecological damage (Daly, 2005). The emergence of "global environmental problems" and the acceleration of planetary "ecological overshoot," along with their unequally shared harmful consequences, cast doubt upon the sustainability of neoliberalism and capitalism per se.

Concerned about the fast pace, intensity, and worldwide reach of anthropogenic climate change and other environmental problems, scientists argue that the climatically stable Holocene (which spanned the last 11,700 years) has ended and the Anthropocene epoch has dawned (Steffen, Broadgate, et al., 2015; Zalasiewicz et al., 2015). They contend that human activity drives overall ecological change, possible runaway climate change, and other ecocatastrophes that loom and threaten to overtake us (Steffen, Crutzen, and McNeill, 2007). In light of copious scientific evidence about rapidly accelerating ecological change, social theorists must ponder interrelations between "material progress" and the larger web of life. Capitalist growth has spurred higher standards of living as well as socioecological disruption and devastation. Today, social theorists need to engage exponential, unplanned growth and the ways of thought and life it shapes and justifies. Employing a wide purview and normative argumentation anchored in empirical-historical knowledge, social theory could mediate between natural science and public life by elaborating overall social impacts of natural-science forecasts, envisioning sustainable socio-economic regimes and strategies to perpetuate democratic institutions in the face of ecological crises, and facilitating communication between specialists, policymakers, and the wider citizenry.

Liberalism's Growth Imperative

Writing when modern industrialism was barely underway, Marx and Engels (1948 [1848]: 12) asserted, "The bourgeoisie cannot exist without constantly revolutionizing the instruments of production, and thereby the relations of production, and with them the whole relations of society." They argued that capitalists had already generated more powerful, varied productive forces and more economic growth than all earlier civilizations together and transformed social life more radically than ever before. Marx and Engels's (1948 [1848]: 11–13) exceptionally prescient analysis about the rise of cosmopolitan, interdependent, concentrated global capitalism highlighted the forces that have driven growth and given modernity its distinctive character today. Marx (1976 [1868]: 247–257) illuminated how capitalism must constantly expand (M-C-M') to avoid crisis, or as Robert Heilbroner (1985: 36) explained, the "continuous transformation of capital-as-money into capital-as-commodities" must be retransformed "into capital-as-more-money." Drawing on Marx, Joseph Schumpeter (1962 [1942]: 81–86, 418–419) held famously that capitalism "never can be stationary" and its "creative destruction" – or competitively driven innovation, obsolescence, renewal, and expansion – provides unparalleled productive power, dynamism, and growth.

The capitalist growth imperative stresses largely unplanned, exponential economic expansion. Market-liberal capitalist regimes treat Gross Domestic Product (GDP), or the monetary value of a nation's finished goods and services, as the standard for measuring growth and evaluating economic performance. Although GDP does not take account of economic inequality, well-being, or ecological sustainability, liberals equate its expansion with "development" and "social progress." They presume that "more is better" – growing productive powers and profits will increase consumer demand and quantity, quality, and diversity of goods and services. They hold that growth benefits everyone, but unevenly, because rewards are merit-based. The growth imperative manifests capitalism's core logic – the competitive drive for profit and accumulation essential for business survival. Investments, job security, debt repayment, retirement, health care, entitlements, lifestyle, and public institutions all depend on continuous growth. Growth becomes the *sine qua non* of electoral politics and manifests beliefs, values, presuppositions, and predispositions operant from the household to the national level in United States–style capitalism and increasingly, global capitalism.

Schumpeter's *Capitalism, Socialism and Democracy* (1962 [1942]), Friedrich Hayek's *Road to Serfdom* (1944), and Karl Polanyi's *Great Transformation* (1957 [1944]) all contributed to an intense debate over whether market liberalism or social liberalism would best avert a postwar return to depression and autocracy. Market liberals argued that regulation and redistribution undercut economic efficiency, weaken property rights and rule of law, sap entrepreneurial and worker motivation, and generate expansive, intrusive bureaucracy and ultimately authoritarianism. They claimed that free-market policies insure individual liberty, mobility, and affluence (Hayek, 1944; Lippmann, 1937). By contrast, social liberals contended that market liberalism precludes the strong state initiative needed for postwar reconstruction and decreased economic inequality, unemployment, and socioeconomic insecurity and instability. Arguing that self-regulating markets are a myth, social liberals supported government regulation, redistribution, and welfare provision (Polanyi, 1957 [1944]). In varying degrees, social liberalism prevailed in the United States and Europe for more than three decades after World War II.

The US postwar expansion generated robust profits, near full employment, increased worker wages and benefits, and a robust middle class. By the late 1960s, however, the United States faced a more competitive international economy that reduced its share of global manufacture. Additionally, the Vietnam War's costs and expanded welfare state increased inflation and reduced corporate profits. Shortly before accepting a Supreme Court nomination, Lewis F. Powell (1971) warned in a secret memorandum to the US Chamber of Commerce that the "American free enterprise system" was under attack from the left and that the Chamber and corporations must start a countermovement. He urged resisting increasing pressure to expand consumer and environmental regulation. Well-funded conservative think tanks (e.g., Heritage Foundation, Cato Institute, American Enterprise Institute) took up his challenge and revived market-liberal thought (i.e., Friedrich Hayek's Austrian School and Milton Friedman's Chicago School). The new "neoliberal" policy elite waged a highly effective ideological war against social liberalism. Big government, high taxes, labor unions, and social permissiveness, they held, strangle growth and destroy capitalism's vitality. They demanded the cutting of the state's social welfare and regulatory arms and that free-market principles be deployed everywhere. Stemming environmental regulation was a core facet of their program.

Neoliberals advocated an extreme version of capitalism's growth imperative, stressing eradicating barriers to profit and externalizing costs. The Thatcher and Reagan elections gave impetus to neoliberal "market fundamentalism" – deregulation, financialization, tax reduction, privatization, de-unionization, and elimination of trade barriers (Antonio, 2012). In a bestselling panegyric about neoliberal globalization, Thomas Friedman (2000: 5, 103–106) declared that free-market capitalism "blew away all the major ideological alternatives." Quoting Marx and Engels's passages mentioned above and Schumpeter's revision, Friedman lauded the vast productive and innovative powers unleashed by the worldwide freeing of markets from political constraints. Neoliberals aimed to relieve the growth imperative from social liberalism's regulatory and redistributive drag on accumulation, expand capitalism's intensity, speed, and scale, and recover and surpass postwar growth. By contrast, social liberals intended to moderate market liberalism's instabilities, market failures, inequalities, and negative social and ecological externalities. Advocates of both regimes contend that they are best equipped to overcome the excesses of the other and to cope with capitalism's profit squeezes, cyclical crises, and negative externalities. Yet both ultimately depend on growth to garner political support and pay for their programs, and neither can escape ecological overshoot and global environmental problems.

The Environmental Movement and Countermovement

In the 1960s and 1970s, the United States enacted major environmental regulatory legislation (e.g., the Clean Water, Clean Air, Wilderness, Endangered Species, Toxic Substances, and Superfund Acts). Fallout from nuclear testing, urban congestion, industrial air and water pollution, and other ecological degradation generated by rapid growth and insufficient regulation during the early phase of the postwar Great Acceleration stirred growing concern about the environment. Warning about ecological damages and health risks caused by indiscriminate use of DDT and other pesticides, biologist Rachel Carson's (1962) *Silent Spring* and hour-long nationally televised special (*CBS Reports*, April 3, 1963) catalyzed public sensibilities about environmental issues. Media coverage of the 1969 Santa Barbara oil spill also spurred these concerns and inspired initiatives such as the National Environmental Policy Act and Earth Day, both in 1970. That year, Republican President Richard Nixon oversaw the creation of the Environmental Protection Agency (EPA), which eventually banned the use of DDT in US agricultural production. Well-publicized environmental disasters (e.g., the Three Mile Island and Chernobyl nuclear accidents, Love Canal toxic waste disaster, Bhopal gas tragedy, Exxon Valdez and Deepwater Horizon oil spills, Hurricane Katrina, and Superstorm Sandy) later heightened awareness of ecological risk, the environmental movement, and regulatory needs.

The Club of Rome's path-breaking *Limits to Growth* (Meadows et al., 1972) explained how exponential economic and population growth would eventually produce ecological overshoot and collapse. This prescient work stressed the interdependent web of nature, put environmental issues in global perspective, and demonstrated that markets and technology could not sustain unlimited growth in perpetuity. It generated a trajectory of debate over environmental policy that continues today. Even Keynesian economists and policymakers bashed the book as misguided neo-Malthusianism. They argued that it exaggerated greatly the severity of resource shortages, which could be resolved routinely by substituting other factors or resources (e.g., Solow, 1974). By the late 1970s, ascendant neoclassical economists and neoliberal policymakers attacked the limits-to-growth thesis more emphatically. Rejecting environmental regulation and efforts to internalize ecological costs, they maintained that unregulated exponential growth is necessary to insure business expansion, job creation, and mitigation of social ills. Despite these concerted attacks, increasing ecological overshoot and worsening global environmental problems have upheld the authors' core claims (Meadows, Randers, and Meadows, 2004).

In the late 1970s and early 1980s, the "Sagebrush Rebellion" sought increased local control over extensive federal public lands in order to open them for greater exploitation by ranchers, miners, developers, and loggers. President Reagan appointed anti-environmentalist conservatives to prominent positions – James Watt as Secretary of the Interior and Ann Gorsuch as head of EPA. They supported business-oriented land use and opposed the usual conservation goals of their posts. Embraced by Reagan and still revered in neoliberal circles today, University of Chicago–trained neoclassical economist Julian Simon (1981) contended that market liberalism's unparalleled power to unleash, motivate, and coordinate creative activity insures that exponential economic and population growth can be sustained indefinitely. Treating nature as an infinitely pliable tablet for human inscription, he ridiculed claims about irreversible ecological problems and helped make anti-environmentalism a touchstone of neoliberal politics. Resource needs, Simon argued, enhance capacities to find and refine them, and to create substitutes. He argued that resource scarcity, measured by price, decreases for all raw materials in the long term, with only brief or local exceptions. Reagan's effort to weaken environmental oversight and to roll back environmental legislation met with stiff resistance and had only limited success. However, his beliefs in costless growth and anti-environmentalism still inspire conservatives today (Oreskes and Conway, 2010).

Climate scientist James Hansen's widely publicized 1988 congressional testimony that climate change is underway and driven by fossil-fuel usage heightened conservative concerns about sweeping regulatory intervention. Their fears intensified with the 1992 Earth Summit and passage of the Rio Declaration on Environment and Development (165 signatories), and its proposed strong sustainability measures (e.g., precautionary principle, polluter pays, binding transnational regulatory legislation, differentiated responsibilities for wealthy and newly industrialized/poor nations). Created at this gathering, the United Nations Framework Convention on Climate Change (UNFCCC) treaty called for collective action to stabilize greenhouse gas (GHG) concentrations. However, even the Rio Declaration suggested harmonizing that environmental protection with neoliberal policies of accelerated economic growth and free trade, which have since trumped the concord's ecological goals. The signatories adhered to a market-friendly conception of "sustainable" development established earlier in the Bruntland Report, which claimed there were no absolute limits to growth, but only temporary technological and organizational constraints (UN World Commission on Environment and Development, 1987).

Reliance on "soft law," voluntary targets, market-based strategies, and nonbinding multilateral agreements has prevented substantial progress in dealing with climate change and other global environmental problems and insuring a responsible approach to the most vulnerable nations, who contribute least to these conditions (Christoff and Eckersley, 2013: 161–189). Nevertheless, fearing comprehensive state-mandated GHG reductions and transformation of capitalism's carbon-based socioeconomic system, conservative think tanks, foundations, politicians, corporate groups, and contrarian scientists made climate science and environmentalism prime enemies. Countermovement advocates of Simonian "free-market environmentalism" disparaged "alarmism" and "junk science" (which it claimed was inspired by hunger for research support and leftist values) and championed "bottom-up" market-based strategies over "command and control" regulation (e.g., Adler, 2013). The "Wise Use" movement asserted the sanctity of private property rights over environmental regulation and called for compensation and cost–benefit analyses to "balance" environmental interests with economic interests. Anti-environmentalism and climate science denial became chief Republican Party battle flags, especially of its conservative base. Free-market anti-environmentalists warned that growing global environmentalism threatened sweeping government regulation and UN incursions on American sovereignty. Conservative critics portrayed environmentalists as closet communists – "green on the outside, red on the inside" (Brulle, 2014; Dunlap and McCright, 2015; Feine, 2012; Jacques, Dunlap, and Freeman, 2008; Oreskes and Conway, 2010).

Polarization between Congressional Democrats and Republicans on environmental matters and climate change increased enormously in the early twenty-first century (Dunlap, McCright, and Yarosh, 2016). The vast majority of conservative Republicans denied the scientific consensus about climate change and that climate scientists understand the process or know how to deal with it (Funk and Kennedy, 2016). "Centrist" skeptics acknowledged that anthropogenic climate change was occurring, but contended that UNFCCC proposals for sharp GHG cuts and decarbonization were too costly, damaging, and politically unrealistic to succeed. They held that mitigation must await the development of new forms of low-price clean energy, much wider reliance on nuclear energy, or yet-to-be-developed costly, risky geo-engineering strategies (Hulme, 2009). Conservative resistance has not been the only blockage to binding measures to cope with fast-moving climate change. Ambivalence, insouciant irresponsibility, and unwillingness of self-interested corporate and state-owned entities (especially fossil-fuel and cement producers), other business and policy elites, and average citizenry to face the risks and bear the costs have contributed substantially to gridlock (e.g., Heede, 2014; Mann, 2013: 361–399; Norgaard, 2011). Despite increasing climate-change impacts, most of the US public have not felt its effects, find it hard to grasp, or doubt it will affect them (Leiserowitz, Maibach, and Roser-Renouf, 2008).

The extension of neoliberal capitalism into populous newly industrializing nations (i.e., transforming hundreds of millions of peasants into wage workers, creating vast new middle classes, and instituting massive development of urban infrastructure) has increased the scale of the global economy relative to the biosphere and consequently the throughput of resources and production of waste (Daly, 2005; Steffen et al., 2011). Millions of contingent workers and rural peoples in these nations and even larger numbers in the poorest nations outside the global capitalist system await integration into it and a share of its material benefits. Neoliberalism's arrant anti-regulatory politics, atomistic cultural impacts (e.g., possessive individualism, consumerism, "personal responsibility"), and powerful allies in civil society, states, and transnational economic governance institutions neutralize proposals to implement obligatory planning and multinational cooperation to deal with global environmental problems. Growth has slowed in wealthy industrialized nations, but consumption and GHG emissions remain high. There is little evidence to support ecological modernist claims about imminent "dematerialization" or absolute "decoupling" of economic output and resource throughput (Jackson, 2011: 67–86). People surveyed in rich nations with the highest per capita carbon-dioxide emissions scored lowest on a climate-change-concern index (Americans had the lowest level of concern) (Wike, 2016). Underemployment and stagnant wages in rich nations, large pockets of immiserated subgroups and pent-up needs in newly industrialized nations, and abject mass poverty in the poorest nations generate calls for greater unleashing of the growth imperative (including in some of the regions suffering most from its negative ecological consequences). The lack of an alternative vision of a regime capable of harmonizing human flourishing and ecological sustainability and providing a new direction and goal of collective action makes the mounting risks daunting. Indian novelist Amitav Ghosh (2016: 11) states, "this era, which so congratulates itself on its self-awareness, will come to be known as the time of the Great Derangement," given the general disregard for climate change's ecological realities. The Trump administration's extreme anti-regulatory posture and appointments of climate deniers Scott Pruitt and Andrew Wheeler to head the EPA stoke these fears.

Anthropocene Planetary Boundaries: Capitalism and the Ecological Wall?

Even in Pleistocene times early humans contributed to significant ecological changes (e.g., fire impacts, megafauna extinction). However, our ecological footprint grew massively during the Holocene epoch, in which a stable, mild climate favored the development of agriculture, complex civilizations, and enormous population growth (Lewis and Maslin, 2015: 173–176). Today, about 43 percent of terrestrial ecosystems have been fundamentally transformed, and, at current rates of land-use change, the 50 percent level will be reached by 2025 (Barnosky et al., 2012: 56). The concept of Anthropocene was popularized shortly after the millennium in response to growing awareness of massive landscape changes and enormous spikes in resource throughput and waste production driven by capitalism's late-twentieth-century global expansion and consolidation. The Millennium Ecological Assessment (2005) tracked how humans have altered ecosystems much faster and more extensively during the Great Acceleration than ever before, substantially degrading ecosystem services (e.g., fresh water, air quality, pollination, pest population control), and consequently slowed realization of UN human development goals. Steffen et al. (2011: 751–752) argue that the *global scale* of environmental damage, *speed* of ecological change, and *complexity* of biophysical, technological, and socio-political interactions are what distinguish the Anthropocene and generate complicated feedbacks that erode ecosystem resilience and risk collapse. They hold that vulnerability to ecocatastrophe substantially increases when a society's "core values" and policy regimes are "dysfunctional" and unadjusted to changed "external conditions." They assert that today's "growth-oriented economy based on neoliberal economic principles and assumptions" poses just such a risk.

Speaking for the International Geological Congress Working Group, Jan Zalasiewicz declared, "The significance of the Anthropocene is that it sets a different trajectory for the Earth system ... ."[1] Scientists warn that the planet is already substantially warmer than in the Holocene era and also has higher sea levels, reduced ice cover, altered precipitation patterns, diminished biodiversity, and other accelerating, dangerous ecological changes. "Business as usual," they argue, threatens a radically degraded planet for human habitation. They urge a turnabout to "planetary stewardship" and ecological sustainability (Lewis and Maslin, 2015: 178; Steffen et al., 2011: 757). Because such efforts require knowledge about the urgency of risks, these scientists strive to define "planetary boundaries" and set targets to avoid overshoot and irreversible diminishment of biological services. They aim to identify "Earth-system processes" (e.g., climate change, biodiversity loss, disrupted nitrogen and phosphorous cycles, land-use changes, toxic pollution) that are approaching thresholds and threatening planetary state changes. They seek to define and measure "safe operating spaces" for these processes that would alert us to imminent, potentially dangerous ecological changes or "tipping points" in major Earth subsystems whereby small disruptions could cause abrupt qualitative changes. They warn that the greatest tipping threats this century are changes to the Arctic sea ice and Greenland ice sheet, which if breached would raise seas, reduce albedo (absorbing solar energy rather than reflecting it back into space), and generate increased water vapor, carbon and methane releases, and warmer temperatures (Lenton et al., 2008; Rockström et al., 2009).

Eco-modernist critics attack planetary-boundary and Earth-system theorists for being unduly pessimistic or "alarmist" about climate change and other global ecological risks. They contend that continued capitalist modernization will culminate in a "Good Anthropocene" if we avert obsession with preserving Holocene conditions, related doubts about growth, and the consequent truncation of resource usage and technical innovation that improve human well-being. Holding that we are "resilient" beings capable of adapting to widely divergent climates and ecosystems, eco-modernists contend that overambitious employment of state power to mitigate environmental problems (especially decarbonization) are far too costly, risky, and complex and would impose much more suffering than will be sustained from ongoing ecological changes. Embracing the capitalist growth imperative, they argue for development of more effective, cheaper types of clean energy, wider employment of nuclear energy, technical innovations that "decouple" economic activity from material inputs and environmental degradation, and geo-engineering as a backup strategy. While deploring regulatory interference, they encourage state support for private-sector energy innovation (Asafu-Adjaye et al., 2015). Eco-modernist critics see climate change as a "wicked problem" that cannot be solved, but only moderated and adapted to (e.g., Hulme, 2009: 322–365). Converging with limits-to-growth skeptics, techno-optimists, and economists and pundits who advocate "green capitalism," they hold that comprehensive state and transnational planning, regulation, and redistribution, if possible at all, could never be as effective as market-based policies and would throttle economic growth, progress, and freedom.[2]

Global policymakers from wealthy nations have not executed the ambitious aims of the 1992 Rio Declaration and UNFCCC treaty for transnational cooperation to curtail climate change and other global environmental problems, but have opted for multitudinous nonbinding multilateral agreements. The "international trading regime" headed by the World Trade Organization and assisted by the World Bank and International Monetary Fund (whose members are UNFCCC signatories) officially supports "sustainable" development, but its trade rules do not (Christoff and Eckersley, 2013: 176–180). They advocate liberalization and make exponential, unplanned growth the first priority. They reject binding regulation to support environmental targets (Christoff and Eckersley, 2013: 171, 161–207). US leadership of the global neoliberal policy regime and tepid support or opposition to global environmental regulation has contributed substantially to policy failure. As growth slows in wealthy market-liberal nations, political and economic elites, often with widespread public support, call for more aggressive deregulation and social welfare cuts to accelerate growth. Advocating market-based strategies, eco-modernists justify forces that produce ecological policy failure.

Eco-modernists comment little on the social forces that would drive their hoped-for decoupling of growth and material throughput. Benefitting from reduced prices for imported commodities, rich nations have not cut their material consumption. Evidence for dematerialization is lacking (Jackson, 2011: 67–102). The global populace now consumes as if it had the restorative capacities of 1.6 Earths; wealthy nations have much higher rates (WWF, 2016: 13). According to updated figures, we have exceeded planetary boundaries for still-accelerating climate change, biodiversity loss, land-system changes, and biochemical flows (Steffen, Richardson et al., 2015). Global vertebrate populations of monitored species have declined by about 2 percent per year and 58 percent overall from 1970 to 2012; freshwater species have plummeted 81 percent; and marine species have declined 36 percent in the same period (WWF, 2016: 19, 30, 36). Scientists warn that a "sixth great extinction" is already upon us, with extinction rates up so sharply and so many species endangered or vulnerable (Ceballos et al., 2015; WWF, 2016: 45–46). Continued climate change, toxic pollution, land-use changes, and other severe environmental degradation will drive extinction rates higher.

The Intergovernmental Panel on Climate Change (IPCC) has targeted an increase of $2°$ Celsius (C), maximum, over the preindustrial average to reduce chances for catastrophic climate change. Comprehensive analysis based largely on "ongoing observation" and "paleoclimate data" by top climate scientists holds that the $2°C$ maximum – impossible to achieve with business as usual – is a "disaster scenario" (Hansen, Kharecha, and Sato, 2013). This team contends that temperature rise needs to be limited to about $1°C$, which we have already reached. Even if we decarbonized immediately, they hold, temperatures will go substantially higher due to release of heat stored in the seas and reduced aerosol pollution. Brysse et al. (2013) demonstrate that climate scientists have tended to underpredict rather than exaggerate the speed and extent of climate change. Political polarization and charges of alarmism and politically motivated bias have intensified scientific reticence. In part to avoid social-media attacks and political and legal harassment, scientists moderate their public reports about urgent climate-change risks and policy changes to accommodate the dominant neoclassical economic and neoliberal priority of accelerated growth. Climatologists Kevin Anderson and Alice Bows (2012) contend that this self-censorship prevents discussion of "the elephant in the room" – that is, that business as usual will lead to a 4°C or more increase and catastrophic impacts that will preclude economic growth. Anderson asserts that IPCC reports, which neoclassical economists and state officials must approve, understate climate risks and provide future scenarios based on unrealistic assumptions. For example, the much-celebrated 2015 Paris agreement emission pathway to hold warming below 2°C and possibly even 1.5°C presumes implementation of yet-to-be-developed large-scale negative emissions technologies to sequester and remove carbon dioxide from the air (Anderson, 2015a; Anderson and Peters, 2016; Hamilton, 2013). Anderson and Hansen charge that the Paris agreement is fraudulent because of these bogus assumptions, its lack of a binding plan of action, and national pledges for carbon reduction that cannot possibly meet the announced targets (Anderson, 2015b; Milman, 2015). Technological-optimist policymakers support business as usual and increased growth as the only path forward, and ignore acceleration toward the ecological wall.

Bringing Social Theory and Environment Back In

> Nature is the mother and the habitat of man, even if sometimes a stepmother and unfriendly home. The fact that civilization endures and culture continues – and sometimes advances – is evidence that human hopes and purposes find a basis and support in nature. As the developing growth of an individual from embryo to maturity is the result of interaction of organism with surroundings, so culture is the product not of efforts of men put forth in a void or just upon themselves, but of prolonged and cumulative interaction with environment.
>
> (Dewey, 1989a [1934]: 34)

Social Theory in the Anthropocene

Later nineteenth- and early-twentieth-century "classical theorists" analyzed the epochal social transformation driven by the rise of industrial capitalism that Marx anticipated in 1848. Theorists drew on empirical-historical knowledge from emergent social science to map new social formations and construct normative arguments about what problems should be the focus of inquiry and of public efforts to adapt, redirect, or mitigate them. More narrowly focused "sociological theory," however, became the dominant theoretical practice after the rise of specialized social science; it stresses strictly empirical and analytical aims of providing hypotheses and conceptual integration for research programs and consequently excludes normative argument. It address exclusively "what is?" and not "what should be?" In leading research institutions today, many and arguably most sociologists see sociological theory to be the only valid type of theoretical practice and view classical theory and its contemporary reincarnations to be moribund facets of the disciplinary history's prescientific phase. By contrast, we see "social theory" to be a living critical theoretical practice that provides vital resources for debating priorities of social science and public life. We need it especially in times of major social transformation and imminent crisis when catastrophic risks demand fundamental shifts in problems, perspectives, and policies that require normative judgments about direction as well as instrumental decisions. Social theorists pose empirical historical arguments about the social consequences of following existent normative and epistemic directions or of developing new ones as well as contextually sensitive rational arguments about the meaning of normative ideals (e.g., rightness or justice). Social theory's empirical-historical moment distinguishes its post-traditional normative argumentation from that based on incontestable transcendental or absolutist claims or the authority of tradition. Social theory makes normative claims public and open to contestation on consequential grounds and provides intelligent contestable means to debate divergent policy regimes and scientific and societal directions.[3]

Prescient works, such as *Silent Spring* and *The Limits to Growth*, did not overturn the postwar phase of the Great Acceleration's widely shared, naturalized, benign vision of the growth imperative. Later neoliberal efforts to accelerate slowed growth at nearly any cost trumped demands to reduce ecological degradation. In 2017, the Trump administration launched an unparalleled attack on environmental regulation, despite scientific warnings about climate change's grave threats to the ecological bases of socioeconomic development and life on the planet. Earth-systems and planetary-boundary scientists, as well as IPCC climate modelers, frame proto-social theories of alternative pathways for adapting to and mitigating climate change and other dangerous, rapidly worsening global ecological problems. Scientists proposed the concept of the Anthropocene motivated by their assessments that an epochal rupture is already underway and that it poses enormous risks; as a result, they initiated efforts to establish planetary boundaries and safe living spaces. Social theorists need to make ecology and global environmental problems and their economic drivers a primary focus, and urge much greater engagement of these issues by sociologists and other specialized social scientists. Currently, relatively few sociology departments have faculty working on these problems or entertaining how they bear on globalization and transnational development.

Socioecological Contradictions of the Capitalist Growth Imperative

As noted above, the growth imperative is central to capitalist accumulation. Any effort to theorize a sustainable alternative to business as usual and ecocatastrophe requires a fundamental rethinking of capitalism as we have known it, or conceptualizing a new political-economic system. Efforts to rein in growth, make capitalism sustainable, or transform it encounter enormous resistance. In the vacuum created by left-leaning and centrist parties' failure to envision a democratic alternative to neoliberalism, nativist populists have posed authoritarian challenges to neoliberal globalization. Neoliberals' relentless efforts to increase growth and accumulation have generated enormous ecological risks and furthered economic inequality. Wealthy nations, which are those most responsible for climate change, block binding climate accords. They refuse to fulfill their commitment to "differentiated responsibilities," such as making greater carbon reductions, paying a larger share of related costs, and providing economic and technological assistance to the poorest, hardest-hit nations who have contributed little to the problem and lack resources to adapt to it. Bangladesh and small island nations face catastrophic damages from rising seas and storm surges. Substantial parts of Africa have suffered prolonged drought, famine, and related warfare. Indigenous people, women, children, and elderly have suffered the most from climate-change-driven conditions. In March 2017, the United Nations warned of the gravest humanitarian crisis since World War II in which 20 million drought-stricken Africans could die without provision of emergency food, water, and medical care. Higher temperatures and reduced rainfall from accelerating climate change will threaten severe drought and likely forced migrations in increasingly extensive portions of Africa, South Asia, South America, and the Middle East (Klare, 2017).

Accelerated by neoliberal tax cuts and other policies favoring the very wealthy, rapidly growing economic inequality within rich and newly industrialized nations undercuts the collective responsibility and cooperation needed to tackle climate change and other global environmental problems. Economist Thomas Piketty (2014) famously explained how wealthy nations made a U-turn from the post–World War II era's meteoric growth and sharply reduced inequality to an insecure, unforgiving new normal of heightened inequality and substantially reduced opportunity, mobility, and fairness. He warned that extreme income polarization threatens return of wealthy nations to a static "rentier society," in which kinship and strategic marriage rule rather than merit (Piketty, 2014: 115–116).[4] Portraying similar growth of sharp economic inequality, economist Robert J. Gordon (2016: 641–652) contended that exceptionally hard-to-reverse "fundamental causes" preclude moderation of the trend. Likewise, Branko Milanovic (2016), an economist, pointed to polarizing incomes, shrinking middle classes, eroding social welfare, and an increasing concentration of income and wealth among the upper 5 percent and especially the 1 percent (half of whom reside in the United States). Predicting a widening, stark divide between a tiny "rich class" and low-paid workers who service them, he sees no significant opposition seeking to resist the trend, or even a plausible alternative political-economic vision, and adds that plutocracy breeds nativist populism (Brexit, Trump, Le Pen) (Milanovic, 2016: 20–23, 70–78, 192–211).[5] Sociologist Wolfgang Streeck (2016: 72–94, 151–163) proposed that postwar "democratic capitalism" is in decline and crisis – its provision by market forces and social need (entitlement) is being displaced by exclusive dependence on markets and trends toward "plutocracy" and "authoritarian liberalism." He held that "slow growth," "mountains of debt," and "oligarchic neo-feudalism" are eviscerating democracy, opening an indeterminate period of instability, and generating a rapidly approaching moment when "the foundations of modern society" and "capitalism will have to be rethought" (Streeck, 2016: 35, 201–203, 250–251).

Already mentioned in passing, Gordon (2016: 633–634) and Milanovic (2016: 232–234) denied that climate change poses severe, urgent threats. They parallel neoclassical economists, whose unflagging belief in the growth imperative and capitalism leads to skepticism or outright denial of climate change. By contrast, Piketty (2014: 567–569), albeit briefly, identified climate change and resource depletion as the "world's principal long-term worry." More recently, he declared, "as a matter of urgency, globalization must be fundamentally re-oriented" to contend with rising "inequality" and "global warming" (Piketty, 2016). Streeck (2016:

60–63) also warned that the growth imperative is unstainable, climate change poses an urgent threat, and that delayed impacts foster denial and inaction. Even Piketty and Streeck do not take full stock of the natural-science evidence of the speed and scope of climate change and the short timetable in which we have to act to avoid catastrophic, irreversible damage.

Anderson and Bows's (2012) point about our inability to come to terms with the threats posed by unregulated growth still holds in most policy circles. The equation of economic growth with progress has put questions about capitalism's sustainability off-limits. Neoclassical economists, neoliberal policymakers, and finance capitalists disembed production from the sociopolitical relations that once directed it toward democratic ends, equality of opportunity, and fulfillment of human needs. Instead, they have fashioned a "market society" that subordinates all aspects of social life to economic growth and capital accumulation. They envision the economic system as an autonomous self-governing force, divorced from socioecological concerns (Longo et al., 2016). Nevertheless, social theorists need to take up the conjoint problems of ecological devastation, sharply increased economic inequality, and the rise of populist racial and ethnic nationalism.

Naturalistic Social Theory Overcoming Dualism

Philosophers and social theorists have long debated Western thought's dualistic features (i.e., body and soul, subject and object, culture and nature, and theory and practice) and consequent subjectivization and individualization. To facilitate the changes of substantive focus suggested above, social theorists must reconstruct their foundations and presuppositions so that they no longer treat social processes and biophysical processes, and the sciences that investigate them, as mutually exclusive domains. Naturalistic social theory takes account of humanity's distinct species capacities and emergent, *sui generis* cultural life, but also addresses the necessary, continuous interaction of social processes with biophysical processes, and consequent need for cooperation between social science and natural science. To engage democratically climate change, we must transcend the chasm erected between normative judgment and empirical judgment that motivates our discussion of social theory, and is rooted ultimately in the culture–nature dualism. We will never breach the propagandistic blockages to serious public debate over ecological problems if the intellectual discourse needed for reaching uncoerced, intersubjective understandings and effective political action and compromise is restricted to factual matters and instrumental decisions about means, while decisions about cultural ends and trade-offs are relegated to the "subjective" individual realm.

In classic articles, William R. Catton and Riley E. Dunlap (1978; 1980) argued that postwar social science and growth-oriented economic policy manifested "human exemptionalist" presuppositions envisioning society as independent from the biophysical world. They held that then-emergent environmental sociology was the harbinger of a "new environmental paradigm" that situates society within the interdependent "web of nature" and acknowledges the fact that humans face ecological constraints like all other living things. Limits-to-growth, Earth-systems, and planetary-boundary scientists all see human systems as embedded within the Earth system and dependent on biophysical processes. Culture mediates human relationships with other facets of the biophysical world, but it does not exempt humans from ecological and biophysical limits. Environmental sociologists examine how growth dynamics, especially population and economic factors, influence the Earth system by altering material conditions and resource availability. They also investigate feedback loops that manifest how the larger biophysical environment constrains and influences social conditions. However, the new ecological paradigm has not yet supplanted widely held dualistic, excmptionalist presuppositions within social science and policy science.

John Dewey held that the split between nature and culture has been a core facet of Western philosophy and religion, rooted in a fundamental divergence between mind (soul) and body (matter) and of the spirit's superiority and imperium over the biophysical domain. Dewey argued that Western dualism goes back at least to Aristotle's metaphysics, was enchanted and diffused by Christianity, and secularized by modern Western philosophy's strong subjectivist thread and epistemological divide between "subject" (inner world) and "object" (external world). He held that the dualism and consequent cultural reductionism originated from ancient ruling classes legitimating their contemplative activities and predatory extractive practices and depreciating the physical work of their slaves and serfs and the unspiritual embodied realm they personified. Dewey contended that this dualism persists today in the corporatized political economy's culturally and politically ascendant market-liberal individualism and in related beliefs about the superiority of professional "mental work" to physical labor and even crafts work.[6]

Drawing on Darwin's conception of naturalistic interdependence, Dewey and George Herbert Mead pitted their naturalism against Spencer's and other Social Darwinists' emphasis on the primacy of the individual struggle for existence and linear socioeconomic progress. Dewey held that acquisitive individualism undercuts the cooperative sociocultural form of naturalistic interdependence vital to human communities, and cannot come to terms with corporately organized society and economy. Dewey's and Mead's "organism-environment" model did not posit a direction to history, but stressed nonlinear adaptive change, locality, unintended consequences, uncertainty, and inquiry into particular conditions of specific situations.[7] They treated "interaction" between the "organism and environment" as a first principle of the life sciences and human sciences. Thinking, speaking, and acting, they argued, are always embodied and the biophysical world is always copresent even in symbolic or mental acts. Our multitudinous, complex instrumentalities, which mediate our relations with each other and the biophysical world, distinguish us from other species, but are *never* beyond nature.

Dewey and Mead saw linguistically mediated sociocultural life to be an emergent, distinctly human facet of naturalistic interdependence. They argued that language has species-specific biological substrates, but, like Marx, they contended that it arose via cooperative and associative practices or social labor.[8] Their position is diametrically opposed to the culturally reductionist "constructivism" criticized incisively by Catton and Dunlap and other environmental sociologists of their persuasion.

Dewey (1986 [1938]: 40) posited the independent natural world but asserted that it is the "*environment* only as it enters directly and indirectly into life-functions." Dewey (1988b [1927]: 245–246) held that human actions (e.g., bank rate manipulation or toxic pollution) seriously impactful to our social and biophysical surroundings can be unnoticed or be misinterpreted. He contended that the scale and complexity of modern corporately organized societies, with their exceptionally complicated inter-dependence and arcane causal chains, make these unknown, unintended, "indirect consequences" more numerous, problematic, and subject to demagogic manipula-tion. Also, Dewey (1989b [1939]: 102–118) saw science as a contested terrain open to diverse uses and manipulation like the rest of culture. In his view, climate science would be a necessary, but insufficient means to cope with climate change; policy-makers and citizenry would have to couple it with effective diffusion of information, normative argument, and collective action for it to contribute substantially to adapta-tion and mitigation. The value of Dewey's and Mead's naturalism is that it takes account explicitly of nature's obdurate and fecund qualities, but in a manner that addresses the vital empirical and normative facets of sociocultural construction that mediate interaction between human organisms and their environments.

Dewey's naturalism shares similarities with Marx's materialist, metabolic analy-sis. Marx theorized socioeconomic systems as embedded in the larger biophysical world and studied interchanges of matter and energy between the environment and society (Burkett, 1999; Foster, 2000; Foster and Burkett, 2016). Following then-current natural-science discoveries, he incorporated the concept of metabolism into his critique of political economy. He denoted "the 'natural' process of production as the material exchange [*Stoffwechsel*] between man and nature" (Marx, 1975: 209). He explained that there is a necessary "metabolic interaction" between humans and the Earth and that labor serves as the nexus (Marx, 1976 [1868]: 283). Marx saw capitalism as a historically specific regime of accumulation that drives the growth imperative, and consequently the social metabolic order. He also contended that social metabolism operates within the broader biophysical world with its specific cycles and processes that produce and regenerate ecological conditions (Foster, 2013: 8; Marx and Engels, 1988: 54–66). Under capitalism, he argued, social metabolism takes on such an alienated form that it generates ecological crises, manifested as "rifts" in socioecological metabolism between society and nature. In his view, sustainability requires scientific exploration of natural limits and efforts to plan social metabolism accordingly. Marx designed his dialectical, metabolic con-ception to avoid subordinating nature to society, as well as to avoid the pitfalls of idealism and reductionist realism (Foster, 2013: 8). His metabolic analysis, like Deweyan naturalism, examines the constant interaction of humans and societies with the rest of nature, including consequent reciprocal influences, impacts, and dependencies.

Dewey and Marx can serve as a departure point for renewing conversations regarding post-exemptionalism and forging "realism without reductionism" (Carolan, 2005; Foster, 2000). The capitalist growth imperative, a deep structure of Western thought, secularized the culture–nature dualism, which assures us that the market and science and their biosocial substrata exempt us from natural limits.

Deterritorialized globalization makes the lived comforts and risks of this belief system a near-universal habitus. Rethinking this dualism is no longer an exclusively metatheoretical project, but is a practical one of reimagining our sociocultural and sociopolitical arrangements and formulating ways to come to terms with climate change. Naturalistic social theory provides languages and analytical tools to address these matters.

Conclusion: A Post-Exemptionalist Anthropocene?

Will the "steel-hard casing" of capitalism's inexorable, frenetic culture of growth at any cost prevail, as Weber warned, "until the last ton of fossil fuel is burned to ashes"? Or will we, as he proposed, pause in an approaching moment of crisis to "consider the streams of events from the heights of thought" and fundamentally rethink our pathway and change course (Weber, 2011 [1920]: 177; 1949 [1904]: 112)? What is evident, as Clive Hamilton and Jacques Grinevald (2015: 67) explain, is that the Anthropocene "is a new anthropogenic rift in the natural history of planet Earth rather than the further development of the anthropocentric biosphere." The window of opportunity for effective action is closing. Yet systemic and cultural blockages to collective global engagement with climate change clash with greatly increased knowledge about the enormous risks, costs, and speed of climate-change processes. Many contingent sociopolitical conditions make it hard to predict what scenario will reign and if our reflexive turn comes too late. Given that the future of the planet is at stake, we do not want to exaggerate the role of social theory. Nevertheless, social theory provides a language and conceptual tools to analyze the social drivers and impacts of climate change and other global environmental problems and to argue for wider attention to them. We must integrate theory and practice on multiple levels to foster development and diffusion of social knowledge within the discipline, between disciplines, and between science and public policy.

Social theorists must reconstruct the epistemic presuppositions of contemporary thought and discourse about nature–culture relations and their impacts. This step requires stripping away ecological blinders and addressing the cultural conditions that gave exemptionalism its distinctive modern form – coming fully to terms with the growth imperative and its connections to the political-economic operating system that drives it. Social theorists must address the culture–nature dualism that remains a profoundly problematic foundation for public policy and a cultural obstacle to mitigation of climate change and other facets of the Anthropocene's distinctive overshoot. Debating, completing, and diffusing post-exemptionalist thought, or a thoroughgoing naturalism, is the core metatheoretical project of social theory directed toward addressing the global ecological crisis. The related substantive project is to facilitate inquiry and debate over capitalism, as we have known it, and entertain alternative futures beyond this regime. This turn revives a long debate, but on new grounds that require fresh thinking and departure from old polarities. Many natural scientists and social scientists resist going there, for mere mention of the topic is often castigated as unscientific, too "political" and "biased," or, worse, a sign that one belongs in the dustbin of history with Marx. The real issue is whether we will dare to grapple with the enormous ecological risks of business as usual, obvious climate changes (e.g., rising seas, retreating glaciers), and the severe impacts already suffered in mostly poor parts of the world.

References

Alder, Johnathan H. 2013. "Conservative Principles for Environmental Reform." *Duke Environmental Law and Policy Review* 23 (2/3): 253–280.

Anderson, Kevin. 2015a. "Duality in Climate Change." *Nature Climate Change* 8 (December): 898–900.

2015b. "Talks in City of Light Generate More Heat." *Nature* 528 (December 24/31): 437.

Anderson, Kevin, and Alice Bows. 2012. "A New Paradigm for Climate Change." *Nature Climate Change* 2 (September): 639–640.

Anderson, Kevin, and Glen Peters. 2016. "The Trouble with Negative Emissions." *Science* (October): 182–183.

Antonio, Robert J. 2005. "For Social Theory, Alvin Gouldner's Last Project and Beyond." In Jennifer Lehmann (ed.), *Current Perspectives in Social Theory, Questioning Social Change*, vol. 23 (pp. 71–129). Amsterdam: Elsevier.

2012. "After Neoliberalism, Whither Capitalism?" In George Ritzer (ed.), *New Blackwell Companion to Sociology* (pp. 588–612). Malden, MA: Blackwell.

Antonio, Robert J., and Brett Clark. 2015. "The Climate Divide in Social Theory." In Riley E. Dunlap and Robert J. Brulle (eds.), *Climate Change and Society, Sociological Perspectives* (pp. 333–368). New York: Oxford University Press.

Asafu-Adjaye, John, Linus Blomqvist, Stewart Brand, et al. 2015. *An Ecomodernist Manifesto.* Available at https://static1.squarespace.com/static/5515d9f9e4b04d5c3198b7bb/t/552d37bbe4b07a7dd69fcdbb/1429026747046/An+Ecomodernist+Manifesto.pdf

Barnosky, Anthony D, Elizabeth A. Hadly, Jordi Bascompte, et al. 2012. "Approaching a State Shift in the Earth's Biosphere." *Nature* 486 (June 7): 52–58.

Brulle, Robert J. 2014. "Institutionalizing Delay, Foundation Founding and the Creation of US Climate Change Countermovement Organizations." *Climatic Change* 114: 169–188.

Brysse, Keynyn, Naomi Oreskes, Jessica O'Reilly, and Martin Oppenheimer. 2013. "Climate Change Prediction, Erring on the Side of the Least Drama?" *Global Environmental Change* 23: 327–337.

Burkett, Paul. 1999. *Marx and Nature.* New York: St. Martin's Press.

Carolan, Michael S. 2005. "Realism without Reductionism." *Human Ecology Review* 20(1): 1–20.

Carrington, Damian. 2016. "The Anthropocene Epoch, Scientists Declare Dawn of Human-Influenced Age." *The Guardian* (August 29). www.theguardian.com/environment/2016/aug/29/declare-anthropocene-epoch-experts-urge-geological-congress-human-impact-earth.

Carson, Rachel. 1962. *Silent Spring.* Boston, MA: Houghton Mifflin.

Catton, William R., Jr., and Riley E. Dunlap. 1978. "Environmental Sociology, a New Paradigm." *The American Sociologist* 13: 41–49.

1980. "A New Ecological Paradigm for Post-Exuberant Sociology." *American Behavioral Scientist* 24(1): 15–47.

Ceballos, Gerardo, Paul R. Ehrlich, Anthony D. Barnosky, et al. 2015. "Accelerated Modern Human-Induced Species Losses, Entering the Sixth Great Extinction." *Science Advances* (June 19). DOI:http://dx.doi.org/10.1126/sciadv.1400253.

Christoff, Peter, and Robyn Eckersley. 2013. *Globalization and the Environment*. Lanham, MD: Rowman and Littlefield.

Daly, Herman E. 2005. "Economics in a Full World." *Scientific American* (September): 100–107.

Dewey, John. 1983a [1904]. "The Philosophical Work of Herbert Spencer." In Jo Ann Boydston (ed.), *John Dewey, the Middle Works, 1899–1924*, vol. 3 (pp. 193–209). Carbondale and Edwardsville, IL: Southern Illinois University Press.

1983b [1909]. "The Influence of Darwinism on Philosophy." In Jo Ann Boydston (ed.), *John Dewey, the Middle Works, 1899–1924*, vol. 4 (pp. 3–14). Carbondale and Edwardsville, IL: Southern Illinois University Press.

1985 [1916]. "Progress." in Jo Ann Boydston (ed.), *John Dewey, the Middle Works, 1899–1924*, vol. 10 (pp. 234–243). Carbondale and Edwardsville, IL: Southern Illinois Press.

1986 [1938]. *Logic, the Theory of Inquiry*. In Jo Ann Boydston (ed.), *John Dewey, the Later Works 1925–1953*, vol. 5–12, 1938 (pp. 41–123). Carbondale and Edwardsville, IL: Southern Illinois University Press.

1988a [1925]. *Experience and Nature*, vol. 1 (1925) in Jo Ann Boydston (ed.), *John Dewey, the Later Works 1925–1953*. Carbondale and Edwardsville, IL: Southern Illinois University Press.

1988b [1927]. *The Public and Its Problems*. In Jo Ann Boydston (ed.), *John Dewey, The Later Works 1925–1953*, vol. 2, 1925–1927 (pp. 235–372). Carbondale and Edwardsville, IL: Southern Illinois University Press.

1988c [1929]. *The Quest for Certainty*, vol. 4 (1929) in Jo Ann Boydston (ed.), *John Dewey, the Later Works, 1925–1953*. Carbondale and Edwardsville, IL: Southern Illinois University Press.

1988d [1929]. *Individualism, Old and New*. In Jo Ann Boydston (ed.), *John Dewey, The Later Works 1925–1953*, vol. 5, 1929–1930 (pp. 41–123). Carbondale and Edwardsville, IL: Southern Illinois University Press.

1989a [1934]. *Art as Experience*, vol. 10 (1929–1930) in Jo Ann Boydston (ed.), *John Dewey, the Later Works 1925–1953*. Carbondale and Edwardsville, IL: Southern Illinois University Press.

1989b [1939]. *Freedom and Culture*. Buffalo, NY: Prometheus Books.

2012 [1941–1942]. *Unmodern and Modern Philosophy*, edited by Phillip Deen. Carbondale and Edwardsville, IL: Southern Illinois University Press.

Dewey, John, and James Hayden Tufts. 1985 [1932]. *Ethics*, vol. 7 in Jo Ann Boydston (ed.), *John Dewey, the Later Works, 1925–1953*. Carbondale and Edwardsville, IL: Southern Illinois Press.

Dunlap, Riley E., and Aaron M. McCright. 2015. "Challenging Climate Change, the Denial Countermovement." In Riley E. Dunlap and Robert J. Brulle (eds.), *Climate Change and Society, Sociological Perspectives* (pp. 330–332). New York: Oxford University Press.

Dunlap, Riley E., Aaron M. McCright, and Jerrod H. Yarosh. 2016. "The Political Divide on Climate Change, Partisan Polarization Widens in the U.S." *Environment* 58(5): 4–23.

Feine, Paul. 2012. "Green on the Outside, Red on the Inside." *Reason.com*. January. http://reason.com/archives/2011/11/20/green-on-the-outside-red-on-the-inside.

Foster, John Bellamy. 2000. *Marx's Ecology*. New York: Monthly Review Press.

———. 2013. "Marx and the Rift in the Universal Metabolism of Nature." *Monthly Review* 65(7): 1–19.

Foster, John Bellamy, and Paul Burkett. 2016. *Marx and the Earth*. Leiden: Brill.

Friedman, Thomas L. 2000. *The Lexus and the Olive Tree*. New York: Anchor.

Funk, Cary, and Brian Kennedy. 2016. "The Politics of Climate." *Pew Research Center* (October 4). www.pewinternet.org/2016/10/04/the-politics-of-climate/.

Ghosh, Amitav. 2016. *The Great Derangement: Climate Change and the Unthinkable*. Chicago, IL: University of Chicago Press.

Gordon, Robert J. 2016. *The Rise and Fall of American Growth*. Princeton, NJ: Princeton University Press.

Gould, Stephen Jay. 2002. *The Structure of Evolutionary Theory*. Cambridge, MA: Harvard University Press.

Hamilton, Clive. 2013. *Earthmasters*. New Haven, CT: Yale University Press.

———. 2015. "The Theodicy of the Good Anthropocene." *Environmental Humanities* 7: 233–38.

Hamilton, Clive, and Jacques Grinevald. 2015. "Was the Anthropocene Anticipated?" *The Anthropocene Review* 2(1): 59–72.

Hansen, James, Pushker Kharecha, and Makiko Sato. 2013. "Assessing Dangerous Climate Change, Required Reduction of Carbon Emissions to Protect Young People, Future Generations and Nature." *Plos One*. 8(12). https://journals.plos.org/plosone/article?id=10.1371/journal.pone.0081648.

Harrington, Brook. 2016. *Capital without Borders*. Cambridge, MA: Harvard University Press.

Hayek, Friedrich A. 1944. *The Road to Serfdom*. Chicago, IL: University of Chicago Press.

Heede, Richard. 2014. "Tracing Anthropogenic Carbon Dioxide and Methane Emissions to Fossil Fuel and Cement Producers, 1854–2010." *Climate Change* 122: 229–241.

Heilbroner, Robert. 1985. *The Nature and Logic of Capitalism*. New York, Norton.

Hulme, Mike. 2009. *Why We Disagree about Climate Change*. Cambridge, UK: Cambridge University Press.

Jackson, Tim. 2011. *Prosperity without Growth*. London: Earthscan.

Jacques, Peter, J., Riley E. Dunlap, and Mark Freeman. 2008. "The Organization of Denial, Conservative Think Tanks and Environmental Skepticism." *Environmental Politics* 17(3): 349–385.

Klare, Michael T. 2017. "Climate Change as Genocide." *Common Dreams*, April 20. www.commondreams.org/views/2017/04/20/climate-change-genocide.

Leiserowitz, Anthony, Edward Maibach, and Connie Roser-Renouf. 2008. *Global Warming's "Six Americas."* New Haven, CT, and Fairfax, VA: Yale University and Center for Climate Change Communication, George Mason University.

Lenton, Timothy M., Hermann Held, Elmar Kriegler, et al. 2008. "Tipping Elements in the Earth's Climate System." *PNAS* 105(6): 1786–1793.

Levins, Richard, and Richard Lewontin. 1985. *The Dialectical Biologist*. Cambridge, MA: Harvard University Press.

Lewis, Simon L., and Mark A. Maslin. 2015. "Defining the Anthropocene." *Nature* 519 (March 12): 171–179.

Lippmann, Walter. 1937. *The Good Society*. Boston, MA: Little, Brown, and Co.

Longo, Stefano B., Brett Clark, Thomas E. Shriver, and Rebecca Clausen. 2016. "Sustainability and Environmental Sociology, Putting the Economy In Its Place and Moving Toward an Integrative Socio-Ecology." *Sustainability* 8(5): 437, DOI: dx.doi.org/10.3390/su8050437.

Mann, Michael. 2013. *The Sources of Social Power (Vol. 4), Globalizations, 1945–2011*. New York: Cambridge University Press.

Marx, Karl. 1975. *Texts on Method*. Oxford, UK: Blackwell.

Marx, Karl. 1976 [1868]. *Capital*, vol. 1. London: Penguin.

Marx, Karl, and Frederick Engels. 1948 [1848]. *The Communist Manifesto*. New York: International Publishers.

Marx, Karl, and Frederick Engels. 1988. *Collected Works*, vol. 30. New York: International Publishers.

Mead, George Herbert. 1962 [1934]. *Mind, Self and Society*. Chicago, IL: University of Chicago Press.

Mead, George Herbert. 1964a [1927]. "The Objective Reality of Perspectives." In Andrew J. Reck (ed.), *Selected Writings* (pp. 306–319). Indianapolis, IN: Bobbs-Merrill Company.

   1964b [1929–1930]. "The Philosophies of Royce, James, and Dewey in their American Setting." In Andrew J. Reck (ed.), *Selected Writings* (pp. 371–391). Indianapolis, IN: Bobbs-Merrill Company.

Meadows, Donella, Dennis L. Meadows, Jørgen Randers, and William W. Behrans III. 1972. *The Limits to Growth*. New York: Universe Books.

Meadows, Donella, Jørgen Randers, and Dennis L. Meadows. 2004. *Limits to Growth*. White River Junction, VT: Chelsea Green.

Milanovic, Barnko. 2016. *Global Inequality*. Cambridge, MA: Belknap.

Millennium Ecological Assessment. 2005. *Ecosystems and Human Well-being, Synthesis* Washington, DC: Island Press. www.millenniumassessment.org/documents/docu ment.356.aspx.pdf.

Milman, Oliver. 2015. "James Hansen, Father of Climate Change Awareness, Calls Paris Talks 'A Fraud.'" *The Guardian* (December 13). www.theguardian.com/environ ment/2015/dec/12/james-hansen-climate-change-paris-talks-fraud.

Norgaard, Kari Marie. 2011. *Living in Denial*. Cambridge, MA: MIT.

Oreskes, Naomi, and Erik M. Conway. 2010. *Merchants of Doubt*. New York: Bloomsbury.

Piketty, Thomas. 2014. *Capital in the Twenty-First Century*. Cambridge, MA: Belknap.

   2016. "We Must Rethink Globalization, or Trumpism Will Prevail." *The Guardian* (November 16). www.theguardian.com/commentisfree/2016/nov/16/globalization -trump-inequality-thomas-piketty.

Polanyi, Karl. 1957 [1944]. *The Great Transformation, the Political and Economic Origins of Our Time*. Boston, MA: Beacon.

Powell, Lewis F. 1971. "Powell Memorandum, Attack on the American Free Enterprise System." Powell Archives, Washington and Lee University School of Law. https://law.wlu.edu/powell-archives

Prins, Gwyn, Isabel Galiana, Christopher Green, et al. 2010. "The Hartwell Paper." Institute for Science Innovation and Society, University of Oxford and LSE MacKinder Programme May. https://eprints.lse.ac.uk/27939/1/HartwellPaper_English_version .pdf.

Rayner, Steve. 2013. "Planetary Boundaries as Millenarian Prophesies, Malthusian Echoes." Oxford Martin School (April 10). www.oxfordmartin.ox.ac.uk/opinion/view/206.

Rockström, Johan, Will Steffen, Kevin Noone, et al. 2009. "A Safe Operating Space for Humanity." *Nature* 461(24): 472–475.

Schumpeter, Joseph A. 1962 [1942], *Capitalism, Socialism and Democracy*. New York & Evanston, IL: Harper Torchbooks.

Simon, Julian L. 1981. *The Ultimate Resource*. Princeton, NJ: Princeton University Press.

Solow, Robert M. 1974. "The Economics of Resources or the Resources of Economics." *American Economic Review* 64(2): 1–14.

Steffen, Will, Wendy Broadgate, Lisa Deutsch, Owen Gaffney, and Cornelia Ludwig. 2015. "The Trajectory of the Anthropocene, the Great Acceleration." *Anthropocene Review* 2(1): 81–98.

Steffen, Will, Paul. J. Crutzen, and John R. McNeill. 2007. "The Anthropocene, Are Humans Now Overwhelming the Great Forces of Nature?" *Ambio* 36(8): 614–621.

Steffen, Will, Åsa Persson, Lisa Deutsch, et al. 2011. "The Anthropocene, From Global Change to Planetary Change." *Ambio* 40: 739–761.

Steffen, Will, Katherine Richardson, Johan Rockström, et al. 2015. "Planetary Boundaries, Guiding Human Development on a Changing Planet." *Science* 347(6232): 1259855-1-10.

Streeck, Wolfgang. 2016. *How Will Capitalism End?* London: Verso.

UN World Commission on Environment and Development. 1987. *Our Common Future*. www.un-documents.net/wced-ocf.htm.

Weber, Max. 1949 [1904]. "Objectivity in the Social Sciences." In Edward A. Shils and Henry A. Finch (eds. and trans.), *The Methodology of the Social Sciences* (pp. 49–112). New York: The Free Press.

    2011 [1920]. *The Protestant Ethic and the Spirit of Capitalism*. New York: Oxford University Press.

Wike, Richard. 2016. "What the World Thinks about Climate Change in 7 Charts." *Pew Research Center* (April 18). www.pewresearch.org/fact-tank/2016/04/18/what-the-world-thinks-about-climate-change-in-7-charts/.

WWF. 2016. *Living Planet Report 2016*. Gland, Switzerland: WWF International. www.worldwildlife.org/pages/living-planet-report-2016.

Zalasiewicz, Jan, Colin N. Waters, Mark Williams, et al. 2015. "When Did the Anthropocene Begin? A Mid-Twentieth Century Boundary Level Is Stratigraphically Optimal." *Quaternary International* 383: 196–203.

Zucman, Gabriel. 2016. "Wealth Inequality." *The Stanford Center on Poverty*. https://inequality.stanford.edu/sites/default/files/Pathways-SOTU-2016-Wealth-Inequality-3.pdf

Notes

1. Zalasiewicz (quoted in Carrington, 2016) presented to the International Union of Geological Sciences the Working Group's proposal that the Anthropocene epoch become an official part of the geologic time scale and that the new epoch began about 1950, at the start of the Great Acceleration. Supermajorities of the Subcommission on Quarternary Stratigraphy and International Commission on Stratigraphy must ratify the proposal to make it official (Lewis and Maslin, 2015: 172).

2. On eco-modernist policy, see Asafu-Adjaye et al. (2015), Prins et al. (2010), and Rayner (2013). For critique, see Antonio and Clark (2015) and Hamilton (2015).

3. Social theorists employ the "best" empirical-historical evidence concerning consequences to support their normative claims, albeit with due consideration to contrary arguments and information. Sociological theory and social theory are ideal types of interdependent

practices that can inform and provide resources for each other. However, actual theoretical practices usually have mixed attributes and often fluid, blurred borders – the two types of theory are often conflated and result in distorted communication (i.e., normative arguments presented as if they were empirical or the converse) (Antonio, 2005).

4. In premodern rentier societies, the upper decile owned 90 percent of the wealth. The US top decile holds 77.2 percent of the wealth. The top 0.1 percent share increased from 7 percent in the late 1970s to 22 percent in 2012. Figures are understated for ultrahigh-income people because a substantial share of their wealth is hidden in offshore tax havens. The bottom 90 percent share declined from 36 percent in the 1980s to 23 percent in 2012 (Harrington, 2016; Zucman, 2016: 40–42).

5. Milanovic (2016: 214–217) stated that robotics will eliminate jobs and increase unemployment and that oversupply of overeducated workers will reduce mobility based on higher education.

6. Dewey held that Western dualism's transcendental realm of spirit provides a comforting myth of certain truths that counter the inherent uncertainty of embodied existence and justify obedience to the status quo. Dewey held that other cultures and religions manifested a mind–body split, but that this dualism has been especially central and widely diffused in the West (Dewey, 1988c [1929]: 3–20; 1988a [1925]: 100–131; 1988b [1927]: 104–110; 2012 [1941–1942]: 3–65, 184–251). See Dewey and Tufts (1985 [1932]: 405–406) on natural resources; Dewey (1988b [1927]; 1988d [1929]; 2012 [1941–1942]: 66–97) on individualism and interdependence; Dewey (1989b [1939]; 1988a [1925]; 2012 [1941–1942]: 304–345) on nature and naturalism.

7. William James's engagement of Darwin deeply influenced Mead and Dewey. Mead (1964b [1929–1930]: 283–284) stated: "But for James the act is a living physiological affair, and must be placed in the struggle for existence, which Darwinian evolution had set up as the background of life. Knowledge is an expression of the intelligence by which animals meet the problems with which life surrounds them." Mead and Dewey saw linguistically mediated human capacity for complex cooperation to be a potentially ascendant force in human evolution that could moderate the struggle for existence. See Mead (1964a [1927]); Dewey (1983a [1904]; 1983b [1909]; 1985 [1916]). Dewey's focus on the interaction between "organism-environment" and associated transformations of this mediate relationship share similarities with the work of dialectical biologists Richard Levins and Richard Lewontin (1985) and with Stephen Jay Gould (2002).

8. Dewey and Mead did not treat meaning as an inner process of mind, but as an interchange between embodied actors and between them and physical objects (Mead, 1962 [1934]: 75–82; Dewey, 2012 [1941–1942]: 184–202).

13 Embodiment

Chris Shilling

Introduction

There has since the early 1980s been an increasing focus on "the body" and embodiment within social theory; a focus that sought to recover from philosophy and classical sociology a subject that had become marginalized within academic thought. Concerned to explicate the collective and individual significance of our incarnate existence, early contributions to this theoretical turn explored how societies managed populations through the structural objectification of the body as *Körper* (the fleshy physical shell) (Turner, 1984). Complementing this approach, other analyses moved away from conceptions of the socially determined body by emphasizing the experiencing, acting and interacting *Leib* (the lived body), and by exploring the relationship between these action-oriented/phenomenal and structural dimensions of embodiment (Frankenberg, 1990; Freund, 1982; O'Neill, 1985; Ots, 1990).

These contrasting approaches advocated distinctive routes to recovering the body, but each engaged in a sustained interrogation of the core and residual categories associated with people's physical being within existing theoretical traditions. From these critiques, moreover, emerged novel analytical frameworks that identified embodiment as foundational to the development of "the social" as an emergent sphere of human existence (e.g. Frank, 1991; Shilling, 1993; Turner, 2006). Moving beyond exploring the body as *Körper* or *Leib*, such writings sought to reconstruct social theory by revisiting and developing past resources.

This identification of embodiment as foundational for social theory developed at a time when grand narratives had become anathema for sociological and cultural thought. Yet its proponents were not advocating an "enfleshed" return to the Archimedean conceit that it was possible to construct a "perspectiveless perspective" on the world, but newly grounded approaches toward long-standing theoretical problems. These included analyzing the history of social relationships through an appreciation of the environmentally emplaced evolution of human attributes (Hirst and Wooley, 1981), inquiring into epistemology by starting from the cultural mediation of the human senses (Stoller, 1989), and reconstructing social ontology by identifying the corporeal foundations of gendered identities (Grosz, 1994).

The significance of these concerns was paralleled within mainstream social theory. The body became opened for investigation within theories of status inequalities (Bourdieu, 1979), the political origins and development of "bare life" (Agamben,

1988), pragmatist reconceptualization of creative action (Joas, 1997), and the generation of emergent phenomena in realist accounts of society (Archer, 2000). Elsewhere, the absorption of human physicality within the expert systems of science, medicine, and technology was seen as an exemplar of nature's abolition within the self-referential parameters of late modern globalization (Giddens, 1991), while the body was also recognized as a battleground for regimes competing to impose religious and secular prescriptions upon this-worldly experiences and actions through the promotion of particular forms of habitus (Mahmood, 2005; Mellor and Shilling, 1997).

Taken together, these theoretical developments exerted a remarkable effect across the social sciences and humanities, displacing the sense that the bodily foundations of human being were biologically determined and irrelevant to the working of societies and cultures. It is no exaggeration, indeed, to suggest that the "rise of the body" – along with associated concerns with the senses and affect – has been one of the most significant developments to occur in sociology and related fields during the last thirty years. During this time a distinctive theoretical terrain has been carved out that includes histories of the body (e.g. Feher, Naddaff, and Tazi, 1989; Sawday, 1995); urban studies of the body (e.g. Sennett, 1994); feminist theories of the body (e.g. Butler, 1990, 1993; Connell, 1987; Diprose, 1994; Frost, 2001; Grosz, 1994; Kirby, 1997); excavations of religious bodies (e.g. Coakley, 2010; Mahmood, 2005), working bodies (e.g. Wolkowitz, 2006), and sporting bodies (e.g. Maguire, Mansfield, and Pike, 2016; Thorpe, 2011); analyses of health, disability, and embodiment (e.g. Frank, 1995; Freund, 2011; Turner, 1987, 1992; Williams, 2003); studies of embodied emotions and affect (Blackman, 2012; Howes and Classen, 2013); diverse readers, reviews, and collections of essays on the subject (e.g. Featherstone, Hepworth, and Turner, 1991; Frank, 1990; Fraser and Greco, 2004; Malacrida and Low, 2008; Scott and Morgan, 1993); a growing number of texts (e.g. Cregan, 2006; Howson, 2012); special editions of such journals including *Sociology of Health and Illness*, and *Societies*; and the launch in 1995 of the international refereed journal *Body & Society*. The fact that this sample only scratches the surface of the proliferation and reach of body studies illustrates the significance of this field.

Exploring the background to this change, and the theoretical advances it facilitated, this chapter examines the historical context for this renewed attention to embodiment, before identifying the contrasting analytical tendencies regarding what the body is and how it should be analyzed that continue to make it such a contested area. The meaning of the body metamorphoses as we move between perspectives, and while this can be viewed as a productive response to Fields' (1995: lvi) call to *go beyond* the body if we are to recognize its social significance, I argue that recent perspectives risk losing sight of the enfleshed actor within their depictions of society and social relationships. Against this background, I conclude by suggesting that revisiting creatively the notion of the body schema can provide us with an essential counterweight to the strong constructionist and materialist orientations of recent writings; a counterweight that allows us to pursue different theoretical options while preventing the facticity of embodied subjects to disappear from view.

The Intellectualist Fallacy in Western Thought

The rise of the body in social theory constituted a reaction against those Western linguistic and philosophical traditions that identified consciousness as the defining characteristic of the human species. In Ancient Greece, for example, "soma" referred to the corpse before signifying "the body." Analytically, Socrates's perishable flesh/immortal soul distinction influenced subsequent oppositions drawn between the "irrational passions" and "rational thought." Even Aristotle's conception of the *hexus*, which continues to shape notions of the habitus, accorded priority to the mind (Mellor and Shilling, 2014a). Reflecting the priorities of Greek philosophy and ethics, these concepts were associated with a more general view that the proper cultivation of the soul was the responsibility of a "healthy thinking" that enabled citizens to rise above the suffering body (Snell, 1960 [1948]).

Mind/body hierarchies continued to flourish in the Judeo-Christian tradition: Augustine's *Confessions* conceptualized physical habits as bondage, while Aquinas held that *deliberative choices* for the good should overcome "unthinking habits" (Davies, 2011). Later, philosophers reinforced this theological devaluation of habit by embracing a dualism that distrusted physical experience. Most influentially, Descartes' "Cogito ergo sum" ("I think therefore I am") suggested that "my mind . . . is entirely and truly distinct from my body and may exist without it" and that "I am . . . only a thing that thinks" (Descartes, 1974 [1634]: 105, 156). Focused on explicating the grounds of ethical action, Kant (1964 [1785]) echoed such sentiments by identifying a rational foundation for universal laws elevating duty above desire, and rejecting the possibility that criterion for the good emerged from humans' natural properties.

These traditions established clear oppositions between cognitive thought and the material body, while also projecting a hierarchy of values onto people's sensory capabilities. In Greek philosophy, the eye was the mind's gateway to knowledge, with the "distant" sense of seeing endorsed as a privileged route to aesthetic appreciation. Descartes ultimately accepted sight as a vehicle of knowledge, yet continued to distrust the other senses, while Kant (1978 [1798]) also identified sight as the noblest and most objective sense.

This philosophical and theological background structured the development of social theory. Weber (1968) identified truly human action as based on rational calculation – with emotionally driven or habitual behavior unworthy of that status – while also attributing to ideas a major historical role (Weber, 1991 [1904–1905]). Durkheim (1938) conceptualized sociology as the study of social/moral "facts" existing "beyond" and "out of reach" of those embodied subjects affected by them. Both distanced social theory from the evolutionary basis of Herbert Spencer's thought. Later, that great synthesizer of sociological theory Talcott Parsons (1937) reinforced these tendencies toward downgrading the body and emotions by interpreting the normative dimensions of Durkheim's and Weber's writings in terms of information-rich values rather than energy-high collective effervescences or charismatic forces, and by neglecting the pragmatists for whom embodiment and environment were central.

As John O'Neill (1985: 18) notes, social theory eventually rejected the "over-socialized" conception of the actor associated with Parsons' commitment to "the study of the rules and normative behavior that proceed from people's beliefs" rather than bodies, but this did not initially prompt a nuanced concern with embodiment. Rational choice theory made residual the "bodily passions" on which its commitment to calculated action depended, while ignoring human frailty and interdependence (Joas, 1997). Symbolic interactionism also marginalized the body, despite claiming roots in pragmatism. Herbert Blumer (1969) exemplified this by reifying the social and material environment transactions in which humans engage into an all-pervasive concern with symbolism, ignoring the interest of Mead and other pragmatists in "forging a socialized conception of nature and human biology for social theory" (Rochberg-Halton, 1987: 195).

Theoretical accounts of specific social sectors also sequestrated the body, none more influentially during the latter decades of the twentieth century than the secularization thesis. Peter Berger (1967), then one of its foremost proponents, exemplifies the cognitive bias of secularizing narratives in suggesting that religious *belief* systems are undermined by science and relativized by sectarianism. Yet his emphasis on "propositional certainties" (Norris and Inglehart, 2004) – echoed in Bruce's (2010: 135) insistence that religious belief is the "bottom line" in secularization debates – ignores how religion becomes embodied through ritualized "pedagogics" centered upon emotion, smell, touch, possession, and material culture (Mellor and Shilling, 2014b).

Excavating the Body from Social Thought

This devaluation of corporeality was not universal. It was rejected firmly by the major Eastern traditions, with Taoist classics such as the *Tao Te Ching* eschewing dualisms, viewing the body as a vehicle of knowledge, and conceptualizing the distinctions evident in human existence through the intertwined cosmic forces of yin and yang. Within the West there also existed a "secret history" of body-relevant writings (Turner, 1991), including Spinoza's monism (based on the notion of an absolute and infinite substance in which thought, feeling, and doing exist within a broader unity of becoming), and Marx's early writings (in which humans developed their physical and cognitive capacities by transforming their environment). In addition, Nietzsche's (1993 [1871]) contrast between Apollonian rationality and Dionysian sensuality assisted explorations of the internally fractured dimensions of human being, as well as struggles between individuals and society.

This marginalized history was not exclusively philosophical, moreover, and three seams of body-relevant writings within the "underbelly" of classical sociological and social theory have proven especially influential in steering body studies. These involve conceptualizations of *historical change* (whereby contrasting modes of embodiment provide a foundation for the emergence of social formations), embodied consciousness (in which the capacity for thought is emplaced within the intentional physical subject and wider environment), and gendered identities (wherein inequalities and prejudices shape the bodily capacities of women and men).

The Embodied Foundations of Historical Change

In opposing idealist conceptions of history, it was Marx who constructed a full-blown materialism based on the recognition that humans remade themselves and their environment through the social relationships entered into, and the tools utilized, in securing the means of subsistence (Marx, 1970: 121; Marx and Engels, 1970: 47). Coupled with his conceptualization of humans as an embodied species-being whose self- and worldly transformations were steered by physical and emotional as well as cognitive responses to oppression, Marx informed later sociological suggestions that contrasting *forms of embodiment* provided a foundation for successive modes of production (Mellor and Shilling, 1997).

This association of embodiment with historical development was complemented by parallels drawn between society and the human organism within the French tradition of social thought. Comte (1853: 150) linked morally harmonious societies with actions informed by mind *and* heart, while Tönnies developed these themes into a theory of social transformation by understanding the shift from medieval to modern societies as the outcome of embodied wills (Levine, 1995). While *Gemeinschaft* was sustained by expressions of instinct, habit, and spontaneity that remained immersed in their social and natural surroundings (*Wesenwille*), *Gesellschaft* was dependent upon a deliberative, calculating, and rational will distanced from and individualized within its surroundings (*Kurwille*). Relatedly, despite his methodological holism distancing theory from biology and psychology through its focus on social facts, Durkheim explored the embodied *internalization* of society. His last major study argued that while bodies generated egoistic appetites, the effervescence circulating in social assemblies demonstrated they were also the source of culturally productive affects and values: the body "conceals in its depth a sacred principle that erupts onto the surface" via markings/adornments that affirm membership of a moral whole (Durkheim, 1995 [1912]: 138, 233).

Emanating from the methodologically individualist German tradition, Weber and Simmel also recruited embodiment to their analyses of social change. Despite focusing on ideas, Weber (1991 [1904–1905]) traced the emergence of an early modern Protestant habitus suited to the rigors of rational action, while also identifying physical and emotional eroticism as shelters from instrumentalism. For Simmel (1971b [1918]), the significance of bodily drives and human vitalism to the creation and transcendence of social and cultural forms ensured that individuals could never be subsumed entirely within society: there is always *more-life* (*mehr-leben*) than the interactions in which an individual is engaged, with people invariably reserving part of themselves from specific exchanges (Simmel, 1971a [1908]).

Seeking to remove sociological thinking from its philosophically categorical moorings, Norbert Elias rejected conceptually "reifying" divisions between "modern" and "pre-modern" societies and bodies, but remained sensitive to the importance of interdependent embodied beings for historical change. His magisterial account of the civilizing process traces how the minutiae of people's behavior and appearances were connected to societally transformational developments in the pursuit of distinction, the division of labor, and governmental monopolies of violence (Elias, 2000 [1939]). Conflicts that used to occur between people developed into intrapersonal struggles, actions motivated by reflexive deliberation and mutual identification rather than impulse became a prerequisite for success, and the body emerged as a sophisticated vehicle for display.

These varied contributions toward embodying historical change informed and have been supplemented by recent additions to this area. These range from Maffesoli's (1996) and Mestrovic's (1994) opposed diagnoses of the character of (post-)modern social groups, to Mellor and Shilling's (1997; 2014b) and Mahmood's (2005) analyses of forms and reformations of embodiment, to Eliasian accounts of the webs of intercorporeal interdependence that drive social developments (Gabriel and Mennell, 2011; Wouters, 2007). Despite variations in the precise meaning of the body, these approaches imparted a facticity to the ontology and meaning of their subject as a consequence of their concern to explore the relationship between the enfleshed subject and society. Each of them invested embodied subjects with a weight that necessitated analyzing them as causally significant.

Embodying Thought

Social change was not the only area in which classical social theory's "underbelly" informed contemporary investigations of embodiment. While dominant philosophical traditions in the West divided mind from body, elevating thought over sensing and feeling, particular writers explored the *embodiment* of consciousness. From a phenomenological perspective, Merleau-Ponty (1962) viewed the body as our "vehicle" of being in the world, examining how our senses interweave themselves into their surroundings when building a multilayered picture of the environment with which we communicate. Cognition/thought/reflexivity is here a bodily activity undertaken by individuals *always already* environmentally emplaced. Elias (1991) also challenged conventional philosophy in identifying the human capacity to reflect, write, and read with symbols as an evolutionary "lift-off" related to the physical and material grounding of our cognitive capacities. It is pragmatist theory, however, that has perhaps exerted most influence in analyses of embodied consciousness. Dewey, Mead, Peirce, and James identified symbolic thought as part of embodied subjects' interconnections with and intentional relations toward their surroundings. In so doing, they suggested that action passes through cycles of habit, crisis, and creativity as individuals experience equilibrium or disturbance within their environment (e.g. Dewey, 2002 [1922]: 194; Mead, 1962 [1934]: 204; Peirce, 1997 [1903]).

Dewey grounded thinking in our embodiment and wider environment, but attributed it with properties "abstracted" from situational immediacy. These enable individuals to contemplate problems by manipulating symbols that represent the environment virtually (Dewey, 2011: 11), yet these symbols continue to resonate with the contexts to which they relate. There are several reasons for this. First, linguistic symbols carry affective weight because their referents can be (imagined as) *encountered*; encounters that are subject to the process of inquiry central to what Peirce (1998) identifies as the sign, object, and interpretant elements involved in signification. Second, thought resonates with those *social relationships* that inform the learning of symbols. This point is central to Mead's (1962 [1934]) account of the reflexive mediation of the I/Me relationship, while intercorporeal communication requires social transaction between at least two communicants capable of taking the attitude of the other toward a third thing (Garrison, 2015). Finally, cognitive thinking is also linked to our bodily location within a wider environment as a consequence of the conditions through which it is stimulated. It is the interruption of habit that provokes thought, circumstances related ultimately to adaptive connections with the environment (Dewey, 1981 [1925]: 212; 2011: 11). Thus, while thought possesses symbolic properties, it occurs within embodied subjects whose abstraction from the contexts in and about which they deliberate is never total.

The mention of an adaptive connection linking cognition to environmentally located embodied subjects suggests that thought is linked to bodily experiences of equilibrium or consternation (Dewey, 1980 [1934]: 35–37). While educated thought is key to conscious knowledge, indeed, the quality of thinking itself relies on the experiential bodily basis it rests upon. In this context, pragmatism emphasizes that people learn not only from symbolic thought but also *directly* from sensory physical activity: the most basic features of embodiment enable people to acquire information about their environment that is irreducible to cognitive symbols and exists outside their bodily topography (Dewey, 1980 [1934]: 13).

This pragmatist reconceptualization of the conventional Western philosophical approach toward (embodied) consciousness exerted most influence on body-relevant writings by shaping the theoretical underpinnings on which the Chicago School of sociology flourished. Pragmatism provided guidance for ethnographically enriched investigations into the symbolism, meanings, and actions of a wide range of groups within the modern metropolis. It not only informed classical studies in the embodiment of culture – ranging from Anderson's (1961 [1923]) *The Hobo* to Wacquant's (2004) *Body and Soul* – but also inspired a vibrant collection of writings on the "body pedagogics" of contrasting social groups (e.g. Grasseni, 2007; Lande, 2007; O'Connor, 2007). Once again, while there exists variation in defining the body subject within these writings, they share a commitment to the idea of causally significant enfleshed individuals able to construct contrasting "ways of life" as a consequence of their emplacement within and intentional orientation toward the wider environment.

Identity and Inequality

A third significant seam of body-relevant theory within social thought involves a long tradition of marginalized women writers sensitive to the embodied dimensions of gender identities and gender stratification (e.g. Astell, 1730; Macauley, 1974 [1790]; Wollstonecraft, 1989 [1787–1797]; see McDonald, 1997: 113). Wollstonecraft (1989 [1787–1797]) criticized the presentation of women as sexualized creatures destined to gratify men, for example, while Germaine de Stael (1798) provided another important early contribution by interrogating Adam Smith's concept of sympathy in order to explore the embodied bonds between mother and children as pre-contractual foundations for human societies.

These and later interventions were not only contributions to social thought, but also constituted critical commentaries on international events: dominant approaches toward sex, gender, and sexuality served historically to *naturalize* social inequalities within imperialist and colonized nations and justify the persecution of those failing to fit physically with the binary divisions at their center. In contrast to the malleable "one sex/one flesh" model of the sexes dominant in earlier eras (Laqueur, 1990), the eighteenth century onward witnessed the aggressive promotion of "heteronormative orders" that treated males and females as biological and cultural opposites, and presented the imposition of partial norms as natural imperatives.

Examining the enforcement of these values, Michel Foucault (1981: 19) highlights how sex was subject to increasingly rigid surveillance involving the church; a surveillance that made it more visible and amenable to state control. Especially significant here was the use of population management as a technology of political power. With the emergence of modernity, governments strengthened the norms associated with sexual identity in order to identify, define, and engineer "the birthrate, the age of marriage, legitimate and illegitimate births" (Foucault, 1981: 25–26). Medical authorities also contributed to this process; equating sexuality during the nineteenth century with "healthy" and "pathological" personalities in a process that validated the nuclear family (Foucault, 1981: 44).

These regulatory regimes persisted well into the twentieth century, yet they were contested. Building on Margaret Mead's (1935) anthropological account of the cross-culturally varied organization of biological maleness/femaleness, feminist theory highlighted the importance of social practices for the classification of intercorporeal relationships. Simone de Beauvoir (1949) emphasized the salience of *socialization* for the bodily dispositions and social roles that sentenced women to be "the second sex," vulnerable to objectification and domination. Her work was complemented later by a focus on the physical work required for heteronormativity to be received as an automatic outgrowth of biology. Newton (1972), for example, argued that sex role behavior was engineered to *appear* natural and reflective of a singular identity (rather than one of many that individuals may choose to express depending on situationally specific factors). Young (1998) explored the naturalized phenomenal experience of such physical roles, while other feminists sought to explain how "compulsory heterosexuality" became embodied through processes of institutionalization (McIntosh, 1968; Rich, 1980; West and Zimmerman, 1987).

Seeking an overarching explanation for these circumstances, Judith Butler (1990: 151) viewed culture as operating through a "heterosexual matrix" that "hails" individuals to assume restricted subject positions and engage in specific types of performativity. It is not just cultural notions of gender that are supported and reproduced by such performances, according to her, but also the very idea there even exist such things as "men's" and "women's" bodies (Butler, 1989; 1993). When repeated sufficiently, these performances manage the physical material they draw on in a manner that suggests there is something essential and unalterable about female and male bodies (Butler, 1990: 22).

Feminist contributions employed different conceptions of the body in their analyses, especially in terms of the ontological weight attributed to the idea of the biologically sexed body (an issue associated with social constructionism, to which we return in the next section). Nonetheless, the embodied subject is, for these writers, kept in view as a result of their broader commitment to engaging critically with how body matters are used to differentiate and maintain structural differences between groups of individuals.

Social/Constructionism

These strands of social theory proved important resources for the theoretically driven rise of body studies, providing a stabilizing set of issues and approaches based around the significance of embodied subjects. Yet body theorists were engaged in a difficult balancing act – exploring how society shaped embodiment without losing their grasp on the material facticity and causal significance of their subject – that was exemplified further by the rising dominance of perspectives informed by strong social constructionism. While all social theories of the body are to some extent constructionist – recognizing the significance of social relations and cultural processes for people's bodily capabilities – strong variants attribute these with overwhelming ontological and epistemological significance. This is exemplified by the writings of Foucault, the individual who exerted the single greatest influence on this approach.

Foucault (1981: 152) described his writings as a "'history of bodies' and the manner in which what is most material and vital in them has been invested." Of particular significance to this history was the shift that occurred during the late early modern period from "heavy" means of discipline to the proliferation of bio-powers operating "through progressively finer channels," gaining access to people's "gestures" and "daily actions" (Foucault, 1975; 1980: 58, 151–152; 2009: 1). Replacing the earlier focus on death with a commitment to the positive management of *life*, this heralded a new "art of government" wherein disciplining the "soul" became more important than punishing the flesh. Evident across hospitals, asylums, prisons, and schools, its recent culmination is exemplified by a consumer culture that eschews "control by repression" in favor of control by stimulation (Foucault, 1981: 140).

Foucault's writings proved enormously influential in steering body theory's concerns with governmentality, medicine, gender, bio-citizenship, education, and a host of other issues (e.g. Armstrong, 1987; Heyes, 2007; Rose, 2007a, b; Sawicki, 1991), but their strong constructionism is characterized by a tension. Taking the body seriously requires identifying what about it is *consequential for* society. Yet while Foucault has a great substantive concern with the subject, his ontological and epistemological view of the body as a discursive product leads him to view it as *always already* amenable to construction by *other* factors. This threatens to rob us of the capacity to recognize that different elements of embodiment (such as death or the morphology of the body) may be variably open to social forces at any point in time. As Dews (1987: 163) points out, failing to include in his writings an account that "makes the corporeal more than a tabula rasa," makes it impossible to reckon the costs imposed by "an infinitesimal power" over the body. In short, Foucault's approach risks vanquishing the body – materially and phenomenologically – behind the impenetrable grids of meaning imposed by discourse (Turner, 1984: 245).

The tension in Foucault's approach has not prevented his substantive analyses being utilized to good effect by those concerned to highlight the significance of the embodied subject. Nevertheless, instead of addressing the tension created by Foucault's strong constructionism, a plethora of analysts who appropriated the body for their own theoretical agendas exacerbated this problem by conceptualizing it as a *product* of those social processes and subjects with which they were concerned. Thus, theorists of discipline (Sawicki, 1991; Turner, 1991), consumer culture (Falk, 1994), aging (Featherstone and Hepworth, 1991), and biopolitics and social policy (Hewitt, 1991), for example, served to multiply the distinctive ways in which the body was viewed as constructed. In so doing, they made even more elusive any sense that the body possessed a distinctive ontological grounding that was itself consequential for society.

Strong social constructionism did not eradicate other approaches to embodiment – including those explored in the previous section – but became enormously influential in directing body writings in the late twentieth century. Yet body theory has since moved on from its at times overwhelming commitment to specifically social variants of constructionism. In particular, alternative approaches associated with what has been referred to as the "new materialism" have highlighted the embodied significance of affect, the assemblage of networks, and vitalism (Coole and Frost, 2010). While these refocus attention on the analytical weight that should be attributed to specific elements of embodied existence, however, they also exhibit centrifugal tendencies that return us to questions about the body subject's meaning and causal significance.

Affectual Bodies

Emerging from influential trends within cultural theory, the turn to affect redirected social thought's concern with embodiment by focusing on what affectual intensities, currents, and flows *make* bodies do (Anderson, 2010; Clough, 2010: 210; Connolly, 2002, 2011; Massumi, 2002). This concern with our embodied capacities "to affect and be affected" can be traced to Sedgwick and Frank's (1995) engagement with emotions as "pre-subjective" hardwired neurological reactions that prompt organismic responses (Leys, 2011: 437), and Blackman (2012: x) has gone so far as to identify it as the "guiding principle" now informing social theories of the body.

Displacing the dominance Foucault attributes to discourse, affect theory traces the body's social salience to its evolutionary heritage. The significance of social relationships, cultural norms, and political campaigns do not from this perspective rest on the ideological effects of discourse, the persuasiveness of arguments, or on individual reflexivity: embodied consciousness arrives too late to influence body-subjects.

Instead, they depend upon the power of elites to manipulate messages and threats that operate "autonomically, bypassing reason and criticality and seizing the body at the level of neural circuits, the nervous system, [and] the endocrine system" (Blackman, 2012: xi). For Massumi (2010: 54), the result of these processes in the American political "war on terror," for example, is such that the "felt reality of threat legitimates pre-emptive action." Just as a fire alarm stirs in us anxiety and a readiness to escape the threat signified, so does the political transmission of warning move us to want preventative action (Massumi, 2010: 64). This is a prime illustration of "how an abstract force can be materially determining" (ibid.).

Contrasting instances of affect's power to prompt incarnate actions exist in discussions of consumer culture. Featherstone (2010: 198) suggests that body images in advertising constitute a material "prosthetic for imaginative work," stimulating in consumers affectually charged "invocations of becoming." Relatedly, Thrift suggests that economies "scoop up affects" and "amplify them in order to produce value" by provoking consumer "fascination" (Thrift, 2010: 290). Commercially profitable forms of allure and glamor are produced here through affectual intensities operating beneath critical consciousness to produce "captivation" (Thrift, 2010: 297).

The turn to affect promotes an account of the body that invests neurologically stimulated basic emotions with an inherent dynamism productive of automatic behavior. Affects here are not personal feelings, but evolutionarily given preconscious responses relevant to the embodied constitution of humans (Leys, 2011: 443). Corporeality remains important, but only in terms of the capacity of authorities to manipulate "subliminal affective intensities" that condition our thoughts and beliefs (Leys, 2011: 436). While affect theory's focus has undoubtedly tempered body theory's emphasis on strong *social* constructionism, however, attributing such causal importance to this dimension of evolution renders embodied subjects captive to forces beyond their intentional control. Yet the powerful remain an exception as a social group possessed of an unexplained ability to "stand back" from affectual intensities in order to mold and direct them toward others; an explanatory gap that leaves affect theory vulnerable to accusations that it lacks a sufficiently sociological account of how emotional flows develop and circulate.

Despite its undoubted popularity, affect theory is not only problematic theoretically, but is also questionable empirically. While those interested in circuits of affect insist reflection arrives too late to influence decision-making, this assumption relies on contentious experimental findings that focus on how brain stimuli can precede conscious intent in specific actions yet fail to take into account the existing intentionality of the embodied subject (Leys, 2011: 455). Isolating the brain from its embodied location and treating it as a director of action outside of those intercorporeal contexts in which thought operates, the conclusions of affect theory also travel way beyond those many neuroscientists are prepared to make about their work (Rose and Abi-Rached, 2013). In short, decentering the embodied and environmentally emplaced subject in favor of affectual intensities replaces the embodied whole with a neurological part of limited analytical value. Seeking to manage the balancing act between taking the body seriously and reaching beyond embodiment to its social and material embeddedness, theories of affect raise the specter of an evolutionary determinism associated previously with politically conservative variants of sociobiology.

Networked Bodies

Emerging during the 1980s from its parent field of science and technological studies, and gaining increasing influence in body theories from the turn of the century, actor network theory (ANT) addressed the overemphasis on *social* constructivism by attending to the *materially assembled* character of embodiment. Specifically, ANT approaches body-subjects as patterned *networks* of *connections* effected between objects and material technologies as well as ideas (Law and Hassard, 1999). To talk about "the body" in isolation is, from this perspective, to miss the work and contingencies involved in making and "holding together" the heterogeneous network of what it is to be embodied; a network open to change that can be "enacted" in various ways (Latimer and Schillmeier, 2009; Mol and Law, 2004: 55). The body is here always multiple, always already connected to and mediated by networks of other objects, ideas, materials, people, and technologies (Latour, 2002: 23; Mol, 2003: viii, 42–43).

ANT has facilitated increasing research into how the body is constituted by its implication within multiple material interdependencies. Michael and Rosengarten's (2012) collection on experimentation, politics, and emergent bodies, for example, argues that bodily capacities, frailties, and diseases are not "givens" but are enacted through the technological and other networks in which they emerge. It is Mol's (2003) theorization of the diagnosis and treatment of atherosclerosis, however, that remains the key exemplar of this approach. How we come to know about disease and illness in medical contexts reveals there are different ways of "choreographing" ontological matter, and that our bodies, identities, and diseases are "more than one" (Cussins, 1996; Mol, 2003: viii. 42–43).

In terms of its capacity to illuminate the causal significance of embodiment, ANT has avoided discursive or affectual reductionism, drawing our attention to the network of interconnections, possessed of their own "modes of existence," that constitute the body (Latour, 2011: 312). Its determination not to overemphasize the significance of social relationships, outside of their emplacement alongside all manner of material interdependencies, firmly contextualizes embodied subjects within their environments. There remain questions, however, about ANT's capacity to provide the embodied subject with either an ontological identity or causal weight sufficient to provide it with enduring theoretical significance.

ANT treats each aspect of a network as an actor or *actant,* highlighting the forms of agency materials as well as people can be said to exercise, but does little to differentiate the ontological qualities of these phenomena. Yet objects do not possess the conscious intentions, habits, internal conversations, desires, or instincts of humans, phenomena key to sociological conceptions of agency (Archer, 2000). This failure of ANT to take seriously the specific properties of embodied subjects is also evident in its tendency to collapse issues of ontology and epistemology.

Michael and Rosengarten (2013: 3) assert that "what the body 'is' and how it emerges depends on the relations of which it is a part and through which it is enacted," but bodies possess properties that themselves *shape* and have to be *included in* or *taken account by* social relations and institutions. Bodies change over time, and there are many epistemological ways of viewing the body, but while the body opens up onto its surroundings in all manner of ways, the embodied subject still confronts the issue that it is their one body that is frail, gets sick and, eventually dies. Without this recognition, there remains the suspicion that ANT fails to attribute the body with sufficient significance for it to warrant a central place in social theory.

Vitalistic Bodies

Vitalistic theories developed from the eighteenth- and nineteenth-century quest within science and philosophy for the *élan vital*, yet have exerted a growing influence on recent body writings. Despite their diversity, vitalistic approaches unite in standing against models of organic closure and equilibrium. For Deleuze (1969), living systems are always reaching beyond themselves: they incarnate pure predicates or potentials that, if carried to their limit, would destroy bounded organisms. The body from this perspective is always becoming something other than itself, possessing a virtual existence, a *body without organs* (BwO) (Deleuze and Guattari, 1972, 1980).

The BwO is not literally deprived of organs, but is removed analytically from any sense that its actions and reactions are formed by patriarchy, the state, social class, or other societal forces in a manner that imposes regularities on or closure to its capacities or development. Instead, the body is "a formation of a relation among potentials," involving a contingent "territorialisation or linking up of organs," with the eye, brain, ear, hand, and so on, and transformed through these connections as it responds to life's vitalism within and outside its permeable borders (Colebrook, 2010). Grosz (1994: 161–162), for example, uses these vitalistic themes to reconceive embodied ontology away from reified conceptions of male and female, toward a concern with "flows," "planes," "intensities," and "becomings." Underpinning these characteristics is a corporeal desire, conceived of as inherent within life, opposed to social constraints (Deleuze and Guattari, 1972). This enables Grosz (1994: 181) to depict female bodies as excessive in relation to patriarchal control – "sites of multiple struggles" from which emerge "unexpected and unpredictable events" – and has allowed those using the vitalistic themes of her work to explore previously fixed notions of difference as phenomena *produced through* and *contingent on* the context in which they emerge (Colls, 2012).

In its concern with the dynamism of life *beyond* the membrane of the organism, vitalism also moves away from the human, throwing into doubt any concern with a social theory that places the embodied subject at its center. Instead, there is more concern with the *deterritorialization* of the organism through imaginings and creations that facilitate extensions of action and movement beyond the present, and beyond embodied life. This deterritorializing vitalism capitalizes on the insight that the body's experience of self must pass through some form of exterior, whether that is the language through which I hear myself speak or an image and expression mediated through new technology and digital media (Colebrook, 2010; Hansen, 2006; Hayles, 2005; Munster, 2006; Wegenstein, 2006).

In discussing the approach to embodiment adopted by such vitalistic writings, Colebrook (2010) emphasizes that those who focus on the dynamism *of* life *beyond* the organism are identifying real conditions associated with what it is to be embodied. As she argues, the living body cannot be self-enclosed but must be open to the needs of life if it is to survive. The logic of evolutionary adaptation, indeed, is such that bodies must constantly be ready to become more than they are if they are to survive and prosper. Yet Colebrook also acknowledges that if the living being is *too* open, failing to attend to the dynamic equilibrium that characterizes its present existence, it is unable to develop, to possess a discernible identity, or even to survive.

In prioritizing the ongoing process of organic change and transformation over a focus on the fixities that can result from socially constructionist approaches, vitalistic approaches continue to confront a problem stemming from the balancing act all body theories must grapple with. As Colebrook (2010) herself suggests, the problem here is that vitalistic theory runs the risk of failing to recognize meaningful continuities within changing forms of embodiment. Turner's (2006) analysis of human rights demonstrates some of the problems with this: regarding the body as fated to constantly become something other than it is makes it difficult to explore inequalities and oppression in relation to embodied subjects in the here and now.

Recentering the Embodied Subject

Having outlined the context from which emerged social theory's interest in the body, I have explored the centripetal and centrifugal tendencies in these writings. If contemporary theories have at times decentered and deterritorialized the incarnate subject, body matters nevertheless remain high profile within the current global era. In governance, for example, the events of 9/11 and the Bush government's subsequent declaration of a "War on Terror" led to a marked expansion in the extent to which the body has been treated as a password (Davis, 2007). The rendition practices to which bodily subjects identified through drone cameras, CCTV, passport control, retinal scanning, and other means as "dangerous" were sometimes subjected, moreover, illustrate the continuing relevance of "heavy" and "ponderous" methods of physical discipline and control.

The body has also been positioned center stage as a result of the molecular reification of racial categories that has occurred since the first draft of the Human Genome Project was completed at the start of the twenty-first century. As Troy Duster (2015) explains, while pharmaceutical, criminological, and other industries and governmental agencies involved in exploiting the findings of "the new genetics" have utilized the varied languages of personalized medicine, law, and individual ancestral genealogy to describe their activities, there has in practice been a wholesale reinscription of race onto the bodies of millions across the globe. This is despite the fact that DNA testing is an imperfect and partial means of tracing ancestral lineages, and is further undermined by a reliance on simplistic notions of "race" and the assumption that substantial populations once existed in states of complete "racial purity," unaffected by ancient migrations (Duster, 2015: 10–11). In the face of recent debates regarding the malleability of embodied identities, this research also locates race in identifiers that supposedly determine the emergent identities of individuals and rules out any possibility that people may enjoy a degree of choice over the groups to which they belong (Brubaker, 2016). The practical implications of this renewed racialization of the body, moreover, echo past forms of discrimination, given their implication in such areas as crime profiling, clinical trials, and research projects that presuppose genetic variations while ignoring cultural differences and social inequalities (Duster, 2015: 10–16).

Elsewhere, embodied subjects have been subjected to intensified commodification processes. David Harvey (2004) has suggested that we are living through a period of primitive accumulation, evidenced not only by the numbers of people still subjected to slavery, but also by the growth of "transplant trafficking" in which value is extracted through "a global billion-dollar criminal industry involved in the transfer of fresh kidneys (and half-livers) from living and dead providers to the seriously . . . ill and affluent or medically insured mobile transplant patients" (Scheper-Hughes, 2011: 58). Extracting bodily processes for value, the biotechnological exploitation of DNA has been associated with potential medical advances that have attracted billions of dollars of capital investment in an attempt to sell "surplus health" to the "worried well" and those seeking to "live life to the full." Involving actions undertaken voluntarily or involuntary, involving the individual as a whole or in part, bodies have never been so multiply entangled in circuits of financial value.

If body matters continue to drag social theory back to the incarnate, analyses still confront the dilemma of needing to travel beyond the confines of the body while ensuring they do not allow the organic dimensions of the embodied to fade from view. In this context, and in conclusion to this chapter, I want to offer a minimal but essential counterweight to help avoid this disappearance by revisiting the notion of the *body schema*. This concept does not make detailed prescriptions about the precise form body theory should take. Nevertheless, while insisting alongside much theory on the importance of social processes and material surroundings for bodily actions, identities, and structures, it also imparts to the intentionally oriented *embodied subject* sufficient ontological weight for it to remain in view.

Research into the body schema was associated initially with developments in neurophysiology at the beginning of the twentieth century (Head, 1920; Schilder, 1978 [1935]) and there have been debates about its theoretical utility. Nevertheless, those neurosociologists and neuroscientists sensitive to the social processes that shape the embodied workings of the brain have usefully restated the necessity for survival of the human capacity to sensorily and preconsciously map and coordinate the body's location within its wider environment (e.g. Damasio, 2010; Pitts-Taylor, 2012). In this context, the body schema can be defined as the embodied template that enables subjects to unify their "postural, tactile, kinaesthetic, and visual sensations so that these are experienced as the sensations of a subject coordinated into a single space" despite the individual not possessing an exhaustive view of themselves or their surroundings (Grosz, 1994: 83). Crucial to the lived experience we have of our bodily selves, and our capacity to coordinate our actions, construct a coherent sense of identity, and engage in as well as reflect on social action, the body schema emerges gradually from its initially fragmented state in infancy shaped as it is by *social relations* and *physical surroundings*, but also by the irreducible facticity of the *body* itself (Merleau-Ponty, 1962: 113, 117).

The significance of *social relations* to the stimulus of the body schema is apparent in the elementary structures of role taking (and the affects and expressions involved in this interaction) engaged in between early caregivers and prelinguistic infants (Joas, 1983, 1997; Schilder, 1978 [1935]). This learning to coordinate and present the body in order to stimulate desired responses continues into adulthood as we become accustomed to projecting ourselves forward, and being evaluated, on the basis of bodily norms and cultural "rules" (McDowell, 2009). The body schema develops not only through social stimuli, however, but also as a consequence of the feelings, perceptions, and movements fostered by our organic being as we "bump into" and problem-solve in the *physical world* (Archer, 2000; Merleau-Ponty, 1962). By engaging with the material environment, individuals learn how to utilize objects that enable them to expand the means with which they project themselves onto the world (Merleau-Ponty, 1962: 234). As Dewey (1980 [1934]: 13) notes, no creature lives within the confines of its skin and our limbs and senses are a "realms of connection" with "what lies beyond [our] bodily frame." With experience, individuals also come to realize how the physical environment changes them, facilitating practical techniques and certain habits, and provoking muscular growth, aches, and pains as the body adjusts to the challenges in its surroundings.

These processes constitutive of the body schema suggest that the biological body is responsive to the social, cultural, and material environment. From our built surroundings, to the latest advances in digital media, to the relationships characterized by various ratios of domination and subordination, to cultural meanings and symbols that assess physical appearance, people's sense of what their bodies are and can do is *irreducible* to the topography of the body itself (Sobchack, 2010). While the body schema may be stretched by social norms, values, and technologies, however, it remains "in conversation" with the bones, flesh, blood, and senses that facilitated its development, and an enfleshed subject that must negotiate the environment on which it depends. Body schemas thus develop on the basis of a *practical* intersubjectivity (Joas, 1997), the interactional effects of bodily selves *on each other* as they are engaged in the manipulation of *physical things* (Mead, 1932: 169). As Mead (1903; 1962 [1934]: 134) and Dewey (1896; 1980 [1934]: 13) note, our biological needs equip us with a "pre-reflective intentionality of the human body," directed initially toward survival, which means that we do not just react to stimuli or internalize permanently and without critical reflection cultural norms, but *engage with them* on the basis of our own desires, aims, and conscious thoughts.

In this context, it is possible for body schemas to be expansive in enabling individuals to reach beyond and extend the horizons of their physical being, recruiting the environment to their plans in a manner that enhances their capacity for exercising agency. Alternatively, when individuals are placed in subordinate positions, subject to oppression or pain, the schema can shrink back to the limits of the physical subject's immediate needs (Scarry, 1985). The capacity of body schemas to expand or contract depending upon the social and material environments in which they develop can, indeed, be seen as a *metric* of the degree of complementarity that exists between social and individual development.

This recognition of the body schema's importance does not attempt to prescribe in detail how theories of embodiment should develop in the future, but does provide one way of ensuring that whatever emphasis may be placed on change, mobility, transformation, connectedness, or other theoretical priorities, the incarnate nature of embodied subjects is held in view. There are many reasons why this recognition is important for social theory in general, but the significance of embodiment to the very existence of humans and to the relationships they forge within and with their wider environments should perhaps be sufficient for us to acknowledge the need for such a move.

References

Agamben, G. 1988. *Homo Sacer: Sovereign Power and Bare Life*. Stanford, CA: Stanford University Press.

Anderson, B. 2010. "Modulating the Excess of Affect: Morale in a State of 'Total War.'" In M. Gregg and J. Seigworth (eds.), *The Affect Theory Reader*. Durham, NC: Duke University Press.

Anderson, N. 1961 [1923]. *The Hobo: The Sociology of the Homeless Man*. Chicago, IL: University of Chicago Press.

Archer, M. 2000. *Being Human: The Problem of Agency*. Cambridge, UK: Cambridge University Press.

Armstrong, D. 1987. "Bodies of Knowledge: Foucault and the Problem of Human Anatomy." In G. Scambler (ed.), *Sociological Theory and Medical Sociology*. London: Tavistock.

Astell, M. 1730. *Some Reflections upon Marriage*. London: Parker.

Beauvoir, S. de. 1949. *The Second Sex*. London: Everyman.

Berger, P. 1967. *The Sacred Canopy*. New York: Free Press.

Blackman, L. 2012. *Immaterial Bodies*. London: Sage.

Blumer, H. 1969. *Symbolic Interactionism*. Berkeley, CA: University of California Press.

Bourdieu, P. 1979. *Distinction: A Social Critique of the Judgment of Taste*. London: Routledge.

Brubaker, R. 2016. "The Dolezal Affair: Race, Gender, and the Micropolitics of Identity." *Ethnic and Racial Studies* 39(3): 414–448.

Bruce, S. 2010. "Secularization." In B. S. Turner (ed.), *The New Blackwell Companion to the Sociology of Religion*. Oxford, UK: Blackwell.

Butler, J. 1990. *Gender Trouble*. London: Routledge.

1993. *Bodies that Matter. On the Discursive Limits of Sex*. London: Routledge.

Clough, P. 2010. "The Affective Turn: Political Economy, Biomedia and Bodies." In M. Gregg and J. Seigworth (eds.), *The Affect Theory Reader*. Durham, NC: Duke University Press.

Coakley, S. (ed.). 2010. *Religion and the Body*. Cambridge, UK: Cambridge University Press.

Colebrook, C. 2010. "Creative Evolution and the Creation of Man." *The Southern Journal of Philosophy* 48: 109–132.

Colls, R. 2012. "Feminism, Bodily Difference and Non-Representational Geographies." *Transactions of the Institute of British Geographers* 37: 430–445.

Comte, A. 1853. *The Positive Philosophy of Auguste Comte, 2 Vols.* Translated by H. Martineau. London: John Chapman.

Connell, R. W. 1987. *Gender and Power*. London: Routledge.

Connolly, W. 2002. *Neuropolitics: Thinking, Culture, Speed*. Minneapolis, MN: University of Minnesota Press.

    2011. "The Complexity of Intention." *Critical Inquiry* 37 (Summer 2011): 792–799.

Coole, D., and Frost, S. 2010. *New Materialisms: Ontology, Agency and Politics*. Durham, NC: Duke University Press.

Cregan, K. 2006. *The Sociology of the Body. Mapping the Abstraction of Embodiment.* London: Sage.

Cussins, C. 1996. "Ontological Choreography: Agency through Objectification in Fertility Clinics." *Social Studies of Science* 26(3): 575–610.

Damasio, A. 2010. *Self Comes to Mind: Constructing the Conscious Brain*. London: William Heinemann.

Davies, D. 2011. *Emotion, Identity and Religion: Hope, Reciprocity and Otherness*. Oxford, UK: Oxford University Press.

Davis, A. 2007. "Body as Password." *Wired*. January, 7. www.wired.com/1997/07/bio metrics-2/.

Deleuze, G. 1969. *The Logic of Sense*. New York: Columbia University Press.

Deleuze, G., and Guattari, F. 1972. *Capitalism and Schizophrenia, Vol. 1. Anti-Oedipus*. New York: Penguin.

    1980. *Capitalism and Schizophrenia, Vol. 2. A Thousand Plateaus*. Minneapolis, MN: University of Minnesota Press.

Descartes, R. 1974 [1634]. *Discourse on Method and the Mediations*. Trans F. E. Sutcliffe. Harmondsworth, UK: Penguin.

Dewey, J. 1896. "The Reflex Arc Concept in Psychology." *Psychological Review* 3: 357–370.

    1980 [1934]. *Art as Experience*. New York: Perigee.

    1981 [1925]. *Experience and Nature*. Carbondale, IL: Southern Illinois University Press.

    2002 [1922]. *Human Nature and Conduct*. New York: Dover.

    2011. *How We Think*. London: Martino.

Dews, P. 1987. *Logics of Disintegration*. London: Verso.

Diprose, R. 1994. *The Bodies of Women. Ethics, Embodiment and Sexual Difference*. London: Routledge.

Durkheim, E. 1938. *The Rules of Sociological Method*. London: Macmillan.

    1995 [1912]. *The Elementary Forms of the Religious Life*. New York: Free Press.

Duster, T. 2015. "A Post-Genomic Surprise: The Molecular Reinscription of Race in Science, Law and Medicine." *British Journal of Sociology* 66(1): 1–27.

Elias, N. 1991. *The Symbol Theory*. London: Sage.

    2000 [1939]. *The Civilizing Process*. Oxford, UK: Blackwell.

Falk, P. 1994. *The Consuming Body*. London: Sage.

Featherstone, M. 2010. "Body, Image and Affect in Consumer Culture." *Body & Society* 16 (1): 193–221.

Featherstone, M., and Hepworth, M. 1991. "Post-Bodies, Ageing and Virtual Reality." In M. Featherstone and A. Wernick (eds.), *Images of Ageing*. London: Routledge.

Featherstone, M., N. Hepworth, and B. S. Turner (eds.). 1991. *The Body: Social Process and Cultural Theory*. London: Sage.

Feher, M., R. Naddaff, and N. Tazi. 1989. *Fragments for a History of the Human Body, 3 Vols*. New York: Zone.

Fields, K. 1995. Translator's introduction, in E. Durkheim, *The Elementary Forms of the Religious Life*. New York: Free Press.

Foucault, M. 1975. *Discipline and Punish*. Harmondsworth, UK: Penguin.

1980. "Body/Power." In C. Gordon (ed.), *Michel Foucault. Power/Knowledge*. Brighton, UK: Harvester.

1981. *The History of Sexuality. Vol. 1: An Introduction*. Harmondsworth, UK: Penguin.

2009. *Security, Territory, Population: Lectures at the College de France, 1977–78*. London: Palgrave.

Frank, A. 1990. "Bringing Bodies Back In: A Decade Review." *Theory, Culture & Society* 7: 131–162.

1991. "For a Sociology of the Body: An Analytical Review." In M. Featherstone, M. Hepworth and B. S. Turner (eds.), *The Body: Social Process and Cultural Theory*. London: Sage.

1995. *The Wounded Storyteller: Body, Illness and Ethics*. Chicago, IL: University of Chicago Press.

Frankenberg, R. 1990. "Review Article: Disease, Literature and the Body in the Era of AIDS – A Preliminary Exploration." *Sociology of Health and Illness* 12: 351–360.

Fraser, M., and M. Greco (eds.). 2004. *The Body: A Reader*. London: Routledge.

Freund, P. 1982. *The Civilized Body: Social Domination, Control and Health*. Philadelphia, PA: Temple University Press.

2011. "Embodying Psychosocial Health Inequalities: Bringing Back Materiality and Bioagency." *Social Theory and Health* 9: 59–70.

Frost, L. 2001. *Young Women and the Body. A Feminist Sociology*. London: Palgrave.

Gabriel, N., and Mennell, S. (eds.). 2011. *Norbert Elias and Figurational Research*. Oxford, UK: Wiley-Blackwell/The Sociological Review Monograph Series.

Garrison J. 2015. "Dewey's Aesthetics of Body-Mind Functioning." In A. Scarinzi (ed.), *Aesthetics and the Embodied Mind: Beyond Art Theory and the Cartesian Mind-Body Dichotomy* (pp. 39–53). Dordrecht: Springer.

Giddens, A. 1991. *Modernity and Self Identity*. Oxford, UK: Polity.

Grasseni, C. (ed.). 2007. *Skilled Visions: Between Apprenticeship and Standards*. Oxford, UK: Berghahn.

Grosz, E. 1994. *Volatile Bodies*. London: Routledge.

Hansen, M. 2006. *Bodies in Code: Interfaces with New Media*. London: Routledge.

Harvey, D. 2004. "The 'New Imperialism': Accumulation by Dispossession." *Socialist Register* 40: 63–87.

Hayles, N. K. 2005. *My Mother Was a Computer: Digital Subjects and Literary Texts*. Chicago, IL: University of Chicago Press.

Head, H. 1920. *Studies in Neurology*. Oxford, UK: Oxford University Press.

Hewitt, Martin. 1991. "Bio-Politics and Social Policy: Foucault's Account of Welfare." In Mike Featherstone, Mike Hepworth, and Bryan S. Turner (eds.), *The Body: Social Process and Cultural Theory* (pp. 225–255). London: SAGE.

Heyes, C. 2007. *Self Transformations: Foucault, Ethics and Normalised Bodies*. Oxford, UK: Oxford University Press.

Hirst, P., and Wooley, P. 1981. *Social Relations and Human Attributes*. London: Routledge.

Howes, D., and Classen, C. 2013. *Ways of Sensing: Understanding the Senses in Society*. London: Routledge.

Howson, A. 2012. *The Body in Society. An Introduction*. Oxford, UK: Polity.

Joas, H. 1983. "The Intersubjective Constitution of the Body Image." *Human Studies* 6(2): 197–204.

1997. *The Creativity of Action*. Chicago, IL: University of Chicago Press.

Kant, I. 1964 [1785]. *Groundwork of the Metaphysics of Morals*. New York: Harper & Row.

1978 [1798]. *Anthropology from a Pragmatic Point of View*. Translated by V. Dowdell. Carbondale and Edwardsville, IL: Southern Illinois University Press.

Kirby, V. 1997. *Telling Flesh: The Substance of the Corporeal*. London: Routledge.

Lande, Brian. 2007. "Breathing Like a Soldier: Culture Incarnate." *The Sociological Review* 51(s1): 95–108.

Laqueur, T. 1990. *Making Sex*. Cambridge, MA: Harvard University Press.

Latimer, J., and Schillmeier, M. (eds.). 2009. *Un/knowing Bodies*. Oxford, UK: Wiley-Blackwell/The Sociological Review Monograph Series.

Latour, B. 2002. *Iconoclash. Beyond the Image Wars in Science, Religion and Art*. Cambridge, MA: MIT Press.

2011. *An Inquiry into Modes of Existence*. Cambridge, MA: Harvard University Press.

Law, J., and Hassard, J. 1999. *Actor Network Theory and After*. Oxford, UK: Blackwell/ The Sociological Review Monograph Series.

Levine, D. 1995. *Visions of the Sociological Tradition*. Chicago, IL: University of Chicago Press.

Leys, R. 2011. "The Turn to Affect: A Critique." *Critical Inquiry* 37(3): 437–472.

Macauley, C. 1974 [1790]. *Letters on Education*. New York: Garland Reprint.

Maffesoli, M. 1996. *The Time of the Tribes. The Decline of Individualism in Mass Society*. London: Sage.

Maguire, J., Mansfield, L., and Pike, E. 2016. *Bodies, Sports and Social Problems*. London: Routledge.

Mahmood, S. 2005. *Politics of Piety: The Islamic Revival and the Feminist Subject*. Princeton, NJ: Princeton University Press.

Malacrida, C., and Low, J. 2008. *The Body: A Reader*. Oxford, UK: Oxford University Press.

Marx, K. 1970. "Theses on Feuerbach." In *Early Writings* (pp. 421–423). Introduced by L. Colletti. Harmondsworth, UK: Penguin.

Marx, K., and Engels, F. 1970. *The German Ideology*. London: Lawrence & Wishart.

Massumi, B. 2002. *Parables for the Virtual: Movement, Affect, Sensation*. Durham, CT: Duke University Press.

2010. "The Future Birth of the Affective Fact: The Political Ontology of Threat." In M. Gregg and J. Seigworth (eds.), *The Affect Theory Reader*. Durham, NC: Duke University Press.

McDonald, L. 1997. "Classical Social Theory and Women Founders." In C. Camic (ed.), *Reclaiming the Sociological Classics* (pp. 112–141). Oxford, UK: Blackwell.

McDowell, L. 2009. *Working Bodies: Interactive Service Employment and Workplace Identities*. Oxford, UK: Wiley-Blackwell.

McIntosh, M. 1968. "The Homosexual Role." *Social Problems* 16(2): 182–192.

Mead, G. H. 1903. "The Definition of the Psychical." In *Decennial Publications of the University of Chicago, First Series, Vol. 3*. Chicago, IL: University of Chicago Press.

1932. *The Philosophy of the Present*. Edited by A. E. Murphy. Chicago, IL: La Salle.

1962 [1934]. *Mind, Self and Society*. Chicago, IL: University of Chicago Press.

Mead, M. 1935. *Sex and Temperament in Three Primitive Societies*. New York: Morrow.

Mellor, P. A., and Shilling, C. 1997. *Re-forming the Body: Religion, Community and Modernity*. London: Sage.

2014a. "Re-Conceptualising the Religious Habitus: Reflexivity and Embodied Subjectivity in Global Modernity." *Culture and Religion* 15(3): 275–297.

2014b. *Sociology of the Sacred: Religion, Embodiment and Social Change*. London: Sage.

Merleau-Ponty, M. 1962. *Phenomenology of Perception*. London: Routledge.

Mestrovic, S. 1994. *The Balkanization of the West*. London: Routledge.

Michael, M., and Rosengarten, M. 2012. "Medicine: Experimentation, Politics, Emergent Bodies." *Body & Society* 18(3–4): 1–17.

2013. *Innovation in Biomedicine: Ethics, Evidence, and Expectation in HIV*. Basingstoke, UK: Palgrave Macmillan.

Mol, A.-M. 2003. *The Body Multiple: Ontology in Medical Practice*. Durham, NC: Duke University Press.

Mol, A.-M., and J. Law. 2004. "Embodied Action, Enacted Bodies: The Example of Hypoglycaemia." *Body & Society* 10 (2–3): 43–62.

Munster, A. 2006. *Materialising New Media: Embodiment in Information Aesthetics*. New York: UPNE.

Nietzsche, F. 1993 [1871]. *The Birth of Tragedy and the Genealogy of Morals*. Harmondsworth, UK: Penguin.

Newton, E. 1972. *Mother Camp: Female Impersonators in America*. Chicago, IL: University of Chicago Press.

Norris, P., and Inglehart, R. 2004. *The Sacred and the Secular: Religion and Politics Worldwide*. Cambridge, UK: Cambridge University Press.

O'Connor, Erin. 2007. "Embodied Knowledge in Glassblowing: The Experience of Meaning and the Struggle toward Proficiency." *The Sociological Review* 51(s1): 126–141.

O'Neill, J. 1985. *Five Bodies. The Human Shape of Modern Society*. Ithaca, NY: Cornell University Press.

Ots, T. 1990. "The Silent Korper, the Loud Leib." Draft paper cited in R. Frankenberg, "Review Article: Disease, Literature and the Body in the Era of AIDS – A Preliminary Exploration." *Sociology of Health and Illness* 12: 351–360.

Parsons, T. 1937. *The Structure of Social Action*. New York: Free Press.

Peirce, C. 1997 [1903]. *Pragmatism as a Principle and Method of Right Thinking – The 1903 Harvard "Lectures on Pragmatism."* Edited by Patricia Ann Turisi. Albany, NY: SUNY Press.

1998. *The Essential Peirce. Vol.2*. Bloomington, IN: Indiana University Press.

Pitts-Taylor, V. 2012. "Social Brains, Embodiment and Neuro-interactionism." In B. S. Turner (ed.), *Routledge Handbook of Body Studies*. London: Routledge.

Rich, A. 1980. "Compulsory Heterosexuality and the Lesbian Experience." *Signs* 5: 631–660.

Rochberg-Halton, E. 1987. "Why Pragmatism Now?" *Sociological Theory* 5(2): 194–200.

Rose, N. 2007a. *The Politics of Life Itself: Biomedicine, Power and Subjectivity in the Twenty-First Century*. Princeton, NJ: Princeton University Press.

2007b. "Molecular Biopolitics, Somatic Ethics and the Spirit of Biocapital." *Social Theory and Health* 5: 3–29.

Rose, N., and J. M. Abi-Rached, 2013. *Neuro: The New Brain Sciences and the Management of the Mind*. Princeton, NJ: Princeton University Press.

Sawday, J. 1995. *The Body Emblazoned: Dissection and the Human Body in Renaissance Culture*. London: Routledge.

Sawicki, J. 1991. *Disciplining Foucault: Feminism, Power and the Body*. New York: Routledge.

Scarry, E. 1985. *The Body in Pain*. Oxford, UK: Oxford University Press.

Scheper-Hughes, N. 2011. "Mr Tati's Holiday and Joaõ's Safari – Seeing the World through Transplant Tourism." *Body & Society* 17(2–3): 55–92.

Schilder, P. 1978 [1935]. *The Image and Appearance of the Human Body*. New York: International Universities Press.

Scott, S., and D. Morgan. 1993. *Body Matters. Essays on the Sociology of the Body*. London: Falmer.

Sedgwick, E. K., and A. Frank. 1995. *Shame and Its Sisters: A Silvan Tomkins Reader*. Durham, NC: Duke University Press.

Sennett, R. 1994. *Flesh and Stone. The Body and the City in Western Civilisation*. New York: W. W. Norton.

Shilling, C. 1993. *The Body and Social Theory*. London: Sage.

Simmel G. 1971a [1908]. "Group Expansionism and the Development of Individuality." In D. Levine (ed.), *Georg Simmel on Individuality and Social Forms* (pp. 251–293). Chicago, IL: University of Chicago Press.

1971b [1918]. "The Transcendent Character of Life." In D. Levine (ed.), *Georg Simmel on Individuality and Social Forms* (pp. 353–374). Chicago, IL: University of Chicago Press.

Snell, B. 1960 [1948]. *Discovery of the Mind: The Greek Origins of European Thought*. Oxford, UK: Blackwell.

Sobchack, V. 2010. "Living a 'Phantom Limb': On the Phenomenology of Bodily Integrity." *Body & Society* 16(3): 51–67.

Stael, G. de. 1798. *The Influence of the Passions upon the Happiness of Individuals and of Nations*. London: Cawthorn.

Stoller, P. 1989. *The Taste of Ethnographic Things: The Senses in Anthropology*. Philadelphia, PA: University of Pennsylvania Press.

Thorpe, H. 2011. *Snowboarding Bodies in Theory and Practice*. London: Palgrave Macmillan.

Thrift, N. 2010. "Understanding the Material Practices of Glamour." In M. Gregg and J. Seigworth (eds.), *The Affect Theory Reader*. Durham, NC: Duke University Press.

Tomas, D. 1995. "Feedback and Cybernetics: Reimaging the Body in the Age of the Cyborg." *Body & Society* 1(3–4): 21–43.

Turner, B. S. 1984. *The Body and Society*. Oxford: Blackwell.

1987. *Medical Power and Social Knowledge*. London: SAGE.

1991. "Recent Developments in the Theory of the Body." In M. Featherstone, N. Hepworth, and B. S. Turner (eds.), *The Body: Social Process and Cultural Theory*. London: Sage.

1992. *Regulating Bodies. Essays in Medical Sociology*. London: Routledge.

2006. *Vulnerability and Human Rights*. Pennsylvania, PA: Pennsylvania State University Press.

Wacquant, L. 2004. *Body and Soul*. Chicago, IL: University of Chicago Press.

Weber, M. 1968. *Economy and Society, 2 Vols*. Berkeley, CA: University of California Press.

1991 [1904–1905]. *The Protestant Ethic and the Spirit of Capitalism*. London: Macmillan.

Wegenstein, B. 2006. *Getting under the Skin: Body and Media Theory*. Cambridge, MA: MIT Press.

West, C., and Zimmerman, D. 1987. "Doing Gender." *Gender and Society* 1(2): 125–151.

Williams, S. 2003. *Medicine and the Body*. London: Sage.

Wolkowitz, C. 2006. *Bodies at Work*. London: Routledge.

Wollstonecraft, M. 1989 [1787–1797]. *Works of Mary Wollstonecraft*. Edited by J. Todd and M. Butler, 7 vols. New York: New York University Press.

Wouters, C. 2007. *Informalization: Manners and Emotions since 1890*. London: Sage.

Young I. M. 1998. "'Throwing like a Girl': Twenty Years Later." In D. Welton (ed.), *Body and Flesh: A Philosophical Reader* (pp. 286–290). Oxford, UK: Blackwell.

14 Sexualities

Stephen Valocchi

Sexuality is a slippery thing. Sociologists who study it, and that study is a relatively recent enterprise, have tried mightily to pin it down: to take what has typically been seen as biological or psychological in nature, and thus standing outside society, and understand it as fundamentally social. As part of that process and as another reason why sexuality is slippery, sociologists parse this concept in several ways. Sociologists consider the role that sexuality plays in the construction of subjectivity and identity, the relationship between desires, behaviors, and identities, the development and shape of sexual subcultures and communities, and sexuality's role in "larger" social structures of the state, immigration, and transnationalism, to name just a few of the institutional arenas in which sexuality has been put to use. Not surprisingly, these diverse uses of sexuality require a similarly diverse set of theoretical frameworks to assist in seeing the "complexly social" and the "complexly sexual" at different levels of interest and analysis.

This chapter will examine the major theories of sexuality that have developed over the past twenty-five years or so, moving from the somewhat micro to the somewhat macro level of analysis. This "moving" requires the modifier "somewhat" because many of the theoretical frameworks focus on both how sexuality affects the self and social interactions (i.e. the micro) and how sexuality is organized in social institutions and culture (i.e. the macro). This "moving" also requires the modifier "interdisciplinary" since these sociological theories are nourished by new work in the area of gender and sexuality that resists disciplinary boundaries. Regardless of these different levels, different emphases, and different sources of nourishment, sexuality is not theorized as a "somatic fact," but rather as a "cultural effect" (Ghaziani, 2017: 13) or alternatively as "a field of meanings, discourses, and practices that are interlaced with social institutions" (Seidman, 1996: 6).

We have traveled quite a distance from the first set of frameworks that attempted to situate sexuality in a social context. In their quest for scientific authority, the sexologists of the late nineteenth century used sexuality or more precisely gendered understandings of sexuality as the basis upon which to classify individuals' bodies, minds, and behaviors and situate these types or species on a spectrum of normality and pathology. The familiar categories of heterosexual and homosexual as well as the less familiar ones such as "invert" and "uranian" were invented by the sexologists to understand the diversity of populations coming increasingly into public view due to urbanization, industrialization, and migration, and thus demanding some sort of regulation and control (Weeks, 1985). To that end, the classification systems were built on the assumptions regarding normative and nonnormative gender presentations, and behaviors and proclivities that supported or undermined the "reproductive instinct" (Dreger, 1998). Although we no longer subscribe to the assumptions and presumptions built into this earlier framework, sexology gave us a few concepts we have continued to rework in theoretical frameworks that are still in use today. For example, we continue to rely on the notion of the heterosexual/homosexual binary to understand an important axis of sexual identity. We of course do not see this binary in natural, biological, or evolutionary terms as did the sexologists. We do nonetheless see identity as an important aspect of sexuality, one captured and in some sense invented by the sexologists, but presented as aspects of either normality or perversion. Sexual identity reappears as an essential component of social-constructionist approaches utilized by sociologists into the present day.

Psychoanalytic Frameworks

Another legacy of the sexologists, albeit from a somewhat more astute observer of early-twentieth-century sexuality, Sigmund Freud, was the "discovery" of the unconscious and the importance of pleasure, fantasy, attachment, loss, risk, and release in the construction of sexual subjectivity (Freud, 1975). Unlike the earlier generation of sexologists, Freud did not view heterosexuality as the natural, normal, and healthy expression of sexuality; instead he viewed heterosexuality and homosexuality as morally and socially equivalent: both constituting "peculiar compromises" between a polymorphous pleasure principle on the one hand and the demands of social life on the other (Seidman, 2015). Although psychoanalytical approaches to sexuality are less popular in sociology than they are in the humanities, they deserve some renewed attention for helping us understand the limits, instabilities, and incoherences that lie below the surface of sexual identities. Psychoanalytical approaches also provide a necessary corrective to theoretical frameworks that focus exclusively on the dynamics of sexual identity. If we return to the capacious nature of sexuality (i.e. its slippery nature) and acknowledge that fantasy and desire are parts of that definition, then we require a theoretical framework that considers their relationship to the other components of sexuality such as behaviors, identities, subcultures, and social institutions.

Psychoanalytical frameworks can provide a guide through this aspect of sexuality. Sociologists have pointed out the problematic aspects of these frameworks, especially the assumptions that the heterosexual, two-parent, nuclear family results in normal, that is, heterosexual, gender-normative children, and the corresponding assumption that the mother is crucial for the successful sexual socialization of the child. Sociologists also remain skeptical about an (unobservable) unconscious that somehow remains outside the realm of the social. We do not have to embrace these assumptions, however, in order to accept the more fundamental insight of the conflicts and ambivalences involved in the creation of a stable sexual subjectivity. Nor do we have to accept these assumptions to acknowledge that the individual's psychic realm has its own logic that interacts with the social in complicated ways.

In the classic formulation of Freudian psychoanalysis, the mind is racked with conflicting desires and painful repressions; it wrestles with the sexual drives of the unconscious due to the interactions between the body, its needs for attachment and nurturance, and its fear of separation on the one hand and the demands of society for restraint and denial on the other (Elliot, 2001). The normative demands of society require a controlled and coherent self while the unconscious pushes against these demands with fantasies and desires only tangentially related to stable sexual identities. As Gamson and Moon (2004: 60) remind us in a review of trends in the sociology of sexualities that focus predominately on identities, institutions, and globalization, we should not lose sight of "our old, raw, ever present concerns," that is, "the sorts of things people like to do with their bodies and with whom, [and] the fantasies of physical intimacy they create . . . ."

Recent research has pointed to the utility of this reminder. In one especially important example of scholarship that utilizes the insights of psychoanalysis, Tim Dean in *Unlimited Intimacy* (2009) examines the barebacking subculture among men (before the advent of PrEP, pre-exposure prophylaxis, an oral medication that significantly reduces the possibility of HIV transmission): the sites and dispositions of men who have premeditated, unprotected sex with men and are indifferent to or actively desire viral exchange. This rich ethnography does many things, but most importantly for this review, it develops a psychoanalytically inflected theory of sexuality to explain this phenomenon and thus demonstrates the usefulness of a psychoanalytic approach as a complement to theories that start from identity. According to Dean (2009), this subculture can be best understood as a communion with others, where the uncertainty and riskiness of sex become an "opportunity" for self-shattering. It is a place where intimacy and pleasure are constructed apart from and against the ego, identity, and the social recognition of stable and respectable sexual subjectivity; a place that acknowledges the psychic pleasures derived from sex apart from the boundaries of identity; and a place that gets its meaning and its danger from the socially created fetish (and fantasy object) of HIV. In this one example, we see the importance of several components of sexuality – fantasy, desire, sexual identity, and the sexual stigmas established by scientists and public health professionals. This example also points to some ways in which sociology can use psychoanalytical insights to study other aspects of sexuality. As we will see below, queer theorists explicitly use psychoanalytical models of subject formation to help understand the incoherence and instabilities inherent in the egocentric concept of identity.

Social Constructionism

While psychoanalytical approaches background identity, or more precisely point to the tensions inherent in the concept of sexual identity, a second set of theories defined broadly as social constructionist do quite the opposite and seek to understand how individuals acquire fairly stable sexual identities. They start from the most basic sociological assumption that we are not born sexual but that we learn to be sexual. We learn what it means to be sexual, what counts as sexual; where to be sexual and with whom; and the relationship of the sexual with other aspects of our lives (Plummer, 1975).

The classic formulation of these frameworks comes from the work of John Gagnon and William Simon (1973), which developed the sexual-scripts approach, and Ken Plummer's work on stigma and homosexuality (1975). Both constructionist frameworks focus on the level of social interactions and the acquisition of a sexual identity on the basis of those interactions. These interactions, moreover, are symbolic or meaning-rich in the sense that individuals "read" the social environment and develop behaviors and self-concepts in reaction to the normative proscriptions embedded in this environment. For Gagnon and Simon (1973) sexual scripts develop at three levels: the cultural level that contains the social norms regarding what is and is not sexual and the meanings attached to the different versions of the sexual; the interpersonal level where those social norms and the personal reactions to these norms meet; and the intrapsychic level where the work of self-processing, desire, and decision-making take place.

Plummer (1975) takes this social-scripts approach and applies it to the process of learning a homosexual role. Like many theorists who developed their symbolic-interactionist perspective in the early deviance tradition in sociology, Plummer interrogates the processes individuals go through in "coming to terms" with a deviant identity. He states: "homosexuality is conceptualized as a form of role playing, juxtaposed constantly with the reactions of society's members, and located in a subjective work where meanings are problematic" (1975: 67). Although the particular language reflects the vocabulary of deviance and does not reflect the social and political changes that have taken place around sexual minorities since the 1970s, Plummer's homosexual role framework, like Gagnon and Simon's sexual-scripts approach, focuses on the same aspects of sexuality: the individual level that tries to theorize the relationship between desires, dispositions, behaviors, subjectivities, and identities. The one consistent criticism of this approach derives from its micro-level focus: the framework's inability to more fully theorize the social structure of sexuality (but see McIntosh, 1968 for the beginnings of this effort within the symbolic-interactionist perspective).

That criticism has been recently addressed by Adam Isaiah Green in his edited book, *Sexual Fields: Toward a Sociology of Collective Sexual Life* (2014). In it, Green integrates the social-field approach of Pierre Bourdieu with the symbolic-interactionist approach of an earlier generation of sexuality scholars to provide a set of concepts that begin to address the "structure problem" in social-constructionist accounts of sexuality. Armed with Bourdieu's concepts of field, capital, and habitus, Green's (2014: 7) sexual-fields approach sees sexual sociality as a kind of social life with its own particular social organization, status hierarchy, and regulative principles. The sexual field essentially acts as the social structure that early approaches were unable to theorize. Green (2014: 2) captures this social structure thusly: a field "is characterized by distinct sets of actors, internal logics, institutionalized modes of interaction and self-management, and positions in social space that conferred advantage on some and disadvantage on others."

One particularly fascinating empirical essay in Green's volume illustrates the utility of the sexual-fields approach, especially its ability to describe social interactions, sexual attractiveness, and desire in structural terms. Situating the sexual field of heterosexual dating among Western foreigners and Chinese in contemporary Shanghai, Farrar and Dale (2014) use the concepts of sexual capital, erotic habitus, and sexual mobility as these are enacted in different sites in the city to understand the differences in desire, gender performance, and dating and mating patterns. The theoretical framework draws their attention to the dynamics of desire, competition, modes of embodiment, and strategies of maneuvering within this field for different groups of men and women (Chinese and Western men; married and single men; Chinese and Western women; married and single women). The differences in these dynamics are explained not only by increased "ethnosexual contact zones" due to globalization but also by macro-level historical processes of colonialism and the racial and gender stereotypes and hierarchies derived from those processes. In accounting for one of their many findings, for example, Farrar and Dale (2014: 166) state: "it is impossible to explain the persisting gender gap in interracial dating in Shanghai without some reference to colonial racial legacies, in particular racial hierarchies of masculinity and femininity." Still, the framework is focused on the structure and function of the sexual fields and focuses on the power of the field itself (i.e. its ability to refashion individuals' erotic habitus) and the agency of actors to achieve sexual mobility within that field. In Farrar and Dale's words (2014: 169): "Historical legacies ... provide cultural raw material for these contemporary local processes, but these interactions are best understood as adjustments to changing positions in existing sexual fields and attempts to acquire and maintain forms of sexual capital therein." Other versions of symbolic interaction would focus more centrally on those "historical [and contemporary] legacies," arguing that various institutional forces such as consumer capitalism, digital technologies, and neoliberalism encourage new sets of sexual scripts. The circulation of these new sexual scripts changes the dynamics by which individuals engage in the symbolic interactional processes of sexual subjectivity and identity formation (Giddens, 1992; Weiss, 2011).

Feminist Theories

Another important set of theories of sexuality come from feminism. One of the criticisms of these aforementioned frameworks of psychoanalysis, social constructionism, and sexual-fields theory has been their neglect or undertheorized understanding of gender and its relationship to sexuality. This is precisely feminism's contribution to the study of sexuality. There are many different kinds of feminism: from psychoanalytical, which locates differences in men's and women's sexual subjectivities in attachment, attraction, and separation anxieties of the mother–child relationship (Chodorow, 1978); to cultural feminism, which understands differences in sexuality as part of men's and women's different "ways of knowing" and the cultures each gender constructs to support those ways (Ryan,

1992); to socialist feminism (Eisenstein, 1980), which locates women's sexual subordination in the profit-maximizing goals of capitalist production and consumption of goods and services and reproduction of labor. Despite these differences, feminism as a theory of sexuality has insisted on the coupling of sexuality with gender and viewing sexuality through the lens of gender inequality and patriarchy. Feminism views patriarchy, the structural dominance of men over women in many social institutions, as crucial in understanding the nature of sexuality. In essence, patriarchy enforces not only gender relations but sexuality as well. For feminist theory, or at least the theoretical framework that took hold in sociology, sexuality is the product of men's power over women to define what desires, behaviors, and feelings are sexual and who has privileged access to pleasure. Sexuality is the site where patriarchy is inscribed; in other words, the site where women's subordination is consolidated (Corber and Valocchi, 2003: 6).

Perhaps the best and most widely cited example of this feminist theory of sexuality is Adrienne Rich's classic 1980 essay, "Compulsory Heterosexuality and Lesbian Existence." In it, Rich makes the provocative claim that the sexual category "heterosexuality" was created and reinforced by men as a way to prevent women's solidarity with other women and ensure men's political and economic power over women. In this way, she collapses the category of sexuality into patriarchy, suggests that women's identification with other women is a form of lesbian identification, and argues that any analysis of sexuality must start with an analysis of the gendered distribution of power in society. This feminist theory of sexuality, for all its limitations, nonetheless reminds us that sexuality at any level (intrapsychic, interpersonal, institutional, or cultural) must be paired with but not collapsed into its close cousin: gender.

Coming out of feminism, anthropologist, Gayle Rubin, in another classic and widely cited essay, *Thinking Sex: Notes for a Radical Theory of the Politics of Sexuality* (1984: 274) was one of the first to makes the point that, though related, sexuality and gender constitute "two distinct arenas of social practice." Using the history of state regulation of sexuality in Great Britain and the United States as her "data," she demonstrates that especially in periods of social anxiety, sexual acts become burdened with an excess of meaning, and individuals are divided up according to a "hierarchical system of sexual value" that operates independently from gender hierarchies (Rubin, 1984: 280). In the words of Carol Vance, the editor of the volume *Pleasure and Danger: Exploring Female Sexuality*, in which Gayle Rubin's essay first appeared, "feminism needs sophisticated methodologies and analyses that permit the recognition of each discrete domain as well as their multiple intersections" (Vance, 1984: 16). Furthermore, as the title of Vance's volume adamantly states, feminism needs to develop models of sexuality that can acknowledge the conditions under which sexuality operates as a domain of female pleasure (as well as a field of danger).

An engaging ethnography of a California high school by C. J. Pascoe, *Dude, You're a Fag: Masculinity and Sexuality in High School* (2007) would meet this challenge and provides an interesting "update" of Adrienne Rich's analysis of compulsory heterosexuality. Pascoe's observations of school rituals, classroom pedagogy, and proceedings at student clubs and sports reveal that, among other things, boys learn heterosexuality as they learn masculinity. As a matter of fact, the omnipresent "fag" discourse is not centrally a homophobic discourse, although it is that, but a gendered one as well, lobbed with ease at other boys as a way to police gender norms. Being a "fag" is failing at masculinity: being incompetent, weak, or lacking sexual prowess. In this way, Pascoe's analysis demonstrates the utility of a feminist theory of sexuality by illustrating the simple but powerful insight that we learn sexuality as we learn gender. Similarly, it demonstrates that this learning takes place at several societal levels: at the interpersonal level of social interactions among boys, between boys and girls, and between students and teachers; at the institutional level, in the pedagogy of the classroom, in the examples teachers use to educate, and the assumptions they use about the aspirations of students; and at the cultural level, in norms and values that are recognized in school-sponsored celebrations, rituals, and assemblies. In essence, Pascoe provides a kind of empirical support for Adrienne Rich's assertions over thirty years ago. In this case, boys are learning masculinity as they learn compulsory heterosexuality. Unlike Rich, however, Pascoe does not assume women's/girls' victimhood (i.e. she describes how high-school girls assert their sexual agency and female masculinity despite boys' sexism and misogyny). Unlike Rich, she does not treat male privilege as a monolithic category (i.e. she points out how the male privilege of the boys depends on their racial and class positions). In these ways, this analysis takes up Carol Vance's call for a feminism that addresses "multiple intersections" and a sexuality that is both a pleasure and a danger.

Intersectional Analysis

Intersectional feminism, or simply intersectional analysis, constitutes another set of frameworks sociologists use to understand sexuality. This framework emerged out of the activism of black feminists in the 1970s during the black and women's liberation movements that refused a monolithic understanding of power, identity, and solidarity. The women of the Combahee River Collective expressed this complexity directly in their classic 1977 "A Black Feminist Statement": "Our situation as Black people necessitates that we have solidarity around the fact of race. We struggle together with Black men against racism, while we also struggle with Black men about sexism" (Hull, Scott Bell, and Smith, 1982: 16). This "lesson in struggle" was also the first salvo in a new way of understanding sexuality from a feminist perspective. Patriarchy as well as maleness, femaleness, and sexuality were inflected by race and class.

This activist perspective made its way into the academy via an influential essay by Kimberle Crenshaw published in 1995 in the *Stanford Law Review*, "Mapping the Margins: Intersectionality, Identity Politics, and Violence against Women of Color." In it, she lays out an exacting analysis of the limitations of antiracism and feminist frameworks in understanding the myriad forms of violence against women of color. These frameworks essentially represent antiracism as a discourse that favors black men, and feminism as a discourse that favors white women. In general, she says that the "experiences of women of color are frequently the product of intersecting patterns of racism and sexism," and these intersections themselves must be fore-grounded in all discussions of sexual violence, particularly for those who occupy multiple marginalizations. Although Crenshaw's analysis references sexuality only in the context of sexual violence against women of color, its "friendly" critique of identity and its careful mapping of an alternative way of analyzing social experience on the margins of multiple identities proved tremendously productive, not only in the sociology of sexuality but in many other subfields of the discipline.

We can distinguish several different components of an intersectional framework. This framework asserts that there are different axes of subjectivity, identity, and power based on one's membership in various marked and unmarked social groups. These groups not only possess different amounts of social, economic, and political power but also are characterized by different cultural representations, stereotypes, and images. As Patricia Hill Collins (1991), another prominent feminist theorist of intersectionality, states in her classic, *Black Feminist Thought: Knowledge, Consciousness, and the Politics of Empowerment*, these groups possess "different combinations of penalty and privilege" (1991: 265). These combinations, moreover, have historical roots and contemporary effects. In Crenshaw's analysis referenced above, for example, sexual violence against women of color – issues of access to shelters, prosecution, reporting, public policy, cultural awareness – can only be understood by means of the multiple ways in which racism and sexism operating together through economics, politics, immigration law, social movements, cultural representations, and history affect black women's sexuality.

Due to its origins in antiracism and black feminist activism and scholarship, an intersectional framework dealing explicitly with sexuality starts from these perspectives. The fairly recent work of Patricia Hill Collins (2006) and Joane Nagel (2003) illustrate these starting points and also the utility of the framework in making sense not only of individuals' identities or sexual assault but also of the discursive construction of racism and racial domination and the historical construction of nation-building, colonialism, and nationalism. Collins (2006) illustrates how racialized, gendered, and homophobic discourses of sexuality are integral to racialized systems of domination, and conversely how these discourses help maintain heteronormativity. Similarly, Nagel (2003: 166) argues that these intersectionalities are crucial in understanding the historical and contemporary processes of nationalism and coloni-alism. She shows that "building nations and national identities involves inspecting and controlling the sexualities of citizens and condemning the sexualities of non-citizens and those considered outside the sexual boundaries of the nation." Similarly, historian Margot Canaday (2009) analyzes the origins and early development of the US welfare/warfare state in terms of the evolving understandings of homosexuality throughout the twentieth century. Interestingly, this research sees sexuality (and its intersections) not primarily as a dependent variable – as something that needs to be explained – but as an independent variable – as an important factor in the explanation of other seemingly "nonsexual" phenomena, for example, state-building, migration, and colonialism. As we will see below, this aspect of intersectional theory moves us closer to the queer approaches to sexuality discussed in the final section of this chapter. These approaches embrace the capacious nature of sexuality and see it as saturating many aspects of social life that have on their surface little to do with sex.

Unlike this previous generation of intersectional theorists, who start from race and bring in gender, sexuality, class, and so on in order to adequately explain various racialized processes, a newer generation of theorists is using intersectional theory to explain processes of sexuality. This tendency has been most obvious in the study of sexual identity and desire. We can see an example of this in the already-mentioned ethnography of gender and sexuality in a California high school, *Dude, You're a Fag* (2007), in which Pascoe observes the sexuality of black boys. Black masculinity (and heterosexuality) is not constructed primarily through the "fag" discourse, as it is among white boys; it is actually constructed using subcultural standards such as dancing, clothing, and cool pose. In some sense, whiteness stands in for the specter of the fag as the feminized term. So, sexual identity is racially inflected. In addition, however, black sexuality is seen as a threat by the school; for example, even though the "fag" discourse is not employed as frequently by African-American boys, when it is, it is punished more severely than when it is employed by white boys. Thus, Pascoe links the concerns of intersectional theorists about the cultural discourse around blackness to the intersectional nature of identity construction.

This intersectional framework has been most recently used to study sexual-identity construction. A very good example of this is Mignon R. Moore's 2011 book, *Invisible Families: Gay Identities, Relationships, and Motherhood among Black Women.* In *Invisible Families*, Moore studies lesbian identities among black women but her intersectional theoretical framework requires that we see these women as embodying same-sex desire in many different ways inflected by race, class, and gender. In order to understand how these women understand and express their desire, the standards they use to evaluate themselves and those around them, and the ways they integrate themselves and their families into their communities, we need intersectionality. In other words, we need to understand the importance of black respectability to middle-class African Americans; the legacy of racism and its impact on social and economic stability; the impact of stereotypes of black womanhood; the alternative standards of femininity forged in black communities; the unique role of women as bulwarks in black communities; and the homophobia which exists in both black and white communities. These factors result in Moore's women demonstrating not a singular lesbian identity but several lesbian identities, to the point that her analysis calls into question the very stability of the identity, or alternatively makes us see that the notion of a singular identity is indeed a limited and biased one built on a middle-class, white, gender-normative model.

Correspondingly, it also makes us question many other assumptions built into previous theoretical frameworks of sexuality. For example, social-constructionist, sexual-fields, and feminist frameworks give conceptual priority to the identity dimension of sexuality: the idea that sexual identity is a unique and unitary set of self-understandings, experiences, and behavioral repertoires and that the dimensions, complexities, consequences, and problems associated with sexual identity are the proper objects of study for a sociology of sexuality. Intersectional frameworks begin to move us away from this assumption in a couple of ways. Most simply, intersectional frameworks refuse analyses based on singular dimensions of subjectivity or human agency. As Gamson (2013: 806) states in his review of recent work in the sociology of sexualities, "In everyday life . . . people do not see gender, race, ethnicity, and age as discrete categories of desire; instead, they experience desire along intersections." In Moore's research, race rather than sexuality emerges as the central force in the shaping of these women's sexual identities. In addition, Moore's intersectional approach perhaps unintentionally also signals a dimension of sexuality apart from identity: sexual desire and the role of gender in shaping it. These black women's same-sex desires were expressed primarily through gender presentation: feminine, gender-blended, or gender-transgressive. Again, intersectionality, when "pushed" beyond the study of identity, gestures toward the queer theoretical approaches to sexuality.

Queer Theoretical Approaches

These queer approaches have several components, many of which can be described in terms of the limitations or silences of the approaches considered above. First and foremost, queer theory rejects the assumption of stable and coherent sexual identities as the primary object of analysis for a sociology of sexuality. In contrast, psychoanalytic, social-constructionist, social-fields, and feminist theories abide by the idea that there exists a patterned ensemble of desires, subjectivities, behaviors, and associations organized by a heterosexual/homosexual binary, and that binary constitutes the starting point of study. In this way, these other approaches start from what Michael Warner (1993: xxvi), a leading scholar of queer theory, calls "regimes of the normal," identity politics and its associated discourse of tolerance. In contrast, queer theory "rejects a minoritizing logic of tolerance or simple political-interest representation in favor of a more thorough resistance to regimes of the normal."

This critique of identity takes many forms. As already anticipated by intersectional theories, individuals may have crosscutting identifications along several axes of social difference and these identifications call into question the salience and coherence of sexual-identity categories. Sex of object choice may be irrelevant to an individual's identity formation: racial, ethnic, and class differences may be more important. In addition, the understanding of sexual identity may be inflected in unique ways depending on racial, ethnic, or class affiliations; thus, the practices, expressions, and interests emergent from this intersection of differences cannot be captured by the dominant categories of homosexual or heterosexual or any other single identity category. Research on "the down low," black men who have sex with men but do not define themselves as gay (Phillips, 2005), and "white dude sex," straight white men who seek out sex with other straight white men (Ward, 2015), illustrates the inability of the hetero/homo binary to represent the complexity of people's lives. In the former example, we need to understand the perils of black masculinity, the racially inflected nature of gay identity, and homophobia in the black community. In the latter example, we need to understand homophobia in the white community, hetero-white privilege, and the role of homoerotic bonding as constructing a hetero-masculinity.

More than simply recognizing the intersectional nature of identity and subjectivity, queer theory goes further and posits that the very idea of identity is a regulatory and disciplining mechanism. Gamson (2013: 807) expresses this critique thusly: "in creating and reproducing sexual categories, people reproduce relations of power; that every social institution, however asexual in appearance, relies on and enforces sexual boundaries and divisions." Unlike other theoretical frameworks of sexuality, identity is not a means of empowerment or a socially constructed "fact of life": rather it is put in place and kept in place by individuals and institutions that construct the boundaries and decide who is inside and outside those boundaries. In a recent example of this multidimensional policing, Brubaker (2016) describes the controversies surrounding Caitlyn Jenner's claim to transgender womanhood and Rachel Dolezal's claim to transracial blackness. Without reviewing the complexities of these two very different identity claims, what is notable in these examples are the myriad efforts by political commentators, activists, and scholars to evaluate them as authentic, fraudulent, legitimate, or dangerous, and in these ways revealing the tensions between "chosenness and givenness" of identity in postmodern life (Brubaker, 2016: 11). Queer theory would intervene in and perhaps derail these debates by pointing out the provisional, unstable, and incoherent nature of *all* identities even as it insists on the profound differences between these identities in terms of their histories and contemporary contexts.

This critique of identity developed from queer theory's encounter with one particular identity formation: gay identity. This is not surprising in light of queer theory's emergence out of gay and lesbian studies. As gay and lesbian studies brought sexuality into the academy as an object of study, and social-constructionist theory made the study of sexual minorities a legitimate topic for research in sociology, these fields narrowed that study to a focus on identity. Part of this enterprise was political in nature: to validate, normalize, and even celebrate this nonnormative identity. As gay studies scholars historicized the idea of gay identity, however, they argued that the binary of heterosexual and homosexual was a fairly recent invention, and that there was a historical (and contemporary) "disconnect" between sexual practices (same-sex and different-sex) and sexual identities (Chauncey, 1994). At the same time, scholars began to listen to AIDS activists who were arguing that gay identity cannot be the focus of HIV prevention efforts: that there were many people who did not abide by the identity but engaged in same-sex practices. In all these ways, queer theory disrupted identity as the focal point of sexuality studies.

Queer theory also disputes another implicit assumption of many of these other theoretical frameworks: that there is a stable and normative alignment of anatomical sex, gender, and sexuality. As Judith Lorber, an important gender theorist who has pushed the study of gender and sexuality in a queer direction (1996: 144) states, "sociology assumes that each person has one sex, one sexuality, and one gender, which are congruent and fixed for life. . . . A woman is assumed to be a feminine female; a man a masculine male. Heterosexuality is the uninterrogated norm." For queer theory, this starting assumption is in itself a form of power, captured by the concept of heteronormativity. Heteronormativity means the set of norms that make heterosexuality seem natural or right and that organize homosexuality as its binary opposite. This set of norms works to maintain the dominance of heterosexuality by preventing homosexuality from being a form of sexuality that can be taken for granted or go unmarked or seem right in the way heterosexuality can (Corber and Valocchi, 2003: 4). As a result, the dominance of heterosexuality often operates unconsciously or in ways that make it particularly difficult to identify. Queer theory's understanding of heteronormativity with its emphasis on meaning systems or discourses has proven useful in research on sexuality. In one important example, Kristin Schilt and Laura Westbrook (2009) examine how gender-"normal" interactions with transgender men at work tend to reinscribe, reinforce, or police the gender binary and (re)connect that binary back to both anatomical sex and heterosexuality. Gender-"normal" men, for example treat trans men as "one of the guys" by engaging in hetero-infused gender rituals such as "back slaps" and sex talk. In other words, they are more comfortable with a gender-conforming (trans) man than a gender-nonconforming (*cis*) woman, and these gender-"normal" men do the "work" to reinforce this alignment. Gender-"normal" women, on the other hand, are more hesitant to include trans men in the category of men since that would directly threaten these women's understanding of heterosexuality based in biological sex. In these ways, queer theory's essential insights about the differences between sex, gender, and sexuality and the forces that keep these differences in normative alignment provide the tools that enable analysis of these discourses in the workplace. These same queer theoretical insights have also proven useful in social movements' research as a way to see gender-conforming, civil-rights seeking, identity-focused LGBT activism as mimicking heteronormativity (Savci, 2016; Ward, 2008).

Although other theories of sexuality do recognize that these alignments are ideological and hence a source of power, they conspire in reproducing them by treating the categories and the normative relationship among them as the starting assumptions on which sexuality research is based and the major lens through which we interpret our data. Rather than study these normative alignments, queer theorists insist that they can learn more about sexuality as a discursive and institutional force by focusing on the nonnormative formations of sex, gender, and sexuality. For these reasons, queer theory focuses on the "deviant" cases, or the anatomies, genders, sexual practices, and identities that do not neatly fit into either category of the binaries or that violate the normative alignment of sex, gender, and sexuality such as sadomasochism, transsexuality, and intersexuality (Corber and Valocchi, 2003). This "sampling on the dependent variable" can be seen as a methodological shortcut for discerning the processes that produce all sexual subjectivities; not just the nonnormative ones.

An important example of research that uses these insights from queer theory is David Valentine's *Imagining Transgender: An Ethnography of a Category* (2007). The subtitle reflects the queer theoretical orientation of the monograph. In it, Valentine does not interrogate the "problems" of being transgender in today's society, although that is indeed part of it; he does not interrogate the process of identity formation among transgender women, although that is also part of it; and he does not interrogate whether and how transgender women reinforce or challenge gender norms, although that is part of it too. These kinds of research questions would be the standard questions for a sociology of sexuality that utilizes many of the previous theoretical frameworks. Instead, Valentine interrogates how the category of transgender emerged, whose interests were represented in the development of the category, and the role that the medical profession, the mainstream gay movement, and trans activism played in creating the boundaries between this form of gender variance and other forms of sex and gender variance. Among other things, Valentine shows how the gay and lesbian movement in its pursuit of a politics of respectability drained the category of homosexuality of gender nonnormativity, how the medical profession pathologized the "residual" category of transsexuality, and how activists "reclaimed" and broadened the category to include various kinds of gender non-normativity under the rubric transgender. In these ways, the research illustrates how categories, even those meant to be empowering, are mechanisms of regulation.

This example also nicely illustrates another component of queer theory: the incoherence and instability of these identity categories. Because these categories are not "facts of life" but cultural constructions or ideological fictions, they incompletely or imperfectly represent a broad range of complicated social processes surrounding the meaning of bodies and the social cues, practices, and subjectivities associated with gender and sexuality (Jagose, 1996; Lorber, 1996). The ethnographic component of Valentine's work clearly captures these instabilities and incoherences. In his encounters on the streets in the Meatpacking District of Manhattan, at drag balls in Harlem and Hell's Kitchen, in transvestite bars in Midtown, attending workshops at the transgender support group in Chelsea or fundraisers for the gay and lesbian community center, Valentine discovers that the category transgender does not and indeed cannot capture the subjectivities, identifications, behaviors, and interests of the people that, according to the category, should possess many commonalities. Some identify as gay, others as butch queens or fem queens. Still others refuse all affiliation and see themselves as transvestites or drag queens. Finally, some recognize that the category, regardless of its incoherence, is embraced by social service providers; so in order to claim services and benefits they claim (but do not own) the identity. These ethnographic encounters suggest that the identity is an ideological construction that may or may not have meaning for individuals who have different relationships to their bodies, gender, sexual desire, race, ethnicity, class, and so on. They also suggest that it serves as a source of discursive and material regulation: you must name yourself thusly to make sense to those who seek to study and help you.

A final component of queer theory is perhaps the least sociological of its starting assumptions, in that the sexual self may not be entirely a socially constructed sexual self or more precisely, may be a more complexly social self than we have hitherto theorized. I am referring here to the use of psychoanalytic models of subject formation that foreground psychic processes of fantasy, desire, attachment, separation, repression, and displacement as accounting for sexual subjectivity. These aspects of the self work to interrupt, short-circuit, or simply shape particular sexual identities and serve as one way in which the neat, normative alignments of sex, gender, and sexuality get destabilized. As the repository of fantasy and desire, the unconscious often conflicts with our conscious construction of our sexual identities, and this conflict between the two different levels may affect the alignment of an individual's sex, gender, and sexuality in ways that cannot be neatly read off the social environment. Tim Dean's analysis of the barebacking subculture discussed above is an excellent example of how queer theory uses psychoanalytic theory to explain how desire is registered in nonnormative ways and how that desire rejects and even emerges in opposition to the dominant constructions of gay identity. In this sense, the pre-social (i.e. fantasy and desire) – if we can even call it that – takes its meaning only in relation to the social (identity).

Michel Foucault

The two theorists most closely associated with queer theory are Michel Foucault and Judith Butler. Many of the components of queer theory described above can be traced to the influence of these two scholars. Michel Foucault's writings on the history of sexuality, the changed nature of power, and the impact of both on the concept of the self is crucial in understanding queer theory's critique of identity and its insistence on seeing sexuality as a disciplining force for the social subject. In some sense, Foucault can be considered a radical social constructionist. In his widely influential *The History of Sexuality* (1980), he argues that discourses around the control of bodies, pleasures, fertility, public health, migration, and labor created a knowledge formation called sexuality. The specifics of this development are complicated and span several centuries. The history is a narrative that travels from the Church, including its discourses in the sacrament of confession and the Christian pastoral, through the rise of science and the sexologist and psychiatrist and their categories of normal and abnormal, to the state and its need to control borders, and create docile citizens and productive workers. In this telling, sexuality is a radical invention, a discursive regime that transformed some subset of pleasures, sensations, appetites, and thoughts into something "really" important, that is, sexuality. And, it made some aspects of this new phenomenon "normal," and others "abnormal," pathological, and dangerous. In these ways, sexuality is an instrument of power.

Foucault (1980: 89) describes sexuality as something that is "economically useful and politically conservative," a truth regime that regulates and controls us from the inside out. Rather than relying on juridico-legal discourse – power from "the outside in" through law and state coercion – modernity requires a new, more subtle and efficient system of control through the internalization of norms. In Foucault's words: "[the judicial system] is utterly incongruous with the new methods of power whose operation is not ensured by right but by technique, not by law but by normalization, not by punishment but by control, methods that are employed on all levels and in forms that go beyond the state and its apparatus." Simply put, sexuality is a discursive regime that does the hard work of social order by encouraging us to internalize the standards of normality and belonging.

Not surprisingly, Foucault saw gay identity very differently from the ways that both activists and social-constructionist theorists of sexuality view it. Rather than a source of empowerment and an instrument of liberation, gay identity was an instrument of power. For Foucault, the "homosexual" was a creation of these above-mentioned historical processes which turned sinful acts into deviant people. The shift from "homosexual" to "gay" was a change in the cultural material that filled up that category (from negative to positive connotations), but the category still exists; and the hierarchy of hetero/homo still exists. Most importantly, the notion that "sexuality" is a truth regime – that it says something important about us – remains.

Judith Butler

Just as Foucault gave queer theory its understanding and critique of sexuality and sexual identity, Judith Butler contributed a new understanding of gender and its relationship to anatomical sex, and sexuality. In *Gender Trouble* (1990) and *Bodies that Matter* (1993), Butler rejects the standard sociological and feminist assertion that first comes anatomical sex and then come the gender norms that the culture ascribes to the categories of male and female. Instead, gender – the discursive regime of norms, performances, and knowledge supported by institutional power – actually creates the binary gender order. Bodies for Butler do not preexist society but are constructed by it through performances. These bodies are constructed by the repeated performance of certain cultural signs and conventions of gender and sexuality. We perform a corporeal style using imitations and idealizations of what we think it means to be a man or woman within the range of cultural representations of sex in the current gender regime.

In Western culture, the gender binary is simultaneously a sexual binary. For Butler, these binaries create and reproduce patriarchy as well as heteronormativity. Learning about gender or engaging in the repeated, always incomplete, and anxious performance of maleness and femaleness becomes recognizable mainly within the context of the heterosexual idiom. Unlike other theories of sexuality that assert a core self able to exercise agency independent of social forces, Butler's analysis of gender performativity rejects that notion and asserts a radical social subjectivity of the self. In other words, rather than the expression of a core self or an essence that defines the individual, identities are the effect of the repeated performance of certain cultural signs and conventions. There is no original from which gender and sexual identities are derived. In this view, sexual and gender identities are "performatively constituted by the very expressions of gender and sexuality thought to produce them" (Corber and Valocchi, 2003: 4). The conscious and unconscious adherence to the norms and cultural signifiers of sexuality and gender both bring the subject into being and constrain the identity enactments of that subject (Butler, 1993).

Sexuality and Transnationalism

A final theoretical framework focuses on sexuality and transnationalism. In some sense it is an extension of queer theory in that it starts from a critique of identity and from the notion that heteronormativity is built into the assumption of the hetero/homo binary. It also shares queer theory's assumptions about the normative and nonnormative configurations of sex, gender, and sexuality in understanding social subjectivity and power. Unlike the "first wave" of queer theory, which was focused on disrupting the domestic gay subject, this "next wave" is focused on the transnational. Of course, "globalizing sexuality" was always part of the queer project, part of the larger attempt to critique identity (Povenelli and Chauncey, 1999). For example, the first wave of queer transnational research reminded us that these categories of sexual identity are Western categories. In many Latin cultures, to take one example, sexual subjectivity is not based on sex of object choice but on the scripted sexual role (i.e., active/passive, masculine/feminine) that one plays in the sexual act, again, pointing to the need to interrogate the gendering of sexuality (Almaguer, 1993; Kulick, 1998). Research in that same vein by Lionel Cantu, *Queer Migrations: Sexuality, US Citizenship, and Border Crossings* (2006) on Mexican and Mexican-American men not only shows the Western bias in our sexual categories of gay and straight but more importantly shows how global processes – the flow of labor, commodities, consumption, tourism, and culture – in conjunction with local norms of sexuality and gender shape sexual subjectivities, migration patterns, state policy regarding borders, and definitions of citizen and alien.

This research moves a queer framework in a slightly different direction: from using queer theory as a tool for interrogating normative and nonnormative alignments of sex, gender, and sexuality, to using it as a vehicle for analyzing other social formations like transnationalism, neocolonialism, and diaspora. Understood in this way, and given the above discussion, queer theory incorporates some of the best insights and analyses from intersectional theory about the importance of racialized, classed, and gendered discourses in the construction of the nation, colonialism, postcolonialism, and global processes of capitalism. As David Eng, Judith Halberstam, and Jose Esteban Munoz (2005) state in the introduction to a special volume of *Social Text*, entitled "What's Queer about Queer Studies Now?":

> Ever vigilant to the fact that sexuality is intersectional, not extraneous to other modes of difference, and calibrated to a firm understanding of queer as a political metaphor without a fixed referent, a renewed queer studies insists on a broadened consideration of the late-twentieth-century global crises that have configured historical relations among political economies, the geopolitics of war and terror, and national manifestations of sexual, racial, and gendered hierarchies. (2005: 1)

Queer-of -color theorists come to a similar position, with analyses that closely map the ways in which a rights-based understanding of sexual identity has been used by neoliberal states to promote military expansion abroad, and Islamophobia and the neglect and persecution of people of color at home (El-Tayib, 2011; Ferguson, 2004; Reddy, 2011). In an excellent summary of the queer-of-color critique, Ferguson and Hong (2012) remind queer theorists of their legacy in the intersectional analysis of women of color and challenge them to incorporate race, racism, and racialized projects of state-building into their analyses. Put in terms of the sociological study of sexuality, it challenges sociologists to see sexuality more as an independent variable than a dependent variable and as intimately connected to other modes of marginalization and difference in society.

An excellent example of this scholarship is the work of Evren Savci (2011, 2016). Her ethnographic research on queer activism in Turkey reveals less about identity deconstruction and more about the workings of power in this Islamic nation, precariously and contentiously situated between the secular and the West on the one hand and the religious and the East on the other. It examines the use of sexuality in constructing the nation state, specifically the role of the regulation of sexual "perversions," the pursuit of heterosexual reproductivity, and the utilization of a liberal discourse of human rights (Savci, 2011: 5). Her work nicely illustrates the starting points and goals of a sociological queer theory of transnationalism: "As subaltern, or abject, queers are not simply evidence of 'deviance,' inequality, and/or difference, but rather tell us about the regimes of truth that govern our lives – 'truths' about neo-liberalism, modernization, secularization, citizenship and legitimacy, and national identity" (Savci, 2011: 6). Somewhat ironically, and perhaps with good intellectual effect, this theoretical framework both moves away from sexuality as a separate object of study and moves toward an incorporation of sexuality as a knowledge and power formation that operates at many different levels of social life and on many different large-scale processes of modernity and postmodernity in a global world.

Conclusion

This discussion of globalization takes us full circle: from the micro to the macro, and from an examination of how the social affects the sexual to how the sexual affects the social. The scope of this review, moreover, reminds us of the daunting nature of the challenge posed at the outset: to "pin down" the slippery nature of sexuality. Perhaps a more fruitful or intellectually productive challenge would be to allow sexuality to travel where it will, use our theoretical tools to track its migration, and be surprised about what it reveals as it bumps into our psyches, identities, communities, institutions, and national and transnational cultures.

References

Almaguer, Tomas. 1993. "Chicano Men: A Cartography of Homosexual Identity and Behavior." In Henry Abelove, Michele Aina Barale, David Halperin (eds.), *The Lesbian and Gay Studies Reader* (pp. 255–273). New York: Routledge.

Brubaker, Rogers. 2016. "The Dolezal Affair: Race, Gender, and Micropolitics of Identity." *Ethnic and Racial Studies* 39(3): 414–448.

Butler, Judith. 1990. *Gender Trouble: Feminism and the Subversion of Identity.* New York: Routledge.

1993. *Bodies That Matter: On the Discursive Limits of "Sex".* New York: Routledge.

Canaday, Margot. 2009. *The Straight State: Sexuality and Citizenship in Twentieth Century America.* Princeton, NJ: Princeton University Press.

Cantu, Lionel. 2006. *Queer Migrations: Sexuality, US Citizenship, and Border Crossings.* Minneapolis, MN: University of Minnesota Press.

Chauncey, George. 1994. *Gay New York: Gender, Urban Culture, and the Making of the Gay Male World, 1890–1940.* New York: Basic Books.

Chodorow. Nancy. 1978. *The Reproduction of Mothering: Psychoanalysis and the Sociology of Gender.* Berkeley, CA: University of California Press.

Collins, Patricia Hill. 1991. *Black Feminist Thought: Knowledge, Consciousness, and the Politics of Empowerment.* New York: Routledge.

2006. *Black Sexual Politics: African Americans, Gender, and the New Racism.* New York: Routledge.

Corber, Robert J., and Stephen Valocchi. 2003. *Queer Studies: An Interdisciplinary Reader.* Malden, MA: Blackwell.

Crenshaw, Kimberle. 1995. "Mapping the Margins: Intersectionality, Identity Politics, and Violence against Women of Color." In Kimberle Crenshaw, Neil Gotanda, Gary Peller, and Kendall Thomas (eds.), *Critical Race Theory: The Key Writings That Formed the Movement* (pp. 357–383). New York: The New Press.

Dean, Tim. 2009. *Unlimited Intimacy: Reflection on the Subculture of Barebacking.* London: University of Chicago Press.

Dreger, Alice Domurat. 1998. *Hermaphrodites and the Medical Invention of Sex.* Cambridge, MA: Harvard University Press.

Eisenstein, Zillah. 1980. "Capitalist Patriarchy and the Case of Socialist Feminism." *Feminist Studies* 6(3): 571–582.

El-Tayib, Fatima. 2011. *European Others: Queering Ethnicity in Post-Racial Europe.* Minneapolis, MN: University of Minnesota Press.

Elliot, Anthony. 2001. "Sexualities: Social Theory and the Crisis of Identity." In George Ritzer and Barry Smart (eds.), *Handbook of Social Theory* (pp. 428–438). London: Sage.

Eng, David, with Judith Halberstam and Jose Esteban Munoz. 2005. "What's Queer about Queer Studies Now?" *Social Text* 84–85 (3–4): 1–17.

Farrar, James, and Sonja Dale. 2014. "Sexless in Shanghai: Gendered Mobility Strategies in a Transnational Sexual Field." In Adam Isaiah Green (ed.), *Sexual Fields: Toward a Sociology of Sexual Life* (pp. 143–169). Chicago, IL: University of Chicago Press.

Ferguson, Roderick. 2004. *Aberrations in Black: Toward a Queer of Color Critique.* Minneapolis, MN: University of Minnesota Press.

Ferguson, Roderick, and Grace Kyungwon Hong. 2012. "The Sexual and Racial Contradictions of Neoliberalism." *Journal of Homosexuality* 59(7): 1057–1064.

Foucault, Michel. 1980. *The History of Sexuality. Volume 1: An Introduction.* New York: Vintage Books.

Freud, Sigmund. 1975. *Three Theories of Sexuality.* Translated and revised by James Strachey. New York: Basic Books.

Gagnon, John, and William Simon. 1973. *Sexual Conduct: The Social Sources of Human Sexuality.* Chicago, IL: Aldine.

Gamson, Joshua. 2013. "The Normal Science of Queerness: LGBT Sociology Books in the Twenty-First Century." *Contemporary Sociology* 42(6): 801–808.

Gamson, Joshua, and Dawne Moon. 2004. "The Sociology of Sexualities: Queer and Beyond." *Annual Review of Sociology* 30: 47–64.

Ghaziani, Amin. 2017. *Sex Cultures.* Malden, MA: Polity Press.

Giddens, Anthony. 1992. *Transformation of Intimacy: Sexuality, Love and Eroticism in Modern Societies.* Stanford, CA: Stanford University Press.

Green, Adam Isaiah. 2014. *Sexual Fields: Toward a Sociology of Sexual Life*. Chicago, IL: University of Chicago Press.

Hull, Gloria T., Patricia Scott Bell, and Barbara Smith (eds.). 1982. *All the Women Are White, All the Blacks are Men, But Some of Us Are Brave*. Old Westbury, NY: The Feminist Press.

Jagose, Annamarie. 1996. *Queer Theory: An Introduction*. New York: New York University Press.

Kulick, Don. 1998. *Sex, Gender, and Culture Among Brazilian Transgendered Prostitutes*. Chicago, IL: University of Chicago Press.

Lorber, Judith. 1996. "Beyond the Binaries: Depolarizing the Categories of Sex, Gender, and Sexuality." *Sociological Inquiry* 66(2): 143–155.

McIntosh, Mary. 1968. "The Homosexual Role." *Social Problems* 16(2): 182–192.

Moore, Mignon. 2011. *Invisible Families: Gay Identities, Relationships, and Motherhood among Black Women*. Berkeley, CA: University of California Press.

Nagel, Joane. 2003. *Race, Ethnicity, and Sexuality: Intimate Intersections; Forbidden Frontiers*. New York: Oxford University Press.

Pascoe, C. J. 2007. *Dude, You're a Fag: Masculinity and Sexuality in High School*. Berkeley, CA: University of California Press.

Phillips, Layli. 2005. "Deconstructing 'Down Low' Discourse: The Politics of Sexuality, Gender, Race, AIDS, and Anxiety." *Journal of African American Studies* 9(2): 3–15.

Plummer, Ken. 1975. *Sexual Stigma: An Interactionist Account*. London: Routledge.

Povenelli, Elizabeth A., and George Chauncey. 1999. "Thinking Sexuality Transnationally: An Introduction." *GLQ: A Journal of Lesbian and Gay Studies* 5(4): 439–449.

Reddy, Chandan, 2011. *Freedom with Violence: Race, Sexuality, and the US State*. Durham, NC: Duke University Press.

Rich, Adrienne. 1980. "Compulsory Heterosexuality and Lesbian Existence." *Signs* 5(4): 631–660.

Rubin, Gayle. 1984. "Thinking Sex: Notes for a Radical Theory of the Politics of Sexuality." In Carole Vance (ed.), *Pleasure and Danger: Exploring Female Sexuality* (pp. 267–319). Boston, MA: Routledge & Kegan Paul.

Ryan, Barbara. 1992. *Feminism and the Women's Movement: Dynamics of Change in Social Movement Ideology and Activism*. New York: Routledge.

Savci, Evren. 2011. "Queer in Translation: Paradoxes of Westernization and Sexual Others in the Turkish Nation." Dissertation, Department of Sociology, University of Southern California.

    2016. "Who Speaks the Language of Queer Politics? Western Knowledge, Politico-Cultural Capital, and Belonging Among Urban Queers in Turkey." *Sexualities* 19(3): 369–387.

Schlit, Kristen, and Laurel Westbrook. 2009. "Doing Gender, Doing Heteronormativity: 'Gender Normals,' Transgender People, and the Social Maintenance of Heterosexuality." *Gender & Society* 23(4): 440–464.

Seidman, Steven. 1996. "Introduction." In Steven Seidman (eds.), *Queer Theory/Sociology*. Cambridge, MA: Blackwell.

    2015. *The Social Construction of Sexuality*. New York: W. W. Norton.

Valentine, David. 2007. *Imagining Transgender: An Ethnography of a Category*. Durham, NC: Duke University Press.

Vance, Carole S. 1984. *Pleasure and Danger: Exploring Female Sexuality*. Boston, MA: Routledge & Kegan Paul.

Ward, Jane. 2008. *Respectably Queer: Diversity Culture in LGBT Activist Organizations.* Nashville, TX: University of Tennessee Press.

2015. *Not Gay: Sex between Straight White Men.* New York: New York University Press.

Warner, Michael. 1993. *Free of a Queer Planet: Queer Politics and Social Theory.* Minneapolis, MN: University of Minnesota Press.

Weeks, Jeffrey. 1985. *Sexuality and its Discontents: Meanings, Myths, and Modern Sexualities.* Boston, MA: Routledge & Kegan Paul.

Weiss, Margot. 2011. *Techniques of Pleasure: BDSM and Circuits of Sexuality.* Durham, NC: Duke University Press.

15 Multiculturalism

Christian Joppke

The *Oxford English Dictionary* (*OED*) defines "multiculturalism" as "the character-istics of a multicultural society" and "(also) the policy or process whereby the distinctive identities of the cultural groups within such a society are maintained or supported." This nearly circular definition still gives away two different meanings of "multiculturalism": as descriptive term for the presence of several "cultural groups" within one society, which in a context of globalization and ever-increasing interna-tional migration has become the dominant reality throughout the world; but also as denoting a "policy," not to counteract, but to "maintain or support" this condition. In fact, the *OED* entry attributes one of the first uses of the term "multiculturalism" to the Canadian "policy of multiculturalism within a bilingual framework." It was introduced by Prime Minister Pierre Trudeau in 1971 to take the heat out of the emergent Quebecois nationalism and anglophone vs. francophone rift through pluralizing it with positively valued and state-supported immigrant diversity. Unsurprisingly, the French-speaking nationalists would never warm to the Canadian multiculturalism policy, and still have not done so to date.

Note, thus, that the historically first reference point of multiculturalism (as policy) is immigrant diversity, while subsequently it also came to denote the claims and policies surrounding national-minority and indigenous groups. Again emblemized by the Canadian situation, the irony is that the strongest policy in the multiculturalism arsenal, which is self-government and special political representation rights, came to be attrib-uted to territorial minorities (both national and indigenous), while these groups have from the start distanced themselves from or even outright rejected "multiculturalism" for diluting their much further-going, nationalist-cum-secessionist ambitions. Conversely, "multiculturalism" came to be associated mainly with accommodating immigrant diversity, particularly as it moved from Canada and Australia (its second official home since the early 1970s) to Western Europe, one to two decades later.[1] While immigrant-targeting multiculturalism policies have everywhere taken a much weaker, integrationist shape and direction, they came to be almost instantly attacked for affecting the exact opposite, segregation and the creation of "parallel societies." Hence the much-touted "crisis" or even "retreat" of multiculturalism, which in fact has been comprised of several crises and retreats (see Joppke, 2017a : 1–2), and which has strangely played out where multiculturalism has remained the least extreme, in the domain of immigrant integration. By contrast, few if any have ever questioned the much stronger provisions for national and indigenous minorities, but minorities who have nonetheless disliked the "multiculturalism" label for not going far enough to satisfy their particular concerns.

The heart of the notorious unhappiness about multiculturalism is its conflict with the principle of nationalism, defined by Ernest Gellner as the norm that "ethnic boundaries should not cut across political ones" (1983: 1), and which is the foundational principle of the modern nation state. The violation of the global nationalism norm can at best only be tolerated by those groups that are in principle ready to form their own state, which by definition are not immigrants, but which at the same time tend to deem their claims too special and too dramatic to see them reconciled by the pluralism-minded "multiculturalism" label.

The cited *OED* entry omits a third meaning of "multiculturalism," next to demographic fact and policy, which is within the realm of political theory and philosophy. Here the word refers to a heterogeneous strand of thinking that either rejects or seeks to amend liberalism for a context of cultural pluralism. Liberalism, if we recall, is the dominant political ideology of Western societies, which stipulates that individuals and their universalist claims of freedom and equality are the basic unit of the social order and their protection the goal of law and public policy. Multiculturalism moves "groups" into the picture of a society of individuals, arguing that culturally marked "minorities" face certain difficulties and disadvantages that "majorities" do not know, and which require us to amend or even to go beyond the individualistic and universalistic precepts of liberalism.

John Rawls famously wrote that "justice is the first virtue of social institutions, as truth is of systems of thought" (1971: 3). Multiculturalism theories articulate what "justice" might mean from the point of view of minorities, which in Rawls' culture-blind picture of society as "self-sufficient association of persons" (1971: 4) has been systematically left out. Will Kymlicka (1995) offers a representative perspective, reflecting the view that multiculturalism theories are about "group-differentiated rights" that go beyond the standard individual rights of the liberal society of individuals. If "rights," "justice," or "liberalism" (particularly its limits) are central concepts and preoccupations of multiculturalism theories, one immediately understands why *social* theory, which has never dwelled in this normative idiom but prefers the nonnormative language of "action," "structure," or "change," has largely been absent from the multiculturalism debates.

As we shall see, multiculturalism theories come in many variants and are differently capacious as to who is included and who not. However, is there anything that multicultural claims have in common?[2] Few would disagree that multiculturalism, whatever it is, is always a politics of identity (often contrasted with a "politics of redistribution"; see the critique by Fraser, 1995). But what is "identity"? The mark of identity is to be simultaneously ascribed and chosen. "Ascribed" is deliberately placed first. Anthony Appiah (2005: xiv) astutely observes that "when asked *who* we are, we are being asked *what* we are as well." The notion of identity refers to persons as "kinds of person" (2005: 65), who live their lives "*as* men and *as* women, *as* gay and *as* straight people, *as* Ghanaians and a*s* Americans, *as* blacks and *as* whites" (2005: xiv). The claims raised in this respect are "ethical claims," pertaining to the good life, as against "moral claims" proper, which pertain to how to treat other people (from which, however, he draws the negative conclusion that third parties cannot be bound to "respect" these claims).[3] Appositely placing the ascriptive moment first, Appiah holds that identity categories are brought into being by the "creation of labels" and "identifications" (2005: 65–66), that is, by external attribution. Only in a second step do they come to be adopted and internalized by the individual herself. In other words, rather than choose an identity category, people find themselves in it. Bhikhu Parekh (2000: 162) argues similarly that the "cultures" that are mobilized in multiculturalism are involuntary: "We do not join but are born into them" (see also Iris Young, 1990, 46, who uses Heidegger's word *Geworfenheit* (thrownness) to mark the condition of her multicultural "social groups"). The assumption is that people identify most with those aspects of their lives that are not entirely chosen by them but that arise through external attribution, often in the form of discrimination – there is an inner relationship between multiculturalism and antidiscrimination, even though in terms of policy they may be far apart from one another (see Joppke, 2018a). These attributions then color most other aspects of a person's life, constituting her "master status" (Hughes, 1945). A compelling account is provided by Howard Becker's "labelling theory": "One will be identified as a deviant first, before other identifications are made" (in Epstein, 1987: 31). As a result, the management of "stigma" comes to preoccupy the individual, becoming her "identity" (Goffman, 1963). According to this model, in which the unmarked dominant majority doesn't really have an "identity," identity is at first negative before it may be positively revalued.

But qua "identity," an identity is also always chosen because it cannot but be a self-reflective, conscious part of the individual. Identity is never implicit or dormant. It requires what 1960s feminists called "consciousness-raising." An identity is always one from the individual's own point of view, who could equally see or define herself otherwise. Short of choice, we are merely dealing with identification by others but not with identity. Relating both aspects of identity, Rogers Brubaker cogently observes: "(T)he opposition between chosenness and givenness is a constitutive and generative tension (of the contemporary politics of identity and difference)" (2016: 434).

The first part of this chapter lays out three major strands of multiculturalism theory, distinguishing between "communitarian," "radical," and "liberal" variants (for more variants, see Song, 2016). Commensurate with the multiple nature of the beast, the second step moves from theory to policy, briefly contrasting the North American (nation-building) with the Western European (more narrowly immigrant-integrating) variants of multiculturalism. Particular attention is given to two developing into a politically discredited multiculturalism, which are "interculturalism" and "diversity." In a third and final step I argue that a thin, individual-centered form of multiculturalism is indispensable to a liberal society, though many will hesitate to call it "multiculturalism" at all.

Multiculturalism Theories: Communitarian, Radical, Liberal

Communitarian

The Canadian philosopher Charles Taylor (1994) delivered the central logo of all multiculturalisms to be a "politics of recognition," and more precisely still, a "politics of difference." He grounds "recognition" in the dialogical, mutually dependent nature of the human species, theorized from Hegel to Mead. Yet he adds a twist in making it a distinctly modern preoccupation, after the demise of the status-fixing feudal order. Moreover, the modern politics of recognition comes in two variants, as a Kantian insistence on the equal dignity of each individual, but also a Herderian insistence on having recognized what makes each individual different from all others.[4] Intriguingly, the second presupposes the first, but also tends to denounce it. However, this paradox came to full blossom only after a game-changing event: colonialism. As Taylor put it, colonialism's "imposition of some cultures on others," colloquially speaking the oppression of the Rest by the West, is multiculturalism's point of departure. Taylor's well-chosen protagonist is the Caribbean psychiatrist and intellectual Frantz Fanon, who sought to liberate colonized people by their "mock(ing)," "insult(ing)," and "vomit(ing)" of the "white man's values" (Fanon, 1963: 43). There is evidently more violence than recognition in Fanon's liberation story, but it has set the agenda for multiculturalism as rejection of the supremacy of "Western values" and having Westerners concede the "equal worth" of the cultures of the colonized (Taylor, 1994: 68).

However, the empirical centerpiece of Taylor's *Programmschrift* is not anticolonialism but a defense of Quebec's "distinct society" project and of its controversial prioritization of the "importance of cultural survival" (Taylor, 1994: 62) over the province's immigrants' interest to have their children educated in the English language, as not just North America's but the global lingua franca. If Quebec's *survivance* is depicted here as an instance of multiculturalism, this multiculturalism is also indistinguishable from old-fashioned nationalism, and Taylor's defense of a special deal for Quebec within an asymmetric federalism is multiculturalist and nationalist in tandem.

Taylor's account of multiculturalism fits with his communitarian philosophy, according to which the group is ontologically prior to the individual. Yet it also contains some liberal elements, such as his insistence that the equal worth of other cultures is at best "presumption" but cannot be "actually judged" on demand (1994: 68). It is no wonder that other authors have sought to resolve the tension in Taylor's communitarian synthesis in either direction, radical or liberal.

Radical

Drawing more on feminism than anticolonialism, Iris Marion Young's radical multiculturalism still starts from the same Fanonian premise of "oppression," which is at its most pernicious when white male power "parade(s) as universal" (1990: 10). While there are many types of oppression in her scenario, the one triggering the "politics of difference," which aims at special group representation rights, is "cultural imperialism." Defined as "universalization of a dominant group's experience and culture, and its establishment as the norm," it exercises power over a specific kind of group, which she calls "social groups." They stand out from other groups through nondominant "cultural forms, practices, or way of life." As the membership in social groups is not chosen but ascribed in stigmatizing intent by the dominant group, Young associates it with "body and feeling," experienced as "epidermalizing of their world" (1990: 123). A body count of the victims of "racism, sexism, homophobia, ageism, and ableism" (1990: 130) paradoxically arrives at 80 to 90 percent of contemporary Americans.

In principle, Young's radical politics of difference rejects "inclusion," because "universal citizenship" appears in its perspective as group power in disguise (see Young, 1989). The model is Black Power and the Brown, Red, or Yellow Power that followed in its wake (Young, 1990: ch. 6). The "whole group" has to move, in "separate organizations" (1990: 167), aiming at nothing less than "cultural revolution" (1990: 153f). But then, even "differentiated citizenship" and "group representation" is still "citizenship" and "representation," whose thrust cannot but be inclusive, with "participation and inclusion possible" as the goal (1989: 273). This flatly contradicts her radical critique of universal citizenship and the Marx-Fanonian framework of repudiating a repressive totality. Only, what alternative is there, particularly for groups that cannot go the separatist road, like women, gays, or the disabled?

A similarly non-liberal, radical multiculturalism has been proposed by Tariq Modood, a rare sociologist in the guild of multiculturalism theorists, but one with a formative background in political theory. Its starting point is the experience of "negative difference" that stands to be "transform(ed) into something for which civic respect can be won" (2007: 41). The model is "race," whereby Modood recovers Fanonian anticolonialism, later borrowed by the American Black Power movement, in which a stigma is revalued as a source of pride. However, for Modood, today perhaps Britain's foremost Muslim intellectual, there are a "plurality of racisms," including the "cultural racism" of "Islamophobia," which call for "customized (arrangements) to meet diverse ... vulnerabilities, needs and priorities" (2007: 46). He thus puts his finger on the importance of religion, which had long been ignored within a color-coded Anglo-American multiculturalism. This multiculturalism is radical in that it refutes mere "integration," asking instead for arrangements that "work differently for different groups" (2007: 48). Modood's quest for "recognition of group difference" captures the orthodox core of multiculturalism, as something that makes it different and distinct from liberalism – much like his intellectual doyen, Bhikhu Parekh, for whom liberalism is merely a "substantive doctrine advocating a specific ... way of life" (2000: 14), Modood surely would not like to be called a "liberal."

However, a strange counterpoint to Modood-Parekhian radical multiculturalism is their parallel insistence that multiculturalism is also a "nation-building project" (Modood, 2007: 147), and one that both pushes for and requires "a plural and inclusive view of national identity" (Parekh, 2000: 236). As the universalist pretensions of liberalism are rejected by them, they both advocate a culturally inflected national identity, which must be more than mere "constitutional patriotism" or "cosmopolitanism" to have "emotional pull," says Modood (2007: 149). Again, its nationalist other is never far away from multiculturalism.

Liberal

The mark of "liberal multiculturalism," whose foremost protagonist is the Canadian philosopher, Will Kymlicka (1995), is to place the claims of the individual above the claims of the group – therefore the adjective "liberal" is attached to it. Culture is not valued here for its own sake, as in Taylor's communitarian defense of the "survival" of francophone culture in Quebec, but for what it does to produce free and equal individuals. Indeed, this multiculturalism is straightforwardly grounded in liberalism's two core principles, freedom and equality.

With respect to freedom, Kymlicka's point is that meaningful choice presupposes a "societal culture," which "provides its members with meaningful ways of life across the full range of human activities" (1995: 76), the prototype being the nation. This dramatically narrows the range of multicultural claimants: women or LGBT people and lifestyle groups are not included, because they are not an "intergenerational community, more or less institutionally complete" (1995: 18). But even immigrants, who are dispersed and lack a distinct territory, do not have an own societal culture, and their only possibility is to "integrate" into majority society. Kymlicka famously argued that immigrants, qua choosing to leave their home country, have "waived" the right to their own societal culture. At most they can ask for "polyethnic rights," which assures them fair terms of integration – the model for this is allowing Sikhs to wear turbans when serving in the Canadian Royal Mounted Police, which signals an integrationist blending of difference with retaining a conventional (though inclusive) national identity. With respect to immigrants, there is no room in liberal multiculturalism for separation and parallel societies, which is the common target in the political attack on multiculturalism. Only national minorities and indigenous groups, who did not exercise choice by moving across borders but, on the contrary, saw the borders of states move above their heads, are attributed stronger "self-government" rights, with the risk of secession always present. The stark gradation between immigrant and national-minority/indigenous rights, weak for the former and strong for the latter, is sanely realistic, also proving Kymlicka to be a so-called "luck egalitarian" (see Song, 2016), the dominant strand in liberal political philosophy that narrows the range of distributive justice to matters over which individuals cannot exercise choice. However, it raises the question why immigrants should have any (if weaker) special "right" to have their culture accommodated. Aren't the "exemptions" from general laws that are granted to them in reality universal individual rights (in the Sikh Mountie's case, religious liberty rights that are due to any citizen and resident in the state), and aren't "special benefits" that may be granted to them (like funding for ethnic organizations) more in the nature of discretionary policies that may be prudent in some contexts but not in others?

Still, in conceiving of culture as a "context of choice" (1989: 166) that is required for individual autonomy, Kymlicka squarely places the concern of the individual over that of the group. He thus escapes the caustic charge of "species conservation" that a liberal Jürgen Habermas (1994: 130) had raised against the communitarian multiculturalism theory of Charles Taylor, and which is a charge that has haunted multiculturalism in general.

With respect to liberalism's second principle, equality, Kymlicka argues that even the liberal state, as hard as it may try, can never quite dissociate itself from majority culture. Witness the inevitable choice of official language, public holidays, and the decorum of flags and hymns that usually reflect the preferences of the majority: "The state unavoidably promotes certain cultural identities and thereby disadvantages others" (1995: 108). The protection of majority culture isn't a problem per se, because an intact "societal culture" is required for people to be meaningfully free. "Liberal states exist," says Kymlicka, "also to protect people's cultural membership" (1995: 125). But justice commands that the same privileges are granted to minorities in the state. Like Modood or Parekh, though on much firmer theoretical ground, Kymlicka is simultaneously liberal nationalist and multiculturalist. "The orthodox liberal view about the right of states to determine who has citizenship rests on the same principles which justify group-differentiated citizenship within states" (1995: 124). In other words, if citizenship is "an inherently group-differentiated thing," liberal justice requires acknowledging this groupness further down the line.

Kymlicka's important move in his "equality" defense of multiculturalism is to reject "benign neglect," which has been the liberal state's classic stance toward cultural difference. Benign neglect may have been possible for religion, he argues, but it is not an option with respect to language and ethnicity: "The state can (and should) replace religious oaths in courts with secular oaths, but it cannot replace the use of English in courts with no language" (1995: 111). This is a powerful argument that seems to wipe out the possibility of liberal state neutrality as a means of obliterating the necessity for multiculturalism.

However, one might question the degree to which contemporary states are still strongly nationalist and nation-building, at least in the West. If minority rights are a concession to the nationalism of the majority, or rather to a Gellnerian nation-building state that Kymlicka sees running at full throttle (1995: 76f), a questioning of these assumptions removes the "equality" case for minority rights. But there are good empirical reasons to do this:

- With respect to immigrants, Western states have long abandoned the goal of "assimilation." The new approach is "integration," which conceives of immigrant incorporation as a "two-way process" and abdicates the necessity for immigrants to change their cultural identities (for Western Europe, see Council of the European Union, 2004). Not even the new era of mandatory and state-tested "civic integration" has changed much in this respect (see Goodman, 2014). Of course, "assimilation," in the sense of making immigrants invisible as such, cannot but be the endpoint of successful incorporation. But contemporary liberal states have few and fewer possibilities to enforce it directly – the new under-standing of assimilation is as "intransitive" process, no longer as a "transitive" project (see Brubaker, 2000).
- With respect to citizenship, it is an anachronism to call it an "inherently group-differentiated notion" (Kymlicka, 1995: 124). In Western Europe, citizenship has become distinctly less nationalistic in the past decades. This is the com-bined result of Europeanization, which reduces the possibilities of member states to privilege their own citizens over other member-state citizens, and the result of a liberalization of access to citizenship at member-state level – ele-ments of it are the rise of conditional *jus soli* citizenship, the toleration of dual

citizenship, and lowered thresholds for naturalization that has become more rule-of-law and less discretionary than in the past (for an overview, see Joppke, 2010: ch. 2).

- A third indicator of the lesser nation-building capacities of contemporary liberal states is the general retreat of morality laws, by means of which states once tried to impose a uniform, most often "Christian" way of life on all members of society (see Frank, Camp, and Boutcher, 2010). The current global victory of same-sex marriage shows an increasing acknowledgment of lifestyle individualism and pluralism in law and public policy.

If the nation is an increasingly multiplex and individualized thing, with less possibility for the state to enforce homogeneity, the equality rationale for minority rights in Kymlicka's theory loses traction. More than being an explicit claim on the part of minorities, to be accommodated by special provisions beyond and apart from the general law, multiculturalism has ever more become a legal-constitutional necessity (see Joppke, 2017b).

Curiously, Alan Patten's (2014) reformulation of liberal multiculturalism as grounded in the principle of liberal neutrality is entirely uninformed by these developments, which, indeed, might lend empirical plausibility to this theoretical choice. Instead, his immediately acclaimed *Equal Recognition* is exclusively a philosophical exercise to show that "liberal principles do mandate specific minority cultural rights." He makes two departures from Kymlicka's liberal multiculturalism, not so much to refute the latter as to put it on firmer theoretical grounds. The first is a "social lineage" account of culture, according to which culture is "shared subjection to a common formative context," a "distinct process of socialization" (2014: 39). This is to fend off one of the commonest charges against multiculturalism of all colors, not just the liberal kind (though here it hurts most), that it "essentializes" culture as a distinct, particular whole, untouched by internal variation and external overlap. By contrast, variation and overlap are compatible with a thin and sociological understanding of culture as shared socializing institutions and experiences, which obliterate the flawed assumption that all of its members think alike and value the same things. The "lineage account" also helps distinguish cultural loss from cultural change: "shared subjection to a common formative context" renders plausible why Quebecois culture did not disappear with the "Quiet Revolution" of the 1960s, while its content changed dramatically (for instance, from Catholic to secular).

Patten's second and really central innovation is to drop the pairing of liberal multiculturalism and liberal nationalism, that is, the argument that nationalism and nation-building require multiculturalism as a compensation. Instead, neutrality is to do the work of justifying multiculturalism. If the liberal state wants to be liberal, it "ought to be neutral in its treatment of majority and minority alike" (2014: xi). In short, the liberal state cannot be a nation state: "Liberal values exclude the notion of a *Favoritvolk*, a privileged religious or cultural group that is given special concern or respect by the state" (2014: 28). Instead, liberal neutrality requires extending "equal recognition to each culture" (2014: 27), all the way up and all the way down. This sounds logical and fantastic at the same time. Patten's anemic view of the "generic liberal-democratic state" has been nicely satirized by Kymlicka: "(T)he state is like a publisher who would prefer to publish without privileging any particular font, but regrettably there is no universal font, and so must sometimes choose between, say, Helvetica and Palatino. This is however simply a technical choice, unrelated to the core values or core identity of the state ... Many of us happen to use Helvetica here, but this has no implications for who we are, or for our political values or aspirations, and so we are happy to give pro-rated funding to users of Palatino" (Kymlicka, 2018: 89). This is how the liberal state should work on paper, but it is not how it operates in the real world. In reality, the users of Helvetica self-define as "Helveticans," and more and more of them are not just unhappy to extend "pro-rated funding" to the "Palatinos," but would prefer them to get lost. [5]

While Patten's grounding of "liberal culturalism" in the principle of neutrality may appear unrealistic, its empirical application to a world of immigrants and national minorities looks much like Kymlicka would have it (see Patten, 2014: ch. 8). He adopts and refines Kymlicka's voluntary vs. nonvoluntary binary to attribute lesser rights to immigrants than to national minorities, and comes to even more hard-nosed conclusions. Citing the example of the gravely ill, who are still expected to consent to the surgery that is their only chance to escape death, Patten considerably widens the scope of "voluntariness," so that even refugees might still be considered to exercise choice (and thus waiving the right to their culture) (Patten, 2014: 278) – something that Kymlicka explicitly negated (1995: 98–99). And "members of the receiving society do have a legitimate interest in requiring that immigrants waive certain cultural rights as a condition of entry into the state on a permanent basis" (Patten, 2014: 281). There is a peculiar disjunction in Patten's multiculturalism theory between an unworldly conception of the state as not beholden to a majority and its cultural imprint and an extreme realism in practice, which raises the question where the "multiculturalism" in all this is.

Patten's important move is still to resurrect "liberal neutrality" as a principle to accommodate diversity, even if one may disagree with its realization. Previously, many liberal philosophers, and all multiculturalists, held it impossible for the state to be neutral, be it with respect to the "intentions" or the "effects" of its policies, at a minimum on the argument that as liberalism is not value-free, policy under its sway could never be "neutral." To this position Patten plausibly retorts that "liberal neutrality" is a second-order, "downstream" value, which presupposes a commitment to the justifiable first-order liberal value of autonomy and "self-determination": "It is *because* one accepts certain nonneutral values that one thinks that, in some limited domain, the state ought to adopt a stance of neutrality" (2014: 109).

The paradox is that Patten engages liberal neutrality for justifying a multicultural politics of recognition. Might one not argue, on the opposite side, that neutrality obliterates the need for recognition and thus of multiculturalism? This is the conclusion drawn by Peter Balint (2017), who also recovers a closely related liberal concept that had been similarly debunked by the multiculturalists as incapable of accommodating diversity: toleration. Multiculturalists have snubbed toleration for being premised on the rejection of what is being tolerated, but forbearing to act on it. Denigration and power, however withheld in this particular instance, is thus held to be the truth of toleration. As the Muslim intellectual Tariq Ramadan put it, "toleration is intellectual charity on the part of the powerful" (in Balint, 2017: 23). Or in the equally dismissive words of political philosopher Wendy Brown, "all objects of tolerance are marked as deviant, marginal, or undesirable by virtue of being tolerated" (2006: 14). Tolerance is thus an "act of power," not "respect" (2006: 25). However, responds Balint (2017: 23), "forbearance tolerance" is a specific form of toleration that does not exhaust its possibilities; the more general form of toleration is based on "indifference" to what is being tolerated. This is the meaning of toleration when, for instance, Sweden is called a "tolerant society" (2017: 23). And this is the liberal state's way of being tolerant, which is not premised on objection but indifference to the ways of life in a diverse society (see also Kukathas, 2003). Thus understood, toleration goes together perfectly with liberal neutrality, leading to the plausible conclusion that "liberal theory does not require radical modification in order to accommodate diversity" (Balint, 2017: 9).

Balint (2017) equals Patten (2014) in mobilizing a long-denigrated liberal neutrality for the purposes of accommodating diversity, though both authors differ in their understandings of neutrality: as indifference to ways of life (Balint) vs. equally recognizing all ways of life (Patten). To be sure, both agree that neutrality does not require people to endorse *all* ways of life, but only "justice-respecting ways of life" (Balint, 2017: 57), commensurate with an understanding of neutrality as a "downstream" value (Patten, 2014: ch.4). And they agree that neutrality needs to be balanced with other values, including the "importance of national cultural identification" (Balint, 2017: 121). But more fundamental than their agreements are the different directions into which they carry the same liberal principle of neutrality: negative "hands-off" (Balint) vs. positive "hands-on" (labeled "evenhandedness" by Patten, who prefers this variant, borrowing the term from Joseph Carens, 2000). Prima facie, it seems odd to load the principle of neutrality with the multicultural language of respect and recognition, which was originally developed as its explicit negation. One thereby catches all the problems of recognition, including false recognition and the reification of identity, which conjoin in the problem of "minorities within minorities" (that typically affects women, see Okin, 1998). But also the sheer extent of diversity makes recognition of each instance of it an unwieldy undertaking (see Balint, 2017: 71; also Joppke, 2017a: 19–20).

Balint's case for "traditional toleration and neutrality" (2017: 10) is also valuable for attributing different types of toleration to "states" and "citizens" as they encounter diversity. As the liberal state is culturally thin and by definition incapable of advocating a particular way of life, it cannot exercise "forbearance tolerance," but only the general toleration that is premised on indifference (within a justice-respecting range). States are reserved in this respect exactly to allow citizens to pursue *their* preferred way of life. Accordingly, the toleration by citizens must be of the specific "forbearance" type, which presupposes a rejection of the ways of life that are not theirs. Moreover, contrary to pedagogical campaigns for (and of) citizens to "respect difference," all that citizens can be reasonably expected to respect is the "sameness" of others, in terms of human dignity and so on, but *not* their difference. Because, "how is the animal activist ... to respect the fox hunter's way of life?" (2017: 17). The limit of citizens' respect for difference is set by their "freedom of conscience" (2017: 104). In sum, toleration on the part of the state means neutrality in the form of "active indifference," while on the part of citizens it implies a "minimal demand of forbearance tolerance" (2017: 121).

Because "neutrality is best realized by the state withdrawing support for favored ways of life" (Balint, 2017: 53), an account that rejects the idea of minority recognition may still have robust "multicultural" consequences – permits for Islamic mosque construction, for instance, are to be "treated equally" to permits for Christian church construction, and even "citizens may need to act tolerantly as well" in this respect (2017: 133). This is incidentally the legal-moral status quo in more and more Western European states, and in North America anyway (see Joppke and Torpey, 2013).

If one goes down the road of endorsing the classical liberal principles of neutrality and toleration, one eventually arrives at the position that liberal constitutionalism itself is sufficiently capacious to accommodate much of the diversity that multiculturalists deem possible only in the form of specific minority rights and policies (see the case for "legal multiculturalism" in Joppke, 2017b). *Nota bene*, this trust in the sufficiency of liberal law applies only to the management of immigrant diversity, not the national-minority and indigenous cases, whose accommodation through special group rights long predates the arrival of "multiculturalism."

Policies, Retreat, and Alternatives

For the multiculturalism theories of all shades, we saw, multiculturalism is a property of minorities. By contrast, where "multiculturalism" was invented as policy, in Canada and Australia, there has been an insistence from the start that multiculturalism is "for all," a new national identity of post-British settler societies after racism fell out of fashion in the early 1970s, and over time all "groupist" elements that may at first have been in it were subsequently purged (for an up-to-date view on Canada, see Winter, 2015; for Australia, Brahm Levey, 2019). Kymlicka pointedly calls Canadian multiculturalism a project of "citizenization" (2010). Its liberal-cum-nationalist hue explains the persistence of New World multiculturalism, immunizing it from the attacks to which an exclusively immigrant-focused Old World multiculturalism would become subjected in the early millennium. In Europe, as Nathan Glazer correctly observed (1999: 186), multiculturalism is something for "immigrants or foreigners." More precisely, multiculturalism in Europe primarily relates to "non-white peoples" immigrating "from outside Europe" (Modood, 2007: 2), with the problems surrounding Muslims and Islam playing a central role in it. The fact that multiculturalism in Europe has not become part of a nation-building project and been considered the property of groups that originally are extrinsic to European society, explains its unique political vulnerability there.

It may well be that the much-touted "retreat" of multiculturalism (e.g., Joppke, 2004) has been greatly exaggerated (as argued by Banting and Kymlicka, 2013; also Vertovec and Wessendorf, 2009). However, it is incontrovertible that the very notion of "multiculturalism" has fallen into disrepute in Europe (see Bowen, 2011), and that other concepts have increasingly taken its place, above all "interculturalism" and "diversity." It is thus apposite to examine whether this is merely a rhetorical change or a change in content.

Interculturalism

An official policy in Quebec and enjoying increasing popularity in Europe, interculturalism grows out of a critique of multiculturalism, which is said to have favored group separation over intergroup exchange and "dialogue" and to have ignored the importance of a common ground, whether in the guise of a particular national identity or a universalist commitment to human rights (see, for instance, Zapata-Barrero, 2017). Multiculturalists have responded that the interculturalist critique thrives on a highly distorted view of multiculturalism that few if any of its protagonists have ever endorsed (Modood, 2017).

Interculturalism comes in two opposite forms, a "majoritarian" variant in Quebec, where the concept was actually invented and first put into practice, and a "diversity" variant in Europe (for more detail, see Joppke, 2018b). In Quebec, "interculturalism" is a code word for "majority precedence," that is, the need for immigrants to respect and accept francophone majority culture (see Bouchard, 2011). This majority culture is defined in particularistic terms, especially (French) language and (Catholic) religion (Bouchard, 2011), which reflects the fact that universalist-political values could not distinguish Quebec from the rest of Canada. Interestingly, Canadian multiculturalism appears from the Quebecois interculturalist optic as a footloose cosmopolitanism in which there is "no recognition of a majority culture" (2011: 441). This is as if Patten's (2014) plea for a neutrality-based multiculturalism without a *Favoritvolk* had come true. This strangely ignores the possibility of multiculturalism having become a central plank of Canadian identity, so that one might speak of a "multicultural nationalism" there (as do Banting and Kymlicka, 2017).

One might think that a majoritarian interculturalism, which operates with a majority–minority dualism, would provide a model for Europe, with its strong ethnic nation-state legacies (see Taylor, 2012). In reality, a different form of "diversity interculturalism" has arisen in Europe. Its key document (Council of Europe, 2008) presents interculturalism as a middle way between a long-denigrated "assimilation" and the more recent "multiculturalism," both of which are found guilty of "the same, schematic conception of society set in opposition of majority and minority, differing only in endorsing separation of the minority from the majority . . . (or) assimilation to it" (2008: 18). The assumption is that "diversity," depicted as "unprecedented and ever-growing," cuts all the way through, obliterating even the category of "majority." If through the lens of Quebec's majoritarian interculturalism (Canadian) multiculturalism was transformed, rather implausibly, into cosmopolitanism, European diversity, interculturalism suffers from the reverse problem of duplicating the grossest stereotypes about multiculturalism, as separatist and "undermining the rights of individuals," especially women (2008: 19). Compared with the majoritarian variant, there is the same emphasis in the diversity variant on fleshing out a common core, only one that is not particularistic but universalistic, consisting of a commitment to human rights and the essentials of liberal democracy. The "common identity" that multiculturalism is accused of having slighted or even violated, is dubbed "equality of human dignity" (2008: 14). Interculturalism thus understood situates itself in the middle between assimilation and multiculturalism, incorporating "the best of both": "It takes from assimilation the focus on the individual; it takes from multiculturalism the recognition of cultural diversity. And it adds the new element, critical to integration and social cohesion, of dialogue and the basis of equal dignity and shared values" (2008: 19).

However, which multiculturalist would deny the "equality of human dignity," which for Charles Taylor (1994) was exactly the starting point for the modern "politics of equal recognition"? Which multiculturalist would advance a total relativism of values and cultures, including honor killings, genital mutilation, and other extreme practices, as seems to be the charge of the interculturalists? Kymlicka (2016) is correct that interculturalism serves mainly "rhetorical functions," namely, to continue multiculturalism's progressive agenda under the mantle of repudiating it in name – with the price that sacking multiculturalism helps legitimize the nationalist populism that helped throw it into crisis.

Diversity

Much like interculturalism, "diversity" is often referred to as "the term now meant to do much of the work that 'multiculturalism' used to" (Vertovec and Wessendorf, 2009: 28). Even more than with respect to interculturalism, this is at best a half-truth, because a new accent is set that leads away from some core assumptions of multiculturalism, particularly the idea of justice-led group recognition. The plausible part of it is that the reality of "super-diversity" (Vertovec, 2007) seems to render obsolete the whole idea of group recognition, which rests on a limited number of such groups. Take London, which currently is inhabited by people from almost 180 different countries, 42 of these nationality groups exceeding the size of 10,000 people, and in which some 300 different languages are spoken. Doing "recognition" with all of them would take too many evenings.

Diversity differs from multiculturalism in two respects: much like interculturalism does, it shifts focus from the group to the individual; and the individual is considered not from a justice but from an efficiency perspective, as set by the requisite functional sphere. Thomas Faist (2009: 173) is right that diversity "straddles many worlds." One could call it multiculturalism adjusted to the logic of functionally differentiated societies, if multiculturalism would not thereby lose what had initially energized it: the idea of justice for historically wronged minorities.

Both elements of diversity, its minority-majority-busting individualism and its replacement of a justice rationale by an efficiency rationale, are patently visible in the US Supreme Court's famous *Regents of the University of California* v. *Bakke* decision of 1978, which invented "diversity" as a legal concept. *Bakke* provided a new and qualified basis for affirmative action in higher education, which had grown out of the 1960s civil rights struggles – and thus shows an element of continuity between the new "diversity" and the old "multiculturalism" eras. However, the continuity was simultaneously disrupted by the new "diversity" formula. Affirmative action had originally been the strongest expression of race-focused American multiculturalism, seeking a remedy to the past injustice against American blacks. *Bakke* put a diminished form of the policy on a new ground, beyond the minority–majority binary on which it had originally rested. For Justice Powell, who delivered the decisive swing opinion in a hung court, there was no dominant "majority" in America – "whites" themselves were in many ways sub-divided, most of whose subgroups could "lay claim to a history of prior discrimination."[6] America was a "nation of minorities," each struggling "to over-come the prejudices not of a monolithic majority, but of a 'majority' composed of various minority groups."[7] But if everyone is a minority, even whites, there is no longer any basis for preferential treatment of nonwhites. Thus the idea of "diversity" was born, in which a "farm boy from Idaho" mattered no less than a black ghetto kid for bringing "educational diversity" to a university campus.[8]

One immediately sees the reason for the meteoric rise of the idea of diversity across functional sectors and also across countries: unlike the multicultural idea of remedying injustice or majority privilege, diversity has no intrinsic, sector-transcending meaning. Instead, it is functionally defined as furthering a sector-specific goal: "educating," as in the *Bakke* case; "democratic decision-making," as in US President Clinton's famous appointment of the first cabinet that "looks like America"; even "profit-maximizing," as in the corporate sector, perhaps diversity's strongest institutional home today (see Joppke, 2017a: 59–60). An advertisement by a corporate investment giant performs diversity's *reductio ad absurdum*: "*Be yourself*. Race. Ethnicity. Religion. Nationality. Gender. Sexual orientation. In the end, there's just one variety of human being. The Individual. All six billion of us. Be bullish. *Merrill Lynch*" (2017a: 57).

After the Retreat: A Multiculturalism of the Individual

Stuart Hall once called multiculturalism a "maddeningly spongy and impre-cise concept" (see Koopmans, 2013: 148). As theory, it means different things, from communitarian to radical to liberal. As policy, it takes different forms in different parts of the world, from New World nation-building to Old World immigrant integration (now largely discarded). Multiculturalism also means different things in different sectors of society, from democratic politics (main site of its "retreat") to constitutional law (where it has survived to the degree that freedom and equality require it) to economics (where "corporate multiculturalism" is well established; see the biting critique by Kymlicka, 2007: 123–132). If one reviews the development of multiculturalism in the worlds of theory and policy alike, one must conclude that an orthodox multiculturalism of groups is in crisis or has even died, whereas a multiculturalism of individuals is alive and well (coming to the same conclusion,

Anne Phillips prefers the heading *Multiculturalism Without Culture* [2007]). Expunging groups from multiculturalism is paradoxical, because a concern for groups had originally called it into existence.

An account of "what is living and what is dead in multiculturalism" has expressed the contemporary condition well (Levey, 2009: 77):

> Liberal democracies today seem to be in somewhat of a state of limbo regarding multiculturalism: retreating from it in certain policy respects and suspicious of the word, but, at the same time, institutionally and attitudinally reshaped by its commitments and norms; reaching for a new idiom and a renewed emphasis on communality, yet reluctant to quash diversity and reinscribe brute assimilationism.

Global Multiculturalism

While notional "multiculturalism" may be in crisis at the domestic level, it is surprisingly strong at the international level, but importantly, largely as an individual-centered undertaking. With a particular eye on South America, Mara Loveman speaks of a "new international norm of multicultural nationhood" (2014: 297), which may be exaggerated because in Africa and Asia, even in the east of Europe, such a "norm" has surely not taken hold. But through a variety of international conventions and backed by international organizations from the United Nations to the World Bank, a new model of "what a normal state looks like" has been established, away from the "older centralized and unitary model" toward a model of "pluralistic, multilingual, and multilevel states" (Kymlicka, 2007: 42–43).

The kind of multiculturalism that flourishes in the "international community" (Kymlicka, 2007) is a liberal multiculturalism of individuals, not of groups. A telling document is the 2004 UN Human Development Report, entitled *Cultural Liberty in Today's Diverse World*. Its novelty is to add "cultural liberty" to the measurable criteria of human development, alongside the conventional indicators of health or economic growth. As a result, to support cultural liberty and minority rights is now a standard condition for receiving credits and development aids from the World Bank or the Inter-American Development Bank. The report stipulates: "People must also be free to be who they are and to choose their cultural identity accordingly – as a Thai, a Quaker, a Wolof speaker, a South African or Indian descent – and to enjoy the respect of others and live in dignity" (quoted in Loveman, 2014: 292). The UN *Cultural Liberty* report emphasizes "choice" and criticizes the "imperialism of identity" that is associated with old-style group-multiculturalism: "(I)t is crucial always to remember that we are not simply black or white or yellow or brown, gay or straight or bisexual . . . we are also brothers and sisters; parents and children . . . let us not let our racial identities subject us to new tyrannies" (in Nederveen Pieterse, 2004: 1267). While Kymlicka is the author most frequently quoted in the 2004 UN report, its promotion of "multiple identities" goes beyond his "liberal multiculturalism," which is still beholden to the crypto-nationalist idea that people belong to one culture and one group only (see the "cosmopolitan" critique by Waldron, 1992). Instead, the UN report moves toward a liberal multiculturalism of the individual.

Multiculturalism of the Individual

Most instances of real, existing multiculturalism in the Western world, even if they are parading under a different name, may be classified as a multiculturalism of the individual. Canada, the one country in the world that most proudly and persistently calls itself "multicultural," has quietly moved from groupist "heritage" multiculturalism to one that is for all Canadians and is stringently liberal-individualist – a proof is the 2005 controversy over sharia law in Ontario, which ended with lifting the arbitration law that had provided the entry for it (see Joppke and Torpey, 2013: ch. 5). In Europe, "interculturalism" is a confusing neologism, because in name it suggests groupism and essentialism, but in reality its whole point is the opposite, to make the individual the starting point. Ironically, the "multi" is a much more plausible linguistic expression for this purpose than the "inter," because "inter" logically requires the stability of boundaries that are to be traversed. "Multi," by contrast, leaves open the possibility of hybrid and multiple identities that underlies radically freedom-centered variants of multiculturalism (such as Appiah, 2005, Sen, 2006, or Waldron, 1992). Interculturalism is a multiculturalism of the individual under a different, unhelpful name. This is only partially true for "diversity," some variants of which, especially the economic, are too radically decoupled from a justice or rights rationale to still count as multiculturalism. If the term "multiculturalism" is at low ebb, and the mentioned alternatives are preferred, this is to fend off the groupism and essentialism that seem to be perniciously associated with multiculturalism.

Can we do without the m-word? Let me respond to this with another question. Is there a better word for describing the reality of pluralistic immigrant societies, which even much of Europe has turned into over the past half-century, and luckily so? This is not to reduce "multiculturalism" to a descriptive term for a demographic reality, because this reality is tied up with policies and laws – in particular, constitutional law – which have brought it into existence, even though these laws and policies rarely (if ever) carry the word "multicultural" in their name. Kissing gays and veiled Muslim women are not only to be seen in the few countries that may have pursued an explicit multiculturalism policy, that is, in Ottawa, Stockholm, or London, but also in countries that did not, such as in Vienna, Berlin, or Zürich – simply because liberal constitutionalism, with its liberty and equality protections that constrain the preferences of the majority, requires that. Liberalism in a context of pluralism, and in no other context is there a need for it, *is* multiculturalism. Of course, it took the post-1960s human rights revolution (see Moyn, 2012) and its social movements (of women, blacks, gays, etc.) to bring liberalism's multicultural dimension to the fore.

Multiculturalist discourse is needed today as a corrective to the possibility within liberalism itself to turn illiberal in the stubborn pursuit of liberal goals, which is only too visible in Europe's current struggles surrounding Muslim and Islam integration and fending off religious fundamentalism and worse. "Illiberal liberalism" (Orgad, 2010) marks some of Western European states' citizenship and immigrant integration policies. What to do with illiberal people is the *crucial question* of multiculturalism, and an increasingly impatient liberal mainstream, whipped up by a populist surge that has not seen its zenith yet, fights multiculturalism in the name of rooting out the illiberal. In Stanley Fish's dark lens, "all of liberalism's efforts to accommodate or tame illiberal forces fail, either by underestimating and trivializing the illiberal impulse, or by mirroring it" (1997: 2255). Faced with this unhappy choice, he sides with "acts of exclusion and stigmatization," which he deems "inevitable in any liberal regime that really wants to be a regime and not an endless philosophy seminar." To ward off this liberal Leninism, liberal multiculturalism is needed, because in the post-2001 era of toughened anti-terror laws the risk of illiberal liberalism is not merely academic.

If we thus need multiculturalism, more for political than for academic reasons, Will Kymlicka's liberal multiculturalism (1995) still remains the benchmark for-mulation to grapple with. No one has theorized more convincingly how and why liberalism's two key principles, freedom and equality, are implicated in the making and justification of multiculturalism properly understood – hence "liberal multi-culturalism." And among all philosophical theories of multiculturalism, his liberal multiculturalism is the one most saturated with empirics, closely reflecting how the real liberal world works.

Kymlicka (2007: 93) concedes that multiculturalism operates "within the larger framework of liberal constitutionalism," but he does not sufficiently consider that, in a context of immigrant diversity, this does not require official multiculturalism policies to be effective. Too sharp a line is drawn between what liberal state constitutions have on offer to protect freedom and equality and "multiculturalism policies" proper, which for Kymlicka require going "beyond . . . rights guaranteed to all individuals" (2007: 16). Do they? Take the perhaps most prominent of his "polyethnic rights" for immigrants, which is to be exempted from general laws that conflict with their cultural (in reality always religious) commitments. Rather than a group-specific right beyond the liberal standard, this is a religious right that in this case trumps other rights or principles, such as animal rights (in the case of ritual slaughter) (see Grimm, 2009 for how that works legally). One can call this trumping "multiculturalism," but it is really the result of a context-dependent balancing of competing rights and principles that might well be lost by the religious claimant (as in the mentioned case of ritual slaughter, if the cause of animal rights advances further).[9]

Rights not granted to all individuals, exclusively reserved for some and withheld from others, will always be rare and potentially contested in a liberal state – the smallish immigrant rights provisions in the liberal multiculturalism theories of Kymlicka and Patten are testimony to this. Whether one needs them, and how much of them, are better taken as prudential and not principled questions, to be decided according to case and context. Admittedly outside the ambit of Kymlicka and Patten's liberal multiculturalism, even accommodating the equality claims of women, which arguably require asymmetric treatment, is contested within rigidly formal and sym-metric antidiscrimination laws in Europe and America alike (see Joppke, 2018a). For ethnic and racial difference, an asymmetric legal-political treatment is in principle within the logic of "reparations" for historical injustice (see Torpey, 2001). But apart from First Nations people or the racially marked descendants of African slaves, it is difficult to find other plausible candidates. The logic of reparations is a stretch for racially unmarked minorities like the French-speaking Quebecois, who feature centrally in Kymlicka and Patten's minority rights schemes, but who can move freely and without stigma within a European-defined Anglo-Canadian majority society and in North America at large. The logic of reparations is altogether implausible and inapplicable for immigrants, wherever they hail from, which has been duly acknowledged in Kymlicka-Pattenian liberal multiculturalism. All known crises, retreats, deaths, and so on of multiculturalism have been with respect to immigrants, for whom the idea of going "beyond . . . rights guaranteed to all individuals," to reiterate Kymlicka's point of entry for multiculturalism, has just never cut much ice. A multiculturalism of the individual knows no such rigid line between "multiculturalism" and its "liberal constitutionalist" presupposition, which also makes it less vulnerable to attack.

The plausibility of Kymlicka's liberal multiculturalism is stronger with respect to its liberty than to its equality rationale. The liberty rationale, according to which culture provides a necessary "context of choice" for the individual, is unabashedly individualist, even though one may bicker about an unnecessarily holist and essentialist understanding of culture (that is not necessarily improved by Patten's somewhat arcane "social lineage" account). By contrast, Kymlicka's equality rationale is rather more groupist. This is perhaps necessarily so, because (unlike "liberty") "equality" is an inherently relative concept that requires a comparing and – in effect – grouping of the units that are deemed "equal" (see Joppke, 2018a). But the assumption of unwaveringly strong nation-building, which justifies minority rights in his scheme, does not quite correspond to reality, at least in the West. It is always the same tired examples of public holidays, official language, and symbolic decorum that serve to validate the claim that states are incurably particularistic, incapable of becoming differentiated from majority culture. The fixation on paltry, at best symbolic matter hides from view a much more important demise of public morality policies and the approximation of a neutrality norm over the past half-century, which has perhaps most dramatically played out in the legalization of homosexuality and related family forms (see Joppke, 2017b). Alan Patten (2014) thinks the neutral state should practice "equal recognition," but the more plausible response to the empirical weakening of the ties between state and majority culture is to drop the entire project of "recognition," for majority and minorities alike, in favor of an indifference of the state to the ways of life of its citizens and residents.

References

Appiah, Kwame Anthony. 2005. *The Ethics of Identity*. Princeton, NJ: Princeton University Press.
Balint, Peter. 2017. *Respecting Toleration: Traditional Liberalism and Contemporary Diversity*. Oxford, UK: Oxford University Press.
Banting, Keith, and Will Kymlicka. 2013. "Is There Really a Retreat from Multiculturalism Policies?" *Comparative European Politics* 11(5): 577–98.
　2017. "Introduction: The Political Sources of Solidarity in Diverse Societies." In Keith Banting and Will Kymlicka (eds.), *The Strains of Commitment: The*

Political Sources of Solidarity in Diverse Societies (pp. 1–58). New York: Oxford University Press.

Bouchard, Gérard. 2011. "What Is Interculturalism?" *McGill Law Journal* 56(2): 435–468.

Bowen, John. 2011. "Europeans against Multiculturalism." *Boston Review* (July–August) www.bostonreview.net/john-r-bowen-european-multiculturalism-islam.

Brown, Wendy. 2006. *Regulating Aversion: Tolerance in the Age of Identity and Empire*. Princeton, NJ: Princeton University Press.

Brubaker, Rogers. 2000. "The Return of Assimilation." *Ethnic and Racial Studies* 24(4): 531–548.

　　2016. "The Dolezal Affair: Race, Gender, and the Micropolitics of Identity." *Ethnic and Racial Studies* 36(1): 414–448.

Carens, Joseph. 2000. *Culture, Citizenship, and Community*. New York: Oxford University Press.

Council of Europe. 2008. *Living Together as Equals in Dignity: White Paper on Intercultural Dialogue*. Strasbourg: Council of Europe.

Council of the European Union. 2004. *Common Basic Principles of Immigrant Integration Policy in the EU*. Brussels: Council of the European Union.

Epstein, Steven. 1987. "Gay Politics, Ethnic Identity." *Socialist Review* 93/94: 117–162.

Faist, Thomas. 2009. "Diversity – a New Mode of Incorporation?" *Ethnic and Racial Studies* 32(1): 171–190.

Fanon, Frantz. 1963. *The Wretched of the Earth*. New York: Grove Press.

Fish, Stanley. 1997. "Mission Impossible: Setting the Just Bounds between Church and State." *Columbia Law Review* 97(8): 2255–2333.

Frank, David John, Bayliss J. Camp, and Steven A. Boutcher. 2010. "Worldwide Trends in the Criminal Regulation of Sex, 1945–2005." *American Sociological Review* 75(6): 867–893.

Fraser, Nancy. 1995. "From Redistribution to Recognition?" *New Left Review* I/212: 68–93.

Gellner, Ernest. 1983. *Nations and Nationalism*. Ithaca, NY: Cornell University Press.

Glazer, Nathan. 1998. *We Are All Multiculturalists Now*. Cambridge, MA: Harvard University Press.

　　1999. "Multiculturalism and American Exceptionalism." In Christian Joppke and Steven Lukes (eds.), *Multicultural Questions* (pp. 183–198). Oxford, UK: Oxford University Press.

Goffman, Erving. 1963. *Stigma: Notes on the Management of Spoiled Identity*. New York: Simon and Schuster.

Goodman, Sara Wallace. 2014. *Immigration and Membership Politics in Western Europe*. New York: Cambridge University Press.

Grimm, Dieter. 2009. "Conflicts Between General Laws and Religious Norms." *Cardozo Law Review* 30(6): 2369–2382.

Habermas, Jürgen. 1994. "Struggle for Recognition in the Democratic Constitutional State." In Amy Gutmann (eds.), *Multiculturalism: Examining the Politics of Recognition* (pp. 107–148). Princeton, NJ: Princeton University Press.

Hughes, Everett. 1945. "Dilemmas and Contradictions in Status." *American Journal of Sociology* 50: 353–359.

Joppke, Christian. 2004. "The Retreat of Multiculturalism in the Liberal State: Theory and Policy." *British Journal of Sociology* 55(2): 237–257.

　　2010. *Citizenship and Immigration*. Cambridge, UK: Polity.

　　2017a. *Is Multiculturalism Dead? Crisis and Persistence in the Constitutional State*. Cambridge, UK: Polity.

2017b. "Multiculturalism by Liberal Law. The Empowerment of Gays and Muslims." *European Journal of Sociology* 58(1): 1–32.

2018a. "Multiculturalism and Antidiscrimination Law." *IDC Law Review* (forthcoming).

2018b. "War of Words: Interculturalism v. Multiculturalism." *Comparative Migration Studies* 6(11). DOI:https://doi.org/10.1186/s40878-0079–1.

Joppke, Christian, and John Torpey. 2013. *Legal Integration of Islam: A Transatlantic Comparison*. Cambridge, MA: Harvard University Press.

Koopmans, Ruud. 2013. "Multiculturalism and Immigration." *Annual Review of Sociology* 39: 147–169.

Kukathas, Chandran. 2003. *The Liberal Archipelago*. Oxford, UK: Oxford University Press.

Kymlicka, Will. 1989. *Liberalism, Community and Culture*. Oxford, UK: Oxford University Press.

1995. *Multicultural Citizenship*. Oxford, UK: Oxford University Press.

2007. *Multicultural Odysseys*. Oxford, UK: Oxford University Press.

2010. "The Rise and Fall of Multiculturalism." *International Social Science Journal* 199: 97–112.

2016. "Defending Diversity in an Era of Populism: Multiculturalism and Interculturalism Compared." In Nasar Meer, Tariq Modood, and Ricard Zapata-Barrero (eds.), *Multiculturalism and Interculturalism: Debating the Dividing Lines* (pp. 158–177). Edinburgh: Edinburgh University Press.

2018. "Liberal Multiculturalism as a Political Theory of State-Minority Relations." *Political Theory* 46(1): 81–91.

Kymlicka, Will, and Sue Donaldson. 2014. "Animal Rights, Multiculturalism, and the Left." *Journal of Social Philosophy* 45(1): 116–135.

Levey, Geoffrey Brahm. 2009. "What Is Living and What Is Dead in Multiculturalism." *Ethnicities* 9(1): 75–93.

2019. "The Turnbull Government's 'Post-Multicultural' Multicultural Policy." *Australian Journal of Political Science* 54(4): 456–473.

Loveman, Mara. 2014. *National Colors: Racial Classification and the State in Latin America*. New York: Oxford University Press.

Modood, Tariq. 2007. *Multiculturalism: A Civic Idea*. Cambridge, UK: Polity Press.

2017. "Must Interculturalists Misrepresent Multiculturalism?" *Comparative Migration Studies* 5. DOI:https://doi.org/10.1186/s40878-017-0058-y

Moyn, Samuel. 2012. *The Last Utopia: Human Rights in History*. Cambridge, MA: Harvard University Press.

Nederveen Pieterse, Jan. 2005. "The Human Development Report and Cultural Liberty: Tough Liberalism." *Development and Change* 36(6): 1267–1273.

Okin, Susan Moller. 1998. "Feminism and Multiculturalism: Some Tensions." *Ethics* 108(4): 661–684.

Orgad, Liav. 2010. "Illiberal Liberalism: Cultural Restrictions on Migration and Access to Citizenship in Europe." *American Journal of Comparative Law* 58(1): 53–105.

Parekh, Bhikhu. 2000. *Rethinking Multiculturalism*. Cambridge, MA: Harvard University Press.

Patten, Alan. 2014. *Equal Recognition: The Moral Foundation of Minority Rights*. Princeton, NJ: Princeton University Press.

Phillips, Anne. 2007. *Multiculturalism without Culture*. Princeton, NJ: Princeton University Press.

Rawls, John. 1971. *A Theory of Justice*. Cambridge, MA: Harvard University Press.

Sen, Amartya. 2006. *Identity and Violence*. London: Penguin.

Simmel, Georg. 1901. "Die beiden Formen des Individualismus." *Das freie Wort* 1(13): 397–403. socio.ch/sim/verschiedenes/1901/individualismus.htm.

Song, Sarah. 2016. "Multiculturalism." *Stanford Encyclopedia of Philosophy.* https://plato.stanford.edu/entries/multiculturalism/.

Taylor, Charles. 1994. "The Politics of Recognition." In Amy Gutmann (ed.), *Multiculturalism: Examining the Politics of Recognition* (pp. 25–73). Princeton, NJ: Princeton University Press.

2012. "Interculturalism or Multiculturalism?" *Philosophy and Social Criticism* 38(4/5): 413–423.

Torpey, John. 2001. "Making Whole What Has Been Smashed: Reflections on Reparations." *Journal of Modern History* 73(2): 333–358.

Vertovec, Steven. 2007. "Super-Diversity and Its Implications." *Ethnic and Racial Studies* 30 (6): 1024–1054.

Vertovec, Steven, and Susanne Wessendorf. 2009. *Assessing the Backlash against Multiculturalism in Europe*. MMG Working Paper 09–04. Göttingen: Max Planck Institute for the Study of Religious and Ethnic Diversity.

Waldron, Jeremy. 1992. "Minority Cultures and the Cosmopolitan Alternative." *University of Michigan Journal of Law Reform* 25(3): 751–793.

Winter, Elke. 2015. "Rethinking Multiculturalism after Its 'Retreat': Lessons from Canada." *American Behavioral Scientist* 59(6): 637–657.

Young, Iris Marion. 1989. "Polity and Group Difference: A Critique of the Ideal of Universal Citizenship." *Ethics* 99: 250–274.

1990. *Justice and the Politics of Difference*. Princeton, NJ: Princeton University Press.

Zapata-Barrero, Ricard. 2017. "Interculturalism in the Post-Multiculturalism Debate: A Defence." *Comparative Migration Studies* 5. DOI:https://doi.org/10.1186/s40878-017-0057-z.

Notes

1. The United States took a different development from Canada or Australia, as multiculturalism never acquired the status of an official policy but came to be associated with accommodating the domestic race problem. See Glazer (1998).
2. For an analysis of how various multicultural claims *differ*, see my comparison of sexual orientation, language, religion, and race claims in Joppke (2017a: 22–33).
3. More on this below, in my discussion of Balint (2017).
4. The duality of the modern self, to be both *allgemein* and *besonders*, has also been captured in Georg Simmel's concept of individualism (1901).
5. "Pro-rated funding" according to population size is Patten's somewhat persnickety scheme for supporting (language) minorities (2014: ch. 6).
6. *Regents of the University of California* v. *Bakke*, 438 U.S. 265 (1978), at 205.
7. *Bakke*, at 292.
8. *Bakke*, at 316.
9. Kymlicka and Donaldson (2014: 120–124), two advocates of animal rights *and* multiculturalism, slight this possibility under the rubric of "cultural imperialism" or "racial bias," which scandalizes dog-eating but happily indulges in pig-eating.

16 Risk

Klaus Rasborg

Introduction

This chapter explores the role of risk in modern society. In order to elucidate this, I first discuss the concept of risk itself, namely from its origin in Ancient Greece, through the Middle Ages and the Renaissance and up to the modern era. Next, the chapter outlines a number of more recent approaches to the analysis of risk in economics, psychology, cultural theory, sociology, and political science. I then discuss in greater depth the sociological approach to risk: here, the leading figure is the German sociologist Ulrich Beck (1944–2015), whose theory of "the risk society" has had a significant impact on contemporary discussions of risk within sociology and the social sciences. In addition, I present the work of two other prominent sociologists who also emphasize the central role of risk in contemporary society, namely Anthony Giddens (b. 1938) and Niklas Luhmann (1927–1998). The chapter also examines the political science-based "governmentality" approach to risk advocated by Michel Foucault (1926–1984), François Ewald (b. 1946) and Mitchell Dean (b. 1957), which in several respects can be seen as a criticism of Beck's and Giddens' views of risk. Finally, the chapter is summarized and concludes that instead of seeing the different approaches to risk as mutually exclusive, we can view them as supplementing one another in various ways and thus as contributing to a more coherent understanding of the interconnections between uncertainty, risk, and insurance in contemporary society.

What Is Risk?

The word "risk" comes from the old Italian word *risicare* which means "to dare" (Bernstein, 1996: 8). Risk thus has to do with the courage to throw oneself into the new and unknown, which indicates that risk is not about destiny but about choice. Thus, according to the American economist and finance historian, Peter L. Bernstein (1919–2009), who charted thinking about risk and insurance from Ancient Greece until the present era, risk has to do with: "The actions we dare to take, which depend on how free we are to make choices." Following Bernstein, risk is such a fundamental feature of human action that the story of risk simply "helps define what it means to be a human being" (Bernstein, 1996: 8; cf. Rasborg, 2014).

In a mathematical sense, risk is associated with the probability of a particular event occurring (Bernstein, 1996: 3). As such, probabilities are neither "positive" nor "negative," but simply a measure of how certain we are that something will happen (Bernstein, 1996: 43). Mathematically, a probability is always greater than (or equal to) 0 and less than (or equal to) 1.. If it is equal to 0, it means that the event has not yet occurred, and if it is equal to 1, it means that the event will certainly occur – and in that case, it is not meaningful to speak of a risk (Giddens, 1999: 22). Probability, and probability theory, can thus be seen as a means to make (mathematically) founded assumptions about uncertainty (Arnoldi, 2009: 21). Normally, we associate the word risk with "adverse" events (Sennett, 1998: 82), for example the likelihood of getting cancer, of losing one's job, or of perishing in a car accident or a plane crash. Hence, risk – in the modern understanding of the term – refers to the calculated probability that something undesirable will occur (Adams, 2001: 8; Arnoldi, 2009: 21). Yet risk can sometimes also refer to something "desired," as in the case of young people who look for excitement in life by actively seeking out risk by gambling, driving too fast, consuming drugs, engaging in extreme sports, or sexual adventurism, and so on. With regard to the economy, a certain amount of risk-taking can be seen as positive as well, since it is a prerequisite for entrepreneurship, innovation, and economic growth (Arnoldi, 2009: 138–157; Giddens, 1999: 23–24). Since the outcome of the events that we associate with risk must necessarily unfold in time, there is an inextricable link between risk and time. More specifically, risk is intrinsically linked to the *future*, as risk refers to events that may take place in an uncertain future: "Risk and time are opposite sides of the same coin, for if there were no tomorrow there would be no risk. Time transforms risk, and the nature of risk is shaped by the time horizon: the future is the playing field" (Bernstein, 1996: 15).

Accordingly, it is not until modern times that the desire to master risk has become predominant. Following Bernstein, the desire to manage or control risks represents a uniquely modern view, which indicates that we have detached ourselves from the belief that our existence is controlled by destiny, or providence, and is thus inevitable:

> The revolutionary idea that defines the boundary between modern times and the past is the mastery of risk: the notion that the future is more than a whim of the gods and that men and women are not passive before nature. Until human beings discovered a way across that boundary, the future was a mirror of the past or the murky domain of oracles and soothsayers who held a monopoly over knowledge of anticipated events. (Bernstein, 1996: 1, cf. 11–12)

Consequently, risk can be seen as a fundamental dynamic in a future-oriented society; that is, a society that sees the future as an arena to be conquered or colonized, which is precisely a defining characteristic of modernity (Arnoldi, 2009: 22–23, 35; Giddens, 1999: 23).

From the outset, the history of risk was associated with various forms of gambling – simple betting, dice games, roulette, and so on – which gave rise to concerns about risk. For instance, it was calculations about games of chance which led to the decisive breakthrough in probability theory. Until then, one had to bet and play games without knowing the odds that could be used to estimate the probability of gain and loss. As a consequence, one had to take risks without having the slightest clue about risk management (Arnoldi, 2009: 28–30; Bernstein, 1996: 11). Apart from gambling, seafaring also plays an important role in the history of risk. Thus, in the sixteenth and seventeenth centuries, the notion of risk was gaining ground among European explorers and traders for whom it meant "sailing into uncharted waters" (Giddens, 1999: 21; cf. Arnoldi, 2009: 25).

With regard to the emergence of the modern perception of risk, we can, roughly speaking, distinguish between four key periods: (1) the period up to the thirteenth century; (2) the period from the thirteenth to the eighteenth century; (3) the period from the eighteenth until early twentieth century; and (4) the period from the beginning of the twentieth century to the present day (Bernstein, 1996: vii–viii).

In the period until about 1200, people still believed that the fate of human existence was determined by providence. At that time, people made decisions without having any real notion about risk:

> In the medieval and ancient worlds, even in preliterate and peasant societies, people managed to make decisions, advance their interests, and carry on trade, but with no real understanding of risk or *the nature of decision-making*. Today, we rely less on superstition and tradition than people did in the past, not because we are more rational, but because our understanding of risk enables us to make decisions in a rational mode. (Bernstein, 1996: 3–4; cf. Giddens, 1999: 21–22)

Thus, the rational, calculated approach to risk based on probability is more recent. More specifically, the modern conception of probability did not emerge until the seventeenth century according to philosopher Ian Hacking (b. 1936) (Hacking, 2006 [1975]: 18–20). In Ancient Greece, the leap into the world of probability had not yet been made, although the notion of probability may have been known (Arnoldi, 2009: 25). Part of the explanation for this may be that the ancient Greeks – like the Romans – were dependent on a number system based on the Greek alphabet which made it difficult to multiply, divide, add, and subtract (Bernstein, 1996: 15–17; Hacking, 2006 [1975]: 6). This obstacle was removed when the modern Hindu-Arabic number system came to the West during the period 1000–1200. However, this was still not enough to pave the way for a modern understanding of risk, which replaces chance with probability and with the belief that the future can be predictable and even, to some extent, controllable. That understanding could not emerge until humans had acknowledged that their existence was neither preordained by fate nor in God's hands (Arnoldi, 2009: 25; Bernstein, 1996: 3, 20, xxx, xxxi).

A precursor of the modern understanding of risk can be found in the Italian mathematician Leonardo Pisano's (1175–1250) book, *Liber Abaci*, from 1202. Here Pisano – who was also known as Fibonacci – demonstrates the superiority of the Hindu-Arabic number system over the Hebrew, Greek, and Roman systems (Bernstein, 1996: xxiii–xxiv). Although measurement here became the decisive factor in risk management, it did not represent a real breakthrough for the modern understanding of probability and risk, since: ". . . most people still thought that risk stemmed from the capriciousness of nature. People would have to learn to recognize man-made risks and acquire the courage to do battle with the fates before they would accept the techniques of taming risk; that acceptance was still at least two hundred years in the future" (Bernstein, 1996: xxviii).

Not until the Renaissance and the Reformation, in around 1300, was the road paved for the modern understanding – and mastery – of risk that rejected the idea that fate or providence determines our lives. Mystery now gave way to science and logic, just as the Reformation helped to weaken the dominance of the Catholic Church, giving rise to an awareness that the future lies in our own hands (Arnoldi, 2009: 26–28; Bernstein, 1996: 20–22). This, together with the introduction of the new number system, formed the basis of attempts to calculate risk. In other words, it marked the emergence of the notion of calculability that is also a key element of the "Protestant ethic" which, according to the German sociologist Max Weber (1864–1920), laid the foundations for modern capitalism (Weber, 1992 [1904–1905]; cf. Bernstein, 1996: 21; Hacking, 2006 [1975]: 18–20).

Hence, the Renaissance departure from medieval superstition led to a breakthrough for probability theory and thus for the possibility of calculating risk. That was the time when Columbus (1451–1506) made his trip around the world, and Copernicus (1473–1543) revolutionized our view of the universe thanks to high-level mathematical knowledge. In the sixteenth century, progress was made within mathematics that became widespread in a range of classic mathematical writings (Bernstein, 1996: 41). In Italy, new ideas were developed about gambling, probability, and risk (Paccioli, Cardano, Galileo), which spread to Switzerland, Germany, and England. In France, progress was also made in the seventeenth and eighteenth centuries within mathematics, arithmetic, and algebra. This went far beyond past empirical experiments with dice rolling, and laid the foundations for the practical application of the concept of probability, especially in insurance, investments, medicine, theories of heredity and molecular behavior, warfare, and weather forecasts (Pascal, Fermat, Méré) (Arnoldi, 2009: 23; Bernstein, 1996: 55).

As a decisive breakthrough, risk is now linked to insurance, which has to do precisely with individual risk equalization, as the total group of policyholders indemnifies each individual member for losses (Bernstein, 1996: 93–95; Boyne, 2003: 10). Financial services and insurance services emerged during the Middle Ages as a result of increasing trade. In the seventeenth and eighteenth centuries, the insurance business gained further momentum due to the increasingly popular coffee-houses that appeared in all major European commercial towns and which, not least among seamen, served as centers for the exchange of news and information. Lloyds, one of Britain's best-known insurance companies, was founded in a coffeehouse that Edward Lloyd (c.1648–1713) opened in 1687 in Tower Street near the Thames. In the late seventeenth century, growing trade also formed the basis for another innovation, namely economic forecasts. These arose in response to the need to be able to estimate future returns – depending on costs, weather conditions, prices, and so on – on investments in goods that had to be shipped over long distances in order to reach their markets (Bernstein, 1996: 88–96). However, the modern insurance business is not only based on probability calculations about future events (risk), but also on projections based on statistical summaries of events that have already taken place, for example the statistical incidence of various diseases in the case of health insurance, or remaining life expectancy for the purposes of life insurance (Adams, 2001: 26; Boyne, 2003: 3).

In the eighteenth century, probability theory also began to take account of utility, since it became clear that there are differences in how people assess risk. Regarding investment risk, for instance, not everyone is equally willing to take a risk, but if no one is willing to take a risk this has negative implications for economic activity. The most important figure with regard to the inclusion of considerations about utility was the Swiss mathematician Daniel Bernoulli (1700–1782), who advanced the hypothesis that the utility of a certain increase in wealth is inversely proportional to the amount of wealth that one already possesses. With this idea, Bernoulli introduced a subjective element in probability theory, namely the motives (risk acceptance) of the people making the choice. He thus laid the foundations for modern decision-making and game theory (Bernstein, 1996: 105–106). However, while Bernoulli conceived utility in numerical (quantitative) terms, more recent researchers conceived it as a set of preferences, pointing out that the statement: "I prefer this instead of something else" is not the same as saying: "This is x utility-units worth to me" (Bernstein, 1996: 189).

In the late eighteenth century, utility theory was rediscovered by the English philosopher, Jeremy Bentham (1748–1832), whose utilitarian moral philosophy defines the morally good act as the act that brings about most benefit, or happiness, for the highest number of people (Bentham, 1970 [1789/1823]). The concept of utility also became popular with nineteenth-century economists, who used marginal utility theory to explain pricing, among other things. With utility theory came an enthusiasm for measurement which rendered ever-more aspects of life subject to quantification, be it pleasure, pain, work, value, wealth, money, or capital, and so on (Bernstein, 1996: 189–193). One thus became aware of the fact that risk is not just about the probability that a certain event – damage – will occur, but also about the possible *extent* of the damage (quantity). In order to be able to account for this, the risk formula has to be extended so that it takes the following form: risk = the probability of p x the extent of p (Adams, 2001: 8, 69).

In the first half of the twentieth century, another important conceptual innovation was made by the American economist, Frank H. Knight (1885–1972): namely the distinction between "risk" and "uncertainty" (Knight, 2006 [1921]: 19–20; cf. Adams, 2001: 25–27; Boyne, 2003: 3–17, 109–110). Knight hereby intervened in the debate on randomness versus statistically calculable probability which dominated most of the twentieth century (Bernstein, 1996: 213–214, 216–230). Due to the experience of World War I – and more recently the knowledge explosion of the information society – ideas about perfect knowledge, and the notion that certainty would eventually replace uncertainty, were increasingly called into question. However, if uncertainty and imperfect knowledge are the rule rather than the exception, risk management becomes difficult, since it presupposes the possibility of being able to rationally calculate the probability of risk (Bernstein, 1996: 205–206, 213–214).

Until that time, classical economists conceived of the economy as a system that was largely risk-free and which always gave optimum results. In contrast to this, Knight abandoned the idea of the economy as a closed system in which probability could be rationally calculated, by pointing out that there will always be uncertainty and unforeseen consequences of action (Knight, 2006 [1921]; cf. Bernstein, 1996: 216–217, 219–222). In order to be able to conceptualize this, Knight introduced a key distinction between randomness that can be probability calculated, which he termed "risk"; and randomness that cannot be probability calculated, which he termed "uncertainty" (Knight, 2006 [1921]: 19–20; cf. Bernstein, 1996: 219–222; Boyne, 2003: 3).

The prototypical example used to illustrate Knight's point is the stock and bond market, in which price oscillations testify to the fact that what is expected does not always occur; on the contrary, uncertainty makes it difficult to calculate investment risk (Bernstein, 1996: 221–222). Knight's distinction between risk and uncertainty is also found, albeit less categorically, in the work of British economist John M. Keynes (1883–1946), who harbored the same skepticism about the foundation of the classic economic theories in mathematical probability laws, including their ideas about certain knowledge as a starting point for decision-making (Keynes, 1948 [1921]; cf. Bernstein, 1996: 222–223). Since, according to Keynes, complete knowledge can never be obtained, it is not always possible to say exactly what the probability is that something will happen – here we are often left to guesswork. Thus, rather than mathematical probabilities, Keynes preferred to speak about "assumptions" in the sense of degrees of rational belief in the possibility of reaching certain conclusions based on given premises (Keynes, 1948 [1921]: 4–5, 8, 15–17; cf. Bernstein, 1996: 226; Hacking, 2006 [1975]: 13–14). Thus, Keynes, like Knight, had serious doubts about statistical averages and probabilities, as he believed that uncertainty, rather than mathematical probability, exists in the real world (Keynes, 1948 [1921]: 24–40; 1949 [1936]: 3, 33–34, 148–150, 152–153, 161–163; cf. Bernstein, 1996: 228–229).

After Knight and Keynes, game theory, among other approaches, has attempted to identify the cause of uncertainty, pointing out that it lies in the "intentions of others." However, this does not mean that game theory rejects mathematical descriptions of human behavior; rather, it is assumed that such descriptions would eventually influence the players themselves and thus help to make them "rational" (Bernstein, 1996: 232, 237–238).

More Recent Approaches to the Analysis of Risk

The question of risk calculability also plays an important role in the second half of the twentieth century, which is reflected in the different approaches to the analysis of risk that can be found in economics, psychology, sociology, and political science from about 1960 until today. More specifically, we can distinguish between: (1) technical-economic, (2) psychological, (3) culture-theoretical, (4) sociological, and (5) political science (governmentality) approaches to the analysis of risk in contemporary society (Breck, 2001: 30; Mythen, 2004: 4 5; Rasborg, 2014: 177–179).

In the 1960s and until the mid-1970s, a stricter technical-economic approach to risk based on statistics, probability theory, and calculations of consequence was predominant within risk research. One of the most important figures in this field was the American engineer Chauncey Starr (1912–2007), who was interested in investigating how much we are willing to pay for safety. In other words, he sought to answer the question: "How safe is safe enough"? (Starr, 1969: 1237; cf. Breck, 2001: 30–32). Starr's point of departure is that we are rational individuals who, in order to achieve a variety of benefits, are willing to take risks such as driving, air travel, smoking, drinking, skiing, and so on. In other words, risk is not just something which is imposed on us "from the outside," but is also something that we take on ourselves (Starr, 1969: 1233–1234; cf. Adams, 2001: 3, 14–16). On the basis of rational choice theory and cost–benefit analysis, Starr thus attempted to determine the level of "acceptable risk" that people are prepared to tolerate, that is, the threshold where the benefits of a given activity would still outweigh the potential risks. One of Starr's findings was that our willingness to take risks is directly proportional to the perceived benefits of a given activity. Moreover, he found that our willingness to accept "voluntary" risks is about 1,000 times greater than our willingness to accept "involuntary" risks (Starr, 1969: 1237; cf. Adams, 2001: 65–67).

In the 1970s and 1980s, researchers became increasingly interested in investigating the subjective experience of risk, since they realized that there are significant differences in how people experience risk. One of the leading figures in this psychological (psychometric) approach to risk was the American psychology professor Paul Slovic (b. 1938), whose research, among others, demonstrated that our subjective experience of risk does not necessarily coincide with expert definitions of "objective" risk (Slovic, 1987; cf. Adams, 2001: 9–14). According to Slavic's studies, many people believe that today's risks are much more extensive than those of the past, and that future risks will be even more serious – in contrast to experts, who typically believe the opposite (Slovic, 1987: 280). Slavic's studies also showed that people's subjective experience of risk is influenced by their social position, education, gender, ethnicity, and so on (Slovic, 2000 [1997]: 396–402). In other words, social differences seem to affect subjective experiences of risk. Lastly, Slovic pointed out a number of paradoxes in subjective perceptions of risk, showing that we are not always as rational in our approach to risk as the technical-economic approach assumes. For example, many people are afraid of traveling by plane, but not of driving a car, even though the former is statistically a much safer form of transport than the latter (Breck, 2001: 35–44). In other words, our subjective perception of risk is not always consistent with the "actual" risk involved. Slavic's response to this apparent paradox is not that experts are necessarily more rational than laymen, but rather that both experts' and laymen's views of risk are mixtures of rational thinking, feelings, and specific worldviews (Slovic, 2000 [1997]: 402–404).

The 1980s represent another turning point, as risk research entered a more culture-theoretical phase where the emphasis was on the "social construction" of risk (Breck, 2001: 47–58). The focus shifted from rational choice and subjectively perceived risk to the culturally specific interpretative frameworks that were assumed to determine how given cultures or societies articulate risk. Here, the leading figures were the British social anthropologist Mary Douglas (1921–2007), and the American political scientist Aaron Wildavsky (1930–1993), who pointed out in their book, *Risk and Culture* (1983), that all societies are characterized by an infinite number of risks. But as it is not possible for any society to relate to all risks at once, some kind of risk selection must take place. According to Douglas and Wildavsky, the interesting question is which social and cultural processes define why a given society focuses on some types of risks and ignores others. In other words, a given society's understanding of risk is, according to Douglas and Wildavsky, culturally determined and constructed through a range of social classifications which define the relationship between "dangerous" and "harmless" (Douglas, 1986; Douglas and Wildavsky, 1983). Furthermore, according to these authors, modern society is characterized by an internal differentiation between various "risk cultures" which have different perspectives on risk, namely an "individualistic" (market) culture, a "hierarchical" (state) culture, a "fatalistic" (individual) culture, and an "egalitarian" (civil society/ social movements) culture (Douglas and Wildavsky, 1983, 90–91, 104–105, 138–139; cf. Adams, 2001: 33–41).

In the 1980s and 1990s, risk research moved into a more explicitly sociological phase where risks were perceived as inextricably linked to the way in which society, not least technology and material production, was organized (Breck, 2001: 61–75). Consequently, the focus turned to how risk was connected with the basic structures of modern society. The leading figure here was Ulrich Beck (1992 [1986]; 2009a [2007]), whose understanding of risk – which I unfold further later in this chapter – was shaped by significant developments in highly developed, industrial, postwar societies. Other key representatives of the sociological understanding of risk are Anthony Giddens (1990; 1991; 1994; 1998a; 1999) and Niklas Luhmann (1990; 1993 [1991]). However, Lehmann's perspective on risk differs from both Beck's and Giddens', since according to Luhmann, risk is associated with the way in which social systems observe themselves and their surroundings, as I shall discuss in what follows.

Finally, we can identify a political science, or governmentality, approach to risk, which gained ground in the 1990s and 2000s. One of the most prominent representatives of this approach is the Australian social researcher Mitchell Dean (b. 1957) who, inspired by the French social philosophers Michel Foucault (1926–1984) and François Ewald (b. 1946), points out that risk is intrinsically linked to insurance, which has to do with making "the incalculable calculable" (Dean, 1999: 184; Ewald, 1991: 204–205). Risk is, thus, associated with insurance technology and the emergence in contemporary society of new forms of reflexive government – governmentality – that are all about making reality calculable and thus controllable (Dean, 1999).

What can we learn from the brief history of risk presented above? First of all, that the notion of risk is closely connected with the advent of modern society, notably the notion that the future is not determined by fate or providence, but can be calculated – and thus controlled – based on probabilities. We also see that the notion of risk differs depending on the historical and social context. Risk, in other words, is not an unambiguous and objective phenomenon, but is a term invented by humans in an attempt to come to terms with the increasing randomness of contemporary society due to its future orientation and high pace of change. As Slovic puts it:

> risk does not exist "out there," independent of our minds and cultures, waiting to be measured. Instead, human beings have invented the concept *risk* to help them to understand and cope with the dangers and uncertainties of life. Although these dangers are real, there is no such thing as real risk or objective risk. Even the simplest, most straightforward risk assessments are based on theoretical models, whose structure is subjective and assumption laden and whose inputs are dependent upon judgment. (Slovic, 2000 [1997]: xxxvi)

In other words, risks are always embedded in a cultural interpretative horizon, and the theoretical models we use to attempt to calculate or estimate risk are always based on certain assumptions.

The "Risk Society" Thesis

With his theory of the "risk society," the German sociologist Ulrich Beck (1992 [1986]) has, as already mentioned, become one of the most influential "risk sociologists" in contemporary sociology. Beck's starting point is the global environmental problems which threaten both humans and animal species, and which are seen as inextricably linked to the organization of modern (industrial) society. Thus, "risks" are, in Beck's view, side effects, or unintended consequences, of industrial society, notably phenomena such as global warming, nuclear disasters, cloudbursts, ozone depletion, CO_2 emissions, global financial crises, and so on (Beck 1992 [1986]: 13–14, 19–20, 21–22). Following Beck, these unintended consequences have today become so predominant that they form the basis for a new type of society, that is, a "risk society." Whereas industrial society, which corresponds to what Beck describes as the "first (simple) modernity," is characterized by the fact that it produces and distributes "goods" (wealth), the risk society, which coincides with what he terms the "second (reflexive) modernity," is characterized by the fact that it produces and distributes "bads" (risks) (Beck, 1992 [1986]: 19–24; 1997 [1993]: 25–28). In his more recent writings, Beck also speaks about risk as the "anticipation of disaster," and furthermore distinguishes between "unintended disasters" (ecological crises, global financial crises) on the one hand, and "intended disasters" (international terrorism) on the other (Beck, 2009a [2007]: 11–14). In this way, it becomes possible for him to include international terrorism, which is deliberate and intentional, in his diagnosis of the (world) risk society (Beck, 2009a [2007]: 13–14; cf. Arnoldi, 2009: 49–50).

Following Beck, industrial society was a "scarcity society" whose main challenge was to overcome material deprivation. Here, struggles over material distribution constituted the main conflict in society, typically taking the form of class conflict. However, the struggle for better living conditions in industrial society has led to an "affluent society," that is, a welfare society where there is almost no limit to what we are able to produce, and where science and technology have reached a high level of development. Still, the flip side of the coin, according to Beck, is that we are increasingly faced with the side effects of the way in which modern welfare is produced (Beck, 1997 [1993]: 129). We are, as Beck puts it, "living in the age of side effects" (Beck, 1994: 175), and these side effects have, in his view, become so extensive that they may signal the advent of a new type of society.

Unlike wealth, which is unevenly distributed, according to Beck risks are characterized by the fact that in principle they affect everybody (Beck, 1992 [1986]: 36–44). The pesticides in drinking water do not distinguish between social classes, and CO_2 emissions cross national boundaries. Of course, we may individually seek to minimize our own risks by buying organic foods produced without pesticides, or by settling in a location where air pollution is not so high. But as pollution today is transnational, and ultimately global, individual risk reduction strategies only have a limited effect (Beck 1992 [1986]: 35–36).

In other words, risks transcend class and are "egalitarian," or put another way: "poverty is hierarchic, smog is democratic," as Beck puts it (Beck, 1992 [1986]: 36). A new distribution pattern – "the logic of risk distribution" – which is linked to the distribution of classless risks, thus becomes more salient than the struggle over material distribution – "the logic of wealth distribution" – which was embedded in class relations (Beck, 1992 [1986]: 19–20). Hence, the risk society is, in Beck's view, a "post-class society," whose pattern of inequality is much more complex than that of industrial society (Beck, 1992 [1986]: 46–48, 100). However, paradoxically, it is not the "crisis," but rather the "triumph" of industrial society – in the form of "egalitarian" risks – that tends to undermine the very same industrial society, according to Beck (1992 [1986]: 78; 1997 [1993]: 25–26).

Whereas wealth, in many ways, is readily observable, Beck points out that risks are characterized by the fact that they often cannot be seen with the naked eye. For instance, we cannot see, taste, or smell the pesticides in drinking water, which can only be identified using scientific methods (Beck, 1992 [1986]: 26–34). Risks are, in other words, knowledge- and hence definition-dependent since they are determined in "definitional struggles," that is, "negotiation games" among polluting companies, public authorities, and citizens concerned about how to determine what is "dangerous" and what is "harmless" (not least by means of threshold values) (Beck, 1992 [1986]: 21–22, 29–30, 46). Thus, risks are not objective and neutral in Beck's view, but "negotiated" and dependent on interpretations, which always take place within a social and cultural context and are interwoven with specific economic and social interests.

As a consequence of the invisibility of risks, we are, in Beck's view, constantly forced to relate to abstract and theoretical matters that cannot be experienced directly. Is it dangerous to eat genetically modified foods? Is mobile phone radiation carcinogenic? Should all women be screened for breast cancer, or does it imply a risk of overdiagnosis that will lead to healthy women having their breasts removed? In order to answer such questions, we depend on expert knowledge, but even experts often cannot agree on the answers (Beck, 1992 [1986]: 71–74).

One of the most obvious objections to Beck's theory of the risk society is that we have always been exposed to all sorts of risks (Lupton, 2013: 110; Mythen, 2004: 2–3). In premodern societies, earthquakes, floods, or crop failure could have disastrous consequences, and diseases and epidemics killed millions of people. The ravages of the plague in Europe in around 1350, for example, wiped out a quarter of the entire population, and the Spanish flu in the years 1918–1919 caused around 50 million fatalities *(Den Store Danske. Gyldendals Åbne Encyklopædi, 2016)*. Of course, Beck would not deny such facts, but he emphasizes that the novelty of the risk society is that whereas risks previously originated from *nature*, they now originate from *ourselves*, as they are the product of modern (industrial) civilization (Beck, 1992 [1986]: 21–24). In order to conceptualize this difference, in his more recent works Beck distinguishes between premodern *dangers*, which originate from unpredictable natural events and are attributed to fate (e.g. earthquakes, floods, and diseases); and modern *risks*, which are side effects of industrial modernization and thus ultimately originate from ourselves (that is, they are decision-dependent) (Beck, 1995 [1988]: 78).

At the same time, however, Beck points out that the highly developed risk society is characterized by the emergence of new threats, which he describes as "large-scale hazards" (*Großgefahren*) (e.g. nuclear accidents, holes in the ozone layer, global warming, etc.). Large-scale hazards, which resemble what Giddens refers to as high-consequence risks (Giddens, 1994: 78, 219–223), display the following features: (1) they are so extensive and complex that they cannot be delimited temporally, spatially, and socially; (2) it is difficult to identify the offender and thus assign responsibility; and (3) it is not possible to insure against them or otherwise compensate for them economically (Beck, 1995 [1988]: 76–77). In other words, large-scale hazards are so extensive, devastating, and irreversible, that they: ". . . undercut the social logic of risk calculation and provision" (Beck, 1995 [1988]: 77).

With Beck's emphasis on the always negotiated – and thus socially constructed – character of risk, his view of risk contains a clear social-constructivist element. At the same time, however, he maintains that risks are real phenomena that play a crucial role in generating a new type of society. Risks are, in Beck's view, complex and composite phenomena that at once have to do with mathematical calculations, technical knowledge, culture, and norms (Beck, 1999: 138). His view on risk thus contains both a realist and a social-constructivist element: ". . . risks are at the same time 'real' *and* constituted by social perception and construction" (Beck, 1999: 143; cf. Lupton, 2013: 79–80). In other words, Beck attempts to find an intermediate position – which he terms "reflexive" or "constructivist realism" – between "naive realism" on the one hand, and "naive constructivism" on the other (Beck, 1996: 4–7; 1999: 134; 2009a [2007]: 88–90; cf. Rasborg, 2012: 13–14).

In his more recent works, Beck emphasizes that the risk society has today become a "world risk society" characterized by global flows of environmental, financial, and terrorism risks (Beck, 1996; 2000 [1997]; 2009a [2007]; 2009c). However, the world risk society not only distributes global risks, but also leads to an increasing awareness of the need to find common solutions to transboundary problems, which in Beck's view creates a breeding ground for the emergence of a "cosmopolitan society" (Beck, 2002; 2006 [2004]; 2009a [2007]; 2009b). Since the problems in question are not confined to particular nation states, they cannot be solved at national level but require the establishment of trans- and/or supranational political structures such as the European Union (EU) and the United Nations (UN). As a consequence we are, in Beck's view, increasingly becoming "global citizens" in a cosmopolitan society which is oriented toward international cooperation based on ideals of human rights, humanity, recognition of diversity, and so on (Beck and Grande, 2010; Beck and Levy, 2013; Beck and Sznaider, 2006).

Another prominent sociologist who has been greatly inspired by Beck and shares his views on the central role of risk in contemporary society is Anthony Giddens (Giddens, 1990, 1991, 1994, 1998a, 1998b, 1999). Giddens endorses the distinction between risk and danger (Giddens, 1998a: 26–27; 1998b: 64) and agrees with Beck that the "external risks" of industrial societies, which were delimited and calculable and could therefore be insured against (Giddens, 1994: 194, 208; 1998a: 27), are supplemented in today's globalized society by new forms of "manufactured uncertainty" and "high-consequence risks" that are incalculable and which, if they materialize, will be so extensive and irreversible that they cannot be insured against (Giddens, 1994: 78–80, 152; 1998a: 28). However, in other areas, as Giddens points out, risks have been reduced. For example, life expectancy increased considerably during the course of the twentieth century in all the highly developed industrial societies, not least due to lower child mortality, improved disease control, improved sanitation, improved living conditions, better diets, hygiene, and housing, and so on. The development of medical science, health technology, and general living conditions have, in many ways, helped to eliminate, or mitigate, a wide range of risks which previously would have been life-threatening (Giddens, 1991: 114–124; cf. Arnoldi, 2009: 8; Douglas and Wildavsky, 1983: 13–14).

Giddens therefore points out that: "In terms of basic life security (. . .) the risk-reducing elements seem substantially to outweigh the new array of risks" (Giddens, 1991: 116). That is, in Giddens' view, the risk society does not necessarily imply an increase in "real riskiness," but rather signals that we have become more aware of risks as a result of late modernity's increasing reflexivity (Giddens, 1991: 123–124, 181–183). Today, Beck seems to have come closer to this view, for instance when he points out that the decisive criterion for whether we live in a risk society is not an objective increase in risk (realism), but whether or not risk plays an increasingly important role on the public agenda (constructivism) (Beck, 2009a [2007]: 11).

A third leading risk sociologist who takes on the full consequences of the constructivist view on risk is Niklas Luhmann, who stresses that risks are basically linked to decisions (Luhmann, 1990: 136, 140; 1993 [1991]: 16–17). For Luhmann, decisions appear as risks when they are observed with an eye to the future, and as the future is inherently unknown (contingent) the possibility – or precisely the risk – of unintended consequences of action (counter-finality) is always present. Any decision – even a decision about safety – is, thus, associated with risk (Luhmann, 1990: 135, 140, 160). As Luhmann points out, since the only thing we can say with certainty is that there is no absolute certainty, certainty cannot be the counter-concept to risk, but must be replaced by the concept of *danger* (Kneer and Nassehi, 1997 [1993]: 175; Luhmann, 1990: 134–135, 164; 1993 [1991]: 20, 28, 220).

The distinction between risk and danger is, according to Luhmann, based on the attribution of harm to decisions, and is connected to who has taken a given decision (Luhmann, 1990: 137–138, 148–149). To the one who decides (ego), the consequences of a decision may appear to involve risk, whereas for those concerned (alter) they appear to involve danger (Luhmann, 1990: 148–149; 1993 [1991]: 21–22, 26–27). Depending on the perspective of the observer, identical matters can, thus, signify risk and danger, respectively. Smokers run the risk of getting lung cancer, but they expose those in their surroundings to danger as they become passive smokers. Car drivers who do not respect the speed limit run the risk of having an accident, but they pose a danger to other motorists.

That notwithstanding, risk and danger can also go hand in hand without being separated into an ego and an alter. Damage caused by an earthquake can, as Luhmann says, be the risk that one takes on board when building in an area that is known to be earthquake-prone. But it is not a risk if you have inherited the house, and it is still a risk if you do not sell the house even if you know that it is located in an earthquake-prone region (Luhmann, 1990: 149–150). As the examples show, it is the element of decision that underlies the distinction between risk and danger, and the more complex modern society's decision-making structures become, the more a given attribution points toward risk (Luhmann, 1993 [1991]: 27, 46).

Where the distinction between risk and danger really becomes sociologically interesting, however, is in cases when one person's risk behavior becomes a danger to others, cf. the examples presented above (Luhmann, 1990: 152). Thus, paradoxically, it can, as Luhmann points out, equally well be argued that increasing decision complexity causes attributions to point more toward danger than risk. The reason for this is that the more complex modern society's decision-making structures become, the more one person's risky decisions become a danger to those affected by them. Moreover, decision makers are themselves ultimately affected by their own decisions. This suggests that society must think about its future not in terms of risk, but rather in terms of danger, since damage, or even disasters, can occur even if it is not possible to accurately identify the decisions that triggered them. Climate change is a good example of this (Luhmann, 1990: 167).

However, the attribution of particular decisions in terms of risk or danger, respectively, presupposes an observation, that is, that there is "somebody" – a social system in Lehmann's terminology – observing and making the attribution in the first place. Consequently, risk becomes a crucial element in modern society's self-observation (Luhmann, 1990: 137–138). And, in his analysis of risk, Luhmann is interested in observing how modern society observes itself with regard to the consequences of increasing decision complexity (Kneer and Nassehi, 1997 [1993]: 176). In other words, we are concerned with the "observation of observation," or, as Luhmann calls it, a "second-order observation," that is, a radical constructivist departure from a realist view of risks as pre-given phenomena ("first order observation") (Luhmann, 1990: 137–138; 1993 [1991]: 14–19, 21).

By applying Lehmann's risk-analysis framework, it becomes possible to highlight a series of paradoxes in contemporary society, not least the fact that there is no necessary link between our own willingness to take risks (risk) and our willingness to accept the consequences of the risk behavior of others (danger). To observe something as a risk or a danger, respectively, may, according to Luhmann, vary socially, since people's willingness to accept a threatening future scenario depends on whether it is considered a danger or a risk. And even if we have a high risk tolerance with regard to our own conduct, we do not readily accept risks caused by the behavior of others (Luhmann, 1990: 154). In other words, we expect, as Luhmann puts it, that we "can live riskily without danger" (Luhmann, 1990: 163). We are thus dealing with a paradox: namely, that independently of our own risk-willingness, we expect a high level of protection from the risk-willingness of others (Luhmann, 1990: 155). It is obvious that the more such expectations are aimed at, for example, the political system and its decision makers, the more the latter will come under pressure and risk falling into a crisis of legitimacy.

Risk, Insurance, and Governmentality

As already mentioned, risk cannot be understood independently of insurance, which is precisely about collective risk sharing. In industrial society, many risks were still relatively confined and calculable and hence, according to Beck and Giddens, it was also possible to insure against them (e.g. unemployment insurance, health insurance, accident insurance, etc.). But because it is hard to define and calculate the large-scale hazards and high-consequence risks of the risk society, it also becomes difficult to insure against them (Beck, 1995 [1988]: 85, 106–110; Giddens, 1994: 152). Although the probability that these risks occur must be deemed to be relatively low, the consequences if they do will be so extensive that they cannot be compensated for economically (e.g. a rise in the global sea level, terrorist attacks, nuclear accidents, etc.) (Beck, 2009c: 293–294; Giddens, 1994: 152). The highly developed risk society is, therefore, for Beck and Giddens, a "post-risk-calculation society" (Dean, 1999: 183) where the insurance principle tends to collapse. For example, after the terrorist attacks in New York on September 11, 2001, it became much more difficult, and considerably more costly, for companies, organizations, and government agencies to insure against the consequences of international terrorism (Arnoldi, 2009: 149–150; Bougen, 2003; Ericson and Doyle, 2004: 161–164).

Both Beck's and Giddens concepts of risk are thus based on the view that industrial society's "calculable risks" are being replaced by risk society's "incalculable risks." However, this contraposition of "calculable" and "incalculable" risks has been criticized by Mitchell Dean (1999) for expressing a realist conception of risk as a "social fact" whose intrinsic properties change during the development of modern society. Dean here draws on Ewald (1991), who rejects such a realist, or essentialist, understanding of risk when he points out that: "Nothing is a risk in itself; there is no risk in reality. But on the other hand, anything *can* be a risk; it all depends on how one analyzes the danger, considers the event" (Ewald, 1991: 199). In other words, according to Ewald, that something is a risk is not an inherent property of a given phenomenon, but rather expresses a certain way of observing it, that is, from an insurance point of view. Consequently, in Ewald's view, there is an inextricable link between risk and insurance (Ewald, 1991: 198). Insurance is, as he says, the technology of risk and this is what makes it meaningful at all to speak of something as a risk. According to this insurance (actuarial) concept of risk, risks are: (1) calculable, (2) collective, and (3) a capital (Ewald, 1991: 201–205).

That is, for something to be a risk it must be possible to subject it to calculation models linked to insurance (statistics and probability) (Ewald, 1991: 201–202). Furthermore, it must be possible to map how damage will be distributed across a given population (Ewald, 1991: 202–204). Lastly, it must be possible, through insurance, to provide financial compensation for damage that cannot easily be priced (e.g. the loss of a body part due to an occupational accident). This is calculated using models that define how much compensation should be awarded for particular kinds of damage (e.g. a given degree of disability) (Ewald, 1991: 204–205). Hence, according to Ewald and Dean, risk should not be seen independently of insurance which, as already mentioned, has to do with "making the incalculable calculable" (Dean, 1999: 184–185).

As a consequence, for Ewald and Dean it does not make sense to speak of "incalculable risks," because if risks are defined in terms of insurance it follows by definition that they must be calculable as otherwise they would not be risks: "It is thus not possible to speak of incalculable risks, or of risks that escape our modes of calculation, and even less possible to speak of a social order in which risk is largely calculable and contrast it with one in which risk has become largely incalculable" (Dean, 1999: 177). Since insurance is exactly about pricing damage that is difficult to quantify economically, everything can, in principle, be turned into a risk from an insurance point of view: "For insurance rationality, everything can be treated as a risk and the task of insurers has been both to 'produce' risks and to find ways of insuring what has previously been thought to be uninsurable" (Dean, 1999: 184–185).

For Dean, then, risk is closely connected with governance, since the attempt to make reality calculable by using risk calculations is precisely an attempt to organize it so that it becomes controllable (Dean, 1999: 177). Unlike Beck and Giddens, who mainly localize the origin of risk in economic and technological development, in Dean's radically constructivist approach risks are associated with the emergence in the modern welfare state of new forms of reflexive government – "governmentality" – which aim at shaping and guiding human behavior ("the conduct of conduct") (Dean, 1999: ch. 9; cf. Foucault, 1991 [1978]; Lupton, 2013: 113–114).

Today, advanced liberal, or neoliberal, forms of governmentality have, in Dean's view, led to an increasing individualization, privatization, and decentralization of the collective risk management of the welfare state, whose aim is to equalize the individual risks associated with unemployment, sickness, and old age (Dean, 1999: 191). These new forms of governmentality do not, however, work through an overt (repressive) power, but rather through a more "concealed," creative and facilitating power which, according to Dean (and Foucault) is about getting individuals to govern themselves ("management through self-management") in terms of taking greater responsibility for their own individual risk management (e.g. minimizing the risk of contracting lifestyle diseases through a healthy lifestyle) (Dean, 1999: 191–197). The exercise of political power is, therefore, in this perspective more about saying "yes" than about saying "no" (Bang and Dyrberg, 2011: 60).

Summary

In summary, a number of insights in the history of risk can be highlighted that have decisively shaped our understanding of what risk is all about, namely: (1) the realization that risk is closely connected with modernity and its secularization and future orientation (the abandonment of belief in fate, providence, God, etc.); (2) the realization that risk in the modern understanding of the term refers to "calculable randomness," that is, incidents whose probability can be calculated, whereas uncertainty refers to "incalculable randomness," which refers to incidents that cannot be calculated by means of probability; (3) the recognition that risks are, to a large extent, knowledge- and definition-dependent phenomena; (4) the realization that risk is not just something which is "imposed on us" from the outside, but also is something that we choose, cf. the familiar term "taking a risk"; (5) the recognition that risk is often part of an assessment of the advantages and disadvantages of a given action, cf. the notion of "acceptable risk"; (6) the realization that our willingness to take risks depends on whether we see advantages or disadvantages in taking the risk in question, cf. smoking, drinking, the annual skiing holiday, and so on; (7) the realization that subjectively perceived risk is not necessarily identical with "objective" risk; (8) the recognition that risk is not just something negative, but can be seen as something positive as well, since taking risks is a key element in embarking on new ventures, including those with no safety net.

The more recent sociological theories of risk (Beck, Giddens, and Luhmann), outlined above, do not merely conceive of risk as a mathematical probability that something undesirable will occur, but also thematize how risk can be seen as part of the social transformation of postwar industrial society in a much broader sense. In Beck's and Giddens' view, the highly developed risk society is, as we have seen, characterized by the fact that risks have increasingly become incalculable and thus uninsurable. This view that we are increasingly confronted with incalculable randomness is in line with Knight's and Keynes' view that it is often difficult to calculate risks in real life (cf. Beck 2009a [2007]: 16–19). However, from the point of view of Knight's and Keynes' distinction between "risk" (calculable randomness) and "uncertainty" (incalculable randomness), Beck's and Giddens' notion of "*in*calculable *risks*," makes no sense, since risk by definition is characterized by being calculable – in contrast to "uncertainty," which precisely refers to "incalculable randomness" (cf. point 2, above).

On the other hand, the view of risks as calculable by definition is, as shown above, a key element in the political science or governmentality approach to risk (Foucault, Ewald, and Dean), which points out that nothing is a risk in itself and that risk therefore first "occurs" when phenomena are viewed from an insurance perspective. From this perspective, risk and insurance have to do with a continuing effort to make the incalculable calculable, or – in Knight's and Keynes' terms – a continuing effort to transform incalculable "uncertainty" into calculable "risks." Above, we have seen how Luhmann, based on his distinction between risk and danger, suggests that in modern society the attribution tends to point toward *danger*, since one person's risky behavior easily becomes a danger to others. Similarly, we can say that according to Beck and Giddens, "the attribution" in modern society tends to point toward incalculable (manufactured) *uncertainty*, whereas according to Foucault, Ewald, and Dean it points more toward calculable (actuarial) *risk* (cf. above; Arnoldi, 2009: 182).

Thus, irrespective of how different these approaches might appear at first glance, they have one thing in common: they all thematize key aspects of the relationship between uncertainty, risk, and insurance in modern society. In modern society, increasing decision complexity (Luhmann) goes hand in hand with new forms of uncertainty (Beck and Giddens); but incalculable uncertainty is also continually transformed into calculable risks which can be insured against and thus compensated for economically (Foucault, Ewald, and Dean) (Arnoldi, 2009: 185). In modern society, this occurs partly through the welfare state, which is about collective risk sharing; and partly through private insurance – and reinsurance – which (to a far greater extent than suggested by Beck and Giddens) transforms uncertainty into actuarial risk – and in some cases takes risks even if the precise odds are not known. Moreover, with regard to extensive "large-scale hazards" (terrorist attacks, floods, etc.), the welfare state acts as a guarantor ("reinsurer") in some cases whereby private "uninsurability" is turned into "governable insurability" (Arnoldi, 2009: 148–152; Bougen, 2003; Ericson and Doyle, 2004). Thus, instead of asserting that *either* risk *or* uncertainty predominates in contemporary society, it seems more meaningful to say that risk and uncertainty *coexist* and are continuously transformed into one another (Arnoldi, 2009: 150–152; Bougen, 2003: 258, 264; Ericson and Doyle, 2004: 140; O'Malley, 2003: 275).

All in all, it can be concluded that although neither the sociological nor the political science – governmentality – approach to risk captures the whole truth about the role of risk in contemporary society, and in some respects may even appear contradictory, if we look at the history of risk, and not least the distinction between "uncertainty" and "risk," it seems possible to "integrate" insights from both traditions into a more coherent understanding of the interconnections between uncertainty, risk, and insurance in modern society. Furthermore, it may – perhaps a little provocatively – be concluded that if one looks at the social dynamics – that is, new forms of incalculable randomness (uncertainty) – which according to Ulrich Beck are becoming increasingly predominant in the new type of society that he describes as a "risk society," then the proper term for that society would not be a "risk society," but rather an "uncertainty society." In retrospect, the most appropriate title for Ulrich Beck's pioneering major work might, thus, not have been *The Risk Society*, but rather *The Uncertainty Society*.

References

Adams, John. 2001. *Risk*. London/New York: Routledge.

Arnoldi, Jakob. 2009. *Risk. An Introduction*. Cambridge, UK: Polity Press.

Bang, Henrik, and Torben Bech Dyrberg. 2011. *Michel Foucault*. Copenhagen: Jurist- og Økonomforbundets Forlag.

Bentham, Jeremy. 1970 [1789/1823]. *An Introduction to the Principles of Morals and Legislation*. Edited by J. H. Burns and H. L. A. Hart. London: The Athlone Press, University of London.

Beck, Ulrich. 1992 [1986]. *Risk Society. Towards a New Modernity*. London: Sage.

1994. "Self-Dissolution and Self-Endangerment of Industrial Society: What Does This Mean?" In Ulrich Beck, Anthony Giddens and Scott Lash (eds.), *Reflexive Modernization. Politics, Tradition and Aesthetics in the Modern Social Order* (pp. 174–183). Cambridge, UK: Polity Press.

1995 [1988]. *Ecological Politics in an Age of Risk*. Cambridge, UK: Polity Press.

1996. "World Risk Society as a Cosmopolitan Society. Ecological Questions in a Framework of Manufactured Uncertainties." *Theory, Culture and Society* 13(4): 1–32.

1997 [1993]. *The Reinvention of Politics. Rethinking Modernity in the Global Social Order*. Cambridge, UK: Polity Press.

1999. "Risk Society Revisited: Theory, Politics, Critiques and Research Programmes." In *World Risk Society* (pp. 133–152). Cambridge, UK: Polity Press.

2000 [1997]. *What is Globalization?* Cambridge, UK: Polity Press.

2002. "The Cosmopolitan Society and Its Enemies." *Theory, Culture and Society* 19 (1–2): 17–44.

2006 [2004]. *Cosmopolitan Vision*. Cambridge, UK: Polity Press.

2009a [2007]. *World at Risk*. Cambridge, UK: Polity Press.

2009b. "Critical Theory of World Risk Society: A Cosmopolitan Vision." *Constellations* 16 (1): 1–22.

2009c. "World Risk Society and Manufactured Uncertainties." *Iris: European Journal of Philosophy and Public Debate* 1(2): 291–299.

Beck, Ulrich, and Edgar Grande. 2010. "Varieties of Second Modernity: The Cosmopolitan Turn in Social and Political Theory and Research." *The British Journal of Sociology* 61(3): 409–443.

Beck, Ulrich, and Daniel Levy. 2013. "Cosmopolitanized Nations: Re-imagining Collectivity in a World Risk Society." *Theory, Culture & Society* 30(2): 3–31.

Beck, Ulrich, and Natan Sznaider. 2006. "Unpacking Cosmopolitanism for the Social Sciences: A Research Agenda." *The British Journal of Sociology* 57(1): 1–23.

Bernstein, Peter L. 1996. *Against the Gods: The Remarkable Story of Risk*. New York: John Wiley & Sons, Inc.

Bougen, Philip. D. 2003. "Catastrophe Risk." *Economy and Society* 32(2): 253–274.

Boyne, Roy. 2003. *Risk*. Buckingham-Philadelphia, PA: Open University Press.

Breck, Thomas. 2001. *Dialog om det usikre – nye veje i risikokommunikation*. Copenhagen: Akademisk Forlag.

Dean, Mitchell. 1999. *Governmentality. Power and Rule in Modern Society*. London: Sage.

Douglas, Mary. 1986. *Risk Acceptability According to the Social Sciences*. London: Routledge & Kegan Paul Ltd.

Douglas, Mary, and Aaron Wildavsky. 1983. *Risk and Culture. An Essay on the Selection of Technological and Environmental Dangers*. Berkeley/Los Angeles: University of California Press.

Ericson, Richard V., and Aaron Doyle. 2004. "Catastrophe Risk, Insurance and Terrorism." *Economy and Society* 33(2): 135–173.

Ewald, François. 1991. "Insurance and Risk." In Graham Burchell, Colin Gordon, and Peter Miller (eds.), *The Foucault Effect: Studies in Governmentality* (pp. 197–210). Hemel Hempstead, UK: Harvester Wheatsheaf.

Foucault, Michel. 1991 [1978]."Governmentality." In Graham Burchell, Colin Gordon, and Peter Miller (eds.), *The Foucault Effect: Studies in Governmentality* (pp. 87–104). Chicago, IL: The University of Chicago Press.

Giddens, Anthony. 1990. *The Consequences of Modernity*. Cambridge, UK: Polity Press.

1991. *Modernity and Self-Identity: Self and Society in the Late Modern Age*. Cambridge, UK: Polity Press.

1994. *Beyond Left and Right: The Future of Radical Politics*. Cambridge, UK: Polity Press.

1998a. "Risk Society: The Context of British Politics." In Jane Franklin (ed.), *The Politics of Risk Society* (pp. 23–34). Cambridge, UK: Polity Press.

1998b. *The Third Way: The Renewal of Social Democracy*. Cambridge, UK: Polity Press.

1999. *Runaway World. How Globalization is Reshaping our Lives*. Cambridge, UK: Profile Books.

Hacking, Ian. 2006 [1975]. *The Emergence of Probability: A Philosophical Study of Early Ideas about Probability, Induction and Statistical Inference*, 2nd ed. Cambridge, UK: Cambridge University Press.

Keynes, John M. 1948 [1921]. *A Treatise on Probability*. London: Macmillan and Co., Limited.

1949 [1936]. *The General Theory of Employment, Interest and Money*. London: Macmillan and Co., Limited.

Kneer, Georg, and Armin Nassehi, 1997 [1993]. *Niklas Luhmann – introduktion til teorien om sociale systemer*. Copenhagen: Hans Reitzels Forlag.

Knight, Frank H. 2006 [1921]. *Risk, Uncertainty and Profit*. New York: Dover Publications, Inc.

Luhmann, Niklas. 1990. "Risiko und Gefahr." In Niklas Luhmann (ed.), *Soziologische Aufklärung 5. Konstruktivistische Perspektiven* (pp. 131–169). Opladen: Westdeutscher Verlag.

1993 [1991]. *Risk: A Sociological Theory*. Berlin-New York: Walter de Gruyter.

Lupton, Deborah. 2013. *Risk*, 2nd ed. London/New York: Routledge.

Mythen, Gabe. 2004. *Ulrich Beck: A Critical Introduction to Risk Society*. London: Pluto Press.

O'Malley, Pat. 2003. "Governable Catastrophes: A Comment on Bougen." *Economy and Society* 32(2): 275–279.

Rasborg, Klaus. 2012. "'(World) Risk Society' or 'New Rationalities of Risk'? A Critical Discussion of Ulrich Beck's Theory of Reflexive Modernity." *Thesis Eleven* 10(1): 3–25.

2014. "Risiko- og frygtsamfund." In Jørgen Elm Larsen, Bent Greve, and Anja Jørgensen (eds.), *Det danske samfund* (pp. 175–200). Copenhagen: Hans Reitzels Forlag.

Sennett, Richard. 1998. *The Corrosion of Character: The Personal Consequences of Work in the New Capitalism*. New York-London: W. W. Norton & Company.

Slovic, Paul. 1987. "Perception of Risk." *Science, New Series* 236(4799): 280–285.

2000 [1997]. "Trust, Emotion, Sex, Politics and Science: Surveying the Risk-assessment Battlefield." In *The Perception of Risk* (pp. 390–412). London: Earthscan.

Starr, Chaunsey. 1969. "Social Benefit versus Technological Risk." *Science, New Series* 165 (3899): 1232–1238.

Weber, Max. 1992 [1904–1905]. *The Protestant Ethic and the Spirit of Capitalism*. London/ New York: Routledge.

Internet Sources

Den Store Danske. Gyldendals Åbne Encyklopædi 2016: "Pest." www.denstoredanske.dk /Krop,_psyke_og_sundhed/Sundhedsvidenskab/Infektions-_og_tropesygdomme/ pest?highlight=pest.

"Spansk syge." www.denstoredanske.dk/Krop,_psyke_og_sundhed/Sundhedsvidenskab/ Infektions-_og_tropesygdomme/spansk_syge?highlight=den%20spanske% 20syge.

17 Trust and the Variety of Its Bases

Barbara A. Misztal

Trust: Anticipation of the Future in Risk Conditions

In the last few decades trust has become one of the most regularly invoked and debated topics in many spheres of life; it has been making newspaper headlines, it has become a popular idea in political and business vocabularies and it has appealed to social scientists. This surge of trust talk raises the question of why modern societies put so much weight on trust. Generally, it can be said that behind today's focus on trust is the recognition of trust as a highly problematic but beneficial feature of social relationships characterized by risk. The popularity of the concept of trust as a precaution against uncertainty and vulnerability reflects the assumption about the omnipresence of trust in social relations and the claim that with trust, societies flourish and "when trust is destroyed, societies falter and collapse"(Bok, 1979: 26). It is also indicative of the reconceptualization of modernity in terms of high levels of risk and uncertainty, which create demand for trust. The status of trust in modern risk society becomes a fundamental resource without which we can make no decisions and take no initiatives. The move from certainty to trust is illustrated, for example, by the shift from "the indisputable certainty" of scientific evidence to "trust in the institution of science" (Latour, 2013: 3). In other words, the visibility of the issue of trust today reflects the current status of trust as both the important condition of societal well-being and the essential asset in conditions of risk.

Although the silent presence of trust was observed in many classical sociological works (Silver, 1985), the proliferation of middle-range theories about trust in social science began in the 1990s. The first wave of sociological writing on trust (Fukuyama, 1995; Gambetta, 1988a; Lewis and Weigert, 1985; Misztal, 1996; Seligman, 1997; Sztompka, 1999) has been followed up by a spread of interest in the topic to other disciplines, such as political science (Warren, 1999), economics (Nooteboom, 1996; Williamson, 1993), organization studies (Kramer and Taylor, 1996; Lane and Bachmann, 1998; Zucker, 1986), and management studies (Nooteboom, Berger, and Noorderhaven, 1997). Numerous attempts to search for explanations of the role of trust in maintaining the viability of democratic forms of governance and enhancing networks of civil associations have also brought the notion of trust to the attention of policy-oriented studies. The second wave of sociological works on trust (Alexander, 2006; Cook, 2001; Edwards and Foley, 1998; Gambetta and Hamill, 2005; Mishra, 1996; Möllering, 2013; Woolcock, 1998) has been the result of attempts to think through implications and challenges posed by the alleged deficit of trust in the working of democracy and the expansion of electronic communication. The growing number of empirical investigations and theoretical works on trust has encouraged many initiatives to develop interdisciplinary forums for discussing the idea of trust and increasing our ability to handle this difficult-to-define and difficult-to-research concept. The creation of the Russell Sage Foundation Series on Trust in 1996 and its publications on empirical research and theories of trust as well as the establishment of the *Journal of Trust Research* in 2011 have added to the popularity of and pluralism in trust research.

The increased recognition of the centrality and new visibility of the issue of trust have resulted in a considerable accumulation of knowledge about trust, its specific problems, and various trust contexts. Yet, notwithstanding the new status of trust studies, trust still remains outside of the interest of mainstream sociology and even now there is a lack of an integrative theory of trust as "the most fundamental debate over *the nature of trust* is yet not effectively settled" (Li, 2015: 104, italics in the original). In spite of the increased number of investigations of the phenomenon of trust, the idea of trust continues to be "one of the most complex, multidimensional, and misunderstood concepts in the social sciences" (Wuthnow, 2004: 146). In fact, many social scientists would agree with Luhmann (1979: 84) that taking into account the varieties of ways of creating trust, it is "fruitless to search for general formulae" of trust construction. They would also agree that trust is a complex, fuzzy, and slippery term which is very difficult to conceptualize. For example, Barbalet (2009: 368) reminds us that the term "trust" is ill-defined, vague, and ambiguous, and points to the *Shorter Oxford Dictionary*'s list of sixteen different definitions of trust, which includes references to trust as faith, confidence, a certain attitude, emotion, belief, a norm of reciprocity or honesty, and telling the truth.

In the academic literature there are also many different definitions of trust; from the conceptualization of trust as a means of overcoming the absence of evidence (Simmel, 1950), and a type of knowledge or social intelligence (Yamagishi, 2003), through "the encapsulated interest" (Hardin, 2001), and "shallow morality" (Messick and Kramer, 2001), to trust seen as refraining "from taking precautions against an interaction partner" (Elster, 2007: 344). The presence of numerous definitions is created, sustained, and expanded by the fact that the social science literature on trust consists of many approaches, which basically are divided into two traditional schools of thought, the first addressing the issue of trust from an individual perspective and the other focused on trust as a "property of society" (Sasaki, 2012: 349). Furthermore, even if we limit our attention to the first perspective, we still need to acknowledge at least two types of trust, namely, interpersonal trust – which can be further split into particular trust and general trust – and institutionalized trust (Zucker, 1986). Moreover, the continuous proliferation of identifications of new types of trust, from strategic, through process-based, calculus-based, role-based, rule-based, and knowledge-based, to the concern with reflexively based trust, provides new bases for the diversity of conceptualizations of the nature of trust, with some authors viewing it as a cognitive trait (Hardin, 2006), others as a behavioral phenomenon (Sztompka, 1999), moral commitment (Uslaner, 2002), or affective experience (Baier, 1986).

Yet, despite the diversity of theoretical explanations and the lack of a general definition which could cover the dynamic, complex, and multifaceted subtleties of the notion of trust, there seems to be "some minimal consensus about its meaning" (Levi and Stoker, 2000: 476). This basic consent involves the recognition of the several main characteristics of trust, namely, the role of trust in the context of uncertainty or risk, its roots in a lack of pertinent knowledge, and the acknowledgment of its capacity to bridge the present and future (Barbalet, 2009). Even more importantly, it is also generally agreed upon that trust involves vulnerability to another affecting one's interests. In other words, one of the key features of trust, understood as "the mutual confidence that no party to an exchange will exploit another's vulnerability" (Sabel, 1993: 1133), is its link with vulnerability. Such a recognition of the connections between trust and vulnerability, by emphasizing that vulnerability creates an opportunity to trust, while at the same time opening the potential for the trusting partner's vulnerability to be exploited, calls for serious consideration of the cognitive and affective components of the trusting relationship as well as norms and values on which trust expectations and commitments are built. This variety of foundations of trust necessitates the conceptualization of trust as a multidimensional phenomenon. It also conveys the importance of accounting for the bases of trust in explaining its mechanisms, and in turn offers a rationale for categorizing the social theories of trust according to their respective identification of its bases.

A classification of social science literature on trust which starts from the assumption that trust is a multifaceted phenomenon, followed up by the assertion that no single model of it offers a sufficient explanation of its production, provides the possibility of making a straightforward distinction between the main theoretical perspectives on trust. Moreover, the recognition that the affective component of trust cannot be separated from other considerations of trust relations allows for further simplifications in the construction of such a categorization (Barbalet, 2009). Thus, I will focus on two main wide-ranging intellectual streams on trust developed in a loosely chronological order. The first perspective is a broadly normative-cultural approach that sees the actor as socialized and actions as governed by social norms, values, commitments, and obligations. The second stream is a broad rational choice perspective that views the actor as purposive, rational, and optimizing their choices. Such a grouping of the main sociological theories of trust emphasizes the contrast between the two different foundations of trust, that is, between values and norms, on the one side, and rational calculation of cost and benefits, on the other side. It also, by emphasizing the role of emotional dimensions in both types of trust, calls for a more comprehensive approach that seeks to overcome this dichotomy.

The following discussion of the dominant theories' explanations of trust production and its deficit starts with attempts to identify the bases of trust within a broad normative-cultural approach that conceptualizes trust as a means of transcending uncertainty. After a presentation of Simmel's (1950) view of trust as a social form involving a suspension of the unknown, and a short summary of Parsons' (1978) identification of familiarity as the main mechanism by which trust is generated, we will focus on Luhmann's (1979: 20) idea that "the complexity of the future world is reduced by the act of trust." It will be followed by a critical analysis of Giddens' (1990) quest for trust as a reflexive project. In the second section we will examine the rational choice concern with self-interest as the basis of trust by discussing Coleman, Gambetta, Hardin, Cook, and Levi's ways of defining trust's role in enabling actors to collaborate and mobilize resources. The final section, while arguing that to explain how trust overcomes vulnerability calls for a bridging between the perspective on trust that views rational calculation as the basis of trust and the tradition that stresses the role of normative routines as its roots, also emphasizes the necessity of taking into account the emotional foundation of trust; that is, the capacity of emotion to underwrite trust.

Trust as a Leap to Commitment

Simmel's perspective on trust is not only the first sociological theory of trust, it has also been one of the most influential approaches to this phenomenon (Möllering, 2001). According to Simmel (1990: 178), trust is a necessary way of coping with the issue of present and future, for without "the general trust that people have in each other, society itself would disintegrate." Simmel (1950: 318) defines trust as a "fundamental attitude toward the other" and asserts that trust is "one of the most important synthetic forces within society." While recognizing that the growing complexity and diversity of the social leads to the increased need for trust, he argues that modern life, "where very few relationships are based entirely upon what is known with certainty about another person," creates complex and differentiated requirements for trust (Simmel, 1990: 178–179). Because of the impossibility of complete knowledge of the other, Simmel (1950: 348) attributes to trust "almost compulsory power," without which interactions would not proceed. However, trust, although being important in social interactions, "cannot be requested" (Simmel, 1950: 348).

While developing a hypothesis regarding future behavior, Simmel (1950: 319) argues that "trust is intermediate between knowledge and ignorance about a man." For a person, trust is "a hypothesis certain enough to serve as a basis for practical conduct" (Simmel, 1950: 318), which suggests that it is possible for the individual to trust in the context of an imperfect informational basis. However, Simmel (1990: 179) does not regard weak inductive knowledge as proper trust (Frederiksen, 2012; Giddens, 1991), but he rather stresses that for social relationships to endure, trust needs to be "as strong as, or stronger than, rational proof or personal observation." In other words, he implies that to trust involves "a state of mind which has nothing to do with knowledge, which is both less and more than knowledge" (Simmel, 1990: 179). Seeing trust as standing "outside the categories of knowledge and ignorance" (Simmel, 1950: 318) means not only that complete knowledge or ignorance would render trust irrelevant, but also that within trust there is a "further element of socio-psychological quasi-religious faith" (Simmel, 1990: 179).

Simmel's (1990: 179) observation that trust "may rest upon particular reasons, but is not explained by them," leads him to suggest that it may be grounded in "some additional affective" element (Simmel, 1950: 318). This element, which is "hard to describe" and which refers to "the feeling that there exists between our idea of a being and the being itself a definite connection and unity, a certain consistency in our conception of it"(Simmel, 1990: 179), is the important factor ensuring the continuation of trust relationships. Thus, it is essential for our understanding of trust to recognize the role of this "further element," which Simmel (1950: 318) calls the "affective, even mystical, 'faith' of man in man." By assuming that trust rests on a kind of "will to trust," and that trust is "an antecedent or subsequent form of knowledge," Simmel (1950: 318) offers a very interesting understanding of trust's unique nature (Möllering, 2001: 412). This defining element of trust, which suspends individuals' reasoning about their vulnerability and uncertainty and therefore stimulates a "faith of man in man," refers to "the mechanism that brackets out uncertainty and ignorance"(Möllering, 2001: 412). A leap to commitment is possible because of the suspension of uncertainty, which by making interpretative knowledge momentarily "certain," enables us to trust (Möllering, 2001: 412).

While Simmel's theory of trust has been a source of inspiration for many, Parsons' theory tends to be limited to the ongoing questioning of a functionalist conceptualization of trust. For Parsons (1978), trust is one of the essential guarantees of social order and system integration, achieved through the institutionalization and internalization of a shared culture. Today, Parsons' (1978) view of trust as the mechanism for co-coordinating social interaction provides only the critical foundation for evaluating to which degree the notion of trust based on norms and values is sufficient to ensure the controllability of a complex, changing, and pluralistic society. In short, the relevance of Parsons' idea of trust for modern society is limited as it is not adequate for the contemporary context, where norms and values are not stable and not commonly shared (Jalava, 2003).

Parsons, who "envisaged society as a system of action, which consists of interdependent phenomena having definite patterning and stability over time" (Cheal, 2005: 99), explained the problem of social integration and order through the voluntary acceptance of norms and the familiar form of trust. For him, the idea of trust describes "a feeling or attitude based on familiarity and common culture" (Jalava, 2003: 178). Thus, trust, as the integrative trait which is learned in the process of socialization, is one of the essential guarantees of the stability of social order. Since trust is based on membership in the societal community and its norms and since these norms define the limits of membership, they also draw the limits of trust (Parsons, 1978). In other words, trust as an attitude which can be activated only between the members of the societal community can only exist inside that community (Cheal, 2005). Therefore, it is expected that people trust only members of their own communities, while strangers are met with distrust. Trust, as the essential part of interaction rooted in common values and common goals, is "a parallel concept to familiarity" (Jalava, 2003: 177). The implication of trust's association with familiarity, ensured by socialization within families and normative training in communities and professions, is that it makes possible stability, order, and system integration (Parsons, 1978). This function of trust can be illustrated by reference to the role-sets of doctor–patient relationships, which prescribe specific types of action to each partner in the interaction system. In such circumstances, trust serves to overcome a competence gap between the expert and the layman and to stabilize the structure of the interaction system.

Parsons' conceptualization of trust as a means for coordinating social interaction and his emphases on the connection between trust and familiarity provided the starting point for Luhmann's neo-functionalist theory of trust. By responding to Parsons' concept of trust as a stabilizer of changing conditions in the societal community, Luhmann (1979) aims to explain the growing demand for trust in contemporary society. His revision of Parsons's approach emphasizes the role of trust in reducing the complexities of the modern system and in bridging the present and the future. Because of trust's ability to increase our "tolerance of uncertainty," it prompts us to "behave as though the future were certain" (Luhmann, 1979: 10). While arguing that the modern world makes familiarity increasingly difficult and asserting that to "show trust is to anticipate the future," Luhmann (1979: 10) rejects Parsons' vision of trust as a taken-for-granted fact of life which is sustained by familiarity and entrenched by the past. Luhmann's (1979: 97) conceptualization of trust as a solution for specific problems of risk also differs from Parsons' idea of trust because Luhmann identifies what American sociologists viewed as the role of trust as a function of confidence.

Within Luhmann's perspective the main difference between the concept of trust and the idea of confidence is connected with their different relationships to the future and risk. Trust is a response to "situations where one must enter into risks one cannot control in advance," while confidence refers to situations where one does "not consider alternatives" (Luhmann, 1991: 129). In the trust situation, you "choose one action in preference to others in spite of the possibility of being disappointed by the actions of others; you define the situation as one of trust"(Luhmann, 1988: 97). In the confidence situation, "you will react to disappointment by external attribution": this means that when you are dissatisfied with the result of your action, you do not attribute responsibility to your behavior for that outcome (Luhmann, 1988: 97). Although confidence, seen as the situation in which you do not consider other options, may also bring discontent, yet such disappointment does not pose a threat to the functioning of the system. For example, when dealing with money, even when we are unhappy with the rate of exchange, we do not consider whether or not to accept money each time we encounter it as we do not have alternatives. Another difference between trust and confidence is that "trust remains vital in interpersonal relations," while it is "confidence, but not trust" that is required for participation in functional systems (Luhmann, 1979: 102). In short, confidence in the system is essential for its functioning. However, it is only the trust situation with its inherent risk where "you choose one in preference to other" (Luhmann, 1988: 97).

Trust, seen as "a gamble, a risky investment" (Luhmann, 1988: 24), always entails the possibility of betrayal, the other's defection from the relationship, or the exploitation of the trust giver (Luhmann, 1979: 4–5). Although there "are obviously some cases which call for trust and other cases which call for distrust"(Luhmann, 1979: 86), yet both trust and distrust are relevant solutions to risk as they are both a bet on the future contingent actions of others. According to Luhmann (1979: 33), "clues employed to form trust do not eliminate the risk, they simply lessen it. They do not supply complete information about the likely behaviors of the person to be trusted. They simply serve as a springboard for the leap into uncertainty." Thus, Luhmann (1979: 26), while seeing trust as a means of transcending uncertainty, drew on Simmel's idea of trust as enabling the leap to commitment. Although Luhmann (1979: 84, 2) doubts the possibility of bridging the gap between reason and trust, as trust is "blending knowledge and ignorance," he views a decision to trust as rational in a "non-calculative sense" (Barbalet, 2009: 376). While describing the rationale for action based on trust as " . . . a movement towards indifference; by introducing trust, certain possibilities of development can be excluded from consideration" Luhmann (1979: 25) follows Simmel's conceptualization of trust as a social form involving both an interpretation and suspension of the unknown. Since our choice to trust cannot be based on applicable knowledge, we "have to conclude, therefore, that whether or not action is founded on trust amounts to an essential distinction [or division] in the rationality of action which appears capable of attainment" (Luhmann, 1979: 25).

According to Luhmann (1979: 69), people not only trust "on the assumption that others trust" but they also evaluate their conditions as more or less encouraging trusting dispositions, calculate the probability of some events, and hold some specific beliefs to justify the specific relations. However, in modern societies, with the increased reflexivity and indeterminability of interaction, the cognitive bases of trust are becoming more problematic and personal trust becomes increasingly difficult to establish (Luhmann, 1979). This decreasing potential of personal trust is overcome by the growing importance of system trust, which adds to people's belief in the stability of the system. Since trust is "indispensable in order to increase a social system's potential for action beyond these elementary forms," it is a property of the system (Luhmann, 1979: 88). Because the function of the performance of trust-worthiness reinforces confidence in relying on social systems, trust rests on "pre-sentational" bases. In other words, trust "rests on illusion" that ensures that everything is seen to be in proper order, which increases our "trust in trust" (Luhmann, 1979: 32).

Luhmann's (1979: 4–5) conceptualization of trust has been incorporated by many scholars, including Giddens. Like Luhmann, Giddens (1990: 19) accepts Simmel's idea that trust presumes "a leap to commitment, a quality of 'faith' which is irreducible" and argues that modernity creates a new social context in which the need for trust is increased and trust becomes reflexive due to the complexity of this setting. Hence, Giddens, in a similar way to Luhmann, considers trust in the context of increased reflexivity and develops definitions of three categories of trust: trust in an abstract system, interpersonal trust, and basic trust. Yet, Giddens, while sharing many of Luhmann's accents on risk and reflexivity, in contrast to neo-functionalist theory, emphasizes the unpredictable, unstable, and contested nature of trust and power relations within complex and open systems. Moreover, for his idea of trust as a type of "faith in the probity or love of another, or in the correctness of abstract principle," Giddens (1990: 34) relies on several other sources. The roots of Giddens' notion of trust as a substitute for knowledge and an adaptive response to uncertain futures and incalculable risks can be found in the works of Erikson, Garfinkel, and Goffman. For instance, Giddens' (1991: 244) conceptualization of trust as "the vesting of confidence in persons or in abstract systems, made on the basis of a 'leap into faith' which brackets ignorance or lack of information," comes very close to Goffman's (1959) concept of bracketing. In this view, the role of trust is to ensure a bracketing-out of possible events that could be a cause for anxiety or alarm. Giddens, like Garfinkel (1963: 188), assumes that people, when confronted with potentially disruptive experiences, tend to resort to "perceived values of typically" and hence also trust. While assigning this essential function of trust in the bracketing of possible issues which could threaten the person, Giddens draws on Erikson's (1959) concept of basic trust.

The platform for basic trust which "forms the original nexus from which a combined emotive-cognitive orientation towards others, the object-world, and self-identity emerges" (Giddens, 1991: 38), is the infant's trust in their early caretakers. Viewing the act of trust as a solution to the problem of uncertainty by anticipating an unknowable future, Giddens (1990) observes that trust presumes a suspension of doubt. As a result of this suspension, the infant develops the ability to reach a state of trust which "brackets distance in time and space and so blocks off existential anxieties" (Giddens, 1990: 97). The faith in the parental figures "is the essence of that leap to commitment which basic trust – and all forms of trust thereafter – presumes" (Giddens, 1991: 95). The infant's anxiety can be generalized to the problem of ignorance that actors face in any social encounter with others whose actions and intentions they cannot fully know or control (Giddens, 1991). This basic trust derived from the confidence in the caretakers offers the basis of "ontological security," which is the foundation of the continuity of our personal identity and our confidence in the constancy of the surrounding environment (Giddens, 1991: 38). It, as confidence or faith learned in infancy, "links self-identity in a fateful way to the appraisals of others" (Giddens, 1991: 38). According to Giddens, the little child's trust in their parental figures is a sort of protection against future dangers which allows her to sustain confidence in the face of whatever threatening circumstances she later confronts. "Basic trust is a screening off device in relation to risks and dangers in the surrounding settings of action and interaction" (Giddens, 1991: 39). Its function is to block off negative possibilities in favor of "a generalized attitude of hope" and to offer the main emotional support allowing for daily functioning (Giddens, 1991: 40). In other words, Giddens (1991: 40) thinks that without basic trust, or without a "protective cocoon" which helps us to get on with our affairs, we may experience existential anxiety and a lack of confidence in the continuity of our identity, as trust presupposes the development of trust in oneself and others.

While emphasizing the role of basic trust at the origin of the experience of a stable external world and a coherent sense of identity, Giddens notes the decline of traditional sources of personalized trust, such as kinship and local communities. The uncontrolled advancement of modernity, with its proliferation, intensification, and globalization of risks, challenges the trust based on familiarity, while at the same time creating a need for trust as a means of controlling the future (Giddens, 1990; 1994a). Trust becomes a "tension management system" (Giddens, 1991: 54) to counteract a growing awareness of risk in the globalized world. This dynamic interplay between trust and risk brings about the deficit of trust as the disappearance of past sources of trust is accompanied by the actual increased in a need for trust. In modern risk culture, which requires and provides us with different means of achieving trust, there is "a fundamental sense in which the whole institutional apparatus of modernity, once it has become detached from tradition, depends on potentially volatile mechanisms of trust" (Giddens, 1994a: 89–90).

The shift from personalized trust to trust in expert systems of technical and professional knowledge follows the transfer from total confidence and certainty to uncertainty and risks of unknowable futures. Abstract systems, while depending on trust, "provide none of the moral rewards which can be obtained from personalized trust" (Giddens, 1991: 136) as they rest on vague and partial understanding. Our willingness to trust abstract systems is predicated on the lack of viable alternatives for those who "have to trust them" (Giddens, 1991). Trust in abstracts systems is conditional, as control is based on claims to "trustworthy" specialist expertise that become contested terrains on which different groups struggle to dominate the terms on which trust will be given or removed. With the growing general awareness of the limitation of expertise, expert knowledge is now "reappropriated" and open to critique and contestation (Giddens, 1994b: 193). In the context of the institutional reflexivity and higher levels of education and access to information, "there is a continuous filter-back of expert theories, concepts and findings to the lay populations" (Giddens, 1994a: 89–90). Since science has lost its previous status in the public eye as a monolithic source of "authority," changes in the nature of the relationship between experts and lay individuals bring about a need for a more active and reflexive type of trust. Consequently, the politics of trust and control become central to the expansion and legitimization of expert systems.

Giddens' three types of trust, as well as his explanations of the role of trust in ensuring actors' self-identity and their relationships with others, have significantly contributed to the development of our understanding of the notion of trust in the context of the increased reflexivity of late modernity. Yet, his view of modern relationships as "ties based on a mutual process of self-disclosure" (Giddens, 1992: 121), while offering an explanation of how trust is to be established as the main feature of intimate relations, overlooks the role of other factors than the search for authenticity in people's assessment of the risk involved in bonding with others. Giddens' theory of trust also fails to provide an adequate account of structural constraints on modern subjects as it seems to suggest that the only form of limitation on agents in social life is that choice is inevitable. Moreover, Giddens does not take into account the impact of cultural and material inequalities on the role of trust in social relationships, while his vision of the agent as knowledgeable, reflexive, and capable of self-determination is overstated.

According to a broad normative-cultural approach, trust is the mechanism for co-coordinating social interactions which helps to overcome the gap between knowledge and ignorance by a leap to commitment. This perspective assumes that the decision to extend or to withhold interpersonal trust does not occur in a "social-vacuum." Trust is seen as embedded in broader social values and norms and viewed as a generalized attitude toward others or familiarity with them. Its conceptualization of the social actor as a part of the social world with all its social norms, rules, and obligations brings to our attention the role of trust in both offering the actor help in overcoming a lack of information and in increasing a social system's integration and its potential for action. However, by concentrating on the normative basis of trust and on positive effects of trust on system functioning and integration, this perspective underestimates the importance of other foundations of trust and overlooks the impact of some essential contemporary changes and trends on the condition of trust production. Hence, because of its concern with the role of norms in constituting the foundation of trust and its limited account of the nature of trust relationships in the context of the diversity and flexibility in people's experiences, the normative-cultural approach's theoretical explanatory power is far from sufficient (Barbalet, 2009; Hardin, 2006).

Trust Based on Rational Choice

Although rational choice theory operates on a minimal set of assumptions about people and produces very general predictions, in the last several decades it has been the most significant theoretical approach to trust. Its underlying consensus that the individual is a rational agent and that one of the main challenges of modern societies is to maintain the production of a common good, along with the strength of game-theoretical analyses of trust, have raised the status of rational choice's trust studies. Rational choice theory sees people as seeking to maximize their chances of achieving a given goal. Thus, it assumes that people are prepared to trust only when the potential gains from trusting are larger than the potential losses. Its studies of empirical differences in achieved levels of cooperation in various contexts aim to explain the role of trust as a supplement to or substitute for contractual and bureaucratic bonds. Its conceptualization of trust as a means of economizing on transaction costs, which identifies the basis of trust as a calculation of benefits from potential future collaboration (Gambetta, 1988a), has become influential in many fields of the social sciences, particularly in economics, organization studies, and political science as well as in empirical studies of the impact of digitalization on social and economic relations.

Rational choice theory's conceptualizations of the social actor and factors behind trust production point to the main differences between this theory and the previously discussed normative-cultural approach to trust. Nonetheless, despite their differences, these two perspectives share several assumptions. For instance, both approaches acknowledge the social importance of trust. Also rational choice theory's recognition of the rationality of trust action is shared by the normative-cultural approach. Both perspectives' reason for the rationality of trust is connected with their admission that it is the incompleteness of our knowledge which makes it logical to trust in trust, as it ensures openness to evidence. Although rational choice views trust actions as "the more or less rational pursuit of interests" (Dunn, 1993: 641), while the normative tradition only acknowledges trust's non-calculative rationality

(Luhmann, 1979), nonetheless both of them emphasize the role of trust in increasing a social system's potential for action.

Rational choice theory provides a set of foundations for the importance of the trust relationship between partners in social, political, and economic exchange. Although following Williamson's (1993) argument that trust should be reserved only for personal relationships, as it is only meaningful if it goes beyond self-interest, there are debates among rational choice theorists as to whether trust is needed in the economy and politics (Möllering, 2013), the mainstream of rational choice theory appreciates the benefits of trust-based exchanges vis-à-vis the costs of defection or betrayal. The dominant perception of trust within this perspective focuses on calculus-based trust and assumes that the decision to extend or to withhold inter-personal trust is based on the evaluation of costs and returns of cooperation. Its argument that mutual trust is essential for cooperation follows Arrow's (1974) view of trust as a lubricant for cooperation and Axelrod's (1984) assertion that trust saves on transaction costs. In his classic text on cooperation, *The Evolution of Cooperation,* Axelrod, while emphasizing the calculative nature of trust and the fact that trust cannot be produced on demand and is difficult to maintain, appreciates its potential to increase efficiency at the system level by reducing costs. Since trust enhances cooperation, thereby productivity and the smooth running of economic or political systems, and since cooperation is difficult without mutual trust, a lack of trust that one's action will be reciprocated represents a loss of economic, social, and political advantage. Thus, the mainstream of rational choice theory views coopera-tion as a result of the actors' calculation that it is to the other party's benefit to behave in a trustworthy manner because the costly sanctions in place for breach of trust exceed any potential benefits from opportunistic behavior (Tschannen-Moran and Hoy, 2000).

James Coleman (1990) was one of the first sociologists to demonstrate rational choice's explanatory power and its usefulness for policy purposes. For Coleman (1990: 91), trust refers to "situations in which the risk one takes depends on the performance of the other actor," while cooperation is enhanced by the development of norms with sanctions. This, together with his basic assumption that "persons act purposively toward a goal with the goal shaped by values or preferences," leads him to conceptualize the notion of trust as a rational calculation of costs and benefits in situations involving risk (Coleman, 1990: 14). Since the decision to trust may be based "not simply on [an] estimate of the probability of the trustee's keeping trust, but also in part on the use of negative sanctions" (Coleman, 1990: 115), reciprocal trusting relationships are mutually reinforcing for each partner. Coleman (1990), while asserting that it is in each partner's interest to be trustworthy, also stresses the importance of reputation for trustworthiness, seen as grounded in the rationality of individual actors and as reinforced by the nature of organizations and networks. For example, closed networks facilitate the flow of information, sustain norms, obliga-tions, and sanctions, and thus provide incentives for cooperation and interpersonal trust.

The idea that long-lasting relationships are established on the basis of exchanges motivated by self-interest allows Coleman (1990) to see trust as connecting the individual and collectivities and to analyze how individuals come together to produce cooperation and benefits for society as a whole. The significance of trust as a social phenomenon is connected with trust's capacity to solve social dilemmas, that is, situations in which individual rationality does not result in collective rationality. Coleman (1990) argues that to prevent situations where individually rational behavior leads to a state in which everyone is worse off than they might have been, we need to rely on interpersonal trust. Since to trust is in the collective interest, trust is a form of social capital, the function of which is "the value of these aspects of social structure to actors as resources that they can use to achieve their interests" (Coleman, 1988: 101). In other words, social capital is a public asset that is embodied in relations among people and that can be capitalized on with social, economic, and political effects. Coleman's idea of trust's links with social capital and his usage of the notion of social capital to explain trust's role as the precaution against uncertainty and consequently in lowering the transition costs have been popularized by Putnam.

The visibility of Putnam's notion of social capital, reinforced by Fukuyama's (1995) message about the importance of trust for economic efficiency, means that since the 1990s there has been an impressive proliferation of theories linking the notions of trust and social capital. Putnam (1993), like Coleman, uses the notion of social capital as a mechanism linking individual behavior and social benefits. However, while Coleman sees trust as a form of social capital and views relations of trust as arising from an underlying system of obligations and expectations, Putnam (1995) conceptualizes trust as the essential element of the ability of social capital to produce civic engagement, increase civil ethics, and make the community more involved, safer, and tolerant. By incorporating trust within the notion of social capital, Putnam (1995) identifies trust as the key to democratic participation and successful collective actions. "For various reasons life is easier in a community blessed with a substantial stock of social capital" (Putnam, 1995: 67). Strong social capital, seen as animated by norms of reciprocity, trustworthiness, and networks, is an active asset and moral resource of the community because it "can improve the efficiency of society by facilitating coordinated action" (Putnam, 1993: 167).

The popular social capital approach's conceptualization of trust as one of three elements of social capital has been criticized (Portes, 1998; Warren, 1999). Without going into the details of these critiques, it can be argued that Putnam's perspective does not clearly differentiate between trust and social capital and between the personal and collective levels of trust. Therefore, it often says nothing more than that informal interactions can facilitate cooperative behavior. Even more importantly, by confusing the notion of interpersonal trust, where the trustee is by definition known, with the idea of social trust, which is directed toward strangers and which entails a willingness to engage in social situations where unknown others are involved, the popular social capital approach overlooks the difference in the nature of the level of risk in each respective situation as well as the fact that these two types of trust operate in different domains. These critical analyses of the social capital perspective, by exposing its tautological outline, its ambiguous view of the consequences of various types of networks for the quality of social life, and its confusing propositions about the factors motivating cooperation, have prompted many theorists to rethink their assertions. Taking into account the criticism of the assumption that trust and social capital are always only beneficial for society, some representatives of rational choice theory, including Gambetta (1988a) and Cook, Hardin, and Levi (2005), have reformulated the relationships between trust and cooperation.

Gambetta, one of the most influential recent proponents of the rational choice theory approach, appreciates the importance of trust for cooperation. Nonetheless, he views trust as "a result rather than precondition of cooperation" (Gambetta, 1988b: 225). According to him, trust "pervades the most diverse situations where cooperation is at one and the same time a vital and fragile commodity, from marriage to economic development, from buying a second-hand car to international affairs, from the minutiae of social life to the continuation of life on earth" (Gambetta, 1988a: 2). Gambetta, (1988b: 217), who shares with Coleman the emphasis on the close relationship between trust, risk, and contingency, defines trust as "a particular level of the subjective probability with which an agent assesses that another agent or group of agents will perform a particular action, both before he can monitor such action (or independently of his capacity ever to be able to monitor it) and in a context in which it affects his own action."

The view of trust as a form of reliance on other people, which involves beliefs about the likelihood of their behaving in a certain way, seems to necessitate the introduction of the probabilistic assessment. To explain how the agent reaches a conclusion about whether the other agent will act in accordance with trust expectations, Gambetta (1988b: 223), who knows that "if evidence could solve the problem of trust, then trust would not be a problem at all," focuses on people's search for reliable signs of trust or distrust. Key here is trustworthiness. Gambetta and Hamill (2005), in investigating how taxi drivers assess their customers' trustworthiness, aim to discover more about how trusters manage to appraise trustees' trustworthiness. Their study demonstrates that taxi drivers, when in a "signalling game" which has a "sorting" or "separating" equilibrium, screen potential passengers, looking for signals that manifest properties that are "trust- or- distrust-warnings" (Gambetta and Hamill, 2005: 9). The success of the technique used by taxi drivers to assess the trustworthiness of their clients depends, however, not only on their capacity to read the recognized signals for trust but also on their ability to process social and contextual cues, thus the importance of drivers' past experiences, attitudes, emotions, and dispositions. In other words, the rational choice model overplays peoples' rationality, the degree to which they engage in conscious calculation, free of their pasts, current worldviews, norms, and moral obligations.

The importance of trustworthiness has also been claimed by Hardin (2002) who, like Gambetta, believes that it is rational to have trust in trust and who, like Coleman, views trust as the rational trait of individual actors and stresses the sense of risk involved. Hardin (2006: 17) has popularized the definition of trust as a form of "encapsulated interest," which points to its cognitive structure and grounds it in the assumption that "the potentially trusted person has an interest in maintaining a relationship with the truster." For Hardin (1999: 26), trust is always a relational concept and means that "I have reason to expect you to act in my interest . . . because you have good reasons to do so, reasons that are grounded in my interest . . . Your interest encapsulates my interest." People trust if they have adequate grounds for believing it will be in that person's interest to be trustworthy, or in other words, if you "know that my own interest will induce me to live up to your expectations, your trust then encapsulates my interests" (Hardin, 1991: 189).

Arguing that the rational account of trust includes two elements, that is, the incentives of the person who is trusted to fulfill the trust and the knowledge that allows the truster to trust another, Hardin (2002) places trustworthiness at the heart of trust decisions. The importance of the differentiation between trust and trustworthiness is connected with the fact that in social exchange "there is no way to assure an appropriate return for a favor; social exchange requires trusting others to discharge their obligations" (Blau, 1964: 4). Only by reciprocating a favor do people prove themselves "trustworthy of continued and extended favor" (Blau, 1964: 4). Hardin (2006: 20), after identifying the respective foundations of trust and trustworthiness and asserting that the context of trustworthiness consists of sustained relations of personal familiarity and monitoring, concludes that the probabilistic assessment of the trustworthiness is always local and trust is inherently a micro-level occurrence. Consequently, since trust "inheres in particular relationships" and depends on ongoing relationships, the nature of its links with social capital cannot be taken for granted (Hardin, 1996: 42).

The realization that trust can fail to motivate cooperation leads Hardin (2006: 97) to observe that "[c]ommunity and social capital are not per se good. It is a grand normative fiction of our time to suppose that they are." In other words, social trust does not necessarily always benefit the collectivity as a whole, there are many negative aspects of social trust or social capital and, moreover, people can collaborate without trust. Hardin's concept of trust as encapsulated interest and his suggestion of the possibility of cooperation without trust are adopted in a book, *Cooperation without Trust.* Its authors, Cook, Hardin, and Levi (2005: 28), argue that cooperation may occur in settings in which there is very little trust, and therefore trust is "not what makes cooperative action occur." According to them, today's society increasingly not only solves the problem of cooperation by setting its foundations in formal rules, but it also substitutes trust with formal rules. Cook, Hardin, and Levi (2005: 1) assert that the actual role of trusting relations has undergone a relative decline and that trust, although important in many interpersonal contexts, can no longer "carry the weight of making complex societies function productively and effectively."

Cook, Hardin, and Levi's view of the role of trust in facilitating cooperation differs from that of many rational choice theorists, who assert that we need trust in order to cooperate. Their main assumption is that we cooperate not because "we have come to trust each other, but because of the incentives in place that make cooperation safe and productive for us" (Cook, Hardin, and Levi, 2005: 15). Today's shift from a customary regulation of daily life to formal rules, expert knowledge, and legal systems makes trust irrelevant. In support of this claim, they refer to empirical evidence suggesting that contemporary societies do not provide a natural environment for trust. Furthermore, they assert that with a growing number of organizations and institutions serving well as substitutes for trust relations, trust is not always preferable as a foundation for cooperation. Yet, they overlook evidence suggesting that the prevalence of distrust is detrimental to cooperation (Dunn, 1988). Moreover, although Cook, Hardin, and Levi disagree with mainstream rational choice theorists on the issue of the role trust in cooperation, their approach shares many of its shortcomings.

The explanatory power of Cook, Hardin, and Levi's (2005) overall line of argument, like the rational choice perspective generally, is weak insofar as it provides an under-socialized conception of trust which does not take into account that people trust others because of their interactional history and that trust is constrained by ongoing social relationships (Granovetter, 1985). The rational choice approach neglects the fact that trust can be based not only on incentives or cost calculation but also on normative attributes. This theory is not only limited in its capacity to address and explain what is empirically observable; there are also many examples of collective action that appear to run counter to what game-theoretical predictions suggest should be the case. For example, people can choose to act more altruistically than predicted (Ostrom and Walker, 2003). Additionally, the existence of empirical evidence of the persistent differences between countries in terms of levels of trust suggests that without taking into account the historical and cultural characteristics of a given context, we cannot comprehend the factors behind trust production (Li, 2015). Finally, rational choice theory overlooks the role of emotions in underpinning trust relationships and the fact that such relations in turn foster social ties, cooperation, and mutual trust.

Thus, any further development of our understanding of the notion of trust requires us to bridge a gap between the rational choice theory of trust and the approach stressing the role of normative routines as the foundation of trust, as well as to reconceptualize trust as an emotional facility. I would argue that such a multidimensional conception of trust can be achieved by rethinking its links with vulnerability, and considering trust-based remedies for vulnerability. Thus, to bring together rational and normative as well as the emotional underpinnings of trust, in what follows we will analyze three types of vulnerability and three trust-based mechanisms for overcoming vulnerability.

Trust and Vulnerability

Vulnerability, like trust, is multidimensional and associated with risk phenomena. Viewing vulnerability as the universal and constant condition of our humanity allows us to emphasize that "we are all 'vulnerable' in some respect and most people are potentially, or actually "vulnerable" with regard to a very wide range of 'risks' and new forms of social exclusion" (Beckett, 2006: 3). The notion of vulnerability is seen as the key element of trust, because the main characteristic of trust is the renunciation of guard or defense. In other words, trust requires us to "allow many other people to get into positions where they can, if they choose, injure what we care about, since those are the same positions that they must be in to help us take care of what we care about" (Baier, 1986: 236). Yet, while trust makes us more vulnerable, vulnerability increases the probability of distrust, as situations of high vulnerability increase the sensitivity of vulnerable parties to the truster's behavior and any higher level of sensitivity has the potential to erode their trust. The main features of situations of high vulnerability, namely, the high levels of uncertainty or risk and increased sensitivity of vulnerable parties, enhance the role of emotions in signaling information to the partner and determining when such emotions are displayed to the other (Lawler and Thye, 1999). In less vulnerable situations, the likelihood that trust will be eroded is lower as such situations do not generate the trustees' attentiveness to the trustor's behavior (Lapidot, Kark, and Shamir, 2007: 27). In other words, trust and vulnerability are locked into a circular relation, where trust reduces vulnerability, while too much vulnerability breeds distrust; which itself further increases vulnerability, which in turn creates a new demand for trust.

Since vulnerability "depends more on a lack of trust in the defenses available than on the volume or nature of actual threats" (Bauman, 2006: 6), the link between trust and vulnerability alters with changes to the nature and scope of risk. If we assume that vulnerability is rooted in three types of risk, the nature of the relationship between trust and vulnerability needs to be viewed in the context of opportunities for trust and distrust as created by these three types of vulnerability (Misztal, 2012). Such a dynamic approach allows us to account for the links between trust and vulnerability by identifying emotional consequences of these risks along a timeline. Hence, the notion of vulnerability can be conceptualized as referring to the insecurity and risks of the present (a fear connected with what is happening), the future (a fear connected with what it might be happening), and to the consequences of past traumas and risks (a fear connected with what did happen). In other words, the notion of vulnerability is seen as rooted in the human condition of dependence on others, in the unpredictability of action, and in the irreversibility of human experiences. These three types of vulnerability present us with three different challenges in terms of how to reduce threats and risks. Trust plays the central role in tackling and reducing all types of vulnerability. Yet such trust-related remedies for vulnerability differ in terms of the type and strength of bases of trust through which we overcome various kinds of uncertainties. In what follows, I will address the issue of the nature and scope of trust by looking at opportunities for trust as expressed by acts of responsibility, promise, and forgiveness (Misztal, 2011).

The first form of vulnerability results from the fundamental dependency of humans on others for protection, care, and recognition. Coping with the vulnerability created by mutual dependency often includes long-term and frequent interactions which can lead to the formation of emotional attachments based upon reciprocal concern and care. As emotion enters into relationships, trustworthiness in a dependent relationship expresses itself in taking responsibility of care for the dependent partner. Although the vulnerability which results from dependency creates the opportunity for affective trust, the asymmetrical dependency also exposes the vulnerable party to an enormous risk and creates a need for self-protection, or in other words makes trust risky and constructs opportunities for deception. Some dependencies pose greater risks or threats of exploitation than do others, and when the risk of harm and exploitation and levels of asymmetry are high, distrust and deceit, rather than trust, offers a better strategy of survival. Yet, acts of protecting self-interest through distrust and deceit can lead to a final erosion of mutual trust, therefore rendering both parties more vulnerable. Because there is a great variety of ways in which people might become dependent upon one another, there are also various ways in which responsibilities might arise. Essentially, however, the principle of taking responsibility for the vulnerable amounts to a feeling that one can rely on one another to reduce one's vulnerabilities by fulfilling trusted obligations. In other words, reasoning in terms of dependency and responsibility makes it possible to show that good care is trust-based, and that trust is supported by "feelings of positive expectation and safe dependency" (Barbalet, 2009: 375).

The second form of vulnerability, seen as a result of the linear experience of time, discloses itself in uncertainty and fear about the future. The unpredictability of human actions, which all occur in a context of plurality, futility, boundlessness, and uncertainty of outcomes (Arendt, 1958), makes us feel afraid, insecure, and fragile. Reducing the vulnerability associated with the inability to predict future risks relies on finding a promise-related type of mechanism. The task of mitigating the scope of vulnerability which underlines our uncertainty about the future can only be performed by promising, because promising, by establishing certain "guideposts of reliability" or "isolated islands of certainty in an ocean of uncertainty" (Arendt, 1958: 224, 244) plays a central role in tackling the unpredictability of action. This promise-related mechanism to cope with vulnerability involves trust in the other party's goodwill and proper use of discretionary power. Thus, it ensures security without undermining freedom (Misztal, 2012). Promises, as sophisticated social devices that guarantee the future by the moral strength of their obligations, are a secured case of mutual trust (Baier, 1986). The moral force of the promissory obligation is explained by the fact that promises carry special obligations which involve trust as a precaution against uncertainty, as it generates confidence with regard to the promisor's future actions. The forward-looking character of trust that underlines promising has important consequences, as offering trust in advance "may increase the objective trustworthiness of the recipient" (Kolnai, 1973: 105). Promising, by reducing some of the uncertainty that would otherwise surround human action, builds trust relations by increasing the feeling of confidence in another's future actions and also confidence concerning one's own judgment of another. Since there is "a double confidence" in promising, seen as trust underpinned by the feeling of confidence in future events, human experience through trust can be made less uncertain and unpredictable and therefore our lives can be more fulfilling and safer.

The third form of vulnerability is grounded in the irreversibility of past action and experiences. This form of vulnerability captures painful experiences which diminish the emotional capacities of individuals, lower possibilities for realizing their individuality, and reduce chances of collaborative relationships with others (Misztal, 2012). The risk associated with this type of vulnerability is that we cannot free ourselves from the consequences of past deeds (Arendt, 1958). The trust-related mechanism for reducing this vulnerability is forgiveness. By refusing to allow the past to determine the possibility of the present and by bringing to an end a process initiated by betrayal, forgiveness creates conditions for cooperation. Only when released from the consequences of what has been done, only by constant willingness to change our minds and start again, can we stop feeling suspicious and mistrustful (Misztal, 2012). As the exact opposite of vengeance, and as the only reaction which does not merely re-act but acts anew, forgiveness is a necessary condition for creating trust in post-conflict situations (Arendt, 1958). Forgiveness entails trust in a common future and enhances the likelihood of cooperation as it stands by the principle that past wrongdoings should not prevent a dialogue. It expresses "that attitude of trust in the world which, unless it is vitiated by hare-brained optimism and dangerous irresponsibility, may be looked upon, not to be sure as the starting point and the very basis, but perhaps as the epitome and culmination of morality" (Kolnai, 1973: 105). Although forgiveness requires a positive feeling of expectation regarding the transgressor's future actions, it does not necessarily mean a return to the previous high level of trust, as a sense of vulnerability tends not to disappear easily. Yet, forgiveness can only be achieved through constructing trust relationships and it can bring both benefits and risk for forgivers, as it can often facilitate reconciliation. Trust, offered for the sake of establishing a new relation based on mutual recognition of each other, involves a suspension of judgment which allows for a dialogue underpinned by the positive feeling about and interest in a common future.

The three mechanisms for reducing vulnerability explain how trust overcomes vulnerability by accounting for the variety of foundations of trust, from values through emotions to self-interest. Moreover, since responsibility, promising, and forgiveness differ in terms of the strength and type of trust involved, they also suggest that in order to explain the operation of trust, we need to be able to differentiate between the types and strengths of uncertainties, risks, and sensitivities that trust attempts to overcome. In the case of responsibility-related mechanisms that enhance strong affective or bonding trust, we are concerned with feelings and emotions connected with confidence in our partners. In the case of the promise-related mechanism, which is helped by and which in turn creates the conditions conducive for the people who are trusted to fulfill their trust obligations, we refer to trust that our partners' action will not harm our interests or disregard our expectations. In the case of forgiveness, we speak about the thinner and bridging form of trust which is the crucial factor in promoting the belief that generally people can be trusted, thereby strengthening the moral foundation of trust (Uslaner, 2002).

To sum up, our discussion reflects the importance of trust as a way of reducing vulnerability in modern complex and diverse societies characterized by compound interdependencies, complementarity, and individualization. The study of the relationship between trust and vulnerability is a good starting point to discuss the variety of foundations of trust and ways to create conditions for a less vulnerable society. By mastering trust-related mechanisms for reducing human vulnerability, we can increase our ability to overcome uncertainties and risks and thus improve societal well-being.

References

Alexander, J. C. 2006. *The Civil Sphere*. Oxford, UK: Oxford University Press.

Arendt, H. 1958. *The Human Condition*. Chicago, IL: University of Chicago Press.

Arrow, K. 1974. *The Limits of Organization*. New York: W. W. Norton.

Axelrod, R. 1984. *The Evolution of Cooperation*. New York: Basic Books.

Baier, A. 1986. "Trust and Antitrust." *Ethics* 96(2): 231–260.

Barbalet, J. 2009. "A Characterization of Trust, and Its Consequences." *Theory and Society* 38: 367–382.

Bauman, Z. 2006 *Liquid Fear*. Cambridge, UK: Polity.

Beckett, A. E. 2006. *Citizenship and Vulnerability*. London: Palgrave.

Blau, P. 1964. *Exchange and Power in Social Life*. New York: Wiley and Sons.

Bok, S. 1979. *Lying and Moral Choice in Public Life*. Hassocks, UK: The Harvester Press.

Cheal, D. 2005. *Dimensions of Sociological Theory*. London: Palgrave.

Coleman, J. 1988. "Social Capital in the Creation of Human Capital." *American Journal of Sociology* 94(1): 95–120.

　1990. *Foundations of Social Theory*. Cambridge, MA: Harvard University Press.

Cook. K. (ed.). 2001. *Trust in Society*. New York: Russell Sage Foundation.

Cook, S., R. Hardin, and M. Levi. 2005. *Cooperation without Trust*. New York: Russell Sage Foundation.

Dunn, J. 1988. "Trust and Political Agency." In D. Gambetta (ed.), *Trust: Making and Breaking Co-operative Relations* (pp. 73–93). Oxford, UK: Blackwell.

　1993. "Trust." In R. Goodin and P. Pettit (eds.), *Companion to Contemporary Political Philosophy* (pp. 638–645). Oxford, UK: Blackwell.

Edwards, B., and M. Foley. 1998. "Civil Society and Social Capital: Beyond Putnam." *American Behavioral Scientist* 42(1): 124–140.

Elster, J. 2007. *Explaining Social Behavior: More Nuts and Bolts for the Social Sciences*. Cambridge, UK: Cambridge University Press.

Erikson, E. H. 1959 [1950]. *Identity and the Life Cycle*. New York: International University Press.

Frederiksen, M. 2012. "Dimensions of Trust." *Current Sociology* 60(6): 733–750.

Fukuyama, Francis. 1995. *Trust, the Social Virtues and the Creation of Prosperity*. London: Hamish Hamilton.

Gambetta, D. (ed.). 1988a. "Forward." In *Trust: Making and Breaking Co-operative Relations* (ix–xii). Oxford, UK: Blackwell.

Gambetta, D. 1988b. "Can We Trust Trust?" In D. Gambetta (ed.), *Trust, Making and Breaking Co-operative Relations* (pp. 213–238). Oxford, UK: Blackwell.

Gambetta, D., and H. Hamill. 2005. *Streetwise: How Taxi Drivers Establish Their Customers' Trustworthiness*. New York: Russell Sage Foundation.

Garfinkel, H. 1963. "A Conception of, and Experiments with, Trust as a Condition of Stable Concerted Actions." In O. J. Harvey (ed.), *Motivation and Social Interaction* (pp. 187–265). New York: The Ronald Press.

Giddens, A. 1990. *The Consequences of Modernity*. Cambridge, UK: Polity.

　1991. *Modernity and Self-Identity*. Cambridge, UK: Polity.

　1992. *Transformation of Intimacy, Sexuality, Love and Eroticism in Modern Society*. Cambridge, UK: Polity.

　1994a. "Living in Post-Traditional Society." In A. Giddens and S. Lash (eds.), *Reflexive Modernization* (pp. 56–109). Cambridge, UK: Polity.

1994b. "Risk, Trust, Reflexivity." In A. Giddens and S. Lash (eds.), *Reflexive Modernization* (pp. 184–197). Cambridge, UK: Polity.

Goffman, E. 1959. *The Presentation of Self in Everyday Life*. New York: Doubleday.

Granovetter, M. 1985. "Economic Action and Social Structure: The Problem of Embeddedness." *American Journal of Sociology* 91(3): 481–510.

Hardin, R. 1991. "Trusting Persons, Trusting Institutions." In R. J. Zeckahuser (ed.), *Strategy and Choice* (pp. 178–193). Cambridge, MA: MIT Press.

1996. "Trustworthiness." *Ethics* 107: 26–42.

1999. "Do We Want Trust in Government." In M. Warren (ed.), *Democracy and Trust* (pp. 22–41). Cambridge, UK: Cambridge University Press.

2001. "Conceptions and Explanations of Trust." In K. S. Cook (ed.), *Trust in Society* (pp. 3–39). New York: Russell Sage Foundation.

2002. *Trust and Trustworthiness*. New York: Russell Sage Foundation.

2006. *Trust*. Cambridge, UK: Polity.

Jalava J. 2003. "From Norms to Trust."*European Journal of Social Theory* 62: 173–190.

Kolnai, A. 1973. "Forgiveness." *Proceedings of the Aristotelian Society* 74: 91–106.

Kramer, R. M., and T. R. Tyler (eds.). 1996. *Trust in Organizations: Frontiers of Theory and Research*. Thousand Oaks, CA: Sage.

Lane, C., and R. Bachmann (eds.). 1998. *Trust Within and Between Organizations*. Oxford, UK: Oxford University Press.

Lapidot, T., R. Kark, and B. Shamir. 2007. "The Impact of the Development and Erosion of Followers' Trust in Their Leader." *The Leadership Quarterly* 18: 16–34.

Latour, B. 2013. *An Inquiry into Modes of Existence*. Translated by Catherine Porter. Cambridge, MA: Harvard University Press.

Lawler, E. J., and S. R. Thye. 1999. "Bringing Emotions into Social Exchange." *Annual Review of Sociology* 25: 217–244.

Levi, M., and L. Stoker. 2000. "Political Trust and Trustworthiness." *Annual Review of Political Science* 31: 475–507.

Lewis, J. D., and A. Weigert. 1985. "Trust as a Social Reality." *Social Forces* 63(4): 967–985.

Li, P. P. 2015. "The Duality of Unity-in-Diversity in Trust Research." *Journal of Trust Research* 52: 103–108.

Luhmann, N. 1979. *Trust and Power*. New York: Wiley.

1988. "Familiarity, Confidence, Trust: Problems and Alternatives." In Diego Gambetta (ed.), *Trust: Making and Breaking Cooperative Relations* (pp. 94–107). Oxford, UK: Blackwell.

1991. *Risk: A Sociological Theory*. Berlin: De Gruyter.

Messick, D. M., and R. M. Kramer. 2001. "Trust as a Form of Shallow Morality." In K. S. Cook (ed.), *Trust in Society* (pp. 89–118). New York: Russell Sage Foundation.

Mishra, A. K. 1996. "Organizational Responses to Crisis: The Centrality of Trust." In R. Kramer and T. Tyler (eds.), *Trust in Organizations: Frontiers of Theory and Research* (pp. 261–287). Thousand Oaks, CA: Sage.

Misztal, B. A. 1996. *Trust in Modern Societies*. Cambridge, UK: Polity.

2011. *The Challenges of Vulnerability: In Search of Strategies for a Less Vulnerable Social Life*. London: Palgrave.

2012. "Trust: Acceptance of, Precaution Against and Cause of Vulnerability." In M. Sasaki and R. M. Marsh (eds.), *Trust: Comparative Perspective* (pp. 209–223). Boston, MA: Brill.

Möllering, G. 2001. "The Nature of Trust: From Georg Simmel to a Theory of Expectation, Interpretation and Suspension." *Sociology* 35(2): 403–420.

2013. "Trust Without Knowledge? Comment on Hardin's 'Government without Trust.'" *Journal of Trust Research* 31: 53–58.

Nooteboom, B. 1996. "Trust, Opportunism and Governance." *Organization Studies* 176: 985–1010.

Nooteboom, B., H. Berger, and N. G. Noorderhaven. 1997. "Effects of Trust and Governance on Relational Risk." *Academy of Management Journal* 40(2): 308–338.

Parsons, T. 1978. *Action Theory and the Human Condition*. New York: Free Press.

Portes, A. 1998. "Social Capital, Its Origins and Applications in Modern Sociology." *Annual Review of Sociology* 24: 1–24.

Putnam, R. D. 1993. *Making Democracy Work: Civic Traditions in Modern Italy*. Princeton, NJ: Princeton University Press.

1995. "Bowling Alone: America's Declining Social Capital." *Journal of Democracy* 6(1): 65–78.

Ostrom, E., and Walker, J. (eds.). 2003. *Trust and Reciprocity: Interdisciplinary Lessons from Experimental Research*. New York: Russell Sage Foundation.

Sabel, C. F. 1993. "Studied Trust: Building New Forms of Cooperation in a Volatile Economy." *Human Relations* 46(9): 1133–1170.

Sasaki, M. 2012. "Cross-National Studies of Trust among Seven Nations." In S. Sasaki and R. M. Marsh (eds.), *Trust: Comparative Perspectives* (pp. 347–376). Boston, MA: Brill.

Seligman, A. 1997. *The Problem of Trust*. Princeton, NJ: Princeton University Press.

Silver, A. 1985. "Trust in Social and Political Theory." In G. D. Suttles and M. N. Zald (eds.), *The Challenges of Social Control* (pp. 52–70). Greenwich, CT: Ablex.

Simmel, Georg. 1950. *The Sociology of Georg Simmel*. Edited by Kurt H. Wolff. New York: Free Press.

1990. *The Philosophy of Money*. London: Routledge & Kegan Paul.

Sztompka, P. 1999. *Trust: A Sociological Theory*. Cambridge, UK: Cambridge University Press.

Tschannen-Moran, M., and W. K. Hoy. 2000. "A Multidisciplinary Analysis of the Nature, Meaning, and Measurement of Trust." *Review of Educational Research* 70(4): 547–593.

Uslaner, E. M. 2002. *The Moral Foundations of Trust*. New York: Cambridge University Press.

Warren, M. E. (ed.). 1999. *Democracy and Trust*. Cambridge, UK: Cambridge University Press.

Williamson, Oliver. 1993. "Calculativeness, Trust and Economic Organization." *Journal of Law and Economics* 36(1): 453–486.

Woolcock, M. 1998. "Social Capital and Economic Development." *Theory and Society* 27 (2): 151–207.

Wuthnow, R. 2004. "Trust as an Aspect of Social Structure." In J. C. Alexander, C. T. Marx, and C. Williams (eds.), *Self, Social Structure and Beliefs* (pp. 145–167). Berkeley, CA: University of California Press.

Yamagishi, T. 2003. "Cross-Societal Experimentation on Trust." In E. Ostrom and J. Walker (eds.), *Trust and Reciprocity* (pp. 352–370). New York: Russell Sage Foundation.

Zucker, L. G. 1986. "Production of Trust: Institutional Sources of Economic Structure." *Research in Organizational Behavior* 8: 51–111.

18 Unities Within Conflict: Mapping Biology's Relevance to Sociological Theory

Douglas A. Marshall

This chapter aims to introduce and orient the interested newcomer to the fields of biosociology and evolutionary sociology. It is neither a grand synthesis of the subdisciplines, an exhaustive inventory of their literature, a history of their development, a refutation of their critics, nor an apologia for their purported crimes. While it may at times touch upon all of these roles, it is best thought of as a map, one that highlights landmarks, delineates borders, and generally aims to render this part of the intellectual landscape more accessible.

Perspective: Unity/Unities

Maps invariably depict their subject as it appears from a particular location. This one's perspective comes courtesy of Simmel, who demonstrates that conflict and unity are mutually constitutive, with apparent conflict belying deeper unity, and vice versa (1971 [1908]). Accordingly, this chapter maintains that the strife between sociology and biology betrays their profound and multifaceted unity.

At the superficial and ontological extremes, such unity is self-evident. Superficially, both biology and sociology emerged as scientific disciplines at about the same time, in response to analogous questions of speciation and socio-cultural diversity (Plotkin, 2004); both are, in effect, historical sciences, explaining phenomena the origins of which precede human memory (Runciman, 2015); and both bear closely enough upon human identity, purpose, and experience to have been the battleground for many an ideological war. At the other end of the spectrum, biology and sociology are ontologically unified in that all known social systems are composed of biological organisms. As such, every social action is ultimately executed via living organs and tissues, and therefore incontrovertibly biological (Rosenberg, 2015).

It is between these extremes that the controversy lies. By some accounts, such unities, however incontestable, hold little explanatory significance for sociological theory. But this chapter maintains the opposing position that such unities entail further continuous, analogous, and topical unities that render biology and sociological theory infinitely and mutually relevant.

Continuous Unity: Human Nature

We begin with the unity of causal continuity: that lower-level, biological factors impact higher-level, social behavior and phenomena (and vice versa) to significant degrees and in theoretically relevant ways. This relationship is commonly debated in terms of "human nature," with the standard sociological position being that there is no such thing – as though the natural and the social are mutually exclusive, or that admitting to a role for biology is tantamount to being reduced thereto.

But humans do have a nature, and far from being at odds with our sociality, that nature is its origin and abode. While human nature produces social behavior and social phenomena only in interaction with cultural and other environmental factors, recognizing and exploiting its contributions – that is, biosociology – makes our theories of the social immeasurably more accurate, powerful, and comprehensive. Consider the role of human nature in sociological theory at the psychological, physiological, and evolutionary levels:

The Psychological Level

As the discipline most directly charged with elucidating human nature, and the form in which sociologists are most likely to encounter it, only psychology can compete with biology's ability to attract the opprobrium of sociologists. Though it is not biology per se, psychology warrants brief consideration here because it: (1) allows us to engage with "human nature" head-on; (2) is an indispensable link in the explanatory chain between biology and sociology, and; (3) previews, in a familiar context, some of the major advantages of including biology in sociological theory.

Despite their pronouncements of its irrelevance, sociologists have long depended upon human nature to define their discipline and undergird their theories. Indeed, the only thing that ultimately unifies sociologists' efforts across all the disparate times, places, and topics that we study into the single entity of "sociology" is that those behaviors and phenomena all emerge from the same substrate: the interaction of organisms possessed of the same human nature. Without this thread, we forfeit any claim to disciplinary integration, identity, or distinctiveness, and have only isolated accounts of episodic sociality to offer.

Good thing, then, that sociological theorists have always found human nature too indispensable to actually eschew, for the simple reason that the engines and gears of a given behavior or phenomena usually operate at a level below it (Coleman, 1990). Consider Marx's dependence upon the putative primacy of materialistic motives in human action, Weber's reliance upon human dispositions for consistency as the motivating force of ideational change and rationality, and the myriad assumptions about human nature pervading Durkheim's entire opus.

Thus, though it has been argued that sociological theory is stymied by the absence of the unifying framework that human nature should provide, the real culprit is the lack of an explicitly acknowledged model thereof. The practical advantages of such are manifold, but four – embodying the explanatory virtues of complete explanations at every level – deserve special mention:

1. First, since only explicit mechanisms are testable, including them increases a theory's disconfirmability, enhancing our confidence in the veracity and validity of those that survive, and providing a sound basis for choosing among competing models (Firat and Hitlin, 2012).
2. Second, explicit models of human nature link a given theory not only to the literatures associated with those theoretical elements, but also to the other, often disparate, phenomena associated therewith. The consolidation of knowledge that theory exists to achieve is thereby advanced, as is its explanatory depth and scope.
3. Third, explicit evocation of their underlying mechanisms increases the resolution, accuracy, and fecundity of sociological theories. To wit, recognizing that prosocial behaviors are mediated by individuals' perceptions of personal responsibility lets us predict how the likelihood of helping varies with circumstance (Latane and Darley, 1968).
4. Finally, specifying the relevant parts of a hypothesized process allows us to control for potential confounds, increasing our ability to detect the signal of the social against the noise of background variation that might otherwise mask it (Conley, 2014).

Since this chapter is about biology rather than psychology, it henceforth takes it as given that the cited biological influences ultimately operate through more proximate psychological mechanisms, without elaborating those mechanisms in detail.

The Physiological Level

Underlying the psychology that makes up human nature are the physiological structures and processes through which those traits and mechanisms are realized. Critics' assertion of an "air gap" between physiology and human behavior is patently untenable on several grounds: Throughout the rest of the animal kingdom, behavior is unequivocally subject to biological influence. From the simplest taxes and tropisms, to personality traits like docility (Belyayev and Trut, 1964) and promiscuity (Insel and Carter, 1995), to such sophisticated behaviors as migration routes (Delmore and Irwin, 2014), the waggle dance of bees, and the elaborate constructions of bower birds, the natural world is replete with social behaviors that are of indisputably biological origin and operation.

Human physiology overlaps so completely with that of these other species (e.g. the same vasopressin receptors that distinguish monogamous from promiscuous voles also populate human brains [Insel and Carter, 1995]), that faith in some bright line of qualitative differentiation between them and us is simply unsustainable. These behavioral capacities and dispositions exist because of their adaptive value over many millennia. Repealing their influence in the short tenure of our species would require not only an inversion of their adaptive value but unprecedentedly powerful selection pressures against them. Moreover, the obvious influence of such patently physiological factors as injury, diet, disease, and pharmaceuticals (both therapeutic and recreational) on human behavior confirms that the biological machinery of behavioral control is by no means missing from human beings. In this light, the burden of proof lies with those who would deny physiology's potential to influence human behavior, evidence which has yet to be produced (Udry, 1995).

This chapter contends that physiology affects human social behavior in ways relevant to sociological theory via: what it makes imperative; what it makes possible, and; what it makes probable.

Human physiology imposes *imperatives* that substantively shape our interactions with one another. Our need for sustenance eventuates in collective procurement and/or production efforts that shape our most basic social arrangements (Lenski, 1966). Our equally pressing need to provision offspring further canalizes us into social structures capable of fulfilling such requirements (Hrdy, 2009). Indeed, the biological imperative to reproduce, and the fact that we do so sexually – necessitating our division into two, numerically closely matched sexes – leaves an indelible imprint upon most of our social and cultural complexes. It is impossible to completely explain phenomena in any of these domains without reference to the essentially biological functions by which they arose and through which they are manifest.

The most profound, yet least visible, physiological influence on behavior is the fact that, out of all the ways that human beings might conceivably behave, our physiology makes some, but not others, *possible*. I call this the "*You can do only what you CAN do*" principle. Though all human action is predicated upon the possession of the necessary physiology, we remain oblivious to its contributions precisely because we are biologically well-equipped to do most of the things we do. The canonical example is walking: until disease or injury incapacitates one of the myriad structures whose coordination makes this miracle possible, we remain blissfully unaware of them (Franks, 2015).

In the same way, even the most basic social interaction relies on a plethora of capabilities that would be impossible without very particular forms of physiological equipage, from the purely morphological (our expressive facial musculature, visible sclera [Kobayashi and Kohshima, 2001], and sophisticated vocal apparatus); to the perceptual (our powers of facial recognition [Kanwisher and Yovel, 2006], prowess at emotion detection [Ekman, Friesen, and Ancoli, 1980], dispositions for physical and emotional entrainment [Hatfield, Cacioppo, and Rapson, 1994], and for gaze-following [Tomasello et al., 2007]); to the cognitive (our capacity for joint attention [Tomasello and Carpenter, 2007], for Theory of Mind (Baron-Cohen, 1991), and spontaneous mapping of social hierarchies [Mazur, 2005]); to the emotional (our ability to form enduring attachments [Crippen, 2015], and to empathize with others [DeWaal, 1996]).

The crucial corollary to the "*You can do only what you CAN do . . . .*" principle is the "*. . . And only in the WAY that you can do it*" principle. That is, the ways in which a behavior is possible are as relevant to explaining social behavior as the fact that it is so. For example, because the instinctive sociality of monkeys was deselected from our ape ancestors, human sociality is built upon the very different foundation of enhanced emotionality, with myriad implications for the ways we form, maintain, and dissolve social relationships (Maryanski and Turner, 2015).

Far from diminishing the importance of the sociological, recognizing the physiological infrastructure of sociality validates and amplifies its foundational assumption: that humans are profoundly and thoroughly social beings. Ironically, it thus turns out to be sociologists who have most egregiously underestimated human sociality by confining its influence to the narrow footprints of language and culture.

Physiology makes it clear that the social dimensions of human nature are much wider, older, and deeper than either of these.

Of all the things they can do, human beings actually engage in only one or two of them at a time. Thus, physiology's relevance to social behavior extends to its role in determining, out of all the things we can do, which are most *probable* at a given time and place. Possibility intertwines with probability in that the same physiology that lets us follow gazes, become emotionally entrained, and form pair bonds simultaneously inclines us to do so. More generally, by orienting attention, and priming certain responses, physiology systematically biases the knowledge we acquire (e.g. we are more likely to learn to fear snakes and spiders than other objects [Öhman and Mineka, 2001]), and exerts even more direct influence on the behaviors we evince (e.g. we are more likely to compete than cooperate in a one-shot prisoner's dilemma game [Van Lange, Liebrand, and Kuhlman, 1990], to be attracted to symmetrical rather than asymmetrical faces [Grammer and Thornhill, 1994], and more likely to forestall a loss than to pursue the gain of the same value [Kahneman and Tversky, 1979]).

Neurosociology – The Physiology of the Social

Charting physiology's pertinence to sociology is the task of neurosociology. It traces the anatomical structures and pharmacological processes through which human sociality is realized (Franks, 2010; Kalkhoff, Thye, and Lawler, 2012). Neuroscience has done much to identify the particular physiologies responsible for various aspects of social cognition and emotion (Lieberman, 2014), and neurosociologists have drawn out the pertinence of such structures for sociological theory, particularly the ways and extent to which it converges with and refines extant constructs in sociological theory (Franks and Davis, 2012).

Among the examples that demonstrate the value of neurological awareness for sociological theory, mirror neurons (Ramachandran, 2011; Rizzolatti and Craighero, 2004) stand out for their ability to consolidate a spectrum of sociological phenomena under a single umbrella. Responsible for both the perception and performance of action, mirror neurons are potentially indispensable to the wildly underestimated feat of human interaction, in that by automatically, instantaneously, and mutually entraining interactants, they make intersubjectivity and solidarity possible (Firat and Hitlin, 2012; Franks and Davis, 2012).

Mirror neurons may be equally integral to social learning, attitudinal transmission, and cultural diffusion, providing a means by which embodied knowledge and affect can bound from mind to mind via mere observation. To wit, the "great leap forward" of human culture – when innovations like fire and language rapidly diffused and accumulated – temporally corresponds with, and may originate in, the accumulation of a critical mass of such neurons in the human brain (Ramachandran, 2011).

The significance of "how" social action takes place is more clearly demonstrated by the finding that the rupture of important social relationships produces a more-than-metaphorical experience of pain, and does so using the same physiological structures and processes as do more prototypical sources of pain, such as injury

(Panskepp, 2003). That the body's premiere system for addressing immanent homeostatic threats has been extended to social loss speaks volumes about the importance of maintaining social relationships throughout our evolutionary history, and sheds light on the singular effectiveness of ostracism as a means of social control. But it also tells us something important about group solidarity, suggesting that groups may be created and maintained less by the carrot of their advantages to the individual than by the stick of exclusion from them, and that social solidarity may be less about loyalty to an abstract group identity than about concrete emotional dependence upon individual group members.

Physiological Unity as a Two-Way Street

To underscore that "unity" is not a euphemism for reduction, note that the relationship between physiology and the social is reciprocal. Clown fish, for example, are known to change their sex as a function of their status in the social hierarchy (Black and Grober, 2003). While nothing so dramatic occurs among humans, our physiology, too, is subject to social influence. For example, even as testosterone impacts a spectrum of social behaviors, culture, behavior, and status, each also influence testosterone levels (Mazur, 2015). Meanwhile, the burgeoning field of behavioral epigenetics is poised to reveal new ways in which "the social gets under the skin" (Meloni, 2014a).

The Evolutionary Level

A family of biological change mechanisms emerging from, and centered on, Darwin's foundational variation/deselection process, evolution supplies the etiology of the physiology that produces the psychology from which the social emerges. As such it constitutes the ground upon which complete sociological theories are constructed, as well as the point at which explanations for social behavior and phenomena can best be consolidated. For what Dobzhansky observed of biology as a whole – that it makes sense only "in the light of evolution" (1973) – extends as well to all of its manifestations, including social behavior.

Thus, for example, to be complete, accounts of gender should at least acknowledge the fact that, beneath and beyond its myriad social meanings and implications, the very construct of sex exists because effectively every one of us belongs to one of two physiologically distinct, reproductively complementary, and biologically determined sexes, a bifurcation that evolved to capitalize on the advantages of sexual recombination as a source of variation.

That such evolutionary origins are relevant to sociological theory is illustrated by yet another example. The human capacity for morality evolved as means of promoting group integration, solidarity, and strength. As such, it is intensely groupish and fickle, unlike the universalist and rationalist morality that Western philosophy has long projected upon human beings, and despaired at our inability to adhere to (DeWaal, 1996; Haidt, 2001). Theorists who proceed from the philosophical ideal of morality thus set out from flawed premises, and the validity, power, and scope of the theories they produce suffer accordingly. More regrettably, in doing so, theorists miss the opportunity to incorporate a more realistic understanding of the extent, limits, and mechanisms of human morality into their formulations so as to construct more illuminating theories.

Three Evolutionary Approaches to Explaining the Social

Just as apparent conflict conceals unity, apparent unity conceals conflict, or at least diversity (Simmel, 1971 [1908]). Despite the tendency to call every evolutionary approach "sociobiology," there are significant differences among the ways that evolution has been applied to social behavior. This section disambiguates three major approaches. All begin by recognizing that the brain, like every other organ, has evolved to increase the fitness of the organisms possessing it but use that fact in different ways.

Sociobiology

"Sociobiology" attained its modern infamy when E. O. Wilson sandwiched his efforts to expand on William Hamilton's revolutionary concept of inclusive fitness (aka kin selection) among insects – the insight that evolution is more concerned with the fitness of the gene than that of the organism carrying it – between an introduction and a conclusion that proclaimed his ambition to likewise explain the social behavior of all species, including human beings. The controversy ignited by Wilson's book is itself fascinating, but beyond the bounds of the present work (see Segerstrale, 2000 for the definitive treatment). Our consideration here is confined to the defining features, shortcomings, and uses of sociobiology in sociological theory.

Along with adopting the "gene's-eye view" of evolution, sociobiology is distinguished by its insistence that evolution is a maximizing process (Lopreato and Crippen, 1999; Wilson, 1975), facilitating a methodology in which a theorist calculates the optimal behavioral strategy for a given organism under given circumstances, and predicts that it will behave accordingly. To the extent that it is found to do so, the theorist claims to have "explained" its behavior.

This maximizing assumption has proved to be sociobiology's Achilles' heel. Early critiques from fellow biologists focused on sociobiologists' blithe presumption that the optimal behaviors thus calculated would necessarily evolve, and much to the benefit of evolutionary biology, they have delighted in demonstrating the fallacy of this belief. Such "panglossian adaptationism" (Gould and Lewontin, 1979) has equally contributed to sociology's antipathy toward sociobiology by inviting theorists to short-circuit its ideally deductive method by starting with observed behaviors and "explaining" these as clever means of maximizing fitness. As with sociology's own forays into functionalism, unless augmented by established mechanisms and etiologies, the fruits of this method easily devolve into dubious "just so" stories.

Although the proliferation of such overzealous and easily ridiculed accounts has undermined the credibility of sociobiology, panglossianism inflicted its most significant damage via its resonance with the "moral reading" of sociobiology initially adopted by many social scientists (Segerstrale, 2000). Implicit in the maximization assumption (and made explicit in the "panglossian" epithet) are shades of the naturalistic fallacy – the presumption that the way things are is the way they should be. To the extent that sociobiology sought to explain assorted social pathologies or inequalities as an optimal solution to some problem, this was understood to mean, at best, that efforts to ameliorate them were futile and, at worst, that extant inequalities and injustices were legitimate or even somehow beneficial.

Sociobiology in Sociological Theory

For these reasons and more, sociobiology per se never found a comfortable niche in sociological theory. But it is worth pointing out that for all of its shortcomings, sociobiology nevertheless contributes to sociological theory. In pioneering the modern application of evolution to social explanation, sociobiology inverted sociology's preoccupation with proximate factors. Even though, by themselves, its answers were thus as incomplete as were sociology's, it provided a counterpoint that opened up productive new ways of thinking about important sociological topics.

Recall, for example, the evolutionary origins of sexual dimorphism. This parceling of reproductive potential made the sexes mutually dependent, but also asymmetric in terms of parental certainty and parental investment. It is implausible that, having produced something as complicated as sexual reproduction, evolution would not equip each morphology with strategies that exploit and/or ameliorate the differences between them. From such "anisogamy," sociobiologists have generated models of optimum male and female reproductive strategies, models which correspond surprisingly well with widespread and empirically documented differences in reproductive behavior (Kanazawa, 2015; Machalek and Martin, 2010).

Sociobiology thus provides something lacking from such essentially descriptive constructs as "patriarchy": an explanatory rubric under which the explanations of multiple sex-based differences (e.g. mate selection, parenting strategies) can be consolidated. In combination with more proximate sociocultural mechanisms of when and how male and female behaviors are differentially canalized toward their respective strategies *in vivo*, the sociobiological approach makes possible a comprehensive, empirically substantiable, and complete theory of sex and gender.

Ultimately, sociobiology's continuing role in sociological theory is that of a Weberian ideal type, one that, like Rational Choice Theory's fictive "rational actor," may only rarely converge with actual behavior, but which provides an often-useful baseline with which to compare it.

Evolutionary Psychology

Evolutionary psychology offers a second means of incorporating biology into sociological theory (Barkow, Cosmides, and Tooby, 1992; Buss, 1999). It differs from
sociobiology by starting not with abstract assumptions of optimality, but with
established psychological traits, the etiology of which it seeks to explain evolutionarily. It dismisses sociobiology's optimality assumption by presuming that: (a) any
given behavioral trait may be a "spandrel" that was never itself selected for, but is
a by-product of other, adaptive, traits (e.g. musicianship, storytelling, religion
[Marshall, 2016; Pinker, 2002]); (b) traits that did themselves evolve did so in an
environment – the "Environment of Evolutionary Adaptedness" (usually identified
with the Pleistocene era; Bowlby, 1969) – so unlike the present, that they may no
longer be adaptive (e.g. our taste preferences for sugar, salt, and fat [Barash, 1982]),
and; (c) the evolution of behavioral traits was multiply constrained (by e.g. limited
cognitive capacity, competing criteria) so that its solutions tend to be satisfying
rather than optimizing – amounting to fast, frugal, and flawed behavioral heuristics
(Barkow, Cosmides, and Tooby, 1992).

In place of optimality, evolutionary psychology holds modularity as its defining
assumption. As per the popular "Swiss-army knife" analogy, it conceives of the mind
as a collection of specialized domain-specific tools, rather than a unified general-
purpose cogitator, and takes uncovering the evolutionary history of those modules as
its primary task. Exactly what constitutes a module is contestable, but generally
speaking, they operate more or less automatically, effortlessly, and outside of
awareness. They are selectively sensitive to relevant inputs, fast, efficient, and
identified with particular, sometimes discrete, neurological structures. Many of
these modules seem to fulfill social functions – cheater detection being a canonical
example (Barkow, Cosmides, and Tooby, 1992), but other well-known candidates
include sexual jealousy (Buss, 1999), language learning (Pinker, 1994), and moral
grammar acquisition (Haidt, 2001).

On the same foundational assumption as sociobiology – behavior as evolved
phenotype – evolutionary sociology constructs a more proximate, individual-level
account of the mechanisms and capacities by which sociality takes place, one that
complements sociobiology's focus on ultimate factors. As such, it is of greater
relevance to sociological theory than is sociobiology, but it is valuable also as
a bridge to, and component of, a third iteration of the evolutionary approach.

Evolutionary Biosociology

Evolutionary biosociology is not a mere relabeling of sociobiology or evolutionary
psychology to make them palatable to sociologists, as it is distinct from both in
several important ways.

Evolutionary biosociology puts little stock in the massively modular mind of
evolutionary psychology, adopting instead a more nominal modularity that, without
dismissing the concept entirely (Turner invites readers to use the term "module," but
only "if one is so disposed" [2015: 184]), assumes a greater degree of hierarchical

and functional linkage among modules, as well as the existence of a general-purpose processor alongside them (Machalek and Martin, 2010; Kanazawa, 2015).

Neither does it share evolutionary psychology's faith that the Pleistocene holds the key to understanding human nature. Beyond the fact that it was in no sense a single environment exerting uniform selection pressures on our ancestors (Plotkin, 2004; Stone, 2008), evolutionary biosociology rejects the conflation of what is perhaps most salient about human beings – our quantitatively unique capacity for language, cognition, and culture – with what is most essential to our nature, and thereby most relevant to explaining our behavior – our qualitatively unique sociality. It thus places the roots of our "humanity" much further back in prehistory. Thus, relative to evolutionary psychology's traditional emphasis on cognition, evolutionary biosociology foregrounds emotion (Franks and Davis, 2012; Machalek and Martin, 2010; Maryanski and Turner, 2015), and is more inclined to see human cognition as an emergent property of our sociality (à la Byrne and Whiten, 1988; Dunbar, 1998) rather than vice versa.

Like evolutionary psychology, evolutionary biosociology eschews sociobiology's optimality assumption, but it expands the evolutionary toolkit by more fully embracing non-optimizing evolutionary mechanisms as exaptation and sexual selection (Maryanski and Turner, 2015). Meanwhile, its extension of evolutionary processes to social entities above the organism level allows it to further incorporate adaptive mechanisms with no clear parallel in the strictly biological realm, but which may be significant factors in understanding the social, that is, "Spencerian" selection, through which social and cultural structures are alterable within a generation via such relatively intentional methods as imitation and innovation (Maryanski and Turner, 2015).

Beyond such divergences from its antecedents, evolutionary biosociology is characterized by two principal traits: its emphasis on group membership, group survival, and group strength as bases of selection in evolutionary history, and its holistic integration of ultimate biological factors with more proximate mechanisms and descriptions at the social level.

Sociologists have long maintained that the isolated human individual is an artificial abstraction absent from nature, so that even individual traits cannot be adequately understood without considering the social context of their origin. Evolutionary biosociology puts flesh on that article of sociological faith by demonstrating that the group is as much an indispensable "vehicle" for the individual organism as that organism is an indispensable vehicle for its cells. Because the ability to obtain and maintain membership in intact and formidable groups is thereby a paramount evolutionary virtue, human evolution has been subject to strong selective pressures for the capacities and dispositions that doing so requires. The resultant repertoire includes not only traits that allow us to get along with one another, but others that increase the robustness – the feeding and fighting efficacy – of the group as a whole (Machalek and Martin, 2010; Maryanski and Turner, 2015; West-Eberhard, 1979). Evolutionary biosociology thus decenters the inter-organism competition featured in most other evolutionary accounts of social behavior. It does so by adopting a model of multilevel selection in which evolutionary processes proceed at different levels – intraindividual, interindividual, interspecific, intergroup, interinstitutional, and intercultural – simultaneously and interactively.

In terms of its integrative potential, evolutionary biosociology excels at locating ultimate (evolutionary) causes, distal (physiological) structures, and proximate (psychological) mechanisms within a thoroughly described and theorized social context of contingency, power, and cultural influence to construct truly comprehensive and complete accounts of social behavior and phenomena.

Consider for example Huber's work on gender, which situates biology-based gender asymmetries in the provisioning of offspring (i.e. lactation) within a sociological understanding of the contexts in which decisions are made and power is allocated (e.g. warfare, hunting) to explain the historical exclusion of women from hierarchies of power (2007). Likewise, Marshall's work on ritual, demonstrates the ways that evolved social dispositions and cognitive heuristics interact with culture – as a tool of emotional manipulation and as a moderating variable – to produce a sociological account of this cornerstone of social life (2008).

Evolution Evolves

Cultures, including science, are always evolving. Thus, evolutionary biology is itself changing, and with it, the explanatory tools available to evolutionary biosociology. Thus, for example, new second-order effects models are transcending the gene/environment dichotomy by attending to the genetic dimension of environmental plasticity (Belsky and Pluess, 2009). That is, in some dimensions, what individuals seem to inherit is a degree of sensitivity to environmental inputs, such that carriers of some alleles are more likely to engage in antisocial behavior given adverse environmental inputs, but also less likely to engage in them given a more congenial environment compared to the carriers of other, less malleable alleles who are relatively unaffected by such environmental variation (Simons et al., 2011). Two other innovations in evolutionary theory are of particular relevance to sociological theory.

Biology Gets Social

While sociology has been undergoing a biological turn in the early twenty-first century, biology is also in the midst of a social turn (Meloni, 2014a), and the domain of sociological theory is thereby expanding. Evolutionary biologists are finding that the consideration and incorporation of social phenomena can help them explain key phenomena. For example, because they are vulnerable to free-riding invaders, dispositions for cooperative behavior are precarious and unlikely to be retained in a population except for the fact that they are stabilized and rendered viable by processes operating at the social level – the assortive association whereby cooperators selectively interact and reproduce with other cooperators (Wilson and Dugatkin, 1997), and the ostracism or violent elimination of noncooperators (Boehm, 2001).

An even more promising expansion of the discipline springs from major transitions theory (Maynard-Smith and Szathmáry, 1995), which demonstrates that the history of life on earth is a thoroughly social one, with each level of biological organization recapitulating a version of the same story, in which competing entities subjugate their divergent individual interests to reap the adaptive advantages of collective reproduction. Thus, genes combine to form chromosomes, prokaryotes combine to form eukaryotes, single-cell organisms combine into multicellular organisms, and complex organisms combine as herds, schools, flocks, and tribes. Sociality is thereby the primary contributor to evolution's ability to create complexity, constituting its "third leg," alongside variation and selection (Nowak, 2011).

In every instance, the "de-Darwinization" of the lower-level entities – the suspension of their individual quests for reproduction for the good of the whole (Godfrey-Smith, 2009) – is essential. Since such sublimation is never complete (because the proliferation of cooperation makes individual defection ever more lucrative), the higher-level entities develop mechanisms to coerce and enforce cooperation among their lower-level constituents, from transcription checks at the genetic level to apoptosis at the cellular level (the failure of which we call cancer), to delegating certain individuals as enforcers at the inter-organism level (Trible and Kronauer, 2017). Sociologists should recognize this tension between the individual and the group, for it is a defining *problematique* of our discipline – that of social order (aka social control, the collective action problem). This patently sociological problem, and the imperative need to solve it, turns out to be a ubiquitous feature of life at every level. Life is itself social, with each of us a walking feat of social cooperation at every level from our genes to our microbiome. Surely sociology has something to contribute to this new view of life.

Less abstractly, the more we learn about the rest of the biological kingdom, the more apparent it becomes that it represents an effectively untapped sociological domain. By confining its focus to the social behavior of human beings, sociology has cut itself off from whole realms of theory and data, and from the explanatory power of a truly comparative method. We are not the only species to possess language or culture (Bonner, 1980), to socialize our young (Gould and Marler, 1987; Lopreato, 2001), to impress slaves, engage in agriculture, police free riders, or rescue combat-wounded comrades (Blatrix and Sermage, 2005; Branstetter et al., 2017; Frank et al., 2017; Trible and Kronauer, 2017).

To be worthy of its name, sociology must study the social in all of its manifestations, across all of the animal (and other [e.g., Wohlleben, 2016]) species in which it obtains. To the extent that the discipline does so, it annexes whole new domains of theory and research.

Epigenetics and "Post-Genomic" Biology

The Darwinian modern synthesis holds that the relationship between genotype and phenotype is unidirectional: though an organism's environment shapes the expression of its genotype, that phenotype does not, in turn, alter the genotype. But while the genotype's immunity to environmental alteration remains undisputed, modern epigenetics provides us with both the evidence that, and the mechanisms by which, environmental forces can nevertheless produce heritable changes by systematically silencing or amplifying the activity of genes in heritable ways (Jablonka and Lamb, 2005).

Epigenetics is but the best known of several approaches (others include Evolutionary Development ("Evo-Devo"), Niche-Construction Theory, and Developmental Systems Theory) that collectively make up what has been called "post-genomic" biology (Meloni, 2014b), which purports to dethrone the gene from its primacy as a determinant of organisms' morphology and behavior.

Critics of evolutionary biosociology have embraced post-genomism as yet new grounds on which to reject its relevance and explanatory utility. Ingold and Palsson, for example, declare neo-Darwinism dead (2013) and Meloni suggests that Developmental Systems Theory renders evolutionary biosociology largely obsolete (2014b). Although the post-genomic approach brings potentially transformational innovations to evolutionary biology, it is overreaching to presume that it obviates biosociology as a whole. Indeed, post-genomic biology is a threat only to a genetically deterministic version of evolutionary biosociology that no longer exists, if it ever did.

Even "post-genomic" biology is still biology. In demonstrating the degree to which genetic influences are intertwined with developmental, cultural, and environmental factors, post-genomic biology equally demonstrates the degree to which these are intertwined with genetics. Ultimately, the very mechanisms post-genomics proffers as alternatives to evolution are themselves either encapsulated versions of it, (e.g. development [Blute, 2015]), or products thereof (e.g. epigenetics [Pembrey, Bygren, and Kaati, 2006]). Thus, what it gives us is all the more reason to believe that explaining even cultural and environmental influences on the social requires greater attention to how those articulate with, and operate through, biological mechanisms, and, conveniently enough, it proffers us new tools with which to do so.

Analogous Unity: Evolutionary Sociology

The earliest attempts to illuminate social life with biology built less upon human nature than upon perceived parallels between biological and social systems. Whether the invoked correspondences were to organisms (e.g. Hobbes), ecosystems (e.g. Ward, Park, Burgess), or a loosely defined "evolutionary process" (e.g. the stage theories of Spencer and Marx), they tended toward the macro-metaphorical. Even after sociology became disillusioned with biology, models of social evolution continued to influence sociological theory from outposts across the border in anthropology, as manifest in Parsonian neo-evolutionism, Lenski's ecological theorizing, general systems theory, and organizational ecology, among others.

In time, Darwinism gave rise to a more literal concept of cultural evolution. Wallace speculated about parallels between biological and cultural change soon after he and Darwin had published their expositions of natural selection, a thread picked up by Darwin himself (Plotkin, 2004), but which then largely lay dormant until Richard Dawkins coined the term "meme" as a cultural analog for the gene (1976).

Together, social evolution and cultural evolution constitute a second, *analogous*, variety of unity (and thereby relevance), between biology and sociological theory. Because this chapter is formally concerned with the application of biology, rather than evolution per se, to sociological theory, and because both social and cultural evolution are themselves expansive fields, they are treated here as collateral cases, and recounted in less detail than was biosociology.

Critics see the purported parallels between evolution and social and cultural change as amounting to, at best, metaphoric restatements of established sociological processes and, at worst, facile and misleading overgeneralizations. Citing the lack of uncontested cultural counterparts to such basic evolutionary concepts as the gene itself, and the lack of clear biological equivalents for culture's capacities for intentional variation and imitative diffusion, they posit that the two domains are too dissimilar for either to illuminate the other.

Such critiques inject a necessary note of caution, but fail to obviate the relevance of these parallels. A metaphor needn't map perfectly onto its referent to illuminate it – indeed, if it did, it would be a recreation, not a metaphor. More substantively, there are good reasons to believe that the relationships between biology and sociology are more than metaphoric. The capacity for culture – to absorb, transmit, and be influenced by it – is neither a fortuitous accident nor a corollary of a general cognitive capacity, but a collection of evolved adaptations (Bonner, 1980; Tomasello, 1999). Put simply, culture is itself both a product of evolution, and an extension thereof, whose very existence is ultimately attributable to its adaptive value in the realm of biology (Rosenberg, 2015; Stone, 2008). Furthermore, as per major transitions theory (Maynard-Smith and Szathmáry, 1995), the history of life on earth is one in which the basic process of variation/selection recapitulates itself at each level. There is no reason to believe a priori that the social level and cultural domain should be an exception to this fractal structure.

The most decisive argument for the applicability of evolutionary change to societies and cultures has to do with just why the process recurs across so many levels. Darwinian evolution is glacially slow (operating across generations), bloodily inefficient (dependent as it is on the reiterated destruction of the less well adapted), and highly unreliable (the fossil record tells of much more extinction than survival). But these disadvantages pale beside its signal advantage – its – for lack of a better term – "parsimony." Evolution is so simple and dependent upon so few prerequisites that anytime a scant handful of basic conditions – variation, competition, and reproduction – obtain in some form, the process commences (Lewontin, 1970; Mesoudi, 2011).

By this "universal Darwinism" account (Dawkins, 1983), evolution is the master etiological mechanism of the known universe, with biological speciation being simply the domain in which it was first discovered. Elsewhere in biology, it manifests itself in the "neural Darwinism" by which the brain is physically and functionally sculpted, in the selectionist modus operandi of the immune system, and bears directly upon behavior in the guise of operant conditioning. Beyond biology, a recognizably Darwinian logic can be discerned in the market economy, in the scientific method, and in the virtual ecosystem of "hits," "likes," and "links" that is the internet. Of particular significance is the realization (extending back through Alfred Russell Wallace, William James, and Jean Piaget, among others) that thought itself manifests much the same variation/selection process (Campbell, 1987). Given this ubiquity of the fundamental evolutionary dynamic, it beggars belief that social or cultural systems alone would be immune to its operation.

Although the disanalogies between biological and sociological systems are real enough, they are neither as great, nor as deleterious, as commonly purported to be. Genes may be the prototypic replicator, but that doesn't mean they constitute some minimum standard for evolution to occur, since even genes had to evolve via some pre-genetic replicator (Rosenberg, 2015). The Punnett squares with which most of us learn Mendelian genetics understate the extent to which genes are blunt instruments: non-particulate, multifocal, and generally unlike the mythical "genes" that other potential replicators are invidiously compared to (Rosenberg, 2015). While cultural evolution involves a kind of intentionality absent from Darwin's original model, it is hardly antithetical to it. In the domestication of crops and livestock, humans have been intentionally directing evolution for millennia. Is a Welsh corgi any less a product of evolution because its stature, personality, and herding instincts were intentionally selected for?

Undoubtedly, evolution, like any other process, will operate differently in different contexts. But it behooves us to recognize not only their differences, but also their convergences and functional equivalences so as to take advantage of the insights these offer.

Social Evolution in Sociological Theory

Eschewing theories that are "evolutionary" only in the nominal sense of positing successive stages, several approaches to social evolution stand out. In *Darwinian conflict theory*, Sanderson extends Marx's invocation of Darwinism as a natural analog of the class struggle (2001, 2015), augmenting conventional sociological approaches (e.g. conflict theory, rational choice) with cultural materialism and sociobiology to erect a deductive edifice of over 300 propositions about sociological phenomena ranging from reproductive behavior to diet, inequality, violence, and religion. It thus vividly demonstrates that the inclusion of biology does not obviate more traditionally "sociological" theories, as well as the comprehensive scope and unification that sociology should aspire to, and which the explicit inclusion of biology alone makes possible.

Thanks to its focus on fairly discrete constituents in explicitly competitive relationships, *organizational ecology* (Hannan and Freeman, 1989) is a relatively unproblematic analogous application of biology to the social. Though not perfectly correspondent, organizations, markets, and economies can be fruitfully modeled as ecosystems. Doing so has previously illuminated the life cycle of firms, and promising future directions include the incorporation of cultural group selection (Johnson, Prince, and Van Vugt, 2013), applications to the institutional sphere (Abrutyn, 2014), and the formalization of Spencerian selection mechanisms among organizations (Maryanski and Turner, 2015).

Superorganism theory builds upon major transitions theory's implication that the organism is not the highest level of biological organization on earth; this is based on the fact that organisms can and do serve as the constituents of larger entities that themselves function like organisms (Holldobbler and Wilson, 2009), such that some social arrangements arguably represent an incomplete transition of human groups into a superorganism, with moral codes functioning as a cultural means of de-Darwinization, aligning individual action with the needs of the group (Aunger, 2017).

Cultural Evolution in Sociological Theory

The most literal transposition of Darwinian evolution into the cultural sphere embraces Dawkins' hypostatization of the "meme" (1976) as a cultural analog of the gene. *Memetics* (Mesoudi, 2011; Stone, 2008) emphasizes that, like any other universal replicator, these snippets of culture, whether ideas or behaviors, are adapted to ensuring their own replication, even at the expense of their carrier organisms – hence both the title of Dawkin's book, *The Selfish Gene*, and "meme's" adoption as a defining neologism of the internet age.

Cultural group selection by contrast, emphasizes a meme's direct value neither to itself nor to the organism, but to the group to which the individual belongs. It argues that groups possessed of some cultural beliefs or habits – especially those that allow them to better cooperate or to better embrace innovations – hold an adaptive advantage over groups that lack those beliefs or habits (Henrich, 2004; Sober and Wilson, 1998).

Within sociology, discussions about cultural evolution typically take place under the umbrella of *dual inheritance theory*, the gist of which is that human beings, and thus their social behavior and social phenomena, are jointly shaped by evolutionary processes in both the biological and cultural spheres. Better known as *gene-culture co-evolution* (Lumsden and Wilson, 1980; Richerson and Boyd, 2005; Runciman, 2009), this approach straddles the line between continuous and analogous unity by focusing on the ways in which culture constitutes a key aspect of the landscape upon which genes evolve, while genes simultaneously constitute a key aspect of the landscape upon which culture evolves (Walsh, 2014). The canonical example is the evolution of lactose tolerance (enzymes of milk digestion) in the dairying culture of Northern Europe, where the cultural practice of raising cattle and drinking milk selected for a continued biological ability to digest milk, which, in turn, led to a proliferation of husbandry/herding cultures and diets (Cavalli-Sforza, 2000).

Along with giving lie to the idea that the onset of cultural evolution, and the onset of cultural forces more generally, means that biological evolution is no longer relevant, gene-culture co-evolution helps us see something important about the interaction of the two domains: that genes and cultures can and often do work together, creating feedback loops that reinforce, backstop, and amplify selective pressures for adaptive behaviors (Chase-Dunn, 2015; Cronk, 2015).

Topical Unity: Biology in Society

One final unity between biology and sociology to be discussed here is topical, in the sense that the issues of greatest concern to sociologists are, ultimately, biological. The importance of sociology's pressing and perennial pre-occupations derives from their impact upon the biological dimensions of persons, something Marx well understood: "The first premise of all human history is, of course, the existence of living human individuals ... The writing of history must always set out from these natural bases" (in Tucker, 1978: 145). Inequalities are most pointed where they impinge upon people's ability to maintain homeostasis and fulfill reproductive imperatives – to eat, hydrate, form pair bonds, raise children, and to keep themselves and their loved ones warm, dry, sheltered, and safe. Note, too, that out of all the disparate dimensions that inequalities in individuals' abilities to fulfill these imperatives could possibly align with, they are depressingly prone to cleave groups along such superficial biologically ascribed traits as sex, sexual orientation, myelination, and age. Less ideologically loaded biological factors like height and attractiveness also remain stubbornly significant determinants of an individual's fate in society. And, as Pinker points out, the very idea of inalienable human rights is dependent upon the assumption that their referent values are not mere constructs, but innate (i.e. biological) aspects of their makeup (2002).

The topical unity of biology and sociology will become only more pronounced in the future, and may well determine the defining *problematiques* of the next generation of sociologists. As the technological revolution pushes its way into the biological realm, its fruits – from 3D organ-printing and other technologies of life extension, to the cheap and easy gene editing of other species, ourselves, and our children – will create whole new orders of inequality, instigate whole new waves of social change, and institute whole new social configurations. At the same time, the looming crises of climate change and overpopulation, in all their manifestations – ecosystem destruction, floral and faunal migration and invasion, drought- and flood-related food shortages, and extreme-event-related depopulations and repopulations – will reiteratively make the biological dimensions of human existence inescapably salient. In particular, between the consequent expansion of disease gene pools, increased contact between pathogens and potential hosts, and the antibiotic-driven evolution of more robust and resistant micro-predators, pandemic disease could become a major renovator of human social structures, cultures, and behaviors.

Sociology's expertise will be indispensable to navigating these developments, but a sociological theory that remains in denial about the extent to which, and/or unenlightened about ways in which, it articulates with biology will neither be effective nor taken seriously in this mission.

Conclusion

This chapter has mapped some of the ways in which its continuous, analogous, and topical unities with sociology make biology vitally relevant to the crafting of complete sociological theories. The stance throughout has been that biology neither intends nor threatens to replace traditional, nonbiological accounts of sociality. Rather, the overarching message has been that the explicit incorporation of biology into sociological theory renders the herculean task of constructing complete explanations for social behavior and phenomena tractable. Metaphorically speaking, while including its biological underpinnings does not by itself unlock any social behavior or phenomenon, doing so does at least provide the first digit(s) of its combination.

But before folding our map, I should point out that the self-handicapping that ignoring biology amounts to is a luxury that sociology can no longer afford. Comte was right to call sociology the "queen of the sciences" since it is where all the causes and contingencies of the lower levels of reality cumulate in a crescendo of complexity. Untangling them is going to require every tool available, especially those proffered by biology in all of its manifestations.

And make no mistake, untangle them we must. The formative dichotomies of mechanical society/organic society, *Gemeinschaft/Gesellschaft*, traditionalist spirit/capitalist spirit, et al., remind us that sociology was born in the struggle to understand whether and how a species naturally suited to (read: evolved for) life in a high-moral-density social environment could thrive, or even survive, in the low-moral-density environment of the modern world. A century of (limited and uneven) "success" at navigating that rift has perhaps lulled us into believing that it is no longer a discipline-defining problem. But it never really went away (Buruma and Margalit, 2005; Herf, 1984; Marshall, 2008) and has of late returned to center stage, with the rise of jihadism, the Brexit vote, and last year's US election each testifying to the enduring motivating potential of the traditional (high-moral density) vs. cosmopolitan (low-moral density) dynamic in human affairs.

Human beings' dualistic nature – our evolved dispositions for life in high-moral-density tribes alongside our capacity to imagine and create low-moral-density societies and organizations – is, I argue, our defining characteristic, and the one most indispensable to sociological theory. Like every other mammal, we are the inheritors of a collection of time-tested, highly effective, fast-acting, nonconscious, emotional, automatic, and effortless behavior-control "modules." But unlike other mammals, we also possess a much newer, limited, slow-acting, conscious, cognitive, controlled, and effortful general-purpose capacity for behaving in accordance with rational calculation and cumulative culture, one often contrary to, and in competition with, its older counterpart (Wegner and Bargh, 1998). Under different names, the conflict between these elements has been a recurrent theme of human literature, art, and philosophy, and as per Durkheim, is the source of much of humanity's grandeur and tragedy (1964 [1914]). But, because both modes are ultimately systems of behavioral control, the conflict between them is of more than experiential relevance.

While the older system is not inexorable, it is primary to the newer one in almost every sense. It is effortless, automatic, and more closely tied to behavior, thus amounting to a "default mode" that requires active effort to overcome. Thus, for example, their evolved-morality-driven preoccupation with the inequity of what they perceive as "line-cutters" reliably leads the voters described by Hochschild to support candidates whom a more demanding and dispassionate analysis reveals to evince no sign of ability or willingness to actually do anything to materially benefit these supporters (2016).

The sociological relevance of *homo duplex* lies not just in such tensions between the modes, but also in the other ways that the two modes interact, a brief inventory of which would include:

- The newer system's need to make sense of the outputs of the older system so as to preserve its *nomos*. This is especially true of the uniquely coercive outputs of the nonconscious moral faculties, the discrepancies between which and conscious expectations may be instrumental to the ubiquity and uniqueness of human religion (Marshall, 2016).
- The newer system's proclivity for finding ways to indulge and exploit the drives and desires of the old system beyond their adaptive utility. Most obvious in this regard are our tastes for fats, sweets, alcohol, and opioids, but consider also the addictiveness of partial reinforcement schedules (e.g. gambling, prayer), our craving for frequent cognitive stimulation and distraction (how far away is your nearest device right now?), and our basic cognitive miserliness – our desire to avoid the hard labor of *nomos* maintenance and recalibration by sequestering ourselves from inconvenient facts (Sunstein, 2017).
- The newer system's ability to bestow upon individuals still possessed of the old system's "rationally irrational" dispositions for retributive justice, violence escalation, and sensitivity to reputation maintenance, technologies that vastly magnify their destructive potential, such that we are each constantly and acutely interdependent with a growing group of anonymous and unaccountable others to not fulfill that potential against us or our loved ones.
- The newer system's ability to construct new species of social actors (organizations, artificial intelligences), that we naturally occurring social actors (individuals, tribes), with our older system of social instincts and moral sentiments, are ill-equipped to interact with – a disadvantage unlikely to go unexploited.

Any sociology that hopes to seriously engage and grapple with the critical issues of twenty-first-century society must be able to address this duality, and every other feature of human nature – that is, biology – head-on (Ellis, 1996; Van den Berghe, 1990).

References

Abrutyn, Seth. 2014. "Religious Autonomy and Religious Entrepreneurship: An Evolutionary-Institutionalist's Take on the Axial Age." *Comparative Sociology* 113: 105–134.

Aunger, Robert. 2017. "Moral Action as Cheater Suppression in Human Superorganisms." *Frontiers in Sociology* 2(2). DOI:10.3389/fsoc.2017.00002

Barash, David P. 1982. *Sociobiology and Behavior*. New York: Elsevier.

Barkow, Jerome, Leda Cosmides, and John Tooby. 1992. *The Adapted Mind: Evolutionary Psychology and the Generation of Culture*. New York, NY: Oxford University Press.

Baron-Cohen, Simon. 1991. "Precursors to a Theory of Mind: Understanding Attention in Others." In Andrew Whiten (ed.), *Natural Theories of Mind: Evolution, development and Simulation of Everyday Mindreading* (pp. 233–251). Oxford, UK: Basil Blackwell.

Belsky, Jay, and Michael Pluess. 2009. "Beyond Diathesis Stress: Differential Susceptibility to Environmental Influences." *Psychological Bulletin* 135: 885–908.

Belyayev, D. K., and L. N. Trut. 1964. "Behavior and Reproductive Function of Animals. II. Correlated Changes Under Breeding for Tameness." *Bulletin of the Moscow Society of Naturalists Biological Series* 69(5): 5–14.

Black, M. P., and M. S. Grober. 2003. "Group Sex, Sex Change, and Parasitic Males: Sexual Strategies Among the Fishes and Their Neurobiological Correlates." *Annual Review of Sex Research* 14: 160–184.

Blatrix, R. S., and C. Sermage. 2005. "Role of Early Experience in Ant Enslavement: A Comparative Analysis of a Host and a Non-Host Species." *Frontiers in Zoology* 2(13): DOI:10.1186/1742-9994-2-13

Blute, Marion. 2015. "Modes of Variation and their Implications for an Extended Evolutionary Synthesis." In Jon Turner, Richard Machalek, and Alexandra Maryanksi (eds.), *Handbook on Evolution and Society: Toward an Evolutionary Social Science* (pp. 59–75). Boulder, CO: Paradigm Publishers.

Boehm, Christopher. 2001. *Hierarchy in the Forest: The Evolution of Egalitarian Behavior*. Cambridge, MA: Harvard University Press.

Bonner, John. 1980. *The Evolution of Culture in Animals*. Princeton, NJ: Princeton University Press.

Bowlby, John. 1969. *Attachment*. New York, NY: Basic Books.

Branstetter, Michael G., Ana Ješovnik, Jeffrey Sosa-Calvo, et al. 2017. "Dry Habitats Were Crucibles of Domestication in the Evolution of Agriculture in Ants." *Proceedings of the Royal Society, B* 284: 20170095. http://dx.doi.org/10.1098/rspb.2017.0095

Buruma, Ian, and Avishai Margalit. 2005. *Occidentalism: The West in the Eyes of its Enemies*. London, UK: Penguin Books.

Buss, David M. 1999. *Evolutionary Psychology: The New Science of the Mind*. Needham Heights, MA: Allyn Bacon.

Byrne, Richard, and Andrew Whiten. 1988. *Machiavellian Intelligence: Social Complexity and the Evolution of Intellect in Monkeys, Apes and Humans*. Oxford, UK: Oxford University Press.

Campbell, Donald T. 1987. "Selection Theory and the Sociology of Scientific Validity." In Werner Callebaut and Rik Pinxten (eds.), *Evolutionary Epistemology: A Multiparadigm Program* (pp. 139–158). Dordrecht, Netherlands: D. Reidel Publishing Company.

Cavalli-Sforza, Luigi. 2000. *Genes, Peoples, and Languages*. Berkeley, CA: University of California Press.

Chase-Dunn, Christopher. 2015. "The Sociological Evolution of World-Systems." In Jonathan H. Turner, Richard Machalek, and Alexandra Maryanski (eds.),

Handbook on Evolution and Society: Toward an Evolutionary Social Science (pp. 267–284). New York: Routledge.

Coleman, James. 1990. *Foundations of Social Theory.* Cambridge, MA: Belknap Press.

Conley, Dalton. 2014. "How I Became a Sociogenomicist." *Contexts* 13(4): 17–18.

Cosmides, Leda, and John Tooby. 1992. "Cognitive Adaptations for Social Exchange." In Jerome Barkow, Leda Cosmides, and John Tooby (eds.), *The Adapted Mind: Evolutionary Psychology and the Generation of Culture* (pp. 163–228). New York, NY: Oxford University Press.

Crippen, Timothy. 2015. "The Evolution of Tenuous Pair Bonding in Humans: A Plausible Pathway and Indicators of design." In Jon Turner, Richard Machalek, and Alexandra Maryanksi (eds.), *Handbook on Evolution and Society: Toward an Evolutionary Social Science* (pp. 402–421). Boulder, CO: Paradigm Publishers.

Cronk, Lee. 2015. "Human Cooperation: Evolutionary Approaches to a Complex Phenomenon." In Jonathan H. Turner, Richard Machalek, and Alexandra Maryanski (eds.), *Handbook on Evolution and Society: Toward an Evolutionary Social Science* (pp. 441–459). New York: Routledge.

Dawkins, Richard. 1976. *The Selfish Gene.* Oxford UK: Oxford University Press.

1983. "Universal Darwinism." In D. S. Bendall (ed.), *Evolution from Molecules to Man.* (pp. 403–428). Cambridge UK: Cambridge University Press.

Delmore, Kira, and Derren Irwin. 2014. "Hybrid Songbirds Employ Intermediate Routes in a Migratory Divide." *Ecology Letters* 17(10). DOI:https://doi.org/10.1111/ele .12326

DeWaal, Franz. 1996. *Good Natured: The Origins of Right and Wrong in Humans and Other Animals.* Cambridge, MA: Harvard University Press.

Dobzhansky, Theodozius. 1973. "Nothing in Biology Makes Sense Except in Light of Evolution." The American Biology Teacher 35(3): 125–129.

Dunbar, Robin. 1998. "The Social Brain Hypothesis." *Evolutionary Anthropology* 6(5): 178–190.

Durkheim, Emile. 1964 [1914]. "The Dualism of Human Nature and its Social Conditions." In Kurt Wolff (ed.), *Essays on Sociology and Philosophy* (pp. 325–340). New York, NY: Harper and Row.

Ekman, Paul, Wallace Friesen, and Sonia Ancoli. 1980. "Facial Signs of Emotional Experience." *Journal of Personality and Social Psychology* 39(6): 1125–1134.

Ellis, Lee. 1996. "A Discipline in Peril: Sociology's Future Hinges on Curing Its Biophobia." *American Sociologist* 27(2): 21–41.

Firat, Rengin, and Steven Hitlin. 2012. "Morally Bonded and Bounded: A Sociological Introduction to Neurology." *Advances in Group Processes* 29: 165–199.

Frank, Erik T., Thomas Schmitt, Thomas Hoverstadt, et al. 2017. "Saving the Injured: Rescue Behavior in the Termite-Hunting Ant *Megaponera Analis.*" *Science Advances* 3(4): DOI:10.1126/sciadv.1602187.

Franks, David O. 2010. *Neurosociology: The Nexus Between Neuroscience and Social Psychology.* New York, NY: Springer.

2015. "The Evolution of the Human Brain." In Jon Turner, Richard Machalek, and Alexandra Maryanksi (eds.), *Handbook on Evolution and Society: Toward an Evolutionary Social Science* (pp. 285–294). Boulder, CO: Paradigm Publishers.

Franks, David O., and Jeff Davis. 2012. "Critique and Refinement of the Neurosociology of Mirror Neurons." In Will Kalkhoff, Shane R. Thye, and Edward J. Lawler (eds.), *Biosociology and Neurosociology* (pp. 77–118). Bingley, UK: Emerald Books.

Godfrey-Smith, Peter. 2009. *Darwinian Populations and Natural Selection*. Oxford, UK: Oxford University Press.

Gould, James, and Peter Marler. 1987. "Learning by Instinct." *Scientific American* 256: 74–85.

Gould, Steven J., and Richard Lewontin. 1979. "The Spandrels of San Marco and the Panglossian Paradigm: A Critique of the Adaptationist Programme." *Proceedings of the Royal Society of London, Series B. Biological Sciences* 205: 581–598.

Grammer, Karl, and Randy Thornhill. 1994. "Human (Homo sapiens) Facial Attractiveness and Sexual Selection: The Role of Symmetry and Averageness." *Journal of Comparative Psychology* 108(3): 233–242.

Haidt, Jonathan. 2001. "The Emotional Dog and Its Rational Rail: A Social Intuitionist Approach to Moral Judgment." *Psychological Review* 108(4): 814–834.

Hannan, Michael, and John Freeman. 1989. *Organizational Ecology*. Cambridge, MA: Harvard University Press.

Hatfield, Elaine, John Cacioppo, and Richard Rapson. 1994. *Emotional Contagion*. New York, NY: Cambridge University Press.

Henrich, Joseph. 2004. "Cultural Group Selection, Coevolutionary Processes and Large-Scale Cooperation." *Journal of Economic Behavior and Organization* 53(1): 3–35.

Herf, Jeffrey. 1984. *Reactionary Modernism: Technology, Culture, and Politics in Weimar and the Third Reich*. Cambridge, UK: Cambridge University Press.

Hochschild, Arlie. 2016. *Strangers in Their Own Land: Anger and Mourning on the American Right*. New York, NY: The New Press.

Holldobbler, Bert, and Edward O. Wilson. 2009. *The Superorganism: The Beauty, Elegance, and Strangeness of Insect Societies*. New York, NY: WW Norton.

Hrdy, Sarah. 2009. *Mothers and Others: The Evolutionary Origins of Mutual Understanding*. Cambridge, MA: Belknap Press.

Huber, Joan. 2007. *On the Origins of Gender Inequality*. Boulder, CO: Paradigm.

Ingold, Tim, and Gisli Palsson. 2013. *Biosocial Becomings: Integrating Social and Biological Anthropology*. Cambridge, UK: Cambridge University Press.

Insel, Thomas R., and Sue Carter. 1995. "The Monogamous Brain: Prairie Voles and the Chemistry of Mammalian Love." *Natural History* 104: 12–14.

Jablonka, Eva, and Marion J. Lamb. 2005. *Evolution in Four Dimensions: Genetic, Epigenetic, Behavioral, and Symbolic Variation in the History of Life*. Cambridge, MA: MIT Press.

Johnson, Dominic, Michael Price, and Mark Van Vugt. 2013. "Darwin's Invisible Hand: Market Competition, Evolution, and the Firm." *Journal of Economic Behavior and Organization* 90: S128–S140.

Kahneman, Daniel, and Amos Tversky. 1979. "Prospect Theory: An Analysis of Decision Under Risk." *Econometrica* 47(2): 263–292.

Kalkhoff, Will, Shane R. Thye, and Edward J. Lawler. 2012. *Biosociology and Neurosociology*. Bingley, UK: Emerald Books.

Kanazawa, Satoshi. 2015. "Evolutionary Psychology and Its Relevance to the Social Sciences." In Jon Turner, Richard Machalek, and Alexandra Maryanksi (eds.), *Handbook on Evolution and Society: Toward an Evolutionary Social Science* (pp. 136–156). Boulder, CO: Paradigm Publishers.

Kanwisher, Nancy, and Galit Yovel. 2006. "The Fusiform Face Area: A Cortical Region Specialized for the Perception of Faces." *Philosophical Transactions B, Biological Sciences* 361(1476): 2109–2128.

Kobayashi, Hiromi, and Shiro Kohshima. 2001. "Unique Morphology of the Human Eye and Its Adaptive Meaning: Comparative Studies on External Morphology of the Primate Eye." *Journal of Human Evolution* 40(5): 419–435.

Latane, Bibb, and John Darley. 1968. "Bystander Intervention in Emergencies: Diffusion of Responsibility." *Journal of Personality and Social Psychology* 8: 377–383.

Lenski, Gerhard. 1966. *Power and Privilege: A Theory of Stratification*. New York: McGraw-Hill.

Lewontin, Richard C. 1970. "The Units of Selection." *Annual Review of Ecology and Systematics* 1: 1–18.

Lieberman, Matthew. 2014. *Social: Why Our Brains Are Wired to Connect*. New York, NY: Crown Publishers.

Lopreato, Joseph. 2001. "Sociobiological Theorizing: Evolutionary Sociology." In Jonathan H. Turner (ed.), *Handbook of Sociological Theory* (pp. 405–433). New York, NY: Kluwer Academic.

Lopreato, Joseph, and Timothy A. Crippen. 1999. *Crisis in Sociology: The Need for Darwin*. New Brunswick, NJ: Transaction Publishers.

Machalek, Richard, and Michael W. Martin. 2010. "Evolution, Biology, and Society: A Conversation for the 21st-Century Classroom." *Teaching Sociology* 38(1): 35–45.

Marshall, Douglas A. 2008. "Sacralization and the Throes of Modernization: Witch Trials, World War, and the WTC." *The New York Journal of Sociology* 1: 26–90.

———. 2016. "The Moral Origins of God: Darwin, Durkheim, and the *Homo Duplex* Theory of Theogenesis." *Frontiers in Sociology* 1(13): DOI:https://doi.org/10.3389/fsoc .2016.00013

Maryanski, Alexandra, and Jonathan H. Turner. 2015. "Evolutionary Sociology: A Cross-Species Strategy for Discovering Human Nature." In Jonathan H. Turner, Richard Machalek, and Alexandra Maryanksi (eds.), *Handbook on Evolution and Society: Toward an Evolutionary Social Science* (pp. 316–332). Boulder, CO: Paradigm Publishers.

Maynard-Smith, John, and Eors Szathmáry. 1995. *The Major Transitions in Evolution*. Oxford, UK: Oxford University Press.

Mazur, Allan. 2005. *Biosociology of Dominance and Deference*. Lanham, MD: Rowman and Littlefield.

———. 2015. "A Biosocial Model of Status in Face-to-Face Groups." In Virgil Zeigler-Hill, Lisa L. M. Welling, and Todd K. Shackelford (eds.), *Evolutionary Perspectives on Social Psychology* (pp. 303–315). Cham, Switzerland: Springer.

Meloni, Maurizio. 2014a. "How Biology Became Social, and What It Means for Social Theory." *The Sociological Review* 62(3): 593–614.

———. 2014b. "Biology without Biologism: Social Theory in a Postgenomic Age." *Sociology* 48 (4): 731–746.

Mesoudi, Alex. 2011. *Cultural Evolution: How Darwinian Theory Can Explain Human Culture and Synthesize the Social Sciences*, Chicago, IL: University Of Chicago Press.

Nowak, Martin. 2011. *Supercooperators: Altruism, Evolution, and Why We Need Each Other to Succeed*. New York, NY: Free Press.

Öhman, Arne, and Susan Mineka. 2001. "Fear, Phobias and Preparedness: Toward an Evolved Module of Fear and Fear Learning." *Psychological Review* 108: 483–522.

Panskepp, Jaak. 2003. "Feeling the Pain of Social Loss." *Science* 302(5643): 237–239.

Pembrey, Marcus, Lars Bygren, Gunnar Kaati, et al. 2006. "Sex-Specific, Male-Line Transgenerational Response in Humans." *European Journal of Human Genetics* 14: 159–166.

Pinker, Steven. 1994. *The Language Instinct*. New York, NY: Harper Perennial Modern Classics.

2002. *The Blank Slate: The Modern Denial of Human Nature*. New York, NY: Penguin Books.

Plotkin, Henry. 2004. *Evolutionary Thought in Psychology: A Brief History*. Hoboken, NJ: Wiley-Blackwell.

Ramachandran, Vilayanur S. 2011. *The Tell-Tale Brain: A Neuroscientist's Quest for What Makes Us Human*. New York, NY: W. W. Norton.

Richerson, Peter J., and Robert Boyd. 2005. *Not by Genes Alone: How Culture Transformed Human Evolution*. Chicago IL: University of Chicago Press.

Rizzolatti, Giacomo, and Laila Craighero. 2004. "The Mirror-Neuron System." *Annual Review of Neuroscience* 27(1): 169–192.

Rosenberg, Alexander. 2015. "The Biological Character of Social Theory." In Jonathan H. Turner, Richard Machalek, and Alexandra Maryanksi (eds.), *Handbook on Evolution and Society: Toward an Evolutionary Social Science* (pp. 28–58). Boulder, CO: Paradigm Publishers.

Runciman, Walter. 2009. *The Theory of Cultural and Social Selection*. Cambridge, UK: Cambridge University Press.

2015. "Evolutionary Sociology." In Jonathan H. Turner, Richard Machalek, and Alexandra Maryanski (eds.), *Handbook of Evolution and Society: Toward an Evolutionary Social Science* (pp. 194–214). London: Routledge.

Sanderson, Steven. 2001. *The Evolution of Human Sociality: A Darwinian Conflict Perspective*. Lanham, MD: Rowman and Littlefield.

2015. "Darwinian Conflict Theory: A Unified Evolutionary Research Program." In Jonathan H. Turner, Richard Machalek, and Alexandra Maryanksi (eds.), *Handbook on Evolution and Society: Toward an Evolutionary Social Science* (pp. 228–266). Boulder, CO: Paradigm Publishers.

Segerstrale, Ulrica. 2000. *Defenders of the Truth*. Oxford, UK: Oxford University Press.

Simmel, Georg. 1971 [1908]. "Conflict." In Donald Levine (ed.), *On Individuality and Social Forms: Selected Writings* (pp. 70–95). Chicago, IL: University of Chicago Press.

Simons, Ronald L. Man-Kit Lei, Steven Beach, Gene Brody, Robert Philibert, and Frederick Gibbons. 2011. "Social Environment, Genes, and Aggression: Evidence Supporting the Differential Susceptibility Perspective." *American Sociological Review* 76: 883–912.

Sober, Elliot, and David Sloan Wilson. 1998. *Unto Others: The Evolution and Psychology of Unselfish Behavior*. Cambridge, MA: Harvard University Press.

Stone, Brad. 2008. "The Evolution of Culture and Sociology." *American Sociologist* 39: 68–85.

Sunstein, Cass. 2017. *#Republic: Divided Democracy in the Age of Social Media*. Princeton, NJ: Princeton University Press.

Tomasello, Michael. 1999. *The Cultural Origins of Human Cognition*. Cambridge, MA: Harvard University Press.

Tomasello, Michael, and Malinda Carpenter. 2007. "Shared Intentionality." *Developmental Science* 10(1): 121–125.

Tomasello, Michael, Brian Hare, Hagen Lehmann, and Josep Call. 2007. "Reliance on Head Versus Eyes in the Gaze Following of Great Apes and Human Infants: The Cooperative Eye Hypothesis." *Journal of Human Evolution* 52: 314–320.

Trible, Waring, and Daniel Kronauer. 2017. "Caste Development and Evolution in Ants: It's All About Size." *Journal of Experimental Biology* 220: 53–62.

Tucker, Robert C. 1978. *The Marx-Engels Reader*, 2nd ed. New York, NY: W. W. Norton and Company.

Turner, Jonathan H. 2015."The Evolution of the Social Mind: The Limitations of Evolutionary Psychology." In Jonathan H. Turner, Richard Machalek, and Alexandra Maryanksi (eds.), *Handbook on Evolution and Society: Toward an Evolutionary Social Science* (pp. 177–193). Boulder, CO: Paradigm Publishers.

Udry, J. Richard. 1995. "Sociology and Biology: What Biology Do Sociologists Need to Know?" *Social Forces* 73(4): 1267–1278.

Van den Berghe, Pierre. 1990. "Why Most Sociologists Don't (and Won't) Think Evolutionarily." *Sociological Forum* 5(2): 173–185.

Van Lange, Paul, Wim Liebrand, and D. Michael Kuhlman. 1990. "Causal Attribution of Choice Behavior in Three N-Person Prisoner's Dilemmas." *Journal of Experimental Social Psychology* 26: 34–48.

Walsh, Anthony. 2014. *Biosociology: Bridging the Biology-Sociology Divide*. New Brunswick, NJ: Transaction Publishers.

Wegner, Daniel, and John Bargh. 1998. "Control and Automaticity in Social Life." In Daniel Gilbert, Susan Fiske, and Gardner Lindzey (eds.), *The Handbook of Social Psychology*, 4th ed. Boston, MA: McGraw-Hill.

West-Eberhard, Mary Jane. 1979. "Sexual Selection, Social Competition, and Evolution." *Proceedings of the American Philosophical Society* 123(4): 222–234.

Wilson, David Sloan, and Lee Dugatkin. 1997. "Group Selection and Assortative Interactions." *The American Naturalist* 149(2): 336–351.

Wilson, Edward. 1975. *Sociobiology: The New Synthesis*. Cambridge, MA: Harvard University Press.

Wohlleben, Peter. 2016. *The Hidden Life of Trees: What They Feel, How They Communicate – Discoveries from a Secret World*. Vancouver: Greystone Books.

19 Civil Society

Simon Susen

The task of defining the concept of civil society is far from straightforward. Within the history of social and political thought, one is confronted with an abundance of conflicting and 'competing definitions' of this term. This lack of definitional clarity indicates that '[i]n the social sciences, there is no consensus as to the theoretical and empirical separation of political, economic and social relations' (Abercrombie, Hill, and Turner, 2000: 48). It is far from obvious in which particular sphere, or set of spheres, civil society is located and on what grounds it can be distinguished from other domains of human reality. Yet, irrespective of its definitional ambiguity and referential elasticity, the concept of civil society has had – and, arguably, continues to have – a significant impact upon contemporary discourses, not only in the humanities and social sciences but also in both mainstream and alternative politics. In a general sense, civil society may be 'best understood as a confrontation with the very possibility of society itself' (Beyers, 2011: 3) – that is, as an intersubjectively constructed, discursively constituted, democratically organized, and publicly accessible participatory realm in which the normative parameters underpinning particular sets of social arrangements are at stake.

Influential Accounts of Civil Society

This section aims to provide an overview of influential accounts of civil society, drawing on analytical frameworks developed by major social and political philosophers. It is therefore important to consider their respective contributions to paradigmatic debates on the concept of civil society.

Aristotle (384 BC–322 BC)

In most studies concerned with the history of intellectual thought, there is widespread agreement that the first theoretically sophisticated and practically significant version of the concept of civil society appears in Aristotle 'under the heading of *politike koinonia*, political society/community' (Cohen and Arato, 1992: 84). Commonly translated by the Latins as *societas civilis*, the use of the concept of *politike koinonia* paved the way for the systematic engagement with the idea of civil society in both classical and contemporary social and political theory. The intimate relationship between 'the social' (*koinonia*) and 'the political' (*politike*), which is stressed in Aristotelian thought, suggests that, in both theoretical and practical terms, *community life* and *decision-making processes* are inextricably linked. The term *koinonia*, which is the transliterated expression for the Greek word κοινωνία, designates specific modes of communion, association, or joint participation. The term *polis* stands for particular types of political involvement and government experienced, and brought about, by human beings. Indeed, whereas the term *koinonia* refers to 'a plurality of forms of interaction, association, and group life' (Cohen and Arato, 1992: 85), the term *polis* describes 'a system where the people governed the people' (Beyers, 2011: 2). In other words, 'the social' and 'the political' can be considered two inseparable preconditions for the possibility of human existence.

In an anthropological sense, the concept of *koinonia* draws attention to the intrinsically social constitution of human existence, just as the concept of *polis* implies that – as famously claimed by Aristotle – 'man is by nature a political animal', that is, a *zoon politikon*. The idea of 'a public ethical-political community of free and equal citizens', peacefully coexisting 'under a legally defined system of rule' (Cohen and Arato, 1992: 84) is expressed in the concept of *politike koinonia*. On this account, *law* can be conceived of as a form of *ethos* that binds people together under the umbrella of a normative framework oriented towards the empirical realization of seemingly abstract principles – such as freedom, equality, and democracy.

It is striking that in Aristotelian thought there is 'no distinction between state and society', just as there is 'no distinction between society and communion (*koinonia*)' (Beyers, 2011: 2). To put it bluntly, we are confronted with the equation *state ≈ (civil) society*, to the extent that 'the Aristotelian notion does not allow for our distinction between state and society', as well as with the equation *state ≈ community*, to the degree that we acknowledge 'the absence of a second distinction ... that between society and community' (Cohen and Arato, 1992: 84). In short, *civil society* can be understood as a *political society*, or indeed as a *political community*, in which 'the social' and 'the political' are so deeply intertwined that they constitute two ontological cornerstones of human reality.

Thomas Hobbes (1588–1679)

'The development toward absolutism represents the watershed between traditional and modern meanings of "civil society"' (Cohen and Arato, 1992: 86). As both his critics and his followers recognize, Thomas Hobbes made major contributions to early modern conceptions of civil society. Arguably, 'the "society" of the Enlightenment, constituting a new form of public life, was the prototype of the early modern concept of civil society' (Cohen and Arato, 1992: 86). Hobbes, unlike several other Enlightenment thinkers, is known for his pessimistic view of the human condition, which is illustrated in his atomistic account of *the state of nature*. According to Hobbes's thought experiment, within the state of nature – which is defined by the absence of government – life is 'solitary, poor, nasty, brutish, and short'. On his interpretation, it is 'the institution of civil society and the state that puts an end to the war of every man against every man' (*bellum omnium contra omnes*). According to this narrative, 'the institution of civil society is ... equivalent to the founding of the political state' (Macey, 2000: 62) Hobbes's theoretical framework, in this sense, is based on the equation *state ≈ civil society*.

With the rise of absolutism and, correspondingly, the consolidation of the authoritarian state, a *functional duality* began to unfold: on the one hand, political power was increasingly monopolized 'in the hands of the *ruler*', epitomized in the monarch representing the ultimate source of sovereign authority over the population living in a given territory; on the other hand, political power was gradually taken away from the hands of 'a depoliticized *society*', whose members had little, if any, influence on the decision-making processes, let alone on the institutional arrangements, by which their lives were directly or indirectly affected. This opposition is both theoretically and practically significant, insofar as it marks the starting point for the development of modern understandings of civil society. At the same time, Hobbes's account entails 'a return to the Ancient Greek concept of no division between state and society' (Beyers, 2011: 2).

In order to avoid a relapse into the state of nature, a strong government needs to ensure that its citizens follow a set of elementary rules, allowing for their peaceful coexistence and preventing them from resorting to physical violence to resolve conflicts that may arise between them. From a Hobbesian perspective, human beings are motivated by their passions, egotistic drives, and narrow self-interests. Hence, within the Hobbesian universe, it is not society that civilizes the state, but, on the contrary, the state that civilizes society. To the degree that individual behaviour is dictated by the permanent prevalence of short-sighted desires, appetites, and selfishness, it is – from a Hobbesian point of view – 'fundamentally impossible for human beings to achieve any measure of self-government' (Dalton, 2014: 44–45).

Even if social practices are shaped by a series of cultural, ethnic, or religious norms, human subjects are in need of a legitimate government, epitomized in the rule exercised by an absolute sovereign, whose power is legitimized on the basis of a *social contract*. Thus, in order to civilize society, 'the state needs to exercise absolute sovereign authority', that is, a form of centralized power that is legitimized by its capacity to guarantee peace as well as social, political, and economic stability. Within the Hobbesian tradition of thought, then, '[t]he absolutism and authoritarianism of Leviathan ... is seen as essential to the necessary civilisation of society' (Dalton, 2014: 45). The alternative to absolutist or authoritarian rule would be, at best, chaos and anarchy or, at worst, violent conflict and war. On this view, '[t]he fusion of society is accomplished only by the power of the state', rather than by the power of civil society.

John Locke (1632–1704)

For John Locke, the social contract can be regarded as vital to protecting both individual and property rights. Indeed, from a Lockean point of view, it is precisely 'this contract that create[s] civil society in contrast to the "state of nature"'. On this account, the social contract can be conceived of as a means of bringing about civil society, enabling its members to liberate themselves from the disempowering aspects of the state of nature. Unlike their Hobbesian counterparts, however, Lockean philosophers defend the idea of a 'slim' liberal-democratic, rather than an author-itarian or absolutist, state. In their eyes, '[l]iberal civil society requires limited government, the separation of powers, the rule of law, and rule by representative government' (Turner, 2006: 70). In brief, liberal civil society cannot dispense with liberal institutions.

While, according to Locke, '[m]en are born free, equal and independent' (Macey, 2000: 62) they are obliged to sacrifice some of their natural freedom when accepting 'the *bonds of civil society*' and agreeing to enter the socially, politically, and legally binding sphere of the Commonwealth, which is established 'for their comfortable, safe, and peaceable living one amongst another' (Locke, 1996 [1689]: 340). Paradoxically, the construction of civil society involves both a decrease and an increase in the amount of liberty that its participants are able to enjoy: on the one hand, they lose a significant degree of their natural liberty to behave as they wish, irrespective of their fellow human beings' concerns, interests, and intentions; on the other hand, they gain a significant degree of their social liberty to behave within the normative framework of rules and norms, defined by a social contract, whose validity and legitimacy they confirm by acting in accordance with its parameters.

'When individuals agree to enter civil society, they adopt the principle of majority rule; they are at liberty to leave civil society but doing so means living in a state of nature that leaves them free but without any defence against others' (Locke as quoted in Macey, 2000: 62). In other words, mutual agreement and democracy constitute integral elements of civil society. Similar to Hobbes, Locke considers civil society and the state as mutually inclusive. Unlike Hobbes, however, Locke makes a case for a state based on the exercise of liberal-democratic, rather than authoritarian-absolutist, power. Thus, in both cases, the establishment of civil society is interpreted as a central evolutionary step away from 'natural society or the state of nature' towards 'civilized society or the state of civilization'. It is, on this account, the 'innate rationality in civil society' that can articulate 'the general good', thereby contributing to the consolidation of relatively peaceful, stable, and predictable life forms, in which humans cannot only flourish and realize their potential but can also reconcile the inevitable tension between individual and collective interests (Sassoon, 1991: 82).

Locke's conception of civilized existence presupposes 'the continuation of the identity of political and civil society' (Beyers, 2011: 2). Despite the intimate nexus between society and state, however, the two spheres *are* separate and, within the Lockean universe, have to be distinguished from one another. According to this – essentially liberal – world view, the most desirable form of modern government is 'constitutional democracy', which is, by definition, designed to protect its citizens' liberty, while guaranteeing the existence of social order and, hence, relative interac-tional predictability. Mediating organizations and institutions – such as unions, churches, associations, schools, and universities – are not only key elements of civil society but also a 'crucial counterweight to the power of government'. On this view, solidified socializing forces 'help keep society civil' (Dalton, 2014: 44). Put differently, there is no civil society without strong organizations and institutions capable of mediating between individuals and the state.

Just as civil society serves a *civilizing* function, facilitating the construction of social networks built on trust, reciprocity, and solidarity, it serves a *democratizing* function, allowing for the emergence of political structures derived from participation, engagement, and debate. Within a Lockean framework, the classical formula *societas civilis sive politicus sive respublica* continues to be valid, to the extent that the identity of 'political society' and 'civil society' is maintained, while both remain separate from 'state power'. In short, from a Lockean perspective, civil society constitutes a political (that is, both a politicized and a politicizing) sphere, whose existence is both fostered and protected by a constitutionally grounded polity, which is committed to guaranteeing its citizens' enjoyment of the civilizing functions of liberty and democracy.

Montesquieu (1689–1755)

Montesquieu's distinction between *public/political law* and *civil law* has had a profound impact upon the development of political and legal institutions in modern societies. *Public/political law* is concerned with 'regulating relations between those who govern and those who are governed'. *Civil law*, by contrast, focuses on 'regulating relations between members of society' (Beyers, 2011: 2). The former provides a *politico-legal* framework aimed at guaranteeing both the existence and the functioning of democratic structures and practices. The latter offers a *civil-legal* framework designed to ensure that citizens of a given society interact with one another in a morally justifiable, normatively sensitive, and practically viable fashion.

This division between these two fundamental socio-legal areas reflects the systematic effort 'to empower society politically, setting it up as a system against absolute rule' (Beyers, 2011: 2). Hence, it may be described as an institutionalized form of 'anti-absolutism'. On this account, members of society can be regarded as 'autonomous individuals' able to make rationally motivated decisions, thereby claiming authorship for their actions and asserting their sovereignty as responsible and accountable subjects. The wider significance of Montesquieu's distinction between public/political law and civil law is illustrated in his corresponding distinction between government (*l'état politique*) and society (*l'état civile*), borrowed from the Italian writer Gravina (Cohen and Arato, 1992: 88). Both conceptual pairs indicate that from the perspective of Montesquieu state and civil society, although they are interdependent, represent two different spheres of large-scale modern life forms.

Montesquieu's (1989 [1748]) unambiguously anti-absolutist conception of society underpins his plea for the separation of state powers: executive, legislative, and judicial. These powers are both relatively interdependent and relatively independent: they are relatively interdependent, insofar as they can be efficiently exercised only in relation to one another; at the same time, they are relatively independent, insofar as each of them possesses an idiosyncratic logic of functioning and, more importantly, needs to be kept separate from the others, in order to guarantee a stable, equitable, and viable balance of power within a democratic political system. Civil society can prosper only to the degree that its protagonists respect the division of public/political law and civil law, as well as the tripartite separation of executive, legislative, and judicial power.

Jean-Jacques Rousseau (1712–1778)

Similar to other social contract theorists, Jean-Jacques Rousseau draws a distinction between natural society or the state of nature, on the one hand, and civil society, on the other. The former is characterized by 'equality amongst people unpolluted by luxury or notions of power and servitude'. The latter is marked by the omnipresence of 'motifs of domination and imitation', triggered by 'the introduction of private property and an increasingly competitive pursuit of commercial gain' (Hall and Trentmann, 2005: 8). In other words, whereas the former represents the natural condition of 'the noble savage', the latter constitutes the artificial condition of 'civilized beings', alienated from their genuine dispositions, inclinations, and desires. In the state of nature, humans have three main preoccupations: food, sleep, and sex. In civil society, humans have become 'slaves to the conventions of social tastes and habits', imposed upon them by the behavioural, ideological, and institutional forces of their culturally codified environment (Hall and Trentmann, 2005: 8). In civilized forms of life, then, humans are estranged from their true nature: 'the savage lives in himself; the man accustomed to the ways of society is always outside himself and knows how to live only in the opinion of others' (Rousseau, 1996 [1755]: 448). This leads to the 'loss of independent consciousness' (Hall and Trentmann, 2005: 8) and, correspondingly, to the thriving of opportunism in the struggle for recognition, status, and prestige.

Hence, Hobbes's and Rousseau's respective accounts of the state of nature are diametrically opposed to one another: anthropological pessimism versus anthropological optimism. Rousseau's (1996 [1755]: 465) famous contention that '[m]an is born free, and everywhere he is in chains', summarizes his optimistic conception of the state of nature and his pessimistic conception of civil society. On this account, inequality between humans is, above all, socially constituted, rather than biologically determined. This view is forcefully expressed in the following passage:

> The first person who, having enclosed a plot of land, took it into his head to say *this is mine* and found people simple enough to believe him, was the true founder of civil society. What crimes, wars, murders, what miseries and horrors would the human race have been spared, had someone pulled up the stakes or filled in the ditch and cried out to his fellow men: 'Do not listen to this impostor. You are lost if you forget that the fruits of the earth belong to all and the earth to no one!' (Rousseau, 1996 [1755]: 431)

Put differently, in collective life forms whose economic organization is based on private property, inequality is due to social – rather than biological or physical – differences between people. Instead of conceiving of private property as a natural right and of social inequality as an inevitable given, Rousseau regarded both as historical products of bourgeois domination. As a result of the epochal transition from the state of nature to the consolidation of society, human beings have gradually distanced themselves from the roots of their existence and, consequently, alienated themselves from their true species-constitutive essence, epitomized in the noble savage.

The state of nature is equivalent to a socio-historical condition characterized by the absence of law, morality, and social conventions. Civil society, on the other hand, is inseparably linked to the emergence of an ever greater division of labour, along with the consolidation of political and legal institutions designed to protect the right to private property. To be clear, Rousseau was sufficiently realistic to recognize that a return to the state of nature, although it might be regarded desirable in some respects, did not represent a viable historical possibility. Similar to other Enlightenment thinkers, however, he was persuaded that, by forming civil society and subscribing to a social contract, individuals would be able not only to preserve themselves as members of their communities in particular and of humanity in general, but also to contribute to their own political emancipation as citizens equipped with basic democratic rights – such as freedom of expression, freedom to form and join organizations, and freedom of assembly. This conviction is articulated in Rousseau's belief in the sociological centrality of citizens' pursuit of a 'general will' (*volonté générale*), based on normative ideals such as popular sovereignty, direct democracy, and fairness of opportunity. His work, then, stands firmly in 'the tradition of civic virtue' (Hall and Trentmann, 2005: 8) understood as an empowering resource of politically conscientious, responsible, and self-determining actors.

Adam Smith (1723–1790)

Adam Smith stands in line with other Enlightenment thinkers, in the sense that the conceptual differentiation between the state of nature and civil society is central to his theoretical framework. On his account, the transition from the latter to the former is indicative of the 'innate rationality' of civil life, allowing for the emergence of a historical formation shaped by the pursuit of 'the general good' (Sassoon, 1991: 82). Within the Smithian universe of human existence, however, individuals contribute to the overall well-being of society without necessarily being aware of the fact that they are doing so when pursuing their own interests. In the Kantian kingdom of moral categorical imperatives, human entities should always be treated as ends in themselves, rather than being reduced to mere means for the pursuit of instrumental or strategic goals. In the Smithian world of wealth creation resulting from everyone's pursuit of their personal interests, by contrast, 'individuals treat one another as means to their private ends', which implies that social relations are sustained by both instrumental and strategic actions. On this interpretation, 'a just moral order is the by-product of that selfish pursuit' to the extent that the latter generates the normative parameters underlying the former (Calabrese, 2004: 318).

Adam Ferguson (1723–1816)

According to Adam Ferguson, civil society, insofar as it constitutes 'a state of civility', represents one of the most significant large-scale consequences of the rise of civilization. The idea of 'civility', on this view, can be employed as a political concept by means of which it is possible, and indeed necessary, to contrast liberal democracies with authoritarian regimes. This conceptual opposition is reflected in the dichotomy of 'the West' and 'the Rest', which refers to the normative antinomy between 'occidental pluralism' and 'oriental despotism', liberal democracy and totalitarian authority, the rule of law and arbitrary power. It is imperative, on this account, to draw a distinction between 'civilization' and 'societies (the barbaric state) in which private property does not exist' (Abercrombie, Hill, and Turner, 2000: 48). The 'history of civil society', therefore, cannot be divorced from the emergence of an ever-more-sophisticated, and universally empowering, civilization (Ferguson, 1995 [1767]).

Immanuel Kant (1724–1804)

For Immanuel Kant, civil society stands for an empowering realm in which rational subjects can ensure that their actions are guided by universal moral principles. 'Kant's redefinition of civil society as based on universal human rights beyond all particularistic legal and political orders' emanates from the ambitious attempt to develop a framework of normativity that, by definition, surpasses the limited scope of claims to moral validity constrained by the situational boundaries of spatio-temporal specificity (Cohen and Arato, 1992: 90). For Kant, then, civil society provides 'an attractive frame for administering *universal* justice' in a theoretically defensible and practically viable fashion (Hall and Trentmann, 2005: 11).

Given its universalistic outlook, civil society – as a reference point of both a collective imaginary and an everyday reality – offers 'people a way of thinking beyond states, communities and ranks' by reminding them of their common human-ity, whose constitutive features transcend the contingency of culturally specific sets of moral standards that vary between communities. To be sure, it would be erroneous 'to project onto civil society a linear view of a growing awareness of cosmopolitan ethics and peace', emerging, in an evolutionary fashion, out of inevitable civiliza-tional progress (Hall and Trentmann, 2005: 11). Yet, from a Kantian standpoint, it is crucial to recognize the emancipatory potential inherent in civil society, notably in terms of its capacity to contribute to the construction of a global ethics whose ultimate objective is to contribute to the empowerment of all members of humanity.

G. W. F. Hegel (1770–1831)

From a Hegelian perspective, the term 'civil society' designates 'an intermediate institution between the family and the political relations of the state' (Abercrombie, Hill, and Turner, 2000: 48) or, rather, 'a specific area of ethical life, which exists or mediates between the family and the state'. Interceding between the domestic demands of the household or *oikos* (ο κος), on the one hand, and the administrative and coercive imperatives of the state, on the other, civil society constitutes a collectively and publicly organized sphere for 'the enjoyment of rights' (Turner, 2006: 70). Thus, '[i]nterposed between the individual (or family) and the state' (Marshall, 1994: 55), civil society represents, above all, a 'market society', in which actors engage in 'infinitely complex criss-cross movements of reciprocal production and exchange' based on legally binding contracts and the inalienable right to private property (Macey, 2000: 62). Owing to the proliferation of and competition between divergent forces, however, civil society is in danger of turning out to be 'an indiscriminate multitude of individuals with conflicting and irreconcilable interests' (Macey, 2000: 62).

In such a context, characterized by potential tensions and frictions, the role of the state is of paramount importance. One of the key functions of the state is to ensure that individual and collective actors with fundamentally different interests can live together not only in a stable and peaceful but also in a fruitful and mutually beneficial manner. The state, then, 'exists over and above civil society, and its agents or civil servants are defined as a universal class serving the interests of society as a whole'. Indeed, in the long run, civil society cannot prevail without 'its absorption into the rational state', thereby expressing the teleology of the world spirit (*Weltgeist*), which is built into the course of world history (*Weltgeschichte*) (Macey, 2000: 62).

In Hegel's work, in other words, the term 'civil society' no longer appears as 'a synonym for political society' (Mautner, 1997: 96); rather, given its intermediate position between family and state, civil society 'is best suited to balancing the diverse range of human needs and interests' within constantly evolving large-scale historical formations (Calabrese, 2004: 319). His conception of modernity is embedded in 'a theory of a differentiated and highly complex social order' (Beyers, 2011: 2) in which civil society has an empowering – and, ultimately, civilizing – influence on the human condition, fostering cohesion, solidarity, 'trust and reciprocity' (Dalton, 2014: 45). To the extent that the mission of civil society is to provide a 'set of institutions or organisations that are held to "mediate" between public and private life', it serves a stabilizing function in creating a social equilibrium (Dalton, 2014: 44).

Ultimately, 'the highest purpose of public life is to generate a rational universal identity' shared by all members of society and epitomized in the emergence of a polity that may be equated with 'the patriotic ethos of the state' (Cohen and Arato, 1992: 113). Paradoxically, however, civil society takes on the function of both an extension of and an opposition to the state. Given the high level of analytical sophistication characterizing his approach, 'Hegel's *conception* of civil society' may be regarded as 'the first modern *theory* of civil society' (Cohen and Arato, 1992: 91).

Finally, it is worth mentioning that, within Hegel's fine-grained account of civil society, the distinction between morality and ethics is crucial: the former is founded on 'the self-reflection of the solitary moral subject'; the latter is based on the normative parameters, standards, and conventions established and negotiated by interacting members of culturally specific communities. Whereas the former concerns the level of autonomous and responsible actors capable of making reasonable decisions, the latter relates to the level of 'the normative content and logic of inherited institutions and traditions', by means of which a socially regulated, and hence culturally codified, life becomes possible in the first place (Cohen and Arato, 1992: 93). From a Hegelian perspective, there is no civil society (*bürgerliche*

Gesellschaft) without both morally motivated subjects and ethically regulated interactions.

Karl Marx (1818–1883)

Within Marxist thought, civil society, far from being reducible to an 'arena of civilized co-operation', represents a realm shaped by 'economic self-interest and the struggle between social classes' (Turner, 2006: 71). Put differently, civil society is located in the economic 'base' or 'infrastructure', rather than in the ideological 'superstructure', of society. As such, it is synonymous with 'the ensemble of socio-economic relations and forces of production', governed by mechanisms of exploitation, competition, and class antagonism (Abercrombie, Hill, and Turner, 2000: 48). To the extent that civil society constitutes 'an arena of particular needs, self-interest, and divisiveness, with a potential for self-destruction' (Sassoon, 1991: 82), it contributes to the fragmentation of modern life and the alienation of human entities from their species-constitutive essence (*Gattungswesen*).

Civil society, according to this account, is the 'site of crass materialism, of modern property relations, of the struggle of each against all, of egotism'. The transition from feudalism to capitalism manifests itself in the replacement of '[t]he old bonds of privilege', honour, and absolutist authority by the new networks of exchange, competition, and exploitation, driven by 'the selfish needs of atomistic individuals separated from each other and from the community' (Sassoon, 1991: 82–83).

The historical irony of civil society, however, consists in the fact that its advocates seek to conceal its particularist essence behind its universalist appearance. In practice, the bourgeois 'idealism of universal interests', expressed in 'the abstractness of the concept of a citizen', translates into the 'materialism of real, sensuous man in civil society', divided by class-specific allegiances and, hence, particular interests. Under the hegemonic influence of capitalism, 'the most universal, moral, social purposes as embodied in the ideal of the state' – and, correspondingly, in the promise of universal citizenship – turn out to be 'at the service of human beings in a partial, depraved state of individual egotistical desires, of economic necessity' (Sassoon, 1991: 83). In the context of modernity, there is no genuine human emancipation unless capitalism is replaced with socialism – that is, unless an exploitative system, sustained by mechanisms of class-based inequality, is superseded by a classless societal formation, founded on the principle 'from each according to his ability, to each according to his needs' (Marx, 2000 [1875]: 615). In a strict sense, this requires the abolishment of civil society, that is, the radical transformation of both the economic base and the ideological superstructure.

Thus, the Marxist account of civil society stands within the Hegelian tradition of intellectual thought, while, at the same time, going beyond it. Both for Hegel and for Marx, civil society constitutes a sphere separate from the state. Yet, their accounts differ in a fundamental way: for Hegel, civil society can successfully mediate between the individual (or family) and the state, thereby transcending group-specific interests; for Marx, by contrast, civil society is dominated by the agenda of the bourgeoisie, thereby reproducing group-specific interests. From a Marxist perspective, one of the key functions of the state, operating in the age of capitalism, is to guarantee 'the property rights that promote and reproduce class divisions', while ensuring that the proletariat, as the oppressed class, exists at the margins of – if not, outside – civil society (Macey, 2000: 62–63).

It is *not* the case that, from a Marxist point of view, the main political achievements of the French Revolution – epitomized in 'the principles of *liberty*, *equality*, and *fraternity* in the 1789 "Declaration of the Rights of Man and the Citizen"' – are historically insignificant, let alone irrelevant to the development of modern society (Calabrese, 2004: 319). It *is* the case, however, that, according to Marxist parameters, the bourgeois defence of these principles is essentially aimed at protecting the right to private property. It is no surprise, then, that 'Marx stressed the negative aspects of civil society, its atomistic and dehumanizing features', focusing on 'the social consequences of capitalist development', notably its detrimental impact on the life conditions of the oppressed classes (Cohen and Arato, 1992: 117). For Marx, genuine human emancipation requires overcoming the division between the 'abstract universal citizen in politics', on the one hand, and the concrete 'materialistic individual in civil society', on the other (Hall and Trentmann, 2005: 9).

Antonio Gramsci (1891–1937)

According to Antonio Gramsci, civil society constitutes the sphere that lies 'between the coercive relations of the state and the economic sphere of production'. As such, it represents 'the realm of the private citizen and individual consent' (Abercrombie, Hill, and Turner, 2000: 49). Compared to Marx's remarkably critical approach, Gramsci's account of civil society is marked by optimism, suggesting that its radical transformation by virtue of 'political education' may contribute to both individual and collective forms of human empowerment. Of course, the principal function of the state – understood as 'a mixture of force plus consent, or hegemony with coercion' – remains to defend the dominant position of the ruling class either by democratic or, if necessary, by authoritarian means (Turner, 2006: 71). One of the main functions of civil society, by contrast, is to realize 'the potential of rational self-regulation and freedom' inherent in modernity, by confronting the coercive power of the state on the basis of counter-hegemonic practices. On this view, civil society is 'not simply a sphere of individual needs', egotism, and self-interest, but, rather, a realm of constellations and organizations capable of undermining the status quo by generating processes of opinion- and will-formation (Sassoon, 1991: 83). This 'ensemble of organisms commonly called "private"' (Gramsci, 1971: 12) then, contains 'self-regulating attributes' (Sassoon, 1991: 83) owing to which non-state actors can pose a serious challenge to the hegemony of the state. Gramsci's narrative differs from orthodox Marxist accounts, therefore, in that it locates civil society in both the economic base and the ideological superstructure, instead of reducing it to one of these two spheres.

Granted, for Gramsci, as for Marx, 'the state's ultimate destiny is its destruction'; that is, eventually, it will wither away. At the same time, for Gramsci 'political society will finally be absorbed back into civil society' when a historical period emerges in which the working class, with the help of its allies, succeeds not only in undermining the hegemony of dominant forces but also in establishing 'a free and self-governing society' (Macey, 2000: 63). What is striking when comparing Marx's and Gramsci's respective interpretations is that the latter is far more optimistic about the normative constitution of civil society than the former. Indeed, from a Gramscian perspective, civil society can be reconquered by the working class in a post-capitalist – that is, socialist or communist – era.

In this sense, civil society constitutes 'a site of struggle for the legitimate use of state power', that is, a realm shaped by the conflict between hegemonic and counter-hegemonic forces (Calabrese, 2004: 320). Arguably, it is one of Gramsci's most significant intellectual achievements to have 'reversed the reductionist trend of the Marxian analysis by concentrating on the dimension of *associations* and *cultural intermediations* and by discovering modern equivalents of Hegel's corporations and estates' (Cohen and Arato, 1992: 117). Within a Gramscian theoretical framework, there is no place for 'the *economistic* reduction of civil society to the political economy' (Cohen and Arato, 1992: 143). For, from a Gramscian perspective, the *raison d'être* of civil society consists in paving the way for the possibility of *self-government* (Cohen and Arato, 1992: 153), thereby converting itself not into the antinomy of political society, but, rather, into 'its normal continuation, its organic complement' – if not its precondition (Gramsci, 1971: 268). As a consequence, we are confronted with the contradiction between civil society 'as a consolidation or normalization of *domination*', sustained by hegemonic mechanisms of control and oppression, and civil society as a sphere of empowerment and *emancipation*, permeated by processes of debate and deliberation (Cohen and Arato, 1992: 157).

The Revival of Civil Society and the Power of Social Capital

'Phrases involving the *resurrection, reemergence, rebirth, reconstruction*, or *renaissance* of civil society' have become a common feature of contemporary social and political agendas (Cohen and Arato, 1992: 29). In the literature, it is widely recognized that the recent revival of the concept of civil society cannot be dissociated from the collapse of numerous military dictatorships across the world, especially in Latin America, and from the disintegration of state socialism, notably in Eastern and Central Europe, at the end of the twentieth century. To this one may add the Arab Spring upheavals in the Middle East. Modern liberal conceptions of civil society are inextricably linked to 'the protection and/or self-organization of social life in the face of the totalitarian or authoritarian state' (Cohen and Arato, 1992: 31). This has led to a novel historical situation in which the political project of liberal democracy represents the normative foundation of most pluralistic societies. Ideologically, this tendency has been reinforced by the gradual consolidation of a capitalist world market. From a liberal point of view, the velvet revolutions in Central and Eastern Europe served as 'the wellspring of a democratic and emancipatory public sphere' (Calabrese, 2004: 321). To the extent that '[t]he idea of civil society was popularized when communist or totalitarian states collapsed in the 1980s', it became increasingly associated with liberal conceptions of civilizational progress and the common good (Ossewaarde, 2006: 199).

In contemporary forms of social and political analysis, it has become prevalent to examine civil society in terms of the production, distribution, circulation, and exchange of social capital. In this respect, three theoretical strands are particularly important: rational choice, critical and neo-Marxist, and liberal.

Rational choice theories are based on the assumption that individuals are driven by self-interest and, hence, guided by instrumental reason, whose preponderance manifests itself in the pivotal role that strategic action plays in the unfolding of social life. On this account, human actors are both utility- and profit-maximizers, capable of making decisions informed by calculative considerations and mediated by instrumental rationality. According to this interpretation, *all* human actions are essentially economic actions, and human entities can be regarded as 'radically individualistic utility-maximizing reasoners'. Within this presuppositional framework, every person's pursuit of self-interest takes centre stage: the ambition to realize one's individual interests constitutes 'the fundamental and governing aspect of *all* human action' (Lewandowski and Streich, 2007: 589).

Critical and neo-Marxist theories draw attention to the unequal distribution of material and symbolic resources in class-divided societies. In particular, Bourdieu's critical sociology suggests that human agents occupy vertically structured positions in different social fields and acquire asymmetrically allocated dispositions by virtue of their habitus. When navigating their way through the social universe, they draw upon multiple forms of capital: social capital, economic capital, cultural capital, political capital, educational capital, linguistic capital, and symbolic capital. Social capital is the most fundamental form of capital insofar as it underlies all forms of capital.

Liberal theories posit that social capital constitutes the ultimate source of social cohesion and stability, allowing for the emergence of networks between citizens based on trust, solidarity, and shared identity. On their account, there are no democratic, participatory, and associational practices and structures unless actors are embedded in, and can rely on, networks of sociality. This Tocquevillian stance – most famously represented by Putnam – insists on the socio-ontological centrality of people's capacity to relate to, count on, and collaborate with one another while engaging in the construction of meaningful lives. According to this approach, the 'habits of acting together in the affairs of daily life' are central to bringing about solidified forms of social interaction sustained by morally binding and intersubjectively recognized norms and conventions (Lewandowski and Streich, 2007: 589).

The concept of 'social capital', then, refers to 'networks, norms and trust ... that enable participants to act together more effectively to pursue shared objectives' (Putnam, 1995: 664–665). In fact, there are major *benefits* to the presence and cultivation of social capital: communities and societies with high levels of social capital tend to have 'lower mortality rates, lower crime and fear of crime, higher educational results, better health and mental health, higher instances of volunteering and democratic voting'. In short, strong normative ties are vital to the empowerment of both individual and society.

Two types of social capital are particularly important. First, bonding (or exclusive) social capital is based on 'a dense layering of norms and trust that is found in homogenous groups and tends to reinforce exclusivity and homogeneity'. As such, it takes on the function of a '"kind of sociological superglue"'. Access to bonding social capital is a precondition for getting by in life. Second, bridging (or inclusive) social capital is founded on 'linkages with groups different from themselves (i.e. heterogeneous relationships), thus creating new spaces' and potentially cross-sectional identities. As such, it serves the function of a 'sociological WD40', capable of contributing to the productivity, creativity, and diversity of individuals and groups, as well as to the communication, collaboration, and solidarity between them. Access to bonding social capital is a precondition for getting ahead in life (Putnam, 2000: 22–23).

To this distinction, one may wish to add a third type of social capital. Linking social capital 'addresses the power differentials within society and allows more marginal groups to link with the resources of powerful groups (i.e. capital, information, knowledge, secondments) as a way of reducing the inherent deficits of influence in civil society'. As such, it assumes the function of a sociological bridge, capable of cross-fertilizing the assets of multiple groups and, in particular, providing socially deprived actors with the opportunity to draw upon resources to which they would not have access otherwise (Baker and Miles-Watson, 2010: 26).

All three approaches have strengths and weaknesses. In terms of their explanatory limitations, the following dimensions are especially noteworthy. Rational choice theories tend to overemphasize the role of economic factors as well as to underemphasize the role of cultural, political, and ideological factors relevant to both reproducing and transforming social networks. Critical and neo-Marxist theories tend to overemphasize the extent to which actors' positions and dispositions are shaped – if not, determined – by access, or lack of access, to symbolic and material resources as well as to underemphasize the extent to which they have both the theoretical and the practical capacity to challenge the power of social structures. Liberal theories tend to overemphasize the empowering effects of democratic, participatory, and associational processes as well as to underemphasize the degree to which these are permeated by relations of power and domination and, hence, by the asymmetrical distribution of material and symbolic resources underlying both individual and collective forms of self-realization.

Outline of a Critical Theory of Civil Society

The task of this section is to propose an outline of a critical theory of civil society. To this end, the key dimensions of civil society shall be identified and examined in subsequent sections.

Civil Society as a Social Sphere

Civil society constitutes a social sphere. As such, it is composed of 'the places where individuals gather together', in order to develop a collective sense of belonging based on solidarity, trust, identity, and connectivity (Jacobs, 2006: 27). The sociality that is built into civil society is reflected in the fact that its very possibility depends on five central components of human coexistence: (1) relationality, (2) reciprocity, (3) reconstructability, (4) renormalizability, and (5) recognizability. First, civil society can come into existence only to the extent that its members relate to one another. As such, it constitutes a form of being-*with*-one-another (*Miteinandersein*). Second, civil society can come into existence only to the extent that its members reciprocate one another. As such, it constitutes a form of being-*through*-one-another (*Durcheinandersein*). Third, civil society can come into existence only to the extent that its members reconstruct one another. As such, it constitutes a form of being-*beyond*-one-another (*Jenseitsvoneinandersein* or *aufhebbares Sein*). Fourth, civil society can come into existence only to the extent that its members renormalize one another. As such, it constitutes a form of being-*about*-one-another (*Übereinandersein*). Finally, civil society can come into existence only to the extent that its members recognize one another. As such, it constitutes a form of being-*within*-one-another (*Ineinandersein*).

In short, since civil society is brought into existence by relational, reciprocal, reconstructable, renormalizable, and recognizable selves, it is based on networks of sociality, mutuality, transformability, signifiability, and identity, which allow for the emergence of individual and collective forms of engagement oriented towards the construction of meaning-laden realities.

Civil Society as a Discursive Sphere

Civil society constitutes a discursive sphere. As such, it is reliant on subjects capable of engaging in symbolically mediated interactions. Civil society is inconceivable without the existence of 'the places where individuals gather together to have conversations' (Jacobs, 2006: 27). There is no civil society that can dispense with communicative action, that is, with human practices oriented towards mutual understanding. Communicative actors learn to reason by arguing with and against one another. Their reasoning capacity (*Verstand*) is embedded in their communicative capacity (*Verständigung*), by means of which they develop not only an interpretive capacity (*Verstehen*) but also a consensual capacity (*Einverständnis*). Civil society, then, can be regarded as a discursively organized realm created by reasoning, communicating, interpreting, and agreement-seeking subjects, whose ability to obtain socioculturally contingent understandings about the world is crucial to their species-distinctive condition. As a 'wise species' (*Homo sapiens*), humans have put themselves in the evolutionarily privileged position of being able to convert both practical knowledge *within* the world and theoretical knowledge *about* the world into the historico-cognitive driving force of their existence. Civil society provides the discursively structured domain in which the collective search for anthropologically valuable knowledge, derived from communicative action, takes place.

Civil Society as an Interest-Laden Sphere

Civil society constitutes an interest-laden sphere. As such, it is composed of 'the places where individuals ... pursue common interests' (Jacobs, 2006: 27). To be precise, within civil society, actors pursue individual, collective, and human interests. They pursue individual interests, insofar as they are driven by personal motives. They pursue collective interests, insofar as they are influenced by social forces, which may be defined in relational terms. They pursue human interests, insofar as they are conditioned by anthropological invariants, which – at least in principle – they share with all other human beings and which, in a broad sense, contribute to the survival of the species. In brief, the term 'civil society' designates a tension-laden realm in which individual, collective, and human interests are incessantly articulated and negotiated and defined and redefined, as well as reproduced and transformed.

Civil Society as a Value-Laden Sphere

Civil society constitutes a value-laden sphere. As such, it can be described as a profoundly normative and, ultimately, political domain of meaningful interactions between discursively equipped actors. It is no accident that, by mobilizing both the symbolic and the material resources available to them within civil society, actors 'try to influence public opinion or public policy' (Jacobs, 2006: 27). In other words, civil society cannot be reduced to an isolated domain centred mainly, or even exclusively, upon itself. Rather, it refers to 'an area of social consensus based on agreements about norms and values' that, potentially, affect the whole of society and, hence, the behavioural, ideological, and institutional patterns by which it is sustained (Turner, 2006: 70). Civil society is a normative realm, which is characterized by 'a different way of existing in the world', 'a different rationality', a different *modus operandi*, according to which cultural and political values are negotiated in a constructive, respectful, and non-violent manner. Viewed in this light, civil society is tantamount to 'the ethical ideal of the social order where the interests of the individual are weighed up against what is best for the community and a balance is established between the two'. Members of civil society, then, are required not only to question the legitimacy of 'existing structures and activities', but also to explore the degree to which these are empowering or disempowering for individual and collective actors (Beyers, 2011: 4). One of the most essential values endorsed by the members of civil society, therefore, is the defence of value-ladenness itself.

Civil Society as a Public Sphere

Civil society constitutes a public sphere. As such, it is shaped by practices taking place in 'public life, rather than [by] private or household-based activities' (Marshall, 1994: 55). Its protagonists may be concerned with a number of public domains: opinion, policy, goods, services, or affairs – to mention only a few. Civil society represents an arena of public encounters. The public/private distinction, which may be regarded as 'a grand dichotomy', possesses a number of binary meanings, three of which are particularly important: society vs. individual, visibility vs. concealment, and openness vs. closure. These three meanings stand for 'hetero-geneous criteria', which have been interpreted in numerous ways. The normative boundaries of civil society are defined by public values – such as solidarity and mutuality, visibility and transparency, openness and accessibility. Yet, the 'constant tension between the private and the public sphere' lies at the core of civil society, for its constitution and development are determined by both individual and collective forms of agency (Beyers, 2011: 4).

Civil Society as a Participatory Sphere

Civil society constitutes a participatory sphere. As such, it is a social domain founded on intersubjectively mediated engagements. In a socio-philosophical sense, 'engage-ment' can be defined as a form of active, purposive, and meaning-laden involvement in the world. In the modern era, human engagements in and with the normative parameters underlying the construction of both small-scale and large-scale realities manifest themselves in 'the way[s] that people participate in civil society' (Jacobs, 2006: 29). The participatory nature of civil society is illustrated in the prevalence of the associational practices by which it is shaped. Indeed, involvement in voluntary organizations is fundamental to the grass-roots spirit permeating civil society. People's committed involvement in the material and symbolic construction of reality, based on the active participation in 'associations and social networks' (Pérez-Diaz, 2014: 812), is central to 'the potential success of civil society's engagement' with challenges faced by humanity (Fioramonti and Thümler, 2013: 213).

Civil Society as a Voluntary Sphere

Civil society constitutes a voluntary sphere. As such, it forms a social realm whose members participate in the meaningful establishment of normative arrangements, which they experience as an empowering process founded on freedom, choice, and emancipation. Participating in voluntary associations, organizations, and networks is a *sine qua non* of civil society. For its emergence as a domain of opinion- and will-formation, undertaken by politically autonomous individuals, is contingent upon its members' ability to make decisions independently of, and without interference from, exogenous forces driven by instrumental rationality.

Civil Society as a Horizontal Sphere

Civil society constitutes a horizontal sphere. As such, it provides a forum in which actors – notwithstanding the sociological variables by which they are divided – relate to one another as individuals guided by normative principles, such as justice, fairness, and equality. To be sure, this is not to deny the fact that, in society in general and in civil society in particular, actors occupy different – vertically structured – positions and are equipped with different – asymmetrically distributed – dispositions. This is to acknowl-edge, however, that, in the modern era, civil society tends to be conceived of as a sphere that gives actors the opportunity to relate to one another on the basis of associations, organizations, and networks capable of challenging the perpetuation of pecking orders and hierarchies by virtue of *inclusive* practices and a broadly egalitarian spirit.

Civil Society as a Transparent Sphere

Civil society constitutes a transparent sphere. It is a space of social interactions guided by the ideals of visibility, accessibility, accountability, liability, and responsibility. This plea for transparency is of paramount importance, notably in historical contexts characterized by major systemic transitions from authoritarian to non-authoritarian types of government. The former are associated with different modes of absolutism, despotism, and totalitarianism. The latter, at least in the modern era, are linked primarily to varieties of liberalism. Transparency is the ultimate currency in civil society, in the sense that its members are committed to challenging arbitrary sources of authority, by insisting that all legislative, executive, and judicial powers must be democratically controlled, and hence publicly accountable, in order to obtain viable degrees of legitimacy.

Civil Society as a Purposive Sphere

Civil society constitutes a purposive sphere. It stands for an arena whose actors seek to 'make a difference' by having a tangible impact upon the world. Regardless of whether they 'try to influence public opinion or public policy' in particular or public affairs in general, individual and collective actors in civil society have a normative purpose, in the sense that their *raison d'être* is to shape behavioural, ideological, and institutional arrangements in such a way that they contribute to the everyday empowerment of human subjects (Jacobs, 2006: 27).

Civil Society as a Consensual Sphere

Civil society constitutes a consensual sphere. As such, it refers to 'an area of social consensus based on agreements about norms and values' underlying behavioural, ideological, and institutional patterns of functioning within a given societal formation (Turner, 2006: 70). Members of civil society are confronted with the challenge of reaching agreements about pressing normative issues. Arguably, one of the most fundamental presuppositional features underlying the daily construction of civil society is the premise that, if necessary, its participants – at least in principle – agree to disagree with one another. In other words, even if they do not share each other's opinions on specific matters, protagonists of civil society are expected to be willing to tolerate disagreements, to the extent that the hermeneutic stances in which they are embedded do not violate basic democratic rights and principles.

Civil Society as a Cooperative Sphere

Civil society constitutes a cooperative sphere. It is a social realm sustained by networks of coordination, collaboration, and mutual support. Thus, 'the potential success of civil society's engagement depends on a sufficient level of problem-work, mobilization and cooperation, the willingness to learn much more about the nature of the problem and possible ways to tackle it' in a collaborative fashion (Fioramonti and Thümler, 2013: 231). The collective spirit pervading quotidian practices in civil society emanates from tireless individual and group efforts to contribute to citizens' well-being and, more generally, to the common good.

Civil Society as a Pluralistic Sphere

Civil society constitutes a pluralistic sphere. As such, it is based on both the recognition and the affirmation of behavioural, ideological, and institutional diversity, permitting the peaceful coexistence of different interests, convictions, and lifestyles amongst socially, culturally, and politically heterogeneous actors. It is reinforced by fundamental humanist principles indispensable to the functioning of highly differentiated societies, whose members, although they may be separated by numerous identity-defining variables, are confronted with the challenge of defining, and pursuing, their common interests when engaging in the daily construction of reality.

Civil Society as a Democratic Sphere

Civil society constitutes a democratic sphere. As such, it tends to be regarded as an integral component of both small-scale and large-scale variants of democracy. The idea of civil society, then, lies at the core of both participatory and representative democracy. In the most general sense, democracy may be defined as government by the people based on the rule of the majority. Thus, democracy requires a governmental system in which all citizens of a polity are directly or indirectly involved in decision-making processes, by means of which they coordinate their actions and shape the social arrangements underpinning their coexistence. Civil society can play a pivotal role in this endeavour in that 'associational membership can shape and inculcate the dispositions necessary to maintain a healthy liberal democracy' (Chambers and Kopstein, 2001: 853), founded on vital normative ingredients such as the following: solidarity; discourse; public life; participation; inclusion; consensus-building; opinion- and will-formation; transparency; pluralism; right to vote; eligibility for public office; fundamental freedoms – notably freedom of conscience, belief, opinion, and expression; freedom of speech; freedom of the press and other media of communication; freedom to form and join organizations; and freedom of assembly.

Civil Society as a Decisional Sphere

Civil society constitutes a decisional sphere. Its very existence is rooted in people's capacity to make decisions that impact their lives. Within civil society, 'decisions should be made locally and should not be controlled by the State and its bureaucracies' (Bell, 1989: 56). Decision-making processes in civil society, therefore, are not colonized by the views and persuasions of hegemonic actors but shaped by a multiplicity of participants from different sectors of the population. Hence, within the dynamic boundaries of civil society, the agendas and objectives of influential groups are no more and no less represented than 'the diverse opinions of marginalized and excluded people' (Batista, 1994: 12). In civil society, actors are empowered to engage in decision-making processes by means of which they not only experience potentially enlightening dynamics of opinion- and will-formation but also gain control over their lives (Batista, 1994: 17). Thus, 'the potential of civil society to operate as a public arena for discussion, mediation, and deliberation' is fundamental to its capacity to equip its participants with decision-making powers by virtue of which they convert themselves into protagonists of their own destiny.

Civil Society as a Resourceful Sphere

Civil society constitutes a resourceful sphere. It stands for a relationally constructed field in which the main source of empowerment is social capital, which is defined by an actor's degree of access to social networks. Within these networks, human transactions are characterized by solidarity, reciprocity, trust, and cooperation. Actors relying upon the use, and contributing to the cultivation, of social capital generate knowledge, goods, and services not exclusively for themselves, but, more importantly, for a common good, the pursuit of which is central to their everyday practices. 'With their clustering and connectivity properties, polycentric forms of civic coordination can enhance the social capital of civic organizations' (Baldassarri and Diani, 2007: 772). Indeed, 'the relationship between associational life and social integration' is so central to civil society that its members cannot experience significant levels of social cohesion unless they coordinate their actions with a sense of shared purpose and common identity (Baldassarri and Diani, 2007: 736). When doing so, however, they draw upon multiple forms of capital: social capital, economic capital, cultural capital, political capital, educational capital, linguistic capital, and symbolic capital. Civil society is unthinkable without actors capable of mobilizing a whole variety of material and symbolic resources, by means of which they contribute to the multifaceted construction of human reality.

Civil Society as a Performative Sphere

Civil society constitutes a performative sphere. As such, it is tantamount to a social space whose constitution and evolution depend on the daily practices undertaken by human actors. The performative nature of civil society illustrates that, as an arena of real-world happenings, it cannot be reduced to a mental abstraction, let alone to an ideological imaginary; rather, it describes an empirically constituted realm whose tangible relevance manifests itself in its impact upon the unfolding of human history. Especially important in this regard is the pivotal role played by social movements, which are firmly situated in civil society and which, owing to their potentially transformative power derived from collective action, have shaped, and continue to shape, the development of modern societies in a fundamental manner.

Civil Society as a Non-Governmental Sphere

Civil society constitutes a non-governmental sphere. As 'a social formation inter-mediate between the family and the state', it intercedes between these two realms without being controlled by any of them (Mautner, 1997: 96). Civil society is located outside of the structures of the states. This is not to suggest that the former is necessarily opposed to the latter. Rather, this is to recognize that, within civil society, decisions tend to be taken locally, thereby escaping the control exercised by the state and large-scale forms of bureaucracy. '[T]he demand for a return to "civil society" is the demand for a return to a manageable scale of social life' (Bell, 1989: 56). It appears that, in the context of emerging postnational constellations, the state is too small for the big problems (such as global terrorism, climate change, migration crises, financial crises, etc.) and too big for the small problems (such as community life, local decision-making processes, neighbourhood and urban developments, etc.). Civil society, by contrast, provides a grass-roots-embedded space 'capable of pre-serving its autonomy and forms of solidarity in face of the modern economy as well as the state' (Cohen and Arato, 1992: 30). It represents an intersubjectively con-structed sphere whose normative contents are shaped predominantly by creative, inclusive, and democratic bottom-up dynamics, rather than by administrative, insti-tutional, and managerial top-down mechanisms.

Civil Society as a Non-Profit Sphere

Civil society constitutes a non-profit sphere. As such, it is a social arena whose actors are driven primarily by value rationality (*Wertrationalität*), rather than by instru-mental rationality (*Zweckrationalität*). To the extent that, within civil society, actions are not motivated by profit, income, or revenue, what takes centre stage is the moral, political, and cultural value of human practices. Irrespective of whether one con-siders 'new' social movements or non-governmental organizations (NGOs), the key players of civil society aim to bypass the functionalist logic permeating not only large-scale bureaucracies but also capitalist economies. The systemic logic under-lying the functioning of both state and economy manifests itself in mechanisms of bureaucratization and commodification, acting in the same way that a colonizing power imposes utility-driven imperatives on communicatively mediated processes of human socialization. In this sense, civil society may be conceived of as an extended lifeworld that resists colonization.

Civil Society as a Civil Sphere

Civil society constitutes a civil sphere. It promotes, and is in turn maintained by, civic values. In this respect, five core tenets are particularly important: (a) self-control, (b) compassion, (c) tolerance, (d) justice, and (e) recognition of the other.

Self-control is crucial to processes of civilization, whereby 'individuals gradually channel, control and moderate their emotions, affects and desires'. On this account, civilization is inconceivable without 'the domestication of the essentially rude nature of

human beings'. 'Civility', which forms part and parcel of modern educational programmes and curricula, can be regarded as the result of this sociologically complex
process oriented towards increasing individual and collective self-control and discipline.

There is no civil society without compassion, for 'the capacity of humans to feel
empathy and compassion with other humans' is central to their ability to develop
a sense of civility that they share with fellow members of society. This cognitive
faculty concerns not only people's ability to experience and to express 'fellow-
feelings with the sorrow of others', but also, in a more fundamental sense, their
willingness to put themselves in someone else's shoes, thereby converting social life
into an intersubjectively constructed arena based on the moral exercise of perspec-
tive-taking (Rucht, 2011: 394). Relatedly, the presence of tolerance is particularly
important 'when sameness is absent' and different members of society are required
to cope with the challenges arising from cultural, political, and moral plurality, which
manifest themselves in ideological, behavioural, and institutional heterogeneity
(Rucht, 2011: 395).

The pursuit of justice can be considered a basic 'principle for social interaction
and the organization of society'. In spite of the interpretive elasticity of normative
standards, the normative constitution of modern civil society is founded on one key
principle: '[e]ach person is to have an equal right to the most extensive total system
of equal basic liberties compatible with a similar system of liberty for all'. The
question concerning the extent to which social inequalities can, or cannot, be
justified represents a contentious issue, which divides actors endorsing different
ideological positions. Yet, the ideal of 'a fair system of co-operation between free
and equal persons' underlies all civil societies, irrespective of their spatio-temporal
specificity (Rucht, 2011: 395).

There is no civil society without recognition of the other, with three modes of
recognition being especially significant: love, right, and esteem (Rucht, 2011: 396).
Insofar as these fundamental forms of recognition are provided by an individual's
social environment, they substantially contribute to his or her capacity to develop
healthy degrees of self-confidence, self-respect, and self-esteem. If, by contrast, an
individual is deprived of access to these fundamental forms of recognition, he or she
may suffer from serious pathological symptoms.

In short, civil society constitutes a social realm sustained by self-control, compassion, tolerance, justice, and recognition of the other. Hence, it is founded on networks
of discipline, empathy, respect, fairness, and identity, which allow for the construction of relatively stable, potentially empowering, and socially sustainable realities.

The Limitations of Civil Society

This final section identifies three broad limitations of civil society. First,
we must recognize the negative dimensions of civil society. Far from constituting a universally empowering sphere of pristine intersubjectivity, civil society is
characterized by numerous problematic aspects – notably those associated with
mechanisms of exclusion, discrimination, inequality, corruption, favouritism,

elitism, and symbolic violence. In many cases, bonding – rather than bridging or linking – forms of social capital predominate, implying that the self-referential reinforcement of preconceptions and prejudices against specific social groups may contribute to the reproduction of closed communities. Second, we must acknowledge the negative contributions of civil society. Not only does it tend to reproduce already existing mechanisms of exclusion, discrimination, inequality, corruption, favouritism, elitism, and symbolic violence; but, furthermore, it produces them, exporting them to other realms of society. Third, we must take into account the limited influence of civil society. In several respects, it is far from clear whether or not civil society can make a substantial difference, even if and where its members make informed, serious, and laudable efforts to do so. Civil society may have too much asked of it, if it is understood exclusively as a sphere of individual and collective empowerment.

The following connects these basic problems to the outline of a critical theory of civil society laid out in the preceding section. Civil society constitutes a social sphere, but it is necessary to explore the extent to which civil society may also represent an asocial or even antisocial sphere, dominated by private and personal, rather than public and collective, concerns and interests. Likewise, though civil society constitutes a discursive sphere, it is crucial to recognize that, within the boundaries of civil society, actors often fail to come to a viable consensus and, hence, frequently do not succeed in taking decisions that all, or at least a majority of, participants may be willing to endorse.

Civil society constitutes an interest-laden sphere. A comprehensive account of civil society needs to draw attention to the fact that it is far from obvious which of these interests – which may, or may not, contradict one another – prevail in a particular situation. Put differently, civil society is a conglomerate of diverse – and, to a large degree, hidden – interests, which cannot always be reconciled. Civil society also constitutes a value-laden sphere. It is vital to concede that civil societies can be marked by both progressive and regressive, emancipatory and reactionary, counter-hegemonic and hegemonic values.

As a public sphere, civil society depends on the daily unfolding of human practices that are situated in the public domain. It would be naïve, however, to underestimate the degree to which the constitution of civil society is contingent upon activities taking place in the private domain. Put simply, civil society is composed of both public and private subjects. Relatedly, civil society is a participatory sphere. The challenging question concerns the extent to which people's – circumstantially or structurally defined – non-participation in collective processes of opinion- and will-formation may convert the critical spirit of civil society into a privilege enjoyed by those equipped with the material and symbolic resources required to contribute to the production, reproduction, and transformation of normative orders. Furthermore, civil society entails a voluntary sphere. Yet, while voluntary associations, organizations, and networks play a pivotal role in the construction of civil society, it is important to account for the fact that exogenous forces that are driven by instrumental rationality have the power to colonize communicative action and, therefore, grass-roots sources of normativity.

Civil society constitutes a horizontal sphere. However, the power of social stratification can be challenged and subverted, but not circumvented, let alone effaced, by civil society. Civil society also represents a transparent sphere. It would be erroneous, however, to lose sight of the fact that, within civil society, actors may not only weaken but also strengthen arbitrary sources of authority, by reinforcing their legitimacy on the basis of corruption and lack of accountability. Transparency is, at best, a laudable ideal affirmed and, at worst, a rhetorical tool employed by both ideologically and strategically driven actors within civil society aiming to play a substantial part in the tension-laden construction of reality.

Civil society is a purposive sphere. But it must be recognized that shaping behavioural, ideological, and institutional arrangements in such a way that they contribute to the empowerment of human subjects is an extremely complex endeavour. Indeed, praiseworthy goals do not always translate into desirable realities, just as counter-hegemonic intentions do not necessarily succeed in subverting the status quo in practice. Civil society similarly is a consensual sphere. We need to admit, however, that the consensus-oriented constitution of civil society is by no means a guarantee of the normative validity of the agreements reached by its members. Consensus-formation is a necessary but not sufficient condition for the construction of emancipatory life forms. Civil society likewise constitutes a cooperative sphere. Just as it would be fatalistic to reduce civil society to a domain of merely instrumental and strategic interactions driven primarily by calculation and self-interest, it would be idealistic to portray civil society as a province of predominantly communicative and cooperative interactions motivated mainly by mutual understanding and collaboration. A realistic conception of civil society acknowledges the tension-laden coexistence of its cooperative and competitive, communicative and strategic, substantive and instrumental aspects.

Civil society constitutes a pluralistic sphere. In other words, the normative integrity of civil society depends on its members' capacity to promote behavioural, ideological, and institutional diversity. It would be reductive, however, to fail to face up to the civilizational challenges arising from elevated levels of social, cultural, and political fragmentation in large-scale interactional formations. Within highly differentiated societies, 'pluralized actors' may find it remarkably difficult to draw upon a horizon of common reference points, enabling them to develop a genuine sense of belonging, cohesion, and solidarity (Susen, 2015: 111–112).

Civil society constitutes a democratic sphere. Arguably, civil society is essential to both indirect/representative and direct/deliberative forms of democracy. Yet, to the degree that it is sustained by vibrant participatory practices, it plays a more pivotal role in the latter than in the former. It is no less important, however, to recognize that, paradoxically, civil society may flourish temporarily under non-democratic regimes, precisely if and when its members aim to subvert, and to transform, them. Indeed, transitions from autocracy to democracy are possible because of, rather than despite, the political pressure exercised by civil society. This fact is connected to the idea that civil society is also a decisional sphere. As critical sociologists, we need to do justice to the empirical complexity of decision-making processes. Decisions take place at different levels: mico-, meso, and macro. Decisions can be classified in terms of different types – such as rational vs. emotional, spontaneous vs. planned, behavioural vs. ideological, intuitive vs reflexive, categorical vs. circumstantial, communicative vs. strategic, proactive vs. reactive, inclusive vs. exclusive, short-term vs. long-term. A critical theory of civil society needs to account for the fact that decision-making processes are not intrinsically but only potentially empowering.

Civil society constitutes a resourceful sphere. There is no civil society without the production, distribution, circulation, and exchange of social capital, which is the most fundamental type of capital, upon which all other types of capital are dependent. Yet, it is crucial to take into consideration not only the interconvertibility between, but also the relative autonomy and forcefulness of, different types of capital. Civil society is shaped by actors who compete over access to resources and whose wider influence, which is reflected in their capacity to set normative agendas, rests on their ability to maximize both the material and the symbolic profits they can gain from their positionally and dispositionally defined access to different forms of capital. This asymmetrical power structure makes civil society strikingly similar to, rather than radically different from, other domains of society.

Civil society is a performative sphere. The global significance of civil society manifests itself in its substantial impact upon the unfolding of human history. Especially noteworthy in this regard is the pivotal role played by social movements. To the extent that 'new' social movements tend to place a stronger emphasis on grass-roots participatory practices than 'old' social movements, the former take on a more central role in the construction of contemporary civil societies than the latter. This is not to deny that most – if not, all – social movements, irrespective of their typological specificity, contribute to setting the agenda in civil society. This is to acknowledge, however, that, in the current era, the following paradigmatic shifts have redefined the role of collective performativity in general and of social movements in particular: (a) from society-as-a-project to projects-in-society; (b) from metanarratives to micronarratives; (c) from relatively homogeneous and monolithic to increasingly heterogeneous and hybrid social bases; (d) from an orientation towards the state to an orientation towards civil society; (e) from formal, bureaucratic, and vertical to loose, flexible, and horizontal forms of organization; (f) from power-affirmative to power-sceptical; (g) from industrial to post-industrial relations and thus, arguably, from a modern to a postmodern context (Susen, 2015: 189).

Civil society constitutes a non-governmental sphere. In terms of its normative outlook, civil society is supposed to be shaped primarily by creative, inclusive, and democratic bottom-up dynamics, rather than by administrative, institutional, or managerial top-down mechanisms. Yet, it would be erroneous to overlook the fact that, in practice, civil society is no less affected by governmental forms of power than other interactional domains and that, more significantly, some key players within civil society – such as lobbyists – seek to influence state actors and others – such as political party delegates and government representatives – are themselves state actors.

Civil society represents a non-profit sphere. Within civil society, actors are expected to be driven primarily by value rationality (*Wertrationalität*), rather than by instrumental rationality (*Zweckrationalität*). Consequently, the worth of their actions and interactions is measured in terms of their moral, political, and cultural value, rather than in terms of their economic value. Yet, it would be inaccurate to disregard the fact that, in practice, civil society is no less affected by economic forms of power than other interactional domains and that, more significantly, some key players within civil society – such as lobbyists – seek to influence economic actors and others – such as businessmen, businesswomen, and entrepreneurs – are themselves economic actors.

Finally, civil society constitutes a civil sphere. As such, it is characterized by five core features: (a) self-control, (b) compassion, (c) tolerance, (d) justice, and (e) recognition of the other. Hence, civil society is founded on networks of discipline, empathy, respect, fairness, and identity. It would be one-sided, however, to focus exclusively on its civil dimensions and, consequently, pay no heed to its non-civil aspects. Within civil society, actors often behave (a) impulsively and irresponsibly, rather than conscientiously and maturely, (b) inconsiderately and egoistically, rather than caringly and altruistically, (c) single-mindedly and chauvinistically, rather than broad-mindedly and benevolently, (d) unjustly and unethically, rather than properly and legitimately, or (e) on the basis of hatred and animosity, disentitlement and disenfranchisement, insult and dishonour, rather than on the basis of love and harmony, right and enfranchisement, esteem and approval. Far from being reducible to a secluded and privileged sphere of mere solidarity and immaculate intersubjectivity, civil society constitutes a field of social struggle that is as shot through with tensions, contradictions, and antagonisms as most other domains of human reality.

References

Abercrombie, Nicholas, Stephen Hill, and Bryan S. Turner. 2000. 'Civil Society.' In Nicholas Abercrombie, Stephen Hill, and Bryan S. Turner (eds.), *The Penguin Dictionary of Sociology*, 4th ed. (pp. 48–49). London: Penguin.

Baker, Chris, and Jonathan Miles-Watson. 2010. 'Faith and Traditional Capitals: Defining the Public Scope of Spiritual and Religious Capital: A Literature Review.' *Implicit Religion* 13(1): 17–69.

Baldassarri, Delia, and Mario Diani. 2007. 'The Integrative Power of Civic Networks.' *American Journal of Sociology* 113(3): 735–780.

Batista, Israel. 1994. 'Civil Society: A Paradigm or a New Slogan?' *The Ecumenical Review* 46(1): 12–20.

Bell, Daniel. 1989. '"American Exceptionalism" Revisited: The Role of Civil Society.' *The Public Interest* 95: 38–56.

Beyers, Jaco. 2011. 'Religion, Civil Society, and Conflict: What Is It That Religion Does for and to Society?' *HTS Teologiese Studies/Theological Studies* 67(3): Art. #949, 8 pages. DOI:10.4102/hts.v67i3.949.

Calabrese, Andrew. 2004. 'The Promise of Civil Society: A Global Movement for Communication Rights.' *Continuum: Journal of Media & Cultural Studies* 18(3): 317–329.

Chambers, Simone, and Jeffrey Kopstein. 2001. 'Bad Civil Society.' *Political Theory* 29(6): 837–865.

Cohen, Jean L. and Andrew Arato. 1992. *Civil Society and Political Theory*. Cambridge, MA: MIT Press.

Dalton, Bronwen. 2014. 'Civil Society: Overlapping Frames.' *Cosmopolitan Civil Societies: An Interdisciplinary Journal* 6(2): 40–68.

Ferguson, Adam. 1995 [1767]. *An Essay on the History of Civil Society*. Edited by Fania Oz-Salzberger. Cambridge, UK: Cambridge University Press.

Fioramonti, Lorenzo, and Ekkehard Thümler. 2013. 'Civil Society, Crisis, and Change: Towards a Theoretical Framework.' *Journal of Civil Society* 9(2): 225–232.

Gramsci, Antonio. 1971. *Selections from the Prison Notebooks of Antonio Gramsci*. Edited and translated by Quintin Hoare and Geoffrey Nowell Smith. New York: International Publishers.

Hall, John A., and Frank Trentmann. 2005. 'Contests Over Civil Society: Introductory Perspectives.' In John A. Hall and Frank Trentmann (eds.), *Civil Society: A Reader in History, Theory, and Global Politics* (pp. 1–25). Basingstoke, UK: Palgrave Macmillan.

Jacobs, Ronald. 2006. 'Civil Society.' In John Scott (ed.), *Sociology: Key Concepts* (pp. 27–29). London: Routledge.

Lewandowski, Joseph, and Gregory Streich. 2007. 'Democratizing Social Capital: In Pursuit of Liberal Egalitarianism.' *Journal of Social Philosophy* 38(4): 588–604.

Locke, John. 1996 [1689]. 'Second Treatise on Government.' In David Wootton (ed.), *Modern Political Thought: From Machiavelli to Nietzsche* (pp. 310–386). Indianapolis, IN: Hackett.

Macey, David. 2000. *The Penguin Dictionary of Critical Theory*. London: Penguin.

Marshall, Gordon (ed.). 1994. *The Concise Oxford Dictionary of Sociology*. Oxford, UK: Oxford University Press.

Marx, Karl. 2000 [1875]. 'Critique of the Gotha Program.' In David McLellan (ed.), *Karl Marx: Selected Writings*, 2nd ed. (pp. 610–616). Oxford, UK: Oxford University Press.

Mautner, Thomas. 1997. *The Penguin Dictionary of Philosophy*, new edition. London: Penguin.

Montesquieu, Charles-Louis de Secondat, Baron de La Brède. 1989 [1748]. *The Spirit of the Laws*. Translated and edited by Anne M. Cohler, Basia Carolyn Miller, and Harold Samuel Stone. Cambridge, UK: Cambridge University Press.

Ossewaarde, M. R. R. 2006. 'Citizenship in Civil Society.' *Journal of Civil Society* 2(3): 199–215.

Pérez-Díaz, Victor. 2014. 'Civil Society: A Multi-Layered Concept.' *Current Sociology* 62 (6): 812–830.

Putnam, Robert D. 1995. 'Tuning In, Tuning Out: The Strange Disappearance of Social Capital in America.' *Political Science and Politics* 28: 664–683.

   2000. *Bowling Alone: The Collapse and Revival of American Community*. New York: Simon & Schuster.

Rousseau, Jean-Jacques. 1996 [1755]. 'Discourse on the Origin and Foundations of Inequality among Men.' In David Wootton (ed.), *Modern Political Thought: Readings from Machiavelli to Nietzsche* (pp. 404–463). Indianapolis, IN: Hackett.

Rucht, Dieter. 2011. 'Civil Society and Civility in Twentieth-Century Theorising.' *European Review of History/Revue européenne d'histoire* 18(3): 387–407.

Sassoon, Anne Showstack. 1991. 'Civil Society.' In Tom Bottomore (ed.), *A Dictionary of Marxist Thought*, 2nd ed. (pp. 82–84). Oxford, UK: Blackwell Reference.

Susen, Simon. 2015. *The 'Postmodern Turn' in the Social Sciences*. Basingstoke, UK: Palgrave Macmillan.

Turner, Bryan S. 2006. 'Civil Society.' In Bryan S. Turner (ed.), *The Cambridge Dictionary of Sociology* (pp. 70–71). Cambridge, UK: Cambridge University Press.

20 Social Movements: Sequences vs Fuzzy Temporality

Kevin Gillan

The chronological story of 'social movement studies' as an interdisciplinary social scientific subfield has been well told a number of times (Crossley, 2002; Edwards, 2014a; Opp, 2009). This is a marker of its maturity as a relatively self-contained area of knowledge with widely recognized central concepts, conceptual frameworks, seminal texts, and (to a lesser extent) methodological preferences. This chapter will not repeat the full chronology but instead pull together some of the most important threads of theoretical development in order to construct – and then critique – a sequential understanding of social movements. I will draw most heavily from the dominant approaches in the self-identified subfield of social movements, especially that associated with the 'contentious politics' framework (hereafter CP; McAdam, Tarrow, and Tilly, 2001; Tilly and Tarrow, 2007), but I will also be arguing that alternative approaches typically demonstrate a similar rootedness in temporal sequences.

Conceptualizing movements sequentially is both heuristically useful and explanatorily powerful. But by presenting the key concepts in this way I will also reveal two systematic weaknesses with this approach. First, I will point to an excessively simplified temporal sequence that (at best) is suitable for the analysis of waves of protest. Waves are generally recognized as including multiple movements, but it is the wave-form sequence that is so often taken as 'social movement theory'. Disentangling waves and movements is a first step to appreciating the temporalities within which movements move. Second, I will examine our conceptualization of 'social movement' itself as an object of study and will point to fuzzy boundaries. This is hardly a new complaint (cf. Melucci, 1989), but I will illuminate the way that the sequential approach relies on our ability to identify a rather definite and bounded set of actions and actors as a social movement. But neither the conceptual definitions we utilize nor the messy reality of empirical applications allow such a stable object to emerge from study. Movements' temporal boundaries are revealed as just as fuzzy as their spatial or ideological boundaries. This point touches on a deeper neglect of the temporal dimensions of both social movements themselves and of the fields in which they move. I will ultimately argue that there has thus far been a failure to apprehend the fact that movements are involved in multiple sequences across distinct timescales, and that their own temporal conditions continuously interact with others. To answer the challenges set forth here I argue that a more nuanced understanding of time is required, for which I develop four concepts: timescale, timescape, velocity, and vector. Vector and velocity indicate directions of travel, speed of transformation, and relative forces. They may apply to movements themselves or their analytically distinct components: the cultural vectors produced, for instance, by new framings or tactical innovations. Simultaneously we should attempt to recognize the other vectors at work in any conflict: economic vectors of increasing precarity, for instance, or political vectors towards greater institutional distrust. Together an analysis of vectors suggests an appreciation of the timescape within which movements move and interact.

Ontological features of the definition of 'social movement' will be explored in more detail later in this chapter. For the sake of a starting point, however, let me offer the following: a social movement is a collective actor – comprising individuals, informal groups, and (often) formal organizations – coordinating voluntarily to pursue a range of values or interests that bring it into conflict with perceived systems of power.

'Social movement' thus refers to both the actor and its action, and both are defined by the conflict in which the movement is engaged. Analytical definitions offered in the literature vary, usually bringing in elements of the broader theory of movements that particular authors are developing (compare, for instance, Diani, 1992: 13; Melucci, 1989: 30; Tilly, 1985: 735–736). Definitional disagreement is to be expected, as 'social movement' is an essentially contested concept in the fullest sense: not only is there a lack of agreement on the concept itself, but the terms with which one defines 'social movement' are themselves contested (Connolly, 1993). Nevertheless, the definition offered here helps to highlight some of the key questions movement scholars typically ask, including: when, where, and how do social movements emerge? What is the identity of the collective and how is it achieved? What forms of coordination are used and to what ends? What systems of power are confronted, and how do those systems react? Much movement scholarship approaches such questions empirically in case studies, or variable-oriented or comparative forms of research that can provide nuanced analytical description of real-world social movements. Common answers to these questions can be brought together into a broader sequential view of action offering a theoretical framework for understanding social movements in a more general sense.

A Sequential View of Social Movements

Underlying the various conceptual apparatuses widely used in movement scholarship there is a sequential view of social movements. This is heuristically useful in so far as it encourages us to explore actions occurring over time, with various precursors and results. In this view movements always have a mobilization phase, which makes demands and generates coordination, competition, and conflict with other social actors, leading to a variety of short- and long-term consequences, but also inevitably to demobilization of the movement (Tarrow, 1998). A theory of social movements, from this point of view, would break the sequence down in search of patterns; an approach that has perhaps reached its zenith in CP (McAdam and Tarrow, 2011; McAdam, Tarrow, and Tilly, 2001; Tilly and Tarrow, 2007). CP reconstructs the conceptual apparatus developed in social movement scholarship over the preceding decades. That 'classic agenda' was initially often driven by US scholars but has undoubtedly achieved significant international interpenetration, at least with Europe, as is evidenced by most chapters in the recent collection *Social Movement Studies in Europe* (Fillieule and Accornero, 2016; Rucht, 2016). CP recasts key concepts such as political opportunities, interpretative frames, and diffusion as mechanisms and processes that, arrayed sequentially, have explanatory power in understanding social movements alongside other periods of contentious political activity. The next three sections will outline the conceptual apparatus of a sequential understanding of movements. Many of these concepts have been subject to wide-ranging debate and development, which cannot be covered extensively; here my focus is specifically on how each concept contributes to a sequential understanding. One caveat in relation to this material is that McAdam, Tarrow, and Tilly do not claim, at least within their CP work, that we should necessarily expect to see mechanisms and processes all appear in the same order over time in different periods of contention, and are thus rowing back somewhat from Tarrow's earlier conceptualization of cycles (McAdam, Tarrow, and Tilly, 2001: 65–67; Tarrow, 1998: 23–25). This may appear contradictory to the following account of a sequential understanding of movements, and will be discussed in the second half of the chapter. First, however, it is necessary to set out the main elements of the sequential view of movements.

Movement Emergence

A great deal of the theoretical development that has taken place in the field of social movement studies has, understandably, addressed the questions of emergence and mobilization. Why does any particular movement appear at the time and place in which it occurs? It is not simply that the existence of a grievance in some population leads directly to the mobilization of a movement, since we can point to many instances of grievances existing without any notable public mobilization (McAdam, 1982). Answering the emergence question for any particular movement often leads the social movement scholar to work with some of the key concepts adumbrated below.

Opportunities, structures, and social change are a focus for those authors who see that any satisfactory discussion of movements requires an appreciation of sociopolitical context. Research focused on 'political opportunity structures' has been an influential route to understanding contextual factors and focus most often on the nation state (Eisinger, 1973; Kitschelt, 1986). Subsequent developments have identified cultural, discursive, industrial, and political-economy opportunity structures among others (Císař and Navrátil, 2017; Motta, 2015; Schurman, 2004; Williams, 2004: 95). The key terms here are suggestive of stable arrangements of institutions and norms that largely form a backdrop for the more dynamic activity in movements. Conceptions of 'political opportunity structure' are most clearly associated with strongly structuralist approaches to movements, although somewhat more culturally oriented interpretations have long been articulated that stress the fact that opportunities are the subject of movement discourse and ultimately must be inter-preted as opportunities in order to be causally effective (Diani, 1996; Gamson and Meyer, 1996; Williams, 2004). In reality, these 'structure' terms are often abbre-viated (e.g. political opportunities, which actually signifies something rather differ-ent). The focus becomes an examination of opening or closure of opportunities (or, indeed, the appearance or disappearance of threats), which gives a much more dynamic appreciation of context (Almeida, 2003). It is, in fact, changes in the political opportunity structure, not the structure per se, which empirical studies tend to stress today (e.g. Josselin, 2007; Piazza and Genovese, 2016), and which were always more central in the broader political process approach in connection with which the concept of opportunity structures gained popularity (McAdam, 1982). In a sequential approach to movements, then, openings or closures – whether political, economic, or cultural – appear as precursors to movement activity; they become an independent variable to be utilized, alongside resource concerns, in the explanation of movement emergence.

The new social movement (NSM) theories developed from the work of Touraine (1981; 1988), Melucci (1989; 1996), and others offer an alternative approach to sociopolitical context. Such theories sought to understand the emergence of new collective actors in relation to large-scale social changes related to (variously) post-industrial, information-centric, or programmed societies in Europe. Today, following the most recent wave of contention and scholarly calls to 'bring capitalism back in' to movement analysis this style of explanation of movement emergence is gaining renewed popularity (Castells, 2015; Cox and Nilsen, 2014; Della Porta, 2015; Gillan, 2017; Hetland and Goodwin, 2013). Without ever seeing movements as emerging in a fully determined manner from structural changes, the NSM theorists always recognized the importance of large-scale societal shifts in both sparking reactive protest and in providing the conditions in which groups come together to autono-mously generate claims to new kinds of interest, value, or identity. Changing social conditions play the same sequential role as political opportunity structure here, but NSM theory gives us a rather broader notion of sociopolitical context wherein we can see more general processes of social change producing certain forms of move-ments, especially through the construction of new collective identities. Since key movement scholars saw themselves as living in a period of great flux any further step in the sequence was an open question: Touraine expected the generation of a grand social movement expressing the dominant conflict of the programmed society (Touraine, 1988; cf. Touraine, 2002), whereas for Melucci the future was much more open.

Aside from sociopolitical context, most accounts of the mobilization phase of movements stress some form of mobilization structure. Early accounts focused on resources and organizations, which more recently has become, for some, a focus on networks. While resource mobilization theory was initially based on a much-critiqued vision of the rational actor (Crossley, 2002) and certainly revelled in economistic metaphors (McCarthy and Zald, 1977), the harnessing of resources and development of organization have been retained as central features in most models of social movements even where the more simplistic assumptions about individual rationality have been dropped. Rational actor models, meanwhile, have continued to develop in sophistication (Oliver, 2013. 200). A notion of the social movement organization (SMO) as a formal, membership-based structure retains influence within an image of movements as multi-organizational fields (Klandermans, 1992). Increasing recognition of the role of other network structures in producing mobilization since the development of NSM theory has led to more network-centric approaches (Diani, 1992; Diani, 2000). Of course a 'multi-organizational field' implies a network in any case, but network-centric approaches focus on the structure of networks (between individuals or collectives) primarily, with consideration of either the attributes of collectives or content of relationships a secondary concern, only really relevant to the extent they affect the network structure itself (but see Krinsky and Crossley, 2014). Despite some notable arguments to the contrary (Edwards 2014a, ch. 8; Haenfler, Johnson, and Jones, 2012; Piven and Cloward, 1979), some minimal level of structured coordination, often conceived as a 'mobilization structure', is ordinarily seen as an essential feature of the mobilization phase of a social movement. In a sequential understanding of movements, the creation of coordination mechanisms is the first agentic step and thus provides a significant part of the explanation for the movement dynamics that follow: the development and promulgation of oppositional ideas, the gathering of essential resources, the emergence of leadership, and the development of strategic action all appear as consequences of coordination.

Movements in Action

We know movements through their action and claims-making. Beyond the study of emergence, movement scholarship has examined what movements do and how they do it. A whole host of concepts have been thrown up in the exploration of different modes of activity. Repertoires of contention describe standard forms of action that are culturally available to movements because participants, opponents, and onlookers understand the significance of, say, a demonstration, petition, or act of civil disobedience (Tilly, 1986). Thus repertoires describe strategies of action as shaped by cultural meaning in historical context; they change rarely over time. More recently, a focus on practices (as culturally inscribed behaviours) drawing broadly on Bourdieu promises a complement to the notion of repertoires because it recognizes that forms of action are not free-floating, but embedded in the everyday activities of individual lives, which in turn reflect broader patterns of constraint and opportunity (Crossley, 2003; Haluza-DeLay, 2008; Yates, 2015a). Whether we understand movement action as shaped by Tillian repertoires, Bourdieusian practices or Foucauldian counter-conducts (Death, 2010), forms of activity can be seen as patterned by the ways in which past activities have shaped culture and patterns of power, with repertoires implying repetition over time rather more than either practices or counter-conducts, which both allow more scope for agency. Examining movement action must also involve a clear sense of what claims are being made. The chief concept for illuminating claims in movements has become the interpretative frame (Snow et al., 1986; Snow et al., 2014). Theoretically, the notion of a frame indicates that beliefs and values tend to hang together in relatively coherent and self-reinforcing ways, such that communication of some elements of a frame carries connotations of other beliefs and values that might be widely understood. Framing the US abortion debate as one between 'pro-life' and 'pro-choice', for instance, offer clear examples of competitive attempts to align the framing of an issue in a way that resonates with more widely held beliefs (McCaffrey and Keys, 2000).

Empirically, repertoires, frames, and other characteristics of movements are often identified in action over short timescales, and it is difficult to ascertain the extent to which they change over time and for what reasons. One way in which this may be approached is through a focus on diffusion, which in CP becomes a particularly important mechanism in the production of contentious action. This is no simplistic uni-causal model, but does highlight an expected sequence. If successful diffusion (of ideas, tactics, or resources) occurs alongside other significant mechanisms, then once combined they set in train a sequential process leading to new forms of coordination of contentious activity (Tilly and Tarrow, 2007: 30–32; cf. Koopmans, 2004: 25–26). Empirical examinations of diffusion often focus on innovative tactics and indicate the importance of attending to local context (understood both in terms of structural and cultural features) of the receiver of a potential diffusion in determining whether diffusion succeeds or not (Edwards, 2014b; Wood, 2012). A second, broader way forward here may be found in a new emphasis on strategic interaction in both CP and in the notions of 'strategic action fields' and 'player and arenas' (Duyvendak and Jasper, 2015; Fligstein and McAdam, 2011). The focus of these approaches is to shift movement analysis away from an overly movement-centric approach. Anywhere we see movements in action there are opponents, state forces, observers, and so on, and we cannot fully understand movement action without the action of these other players. Strategic interaction introduces a temporality within movement activity that is often missing, so that it becomes possible to view more clearly the processes by which movements adapt their actions on the basis of an analysis of the interactions in which they have already participated (McCammon et al., 2008; Williams, 2016).

Both strategic interaction and diffusion approaches allow recognition of a temporality that is tied to a movement's own timescale. This is certainly an advantage over snapshot descriptions of repertoires, frames, and other movement-focused concepts. They are both inherently sequential in nature, although they risk producing a rather one-dimensional temporal sequence, wherein, for instance, context is held constant while the action and reaction of strategic players plays out according to its own logic. In the second half of the chapter I will argue that appreciation of a longer temporality would be helpful here, although it is worth noting at this point that this does not necessarily mean that we should reinvent the wheels of movement analysis. For instance, not all approaches to interpretative frames are so wedded to the notion of short-term strategic attempts to find resonance in a particular political moment: one way of appreciating the historical input to movement frames is to recognize their dialogic relations with longer-term ideological or discursive reference points (Gillan, 2008b; Steinberg, 1998). Similarly, approaching tactics as modes of action selected within particular strategic contexts can be temporally enriched by close attention to the ways in which different cultural traditions influence the adoption (or not) of particular practices (Doherty and Hayes, 2012).

Consequences and Demobilization

Movement scholars naturally assume that movements matter in some way: they have consequences of social import that may (or may not) flow from their own stated goals and modes of activity. Aside from some important work on movement strategies (Gamson, 1989), however, that assumption went surprisingly unexplored until the mid-1990s. As work began to coalesce around the question of movement conse- quences (or outcomes) it suggested the need for a view that was broader than simply identifying whether stated goals of movements had been met, because, firstly, move- ments are often heterogeneous in their goals, and, secondly, many important out- comes of movement activity are likely unintended (Giugni, 1998). As a result, the focus of studies of the consequences of movements has broadened considerably, taking in not only issues of policy and political inclusion, but personal and biogra- phical factors, cultural trends, repressive behaviour, political parties, and much else (the breadth can be seen in edited collections, e.g. Bosi, Giugni, and Uba, 2016; Giugni, McAdam, and Tilly, 1999). Unsurprisingly, movement scholars investigat- ing outcomes often do so using the kinds of conceptual approaches already described: just as political opportunity structures may be more or less conducive to mobilization, for instance, so too might they be more or less conducive to various kinds of outcome. Without detailing either the multiple types of consequence or the various methodological debates raised by this focus in movement scholarship, it is possible to identify three elements of this research agenda that have relevance here. First, research on consequences is by necessity tied to the sequential view of move- ments: if mobilization and action are the first two analytical phases then this is the next logical step. Second, one of the key findings in studying movement outcomes is that the timescales may be relatively long. Andrews (1997: 815) for instance, argues that 'civil rights mobilization shaped electoral outcomes 10 to 20 years after the peak of the movement', although given interest in topics such as the transfer of activist experience across generations, the timescale could extend much further (Masclet, 2016). Third, increasing focus on movement outcomes has been a significant push factor in the field's search for ways to understand strategic interaction because, especially when focused on policy change, it is impossible to understand outcomes without examining the actions of targeted institutions. Potentially this could also provide a useful spur to extend the timescale of attention on interaction beyond those brief peak years of movement activity.

We can see consequences as the third analytical stage in social movements; empirically, however, the third phase is more likely to be described as demobiliza- tion. It is reasonable to claim that, even more than the question of consequences, this is an area that scholars have shied away from until recently (Koopmans, 2004). Davenport offers a useful review of the existing literature, noting that explanations of demobilization have tended to focus on various internal factors (e.g. burnout, factionalization, reduced commitment) or external pressures (resource deprivation, problem depletion, state repression) before suggesting the ways in which these might interact (Davenport, 2007). Most such factors more clearly relate to bounded SMOs than movements in general. While some movements' fortunes are clearly linked to key organizations, most significant movements become multi-organizational fields. Moreover, it should be noted that there is nothing necessary about a demobilization phase when applied to movements. Many movements have become apparently permanent fixtures (as have, for instance, environmentalism or feminism in many countries), even if during times of lowered contention their activity may mostly be within 'abeyance structures' or 'submerged networks' (Melucci, 1989; Taylor, 1989). The notion of demobilization as decline in public protest activity (rather than as death of an organization) is particularly tied to concepts of cycles of contention or protest waves, and will be discussed shortly.

Temporal Complexities

The preceding section has set out a range of concepts that are often used in understanding social movements, with a particular focus on the way in which they are arrayed in a temporal sequence of movement development. Often these are treated as a 'toolkit', with concepts selected according to particular research questions. Rucht (2016) rightly criticizes the toolkit approach for failing to take into account the theoretical assumptions made in the development of each concept. CP is the most ambitious attempt at a more theoretically consistent synthesis yet, although I have deliberately aimed here at a more inclusive selection of theoretical bases. Here I set most issues of theoretical consistency to one side and merely note that the purpose of this review has not been to suggest that all of these conceptual developments are necessarily congruous. However, as is evident above, each concept has a clear position in an overarching temporal sequence. It is my contention below that attention to the appropriate temporality of our conceptual apparatus is a valuable first step in further work on building a more coherent framework. I will develop this argument through, firstly, a critical examination of the ways in which the temporal nature of the sequence set out above is typically conceptualized; secondly, examining the ontology of movements to point to the temporal indeterminacy of our object of study; and thirdly, introducing the notions of timescale, timescape, vector, and velocity as potentially valuable correctives.

Cycles and Waves

The foregoing account of movements as sequence is similar in nature to Tarrow's influential depiction of cycles of contention. In that formulation the cycle encompasses a mobilization phase, during which initial conflicts diffuse across a range of sectors of society. Cycles bring about new repertoires of action and interpretative frames, bring together established organizations and new ones, and increase the rate of information flow and interaction among challenging groups. As the cycle experiences a downturn it involves a complex of processes, although Tarrow accepts that this stage will be rather unpredictable (Tarrow, 1998: 145–155). In their CP work Tarrow and colleagues row back from the 'cycles' approach somewhat, arguing that this is only one possible sequential arrangement of mechanisms and processes of contention. This aligns with their overarching move,

> away from static variables to dynamic mechanisms … In place of an objective accounting of the opportunities, the organizational capacity, the available frames and repertoires of a given 'mobilizing structure', we substitute a dynamic analysis of the internal debates and interactive processes through which social groups seek to define and act on a shared sense of collective purpose and identity. (McAdam, Tarrow, and Tilly, 2001: 50)

In my depiction of movement scholarship above I have paid little attention to the distinction identified here. In some ways I am being more generous to the 'classic agenda' of movement scholarship than McAdam et al. By presenting that agenda (alongside various additional concepts) in its sequential form there is an implicit dynamism. Individual studies that focus on one phase or another can appear more static – particularly when zoning in on one particular concept or taking a snapshot cross-national methodology – but the field as a whole, appropriately read, can contain dynamism between the parts. Where CP offers greater advantages is in making visible the possible feedback between different phases, so that, for instance, the various mobilization mechanisms are recognized as occurring throughout an episode of contention, not merely in an opening phase (McAdam, Tarrow, and Tilly, 2001: 45). By broadening the object of study to 'contentious politics' in general, one can also recognize that the end phase may not be simply demobilization, but the transformation of activity into a different form, of the kind recently seen in Spain when much of the energy of the 15-M movement transferred into electoral politics through Podemos (Martínez-Arboleda, 2016).

The notion of cycles of contention was always based on the observation that protest occurs in waves: periods of heightened mobilization when, often, the 'usual suspects' who organize demonstrations find themselves surprised by the sudden scale of participation when thousands of 'new faces' line the streets. Waves may make more appealing metaphors than cycles, since they are often visible in empirical data and do not carry an implicit notion of cycling back to an identical starting state. Protest event analysis offers us images of protest waves that are visible in graphical form. This is increasingly popular thanks to the availability of new data sets and analytical approaches (Hutter, 2014; Koopmans and Statham, 1999; Quaranta, 2016). At their most powerful, such accounts can give a sense of connections and differences between different waves (Almeida, 2008). Where 'waves' are considered in more abstracted theoretical terms they are often synonymous with 'cycles', *pace* Tarrow (Barker and Dale, 1998; cf. Koopmans, 2004). By comparison it is worth considering comments in Freeman and Johnson's (1999) edited collection, *Waves of Protest: Social Movements since the Sixties*. Here the editors posit three long-term protest waves in modern American history, each composed of,

> wave after wave of protests [that] have reshaped our policies, priorities, and values ... While each period has its own theme, there are some common characteristics. They last roughly twenty to thirty years. While there are a few major movements that set the tone of the period, there are many minor ones that vary the theme. (Freeman and Johnson, 1999: ix)

Clearly, these waves are historic periods of significant social change with movements as central actors. As with Tarrow's account (and emphasized more recently by Koopmans, 2004), waves include multiple interacting actors and, as such, although there may be some recognizable internal dynamics to protest waves, the way these dynamics play out will be rather unpredictable. Where Freeman and Johnson differ from Tarrow is on a notion of timescale. Tarrow's example cycles are short compared to Freeman and Johnson's 'twenty to thirty years', although the latter allow for 'wave upon wave' within their long waves. This is a matter of analytical resolution: '*Viewed from a distance*, waves of collective action from the 1848 revolutions onward describe parabolas from institutional conflict to enthusiastic peak of contention, to ultimate collapse or ... the consolidation of new regimes' (Tarrow, 1998: 160, italics added).

There is much potential to develop from the literature on waves of protest a more attuned sense of the different timescales on which different movements work. Freeman and Johnson's selection of waves, each containing 'wave after wave' of protest rolling in approximately the same direction, is suggestive that waves of protest might be understood as temporally nested. This can be clarified by application to recent decades. The years 2010–2012 witnessed a wave of protest marked by the context of austerity politics (Della Porta, 2015). This might also be understood as the latest in a series of waves confronting neoliberal globalization that emerged with the alter-globalization movement in the early 1990s; transformed into an anti-war movement in the early 2000s; and re-emerged as the Arab Spring, 15-M, and Occupy in the 2010s (Della Porta, 2006; Hutter, 2014). Periods of heightened mobilization have temporal and geographical specificities, but two features are pervasive. First, the context of expanding neoliberalism has been used to account for most of the grievances that have motivated left-leaning protest movements since the mid-1990s (e.g. Cox and Nilsen, 2014). The argument is less direct in relation to the anti-war mobilizations. Yet many of the same protest networks formed in the alter-globalization movement fed in to the anti-war movement, which is why it mobilized so rapidly (Gillan, Pickerill, and Webster, 2008). The invasion was often framed as a 'war for oil' and critics pointed to the corporate interests present in the US administration's drive to war, with Halliburton's economic interest in Iraq, for instance, seemingly personified in Vice President Dick Cheney. While the realities of war brought in a new diversity of participants to protest, therefore, those framing it with reference to the influence of corporations over governments in the neoliberal age were an important grouping (Gillan, Pickerill, and Webster, 2008; Walgrave and Verhulst, 2009).

The second pervasive feature of the recent period is that of organizational innovations in the construction of global networks of action. The construction of Indymedia at the Battle of Seattle in 1999 was a watershed moment in giving activists direct and easy access to rapid internet publication (Pickerill, 2007; Wolfson, 2014). Indymedia enabled 'user-generated content' long before business circles had begun to discuss the power of user-generated content in Web 2.0 and, moreover, demonstrated a productive connection between autonomist politics and the hacker ethic developed in subcultures of software design (Gillan, 2008a). The development of the World Social Forum and its regional and local variants indicated that while information technologies were clearly important, it was perhaps the central role of a new cultural logic of networking that was the central innovation during this period (De Angelis, 2005; Juris, 2005; Juris, 2008). Analyses of the Arab Spring and the following 'movement of the streets and the squares' has also tied this movement both to neoliberalism as a source of grievances and globally networked forms of action as the source of coordination (Benski et al., 2013; Castells, 2015; Fominaya, 2014). Linking these three waves as instances of a longer-term wave convincingly may take a longer empirical account. However, the preceding material should suffice to indicate significant potential in attempting to understand the nested timescales within which movement action occurs.

The sequential framework set out above has a good fit with waves of protest but may be less suited to movements themselves. When measured as a series of public events, such waves do clearly have phases of mobilization, action, and demobilization. Koopmans reiterates this point, re-describing the phases as ones of expansion, transformation and contraction of contention. Recognizing the interplay between movements in waves he argues that 'we must move beyond single movements, and consider dynamic interactions among a multitude of contenders' and that the key questions are 'what accounts for the destabilization of social relations within the polity, and what explains their ultimate restabilization' (Koopmans, 2004: 21, 42). More than most, then, Koopmans is clear that the study of waves is different from the study of movements. That this distinction is important can be shown to be evident simply by comparing well-known examples. European environmental movements, for instance, were already sufficiently mature to influence the United Nations by the time of the 1972 Stockholm conference that set the agenda of sustainable development that remains vital today. Since then, environmental movements have existed continuously in most major European nations, although, of course, the levels of visible protest activity have varied widely across country and over time (Rootes, 1997). During that time, countless short-term movements have sprung up with a significantly time-delimited purpose. Consider the anti-poll-tax movement in early-1990s Britain, for instance, which generated widespread protest and a coordinated campaign of non-payment of the regressive council-level tax. The campaign led to 6.1 million non-payment summonses in England, and a combined value of £2.4 billion of poll tax was left unpaid by the time it was abolished in 1993 (Bagguley, 1995; Tonge, 1994). The latter movement can be described as a short-term wave of protest related to a particular political threat; while within the afore-mentioned environmental movement we could talk about successive waves of protest that respond partly to the timetables of institutional actors. But reducing the environmental movement to a series of waves of protest would miss much of the vital underlying activity that has had an effect on both the everyday lives of millions of people and on the acceptable discourses of political and economic organizations. Alternatively, studying anti-poll-tax action as an isolated wave would make it inexplicable because it would miss the highly contentious period of British politics in which it emerged: the longer-term wave of protest against the imposition of Thatcherism.

Attention to temporality clarifies that waves are simply different kinds of phenomena to movements. Too often in movement scholarship the two are conflated, such that the development of 'theories of movements' is in fact tied to wave-like sequences. The dominant approaches to movements were generally developed in the study of waves, even if their named objects of study have been movements that at some point became permanent actors whose composition and character may change over time. The US civil rights movement, for instance, as a classic case study for so much US literature, is generally studied in its main upswings in the 1950s and 1960s. But it has had a permanent organizational presence in American politics ever since, and the recent Black Lives Matter campaign must – in the *longue durée* – be seen as a continuation of that movement. We cannot, in fact, understand waves without attention to movements. Abeyance structures keep the ideas of the last wave alive, while it is within submerged networks and ongoing movements that groups develop the critical ideas, networks, and tactics that will appear characteristic of the next wave (Melucci, 1989; Taylor, 1989). The sequential understanding of movements set out in the first half of this chapter is most suited to understanding short-term waves of protest or, as CP's authors have it, periods of contentious politics. When one attempts to disentangle movements from the waves they participate in, the temporal character of movements is revealed as decidedly fuzzy; for this reason it is necessary to return to the ontological character of movements.

The Indeterminacy of Movements

As noted above, 'social movement' is an essentially contested concept. But the impossibility of finding a 'correct' definition does not, of course, mean that definitional work is unimportant: 'Definitions cannot be true or false, but they can be more or less useful' (Tilly, 1999: 258). For Tilly, the utility to be found in a definition is in identifying a set of phenomena sharing particular causal processes that need to be distinguished from adjacent phenomena (electoral politics, say), which may have different causal properties. However, this appears to puts the epistemological cart before the ontological horse – one does not need to be a pure empiricist to seek to identify by 'social movement' some recognizable features shared by most, if not all, of those phenomena to which we commonly (and atheoretically) apply the label 'movement', and only subsequently investigate underlying properties, mechanisms, or relationships with other aspects of society. The most obvious alternative is simply resting on the common-sense invocation of the term 'movement', but this unearths a different problem. To point at a set of groups, individuals, ideas, or events and say 'the movement' is to reify complexity in an analytically unhelpful way. The problem is that reification gives the aggregation of individual and collective behaviours an undeserved 'ontological weight and qualitative homogeneity; collective reality, as it were, exists as a unified thing'.

As a result, 'the collective dimension of social behaviour is taken as a given, as a datum obvious enough to require no further analysis' (Melucci, 1989: 13–15). For Melucci, it is precisely the achievement of the collective appearance lent to a variety of processes, groups, and so on that should be questioned in the study of social movements. The Meluccian challenge, therefore, is to analyse a movement without starting with an assumption of its unity (Gillan, 2008b). Tilly was certainly not unaware of this problem, and one impressive summary of his career output argues, 'The problems of actor constitution – that is, the illusory unity of motivations and forms of action, the unruly association of identities with relations – were all issues with which he wrestled for more than 40 years' (Krinsky and Mische, 2013: 2). For Melucci the problem of the unity of the collective actor should be apprehended through the study of the unending process of collective identity, whereas for Tilly (with a somewhat different formulation of the issue), the solution was rather to sidestep the problem by separating out movement bases from demands to focus on what he saw as more important questions. Within a sequence-oriented approach to movements, the latter approach has been highly productive, leading to the development of an array of concepts describing a range of important features of movement activity and (latterly) contentious politics more broadly. Collective identity has slipped into that array of concepts, but in doing so is converted to something rather static (deliberately so in, for instance, Saunders, 2008). Retaining a dynamic view of collective identity as an unending process in the temporary achievement of (the appearance of) unity of action is challenging, but retains significant appeal, especially for those whose approach to movements is ethnographic or embedded (e.g. Fominaya, 2010; Maeckelbergh, 2009).

Despite the ontological difficulties of identifying movements as collective actors, a great deal of movement scholarship begins with the selection of a named movement (or a set of movements) for study, or else particular SMOs, events, waves, or frames may be selected as emblematic of the named movements which the analysis is purported to be about. Given Melucci's point on reification above we must recognize that the naming of a particular movement can be a decisive analytical step. Yet it is one that scholars rarely control as we adopt or adapt, more or less consciously, the names used in public or movement discourse. Movements are typically named for their field of conflict (i.e. pro- or anti- movements) or by the identity claimed by the collective actor itself (e.g. women's movements). The recent 'Occupy' movement was relatively unusual, but not unique, in being named instead for a characteristic tactic (c.f. Doherty, Plows, and Wall, 2003). Names are deeply political, however, as was obvious in attempts to agree a name for what is variously known as the anti-globalization, alter-globalization, anti-capitalist, or global justice movement (among other names). Different ideological currents within the movement always had a vested interested in one or other label, which signals as well the fact that from certain perspectives different groups may be included or excluded as legitimate parts of the movement (Gillan, 2006: 77–82). That movement had been particularly marked by its ideological diversity. But even in the movement against the invasion of Iraq, which had a clear goal, delimited by policy and timing, some participants decried the given name 'anti-war movement', since most involved actors were expressing a limited (in the view of pacifists) 'anti this particular war' position (Gillan, Pickerill, and Webster, 2008, ch. 5). This issue has clear methodological ramifications, since social movement scholarship so often proceeds in a case-oriented fashion, with movements as 'cases'; the analytical construction of cases is thus an important step over which scholars are often silent (cf. Ragin, 1992). Our analytical boundary-drawing in the study of movements is – whether we acknowledge it or not – loaded with political implication.

When 'casing' movements we decontest, for the purpose of a specific analysis, the ideological and organizational boundaries of a complex set of individual and collective activity. But we also decontest temporal boundaries. When studying waves, observers typically point to upsurges in publicly recorded activity. However, in searching for a beginning to a particular movement there is a danger of infinite regress. To return to our familiar example, we can ask, when did the alter-globalization movement start? We can attempt to answer this by drawing on movement histories written by participants and sympathetic observers. But to do so simply highlights the fuzzy temporal boundaries of the movement. For instance, revolutionary socialists typically refer to the 'summit-hopping' phase of the alter-globalization movement as an anti-capitalist movement that began in 1999 with the Battle of Seattle (e.g. Bircham and Charlton, 2001). Seattle was an important marker within that political standpoint, because it marked the first mass involvement of trade unions from the global North in militant protests against international financial institutions. For the more autonomist strand of the alter-globalization movement however, it is possible to point to either the June 1999 'Carnival Against Capitalism' in London, which was marked by a distinctly anarchic style of action, or the Zapatista uprising of 1994, with its decidedly autonomous ideological statements (Notes from Nowhere, 2003; Petras, 1999).

The alter-globalization protests always involved a strong strand of development and environmental NGOs with a more liberal ideological background. From this point of view, more obvious starting points may be the campaign against the Multinational Agreement on Investment, a treaty planned by the OECD but dropped in 1998 after three years of negotiations were met with consistent opposition by NGO-led campaigns (Griffin, 2002). And this ignores the wave of IMF riots in developing countries in the 1980s (Walton and Seddon, 2008); are these 'precursors' or the beginning of the movement proper? Not only are the starting points debatable, so too are the endings. The summit-hopping phase was heavily impacted by the devastation of the 9/11 terrorist attacks on America. The immediate response was the cancellation of a protest planned against the IMF and World Bank in Washington later that month, and some commentators were moved to pronounce the death of the movement. Much movement energy was diverted to opposing the invasions of Afghanistan and then Iraq. But subsequent summit protests such as that in Gleneagles in 2005, as well as the continuation of the World Social Forum in networking activists from North and South in struggles against neoliberal capitalist organizations, suggest the movement continues, albeit in somewhat altered form

(Cumbers, Routledge, and Nativel, 2008; Smith et al., 2015). The links in personnel, organizations, and ideas between the alter-globalisation movement and Occupy have been outlined, but Occupy never took on any of the original names attached to the previous wave of mobilization (Graeber, 2014).

In sum, social movement scholarship has an exceedingly fuzzy entity at its heart. This problem is often sidestepped by switching to other units of analysis: SMOs, waves, contentious politics, players and arenas, and strategic action fields have already been outlined and offer solutions that, depending on particular research goals, may be more or less workable. But even when utilizing these approaches, movements appear (perhaps indirectly) as collective actors associated with an over-arching sequence of mobilization, (inter)action, and demobilization. That sequence requires that we can associate a relatively simple temporality with a named move-ment, and it is against this notion that the last two subsections argue. In the final section I suggest that opening up our understanding of the multiple temporalities that are associated with movement activity may offer a productive way forward.

Timescales, Timescape, Velocity, and Vector

The critique of a sequential view of social movements presented above is not intended to argue that sequence is unimportant. Quite the opposite: the sequencing of events and interactions is vital to our understanding of both waves of protest and the social movements involved in them. But sequences have often been a background condition in movement theories, given little sophisticated analysis. This reflects broader weaknesses in (especially variable-oriented) social scientific agendas that have been subject to both theoretical and methodological critique for ignoring the temporal dimensions of social and political life (Abbott, 2001; Pierson, 2004). Even where sequences are brought to the fore – as in CP – the sequences are relatively micro-scale, focused on the concatenation of mechanisms into processes. This final section highlights four ways in which we can approach temporality. This is not an exhaustive account; my aim is simply to offer a constructive beginning for a research agenda on the fuzzy temporalities of social movements.

The importance of *timescale* has been noted above as an issue of analytical resolution. While many movement studies examine the fortunes of a movement over a few years, historical work on movements too has been very productive (e.g. Tilly and Wood, 2015). Long timescales can indeed illuminate processes that are lost with a shorter-term focus. More revealing than that, however, may be a simultaneous focus on multiple timescales. Markoff (2015) for instance shows the importance of annual rhythms of agricultural work and weekly rhythms of church gatherings which impacted on protest occurrences during the French Revolution. This intersects with longer-term processes such as the decline of agriculture or production of different means by which individuals can coordinate in generating new repertoires of conten-tion (Tilly, 1986). Switching between timescales is used to good effect by Haydu and Skotnicki (2016) in tracing three periods of food activism in America, crossing a period of 120 years. Three movements during that time each contested commer-cialized food production as unnatural and unhealthy. By examining all three it is possible to see that each is shaped by its own historical temporality (with, for instance, the most recent organics movement connected to wider countercultural trends), but each also engages with long-term dynamics in the development of the food industry and capitalist production in general. Moreover, the organics movement has clearly drawn on past strategies and tactics (the valorization of the 'natural', the pursuit of labelling legislation and alternative forms of production), which were not only cultural memories of past struggle but also shaped by 'regulatory institutions constructed in large part by their early-twentieth-century ancestors' (Haydu and Skotnicki, 2016: 359). So, it is not simply the case that different analytical timescales highlight different kinds of process, though that is important, but also that these different timescales interact culturally, economically, and politically. Not all movement analysis need be historical in nature, but even broadening one's purview from a specific wave of contention to the decade or so that preceded – that is, its temporal context or *timescape* (described further below) – would reveal a great deal of analytically important information.

Attention to different timescales indicates that processes occur with different *velocities*. In a global information age many kinds of interactions are speeded up and activists interact with broader information circuits that keep to the pace of instant news. Analyses of movement uses of new communications technologies often point to speed of communication as a vital affordance, especially where fast communication leads to fast mobilization, but also note that this cannot wholly replace slower processes of face-to-face trust building and resource sharing (Gillan, Pickerill, and Webster, 2008). Nicholls and Uitermark (2015) argue that 'wildfire movements' such as Occupy spread rapidly by promoting very generalized frames via social media, but that these features limit their possible relations with other movements and local activists, and thus lead to an equally rapid demise. The apparently high-speed processes of mobilization via social media interact with even slower processes, such as demographic shifts, the spread of education, or the transformation of employment structures. Indeed, many movements of the most recent wave seem at some stage to have depended on people who were young, highly educated, but precariously (under)employed (Castells, 2015). This confluence of characteristics rests on slower trends such as flexibilization and the massification of higher education as well as the (faster) working through of economic crisis and adoption of new technologies.

Processes move with varying speeds and also in varying directions: velocity comes with *vector*. One way we might see this is through the notion of path dependence, which Pierson describes by emphasizing that earlier points in a path-dependent sequence may have a much greater influence than later ones because they set in motion positive feedback mechanisms which keep developments on a particular trajectory (2004: ch. 1; cf. Haydu, 1998). Consider, again, the summit-hopping phase of the alter-globalization movement. Its image throughout was militant and confrontational: British activist magazine Schnews (2004: 192) approvingly quoted then Prime Minister Tony Blair's depiction of an 'anarchists' travelling circus ... causing as much mayhem as possible'. Although many arguments were waged over the definition and role of violence in the movement, the uneasy settlement for many years was that a 'diversity of tactics' must be respected: black-bloc confrontation with the police was acceptable so long as there were options for more pacifist elements of the movement to participate in peaceful demonstration (Conway, 2003). We can hypothesize that the confrontational nature of protests in both London and Seattle may have set up two feedback mechanisms within the movement. Firstly, widely circulated images of confrontation with the authorities encouraged further participation by individuals who were already inclined to confrontational styles of activity, who participated in subsequent action decisions, thus setting in train a repeated preference for confrontation. Second, a narrative of the success of such tactics was developed and diffused in activist discourse. Accounts of 'diffusion' in the movement literature capture the spread of tactics across geographical distances and sometimes offer a nuanced account of the ways that deliberation within local contexts can alter the characteristics of the tactics (Wood, 2012). Nevertheless, such deliberation is already shaped strongly by the origins of the diffused tactic and such accounts might be improved by further sensitivity to the importance of temporal sequencing and path dependence. It is worth noting that at the same time processes were going on within and between state agencies as, for instance, when 'best practices' for policing protest were shared across police forces, setting up a process of militarization (Wood, 2014). Here too we may well find path dependence in action.

So, early decisions and interactions in a movement may set a particular vector for the actors and processes involved. In political science path dependence is often traced through formal rules in institutions, where it is easier to see the influence of earlier choices ossified in structures. However, as Pierson (2004) intimates and I suggest above, positive feedback mechanisms may well exist in other kinds of social process. It is not that path dependence is wholly determining, however. Movement actors may deliberately break from a path as when, for instance, the World Social Forum was set up to put alter-globalization activists in a less conflictual space to devise alternative solutions to the problems the movement had identified (Keraghel and Sen, 2004). Two separate cultural vectors – one oriented towards conflict and one towards the construction of open deliberative spaces – thus coexisted in the alter-globalization movement.

One way we can understand the roots of Occupy is to recognize the re-emergence and combination of both vectors in the same space and time: occupation as a tactic generated conflict precisely by creating, in public, spaces for open deliberation. While that innovation was not an outcome of a path-dependent process, we can see the continuing relevance of vectors (as directions of travel over time) in producing a particular combination of movement characteristics. Path dependence is tightly bounded with temporal sequences, which can be the source of its explanatory power. But the kinds of mechanisms that produce path dependence in institutional settings may be absent from looser social movements, in which agency must always be a central focus because of the degree of reflexivity about action evident when individuals are deliberately trying to change the 'rules of the game'. Movement participants imagine alternative futures. The label 'utopian' is often rejected by those who would rather not be seen as idealists; nevertheless, movement arguments about both principles and strategies rely on some sense of what a preferable future might look like. 'I have a dream' remains the inspirational beginning of much movement thought. The long emphasis on prefiguration within some movements indicates conscious attempts to bring that future into the present (Maeckelbergh, 2011; Yates, 2015b). Thus even the basic sequential notion of time (flying like an arrow) might be troubled by the realities of activist practices; a looser notion of vector may be preferable to a tighter focus on path dependence.

As noted in the first half of the chapter, the sociopolitical context of movement activity is often theorized through a number of 'opportunity structure' terms that are sometimes apprehended as static conditions, and sometimes as moments of change. Even where change is emphasized it is often momentary, and rather different from the notion of temporal context or *timescape* mentioned above. By timescape I intend a focus on velocities and vectors associated with multiple processes and actors in a range of timescales. This neologism may be illuminating. Like landscapes, we should recognize that our position and perspective will frame the image and highlight some important features over others – as analysts we must explicitly choose a vantage point. Within these bounds, however, we can achieve a degree of realism in our representation of important contours and landmarks. Like cityscapes, we can imagine how the key features of timescapes are representative of human activity. If one were to imagine stop-motion photography of a familiar city over the course of decades one would see patterned changes over time, without seeing the detail of the human activity that produced it. Nevertheless, the changing image would raise important questions about what determines the shapes and trends that we can see: new edifices raised, different materials appearing, loci of gentrification shifting. Explanation of any of those would require a focus on human activity, both individual and collective. One might also spot the impact of key events (or critical junctures) that have immediate and longer-term impacts: imagine economic crisis as a terrorist bomb, with very immediate devastation followed by slower processes of adaptation and reconfiguration. To focus on timescapes is akin to focusing on 'the macro', but instead of seeking durable structures, one's eye should be attuned to the processes – sometimes gradual, sometimes sudden – of social change that, over time, alter the contours, landmarks, and arrangements of power in a society.

Timescapes can be conceived as the product of a multitude of vectors moving at different velocities and with different force, sometimes against each other, sometimes together. We might analytically separate cultural vectors (frames, repertoires, and practices), social vectors (demographics, organization), political vectors (power elites, party platforms), or economic vectors (production processes, markets) with the aim of showing the degree to which each is pushing society in similar or different directions. Social movements are driven by vectors carrying meaning, organizational form, strategic preferences, and tactical know-how. In turn, as individuals and groups construct their collectivity, they intentionally ride and redirect these vectors against other directions of travel evident in their temporal context. When movements *move against*, it is because they have identified a target that is, itself, moving in a conflicting direction – this is evident in the examples above of movements against war or neoliberalism. When they *move for*, it may be because they are harnessing broader vectors of change and redirecting them to achieve specific goals – consider the achievements of women's suffrage or the campaign for the right of homosexuals to marry. While this chapter cannot empirically ground such observations, it is my hope that this kind of imagery is at least intriguing because it promises a genuinely dynamic view of the traditional concepts of movement scholarship and simultaneously contains an invitation to broaden the field of study.

Conclusion

This chapter began with an overview of some of the most important conceptual frameworks used in the study of social movements. I argued that although many individual concepts can appear rather static in nature, the field as a whole has produced a dynamic view of social movements. It is, however, a narrow dynamism tied to an overarching three-step sequence. CP has intentionally sought a more dynamic combination of past conceptual work and, in doing so, has emphasized sequences at a different scale: the concatenation of mechanisms into processes. Connected scholarly trends, such as work advancing strategic interaction and diffusion, were highlighted because not only do they rightly increase the importance of seeing movements as developing within interconnected fields, but they also imply a sequence of move and countermove by interacting actors. I constructed two challenges to the sequential understanding of movements. First, I argued that the overarching sequence is much more appropriate to the study of waves of protest than movements per se and that the two are distinct phenomena, too often conflated, that encompass different kinds of sequence. While the study of waves of protest (or indeed episodes of contentious activity) is important in its own right it is insufficient from the perspective of those who wish to understand social movements. Moreover, to explain any particular wave it is necessary to comprehend the movements that contribute to that wave in a longer timescale. This means, on the one hand, studying those movements in their own right and, on the other, attending to the potentially nested temporality of the wave. The second challenge was the inherent indeterminacy of social movements, both as a social scientific category and as empirical phenomena. Movements' boundaries – whether we consider them organizationally, ideologically, geographically, or temporally – are decidedly fuzzy. We can, of course, make analytically justifiable decisions to bound named movements in particular ways, but doing so is always a politically loaded move and one that must be left ever open to critique. This can throw doubt on claims that are based on movements as 'cases', either within single case studies or within variable-oriented approaches that depend on identifying variables attached to a named movement.

My response to these challenges is to suggest a temporally focused terminology to combine the dynamic elements already present in social movement theory and to highlight areas where further development – perhaps through conversation with other disciplinary subfields – would be valuable. Thus I suggest we examine vectors and velocities of action to get a sense of directed movement over time. Particular vectors may represent what movements do. For instance, Occupy generated a particular cultural vector in the reframing of class as inequality of power between the 99 per cent and the 1 per cent. It took on vector properties because it diffused rapidly across different contexts. Movement-generated vectors also encompass and interact with other vectors. Most obviously, in this case, socio-economic vectors (increasing economic inequality) and political-economic vectors (corporate influence on government) meant that this reframing resonated, not only across US cities but across advanced capitalist democracies in general. In Europe one might also point to a long-term sociocultural vector – the declining willingness of individuals to claim a class identity – that opened cultural space into which the 99 per cent reframing could move. In this example any account that depends on the interactions of bounded organizations would struggle to make sense of either the diffuse nature of action or the combination of cultural, social, economic, and political influences in shaping the overall direction of travel. A multitude of vectors – with different velocities, directions of travel, and degrees of force – can be conceived together as the timescape within which movements are located. Scholars of movements have largely begun to accept the need to move away from movement-centric theories but as yet are often limited to conceptualizations of 'context' in terms of 'opportunity structure'. NSM theory had presented a richer alternative in its attempt to depict the shaping of movement action by long-term social change, but its context-specificity meant that it never travelled well across space or time. 'Timescape' may appear abstract but the intent is to produce a placeholder, to be filled out by a rich understanding of the dynamic nature of the social location of any movement we wish to subject to study. Movements move, of course, but the grounds they cross are already shifting.

References

Abbott, Andrew. 2001. *Time Matters: On Theory and Method*. Chicago, IL: University of California Press.

Almeida, Paul D. 2003. 'Opportunity Organizations and Threat-Induced Contention: Protest Waves in Authoritarian Settings.' *American Journal of Sociology* 109(2): 345–400.

2008. *Waves of Protest: Popular Struggle in El Salvador, 1925–2005*. Social Movements, Protest and Contention Series. Minneapolis, MN: University of Minnesota Press.

Andrews, Kenneth T. 1997. 'The Impacts of Social Movements on the Political Process: The Civil Rights Movement and Black Electoral Politics in Mississippi.' *American Sociological Review* 62: 800–819.

Bagguley, Paul. 1995. 'Protest, Poverty and Power: A Case Study of the Anti-Poll Tax Movement.' *The Sociological Review* 43(4): 693–719.

Barker, Colin, and Gareth Dale. 1998. 'Protest Waves in Western Europe: A Critique of "New Social Movement" Theory.' *Critical Sociology* 24 (1–2): 65–104.

Benski, Tova, Lauren Langman, Ignacia Perugorría, and Benjamín Tejerina. 2013. 'From the Streets and Squares to Social Movement Studies: What Have We Learned?' *Current Sociology* 61(4): 541–61.

Bircham, Emma, and John Charlton (eds.). 2001. *Anticapitalism: A Guide to the Movement*. London: Bookmarks.

Bosi, Lorenzo, Marco Giugni, and Katrin Uba (eds.). 2016. *The Consequences of Social Movements*. Cambridge, UK: Cambridge University Press.

Castells, Manuel. 2015. *Networks of Outrage and Hope: Social Movements in the Internet Age*, 2nd ed. Cambridge, UK: Polity Press.

Císař, Ondřej, and Jiří Navrátil. 2017. 'Polanyi, Political Economic Opportunity Structure and Protest: Capitalism and Contention in the Post-Communist Czech Republic.' *Social Movement Studies* 16(1): 82–100.

Connolly, William E. 1993. *The Terms of Political Discourse*, 3rd ed. Oxford, UK: Blackwell.

Conway, Janet. 2003. 'Civil Resistance and the Diversity of Tactics in the Anti-Globalization Movement: Problems of Violence, Silence, and Solidarity in Activist Politics.' *Osgoode Hall Law Journal* 41: 505–530.

Cox, Laurence, and Alf Gunvald Nilsen. 2014. *We Make Our Own History: Marxism and Social Movements in the Twilight of Neoliberalism*. London: Pluto Press.

Crossley, Nick. 2002. *Making Sense of Social Movements*. Buckingham, UK: Open University Press.

   2003. 'From Reproduction to Transformation: Social Movement Fields and the Radical Habitus.' *Theory, Culture & Society* 20(6): 43–68.

Cumbers, Andy, Paul Routledge, and Corinne Nativel. 2008. 'The Entangled Geographies of Global Justice Networks.' *Progress in Human Geography* 32(2): 183–201.

Davenport, Christian. 2007. *State Repression and the Domestic Democratic Peace*, 1st ed. Cambridge Studies in Comparative Politics. Cambridge, UK: Cambridge University Press.

De Angelis, M. 2005. 'PR like PRocess! Strategy from the Bottom-U.' *Ephemera* 5(2): 193–204.

Death, Carl. 2010. 'Counter-Conducts: A Foucauldian Analytics of Protest.' *Social Movement Studies* 9(3): 235–251.

Della Porta, Donatella. 2006. *Globalization from Below: Transnational Activists and Protest Networks*. Minneapolis, MN: University of Minnesota Press.

   2015. *Social Movements in Times of Austerity: Bringing Capitalism Back into Protest Analysis*. Cambridge, UK: Polity.

Diani, Mario. 1992. 'Analysing Social Movement Networks.' In Mario Diani and Ron Eyerman (eds.), *Studying Collective Action* (pp. 107–136). London: Sage.

   1996. 'Linking Mobilization Frames and Political Opportunities: Insights from Regional Populism in Italy.' *American Sociological Review* 61(6): 1053–1069.

   2000. 'Simmel to Rokkan and Beyond: Toward a Network Theory of "New" Social Movements.' *European Journal of Social Theory* 3(4): 387–406.

Doherty, Brian, and Graeme Hayes. 2012. 'Tactics, Traditions and Opportunities: British and French Crop-Trashing Actions in Comparative Perspective.' *European Journal of Political Research* 51(4): 540–562.

Doherty, Brian, Alex Plows, and Derek Wall. 2003. '"The Preferred Way of Doing Things": The British Direct Action Movement.' *Parliamentary Affairs* 56(4): 669–686.

Duyvendak, Jan Willem, and James M. Jasper (eds.). 2015. *Players and Arenas: The Interactive Dynamics of Protest*, 1st ed. Amsterdam: Amsterdam University Press.

Edwards, Gemma. 2014a. *Social Movements and Protest*. Cambridge, UK: Cambridge University Press.

   2014b. 'Infectious Innovations? The Diffusion of Tactical Innovation in Social Movement Networks, the Case of Suffragette Militancy.' *Social Movement Studies* 13(1): 48–69.

Eisinger, Peter K. 1973. 'The Conditions of Protest Behavior in American Cities.' *American Political Science Review* 67(1): 11–28.

Fillieule, Olivier, and Guya Accornero (eds.). 2016. *Social Movement Studies in Europe: The State of the Art*. New York: Berghahn Books.

Fligstein, Neil, and Doug McAdam. 2011. 'Toward a General Theory of Strategic Action Fields.' *Sociological Theory* 29(1): 1–26.

Fominaya, Cristina Flesher. 2010. 'Creating Cohesion from Diversity: The Challenge of Collective Identity Formation in the Global Justice Movement*.' *Sociological Inquiry* 80(3): 377–404.

  2014. *Social Movements and Globalization*. Basingstoke, UK: Palgrave Macmillan.

Freeman, Jo, and Victoria Johnson (eds.). 1999. *Waves of Protest: Social Movements since the Sixties*. Lanham, MD: Rowman & Littlefield Publishers, Inc.

Gamson, William A. 1989. *The Strategy of Social Protest*. 2nd rev ed. Belmont, CA: Wadsworth Publishing Co Inc.

Gamson, William A., and David S. Meyer. 1996. 'Framing Political Opportunity.' In Doug McAdam, John D. McCarthy, and Meyer N. Zald (eds.), *Comparative Perspectives on Social Movements: Political Opportunity, Mobilisation Structures and Cultural Framings* (pp. 275–290). Cambridge, UK: Cambridge University Press.

Gillan, Kevin. 2006. 'Meaning in Movement. An Ideational Analysis of Sheffield-Based Protest Networks Contesting Globalisation and War.' PhD thesis, University of Sheffield. http://kevingillan.info/tag/thesis

  2008a. 'Diverging Attitudes to Technology and Innovation in Anti-War Movement Organisations.' In Tapio Häyhtiö and Jarmo Rinne (eds.), *Net Working/ Networking: Citizen Initiated Politics*. Tampere: Tampere University Press.

  2008b. 'Understanding Meaning in Movements: A Hermeneutic Approach to Frames and Ideologies.' *Social Movement Studies* 7(3): 247–63.

  2017. 'Review Essay: 2010+: The Rejuvenation of New Social Movement Theory?' *Organization* 24(2): 271–74.

Gillan, Kevin, Jenny Pickerill, and Frank Webster. 2008. *Anti-War Activism: New Media and Protest in the Information Age*. New Security Challenges. Basingstoke, UK: Palgrave Macmillan.

Giugni, Marco. 1998. 'Was It Worth the Effort? The Outcomes and Consequences of Social Movements.' *Annual Review of Sociology* 24: 371–393.

Giugni, Marco, Doug McAdam, and Charles Tilly. 1999. *How Social Movements Matter: Past Research, Present Problems, Future*. Minneapolis, MN: University of Minnesota Press.

Graeber, David. 2014. *The Democracy Project: A History, a Crisis, a Movement*. London: Penguin.

Griffin, M. 2002. 'Globalization and Its Critics. An Examination of the "Anti-Globalization" Movement.' In R. C. Meier-Walser and P. Stein (eds.), *Globalisierung und Perspektiven Internationaler Verantwortlichkeit*. Baden-Baden:NOMOS.

Haenfler, Ross, Brett Johnson, and Ellis Jones. 2012. 'Lifestyle Movements: Exploring the Intersection of Lifestyle and Social Movements.' *Social Movement Studies* 11(1): 1–20.

Haluza-DeLay, Randolph. 2008. 'A Theory of Practice for Social Movements: Environmentalism and Ecological Habitus.' *Mobilization: An International Quarterly* 13(2): 205–218.

Haydu, Jeffrey. 1998. 'Making Use of the Past: Time Periods as Cases to Compare and as Sequences of Problem Solving 1.' *American Journal of Sociology* 104(2): 339–371.

Haydu, Jeffrey, and Tad Skotnicki. 2016. 'Three Layers of History in Recurrent Social Movements: The Case of Food Reform.' *Social Movement Studies* 15(4): 345–360.

Hetland, Gabriel, and Jeff Goodwin. 2013. 'The Strange Disappearance of Capitalism from Social Movement Studies.' In Colin Barker, Laurence Cox, John Krinsky, and Alf Gunvald Nilsen (eds.), *Marxism and Social Movements* (pp. 83–102). Leiden: Brill.

Hutter, Swen. 2014. *Protesting Culture and Economics in Western Europe: New Cleavages in Left and Right Politics*. Minneapolis. MN: University of Minnesota Press.

Josselin, Daphné. 2007. 'From Transnational Protest to Domestic Political Opportunities: Insights from the Debt Cancellation Campaign.' *Social Movement Studies* 6(1): 21.

Juris, Jeffrey S. 2005. 'The New Digital Media and Activist Networking within Anti-Corporate Globalization Movements.' *Annals of the American Academy of Political and Social Science* 597 (January): 189–208.

2008. *Networking Futures: The Movements against Corporate Globalization*. Durham, NC: Duke University Press.

Keraghel, C., and J. Sen. 2004. 'Explorations in Open Space. The World Social Forum and Cultures of Politics.' *International Social Science Journal* 56(4): 483–493.

Kitschelt, Herbert. 1986. 'Political Opportunity Structures and Political Protest: Anti-Nuclear Movements in Four Democracies.' *British Journal of Political Science* 16(1): 57–85.

Klandermans, Bert. 1992. 'The Social Construction of Protest and Multiorganizational Fields.' In Aldon D. Morris and Carol McClurg Mueller (eds.), *Frontiers in Social Movement Theory* (pp. 77–103). New Haven, CT: Yale University Press.

Koopmans, Ruud. 2004. 'Protest in Time and Space: The Evolution of Waves of Contention.' In David A. Snow, Sarah A. Soule, and H. Kriesi (eds.), *The Blackwell Companion to Social Movements* (pp. 19–46). Oxford, UK: Blackwell.

Koopmans, Ruud, and Paul Statham. 1999. 'Political Claims Analysis: Integrating Protest Event and Political Discourse Approaches.' *Mobilization: An International Quarterly* 4(2): 203–221.

Krinsky, John, and Nick Crossley. 2014. 'Social Movements and Social Networks: Introduction.' *Social Movement Studies* 13(1): 1–21.

Krinsky, John, and Ann Mische. 2013. 'Formations and Formalisms: Charles Tilly and the Paradox of the Actor.' *Annual Review of Sociology* 39(1): 1–26.

Maeckelbergh, Marianne. 2009. *The Will of the Many: How the Alterglobalisation Movement Is Changing the Face of Democracy*, 1st ed. London; New York: Pluto Press.

2011. 'Doing Is Believing: Prefiguration as Strategic Practice in the Alterglobalization Movement.' *Social Movement Studies: Journal of Social, Cultural and Political Protest* 10(1): 1–20.

Markoff, John. 2015. 'Historical Analysis and Social Movement Research.' In Donatella della Porta, Mario Diani, and Klaus Eder (eds.), *The Oxford Handbook of Social Movements* (pp. 68–85). Oxford, UK: Oxford University Press.

Martínez-Arboleda, Antonio. 2016. 'Podemos and the 15 M Language Community.' *New Politics* 15(4): 99–107.

Masclet, Camille. 2016. 'Examining the Intergenerational Outcomes of Social Movements: The Case of Feminist Activists and Their Children.' In Lorenzo Bosi, Marco Giugni, and Katrin Uba (eds.), *The Consequences of Social Movements*. Cambridge, UK: Cambridge University Press.

McAdam, Doug. 1982. *Political Process and the Development of Black Insurgency,
1930–1970*. Chicago, IL: University of Chicago Press.

McAdam, Doug, and Sidney Tarrow. 2011. 'Introduction: Dynamics of Contention Ten Years
On.' *Mobilization: An International Quarterly* 16(1): 1–10.

McAdam, Doug, Sidney Tarrow, and Charles Tilly. 2001. *Dynamics of Contention*.
Cambridge, UK: Cambridge University Press.

McCaffrey, D., and J. Keys. 2000. 'Competitive Framing Processes in the Abortion Debate:
Polarization-Vilification, Frame Saving and Frame Debunking.' *Sociological
Quarterly* 41(1): 41–61.

McCammon, Holly J., Soma Chaudhuri, Lyndi Hewitt, et al. 2008. 'Becoming Full Citizens:
The U.S. Women's Jury Rights Campaigns, the Pace of Reform, and Strategic
Adaptation.' *American Journal of Sociology* 113(4): 1104–1147.

McCarthy, John D., and Mayer N. Zald. 1977. 'Resource Mobilization and Social
Movements: A Partial Theory.' *American Journal of Sociology* 82(6): 1212–1241.

Melucci, Alberto. 1989. *Nomads of the Present. Social Movements and Individual Needs in
Contemporary Society*. London: Century Hutchinson.

1996. *Challenging Codes – Collective Action in the Information Age*. Cambridge, UK:
Cambridge University Press.

Motta, Renata. 2015. 'Transnational Discursive Opportunities and Social Movement Risk
Frames Opposing GMOs.' *Social Movement Studies* 14(5): 576–595.

Nicholls, Walter, and Justus Uitermark. 2015. 'Wildfire Movements Crashing on the Local
Trenches: A Comparison of Occupy Los Angeles and Occupy Amsterdam.' In
Nahide Konak and Rasim Özgür Dönmez (eds.), *Waves of Social Movement
Mobilizations in the Twenty-First Century: Challenges to the Neo-Liberal World
Order and Democracy* (pp. 115–128). Lanham, MD: Lexington Books.

Notes from Nowhere. 2003. *We Are Everywhere: The Irresistible Rise of Global
Anticapitalism*. London: Verso.

Opp, Karl-Dieter. 2009. *Theories of Political Protest and Social Movements:
A Multidisciplinary Introduction, Critique, and Synthesis*. London: Routledge.

Petras, J. 1999. *The Left Strikes Back: Class Conflict in the Age of Neoliberalism*. Boulder,
CO: Westview Press.

Piazza, Gianni, and Valentina Genovese. 2016. 'Between Political Opportunities and Strategic
Dilemmas: The Choice of "Double Track" by the Activists of an Occupied Social
Centre in Italy.' *Social Movement Studies* 15(3): 290–304.

Pickerill, J. 2007. 'Autonomy Online: Indymedia and Practices of Alter-Globalisation.'
Environment and Planning A 39: 2668–2684.

Pierson, Paul. 2004. *Politics in Time: History, Institutions, and Social Analysis*. Princeton, NJ:
Princeton University Press.

Piven, Frances Fox, and Richard A. Cloward. 1979. *Poor People's Movements: Why They
Succeed, How They Fail*. New York: Random House Inc.

Quaranta, Mario. 2016. 'Protesting in "Hard Times": Evidence from a Comparative Analysis of
Europe, 2000–2014.' *Current Sociology* 64(5): 736–756. DOI:0011392115602937.

Ragin, Charles C. 1992. '"Casing" and the Process of Social Inquiry.' In Charles C. Ragin and
Howard S. Becker (eds.), *What Is a Case?* (pp. 217–234). Cambridge, UK:
Cambridge University Press.

Rootes, Christopher A. 1997. 'Environmental Movements and Green Parties in Western and
Eastern Europe.' In M. R. Redclift and G. Woodgate (eds.), *The International*

Handbook of Environmental Sociology (pp. 319–346). Cheltenham, UK: Edward Elgar.

Rucht, Dieter. 2016. 'Conclusions: Social Movement Studies in Europe: Achievements, Gaps, and Challenges.' In Olivier Fillieule and Guya Accornero (eds.), *Social Movement Studies in Europe: The State of the Art* (pp. 456–487). New York: Berghahn Books.

Saunders, Clare. 2008. 'Double-Edged Swords? Collective Identity and Solidarity in the Environment Movement.' *British Journal of Sociology* 59(2): 227–253.

Schnews. 2004. *Schnews at Ten: A Decade of Party and Protest*. London: Calvert Press.

Schurman, R. 2004. 'Fighting "Frankenfoods": Industry Opportunity Structures and the Efficacy of the Anti-Biotech Movement in Western Europe.' *Social Problems* 51 (2): 243–268.

Smith, Jackie, Ellen Reese, Scott Byrd, and Elizabeth Smythe. 2015. *Handbook on World Social Forum Activism*. London: Routledge.

Snow, David A., Robert D. Benford, Holly McCammon, Lyndi Hewitt, and Scott Fitzgerald. 2014. 'The Emergence, Development, and Future of the Framing Perspective: 25+ Years since "Frame Alignment."' *Mobilization: An International Quarterly* 19(1): 23–46.

Snow, David A., E. Burke Rochford, Steven K. Worden, and Robert D. Benford. 1986. 'Frame Alignment Processes, Micromobilization, and Movement Participation.' *American Sociological Review* 51(4): 464–481.

Steinberg, M. W. 1998. 'Tilting the Frame: Considerations on Collective Action Framing from a Discursive Turn.' *Theory and Society* 27: 845–872.

Tarrow, Sidney. 1998. *Power in Movement: Social Movements and Contentious Politics*, 2nd ed. Cambridge, UK: Cambridge University Press.

Taylor, Verta. 1989. 'Social Movement Continuity: The Women's Movement in Abeyance.' *American Sociological Review* 54(5): 761–775.

Tilly, Charles. 1985. 'Models and Realities of Popular Collective Action.' *Social Research* 52 (4): 717–747.

    1986. *The Contentious French: Four Centuries of Popular Struggle*. Cambridge, MA: Harvard University Press.

    1999. 'Conclusion: From Interactions to Outcomes in Social Movements.' In Marco Giugni, Doug McAdam, and Charles Tilly (eds.), *How Social Movements Matter* (pp. 253–270). Minneapolis, MN: University of Minnesota Press.

Tilly, Charles, and Sidney Tarrow. 2007. *Contentious Politics*. Boulder, CO: Paradigm.

Tilly, Charles, and Lesley J. Wood. 2015. *Social Movements 1768–2012*, 3rd ed. London: Routledge.

Tonge, Jon. 1994. 'The Anti-Poll Tax Movement: A Pressure Movement?' *Politics* 14(3): 93–99.

Touraine, Alain. 1981. *The Voice and the Eye*. Cambridge, UK: Cambridge University Press.

    1988. *Return of the Actor: Social Theory in Postindustrial Society*. Minneapolis, MN: University of Minnesota Press.

    2002. 'The Importance of Social Movements.' *Social Movement Studies* 1(1): 89–95.

Walgrave, Stefaan, and Joris Verhulst. 2009. 'Government Stance and Internal Diversity of Protest: A Comparative Study of Protest against the War in Iraq in Eight Countries.' *Social Forces* 87(3): 1–33.

Walton, John K., and David Seddon. 2008. *Free Markets and Food Riots: The Politics of Global Adjustment*. Hoboken, NJ: John Wiley & Sons.

Williams, Matthew S. 2016. 'Strategic Innovation in US Anti-Sweatshop Movement.' *Social Movement Studies* 15(3): 277–289.

Williams, Rhys H. 2004. 'The Cultural Contexts of Collective Action: Constraints, Opportunities and the Symbolic Life of Social Movements.' In David A. Snow and Sarah A. Soule (eds.), *The Blackwell Companion to Social Movements* (pp. 91–115). Oxford, UK: Blackwell.

Wolfson, Todd. 2014. *Digital Rebellion: The Birth of the Cyber Left*. Urbana, IL: University of Illinois Press.

Wood, Lesley J. 2012. *Direct Action, Deliberation, and Diffusion: Collective Action after the WTO Protests in Seattle*. Cambridge, UK: Cambridge University Press.

    2014. *Crisis and Control: The Militarization of Protest Policing*. London: Pluto Press.

Yates, Luke. 2015a. 'Everyday Politics, Social Practices and Movement Networks: Daily Life in Barcelona's Social Centres.' *The British Journal of Sociology* 66(2): 236–258.

    2015b. 'Rethinking Prefiguration: Alternatives, Micropolitics and Goals in Social Movements.' *Social Movement Studies* 14(1): 1–21.

21 Immigration

Ewa Morawska

During the last half-century the study of international migration has become an academic specialization of its own, first in North America, then in Europe, and most recently and still in the making, also in Asia and Africa. With its rapid expansion, the study of people's cross-border travels and their subsequent accommodation in the receiver societies has developed its own field-specific problem agendas, theories, meetings, specialized journals, and research networks. It has also fragmented into several subfields, such as economic migration, family-reunification movement, educational travels, refugee flights, criminal (human trafficking and terrorism) migration, international tourism of different kinds (pastime tourism, health tourism, voluntourism), and lifestyle migration. In this essay I review the main concepts and theories informing 'mainstream' social-science research on immigration, that is, economic, political-economic, educational, and family-reunification cross-border population movements. Reflecting the current problem agenda in this field of study, the considered issues include: (i) most numerous and systematically elaborated, theories of international population movement; (ii) different models of immigrants' and their offspring's assimilation into the host society vs. retention of ethnicity, and the current debate concerning the so-called super-diversity and multiculturalism of present-day societies with their implications for newcomers' adaptation; and (iii) concepts and debates concerning immigrants' and their offspring's transnationalism and its implications for their assimilation (integration) into the host society.

International Migration

Reflecting the enduring division in mainstream social-science theorizing between explanatory frameworks focused on micro-level and those emphasizing macro-level causal mechanisms of the examined issues, the so-called classical theories of international migration have replicated this micro–macro gap. This section consists of three parts. I first present the main premises/arguments of the early, micro-, and macro-level models of international migration. In the third part I offer an overview of recent theories of international migration that bridge the micro–macro gap in accounting for this phenomenon.

433

Micro-Level Theories

The earliest of this type of theory of international migration has been the neoclassical economics or rational choice model founded on the premise of individuals' rational choice in pursuing their goals (Sjastad, 1962; Todaro, 1976, 1989). It was designed to account for economic/wage-seeking cross-border population movements. In this approach, individual rational actors decide (or not) to migrate because a cost–benefit calculation leads them to expect a positive (or negative) return, primarily monetary but also in terms of employment opportunities, from the movement. Potential migrants estimate the costs and benefits of moving to alternative international locations and migrate to where the expected net rewards are greatest over some time horizon. In this model, aggregate migration flows between countries are simple sums of individual moves undertaken on the basis of individual cost–benefit calculations.

A more recent variant of microeconomic model, human capital theory, also primarily focused on economic migrations, views the likelihood of international movement as dependent on such components of individual capital as age, gender, education, skill, experience, and marital status, as well as on personality features such as ambition to succeed and 'entrepreneurial spirit' or a willingness to take risks by changing language, culture, and social habitat (Boeri et al., 2012; Dierx, 1988). The human capital theory holds international migration to be selective, drawing out people with certain socio-demographic and personal characteristics. Because international migrants are positively selected with respect to their human capital, the theory holds, these transnational relocations create a 'brain drain' from sending countries, which cannot meet the income and career expectations of their highly skilled elites.

The new economics-of-migration model challenges the basic premise of the micro-level theories that hold that migration decisions are made by isolated individual actors. Rather, advocates of the new economic of migration model argue, migration/non-migration decisions are made by larger units of related people – typically families or households – in which people act collectively not only to maximize expected returns from undertaken actions, but also to minimize risks and to loosen constraints associated with a variety of potential failures, not only those in the labour market (Katz and Stark, 1986; Stark, 1984, 1991; Taylor, 1986). Thus, families, households, or other culturally defined units of production and consumption are the *locus classicus* of the causal mechanisms of international migration and, as such, the appropriate units of analysis for migration research, not the autonomous individuals. Wage differentials are not the only or even the necessary condition for cross-border movement of such units' members as they collectively try to minimize the overall risks/maximize rewards in terms of their group's well-being. Although originally created to account for economic/wage-seeking migrations, the new economics theory and, specifically, its premise of the social nature of migration decisions, has also been used to account for political, educational, and family-reunification population movements.

Unlike the previously considered theories of international migration which focus, usually implicitly, on the mechanisms triggering cross-border population flows, the social network approach concerns the factors that sustain rather than initiate people's transnational travels (Gurak and Caces, 1992; Hugo, 1981; Taylor, 1986). In models falling into this category, migration networks are understood in two ways. First and most commonly, they denote transnational interpersonal connections that link those at home with migrants in destination countries through ties of kinship, friendship, and mutual obligations stemming from the shared community of origin. In the second meaning – alternately referred to as the institutional theory of international migration – the term denotes formal or institutional (ethnic churches and associations, immigrant travel, credit, and counselling agencies and, broader in scope, host-country institutions catering to immigrants) networks of information and assistance that emerge as an outcome of the ongoing migratory processes.

The network/institutional theories hold that the existence of such information and assistance networks/institutions, otherwise called social capital, significantly increases the likelihood of continued international migration between places of origin and destination. To emphasize the autonomous effect of migration networks/support institutions in sustaining cross-border movement, the advocates of the network/institutional theories point out that whereas these international population flows are triggered by adverse macroeconomic or political conditions, they usually continue even when the circumstances that activated them considerably improve, as long as the translocal support networks/agencies sustaining them make it possible for those interested in moving to do so without difficulties. Like the new economics-of-migration model, the network/institutional theories of the persistence of international migration have been used to account for different types of transnational population movements. The assessment of micro-level models of international migration presented below is limited to their main theoretical premises and arguments (for an evaluation of these theories' empirical testability, see Massey et al., 1993).

The uncontested strength of micro-level theories of international migration, especially the rational choice and human capital models, is their recognition of the causality of human actors in decisions regarding transborder movement. Their weaknesses, however, prevail over their merits. The basic criticism of all these micro-level models has been twofold: their insufficient attention to the macro-level contexts shaping international migration on the one hand, and, on the other, their single-factor explanatory schemes, which are insufficient, it has been argued, to account for the complexity of the mechanisms triggering as well as sustaining transnational population movements. Regarding, specifically, the rational choice model, its very premise – that is, rational calculation or the maximization of profit as the mobilizer of migration – has been challenged by arguments that, first, not all potential migrants have equal and unlimited access to relevant information on the basis of which to make well-grounded decisions about the move (or non-move). Second and particularly important has been the criticism of the rational choice model's limited definition of rationality understood exclusively in instrumental terms without the recognition of other types of rational thinking, such as, for example, Weberian value-rationality as a mediator of decision making regarding migration. Obviously apt, this criticism can also serve to motivate (im)migration scholars to expand the definition and elaborate theoretically the notion of rational choice as the/a mechanism triggering/sustaining people's transnational travels.

The explanatory framework proposed by the human capital theory has drawn criticism for its lack of acknowledgement of the culturally specific and variable human capital values and, therefore, for using a basic unit of analysis that is hardly comparable across time and space. The only general prediction derived from the human capital model, its critics complain, is that human capital is somehow related to the likelihood of international migration, but the intensity and direction of this relationship remain unspecified.

The new economics-of-migration model, appreciated for its breaking with the individual-in-the-social-vacuum treatment of the migration issue, has been nevertheless challenged by scholars working on economic/wage-seeking cross-border population flows for neglecting to isolate the influence of sender-locality market imperfections (the necessary context of pro-migration family decisions) from other potentially contributing factors such as expected employment and income in the destination.

The main contribution of support network/institutional theories of cross-border population movements has been their recognition of international migration as a process extended over time and of its different phases requiring different explanations, accompanied by an attempt to account for one of them, the continuation of migratory flows. Two limitations of these theories have been pointed out in the subject literature. First, their fragmentary account of the migration process, focusing only on its sustaining phase; and second and more detrimental to these models, their asserted rather than demonstrated – theoretically or empirically – claim that interpersonal networks and/or institutional agencies of information and assistance indeed represent the most powerful predictors of transnational movement of people.

Macro-Level Theories

As in the section dealing with micro-level theories, this assessment of macro-level models of international migration presents their premises and basic arguments followed by identification of the main theoretical strengths and weaknesses of these explanatory frameworks (Massey et al., 1993 provide an evaluation of these theories' empirical testability).

The oldest among macro-level theories of international migration, the neoclassical economics or push-and-pull model, was originally developed to explain labour migration in the process of economic development (Harris and Todaro, 1970; Lewis, 1954; Ranis and Fei, 1961). Advocates of this model view international population flows as generated by macro-level disequilibria between regions/countries in the supply of and demand for labour and the resulting wage differences these imbalances create. The 'push' forces operate in the economically un(der)developed areas affected by oversupply of labour and low wages, sending people in search of livelihoods. The 'pull' forces operate in the economically more developed areas where the labour demand and wages are higher, attracting migrants pushed out of their economically depressed regions/countries. The push and pull model assumes that international labour migrations will, over time, equalize the forces of economic growth between regions/countries that display economic imbalances. After the departure of sufficient numbers of labour migrants raises wages in the sending areas, and after wages are lowered in receiving areas as the result of migrants' joining the labour market, international migration between these regions/countries is expected to cease.

Although it also focuses on macroeconomic mechanisms of transnational labour migration, the segmented- (also known as dual-) labour market theory (Piore, 1979) differs from the push-and-pull model in two important aspects. First, it does not assume that the relocation of people from less to more developed regions will balance out the world's economic disequilibria over time. And second, it views international labour migration as primarily demand- (or 'pull') based, responding to the structural needs of the world's contemporary highly developed economies. These structural needs, founded on the inherent duality between capital and labour in highly developed capitalist economies, stem from the bifurcation of the economically advanced regions/countries into the capital-intensive primary sectors offering high-skilled, well-paid jobs with good advancement opportunities, and labour-intensive secondary sectors with expendable, low-paid, unskilled jobs. The continued demand for low-skill and dispensable labour in secondary sectors of the economies of advanced regions/countries is satisfied by immigrants from un(der)developed parts of the world recruited by the receiver firms; desperate to earn the basic livelihoods for themselves and their families, these immigrants accept such bottom-level jobs and substandard wages.

The last and most recent among macro-level models is the world-system theory of international migration (Petras, 1981; Sassen, 1988; Sklair, 1990). While it shares with the segmented-labour-market model the Marxism-inspired view of the world as characterized by a profound inequality in economic development, the world-system theory of cross-border population flows is theoretically more innovative than the dual-market one. Rather than linking the origins of international migration to the demands of segmented labour markets in economically advanced regions/countries, it holds that these transnational relocations of people are generated by the structure of expanding global capitalism. Global capitalism is conceived of as the interrelated whole composed of the unequal parts referred to, according to the founder of the general world-system theory, Immanuel Wallerstein (1974), as the economically advanced core (North-West or NW) and the un(der)developed periphery (South-East or SE), linked by the exploitation by the former of the resources and labour of the latter parts of world capitalist market. Reflecting this unequal global economic relationship, the bulk of international labour migration moves in a compass direction, from SE un(der)developed to NW (advanced) parts of the world and, in within this pattern, towards the so-called global cities or the command centres of global capitalism. 'The international flow of labour follows international flows of goods and capital, but in the opposite direction. Capitalist investment foments changes that create an uprooted mobile population in (semi-)peripheral countries while simultaneously forging strong material and cultural links with core countries, leading to transnational movement' – Massey et al. (1998: 41) aptly summarize the main argument of the world-system theory of international migration.

While micro-level theories of international migration have been appreciated for their recognition of the role of human actors in this process and at the same time criticized for their negligence of macro-structural factors that generate and sustain people's cross-border travels, the macro-level models attracted the opposite evaluations: praised for the acknowledgement of the causal importance of structural contexts of transnational population flows, they have been challenged on their inattention to the role of human actors and, generally, micro-contexts in triggering/ sustaining these movements. Like micro-level theories, their macro counterparts have also been criticized for single-factor explanatory frameworks, in this case, a tendency towards economic reductionism.

In terms of specific contributions and limitations of the macro-level theories presented here, by focusing the analysis on structural – labour market – forces, the push-and-pull model, the earliest of macro-level theories, provided a new and important perspective on international migration that had been traditionally explained in individualistic terms. This contribution should be acknowledged. It has, however, been correctly criticized for treating wage disparities by themselves, taken out of the broader context of the economic dynamics of the involved regions and, in particular, for the disproven assumption that international labour migrations lead to the balancing of the forces of economic growth in different regions.

The major strength of segmented-labour-market theory has been, besides its emphasis on the structural mechanisms of international migration, the recognition of the context-dependent and, thus, changing circumstances of industrial capitalism or, of concern here, its evolution from the industrial to post-industrial phase characterized by the dual-labour market and the consequences of this transition for the transnational movement of labour. By recognizing the context-dependency of the constitutive forces of capitalism, the model also implicitly acknowledges the historical: the time- and place-specific nature of the mechanisms responsible for international migration. In addition to misgivings concerning its narrow applicability to labour migrations, three main weaknesses of the segmented-market theory of cross-border labour movements have been noted. One of them is its unjustified focus on the demand ('pull') side of the transnational population flows with inadequate attention to the role of the supply ('push') circumstances co-determining this movement. The second weakness is the model's premise of two separate (primary and secondary) sectors of employment, which overlooks the existence of growing informal sectors of post-industrial economies on the one hand, and, on the other, ethnic economic enclaves in large, concentrated ethnic communities that employ significant numbers of immigrants and offer security and advancement opportunities to a considerable number of them. Related to the above, the third criticism has challenged the segmented-labour-market theory's assumption that it is formal recruitment by receiver-country companies that leads most migrants to undertake their international travels by demonstrating the predominance of other (in-group) channels.

The world-system theory's innovative global approach to the analysis of the examined phenomena and its long-term 'processual' explanatory framework have been, in my opinion, its greatest contributions to theorizing international migration. Another strength of this model – the world-system theory in general and its application to international migration – has been its flexibility in modifying its claims in response to criticisms, and – importantly – its amenability to combining with theoretical approaches informed by other analytic priorities. Thus, criticized for their sole concern with the economic factors in shaping transnational population movements, the world-system theorists have allowed for macro-political (state-, region-, and global-scope) mechanisms to mobilize/ hinder and (re-)direct these travels – a 'creative' modification which permits, for example, accounting in the world-system political economy for the so-called *Gastarbeiter* migrations from SE to NW regions, in this case the United States and European Union, initiated and controlled by political institutions and legal arrangements. And, because of its broad scope or global framework, world-system theory can be used in combination with elements of micro-level social and individual models in deliberately multilevel accounts for the economic as well as political, educational, and family-reunification migrations.

Micro–Macro Theories

It has been exactly with the purpose of creating an encompassing theoretical framework that some immigration scholars have moved to bridge the micro–macro gap in accounting for transnational population movements – a concern that, again, reflects a similar trend to that of mainstream social theorizing at the turn of the current century. There have been thus far two such attempts: the cumulative causation theory and the structuration model of international migration.

The cumulative causation model (Massey et al., 1998) holds that distinct constellations of macro- and micro-level structural and individual factors first trigger and then sustain cross-border population flows. 'Causation is cumulative in that each act of migration alters the social context within which subsequent migration decisions are made, typically in ways that make additional movement more likely'(Massey et al., 1993: 452). Thus, the initiation of wage-seeking migratory flows is best accounted for by a combination of propositions from the following theories of international migration: world system (incorporation of un[der]developed parts of the world into the global capitalist system and the economic transformation and dislocation of people it generates in those regions); segmented labour market (demand for low-skill immigrant workers in post-industrial economies of core receiver societies); political economy (reflecting this demand, immigration policies of receiver governments); neo-classical economics (wage differentials between sending and receiving countries/regions stimulating periphery-to-core flows of labourers seeking better livelihoods); and the new economics of migration (sending households' calculated efforts to maximize their income by engaging in international labour markets).

The perpetuation of international migration is explained, in turn, by a combination of the propositions derived from the political-economy and segmented-labour-market models at the macro-level, and, at the micro-level, social-capital (network/institutional) theory positing the formation of informal and organized transnational information and assistance networks that facilitate people's cross-border travels. This multilevel mechanism perpetuating migration is further enhanced by the cumulative causation effect: over time, transnational movement from sender to receiver locations becomes more likely to be sustained by established support networks, increasing discrepancies in the distribution of income and material affluence in home-country sending communities, and by the 'culture of migration' created during continued transnational travels. Although in its original formulation the cumulative causation model has been constructed to account for wage-seeking cross-border movements, as it allows for the construction of different constellations of macro- and micro-level factors triggering and sustaining transnational population flows, it can also be used to account for different types of international migration.

Founded on a similar premise as that informing the cumulative causation theory, which holds that different constellations of both structural and individual circumstances play a role in shaping international migration, the structuration model of transnational population flows offers a more theoretically elaborated account of these processes (Morawska, 2001a). Like the general structuration theory, it posits the ongoing process of 'becoming' of human agency and (multilevel) societal structures which (re)constitute each other through mutual engagements. Structures, conceived of as more or less enduring patterns of social (including economic and political) relations and cultural formations (re)constituted through the everyday practice of social actors are plural in purposes, modes of operation, and dynamics. This multiplicity imbues them with the inherent tensions or even direct contradictions that create 'gaps' and 'loopholes' between different structural arrangements and, resulting from these imperfections, an inconsistent and mutable capacity to enable and constrain human agency. Human agency refers to everyday engagements with their structural environment by individuals whose pursuits are informed by the available 'cultural kits' or repertoires of basic guideposts for action and actual resources (knowledge, skills, positions in societal structures). These daily engagements can both reproduce and transform the surrounding structures through individuals' interactive responses to the problems posed by changing situations.

As they adjust their accustomed reactions and future-oriented projects to a practical assessment of the situations they find themselves in, human actors create and recreate different structures of social life. New situations, in particular, such as the prospects of international migration, enable actors to reinterpret the existing schemas and redesign the resources. Interpreted in this framework, immigrants' cross-border movement is not simply the product of structures nor of their agentic volitions but of the time- and place-specific contexts of the interactions between the two. The conceptualization of international migration as a structuration process can be summarized thusly. Whereas the long-term and immediate configurations and pressures of forces at the upper structural layers (global/regional/national economies and political-military arrangements) set the dynamic limits of the possible and impossible within which people act, it is at the level of their more proximate, local social surroundings that individuals evaluate their situations, define purposes, and undertake actions – in this case, cross-border travel – the intended and, often unintended consequences of which, in turn, affect these local-level and, over time, large-scope structures.

A joint micro–macro account of international migration and, in this framework, the identification of different constellations of structural and agentic factors shaping this movement depending on its phase, have been the most valuable contributions of the cumulative causation model. It does not, however, integrate the structural and agentic mechanisms it identifies into a theoretically coherent account of transnational population movement as a dynamic process of reconstituting over time causes and effects. The treatment of international migration as a structuration process improves on Massey et al.'s ground-laying work by elaborating analytically the categories of societal structures and human agency, and accommodating in one theoretical framework the reciprocal influences of migrants' purposeful activities and plural in kind, multilevel societal structures. And, because of its broad scope, the structuration model of international migration can be used to account for different kinds of transnational population movement. Reflecting the limitation of the 'mainstream' structuration theory, one of the main imperfections of this model in its application to transnational population movements has been its still-insufficient theoretical elaboration of the 'how' of the translation of human activities into societal structures. The other weakness – shared, for that matter, with all other theories of international migration – has been the structuration model's inattention to the inherently gendered nature of people's cross-border movement (for appeals, thus far unsuccessful, to engender international migration theories, see Hondagneu-Sotelo and Cranford, 1999; Morokvasic, 2011).

Assimilation

Two overlapping but not identical concepts – assimilation and integration – have been used in immigration studies to denote the process of newcomers' and their offspring's adaptation to the receiver society. Commonly used in Europe, the latter term refers to the process through which immigrants and their descendants gradually increase and eventually achieve parity with the natives in life chances (primarily educational and socio-economic) and representation/participation in the major public institutions (such as schools, workplaces, and government and its agencies) of the host society. More common in North American studies, the concept of assimilation is broader in scope in that it includes, besides socio-economic and civil-political aspects of the integration, sociocultural ones as well, that is: immigrants' and their offspring's acceptance into/participation in mainstream formal and informal social circles/networks; absorption of the receiver society's cultural values, life orientations, customs, and traditions; and the acquisition of the host-country national identity. Because it is more encompassing, and also because it has been the foundation of most of the available theoretical models proposed by the sociologists, this presentation focuses on the concepts/models of assimilation and, conceptualized in reference to it, ethnic resilience/pluralism (for a good selection of theoretical reflections on immigrants' and their descendants' civic-political integration into the host society, see Hochschild et al., 2013).

This section consists of two parts. I present, first, the classical, straight-line theory of assimilation and, next, three major directions in which it has been challenged: (i) conceptualization of immigrants' and their offspring's incorporation into the host society not as a linear-progressive development as in the classical model, but as a 'bumpy' process with turns and reverses contingent on the changing circumstances of the participating actors and their environment; (ii) replacement of the classical model's conceptualization of assimilation as the single-trajectory, upward main-stream socio-economic mobility of immigrants and their offspring, with a segmented, class- and race-contingent assimilation process with different outcomes; and (iii) a view of the assimilation process as transforming immigrants and their descendants as well as the host society itself, instead of the classical model's exclusive focus on changes experienced by the newcomers and their offspring. (For a representative selection of the classical and contemporary formulations of assimilation models, see Kivisto, 2005.) In the second part of the section, I present the classical and contemporary concepts of ethnic persistence/pluralism, and the current debate about the super-diversity of present-day societies and the possibility of a multicultural trajectory of immigrants' and their descendants' adaptation to such super-diverse environments.

Classical Straight-Line Model

The earliest straight-line model of assimilation, formulated in the 1920s by the Chicago school sociologists Robert Park and Ernest Burgess (1969 [1921]; see also Thomas and Znaniecki, 1927), posited the progressive, irreversible weakening, and ultimate disappearance of foreign cultural orientations and identities and social bonds of immigrants and their offspring as they 'melted' into the receiver (here, American) society, voluntarily adopting the latter's traits, identities, and commitments. This view of assimilation – later elaborated by W. Lloyd Warner and Leo Srole (1945) and Tamotsu Shibutani and Kian Kwan (1965), who specified the adaptation trajectories of different class and ethno-racial groups, and, in the canonical formulation, Milton Gordon (1964), who identified the necessary stages of integration all types of immigrants and their children go through – constituted the hegemonic model in immigration/ethnic studies in the United States through the 1960s.

'Bumpy' Assimilation Process

Replaced in the 1970s by a 'resilient ethnicity' perspective, the assimilation model fell out of use in American immigration/ethnic studies for about a decade and a half, to return in the 1990s in a different formulation as the multitrack process of a 'bumpy' (Gans, 1992) or non-linear incorporation of different types of immigrants and their descendants into the host society, allowing for variable degrees and aspects of similarities, differences, and 'boundary-crossing' among foreign and native-born groups, twists, (re)turns, and 'paradoxes' (Alba and Nee, 2003; Brubaker, 2003; Morawska, 1994; Rumbaut, 1997). The non-linear progress of assimilation has been ascribed to time- and place-contingent and, thus, shifting local and more remote circumstances, which immigrants and their offspring creatively negotiate.

Also founded on the premise of assimilation evolving in a multitrack, non-linear fashion have been the concepts of 'symbolic ethnicity' (Gans, 1979) and 'ethnic options' (Waters, 1990). They describe the situation of later-generation American-born (white) ethnics who are basically assimilated into the mainstream society in terms of economic position, social participation, cultural orientations and practices, and identities, but voluntarily 'pick and choose' from their ancestral traditions the elements which suit them. (As the originators of these concepts argued, the main purpose of opting for ethnic symbols as part of their carriers' identities was to maintain boundaries between their – white – groups and blacks and new immigrants of colour; but the notions of symbolic ethnicity and ethnic options can also be used to account for behaviours of later-generation members of mainstream society with immigrant origins which have other purposes: nostalgic, aesthetic, identity- or status-seeking.) While the concepts of symbolic ethnicity and ethnic options were coined to explain the choices of (some) otherwise well-integrated later-generation ethnics and, thus, have been presented under the theme of assimilation, to the extent that they describe the endurance of ethnic orientations and practices, they can also be also treated under 'ethnic pluralism' (see the section 'Ethnic Pluralism').

Segmented Assimilation

The segmented assimilation model was formulated by Alejandro Portes and Min Zhou (1993; also Portes and Rumbaut, 2001) to account for the experience of native-born, second-generation immigrants' offspring whose incorporation into the host society has evolved along three distinct trajectories rather than in the single, upward-into-the-white-mainstream, middle-class pattern posited by the classical assimilation theory. In addition to the mainstream white middle-class trajectory, a significant number of immigrants and their offspring, especially members of non-white ethnic minorities with limited human capital incorporate downward into the underclass in the secondary sector of the mainstream economy; while others, members of numerically large and residentially concentrated ethnic groups, remain in their ethnic-group enclaves, which provide not only employment but also opportunities for socio-economic advancement.

While it draws on the segmented-labour-market theory in explaining the structural mechanisms of incorporation of members of ethnic minorities into the host-country economy, the segmented assimilation model recognizes other, non-economic structural and individual factors in tracking people along different integration trajectories. By incorporating into different sectors of the receiver society's economic/class structure, advocates of this approach argue, immigrants and their descendants participate in different social circles and adopt different subcultures.

Transformative Effects of Assimilation

Another recent challenge to the classical model concerns its implicit understanding of assimilation as the transformation of identities, values, life orientations, and practices of immigrants and their offspring. A more adequate approach, it has been argued, is to conceive of assimilation as the process transforming *both* immigrants and their descendants and the host society through the ongoing reciprocal influences (for early advocates of this approach in the United States, see Crevecoeur, 1962 [1782]; Emerson, 1971 [1845]; contemporary formulations in Alba and Foner, 2015; Alba and Nee, 2003; Zolberg and Woon, 1999). The impact of immigrants/ethnics on the host society includes the emergence of new customs, consumer patterns, and self-representations. The Turkish doner kebab and Indian samosa have become popular mainstream foods in German and English towns, respectively, and – in the symbolic sphere – the idea of the American nation, which until the mid-twentieth century denoted white Anglo-Saxon Protestants, has since expanded to include members of other ethno-religious and racial groups.

By way of concluding this section, I would summarily evaluate as follows the assimilation models presented above. While the classical straight-line model has been convincingly discounted on several grounds, its premise of immigrants' and their offspring's gradual incorporation into the host society has proven by and large correct. The process of assimilation is conceived today as a multi-trajectory, non-linear development impacted by and impacting immigrants' and their offspring's human capital, socio-economic position(s), life orientations, and sociocultural practices as well as the local and macro-level socio-economic, cultural, and civic-political host-society arrangements. Varied, time- and place-specific combinations of bumpy, segmented, and two-way-effects explanatory approaches seem most promising for making sense of assimilation processes. They still require improvement however. To note just one persistent limitation of these models, as in the case of international migration theories, although there exists abundant empirical evidence of gender-specific patterns of certain aspects of immigrants' and their offspring's incorporation into the host society, all the different theories of assimilation remain genderless. More precisely, while each of the three perspectives challenging the classical model allows for the treatment of gender as a factor in channelling adaptation trajectories, unlike other basic societal dividers such as class and race, it has not thus far been treated as the integral part of a theoretical account of assimilation (on the need for such work, see Anthias, Kontos, and Morokvasic, 2013; Ehrenreich and Hochschild, 2002).

Ethnic Pluralism

In most formulations of this thesis (it is a proposition rather than a full-fledged theory), the retention by immigrants and their offspring of different aspects of their ethnic groups' traditions and commitments coexists with the process of their assimilation to the host society. The earliest pluralist propositions date back to the fierce debate in the early-twentieth-century United States about how to absorb the millions of 'culturally other' South and East European immigrants settling in the country. Some participants in this exchange, such as Randolph Bourne (1916), Horace Kallen (1915), or Louis Adamic (1940), viewed the diversity of people's lifestyles and ethnic subcultures as vital for the prosperity of a common American civilization (see Meyer, 2008 for a good review of the early pluralists' arguments discussed against the background of the Americanization debate). This approach was revived in a revised version in the mid-twentieth century, which noted earlier criticisms of the classical assimilation model and its replacement by the 'ethnic resilience' thesis (Gans, 1997; Glazer and Moynihan, 1963; Greeley, 1974). Two alternative accounts of the persistence of ethnicity were proposed: one of them conceived of ethnic attachments and identities as the primordial forces stemming from deeply rooted psychological and emotional needs, while the other, more popular among advocates of ethnic pluralism, treated these commitments as contingent on specific contexts or situationally mobilized/sustained. In a different version, the ethnic pluralism-cum-assimilation perspective has been represented by the notion of ethnicization understood as the process of mixing and blending from inside the ethnic groups of the old (country of origin) sociocultural patterns with the new customs and life orientations of the dominant host society (Sarna, 1978).

Most recent and often formulated/tested in the emergent collaboration between American and European immigration scholars has been a promising proposition to reconcile assimilation with ethnic pluralism, which derives, basically, from the 'bumpy' and multidirectional conceptualization of the former, but emphasizes the enduring coexistence of the two phenomena while at the same time debating the conditions which sustain/weaken the integrative values of the common society (Alba and Foner, 2015; *Ethnic and Racial Studies*, 2014; Glazer, 1997: 450). Like models of international migration and assimilation, the joint accounting for assimilation-cum-transnationalism has thus far been more class- and race- than gender-sensitive. Applying an encompassing structuration model as outlined in the previous section whose strength lies, precisely, in accommodating complexities, to the analysis of these multitrack, specific situation-contingent processes, might be promising.

Recognition of the enduring or even increasingly diversity of contemporary societies has been reflected in the current debate among immigration experts – here, the Europeans have led the way – centred around the recently coined notions of 'super-diversity' and 'multiculturalism'. Originating with Steven Vertovec (2007), the concept of super-diversity denotes not only the recognition of the ethno-religious aspect of multilevel social differentiation, to which increased transnational migratory flows significantly contribute, as the taken-for-granted feature of contemporary societies, but also an appreciation of this diversity as a 'constructive' force in the lives of their members (see the 38 [4] 2015 special issue of *Ethnic and Racial Studies* on super-diversity Ethnic and Racial Studies, 2015a).

Two different conceptualizations of the notion of multiculturalism have informed the quickly growing literature on this subject. In one of them, used by political sociologists and philosophers, and political scientists in general, multiculturalism refers to a set of civic-political programmes and their (mal)functioning in legal and institutional arrangements recognizing the existence of different ethnic/religious/

racial groups and their collective and individual-member civil rights (Kymlicka, 1996; Modood, 2007; Parekh, 2000). In the course of a debate (also in political and media forums) about the negative implications of thusly understood and implemented multiculturalism for the cohesion of a nation state fragmented into separate groups defined by the essentializing criteria of their ethnic/racial origins, the notion of 'interculturalism' was launched (for a review, see Bouchard, 2011) to denote the ongoing exchange among members of different groups/institutions, including host-country agencies. It was followed by a modification of the original concept of multiculturalism to account for the reciprocal engagement among people of different backgrounds on one hand and, on the other, to recognize the importance of 'a sense of whole' and 'the unifying potential of renegotiated inclusive national unity' (Meer and Modood, 2012: 190; Uberoi and Modood, 2015).

In the other conceptualization of multiculturalism, also referred to as 'conviviality' and popular among the anthropologist/ethnographer, urban geographer, and community- and cultural-sociologist students of this phenomenon, it denotes a set of orientations and practices guiding everyday intergroup relations (Nowicka and Vertovec, 2014; Vertovec, 2011; Wise and Velayutham, 2009). Discussions informed by this understanding of multiculturalism have primarily focused on the specification of conditions which facilitate or hinder amicable mutual perceptions and reciprocal engagements among members of different groups in local settings.

As super-diversity and multiculturalism have entered the lexicon of immigration studies, initial attempts have been made to (re-)consider assimilation in the context of these concepts' sociocultural implications. Thus, Thomas Faist (2009) and Paolo Boccagni (2015) propose to treat (super-) diversity as a mode of immigrants' and their descendants' incorporation, understood as the 'supportive recognition' of diversity by legal systems, policies, and public institutions of the receiver society. In a more encompassing, structures-and-actors approach, Peter Kivisto (2002) argues for the possibility of treating multiculturalism – understood in the first of the two meanings specified above – as a path of immigrants' and their offspring's civic integration through the joint engagement of host-society institutions and the collective and individual immigrants/ethnic actors themselves. None of these authors, however, offer theoretical elaborations of their propositions. This has been done by Ewa Morawska in her article entitled 'Multicultural Modes of Immigrants' Integration into the Host Society: Exploring the Proposition' (2018).

A multicultural trajectory of immigrants' integration, in Morawska's conceptualization, consists of four components founded on the base orientation of appreciation of diversity, yet varying in scope and intensity over time and situations: (i) symbolic identification with plural national/ethnic/religious groups resident in the host society and their traditions; (ii) internalization and practice of extrinsic (language, customs) and intrinsic (values, normative expectations, beliefs) components of cultures of different national/ethnic-religious groups resident in the host society; (iii) regular social engagement with members of different national/ethnic/religious groups resident in the host society in formal, semi-formal, and/or informal settings including neighbourhood public places such as streets, shops, pubs, and eateries; workplaces; kindergartens and schools; and homes and gardens; and (iv) civic commitment to/

responsibility for the well-being of the body politic of several national/ethnic/religious communities resident in the host society. Last and most important, emerging from the above processes is the involved actors' experience of the host country/locality of their residence as inherently diverse in people, languages, tastes, smells, and customs.

As the above understanding of a multicultural trajectory of immigrants' incorporation indicates, it is conceived in terms of diverse forms and 'contents' rather than as present-or-absent condition. It is, therefore, more adequate, Morawska argues, to think of it in the plural as multicultural trajectories rather than as a single-track development. Different components of these trajectories may also display different scopes and intensities due to the changing circumstances of immigrants' and their descendants' lives that alter their interest, perceptions, and everyday involvements. Also, importantly, because they take shape, persist, or are reconstituted through everyday felt, heard, tasted, and smelled intergroup relations, multicultural trajectories of incorporation into the host society evolve at the *local* level or in the concrete settings where people live, although the components of these adaptation processes may well include broader imagined communities such as the nation state. This proposition of multicultural modes of assimilation does not imply that these are *the* trajectories of present-day newcomers' integration into diverse receiver societies. Rather, it holds them to be contingent on the specific constellations of conducive circumstances which, drawing on the available studies of intercultural encounters in local settings, Morawska identifies. Although more elaborate than the earlier-noted parallel ideas, this conceptualization of multicultural trajectories of immigrants' and their offspring's assimilation is exploratory and awaits further analytic refinement.

Transnationalism

A vigorous academic industry has developed since the 1990s around the idea of transnationalism. It has attracted adherents among political scientists, international-relations and legal scholars, sociologists, and anthropologists and has already produced a crop of specialists in transnational cultural studies. All agree that the mass migrations of different kinds now criss-crossing the globe are an important, even central, agent in diffusing transnationalism. Expectedly, immigration scholars have actively participated in the debates about this phenomenon. Representatives of different disciplines among immigration scholars have assigned different meanings to the idea of transnationalism – a concept-cum-argument, rather than a coherent theory or set of theories. In particular, they have used different interpretations of the prefix trans.

Vertical and Horizontal Transnationalism

The first interpretation, common among political scientists, lawyers, and international-relations specialists, understands transnationalism as a shift beyond or, as it were, vertically over (rather than horizontally across) the accustomed territorial state-national memberships and national identities, and civil-political claims. This new realm inscribes more encompassing involvements and identities resting on higher-order universal humanity or human rights, supra-statal memberships and entitlements (evident, for example, in the European Union), and pan-ethnic or pan-religious solidarities (for example, Hispanic or Asian in the United States, or Muslim in Europe) which, argue the advocates of this interpretation, undermine the nation states' abilities to control and regulate activities within their borders (see Sassen, 1996; Soysal, 1994; for a critical discussion, Brubaker, 1996). The other interpretation of transnationalism – used by immigration sociologists, social geographers, and anthropologists, and the focus of this discussion – treats it as consisting of loyalties and engagements that stretch horizontally across state-national borders and link people and institutions in two or more nation states in diverse, multilayered patterns (Basch, Glick Schiller, and Szanton Blanc, 1994; Glick Schiller, 1996; Levitt, 2001; Smith and Guarnizo, 1998; also Faist, Fauser, and Reisenauer, 2013).

These transnational involvements, maintained through letters, internet, websites, phone calls, and personal visits, include immigrants' economic/financial investments in their home countries/locations such as remittances and business and communal investments; civic-political activities on behalf of the home countries, such as voting (where it is allowed) and group lobbying in the receiver and sender societies; and a plethora of sociocultural activities, such as sustained transnational management of family matters by the immigrants, cross-border friendships, import and consumption of home-country commodities, and reading of/listening to home-country media. While a number of these cross-border involvements are shared by immigrant men and women, some transnational pursuits are detectably gendered: for example, civic-political activities tend to be pursued by men, while care of families and maintenance of transnational community information networks falls into the domain of women. These transnational engagements on the part of immigrants display different intensities: regular or occasional, depending on their length of stay, socio-economic situation, and prospects in the host country, intentions (or not) to return home, position in the life cycle and family situation, and the presence/absence of mobilizing events in the home country (Guarnizo, Portes, and Haller, 2003). Regular and enduring transnational economic and civic-political investments of immigrants in their home-country localities bring about visible transformations of those places' consumer standards and lifestyles, business activities, the condition of the public infrastructure, and often also the level of civic mobilization on the part of the residents.

Transnationalism: Original Conceptualization and Subsequent Challenges

Introduced into the field of immigration studies by Linda Basch, Nina Glick Schiller, and Cristina Szanton Blanc in their now-canonical study entitled *Nations Unbound: Transnational Projects, Postcolonial Predicaments, and Deterritorialized Nation-States* (1994), the original formulation of ('horizontal') transnationalism can be summarized as follows. Due to the improved transportation and communication technologies and the related globalization of the world in the post-industrial era of capitalism, new transnational social spaces are created that transcend state-national boundaries linking émigrés with those who stayed behind in their home countries/ regions through economic, political, and sociocultural connections. These transnational connections sustain immigrants' home-country identities and commitments and, by implication, undermine their assimilation into the host national society. This conceptualization of transnationalism and its workings has since been challenged on three major accounts (for overviews, see Faist, Fauser, and Reisenauer, 2013; Kivisto, 2012).

Basch and collaborators' notion of transnationalism was premised on the idea that the surrounding social contexts and, within them, life orientations and practices of past and present immigrants are qualitatively different. Of concern here, they viewed immigrants of the past as detaching themselves from their homelands upon arrival in the receiver society; in contrast, due to the rapid globalization of the world fostered by the revolution in transportation and communication technologies, their contemporary successors, whom the authors named 'transmigrants', create and maintain dense cross-border links with their countries of origin. This representation of immigrants' transnationalism as a new phenomenon has been challenged by demonstrations of turn-of-the-twentieth-century East and South European immigrants in America having maintained multilevel, enduring connections with their home countries. Present-day immigrants' transnationalism, therefore, the challengers have argued, is not new but is, due to the changed circumstances in which it occurs, different from its counterpart in the past. On one hand, facilitated by advances in communication and transportation technologies, contemporary immigrants' transnationalism has significantly increased in scope and frequency and, on the other, resulting from more openness towards and tolerance of foreigners and their ethnic cultures in the public climate and legislation in present-day receiver societies, it has become public and assertive. In comparison, turn-of-the-twentieth-century immigrants, expected to melt into the mainstream host society as soon as possible, kept their transnational engagements in the 'closet' (Bryceson, 2002; Foner, 1997; Morawska, 2001b).

A second criticism has been directed at Basch et al.'s claim that immigrants' sustained participation in transnational social spaces undermines their assimilation into the host society. As empirical studies of different types of immigrants' cross-border involvements have demonstrated, such engagements do not necessarily hinder their assimilation, but can – and actually do – coexist with this process in different arrangements (see, e.g., Levitt, 2003; Morawska, 2003; Portes, 2001). A third and important challenge to the original formulation of the idea of transnationalism has been the issue of the endurance of those cross-border commitments – implied as permanent in Basch et al.'s argument about the deterritorialization of the nation state in the global era – beyond the immigrant generation. A number of studies of the identities and pursuits of second and later generations suggest that transnational practices decline in successive generations with the progressive mainstream – upward or downward – assimilation of their members (for the most persuasive recent argument on behalf of this thesis, see Waldinger, 2015). Still, evidence of the persistence of (even weakened) transnational connections among the offspring of immigrants in groups whose members draw material and/or symbolic benefits from such links indicate that the answer(s) to the question of their endurance/decline over time/across generations should be sought in terms of middle-range or time- or place-specific propositions, or those based on main societal dividers (class-, race-, or gender-specific), rather than general claims. (For the evidence and arguments, see Bauböeck and Faist, 2010; Levitt, 2001; Levitt and Waters, 2002; Smith, 2006; Smith and Guarnizo, 1998; and the special section of 38 (13) 2015 *Ethnic and Racial Studies* (2015b), entitled 'Towards a Systematic Understanding of Cross-Border Linkages'.)

Directed at the current state of the art in social-science studies of immigrant cross-border engagements, rather than Basch and collaborators' original conceptualization of this phenomenon, have been recent appeals for an extension of the understanding and analysis of transnational social spaces as affecting not only immigrants but also their host society. This postulate overlaps with the earlier-noted suggestion of broadening the study of assimilation to include the transformation of the receiver society under the impact of immigrants' adaptation. Thus far, however, these parallel initiatives have not been pursued in joint, systematic analyses beyond such general conceptual guideposts as the multi-sitedness and interconnectedness of (im)migration processes – and thus this is a challenge that still awaits work by immigration scholars. (On the need to consider the impact of immigrants' activities in transnational social spaces on the host-country localities they inhabit, and empirical evidence thereof in the labour markets and business cultures, civic-political agendas, and cultural orientations and practices, see Faist et al., 2013; and Morawska, 2014 for a more theorized attempt to interpret these effects in terms of glocalization processes.)

Last to note in this section is the ongoing debate among immigration scholars about the methodological implication of the recognition of the multi-sitedness of immigrants' assimilation into the host society and their involvements in the home one. Specifically, this debate has engaged advocates of abandoning what they call a 'methodological nationalism' of immigration studies or the replacement of nation-state-bound conceptualizations and analyses of migration-related phenomena with a multi-scalar, mobile perspective (Faist et al., 2013; Glick Schiller, 2010). Their opponents recognize immigrants' multiple anchoring in their home and host societies, but argue that the nation states still maintain considerable control over the processes of those cross-border travellers' assimilation and transnational engagements, and, therefore, should not be discarded from the analysis (Waldinger, 2015; see also a discussion of the pros and cons of these two arguments in the special section of *Ethnic and Racial Studies* of 38 [13] 2015 (2015b)). The debate is ongoing and the jury is still out, but my preference would be not to posit these two propositions as either/or alternatives, but, rather, to allow theoretically for both possibilities and test them in empirical studies in order to see in which time- and place-specific situations one or the other prevails.

References

Adamic, Louis. 1940. *From Many Lands*. New York: Harper & Brothers.

Alba, Richard, and Nancy Foner. 2015. *Strangers No More. Immigration and the Challenges of Integration in North America and Western Europe*. Princeton, NJ: Princeton University Press.

Alba, Richard, and Victor Nee. 2003. *Remaking the American Mainstream; Assimilation and Contemporary Immigration*. Cambridge, MA: Harvard University Press.

Anthias, Floya, Maria Kontos, and Mirjana Morokvasic (eds.). 2013. *Paradoxes of Integration: Female Migrants in Europe*. London: Springer.

Basch, Linda, Nina Glick Schiller, and Cristina Szanton Blanc. 1994. *Nations Unbound: Transnational Projects, Postcolonial Predicaments, and Deterritorialized Nation-States*. New York: Gordon and Breach.

Bauböck, Rainer, and Thomas Faist (eds.). 2010. *Diaspora and Transnationalism: Concepts, Theories, and Methods*. Amsterdam: Amsterdam University Press.

Boccagni, Paolo. 2015. '(Super)Diversity and the Migration-Social Work Nexus: A New Lens on the Field of Access and Onclusion?' *Ethnic and Racial Studies* 38(4): 608–620.

Boeri, Tito, Herbert Brueckner, Frederic Docquier, and Hillel Rapoport (eds.). 2012. *Brain Drain and Brain Gain: The Global Competition to Attract High-Skilled Migrants*. Oxford, UK: Oxford University Press.

Bouchard, Gerard. 2011. 'What Is Interculturalism?' *McGill Law Journal* 56(2): 436–468.

Bourne, Randolph. 1916. 'Trans-national America.' *Atlantic Monthly* 7: 86–97.

Brubaker, Rogers. 1996. *Nationalism Reframed*. New York: Cambridge University Press.

   2003. 'The Return of Assimilation? Changing Perspectives on Immigration and Its Sequels in France, Germany, and the United States.' In Christian Joppke and Ewa Morawska (eds.), *Toward Assimilation and Citizenship: Immigrants in Liberal Nation-States* (pp. 39–58). Basingstoke, UK: Palgrave Macmillan.

Bryceson, Deborah. 2002. 'Europe's Transnational Families and Migration: Past and Present.' In Deborah Bryceson and Ulla Vuorela (eds.), *The Transnational Family: New European Frontiers and Global Networks* (pp. 31–59). Oxford, UK: Berg.

Crevecoeur, Jean. 1962 [1782]. *Letters from an American Farmer*. London: Dent.

Dierx, A. H. 1988. 'Estimation of a Human Capital Model of Migration.' *The Annals of Regional Science* 22: 99–110. https://link.springer.com/article/10.1007/BF01283655

Ehrenreich, Barbara, and Arlie Hochschild. 2002. *Global Woman: Nannies, Maids, and Sex Workers in the New Economy*. London: Granta.

Emerson, Ralph Waldo. 1971 [1845]. *The Collected Works*. Cambridge, MA: Belknap Press.

Ethnic and Racial Studies. 2014. Special section on 'Herbert Gans Symposium'. 37(5).

   2015a. Special issue on super-diversity. 38(4).

   2015b. Symposium, 'Towards a Systematic Understanding of Cross-Border Linkages.' Edited by Peter Kivisto. 38(13).

Faist, Thomas. 2009. 'Diversity – a New Mode of Incorporation?' *Ethnic and Racial Studies* 32(1): 171–190.

Faist, Thomas, Margit Fauser, and Eveline Reisenauer. 2013. *Transnational Migration*. Cambridge, UK: Polity.

Foner, Nancy. 1997. 'What's New about Transnationalism? New York Immigrants Today and at the Turn of the Century.' *Diaspora* 6(3): 355–375.

Gans, Herbert. 1979. 'Symbolic Ethnicity: The Future of Ethnic Groups and Culture in America.' *Ethnic and Racial Studies* 2(9): 1–20.

1992. 'Comment: Ethnic Invention and Acculturation, a Bumpy-Line Approach.' *Journal of American Ethnic History* 12(1): 42–52.

1997. 'Toward a Reconciliation of "Assimilation" and "Pluralism": The Interplay of Acculturation and Ethnic Retention.' *International Migration Review* 31(4): 875–893.

Glazer, Nathan. 1997. *We Are All Multiculturalists Now.* Cambridge, MA: Harvard University Press.

Glazer, Nathan, and Patrick Moynihan. 1963. *Beyond the Melting Pot: The Negros, Puerto Ricans, Jews, Italians and Irish of New York City.* Cambridge, MA: MIT Press.

Glick Schiller, Nina. 1996. 'From Immigrants to Transmigrants: Theorizing Transnational Migration.' *Anthropological Quarterly* 68(1): 48–63.

2010. 'A Global Perspective on Transnational Migration: Theorizing Migration without Methodological Nationalism.' In Rainer Bauböck and Thomas Faist (eds.), *Diaspora and Transnationalism: Concepts, Theories, and Methods* (pp. 109–130). Amsterdam: Amsterdam University Press.

Gordon, Milton. 1964. *Assimilation in American Life.* New York: Oxford University Press.

Greeley, Andrew, 1974. *Ethnicity in the United States: A Preliminary Reconnaissance.* New York: John Wiley and Sons.

Guarnizo, Luis, Alejandro Portes, and William Haller. 2003. 'Assimilation and Transnationalism: Determinants of Transnational Political Action among Contemporary Migrants.' *American Journal of Sociology* 108(6): 1211–1248.

Gurak, Douglas, and Fe Caces. 1992. 'Migration Networks and the Shaping of Migration Systems.' In Mary Kritz, Lin Lean Him, and Hania Zlotnik (eds.), *International Migration Systems* (pp. 150–176). Oxford, UK: Clarendon Press.

Harris, J. R., and Michael Todaro. 1970. 'Migration, Unemployment, and Development: A Two-Sector Analysis.' *American Economic Review* 60: 126–142.

Hochschild, Jennifer, Jacqueline Chattopadhyay, Claudine Gay, and Michael Jones-Correa (eds.). 2013. *Outsiders No More? Models of Immigrant Political Incorporation.* New York: Oxford University Press.

Hondagneu-Sotelo, Pierette, and Cynthia Cranford. 1999. 'Gender and Migration.' In Janet Saltzman Chafetz (ed.), *Handbook of the Sociology of Gender* (pp. 105–126). New York: Kluwer.

Hugo, Graeme. 1981. 'Village-Community Ties, Village Norms, and Ethnic and Social Networks: A Review of Evidence from the Third World.' In Gordon DeJong and Robert Gardner (eds.), *Migration Decision Making: Multidisciplinary Approaches to Microlevel Studies in Developed and Developing Countries* (pp. 186–225). New York: Pergamon Press.

Kallen, Horace. 1915. 'Democracy versus the Melting-Pot: A Study of American Nationality, Parts I and II.' *The Nation*, February 18: 190–194 and February 25: 217–220.

Katz, E., and Oded Stark. 1986. 'Labor Migration and Risk Aversion in Less Developed Countries.' *Journal of Labor Economics* 4: 131–149.

Kivisto, Peter. 2002. *Multiculturalism in a Global Society.* New York: Wiley-Blackwell.

Kivisto, Peter (ed.). 2005. *Incorporating Diversity: Rethinking Assimilation in a Multicultural Age.* Boulder, CO: Paradigm Publishers.

Kivisto, Peter. 2012. 'Integration and Assimilation: The Core Concepts and Three Contemporary Developments.' In Elliott Barkan (ed.), *Immigrants in America* (pp. 1621–1636). Santa Barbara, CA: ABC-Clio.

Kymlicka, Will. 1996. *Multicultural Citizenship: A Liberal Theory of Minority Rights.* Oxford, UK: Oxford University Press.

Levitt, Peggy. 2001. *The Transnational Villagers*. Berkeley, CA: University of California Press.
    2003. 'Keeping Feet in Both Worlds: Transnational Practices and Immigrant Incorporation
    in the United States.' In Christian Joppke and Ewa Morawska (eds.), *Toward
    Assimilation and Citizenship: Immigrants in Liberal Nation-States* (pp. 177–194).
    Basingstoke, UK: Palgrave Macmillan.
Levitt, Peggy, and Mary Waters (eds.). 2002. *The Changing Face of Home: The Transnational
    Lives of the Second Generation*. New York: Russell Sage.
Lewis, Arthur. 1954. 'Economic Development with Unlimited Supply of Labour.' *The
    Manchester School of Economic and Social Studies* 22: 139–191.
Massey, Douglas S., Joaquin Arango, Hugo Graeme, et al. 1993. 'Theories of International
    Migration: A Review and Appraisal.' *Population and Development Review* 19(3):
    431–466.
    1998. *Worlds in Motion: Understanding International Migration at the End of the
    Millennium*. Oxford, UK: Clarendon Press.
Meer, Nasar, and Tariq Modood. 2012. 'How Does Interculturalism Contrast with
    Multiculturalism?' *Journal of Intercultural Studies* 33(2): 175–196.
Meyer, Gerland. 2008. 'The Cultural Pluralist Response to Americanization: Horace Kallen,
    Randolph Bourne, Louis Adamic, and Leonard Covello.' *Socialism and Democracy*
    22(3): 19–51.
Modood, Tariq. 2007. *Multiculturalism*. London: Verso.
Morawska, Ewa. 1994. 'In Defense of the Assimilation Model.' *Journal of American Ethnic
    History* 13(2): 76–87.
    2001a. 'Structuring Migration: The Case of Polish Income-Seeking Travellers to the West.'
    Theory and Society 30: 47–80.
    2001b. 'Immigrants, Transnationalism, and Ethnicization: A Comparison of This Great
    Wave and the Last.' In Gary Gerstle and John Mollenkopf (eds.), *E Pluribus Unum?
    Contemporary and Historical Perspectives on Immigrant Political Incorporation*
    (pp. 175–212). New York: Russell Sage Foundation.
    2003. 'Immigrant Transnationalism and Assimilation: A Variety of Combinations and the
    Analytic Strategy It Suggests.' In Christian Joppke and Ewa Morawska (eds.),
    Toward Assimilation and Citizenship: Immigrants in Liberal Nation-States
    (pp. 133–176). Basingstoke, UK: Palgrave Macmillan.
    2014. 'Glocalization Effects of Immigrants' Activities on the Host Society: An Exploration
    of a Neglected Theme.' In Roland Robertson (ed.), *European Glocalization in
    Global Context* (pp. 103–128). Basingstoke, UK: Palgrave Macmillan.
    2018. 'Multicultural Modes of Immigrants' Integration into the Host Society:Exploring the
    Proposition.' *Sociology and Anthropology* 6(10): 764–774.
Morokvasic, Mirjana. 2011. 'L'(in)visibilité continue.' *Cahiers du Genre, Migrantes et
    Mobilisées* 51: 25–47.
Nowicka, Magdalena, and Steven Vertovec, 2014. 'Comparing Convivialities: Dreams and
    Realities of Living with Difference.' *European Journal of Cultural Studies* 7(4):
    341–356.
Parekh, Bhikhu. 2000. *Rethinking Multiculturalism: Cultural Diversity and Political Theory*.
    Basingstoke, UK: Palgrave Macmillan.
Park, Robert, and Ernest Burgess. 1969 [1921]. *Introduction to the Science of Sociology*.
    Chicago, IL: University of Chicago Press.
Petras, Elizabeth. 1981. 'The Global Labor Market in the Modern Word-Economy.' In
    Mary Kritz, Charles Keely, and Silvano Tomasi (eds.), *Global Trends in*

Migration: Theory and Research on International Population Movements (pp. 44–63). Staten Island, NY: Center for Migration Studies.

Piore, Michael. 1979. *Birds of Passage: Migrant Labour and Industrial Societies*. Cambridge, UK: Cambridge University Press.

Portes, Alejandro. 2001. 'Introduction: The Debates and Significance of Immigrant Transnationalism.' *Global Networks* 1(3): 181–194.

Portes, Alejandro, and Rubén Rumbaut. 2001. *Legacies: The Story of the Immigrant Second Generation*. Berkeley, CA: University of California Press.

Portes, Alejandro, and Min Zhou. 1993. 'The New Second Generation: Segmented Assimilation and Its Variants.' *The Annals of the American Academy of Political Sciences* 530: 74–96.

Ranis, Gustav, and J. C. H. Fei. 1961. 'A Theory of Economic Development.' *American Economic Review* 51: 533–565.

Rumbaut, Rubén. 1997. 'Paradoxes (and Orthodoxies) of Assimilation.' *Sociological Perspectives* 40(3): 483–511.

Sarna, Jonathan. 1978. 'From Immigrants to Ethnics: Toward a New Theory of Ethnicization.' *Ethnicity* 5: 73–78.

Sassen, Saskia. 1988. *The Mobility of Labor and Capital: A Study in International Investment and Labor Flow*. Cambridge, UK: Cambridge University Press.

1996. *Losing Control? Sovereignty in an Age of Globalization*. New York: Columbia University Press.

Shibutani, Tamotsu, and Kian Kwan. 1965. *Ethnic Stratification: A Comparative Approach*. New York: Macmillan.

Sjastad, Larry. 1962. 'The Costs and Returns of Human Migration.' *Journal of Political Economy* 70S: 80–93.

Sklair, Leslie. 1990. *A Sociology of the Global System*. London: Harvester Wheatsheaf.

Smith, Michael, and Luis Guarnizo (eds.). 1998. *Transnationalism from Below*. New Brunswick, NJ: Transaction Publishers.

Smith, Robert. 2006. *Mexican New York: Transnational Lives of New Immigrants*. Berkeley, CA: University of California Press.

Soysal, Yasemin. 1994. *Limits of Citizenship: Migrants and Postnational Membership in Europe*. Chicago, IL: University of Chicago Press.

Stark, Oded. 1984. 'Migration Decision Making: A Review Article.' *Journal of Development Economics* 14: 251–259.

1991. *The Migration of Labor*. Cambridge, UK: Basil Blackwell.

Taylor, Edward. 1986. 'Differential Migration, Networks, Information and Risk.' In Oded Stark (ed.), *Research in Human Capital and Development*. Greenwich, CT: JAI Press.

Thomas, William I., and Florian Znaniecki 1927. *The Polish Peasant in Europe and America*, 5 vols. Boston, MA: Knopf.

Todaro, Michael. 1976. *Internal Migration in Developing Countries*. Geneva: International Labor Office.

1989. *Economic Development in the Third World*. New York: Longman.

Uberoi, Varun, and Tariq Modood (eds.). 2015. *Multiculturalism Rethought: Interpretations, Dilemmas and New Directions*. Edinburgh: Edinburgh University Press

Vertovec, Steven. 2007. 'Super-Diversity and Its Implications.' *Ethnic and Racial Studies* 30: 1024–1054.

Vertovec, Steven (ed.). 2011. *Anthropology of Migration and Multiculturalism*. London: Routledge.

Waldinger, Roger, 2015. *The Cross-Border Connection: Immigrants, Emigrants, and Their Homelands*. Cambridge, MA. Harvard University Press.

Wallerstein, Immanuel. 1974. *The Modern World-System*. New York: Academic Press.

Warner, W. Lloyd, and Leo Srole. 1945. *The Social Systems of American Ethnic Groups*. New Haven, CT: Yale University Press.

Waters, Mary, 1990. *Ethnic Options: Choosing Identities in America*. Berkeley, CA: University of California Press.

Wise, Amanda, and Selvaraj Velayutham. 2009. *Everyday Multiculturalism*. Basingstoke, UK: Palgrave Macmillan.

Zolberg, Aristide, and Litt Woon. 1999. 'Why Islam Is Like Spanish: Cultural Incorporation in Europe and the United States.' *Politics and Society* 27(1): 5–38.

Index

Horkheimer, Max, 132–4, 136–7, 138, 151–2
Huber, Joan, 364
human capital theory of immigration, 434, 436
Human Genome Project, 262
humanitarian aid, cultural sociology and, 49
human nature
  physiological level, role of at, 356–8, 359
  psychological level, role of at, 355–6
human trafficking, 191
Hume, David, 171, 183
Humean causation, 171, 183
Hungary, populism in, 185, 198
Hurricane Katrina, 230

identity theory
  age and, 67
  change of identity, 71–2
  college students and, 67
  commitment in, 65, 66
  content of identities, 66–7
  emotion theory and, 86
  ethnicity and, 67
  gender and, 67
  identity standard and, 69
  identity verification and, 69–71
  individual as basis of identity, 68
  leadership and, 67
  Mead and, 64, 65, 70–1
  multiple identities, 74–6
  origins of, 64–5
  overview, 63, 76
  prominence in, 65, 66
  role as basis of identity, 68
  salience in, 65–6
  self-esteem and, 72–4
  social category as basis of identity, 68
  spouses and, 67
  symbolic interaction and, 64–5
Ikegami, Eiko, 46
immigration
  assimilation (See Assimilation)
  in Australia, 190
  in Canada, 190
  citizenship and, 298–9
  cumulative causation model of, 439–40, 441
  dual-labour-market theory of, 437, 438
  in France, 190
  in Germany, 190
  globalization and, 189–90
  human capital theory of, 434, 436
  macro-level theories of, 436–9
  Marxism and, 437
  micro-level theories of, 434–6
  micro-macro theories of, 439–41
  morality and, 299
  multiculturalism and, 292, 298, 300, 302
  network/institutional theories of, 435, 436
  new economics of migration model of, 434, 436

  overview, 433
  push and pull model of, 436–7, 438
  rational choice theory and, 434, 435–6
  segmented-labour-market theory of, 437, 438
  social network approach to, 435, 436
  structuration model of, 440–1
  transnationalism and, 447–50 (See also
    Transnationalism)
  in United States, 190
  world-system theory of, 437–8, 439
indigenous peoples, multiculturalism and, 292,
    308–9
individualism
  emotion theory, centrality of individuals, 82–8
  identity theory, individual as basis of identity,
    68
  modernity, individual autonomy and, 151–2
  multiculturalism of individual, 305–6, 307–9
  Simmel and, 312
Industrial Revolution, 148, 151
Indymedia, 416–17
Inglehart, Ronald, 157
Ingold, Tim, 366
Institute for National Strategic Studies (INSS),
    187–8
integration. See Assimilation
Interaction Ritual Chain (IRC) theories, 85
Interaction Ritual (IR) theories, 85
Inter-American Development Bank, 306
interculturalism, 303–4
Intergovernmental Panel on Climate Change
    (IPCC), 235–6, 237
International Air Transport Association (IATA),
    189
International Criminal Tribunal for Rwanda, 197
International Criminal Tribunal for the former
    Yugoslavia, 197
International Geological Congress Working
    Group, 233
international governmental organizations (IGOs),
    191
International Monetary Fund (IMF), 193, 195,
    199, 234–5, 420
International nongovernmental organizations
    (NGOs), 191
International Planned Parenthood Federation, 191
International Red Cross, 53, 191, 193
international relations (IR) theory, 190
International Telecommunication Union, 193
International Union of Geological Sciences,
    247
interpersonal trust, 340–1
intersectionality
  academic environment, limitations of, 126–7,
    129
  activist nature of, 122–3
  African-American women and, 126–9,
    278–81

network theory and, 26
realism and, **173**
time and space and, 210
trust and, 335–6, 337–8
Pascoe, C.J., 277–8, 280
Patten, Alan, 299–301, 303, 308–9
Peirce, Charles Sanders, 254
Peterson, Richard, 46
Phillips, Anne, 305–6
Piaget, Jean, 368
Pierson, Paul, 423
Pieterse, Jan Nederveen, 196
Piketty, Thomas, 238–9
Pinker, Steven, 370
Pinter-Wollman, Noa, 29
Pisano, Leonardo, 315
Plato, 79
Plummer, Ken, 275
Poland, populism in, 198
Polanyi, Karl, 146, 150, 228
Polybius, 192
Pomeranz, Kenneth, 147
Popper, Karl, 18
populism, 185
Portes, Alejandro, 443
positivism
    logical positivism, 183
    realism versus, 166, 175, 178–9
postculturalism
    feminist social theory and, 111, 113
    intersectionality and, 134–6
"post-genomic" biology, 365–6
postmodernism
    feminist social theory and, 111
    modernity versus, 143–4
    rational choice theory versus, 18
    realism and, 163
Postone, Moishe, 208
poststructuralism, realism and, 163
Powell, Lewis F., 229, 305
Powell, Walter W., 27
Power
    cultural sociology and, 55
    intersectionality, power relations and, 121–2, 123–4, 129–30
Powers, William T., 70–1
power-status theory, 86
pragmatism
    cultural sociology and, 45, 51
    embodiment and, 254–5
    intersectionality compared, 121
    realism and, 164
Preciado, Paul, 33
Preda, Alex, 217
prisoner's dilemma, 9–10
prospect theory, 7–9
Protestantism
    capitalism and, 11–13

Reformation, 153, 316
    Weber and, 11, 12, 208
Pruitt, Scott, 233
psychoanalytical frameworks of sexuality, 273–4, 284–5
Puetz, Kyle, 26
push-and-pull model of immigration, 436–7, 438
Putnam, Robert D., 391

queer sexuality
    African-American lesbians, 281
    barebacking subculture, 274, 285
    Butler and, 286
    Foucault and, 285–6
    gender normativeness, rejection of, 282–3
    globalization and, 286–8
    identity normativeness, rejection of, 281–2
    in Mexico, 287
    psychoanalytical frameworks, 284–5
    Queer of Color Theory, 287
    sexual scripts and, 275
    transgender persons, 114–16, 283–4
    in Turkey, 288
Quintane, Eric, 29–30

race
    African Americans (*See* African Americans)
    intersectionality and, 126–9, 278–81
    multiculturalism and, 295–6
    racialization of space, 207
radical feminism and, 106, 107–8
radical multiculturalism, 295–6
Ramadan, Tariq, 301
rational choice theory
    agent-based modeling and, 10–11
    analytical sociology (AS) as alternative, 18–19
    basic version, 1–2
    behavioral economics and, 3
    beliefs, criticism based on, 17
    Bourdieu and, 18
    circular explanations, criticism based on, 13–14
    civil society and, 391, 392
    computer simulation and, 10–11
    constraints and, 2, 4–5
    costs and benefits and, 5
    critical social theory versus, 18
    deliberate versus spontaneous behavior in, 2
    dual-process theories as alternative, 19–20
    economics and, 3
    egoism and, 2, 15
    emotion, criticism based on, 16–17
    emotion theory and, 84
    falsification, criticism based on, 15
    functionalism versus, 18
    game theory as variant of, 3, 9–10
    immigration and, 434, 435–6